THE CRASH DETECTIVES

Journalist, aviation blogger, television commentator and crash investigator Christine Negroni has twenty years' experience observing and participating in the international effort to create safer skies. She currently reports for the *New York Times*, ABC News and *Air & Space* magazine, and she writes the popular blog *Flying Lessons*.

'A lively dissection of history-making accidents. . . Negroni tracks the astonishing progress in understanding the combination of mechanical flaws and human frailties that bring down aircraft.' *The Times*

'Fascinating. . . For all the horror stories in *The Crash Detectives*, the reasonable reader will leave the book more sanguine about modern commercial airline travel than before.' *Wall Street Journal*

'Christine Negroni is a talented aviation journalist who clearly understands the critically important part the human factor plays in aviation safety. She "gets it".' Captain Chesley 'Sully' Sullenberger, pilot of US Airways 1549 the 'Miracle on the Hudson', *New York Times* bestselling author of *Making a Difference* and *Highest Duty*

'Christine Negroni's book is a refreshing take on airplane accidents. . . [Negroni] brings the dual perspectives of an experienced air safety invest ne

'In *The Crash Detectives*. . . journalist and crash investigator Christine Negroni looks at numerous air crashes – from Earhart's in 1937 to the 2014 disappearance of Malaysia Airlines Flight 370 – and explores the different theories about what might have happened and why it can be so difficult to get to the truth.' *Chicago Tribune*

[*The Crash Detectives*] makes a compelling case. . . It puts [MH370] into context by chronicling a string of. . . mysterious air disasters. . . And it plumbs the reasons why some accidents are particularly hard to crack.' *Condé Nast Traveler*

'The evolution of air safety is rooted in catastrophe. Christine Negroni pulls back the curtain on the people, the places, and the tragedies that have shaped this process over the decades – an unflinching look at a system that most of us take for granted.' Patrick Smith, bestselling author of *Cockpit Confidential*

'Mysteries are always fascinating; aviation mysteries are especially so because they involve ordinary people. In *The Crash Detectives*, Christine Negroni combines her investigative reporting skills with an understanding of the complexities of air accident investigations to bring to life some of history's most intriguing and heartbreaking cases, reminding us that even in the 21st century, aviation still holds elements of the unknown.' Bob Woodruff, ABC News

'This is a completely fascinating book that will interest everyone and belongs in every aviator's library.' Patty Wagstaff, aerobatic national champion pilot

THE CRASH DETECTIVES

INVESTIGATING THE WORLD'S
MOST MYSTERIOUS AIR DISASTERS

CHRISTINE NEGRONI

Atlantic Books
London

Published by arrangement with Penguin Books, an imprint of Penguin
Publishing Group, a division of Penguin Random House LLC.

First published in Great Britain in 2016 by Atlantic Books,
an imprint of Atlantic Books Ltd.

This paperback edition first published in Great Britain
in 2018 by Atlantic Books.

1 2 3 4 5 6 7 8 9

A CIP catalogue record for this book is available from
the British Library.

E-book ISBN: 978-1-78239-642-0
Paperback ISBN: 978-1-78239-643-7

Designed by Elke Sigal

Printed in Italy by 🦁 Grafica Veneta

CONTENTS

O Trinity of love and power
All travelers guard in danger's hour;
From rock and tempest, fire and foe,
Protect them whereso e'er they go;
Thus evermore shall rise to Thee
Glad praise from air and land and sea.

—WILLIAM WHITING, 1860
PRESBYTERIAN HYMNAL

INTRODUCTION

This I can say about Malaysia Airlines Flight 370: there is little to suggest the pilots were involved in hijacking or crashing the plane they were flying from Kuala Lumpur to Beijing on March 8, 2014. One need only look at the shocking, intentional crash of a GermanWings* flight one year later to see how quickly, and how many, clues emerge when a pilot plots to bring down an airliner. My theory about what happened to MH-370 began to form within a week of arriving in Malaysia to help ABC News cover the story.

When I first heard about the missing flight, I was at sea in Vietnam's Gulf of Tonkin. The fact that the news reached me in such a remote place was a new high in communications technology. That years later we do not know what happened to the airliner and its passengers demonstrates the shallows.

I hurried to Kuala Lumpur and spent five weeks there. Each night, I went to bed pretty sure I'd wake up to hear that

---

* A subsidiary of Lufthansa, GermanWings became Eurowings in 2016.

the airliner had been found. When it was not, I was swept along with everyone else in believing that this was "unprecedented," as Malaysia's transportation and defense minister was fond of saying.

In fact, over the past century of commercial aviation, more than a dozen airliners have disappeared without a trace. And even when a missing plane is found, it is sometimes impossible to determine what went wrong.

When I returned to the United States and started the research for this book, I came across the trailer for a documentary produced by Guy Noffsinger, a media specialist at NASA. "What happened to the most high-tech commercial airliner in the world and those people aboard it?" the narrator asked ominously. Was it structural failure, pilot error, or something more sinister?

In a similar vein, author Edgar Haine in *Disaster in the Air*, writes, "Of particular concern to everyone was the sudden termination of normal radio contact" and "the absence of subsequent communications."

Yet Noffsinger and Haine weren't referring to MH-370; they were talking about the Pan American Airways flying boat the *Hawaii Clipper*.* It disappeared seventy-six years before MH-370 and was one of the first mysteries in commercial aviation. It remains a subject of fascination to this day.

After two decades writing about air safety and working as an accident investigator, I have learned that most accidents are variations on a limited number of themes, and in this book I explore some of them: communication failures, overreliance on or misunderstanding of technology, errors in the design of

---

* Pan American Airways became Pan American World Airways in 1950.

airplanes and engines, and lapses in the performance of flight crews, operators, and mechanics. The tie that binds the accidents (and incidents*) in this book is that they confounded the crash detectives looking for answers.

Why conduct investigations anyway? It is not to provide "closure" for families of victims, though that's a compassionate side benefit. It is not to assign blame so people can be prosecuted and lawyers can sue. Investigations help illuminate how machines and humans fail, which in turn shows us how to prevent similar events. Because the aviation community has been so conscientious about this over the years, hurtling through the air at five hundred miles an hour and seven miles high is far less likely to kill you than almost any other type of transportation.

From pilot training and airplane and engine design to dropping crash test dummies on their rubberized and sensor-equipped bottoms to the floor of a test lab, every decision in commercial aviation is based on lessons learned from disaster. That's why it is so important to discover what happened to Malaysia 370, even if the plane is never found.

An unsuccessful search is still not the end of the story; thinking through scenarios of what might have happened can identify hazards that need to be fixed. So while it is possible that one or both of the pilots—in an uncharacteristic act of hostility and without any of their friends or family noticing anything amiss—purposefully took the plane on a flight into oblivion, other theories better fit the available facts.

My theory is that an electrical malfunction knocked out systems on the Boeing 777 and that the plane lost pressurization,

---

* Incidents do not involve serious injury, loss of life, or substantial damage to the airplane.

incapacitating the pilots. Whatever happened, it could not have caused damage serious enough to affect the airworthiness of the plane, since it flew on until running out of fuel many hours later. Likely, the men in the cockpit were overcome by the altitude sickness known as hypoxia, which robbed them of the ability to think clearly and land the plane safely. Many of the links in the bizarre chain of events that night can be explained by hypoxia because past cases have shown how rapidly those who fall victim to it turn imbecilic.

As soon as a plane crashes, people begin to speculate about what happened. Horace Brock, who became a Pan Am pilot shortly after the *Hawaii Clipper* disappeared, noted in his book, *Flying the Oceans*, "The public will not tolerate a mystery. They always sense a conspiracy. They will never believe in coincidence or even a predictable tragedy."

Alternative theories abound in many notable accidents, including the disappearance of Amelia Earhart in 1937, the death of United Nations secretary-general Dag Hammarskjöld in Northern Rhodesia* in 1961, and the 1996 in-flight explosion of TWA Flight 800 off the coast of New York.

Questioning the official version of events can be a good thing. The loss of an Air New Zealand DC-10 on a sightseeing flight over Mount Erebus in Antarctica in 1979 was first attributed to pilot error. Only after people outside the investigation presented their own evidence did a special court of inquiry discover what it called "a litany of lies" by an airline and a government trying to hide their culpability. More on that crash later.

The tradition of doubt in aviation goes back to Orville and Wilbur Wright's successful first flights, which prompted an edi-

---

* Now Zambia.

torial writer to say of the brothers three years later, "They are in fact either fliers or liars. It is difficult to fly. It is easy to say, 'We have flown.'"

If skepticism was a gnawing mouse in flying's early days, it is a roaring lion now that anyone with an Internet connection can access information and review the evidence. Invited or not, independent analysts and armchair investigators are contributing to the discussion on TV news, blogs, and pop-up crowdsourcing sites. For the first time in history, technology is connecting hyper-specialists with geeks, skeptics, and advocates. Information can be scrutinized and analyzed in ways not previously possible, and this Internet-enhanced coalescing of the world's brain power will certainly continue to grow.

This book is a part of that evolution as I hypothesize about MH-370 and other disasters that have mystified the world.

PART ONE

Mystery

I have approximate answers and possible beliefs and
different degrees of uncertainty about different things.

—NOBEL PRIZE–WINNING THEORETICAL
PHYSICIST RICHARD FEYNMAN

The Clipper

On the last leg of a journey halfway around the world, Pan American Airways captain Leo Terletsky began to worry. And when Captain Terletsky worried, everybody else on the flight deck worried, too. "His anxiety caused him to shout at copilots, issue orders and immediately countermand them. He infected his crews with his own anxiety," wrote Horace Brock, who flew a few times with Terletsky and didn't much like it.

At noon on July 29, 1938, there was plenty to be anxious about. Having spent fifty-six hours over five days flying Pan Am passengers from San Francisco to the Far East, Terletsky and his nine-man crew were deep into bad weather as the Martin 130 flying boat approached the Philippine archipelago.

The plane was "sandwiched between two layers of clouds," explained Pete Frey, a captain with a large American carrier and a safety investigator with his union, who reviewed for me the weather reports submitted by the crew on that miserable summer morning. The stratocumulus clouds that Terletsky encountered are often at the beginning or end of worse weather, including rain and turbulence. Terletsky was dealing with both as he threaded the four-engine plane through the bands of clouds above and below where he was flying at 9,100 feet, 586 miles east of Manila. As Frey explained it to me, the rocky ride was not the crew's biggest problem.

"They are inside the clouds half the time, flying on instruments. This would make navigating by observing landmarks below impossible. It would also make getting a fix from the sun or other celestial object impossible as well.

"They are navigating with dead reckoning," Frey said. Dead reckoning is the most basic form of navigation: essentially a mathematical calculation involving weather, wind, time, speed, and direction. "You make an assumption of wind correction and simply hold a heading and course for a fixed period of time. At the end, you hope to be where you planned," Frey explained. Yet considering their inability to see the earth below, the crew would have had little on which to base their position; or as Frey imagined flying under the circumstances, "You are lost."

Around noon local time, radio operator William McCarty, thirty-three, sat at his desk behind the copilot, tapping the keys of his Morse code machine. He was sending a message to the Pan Am ground station on the Philippine island of Panay. Even if the crew was uncertain of its position, Pan Am's ground personnel would try to use radio wave direction finding to pinpoint the flying boat's location. They could also provide the crew with information about the weather ahead.

McCarty reported the weather and the winds, the temperature, and the crew's approximation of where they were, along with their speed. Morse code could get through even when the plane's radio signal was not strong enough to transmit a voice. By the time McCarty was done, about ten minutes had passed, and Edouard Fernandez, the operator at Panay, wanted to pass the weather news on to the crew. McCarty asked him to wait. "Stand by for one minute before sending as I am having trouble with rain static." When Fernandez tried later to contact the Clipper, there was no reply.

Nothing was ever again heard from the *Hawaii Clipper*. No piece of the plane, no human remains, no luggage or cargo, and no airplane fluid or fuel would show up. As with Malaysia 370 seventy-six years later, only the evidence still on the ground would be available for investigators to consider. They could scour the maintenance records and operational history of the plane and review the performance and training of the crew along with the information sent by McCarty during the flight, but it might not be enough to determine conclusively what happened. It could be illuminating; it might be baffling. It turned out to be both.

Thin Air

No one knows for sure what happened aboard Malaysia 370. The scenario I am about to describe is based on a framework of events put forward by Malaysian and Australian investigators and other sources who participated in gathering or analyzing the known data. To this I have applied Occam's razor, the principle that suggests that if there are many possible explanations for something, the simplest is the most likely.

Shortly after midnight on March 8, 2014, and seemingly without warning, what had been an entirely normal flight devolved into an illogical series of events. That kind of wacky has been seen before when pilots are afflicted with altitude sickness, known as hypoxia.

An inability to get enough oxygen into the lungs to sustain cogent thought happens when planes lose pressurization, and that can happen for a variety of reasons. It can be triggered by an electrical problem or some mechanical difficulty. Pilots sometimes fail to turn the pressurization on at the beginning of the flight, but even when the pressurization is working as it should, there's no way to keep a plane pressurized if there is a hole in the fuselage or if leaks at the seals of doorways, windows, or drains from the galley and bathrooms allow the denser air to escape.

If the pilots on Malaysia Flight 370 experienced oxygen deprivation because something happened to cause the plane to lose pressurization, they would have behaved irrationally, perhaps turning a moderate problem into a catastrophic one. The passengers and crew would have become feebleminded and helpless.

At the time of the MH-370 disaster, people were boarding airplanes around the world at a rate of eight million a day. Few air travelers then (or now) gave a thought to the fact that outside those aluminum walls the air is too thin to sustain coherent thought for more than a few seconds. Life itself is extinguished in minutes. While the percentage of oxygen in the air (21 percent) is the same as on the ground, the volume of air expands at higher altitudes. We rely on air density for the pressure that drives oxygen into our bodies. Miles above the earth and absent this pressure, oxygen will rush out like air racing out of a balloon.

What keeps us air travelers alive and, for the most part, in our right minds is a relatively simple process that pumps air into the plane as it ascends, like air filling a bicycle tire. The air comes off the engines and is distributed via ducts throughout the plane. In most airliners, the cabin pressure is set to mimic the pressure density of about eight thousand feet. So to your body, flying is like being in Aspen, Colorado, or Addis Ababa, Ethiopia.

When it is time to land, the valves that closed on takeoff to maintain that air density in the cabin begin to open, allowing it to escape gradually until the inside of the plane is equalized with the outside, or generally, to 190 feet above the altitude of the airport. You'll know this process is happening when your ears start to pop in the last twenty to thirty minutes of your flight. If this extra pressure weren't allowed to vent, the door of the plane might explode outward. It happened as recently as 2000, when an American Airlines Airbus A300 made an emergency landing at Miami International. Insulation blankets blocked the outflow valves, so the differential pressure inside the cabin was still high even after landing. It is not clear if the flight attendants realized it, because they had other problems. A smoke alarm had triggered, and they were worried about a fire. So they were trying to evacuate the plane, but the doors would not budge. Finally, thirty-four-year-old senior flight attendant José Chiu pushed hard enough, and the door blew out. Chiu was jettisoned off the airplane and killed.

On most flights the automated system works as designed. Still, at least forty to fifty times a year, an airliner somewhere in the world will encounter a rapid decompression, according to a study for the Aviation Medical Society of Australia and New Zealand. James Stabile Jr., whose company, Aeronautical Data Systems, provides oxygen-related technology, said that when slow depressurizations are figured in, the rate increases even more. And because not all events require that regulators be notified, the problem is "grossly underreported."

When planes fail to pressurize after takeoff or lose cabin altitude in flight, it is potentially life-threatening. The reason we don't see tragedies more often is because pilots are taught what to do. First, they put on their emergency oxygen masks. Then they verify that the system is on. There are numerous cases of pilots discovering that they failed to set cabin altitude upon takeoff, which I liken to finding the laundry I loaded in the washer unwashed hours later because I forgot to start the machine.

If pressurization was set correctly and is still not working, pilots immediately begin a rapid descent to an altitude where supplemental oxygen is not necessary. When pilots do not follow these steps, the situation spins out of control quickly.

To be clear, pilots don't intentionally ignore the procedures. When they do, it is usually because their mental processes are already compromised by oxygen starvation. Sometimes the effect is unfathomable; pilots faced with an alert that the cabin altitude is exceeding twelve thousand feet have been known to mistakenly *open the outflow valves*, completely depressurizing the cabin and ratcheting up the problem.

On an American Trans Air flight in 1996, a mind-boggling sequence of events brought a Boeing 727 a hairbreadth from catastrophe. The miracle is that despite the lunacy in the cockpit, the plane landed safely.

ATA Flight 406 departed Chicago's Midway Airport bound for St. Petersburg, Florida. At thirty-three thousand feet, a warning horn sounded because the altitude in the cabin was registering fourteen thousand feet. First Officer Kerry Green was flying. He immediately put on his emergency oxygen mask. Capt. Millard Doyle did not, opting to try to diagnose the problem. He instructed the flight engineer, Timothy Feiring, who was sitting behind and to his right, to silence the alarm. Doubtless already feeling the effects of altitude that was steadily increasing, Feiring could not find the control button, and more time passed.

As he looked around, the captain evidently thought he'd discovered the source of the problem, an air-conditioning pack switch that was off, and he pointed it out to Feiring. Then he turned his attention to the flight attendant in the cockpit, asking her if the passenger oxygen masks had dropped.

They had, she replied, and promptly collapsed in the doorway. Now Captain Doyle reached for his own mask, but it was too late. Disoriented and uncoordinated, he could not place it over his head, and he passed out, too.

Two of four people in the cockpit were now incapacitated, and Feiring was having trouble thinking. He mistakenly opened an outflow valve, creating a rapid and total decompression of the airplane.

He put on his mask and then got up to attend to the unconscious flight attendant, placing the flight observer mask on her face, but dislodging his own in the process. He passed out, falling over the center console between the two pilots' seats.

Through all this, First Officer Green, with his mask on, was taking the plane down to a lower altitude at a speed of about four to five thousand feet per minute.

Back in the passenger seats, the cabin crew had not been given any instructions from the cockpit, but the flight attendant seated at the front of the plane made a pantomime with her mask to demonstrate what the passengers should do. Some travelers followed her example; others did not. Through it all, the flight attendants reported that the plane was pitching up and down and side to side, and there was a brief, incomprehensible announcement from the cockpit.

Passenger Stephen Murphy of San Diego thought he was going to die and remembers feeling a sense of peace as he recited his prayers. Then the woman seated behind him started having convulsions, and the man across the aisle began to claw at his ears.

"What bothered me was there was nothing I could do for him. It's not like you see on TV; people don't grab portable oxygen bottles and walk around the cabin helping people,"

Murphy told me years later. "Had I had my full senses, I'd like to think I could have helped somebody. But based on what was going on, I didn't. I knew I couldn't."

On the flight deck, Green was trembling, a common symptom of hypoxia. Something was wrong with the microphone in his mask, and he had to pry the compressible seal away from his face to contact air traffic control.

When the oxygen mask Feiring had placed on her face rejuvenated the flight attendant, she got up and returned the favor, replacing the mask that had come off him as he moved away from the flight engineer console. She also got a mask on Captain Doyle. Soon they both came to. American Trans Air Flight 406 landed safely in Indianapolis, but the episode could have ended in catastrophe.

The story, equal parts chilling and absurd, tells me that knowing what to do does not mean pilots will actually do it if their ability to think has begun to deteriorate.

Nine years after American Trans Air 406, on August 14, 2005, a Boeing 737 took off from Cyprus on a flight to Athens, but it never arrived. Helios Flight 522 ran out of fuel and crashed into a mountain south of the airport after flying on autopilot for more than two hours—long after the pilots and nearly everyone else on board had fallen into deep and prolonged unconsciousness. They had been starved of oxygen, presumably because the pilots failed to pressurize the aircraft after takeoff. The pilots were hypoxic before they realized what had gone wrong.

The Helios 522 disaster started about five and a half minutes after takeoff, as the plane climbed through twelve thousand feet. A warning horn alerted the pilots that the altitude in the cabin had exceeded ten thousand feet.

Less than two minutes later, the passenger oxygen masks

dropped, but Capt. Hans-Jürgen Merten and First Officer Pambos Charalambous did not put on their masks, deciding instead to try to figure out what was wrong: a classic case of impaired judgment due to hypoxia.

For nearly eight minutes, Captain Merten, a pilot with five thousand hours of experience on the 737, conversed with the Helios operations center in Cyprus in an exchange that grew increasingly confusing to the men on the ground. One thing was certain. The horn warning of *altitude* did not direct the pilots to focus on the cabin altitude, and here's why: the alarm's insistent staccato is also used on the runway when an airplane is incorrectly set for takeoff. At that time in the flight, the same alarm is called a takeoff configuration warning. This case of one alarm for two hazards relies on the pilots' knowing to which hazard they are being alerted.

On the ground, it seems straightforward. The takeoff configuration alarm will sound only prior to takeoff. The distinction is not so obvious, however, when the pilot's ability to think is already fading. And we know this because, when the alarm on Helios 522 went off, Merten told his airline's operations desk that the takeoff configuration horn was sounding. He did not associate the warning with cabin altitude. That mistake has been repeated on passenger flights around the world, including ten instances over ten years found in the files of the NASA Aviation Safety Reporting System, or ASARS.

"The simplicity of the error" is what struck Bob Benzon, an accident investigator with the National Transportation Safety Board at the time, who was helping the Greeks on the Helios accident. "There were one hundred twenty-one people who died on a modern airliner, and all through a simple error. That was the thing," he said.

Six years earlier Benzon had been assigned to investigate a similar accident, involving a private jet and a popular American athlete. Payne Stewart was one of the most famous golfers on the pro circuit, beloved for the weird collection of tam-o'-shanters and knickerbockers he wore at tournaments. He suffered hypoxia on October 25, 1999, in the early stages of a four-hour flight from Florida to Texas.

Not long after departing from Orlando, the first officer, Stephanie Bellegarrigue, failed to respond to calls from air traffic control. She sounded fine in her last radio communication, but the plane failed to turn as planned, and no one on the ground could raise the crew as the plane passed thirty-two thousand feet.

"Somewhere west of Ocala, the crew became incapacitated. Maybe not dead, but they couldn't answer the radio," Benzon told me. The investigation never determined when or why the plane lost cabin pressure.

The plane continued straight from its last heading until it ran out of fuel and crashed in a field in South Dakota. From his office in Washington, DC, Benzon watched live news coverage of the runaway flight. Fifty years old at the time, he had worked nearly two hundred airplane accidents, but he had never seen one unfold before his eyes.

In the months after the Helios accident, aviation authorities in several countries shared their experiences with the investigators. Just eight months before the Helios accident, NASA had sent a special bulletin to Boeing and the FAA, concerned that several flight crews reported they had been confused by the dual use of the pressurization warning horn. Even earlier, in 2001, there had been an event in Norway when pilots disregarded the warning horn and continued to ascend. The Norwegian Air Accident Investigation Board sent a safety recommendation to

Boeing also in 2004, calling for it to discontinue the dual-use alarm.

As Helios 522 ascended over Cyprus, Captain Merten's thoughts were scattering, and his brain was going dim. He collapsed at his last position, checking a switch panel behind his seat. First Officer Charalambous passed out against the airplane control yoke.

Using the experience of the survivors of American Trans Air Flight 406 as a reference, we can assume that the passengers on the Helios 737 were uneasy once their masks dropped, everyone waiting for news from the flight deck. But that uneasiness would not have lasted for more than twelve to fifteen minutes, because those masks have only a limited supply of oxygen; after that, the passengers would have passed out. This is why pilots quickly have to get the airplane to a lower altitude, but the pilots on Helios 522 were unconscious, and they weren't going to recover. There was no one to initiate a descent, and the plane flew on, northwest past southern Turkey and high above the Greek islands.

The flight attendants had higher-capacity emergency oxygen bottles and portable oxygen masks. With more than an hour's supply in each, they were likely conscious longer than the passengers. Twenty-five-year-old Andreas Prodromou was a flight attendant who also happened to be a private pilot. He may have waited for word from the cockpit, but at some point he got up from his seat by the back galley and took action.

What we know from this point comes from two sources: recordings in the cockpit documenting Prodromou's arrival on the flight deck and the observations of two Greek fighter pilots who were dispatched to see what was happening with the airliner that had silently, and without contacting controllers, entered Greek air space.

Two air force F-16s were flying on either side of the airliner. It was just four years after terrorists had crashed four commercial jets into landmarks in New York and Washington, DC, and the Greek Air Force pilots expected to find something similar. Instead, they saw the first officer unconscious in the right-hand seat. One of the air force fliers saw Prodromou enter the cockpit. This means that Prodromou waited more than two hours after the depressurization.

He may have suspected the incapacitation of the crew, but the sight of the vacant captain's seat and the copilot lifeless at the controls must have been terrifying. Captain Merten was partially on the floor and partially on the center console. Prodromou probably had to step over him to get to the left seat, where he removed Merten's unused oxygen mask from the storage compartment and put it on. Lifting the mask activates the flow of oxygen through a thick gray umbilical cord that also contracts the face straps. This design keeps the mask fitted tightly to the head.

Prodromou put on the mask as the last of the left engine's fuel was spraying into the combustion chamber. In moments, the engine would stop producing power.

Bank angle, bank angle. A computerized voice warned that the airplane's left wing was losing lift. The Boeing 737 can fly with only one engine, but control surfaces have to be adjusted to compensate.

Prodromou searched the control panel for something familiar— something that connected this complicated aircraft to the small planes on which he had learned to fly. Then the control wheel in front of him started to vibrate. The stick shaker warning is as

15

dramatic as it is urgent, an attention-getting, multisensory advisory that the plane is about to stall. For two and a half minutes Prodromou scanned the instrument panel while the airplane picked up speed in descent. The sound of rushing air joined the cacophony of warnings. Finally, hope extinguished, he called for help in a frail and frightened voice.

"Mayday, mayday, Helios Flight 522 Athens . . ."

And forty-eight seconds later:

"Mayday."

"Mayday."

Traffic, traffic. He heard only the mechanized voice of the 737.

The radio was not set to the proper frequency to transmit the message. Prodromou's mayday would be heard only in the postcrash examination of the cockpit voice recorder.

As the plane approached the ground and ambient air pressure increased, the cabin altitude warning horn turned off and one contributor to the din in the cockpit subsided. It was then that Prodromou first noticed the fighter jet escort.

Years later, one of the fighter pilots explained that he gestured for Prodromou to follow him to a military airfield nearby. To this signal, the young flight attendant raised his own hand and, with weary resignation, pointed downward. Even if he could have figured out how to follow the F-16, it was too late. The right engine was shutting down. The plane was seven thousand feet above the ground with three and a half minutes left. Helios Flight 522 crashed into the countryside near Athens International Airport, not far from where it had been programmed to fly, killing the last of the travelers on this terrible journey.

When Prodromou's role in the story made the news in Cyprus, many wondered: what if the young man had entered the cockpit earlier? Many factors could have changed the course of Flight

522. But at its heart, what claimed Prodromou and the others was a simple truth.

"Inherent in aviation is the exposure to altitude," said Robert Garner, an aviation physiologist and director of a high-altitude training chamber in Arizona, "and the risk of hypoxia is always present."

Emergency

In the early days of the Malaysia 370 mystery, I thought of these episodes. After all, it was an ordinary flight—under the command of an experienced and well-regarded captain—that suddenly turned baffling.

The Boeing 777 departed Kuala Lumpur International Airport on March 8, 2014, on an overnight trip to Beijing. There were 227 passengers and 12 crew members on board. In the cockpit, Capt. Zaharie Ahmad Shah, a thirty-three-year employee of the company, was in command. He had eighteen thousand flight hours. As a point of reference, that's just fifteen hundred hours fewer than Chesley Sullenberger had in his logbook when he successfully ditched a disabled US Airways airliner into New York's Hudson River, and Zaharie was five years younger than Sully.

Zaharie spent even more untallied time flying his home-built flight simulator. He took so much pleasure in this activity that he made videos and posted them on his Facebook page, offering tips and instructions to other simulator enthusiasts. *Obsessed much?* you might think when I tell you he also owned and flew radio-controlled airplanes. There just wasn't enough flying, as far as Zaharie was concerned.

Professionally speaking, First Officer Fariq Abdul Hamid was everything Zaharie was not. Inexperienced on the Boeing 777, he was still training on the wide-body while Zaharie supervised his performance. The flight to Beijing would bring the young pilot's total hours on the airplane to thirty-nine. Fariq had been flying for Malaysia for four years. From 2010 to 2012, he was a copilot on Boeing 737s. He was moved to the Airbus A330, where he flew as a first officer for fifteen months until he began his transition to the even bigger Boeing 777.

The moonless night was warm and dark with mostly cloudy skies when the jetliner lifted off at 12:41 a.m. on Saturday morning. Fariq was making the radio calls, so we can assume Zaharie was flying the plane.

On board were business travelers, vacationers, and students. There were families, couples, and singles from Indonesia, Malaysia, China, Australia, America, and nine other countries; a global community common on international flights. Because Kuala Lumpur and Beijing are in the same time zone and the flight was to arrive at dawn, many travelers were probably sleeping when things started to go wrong.

Flight 370 was headed north-northwest to Beijing. Twenty minutes after takeoff, at 1:01 a.m., the plane reached its assigned altitude, thirty-five thousand feet, and Fariq notified controllers.

"Malaysia Three Seven Zero maintaining flight level three five zero."

Independent of what the pilots were doing, the twelve-year-old Boeing 777 was transmitting a routine status message via satellite with information about its current state of health. In the acronym-loving world of aviation, this data uplink is called ACARS, for Aircraft Communications Addressing and Reporting System. Messaging can be manual if the pilots want to request or send information to the airline. It can also be triggered by some novel condition on the plane requiring immediate notice. Absent either of these conditions, an automatic status report is transmitted on a schedule set by the airline. At Malaysia, it was every thirty minutes.

Pilots may not be aware of when or how often the aircraft makes scheduled status transmissions, but they certainly know about them. They use ACARS often, for both the serious and the mundane things that happen in flight, from requests for weather updates to the latest sports scores. A pilot who needs a minor repair or a wheelchair on arrival can simply send a text through ACARS.

Neither Zaharie nor Fariq had anything to add to the 1:07 a.m. scheduled report, and the message showed nothing amiss. The engine performance indicated how much fuel had been consumed by the Rolls-Royce Trent 892 engines.

Around the time the ACARS message was being sent, it appears control of the flight was transferred to the first officer because Captain Zaharie was now making the radio calls. He confirmed to air traffic control that the plane was flying at cruise altitude. "Ehhh . . . Seven Three Seven Zero* maintaining level three five zero."

Eleven minutes later, as the airplane neared the end of Malaysian airspace, the controller issued a last instruction to the men in

---

* This was an error, as the flight was Three Seven Zero, not Seven Three Seven Zero.

command of Flight 370, giving them the frequency to which they should tune their radio upon crossing into Vietnam's area.

"Malaysian Three Seven Zero contact Ho Chi Minh one two zero decimal niner, good night."

"Good night, Malaysian," Zaharie said. It was 1:19. His voice was calm, according to a stress analyst who listened to the recording as part of the Malaysian probe. There was no indication of trouble.

Zaharie, fifty-three, had been in his seat since around 11:00 p.m., ordering fuel, entering information in the onboard computers, arming systems, checking the weather en route, and discussing the flight with the cabin attendants. He had also been supervising Fariq, who, after landing in Beijing, would be checked out on the Boeing 777. That was sure to be a heady and exhilarating new assignment for the young man, as Zaharie certainly recognized, having three children of his own around the age of Fariq, who was twenty-seven.

The airliner was at cruise altitude, flying a preprogrammed course. There was very little difference at this point between the Boeing 777 and every other jetliner Fariq had flown. So, in the scenario I envision on Malaysia 370, this would have been the perfect time for Zaharie to tell Fariq, "Your airplane," leaving the triple seven in the first officer's hands so he could go to the bathroom. And so he did.

Alone on the flight deck, Fariq must have enjoyed these moments. He was in sole command of one of the world's largest airliners, responsible for taking his passengers to their destination.

Seven years earlier, he had graduated from junior science college, a boarding school three hours north of his family home in Kuala Lumpur. He was accepted into Malaysia Airline's pilot cadet program, at the Langkawi Aerospace Training Centre, on the northwest coast of the Malay Peninsula. He would get more than flying lessons at the training center. He had a guaranteed job flying for his nation's flag carrier, which served sixty destinations around the globe and operated the Airbus A380, the world's largest airliner.

His professional future was full of promise and so was his personal life. During cadet training he met and fell in love with a fellow student, Nadira Ramli, who became a first officer with AirAsia, a Kuala Lumpur–based low-cost carrier. Ramli, one year younger than Fariq, was so charming that she was selected by AirAsia to represent the company on a public relations and marketing campaign that included a drive across China in 2012. In March 2014, Fariq and Ramli were engaged to be married.

While Zaharie was out of the cockpit, it would be Fariq's job to tune the radio to the Ho Chi Minh air traffic control frequency. Once he established contact, he would change the transponder's four-digit squawk code from the one used in Malaysia to one for transiting to Vietnam-controlled airspace. But instead of making that switch, the transponder stopped transmitting entirely. The question is why.

A transponder is critical for airliners. It links altitude, direction, speed, and, most significantly, identity to what otherwise would be a tiny anonymous green dot on an air traffic control screen. The transponder provides what is called a secondary return: a data-rich reply to a radar interrogation. Controllers need the transponder to keep planes from colliding in increasingly crowded skies. Airlines use it to track the progress of flights. Pilots depend on it for a timely warning if another plane winds up in their flight path.

Turning the knob on the lower-right-hand side of the device to the left—to the "standby" mode—effectively shuts off the transponder. This stops sending the plane's identification information and eliminates the plane's ability to be seen on the collision avoidance systems of other aircraft. Standby is used mostly while airliners are taxiing at the airport, so all the planes don't trigger the collision avoidance system. For all intents and purposes, standby is "off."

In flight, however, pilots have little reason to turn off the transponder, though there have been cases in which it has stopped transmitting for undetermined reasons. In one perplexing flight in 2006, the lack of secondary radar contributed to a catastrophic collision. An Embraer Legacy business jet was being delivered to New York from Manaus in Brazil. While flying over a remote jungle region, it hit a GOL Airlines Boeing 737 flying in the opposite direction at the same altitude. The pilots of the Legacy said they did not intentionally shut off the transponder, but it was in standby mode, so as they flew westward at thirty-seven thousand feet, an altitude normally reserved for eastbound flights,* the plane was invisible to the GOL Airlines collision avoidance system. These systems require both planes to have a transponder operating to issue an alert.

The winglet of the small business jet sliced through the left wing of the 737, and the airliner fell from the sky and into the jungle, killing all 154 people on board. The little jet made an emergency landing, and no one aboard was injured. When

---

* Commonly, eastbound flights fly at odd-numbered altitudes, and westbound flights at even-numbered altitudes.

questioned, neither pilot on the business jet was able to explain what had happened.

On the captain's side of the Embraer, the switches for the Honeywell transponder are positioned below a bar that is also used as a pilot footrest. Investigators suspected the captain might have kicked the switch into standby mode. There was also a theory that the lid of the laptop both pilots had been using might have pushed the button into standby. Less than a year earlier, Honeywell discovered a software glitch on more than thirteen hundred devices that could make them go into standby mode if pilots failed to dial the squawk code in less than five seconds. So there were plenty of theories about what might have happened. Ultimately, though, the Brazilians concluded that the software problem was not an issue on the Legacy involved in the collision, and what happened in that case remained a mystery.

In the United States, however, the Brazilian accident led the safety authorities to one unequivocal conclusion: something needed to change. The FAA issued a rule in 2010 that on new airplanes, the warning of an inoperative transponder should be more obvious to the pilots. Planes produced before the rule, including 9M-MRO, the registration for the plane that was flying as Malaysia 370, would not be affected.

Zaharie left the cockpit for what is delicately called a "biological break." Perhaps he would have stopped by the galley for a cup of coffee or a snack. It's a long flight at cruise altitude, so there would have been no rush to get back to the flight deck. The tasks that First Officer Fariq had to take care of were routine. Easy peasy, as they say.

Fariq knew he had to get the squawk code from Ho Chi

Minh—but first he had to tune the radio to that frequency. This is about the time when, I think, a rapid decompression happened near or in the cockpit. It would have made a deep and startling noise, like a clap or the sound of a champagne bottle uncorking, only much, much louder and sharper. This would have been followed by a rush of air and things swirling everywhere. Zaharie's nearly empty coffee cup, pens, papers—everything loose—would have been tossed about in the wind, including the shoulder straps of Fariq's seat restraint, which he would have unfastened for comfort not long after the plane's wheels left the runway at Kuala Lumpur. A white fog would have filled the space as the drop in temperature turned the moist cabin air into mist. The first officer would have realized immediately, *This is an emergency*. It would have been a neon light in his brain, but it would also have been competing with other lights and sounds, physiological sensations that had to have been both disconcerting and overwhelming.

The denser air inside Fariq's body would have rushed out through every orifice, an effect that can be particularly painful in the ears, as anyone who has flown with a head cold already knows. His fingers, hands, and arms would have started to move spastically. Fariq would have struggled to understand this rapid change from normal to pandemonium while irretrievable seconds of intellectual capacity ticked away.

Emergency, have to get down, have to let someone know. What first? He would have reached over to the transponder to enter 7700, the four digits that will alert everyone on the ground and in the air that something has gone wrong with the plane. His fingers would still have been trembling as he clutched the small round knob on the bottom left of the device and turned it to Standby. It is not what he would have intended, but he would already have begun to lose his mental edge. In an attempt to transmit a message of distress, he would have inadvertently severed the only means air controllers had of identifying his airplane and the details of his flight. It was half a minute past 1:20 in the morning.

A Fading Glimmer

It is not difficult to imagine Fariq responding inappropriately. As the Greeks investigating the Helios disaster discovered, only a small portion of pilots has experienced the dangerous seduction of hypoxia. Military aviators in many countries are trained to recognize the symptoms of oxygen deprivation by spending time at twenty-five thousand feet in high-altitude chambers. Yet even military pilots, astronauts, and soldiers are not subjected to the kind of rapid decompression that could have happened on MH-370. The onset of hypoxia above twenty-five thousand feet is too quick, and the health risks too high, to duplicate it in a high-altitude chamber.

When MH-370 lost secondary radar and disappeared from controllers' screens at thirty-five thousand feet, the plane wasn't exactly invisible. A two-hundred-foot blob of metal can hardly be missed by the sweep of a radar signal, even if the antenna is as far as two hundred miles away. However, the signal sent back, called an echo, does not transmit the precise information provided by the transponder. The object is picked up on the radar sweep in what is called "primary" mode. Things as different in size and nature as a flock of geese, a cloud, or a ship can all cause the radar signal to ricochet, and show up on the screen as a green blip.

Primary radar is a "no-frills" target. Viewing these kinds of blips over time allows calculation of an object's speed, which can help determine if it is an airplane, as few things move as fast as an airliner. Sometimes it is possible to tell what kind of plane it is because different planes move at different speeds. The Boeing 777 cruises at around five hundred seventy-five miles per hour.

Altitude is a different story. It is much more complicated to judge height, and altitude cannot be determined from primary civilian radar. Only military radar has this capability.

After MH-370 went missing, stories and theories emerged based on a Reuters wire service report that the airliner went on a wild ride of ascents and descents after turning back toward Kuala Lumpur. While this was based on real information collected and reviewed by international military and civilian radar specialists, some of the data was "essentially useless," according to one of the men who participated in the evaluation and who wishes to remain anonymous.

Not all the air defense systems capable of capturing altitude actually got it, and among the altitude data collected were indications that the target thought to be the plane was dropping thousands of feet in a few seconds. This had to be considered erroneous, because the plane could not move that quickly.

"It was being reported accurately as far as it went. It was showing a forty-thousand- to twenty-five-thousand-foot descent, but to make an airliner do that would require a ten-thousand-foot-per-minute descent," I was told by my source, more than twice even a rapid ascent rate. "A lot of the numbers were not reasonable."

What was never reported is that this questionable altitude information caused a controversy among those reviewing the tapes, because some civilian radar specialists thought it indicated that the plane had been hit by a missile. This dominated the discussion for several days, with the Malaysian Air Force arguing against the theory. What settled it, according to the participant who told me about it, was the lack of wreckage in the South China Sea. "The search was going on in that area, the last place the airplane was seen, but they weren't finding anything," this person said. "If it had been shot down you would have found pieces of stuff, but there was no evidence to back up that theory, so we came to a consensus that's not what happened."

That consensus got another boost when the engineers from the satellite company Inmarsat showed up in Kuala Lumpur a few days later to share with the team information that the airplane had not come to a sudden end after disappearing from radar, but flew on a lengthier and far more puzzling journey. They knew this because the airplane was exchanging digital handshakes with a communications satellite. The logs of those exchanges also provided a small slice of data about 9M-MRO's final hours.

Before the plane departed Kuala Lumpur it was loaded with just under 111,000 pounds of jet fuel. Based on fuel consumption between 15,000 and 17,000 pounds per hour on a Boeing 777-200, at best the plane had 7.2 hours of flying time. The Inmarsat data showed the plane did fly slightly longer, for 7.5 hours, meaning it could not have engaged in steep ascents or low-altitude flying, both of which burn more fuel.

The satellite data also indicated that nothing could have happened to the airplane to cause a decrease in its performance, such as a debilitating fire or structural damage. These would have caused more drag or prevented the plane from remaining aloft as long as it did.

Like the no-frills radar data, the equally unpretentious signals between the airliner and the satellite communication network would become a significant source of information, providing facts even the experts didn't know they had.

While the radar intermittently picked up the presence of something moving at the speed of a 777 heading southwest over the peninsula, inside the cockpit of 9M-MRO, Fariq's brain would have been hovering in a state of befuddlement. He would have been not in the game but not entirely out of it, either. When the interior atmosphere of the 777 suddenly zoomed from eight thousand to more than thirty thousand feet, the young pilot did the wrong things as his rapidly diminishing mental state was telling him he was doing the right things. He would not have become aware of his error: hypoxia victims think they are performing brilliantly.

When I try to imagine Fariq's compromised intellectual state, I recall an army aviator in an altitude chamber training session, later posted on YouTube. I could not stop watching the astonishing transformation of the man in the video, identified as Number 14.

The young soldier is flanked by two others using supplemental oxygen, but Number 14 has his regulator off in order to experience hypoxia. He holds a deck of cards and has been asked to flip through them one by one, announcing the number and suit before moving on to the next card. The altitude in the chamber is twenty-five thousand feet.

"I feel really good right now," Number 14 says as he begins announcing, "Six of spades," and showing a six of spades to the camera. "No symptoms yet." In twenty-four seconds he reports feeling tingling "in my toes and in my toes." One minute in, Number 14 gets his first card wrong. He identifies a five of spades as a four of spades. After being asked twice to look again and making the correction, he calls every card the four of spades.

After two minutes, as his thinking gets increasingly sloppy, Number 14 is asked, "Sir, what would you do if this was an aircraft?" to which he replies, "Four of spades, four of spades." Ninety seconds later, after ignoring several requests that he put on his regulator, a seatmate does it for him.

Sessions like this are intended to demonstrate to future pilots the danger of hypoxia. Like the drunk who's convinced he's the funniest guy in the room, a pilot suffering from hypoxia can feel a heightened sense of competence and well-being, what one pilot called "a lightheaded euphoria."

This is a tricky issue, because hypoxia can lead to brain death. People experiencing it ought to be trying to get some oxygen STAT, but they often don't. Hypoxia creates a state of idiotic bliss. One commenter on the YouTube video wrote, "Make this legal," because it sure does look like silly fun.

I expected to have a similar experience when I joined two dozen pilot cadets from Taiwan's EVA Air for a daylong hypoxia awareness training session at the Del E. Webb High Altitude Training Chamber at Arizona State University Polytechnic at Mesa, run by hypoxia specialist Dr. Robert Garner.

Prepared for the goofy, loopy, playful effects of oxygen deprivation, I removed my mask when the hypobaric chamber reached the atmospheric equivalent of twenty-five thousand feet. I began carefully doing the simple math problems on the clipboard given to me and smugly noted that I was getting them right. Some of my classmates were also diligently writing, but others were looking around grinning. My fellow student Shih-Chieh Lu said the sensation was like that of being drunk. After about one minute, my breathing was labored. The head lolling started two minutes in.

"Hot," I said, more an exhalation than a statement, because it required a lot of effort just to push the microphone button to speak to the chamber operator. That was it. I passed out, and chamber attendant Dillon Fielitz got an oxygen mask on my uncooperative head. In another minute, the oxygen worked its magic and I was roused from my oblivion. I was unaware that I had lost consciousness and had no recollection that Fielitz had come to my aid.

"This high-altitude chamber training experience is quite helpful to the pilot," another cadet, Yuchuan Chen, told me in an e-mail later. "It will become a hazardous situation if pilots encounter the loss of pressurization without any correction." Silliness or unconsciousness, the symptoms can vary, but Yuchuan's impression is the hoped-for takeaway of altitude chamber training, Dr. Garner said.

Hypoxia was responsible for at least seven fatal aviation accidents since 1999, and many more near disasters. In 2008, both pilots on a Kalitta Flying Service Learjet became hypoxic at thirty-two thousand feet. The flight had just been handed over to Cleveland ATC (air traffic control) when the controller became concerned about the halting transmission of the pilot and the sound of an alarm in the background. In what seems like farcical overenunciation that makes a lot of sense to me now, the captain explained to the controller that he was "Unable . . . to . . . control altitude. Unable . . . to . . . control . . . airspeed. Unable . . . to . . . control heading." He added, "Other than that, everything . . . A-OK."

It must have taken extraordinary effort for the Kalitta pilot to pierce his mental fog enough to make the emergency call. Recognizing the problem, controllers cleared the Learjet to an immediate descent to eleven thousand feet. What made the pilot perceive and react to the instruction remains a mystery and a miracle, as it certainly saved lives. The plane flew lower, the crew revived, and the plane landed safely.

A similar scenario on Malaysia 370 doesn't explain everything, but it does explain a lot. Fariq would have known right away that he had a problem, even without the steady high/low electronic sound of the altitude warning horn. And at some point he must have remembered to put on his oxygen mask. It was stored in a chamber the size of a car glove compartment, below his armrest. He may have been slowed by his sluggish movements or confounded by the difficulty of squeezing the red tabs together with his thumb and middle finger so that the huge circle of rubber would expand enough to go over his head before he released the tabs to shrink it back to secure the regulator tightly over his nose and mouth. Thick clear plastic goggles covered his eyes, and a gasket should have created a seal.

So what happened? Why did it fail to revive him? Why didn't Captain Zaharie return to the cockpit? Everything was in chaos, the altitude warning alarm still clanging.

I find it logical to assume that Zaharie visited the business-class bathroom near the flight deck that is also used by the flight crew. In this and all the airline's 777s' bathrooms, a drop-down mask is there to provide oxygen in the case of depressurization. Imagine what it would have been like for Zaharie to see the yellow plastic cup bob down after the depressurization. He would have been momentary rattled, but with his experience, he would have realized immediately what had happened and what needed to be done.

Still, he had to make a choice: try to get back to the cockpit without supplemental oxygen, or remain in the bathroom and wait for Fariq to get the airplane to a lower altitude and then rejoin him on the flight deck. I'm guessing Zaharie wasn't confident in Fariq's ability to handle the emergency and chose the former course of action. But the effect of oxygen deprivation would have been crippling for Zaharie, too. Air would have been exploding from his respiratory and digestive systems. His extremities would have been shaking. He would have struggled to get out of the bathroom. Perhaps he looked for a flight attendant or a portable oxygen tank. Perhaps he stopped to assess the situation in the cabin. Perhaps he retained focus and moved quickly to the cockpit door.

The distance between the bathroom and the cockpit is just a few steps, but like Fariq, Zaharie was a smoker and probably more susceptible to the effects of oxygen deprivation. If he got out of the bathroom, if he got down the narrow corridor, if he got to the door of the cockpit without losing consciousness or cognitive function, another challenge would have awaited him.

The cockpit door unlocks automatically when cabin altitude is lost. Would Zaharie have remembered that? Or did he, by force of habit, stop outside the door and try to enter the code? Did he lose precious seconds struggling to remember a passcode he did not need? Or did he just grab the handle and open the door, but succumb to the lack of oxygen before getting into his seat? Pilots at Malaysia Airlines tell me that in a rapid decompression, it would have been very difficult for Captain Zaharie to get back onto the flight deck. All the previous cases of rapid depressurization on airliners, those that successfully landed and the few that crashed, bring home with chilling clarity that physical exertion eats away at the too-few seconds of useful consciousness.

The captain was unable to regain command of the airplane. If he had, things might have turned out very differently.

Incomprehensible

On the flight deck, Fariq was wearing his oxygen mask. He was getting enough oxygen to sustain some level of intelligent thought. *Why hasn't Captain Zaharie returned?* he must have thought. And he must have realized that he needed to get the plane back on the ground.

The control panel for the flight management system is located between the two pilot seats, above the throttles, where it is easily accessible to whichever pilot is programming it. The FMS has many functions, including allowing the crew to send text messages to the airline's operations desk. We know no messages were sent. Yet in an emergency, the FMS stores navigational information for the closest airports, so that in seconds the pilots can select a destination and head there.

From where the 777 was flying, between the Gulf of Thailand and the South China Sea, if Fariq turned the plane around, the divert airports would include Penang and Langkawi, according to pilots who fly in the region. These choices would have appeared on the screen in a list, waiting for the pilot to select one of them.

Who knows how much actual thinking Fariq was able to accomplish, but for some reason he selected Penang, Malaysia's third-busiest airport, with a ten-thousand-foot runway. The next choice appeared on the screen. DIVERT NOW? Fariq selected, EXECUTE.

The plane immediately began a slow, orchestrated turn, and by 1:30 it was headed south-southwest to Malaysia, once again.

The amount of time a person can remain conscious and thinking at high altitudes is called the time of useful consciousness. While that time varies depending on many factors, including health, age, and a genetic predisposition, the ballpark figure for how long Fariq had before he lost his ability to think clearly would be fifteen to thirty seconds. We know that Fariq, or whichever pilot was in the cockpit, maintained sufficient intellectual capacity to turn the airplane around and select a course toward Penang. Yet that these maneuvers were made without a radio call and after the transponder became inoperative leads me to conclude that the pilot handling the airplane was compromised to such an extent that while he could make simple decisions about the direction of the airplane, not much more sensible action could have been expected of him.

Fariq was breathing through a mask. The default position should have given him 100 percent oxygen, and at thirty-five thousand feet, positive pressure actually pushes the oxygen into the wearer's nose. I experienced this during my time at the ASU high-altitude training chamber. It felt like an air-conditioning vent was being pressed to my face.

When all is working well, the mask should rejuvenate. Fariq's vision would have been clear again and his thoughts solidified, except, judging from what happened next, he did not return to his senses. The primary indicator of that is that the plane did not start to descend.

Because of the seriousness of loss of pressurization in flight, the modern airliner has a belt-and-suspenders approach to the hazard. The oxygen mask is the belt, and emergency descent is the suspenders. They are equally important, two routes to the same destination: clearheadedness.

In his book *Of Flight and Life*, Charles Lindbergh tells of testing an unpressurized fighter plane at thirty-six thousand feet in 1943 when his oxygen supply abruptly stopped. "I know from altitude-chamber experience that I have about 15 seconds of consciousness left at this altitude—neither time nor clearness of mind to check hoses and connections. Life demands oxygen and the only sure supply lies four miles beneath me," he writes.

As he recounts in the book, Lindbergh sent the airplane into a dive, rocketing toward earth as he passed out. Not until he was at fifteen thousand feet did he come to and witness the clarity of "the cockpit, the plane, the earth and sky."

That was not Fariq's experience. The razor's edge was dull. His mask was providing him with enough oxygen to maintain some awareness, but he was not thinking clearly.

Any number of problems may have prevented Fariq from getting enough oxygen even while wearing his mask. Something wrong with the mask, the oxygen supply, or the connection between the two could explain why he might not have experienced what Lindbergh called "the flood of perception through nerve and tissue."

In the hours before MH-370 departed for Beijing, mechanics had serviced the two oxygen containers for the cockpit, topping them off and restoring the pressure to eighteen hundred pounds per square inch. After reinstalling the bottles, mechanics must reopen the valve fully, or the proper supply of air will not flow to the mask. "One or two times a year out of the hundreds of times oxygen bottles are changed at a major U.S. airline, a mechanic may fail to do this," according to a mechanic who agreed to discuss the issue if I did not identify him.

"It's a lapse in memory, and it's embarrassing," he told me. I was asking my contact about this because of a story I heard from a pilot who flies for a different U.S. carrier. The pilot was conducting his preflight check when he discovered there was little oxygen flowing to his mask. "I had the mechanic come to the cockpit," he told me—again, as long as I did not use his name—and it was then that they discovered the supply valve was barely open. "He was shocked; he was ashen," the captain said, describing the mechanic, who then got a little spooky. "You all would have died," the mechanic told him.

On many airliners, this important final action after servicing the oxygen is not left to a mechanic's memory. A message appears on a flight deck monitor notifying the pilots if the oxygen pressure drops between the tank and the mask. If the supply line between the tank and the mask is full, the indicator will show that the oxygen system is working properly, but it does not indicate if the valve is only partially open, which would reduce the oxygen available to the pilot in a depressurization event.

"To the pilot doing the preflight, it looks, because of the trapped air in the supply line, that the system it is fully pressurized, and if he looks at the monitor it will show the tank is fully charged," this pilot told me. If the crew needs oxygen during the flight, that restricted flow could cause a problem for the pilots. "Once that stored volume of oxygen in the supply line flows out, the pressure will drop within this line to some value that is insufficient. It won't supply full oxygen, so no matter how hard he breathes, he is not going to get enough oxygen."

There are other potential pitfalls. Leaks in the supply tubes or in the seal holding the mask on the face can diminish the supply to the pilot. While working for the NTSB, Dr. Mitch Garber said he would sometimes fly in the cockpit observer seat. On three occasions he discovered a problem with his oxygen mask. Once, the air-filled tubes that contract to hold the mask to the head were leaking. Another time, the inflation of the tubes was followed by a loud pop and no air flow. The one he remembers best is the time the mask worked fine in the box, but when he pulled it out of the holder, it fell apart. "That was the one that got me kicked off the plane, because there were no other masks," he said, adding, "These things sit in these boxes for a long time."

Another factor that could have kept Fariq from regaining full cognitive function was if the aneroid barometer in the regulator of his mask failed so that it did not correctly sense cabin altitude. Above thirty-five thousand feet, this small bellows-like device triggers the mask to provide not just a mix of pressurized air but 100 percent oxygen under pressure.

In a decompression at higher altitudes there is a delay between a pilot's first breath of supplemental oxygen and its arrival in the brain. James Stabile, an airline pilot and a longtime member of the industry committee overseeing standards for aircraft oxygen systems, asked me to imagine little boxcars loaded with oxygen, chugging first from the lungs, where oxygen will enter the bloodstream, then to the heart and then to the brain.

When the oxygen pressure drops suddenly, as in a rapid decompression, gas races out of the body, including out of the lungs. The time it takes for this oxygen shortage to reach the brain is about ten to twelve seconds. That's the time of useful consciousness at high altitudes. Pushing 100 percent oxygen into the lungs will enable the next several boxcars to resupply the brain, switching it back on, and "quite often the individual will not even be aware of this cognitive lapse," Stabile said.

The difference between what happened on Helios Flight 522 and the private jet carrying Payne Stewart and what I believe occurred on 9M-MRO (the plane that was Malaysia Flight 370) is that when it departed Kuala Lumpur, the cabin was pressurized. Had it not been, the pilots' exchange with air traffic control at 1:19 a.m. would have indicated that something was amiss. The problem would also have been transmitted via the 1:07 a.m. normal ACARS status report. What happened on Flight 370 happened suddenly.

Because pilots succumb to hypoxia so quickly at cruise altitude, some government aviation regulators require that if one pilot leaves the cockpit, the crew member remaining wear the emergency oxygen mask. And while the intent is good, the execution is inconsistent. Crews frequently ignore the rule. One pilot told me he had not put on his oxygen mask in five years; nor had he been asked to by a fellow pilot vacating the cockpit. "It is incredibly cumbersome," he told me.

John Gadzinski, a pilot with a U.S. airline and a private safety consultant, told me why so few pilots comply. "You have to take off your headset and put it back on and maybe even take your glasses off. You then have to speak through the microphone in the mask and reset the communications when you stow the mask again," he told me. "Pilots are human, and ninety-nine-point-nine percent of the time, nothing bad ever happens on a flight."

So I think that when Zaharie left the cockpit, leaving Fariq at the controls, the young first officer did not put on his mask. Neither pilot anticipated the number of things that could have gone wrong, from the banal to the bizarre. Here are a few:

In 2011 a rupture in the roof of a Southwest Airlines Boeing 737 at thirty-four thousand feet caused a rapid loss of pressure on a flight in Arizona. Passenger masks dropped, but one flight attendant who was trying to use the public address system before putting on his mask lost consciousness, as did the passenger who tried to help him. The pilots made an emergency descent and landed without further problems.

Faulty door seals and breaks in the structure of an airplane have been known to cause decompressions. In one case, a passenger oxygen bottle exploded on a Qantas Boeing 747 in 2008. The bottle shot through the side of the airplane like a small missile, leaving a hole large enough to cause a rapid decompression. No one was injured.

Sometimes, however, decompressions do turn deadly. In one horrific case in 1988, an eighteen-foot section of an Aloha Airlines 737 tore off on a flight to Honolulu, sucking a flight attendant out of the airplane.

British Airways Flight 5390 is another macabre story. This was an early morning trip from Birmingham, England, to Málaga, Spain, on a sunny day in June 1990. As the BAC-111 jet with eighty-one people on board passed through seventeen thousand feet, the cockpit windshield blew out. Capt. Tim Lancaster was partially sucked out of the hole, but his legs got tangled in the flight controls.

Flight steward Nigel Ogden had just turned to leave the flight deck, after checking to see if the pilots wanted tea, when he heard the blast. He thought a bomb had gone off. When he turned around, he saw the captain's legs.

"I jumped over the control column and grabbed him round his waist to avoid him going out completely," Ogden wrote in a first-person account for a local newspaper.

In his unexpected exit through the cockpit window, Lancaster had kicked off the autopilot. While another flight attendant raced in to help keep the captain from disappearing, First Officer Alistair Atcheson regained control of the airplane, and then prepared for an emergency landing, which he accomplished just eighteen minutes later. Captain Lancaster survived, and returned to flying. An examination of the airplane showed that while replacing the windshield days earlier, a mechanic had used screws slightly shorter than those required, so the new window was not effectively secured.

So you can see that in the case of Malaysia 370, a loss of pressurization mishandled by the pilot is neither farfetched nor unprecedented. It fits the facts we know.

By 1:52 a.m., Fariq had taken the plane back across Malaysia and to Penang. Here he made yet another decision explicable only by a hypoxia-induced, half-witted state. He turned the plane north. Perhaps he had the intention of landing at Langkawi International Airport, where he'd learned to fly. Surely the airfield was as familiar to him as his own driveway, and the runway was nearly two thousand feet longer than that at Penang. He would be coming in heavy, with much of the fuel loaded on the plane in Kuala Lumpur still in the tanks. If Fariq did any mental processing at all, he may have concluded the more runway, the better, and Langkawi had a lot of it. Yet I think he was no longer doing much reasoning, because his ability to do that was long gone. Turning to the northwest, 9M-MRO continued to fly. There was no effort to descend or to begin an approach to the airport. Fariq had been flying for thirty-two minutes since the occurrence of whatever had caused the flight to go amiss. Still at cruise altitude, the plane passed over VAMPI—one of the many navigational waypoints in the sky, all of which have five letter names. Then the plane flew north of the next one, MEKAR, disappearing for good somewhere at the northernmost part of Sumatra.

Intermittent Power

Fariq's mental incapacitation explains a series of perplexing events that began with a sudden and unknown catastrophic occurrence. Some have theorized it was related to the load of lithium-ion batteries the plane was carrying. That's an iffy theory to me, for two reasons. First, a lithium-ion battery fire is a frightening thing, which you will read about later in this book. I have little doubt that in such an alarming circumstance, the pilots would have understood the need to get the airplane on the ground quickly. Moreover, had there been a fire, it is unlikely it would have disabled the crew without causing significant damage to the structure of the airplane, and we know the plane continued to fly with notable efficiency for many more hours after the initial problem.

Whatever happened to Flight 370 probably caused both the depressurization and an encompassing failure in the airplane's electrical system. It is not knowable if Fariq accidentally turned off the transponder or if it failed on its own. The same is true for the loss of the ACARS reporting system: did it fail or was it intentionally switched off for some reason? Yet an even more intriguing clue is the loss of regular transmissions from the plane to the satellite sometime between 1:07 a.m. and 1:37 a.m., with the return of the signal at 2:25 a.m. Even those paying attention to the Flight 370 story have heard little about this peculiar lapse.

During the ongoing news coverage, people learned that airliners regularly transmit a status message: a "ping" or "handshake" in the same way a mobile phone that is powered on sends out signals to nearby cell towers even when it is not being used to make a call. A phone would stop doing this only if it were turned off or in aircraft mode.

This is the analogy used by the engineers at Inmarsat to explain what happened on MH-370 at the same time that so many other inexplicable events were occurring. The airplane's signal to the satellite stopped, and returned only when the airplane logged back on at 2:25, as if powering on at the beginning of a flight.

There are only a few ways this can be explained: there was a power failure on the airplane, the software failed, or something interfered with the connection between the antenna and the satellite, such as the plane flying upside down so that the fuselage was between the antenna and the satellite. All three possibilities are extremely remote. Some clues, however, have not been pursued.

One week into 2008, a Qantas Boeing 747 was on approach to Bangkok from London with 365 people on board. It was a clear and sunny afternoon—which was fortunate because as Qantas Flight 2 passed through ten thousand feet, it lost electrical power. The autothrottle, autopilot, weather radar, and many other systems, including the automatic control for the pressurization system, simply stopped. Only the captain's flight display worked, albeit in "degraded mode." The plane landed safely, but once it was on the ground, its doors could not be opened because the outflow valves failed to automatically release the cabin pressure.

On the Boeing 747 and other Boeing jetliners, including the 777 and the 767, there is a galley located above the electronics and equipment room, called the E&E bay. On Qantas Flight 2, a flood from the galley above caused water to flow into this area. This was not a one-time event. During its investigation, the Australian Transport Safety Bureau discovered that electronics equipment in the bay had been "repeatedly subjected" to liquid beyond what it was designed to handle. When the ATSB set out to find similar events, it turned up five on large jetliners, four on Boeings, and one on an Airbus A300—and those were just the ones serious enough to have caused a safety event in flight.

I've learned that on airplanes with galleys located above electrical equipment, mechanics often see leaking.

"The 777 has an avionics bay below the first-class galley. When a crew reports water, it is required by the manual to inspect the avionics bay for leaks from water penetration," I was told by a mechanic for a major American airline—I'll call this mechanic Fred because he does not want me to use his real name. A few days after Fred told me this, he sent a video in which I could clearly see water dripping onto the floor of a cramped and noisy equipment room.

"Where did you get this?" I asked, thinking Fred had found the footage on a YouTube-like service for aircraft mechanics. But no, he'd shot the video himself, on a Boeing 767 that came under the care of his wrench shortly after our initial conversation about Qantas Flight 2.

I started to think that maybe some water-induced intermittent electrical problem could have produced the various failures on Malaysia 370, including the puzzling power down and subsequent restoration of communication at 2:25 a.m. that no one has yet been able to explain.

So I asked the ATSB, when Flight 2 lost most of its power on January 7, 2008, did it cause a termination in the link to the satellite? Could this issue with water damaging the electronics affect satellite communication? The ATSB did not know.

"I am unable to provide you with a definitive answer as we would need to establish a detailed understanding of the load-sharing arrangements on the aircraft, interaction with AC BUS 4, not to mention the electrical system that supports the SAT-COM," Julian Walsh, the acting chief commissioner, replied in an e-mail. "This was not an aspect of the original investigation," he told me.

I do not know if it is part of the Malaysian investigation into what happened to the plane, which had the registration ID 9M-MRO, because the team doing that investigation does not answer questions.

Once Malaysia 370's last radar echo faded—the one showing it somewhere at the northern tip of Sumatra—Fariq made a final turn. No data suggest when, but the plane turned south and flew on for five hours more until it ran out of fuel. This final turn is the point where I believe Fariq's deprived brain reached its limit. Like Number 14 fixed on the four of spades, Fariq was locked onto some thought. I asked airline captain Pete Frey to try to explain Fariq's last action. I wasn't intending to insult Pete, a longtime friend, by suggesting he might know what it is like to be without cogent thought, and thankfully, Pete didn't take it that way.

"Who knows what he's doing? *He doesn't know what he's doing*," Frey said after considering my question. "He's lost sense of time, so now he thinks he's back there. Maybe he's thinking, 'I've got to head north, and where am I? I'll go this way.' By the time he realizes he's lost, he says, 'Now I'll turn around and go back, but I don't know where I'm going back to, so I'll just head south. I'm too far north.'"

When you consider how muddled Fariq's mind must have been, you can see many ways in which MH-370's bizarre flight path can be explained.

"All you really have to say is at this point," Frey told me, "he's struggling with intermittent abilities, and it's not enough."

Center of Confusion

Commercial aviation is both more and less advanced than people think. The pilot's preflight programming can enable the machine to take off, fly, and land, though any pilot will tell you there's a lot more to the job than just getting the airplane into the sky and back down again (as you will see in part 5 of this book).

"If we have it set up for where the plane is going to fly the flight plan, we could go to first class and have a meal, and it would do those things," said James Blaszczak, now retired, who flew the Boeing 777 for eight years for United before going on to fly the 787 Dreamliner. Yes, that's pretty impressive. Yet at any hour around the world, hundreds of planes are flying isolated in the sky, communicating only sporadically with the ground. In this respect, MH-370 is more like the *Hawaii Clipper.*

The 1930s-era, four-engine Martin 130 flying boat was robust and comfortable enough that up to thirty-two passengers, seated in bamboo and rattan chairs in the lounge, could be served hot meals prepared in the galley by uniformed and gloved stewards. After dining, they could retire to berths made up with blankets and pillows.

A nine-man flight-deck crew was responsible for operating the flight that would get travelers from California across the Pacific to Manila, a five-day journey with overnight stays in island hotels built and operated by the airline.

The crew consisted of a captain, four copilots, a flight engineer, a radio operator, a navigator, and a pilot studying basic navigation from him. Navigation was by celestial observation combined with a calculation of elapsed speed and time, the dead reckoning Pete Frey explained earlier. The navigator could get an assist by using a direction-finding system, antennas that locked onto broadcast radio stations.

"We would tune in certain stations we knew we could use. In those days, one of our favorite things were the high-powered commercial stations along the California coast," said Ed Dover, a radio operator with Pan Am from 1942 until 1948, who later spent thirty-three years as an air traffic controller. "KGO broadcast such a strong signal we could hear them out to sea."

Using an antenna shaped like a figure eight, radio operators like Dover could note the areas of strongest and weakest signal and use that information to determine the direction of the station. "You could draw a line on the map. We knew where the station was; on land, the transmitter was on the map, so we could match the direction in terms of compass direction and say, 'Okay, down that way, that's where we are in relation to where the station was.'" You have to love the term used when navigators and radio operators shared their information to ratify their calculation of position: they called it the center of confusion.

If that kind of direction finding seems like something from the Stone Age, communication technology wasn't much better. The weekly Pan Am transpacific flight from San Francisco to Manila left California on a Wednesday in coordination with two ships leaving on Monday, one from San Francisco, the other from Honolulu. The ships would be midway through their cruises when the Pan Am Clipper passed overhead, giving the airliner a navigational fix and, as significantly, a degree of comfort that someone—even someone eight thousand feet below, in a dark ocean—knew where the airliner was.

Still, darned if those big airships didn't land right where they should have, without a single computer assist.

It is easy to be dismissive of the early rudimentary systems when air travel began. But that a twenty-six-ton flying boat could take off from San Francisco and arrive in Honolulu eighteen hours later was nothing short of a miracle. It was state of the art, as they say.

So people were shocked to learn, four generations later, that with all their fancy navigation and communications equipment, many airlines were still in the dark when it came to knowing exactly where their airliners were when crossing the oceans. As with the Pan Am Clippers, the challenge for overwater flights remains that airplanes are outside the range of land-based radar. If they are going to communicate their position, it will have to be via satellite, which is expensive. As Daniel Baker, the founder and CEO of FlightAware.com explained, the "center of confusion" has given way to the "cone of ambiguity."

An airline sending a position report via satellite every fifteen minutes can cover one hundred fifty miles before sending the next position report, Baker said. Should the location be more precise?

"Satellites don't know where the airplane is. The airplane sends the signal, and that requires the airplane be pointed in the right direction, that is, belly down. If there is an upset on board—a loss of control, the plane is headed straight down or upside down—it can't get a satellite signal, because it is pointed in the wrong direction," he said, adding, "That's a big challenge." And just in case you are thinking, as I did, that he was talking about really unlikely possibilities, he ticked off a few disasters to illustrate his point: EgyptAir Flight 990 and Air France 447. "We are at the limits of technology," he said.

Acausal Connections

Seventy-six years separate the *Hawaii Clipper* and Malaysia Flight 370, and yet we see striking similarities. Both airliners were modern and spacious, and the pilots in command were highly trained and experienced. Upon closer look, however, we see that maybe all wasn't as it seemed. Was Leo Terletsky, forty-three, "one of the most distinguished flight commanders,"* as Pan Am claimed—or was he afraid of flying and so volatile that most pilots were unwilling to work with him, as Horace Brock wrote?

Pilots who flew with Zaharie Ahmad Shah, captain of Malaysia 370, said he was a passionate aviator and a mentor to younger pilots. "A gem of a guy, a real professional, enjoying the best time of his life," one of them told me. Yet a few journalists—quoting unidentified sources, mind you—painted a picture of a political fanatic.

Pan Am's Martin 130 flying boat was a marvel of aviation;

---

* *Airways*, Pan Am employee magazine, no. 5 (July–August 1938).

custom-built to help the airline span the oceans, but the company's chief pilot in the thirties complained that it was "unstable on every axis and a pig to fly."* While the Boeing 777 airliner is widely used and considered by pilots to be pleasurable and reliable, the list of things that could have contributed to the 2014 disaster exposes unappreciated hazards on the airplane.

If the Pan Am Clipper experienced something catastrophic, the area where it could have gone down is relatively small. If it was hijacked, though, the search zone becomes enormous, because the amount of fuel on board allowed the plane another eleven hours of flight. With Malaysia 370, the plane's satellite indicated the Boeing 777 flew for five hours and fifty-four minutes after mysteriously powering up at 2:25, so predictions about where it ultimately came down could be no more precise than an area from sixty thousand to six hundred thousand square miles.

On a stormy night above the Atlantic Ocean on June 1, 2009, an Air France Airbus A330 with 228 people on board disappeared on a flight from Rio de Janeiro to Paris. Though the plane was five hundred miles outside radar coverage, investigators had a last-known position based on an ACARS message transmitted via satellite. The plane must have entered the water within forty miles of that. Even so, it took five days for the first bodies and floating debris to be discovered, and two years to locate the plane.

Some of the credit for finally finding the submerged airliner goes to Metron Scientific Solutions, a company staffed with pencil-wielding mathematicians who used probability, logic, and numbers to conclude that the likely resting place of the plane was a narrow slice of ocean that had already been checked.

---

* *Flying the Oceans*, by Horace Brock.

"A lack of success tells you about where it is not, and that contributes to knowledge," said Larry Stone, chief scientist at Metron. Talk about having a positive point of view. The Metron method is based on Bayesian probability, the theory of eighteenth-century statistician and philosopher Thomas Bayes, whose first published work, *Divine Benevolence*, was equally optimistic because it attempted to prove that God wants us to be happy.

Using Bayesian logic to look for missing airplanes, as interpreted by Metron, involves taking all kinds of input about the missing thing (even conflicting input) and assigning levels of certainty or uncertainty to each. Everything gets a weight, and everything gets revised as things change. New information, as Stone so cheerily described it to me, is often negative.

In the search for Air France 447, scientists, mathematicians, and underwater technologists were involved in a very difficult bit of detective work. They covered a surface area of eighteen thousand square miles and a debris field nearly three miles deep. Two search seasons after they started, the wreckage of the Airbus was found on the edge of a plain not too far from the beginning of a steep and rugged underwater mountain range.

Many smart people contributed to the search but Olivier Ferrante, then the investigator in charge of the Air France 447 probe for France's Bureau d'Enquêtes et d'Analyses, said they benefited from an additional, highly uncertain element: luck. "The fact that the airplane was on flat terrain" was important to seeing the debris on the sonar pictures, Ferrante told me. "We saw man-made debris, and we identified it in the picture. That was luck. If it had been a couple of kilometers to the east or north, or close to the cliff, we wouldn't have seen it."

I bring up the Air France search in this context because it is the event most like Malaysia 370 in terms of how the newest technological developments are being pushed to do even more within the cone of ambiguity, defined earlier by FlightAware's Daniel Baker as the number of miles a plane can travel between satellite position reports.

While the ACARS messages helped to narrow the area where the Air France 447 airliner might be located, the difficulty in getting a more precise location prompted the satellite company Inmarsat to beef up some of its network by adding new data to the communication transmission. Two additional tidbits of information enable calculations of a plane's location based on how long it takes a message transmitted from the plane to arrive at its destination.

"Inmarsat did modify its systems to add the so-called timing and frequency information to the handshake messages," Ruy Pinto, an engineer and the chief operating officer at Inmarsat, told me at the company's futuristic high-rise headquarters in London. This newly added information would become useful the weekend Malaysia 370 went missing. First, it showed that the plane had not crashed right away, but had flown for hours. Later, the timing and frequency data allowed the company to determine that the plane flew south into the Indian Ocean.

"If MH-370 had occurred at the time of the Air France disaster it would not have been possible to make the analysis that we ended up doing," Pinto told me.

What's missing with Malaysia 370 is even the basic information used by the French, because in the case of MH-370, no ACARS messages were sent after 1:07 a.m. This meant the search area would be massive.

It would be nearly a year and a half before the first debris from Malaysia 370 was found on a beach on Réunion Island, off the coast of East Africa. By then, the wing section had traveled too far and arrived too late to provide any clue as to where the airplane landed in the water. At its smallest, the search area is three times larger than the one in which Air France 447 was found.

Still, the discovery of the wing flap was useful in one way: it shut down the theory that once it disappeared from radar, the plane had turned north, toward Asia and the Caucasus Mountains. One of the more popular proponents of that line of thinking was Jeff Wise, a CNN talking head who wrote a book, *The Plane That Wasn't There*, describing an elaborate plot that required dismissing some of the data from Inmarsat.

"All the inexplicable coincidences and mismatched data went away," Wise wrote about his alternative scenario, getting a big spread in *New York* magazine. "The answer became wonderfully simple."

He was not the only person who thought the plane was hiding in a remote part of the world. Thomas McInerney, a retired lieutenant general and military analyst for Fox News, told the network's morning news program in 2015 that the plane could be in the "the Stans," referring to the countries whose names include the suffix -*stan*. "That airplane can fly nonstop from the Stans to the United States, New York, or Washington, DC. It could be a future trigger for events against the country."

I'll leave that kind of worrying for Fox News watchers. I'm more concerned with a disturbing discovery made while working on this book: for all the apparent effort to try to solve the mystery of MH-370, authorities may not be as committed to finding out what went wrong. That also would not be unprecedented.

Cover-Up

Air crashes have the potential to reveal government secrets and failures, company malfeasance, or all the above. This is even more pronounced if the airline is owned by the government, as is the case in Malaysia and many other countries.

In the case of Malaysia 370, the airline seems to have had a most embarrassing secret to keep: that before the plane flew off into oblivion, the company already knew it was unable to track its airplanes as frequently as required. After the plane went missing at the end of March 2014, twenty-six countries were donating personnel, aircraft, and ships to look for the jet. What would they say if they knew that a year earlier, Malaysia Airline executives had been warned about just this kind of problem? In fact, they had.

In April 2013, and again in June, several company auditors looking at the flight operations discovered a number of problems with the airline's compliance with government and international aviation standards. Most significant was that on

Malaysia's wide-body, long-haul Boeing 747s* and 777s, which would include the plane flying as MH-370, flights could be tracked only every half hour, even though the airline was required to know on a more frequent basis the whereabouts of each plane.

In a presentation to the executives in August, the auditors from Quality Assurance and Regulatory Affairs said that flight following and flight watching could "not be achieved . . . at intervals stated" in the flight dispatch manual. According to the auditors, by law the planes should not have been dispatched.

In a warning that was prescient, the auditors reminded executives that airlines were required to actively watch and track their airplanes "throughout all phases of the flight to ensure that the flight is following its prescribed route, without unplanned deviation, diversion or delay," in order to satisfy government regulations.

So while the rest of the world was shocked that a plane carrying 239 people could just vanish, it could not have been totally surprising to those within the airline's flight operations office, who had been warned seven months earlier.

In the chaotic months that followed MH-370's disappearing act, information about these audits was presented to Hishammuddin Hussein, who was the acting transport minister at the time, by airline employees who were concerned about the implications for future flights. When I was given the audit documents, which are marked "Confidential," I was told it was because Hussein and others in government, even after being told about the issue, had failed to respond.

Malaysia Airlines and the Department of Civil Aviation also

---

* Malaysia Airlines no longer flies the Boeing 747.

failed to reply to my inquiries about the audits, despite repeated requests.

Certainly, an investigation means the arrival of countless busybodies just like me asking all sorts of questions about what would not necessarily be public information absent an accident.

Another example is the five hundred pounds of lithium-ion batteries that were packed onto the Malaysia flight. There is much interest in whether this highly flammable cargo might have contributed to the crash. The pallets of Motorola walkie-talkie batteries were not declared hazardous because the Malaysians said they had complied with international guidelines for the safe transport of dangerous goods. But had they? And what about the curiously large amount of mangosteens also in transit to China? Some five tons of this tropical fruit were loaded into the hold. No matter how scrumptious they are or how large the appetite for them in China, they are a notably large item on the cargo manifest, because mangosteens were at the tail end of the small and secondary fruiting season in Malaysia, which runs from November to February.

If the plane hadn't gone missing, the contents and veracity of the airline's cargo manifest, and even the airline's failure to meet standards for knowing where its planes are during flight, would have remained the airline's business. Now the world is demanding answers.

How much attention could the airline and the government have been paying if they failed to notice a Boeing 777 flying off course over the country's most populated cities? For all anybody knew, the plane might have been on its way to fly, 9/11-like, into the pride of Kuala Lumpur, the Petronas Towers. Then there is the embarrassing revelation that after MH-370 stopped communicating, it took five hours for controllers to raise an alarm and begin a search for the plane.

Global attention paid to these questions did not bring out the best in Malaysia's leaders, who were alternately confused and combative, and mostly nonresponsive to questions about their investigation. At the time, all information was provided by Hishammuddin Hussein, who had the most reason not to be forthcoming. When the jetliner disappeared, Hussein was not only the acting minister of transportation but also minister of defense. The performance of both departments on March 8 could be kindly described as deficient or, less kindly (if more accurately), derelict. When it came to hyperbole, however, the minister was a master. At one point he described the search as "the most difficult in human history." So one has to wonder if the daily press conferences, conducted in three languages but delivering little new information, were intended to obfuscate, or whether that was just an unintended side benefit.

A lack of transparency leads to one thing: "You're going to have conjecture," explained Jesse Walker, an editor at *Reason* magazine and the author of the 2014 book *The United States of Paranoia: A Conspiracy Theory.* "When you have a blank slate to play with, people will fill in the blanks with stories that interest and excite and feel plausible to them—even apart from the evidence, because this is the way they expect the world to work," he said. "They draw on the narratives they know and find appealing."

After studying a number of accidents with intransigent conspiracy theories attached, I've come to the conclusion that there can be no better tactic for an investigator with something to hide than to encourage those theories. The story doesn't have to be convincing; it need only gain a toehold, after which the public does the rest.

When McInerney, the Fox News commentator, worried about the "Stans" on the one-year anniversary of the loss of MH-370, the ATSB had long ago discounted the Reuters report that the plane had engaged in a series of altitude climbs and descents in an attempt to hide from radar. The length of the plane's flight indicated that it had operated at maximum fuel efficiency. That simply doesn't allow for those kinds of gas-guzzling up-and-down maneuvers, or it would have run out of fuel earlier. Yet there was McInerney, with the credibility of a military general, describing the pilot's intentional acts to the network's 1.6 million viewers.

"He makes his turn at the checkpoint, and all of a sudden he climbs to forty-five thousand feet, which means he's depressurizing the airplane, then he goes down to twenty-three thousand feet and then back to thirty-five [thousand] again," McInerney said, while a simulation of the flight he was describing was shown on the split screen. "He eliminated the people in the back to be a threat," he said, by which I assume he meant to tell his audience that the pilot planned to kill the passengers by depressurizing the airplane. "And now," McInerney continued, "all of a sudden the airplane disappears."

Jesse Walker describes fill-in-the-blanks conjecture as the inevitable result of an information vacuum. The airplane's roller-coaster flight is one example. I'm not suggesting that creating stories was a premeditated effort by Malaysia, but the effect, intended or not, was to create uncertainty about the facts that lingers to this day.

The first major accident I wrote about was the crash of TWA Flight 800 in 1996, which I covered as a correspondent for CNN. My book *Deadly Departure* dealt largely with what caused the plane to explode while climbing out of New York airspace on a flight to Paris. One could not write about TWA 800 without getting into alternative theories, including that it had been shot down by the U.S. Navy or by an Iranian submarine.

On the seventeenth anniversary of the crash, an online television network released a documentary that would, the advertising promo claimed, "blow the lid off an alleged multi-agency cover-up of what really happened." According to the ninety-minute program, objects fired at the plane caused it to blow up, though what, how, and why were not explained. The point of the film was to suggest that two hundred thirty people were murdered and the National Transportation Safety Board and the Federal Bureau of Investigation hid the truth from the public.

The documentary was part of a salvo that included a petition that the NTSB reconsider its probable cause report on the disaster. The safety board had spent four years and twenty million dollars investigating. It had consulted thousands of people from academic, commercial, and research organizations and concluded that the 747's design had allowed the vapors in the plane's center fuel tank to get so hot that the tank could explode. This hazard existed on many airliners during normal flights. From the tests performed by the safety board at a lab at the California Institute of Technology, the NTSB determined that the amount of time a jetliner fuel tank could be in this volatile state, just a spark away from going *kaboom*, was about one-third its operational time.

While the NTSB never determined exactly what set off the blast on TWA 800, the realization that airliners were at considerable risk prompted the Department of Transportation to order changes.

The NTSB denied the request to reopen the TWA Flight

800 investigation, but all the news hype had served its purpose, driving traffic to the online channel where the documentary* was posted.

Deadly Departure was published years before the documentary was produced, and suggested a different kind of cover-up, the cover-up of a design flaw you will read about later in this book and one that is now recognized in the industry. But if you ask people what they remember about TWA 800, most will say something about a missile shooting it down.

---

* Spencer Rumsey, "TWA Flight 800 Exposé Takes Off at Stony Brook Film Festival," *Long Island Press*, July 8, 2013, http://www.longisland press.com/2013/07/08/twa-flight-800-expose-takes-off-at-stony-brook-film-festival/.

Lost at Sea

Theories about what happened to the *Hawaii Clipper* and Malaysia 370 have another element in common: provincialism. Malaysia's largely Muslim population caused some nervousness in the West that the loss of MH-370 might be the work of Islamic extremists. In 1938, when the *Hawaii Clipper* disappeared, the Japanese were suspected of having played a role.

Between World Wars I and II, the Pacific Ocean was a zone of geopolitical intrigue. America was eager to strengthen its presence in the Pacific, but was prevented by the 1922 Washington Naval Treaty from any military buildup on the islands west of Hawaii. So when Pan American Airways applied to the U.S. government to develop facilities for civilian seaplane service on Midway, Wake, Guam, and the Philippines, the airline's and the military's interests were aligned. Pan Am would build bases complete with radio stations, power plants, fuel supplies, maintenance operations, and housing, so it could have stopover points for its transpacific flights. After the treaty restrictions expired in 1936, the military could take advantage of that infrastructure.

America was also eager for land-based airfields in the region, a project of aviation pioneer Gene Vidal, director of America's Bureau of Air Commerce. Vidal had already participated in the creation of three airlines—Eastern, Trans World, and Northeast—and he thought that flying boats had a limited future. In 1935 he oversaw the colonization of three small islands that could provide southern Pacific air access to Australia, New Zealand, and Singapore, and he arranged federal funding for an airfield to be built on one of them, Howland Island.

The first use of this airfield would be to provide a refueling stop for the upcoming around-the-world journey of Amelia Earhart. The much-anticipated flight provided perfect justification for building a runway with fuel and service support in an area where Japan had a strong presence.

Combine the star power of Angelina Jolie with the ceaseless trending of the Kardashians to get an idea of the level of celebrity adoration Earhart enjoyed during the 1930s. She was a woman in what was perhaps the first extreme sport of the industrial age.

Sure, within the small world of early aviators, there was grumbling about her flying skills, her occasional errors in judgment, and her pushing on when waiting might have been wiser. She also never became fluent with the radio, which was critical because it was more than a form of communication; it was a source for determining direction. Still, these are ordinary shortcomings. Amelia Earhart made history because of her extraordinary strengths, tenacity and fearlessness among them. And she married a man willing to do more than support her unconventional career. George Putnam was Mr. Amelia Earhart, devoted to promoting the First Lady of Flight.

Earhart was the first woman to fly across the Atlantic Ocean and the first pilot to cross the Pacific solo from Honolulu to the U.S. mainland. While she was not the first woman pilot, she was the one who most famously used her career in the sky to promote women's equality on the ground.

Always pushing to accomplish one more feat, Earhart set out from Miami on June 1, 1937, to circle the globe at the equator. It was an undertaking punctuated with problems, one of which was that her navigator, Fred Noonan, had a drinking problem. Well into the endeavor and one week before crossing the Pacific, the most difficult part, she complained about Noonan's drinking to her husband. In his book, *Amelia Earhart: The Final Story*, author Vincent Loomis said Earhart told Putnam on June 26 that Noonan was "hitting the bottle again, and I don't even know where he's getting it!"

Noonan had been Pan Am's chief Pacific navigator, a licensed pilot and a master mariner, charting and mapping the routes pilots would use to Asia. He navigated the *Hawaii Clipper* on its first flight with fare-paying passengers. So his drinking must have been pronounced for it to have cost him his job at Pan Am, which several accounts claim it did. Yet his leaving Pan Am made him available for Earhart's round-the-world flight.

Noonan's direction-finding skill was top-notch. It would need to be, because the last portion of the exhausting trip would be the 7,000-mile transpacific flight to Vidal's new airstrip on Howland Island, one by two miles in size. From Lae, New Guinea, it was a 2,556-mile, eighteen-hour journey.

After two days preparing the plane and waiting for suitable weather, Earhart and Noonan took off from the jungle runway at Lae at 10:00 a.m. on July 2. In her diary of the trip, published posthumously as *Last Flight*, Earhart wrote that she was still hoping to arrive in California in time for the Fourth of July.

Earhart and Noonan flew through the day and into the night, crossing the international dateline and passing a ship that confirmed to radio operators on the ground that the plane was right on course.

At 2:45 a.m., the radio operator on the U.S. Coast Guard cutter *Itasca*, which was waiting by the island to guide Earhart's Lockheed Electra to land, began receiving radio messages. By 7:42 a.m., which was close to Earhart's estimated arrival time, the messages were getting disturbing. *We must be on you but cannot see you. But gas is running low. Been unable to reach you by radio. We are flying at altitude one thousand feet.* The next was also troubling: *We are circling but cannot hear you.*

Earhart and Noonan never found Howland Island. Their last message was sent at 8:44 a.m.

By circumnavigating the equator west to east, Earhart knew she had left the most difficult part of the trip for last. "Howland is such a small spot that every aid to locating it must be available," she wrote. She would be "glad when we have the hazards of its navigation behind us."

Earhart was not expressing just her own concerns. During the planning stages, others advised that her plan was not workable. Navigator, explorer, and Harvard professor Brad Washburn spent an evening reviewing details with Earhart. He worried about her trying to find Howland without radio signals to home in on. Mark Walker, the Pan Am first officer who would go missing on the *Hawaii Clipper* one year later, said the challenge was insurmountable. In a letter to *Shipmate*, the alumni magazine of the U.S. Naval Academy, Walker's cousin Robert Greenwood wrote that early in 1937, Walker was assigned by Pan Am to help Earhart and Noonan in planning the Pacific phase of the trip. Greenwood said his cousin urged Earhart not to risk "such a foolhardy publicity stunt," and that "her equipment was barely adequate."

In addition to his concern that Earhart was ill-equipped, Walker was especially troubled about Japanese kidnappers and hijackers. Okay, maybe he was a worrywart. He told his younger sister, Mary Ann Walker, that his role in protecting newsreel footage taken of a Japanese air attack on the U.S. gunboat *Panay* in 1937 had resulted in personal threats from the Japanese. Even so, he was not the only person to imagine a sinister turn of events when Earhart failed to arrive at Howland Island.

Earhart and Noonan had personal histories that, from a skeptic's point of view, suggest that they could have been carrying out a secret agenda during the flight. Charles Hill, author of *Fix on the Rising Sun*, proposes that Earhart defected to Japan, delivering Noonan, his valuable navigational skills, and insider knowledge of Pan Am's Pacific air routes as a gift to the Japanese. Other theories suggest the opposite: that Earhart was an American spy, having accepted a mission to fly over the Japanese islands in the Pacific to photograph them and assess troop buildup.

Regardless of how preposterous the theories, they demonstrate that people were already on edge and prepared to believe practically anything when the Pan Am *Hawaii Clipper* vanished in the Pacific just as Earhart had less than a year earlier. Beyond the basic facts of the flight (the who, the when, and the where), there was little information about what happened to the flying boat, and that fueled speculation.

Horace Brock was in Manila awaiting the arrival of the *Hawaii Clipper*. As he tells the story in his autobiography,

Flying the Oceans, when he heard that the plane was overdue and probably down, he took a cab to the U.S. Army air base at Clark Field. He barged into the commander's office, wanting to know why military planes weren't being sent to search for the missing Clipper. The commander was apologetic but firm, according to Brock. "Son, my men have families, too, wives and children. They have no navigation experience. I doubt if any one of them could find his way back." Flying over vast amounts of ocean in the decades before GPS was not for the fainthearted.

As far as Brock was concerned, a combination of bad weather and Captain Terletsky's lack of the right stuff was to blame for the tragedy. All over Manila, however, Pan Am crews were accosted by people insisting that the Japanese had taken the plane.

The search for the Clipper was still under way on August 4, 1938, when the Hearst International News Service reported a blockbuster story. FBI agents had been undercover at the Pan Am Alameda base since January in an attempt to "thwart any sabotage" at the company and "protect the nation's most ambitious private air route." A memo to FBI director J. Edgar Hoover dated February 5, and obtained through a Freedom of Information Act request by Clipper researcher and documentary filmmaker Guy Noffsinger in his ongoing effort to find out what happened, confirms that seven months before the *Hawaii Clipper* went missing, the bureau was investigating the possibility of vandalism of Pan American Airways flying boats. After the loss of the Martin 130, the acting secretary of commerce sent a letter to Hoover thanking him for information "relative to possible sabotage in connection with Pan American Airlines [*sic*] ships." Through it all, Pan Am was circumspect; "all lines of merit" were being investigated, the company told the Hearst reporter.

The elaborate theories about the *Hawaii Clipper* didn't get fleshed out for many years, and when they did, it was almost by accident. In 1964 an Earhart searcher named Joseph Gervais was investigating whether the wreckage of an old airplane on the Pacific island of Truk was Earhart's Electra. It was not, but having come five thousand miles, he had nothing to lose by sitting down with the locals and listening to their stories. According to them, fifteen people arrived on the airplane before the start of the war, and they were escorted by the Japanese, who were using Truk as an air base. The travelers were executed, and their bodies buried below a concrete slab.

Remarkably, after hearing the story, Gervais's response was "I'm not interested in a plane with fifteen people. I'm interested in a plane with two people, a man and a woman." Then, in 1980, he had a change of heart after reading Ronald W. Jackson's *China Clipper*, a book that sets the loss of the *Hawaii Clipper* against the backdrop of the conflict in the Pacific.

The Japanese were apprehensive about the development of Pan Am's island seaplane bases. They understood how the American military could use them to dodge international prohibitions on arming in the Pacific. When the first Pan Am survey flight from San Francisco to Honolulu was flown, a Japanese newspaper editorial noted the worry: "Even if the route is restricted to commercial flights, who can assure that it would not be used for military purposes in case of emergency?"

Jackson writes that the Japanese set out to disrupt the Clipper service. On the eve of November 22, 1935, the inaugural transpacific flight, FBI agents arrested two Japanese nationals who had slipped on board the *Hawaii Clipper* as it sat in the harbor at the Alameda base, across the bay from San Francisco. The men had been tampering with the plane's radio direction finder, key to navigating across the vast ocean. The airline kept the arrest quiet. On January 5, 1936, as another Pan Am captain was sailing the same flying boat through a channel in San Francisco Bay, the hull was sliced by several concrete pillars studded with iron rods that sat just below the water's surface. Who had placed them there was not known. Once again, the suspected vandalism was hushed up.

From these accounts, Jackson concluded that the *Hawaii Clipper* was hijacked by Japanese stowaways who'd boarded the plane on its overnight in Guam. Backing up his scenario is an FBI report from William L. MacNeill, a former U.S. Marine who worked for the military and Pan Am in the village of Sumay for three years in the mid-1930s. MacNeill claimed that a spy ring operated in Guam and that the Japanese had "all the chance in the world to plant a time bomb on any ship or clipper that comes in." All this convinced Gervais that the Pan Am mystery was worth another look. His narrow focus on Earhart broadened.

I pause here to point out that ten years before deciding he had stumbled on the final destination of the *Hawaii Clipper*, Gervais cowrote* *Amelia Earhart Lives*, a book claiming that she survived capture by the Japanese during the war and afterward returned to the States to assume a new identity as Irene Bolam. Gervais met Bolam, a private pilot in her youth, through a mutual friend at a flying club meeting in Long Island. Bolam was said to look a lot like Earhart, leading Gervais to believe that she actually *was* Amelia Earhart. There were several problems with his theory, the most significant of which was that Bolam insisted she was not Earhart. So bear this in mind when I refer to Gervais's findings.

---

* With Joe Klaas.

In 1980, Gervais was invited to meet with a group of retired World War II–era Pan Am mechanics who would view the photos of the airplane he saw in Truk sixteen years before and consider the possibility that the passengers and crew of the *Hawaii Clipper* ended up interred there. The sixteen former Pan Am men quickly concluded that the plane was not a Martin 130, and two days later they sent a recommendation to airline management advising against an investigatory visit to the island, according to documents in the airline's historical archives at the Richter Library at the University of Miami.

To me, the meeting with Gervais gives the impression that the company was trying to get at the truth, but in a memo to executives, Pan Am's then-director of corporate public relations, James Arey, wrote that the official position had not changed. As ever, "the Clipper was lost during a storm."

Ten years earlier, however, Pan Am founder and chairman Juan Trippe had a very different view.

In a memo Guy Noffsinger found in the airline's archives, Harvey L. Katz, who preceded Arey in the Pan Am public relations department, details a meeting with Trippe on August 26, 1970, at which the recently retired former CEO dropped this startling tidbit. "Mr. Trippe said that after the war, he was told by the Navy department that the Japanese hid in the aircraft and commandeered it in mid-flight," wrote Katz. There was more: "The aircraft then was flown to a Japanese base where the engines were studied and, according to Mr. Trippe, were copied in detail for use on Japanese fighter aircraft. He said passengers and crew were killed." Katz wrote the memo to John C. Leslie, a senior VP for Pan Am international affairs.

So why was the airline not receptive to Gervais's account? The crash hunter's mistake, according to Charles Hill, was hanging the entire hijacking theory on the aircraft wreckage he photo-graphed in Truk in the 1960s. The Pan Am review committee said it was a British Sunderland, a four-engine flying boat of the same era used by the Royal Air Force during the war. The mis-identification of the plane allowed the committee to dismiss all Gervais's claims.

Hill's *Fix on the Rising Sun* is at times complimentary to Jackson's and Gervais's accounts and at other times contradic-tory; and the book is often incomprehensible. It does include some of the same details Trippe revealed, and Hill's theory is eerily similar to the one proposed by Jeff Wise in the disappear-ance of Malaysia 370.

Both these armchair investigators, Hill and Wise, proposed that the flights were skyjacked by technically savvy interlopers who took control of the planes and then made deceptive trans-missions. With the *Hawaii Clipper*, the theory goes, hijackers forced the pilots to fly to a Japanese-controlled island. In Malaysia 370, the hijackers were Ukrainian, and the destina-tion was Russian-controlled Kazakhstan. In Hill's version of events, the crew was desperate to communicate their plight sur-reptitiously to ground stations while under the watchful eye of the Japanese skyjackers—so Pan Am's radio operator, McCa-rty, transmitted false navigational fixes, a kind of code that, when deciphered, would point the listener to the location of three Japanese seaplane bases in the Pacific. The message being "The Japanese have us."

In the Malaysia 370 scenario Wise proposed (before the discovery of the wing flap convinced him he was wrong), the skyjackers slipped through the floor hatch leading to the air-craft's electronics bay near the cockpit. Having accessed the plane's satellite data unit, they reprogrammed it to transmit signals that would send out phony information about where the plane was heading, sending the search-and-recovery teams on a wild goose chase on the wrong side of the equator. With access to the plane's brain, the hijackers seized the flight controls from the pilots and remotely flew the plane to their target destination.

In the case of the *Hawaii Clipper*, was McCarty's ingenious code lost on the recipients? Did the airline's ground operators figure out the message but were subsequently told to keep its significance to themselves? Hill does not say. The official statement was then, and still is to this day, that no one knows what happened to the plane—just as with Malaysia 370.

"I'm considered among the whack-a-doodles," Wise told me when journalists were still interested in what he called his "spoof theory" of MH-370. A charmingly self-effacing science writer with a private pilot's license and a penchant for the technical, Wise is not a basement-dwelling nerd spinning plots involving hostile foreign powers and Ernst Blofeld–style, computer-hacking villains. Well, maybe he is a little, but Wise didn't expect the world to embrace his view. He just wanted the possibility considered.

I never bought Wise's "north to Kazakhstan" idea, but we did agree on one thing. The most troublesome piece of data, the one that opens the door to consideration of some kind of hacking into the electronic system, is that after MH-370 disappeared from radar, the signal to the satellite was inexplicably lost for as long as an hour and twenty minutes. Something interfered with the satellite data unit, or SDU. This is why I was so interested in the water damage to the E&E bay on the Qantas flight to Bangkok in 2008 and in similar events.

"Nobody has tried to grapple with the key data point, the

reboot of the SDU," Wise told me, noting that deactivating the satellite communication system is not something most pilots would know how to do. To Wise, this cries out for further study. "This indicates to me that there was tampering by somebody, and a tampered piece of equipment—you have to put an asterisk by that."

Wise's spoof theory required imagining a state-backed plot involving a number of people with detailed knowledge of the inner workings of a sophisticated, computer-driven machine. It points out the alarming possibility that airliners can be digitally commandeered. In this respect, Wise is the voice of a small community of people who warn that it is indeed possible. The digital airliner has outpaced the industry's ability to protect against all cyber threats.

In a presentation to the 2014 Black Hat, a computer security conference, Madrid-based cyber security expert Ruben Santamarta demonstrated how he hacked into an airliner's SDU through Inmarsat's SwiftBroadband connection. Santamarta said he was able to bypass normal security gates and log on using the industry standard naming protocol of the aircraft.

Once in the satellite data network, a hacker can "modify settings, reboot the terminal, turn off the terminal, and do nasty things," he told the crowd. "Obviously we are not crashing airplanes with these vulnerabilities, that has to be clear," Santamarta said. "These attacks—one can be used to disrupt or to modify satellite data links."

Santamarta's claim has been challenged by those who argue that his lack of access to actual equipment used by airlines casts doubt on his conclusions. Still, if it could theoretically happen, it must be considered a hazard; one the industry should be dealing with—yesterday.

Wise is the lucky alternative theorist whose scenario has been disproven to his satisfaction. Being wrong isn't too bad if it provides closure. It is a different story for Guy Noffsinger. "I'm in it for the long haul," he told me well into the second half of a decade spent wandering down the many side roads of the Pan Am Clipper enigma. He is waiting for some kind of satisfying ending, which, like the missing flying boat, is nowhere to be found.

PART TWO

Conspiracy

Just because you're paranoid doesn't mean
they aren't after you.

—JOSEPH HELLER, *Catch 22*

A Little Mistrust

f Juan Trippe, with all his political connections, knew that the *Hawaii Clipper* had been taken by the Japanese in 1938, choosing to share it in a conversation with a public relations executive in 1970 was a very understated way of setting the record straight. So while his astonishing confirmation of the long-held theory about the *Hawaii Clipper* added another curious element to the story, it fell short of providing certainty.

Ah, certainty. Before I started writing this book, I had no idea how elusive certainty could be in investigating air crashes. Yet the more accidents I looked at, the more odd elements I found.

The Helios 522 case seemed straightforward until 2011, when consultants hired by a Helios mechanic and three executives of the airline, all facing criminal charges in the accident, reexamined the wreckage as part of their defense and came to a conclusion that differed from the official report. With the assistance of Ron Schleede and Caj Frostell, now retired from the International Civil Aviation Organization, they asked to reopen the investigation.

Schleede and Frostell had questioned whether the pilots failed to pressurize the aircraft, based in part on their examination of the system-selector knob found at the scene in the Off position. When the consultants examined it, they thought the scoring on the back was evidence it might have been pushed to the Off position upon the airplane's impact with the ground, rather than because the pilots failed to pressurize the plane on takeoff. That would have meant a case of mechanical failure rather than pilot error. Boeing disagreed; the Greeks and the Americans opted not to reopen the case. The official report had been published; public attention had moved on.

An air disaster dominates the news until the next story. For those involved, however, the investigation, in all its gritty, tedious detail, is enormously important. People can face jail, as the Helios workers did. Airlines and manufacturers can be sued and fined, ordered to make expensive design or operational changes, and subjected to new regulations. Aviation authorities can be exposed as derelict, and government secrets can be exposed.

In air accident investigations in some countries, unlike in criminal cases, people with an interest in the outcome take part. The airline, pilots, maintenance workers, air traffic controllers, flight attendants, product manufacturers, and government officials work together. The idea is that that their conflicting interests keep them all in check.

Still, there is a real knowledge disparity. For example, when Inmarsat arrived in Malaysia with the news that its satellite data could be used to help locate the airplane, its calculations showed that the 777 flew into the South Indian Ocean. This news was met with skepticism.

Inmarsat's vice president for aviation, David Coiley, kept defending the company's research, telling me that the calculations and conclusions were peer reviewed. But seriously, who were the company's peers? This was new to everybody. Coiley said even his own people didn't understand completely. "We could tell [only] so much from a simple handshake or logon."

An experienced tin kicker is a generalist—a mile wide and half an inch deep. Conversely, the designer of a microprocessor or satellite communication system is a specialist—half an inch wide and a mile deep. The trend for future investigations will be toward more sophisticated, niche areas of specialization, according to Robert MacIntosh, former NTSB chief of international aviation affairs. "We're going to have to depend more and more on the technical expertise we get from the manufacturers."

Cue the menacing *Jaws* theme music here, because this approach calls for trusting the untrustworthy, those with a stake in the outcome, said Florida State University professor Lance deHaven-Smith. A fervent contrarian, deHaven-Smith said people who will suspect the activities of foreign governments are reluctant to doubt their own, even though they should. "We got enough events where the government is not giving us an adequate explanation," he said. When accidents happen that benefit the powerful, or happen with a frequency that defies the odds, a little mistrust can be a good thing.

There were many reasons to question the cause of the crash that killed Dorothy Hunt, wife of White House fixer E. Howard Hunt, in 1972. Ms. Hunt was a former CIA operative who was said to have delivered hush money to the Watergate burglars in the scandal that led to President Richard Nixon's resignation.

On an overcast afternoon in December of that year, she was flying on United Flight 553 from Washington to Chicago.

Snow and freezing rain fell as the Boeing 737 stalled on approach to the city's Midway Airport and plowed into a residential neighborhood. The NTSB said in its final report that it found no evidence of "any medical condition that would have incapacitated the crew, or of any interference with the crew in the performance of their duties," in short, no evidence of foul play. Still, there were several eyebrow-raising details. Hunt was carrying $10,000 and had bought $250,000 of flight insurance before boarding.

"It's pretty wild when you have the White House being blackmailed by a former CIA agent to keep quiet about a crime," deHaven-Smith said of the circumstances. "Then she dies in a plane crash with ten thousand K? If you're not suspicious of that, you're crazy."

The investigation was more difficult because the flight data recorder was not working. Despite that, the NTSB found oversights by the crew during the critical period as the plane neared the airport.

By analyzing the engine noise and other sounds captured by the cockpit voice recorder and time-syncing them with the air traffic control radar, the investigators deduced that the pilots were trying to comply with requests from ATC to slow their arrival so that another plane could clear the runway. With gear down and spoilers deployed, the crew did not maintain enough speed after leveling the airplane and got dangerously close to a stall.

Flight 553 was at one thousand feet, just below the minimum decision height, when the controller asked the crew to execute a missed approach. At precisely that time, the stick shaker started and the pilots retracted the flaps to fifteen degrees and applied takeoff power.

The 737 descended through the cloud cover in a level attitude and then quickly went nose high as it slammed into a number of homes, killing two residents inside one bungalow and forty-three people on board the airplane.

Charles Colson, once special counsel to Nixon and another character who was jailed for his role in Watergate, would later tell *Time* magazine that Dorothy Hunt was murdered by the CIA. The charge remains alive among those of a conspiratorial bent. Yet as a murder plot, it falls short on the credibility scale.

Too many people would have had to be involved to carry off a complex plan that also had to factor in the unforeseeable conditions that would lead to the plane's speed getting away from the pilots. Murder by airplane is a concept more likely to succeed in crime fiction than in reality.

In the movies, the bad guy tampers with the victim's car, which then goes off a cliff. In aviation, however, sabotage must do more than create the failure mechanism; it must make sure it goes undetected while triggering the catastrophe at just the right time so that it can also penetrate a highly developed safety net. Short of commandeering the airplane and purposely crashing it, detonating a bomb, launching a missile, or setting a fire—all of which leave evidence in the wreckage—intentionally causing a crash is not so simple.

"What's possible and what's not?" asks retired airline pilot and novelist John Nance, whose books sometimes feature crime at thirty-five thousand feet. He knows how tricky it is to come up with a credible murder plot where an airliner is the weapon. "The linchpin is predictability; how certain are you that A is going to produce B? That's what you must have."

Parts can be tampered with to create a crime novel plot, such as slicing the brake line, but in aviation, the most capricious elements of all, according to Nance, are sitting at the front of the airplane. Pilots can rise to the challenge and save the day or they can founder and become another link in an unbroken chain to disaster. There are fascinating examples of both pilot heroics and failures, which you will read about later in this book. Yet rare is the would-be assassin who can orchestrate all the instruments of destruction in advance. Sometimes an air accident is just an accident. Other times, however, it is an enigma.

A Diplomat Dies

One thing investigators don't expect to find on the scene of an air disaster is passengers with gunshot wounds. Yet two of the fifteen people on the plane with United Nations secretary-general Dag Hammarskjöld had been shot, and that was just one of many surprising discoveries. There are various theories about what caused the plane to fly into the trees on a dark night in September 1961. It could have been an assassination or kidnapping plot or an attempted interception by mercenaries to divert Hammarskjöld from his peace mission. It could have been a mechanical problem or an error by the crew. Although the accident has been investigated four times, what really happened remains a mystery.

The UN-chartered DC-6 was approaching the airport at Ndola, in Northern Rhodesia,* during a violent interlude in the decolonialization of the Congo. The Belgians had ostensibly pulled out of the country, but in the resource-rich state of

---

* Now Zambia.

Katanga, European-backed mercenaries were still around supporting its attempt to secede from the Republic of the Congo.* Hammarskjöld wanted a cease-fire between the mercenaries and the UN troops that were there to assist the Republic of the Congo. Stopping the violence was to be the first of a two-step effort to reverse Katanga's secession. Because of their commercial interests in the region's resources, Africa's colonial powers, Belgium, Britain, and France, opposed the UN plan. The Americans had a different concern: in these Cold War days, certain factions in the U.S. government worried that the Soviet Union would take advantage of the turmoil in Africa to gain an advantage.

So when Hammarskjöld died in a plane crash, it was like an Agatha Christie novel. There were plenty of suspects.

Accompanying the secretary-general on the flight were two UN executives, four security officers, two soldiers, and a secretary. Six men, all Swedes, made up the flight crew.

For security reasons, Hammarskjöld's trip to Northern Rhodesia to meet with Katanga leader Moise Tshombe was hush-hush: The plane would follow a circuitous route. The crew would maintain radio silence, using only an emergency channel staffed by an operator communicating with them in their native Swedish.

But if the Hammarskjöld visit was a secret, it was badly kept. Journalists, protesters, and mercenary pilots were waiting at the airport, along with Lord Cuthbert Alport, the region's British high commissioner. Tshombe was there, too, under a special exception to the whites-only rule imposed in British-controlled Northern Rhodesia.

---

* Now the Democratic Republic of the Congo.

The Swedish DC-6, known as *Albertina*, was on final approach to the Ndola Airport at around midnight on September 18. During the last bank, a wing hit the trees and then the ground not far from a twelve-foot anthill. The plane plowed into it and cartwheeled to the right. The still-spinning propellers on the right wing dispersed fifteen hundred gallons of fuel along a three-hundred-foot path as the plane slowed and came to rest. There was a fire on the ground, but it could not be determined when it started. Evidence, autopsies, and eyewitnesses offered conflicting information. The plane could have been on fire as it flew; it could have caught fire when it crashed; or the fire could have been rekindled after the crash. There was testimony to back up all three possibilities.

The captain of the *Albertina*, Per Erik Hallonquist, had radioed the tower of his anticipated arrival at 12:20 a.m. Why the air traffic controller waited until 2:20 to issue an alert when the plane did not arrive is not clear. Maybe he was reassured by Lord Alport, who for some reason told the tower staff not to worry about the missing plane because Hammarskjöld had probably changed his plans.

That night, John Ngongo and Safeli Soft were camping in the forest not far from the airport, tending a charcoal-making kiln. It was clear and sometime after 10:00 p.m., Ngongo said, when he and Soft saw a large aircraft fly overhead, followed by a smaller plane that sounded like a jet. The engine and the wings of the big plane were on fire, according to Ngongo. The two men got to the crash scene at dawn, where they found the plane smoldering and the body of a man, whom they later learned was Dag Hammarskjöld, lying apart from the plane, propped up against an anthill.

Susan Williams, author of *Who Killed Hammarskjöld?*

The UN, the Cold War, and White Supremacy in Africa, writes that the men went to Timothy Kankasa, the township secretary, to report what they had found. Kankasa went to the scene with them and returned to call the police. Kankasa said it was between 9:00 and 9:30 a.m., but it wasn't until afternoon that he heard ambulances. By contrast, a number of other locals say they came upon the wreckage that morning and that it was surrounded by uniformed soldiers and police and cordoned off with red tape.

Obviously, it couldn't be both. The Federation of Rhodesia authorities' story doesn't match either of the bystanders' accounts. The authorities said the plane wasn't discovered until 3:15 p.m., fifteen hours after it crashed eight miles from the airport. The mysteries were multiplying.

If Kankasa called the police in the morning, why did it take them so long to get to the site? If police were there early on, what were they doing and why was 3:15 p.m. given as the time of their arrival? These are not academic questions because there was a surprise in the middle of the charred wreckage: a survivor.

Harry Julien, Hammarskjöld's director of security, was suffering from first- and second-degree burns, sunburn, a fractured ankle, and a head injury, but he was very much alive. If the authorities had deliberately slowed getting him medical treatment, why?

"We know that the crash was known; Timothy Kankasa reported it early on to the authorities, but nobody came," Susan Williams told me. "The authorities knew about the crash. We know there were people there. We know the ambulances didn't come." The sun was blazing, it was September, and Julien had been suffering for fifteen hours.

"I am Sergeant Harry Julien, security officer to the OUN," he told his nurse at Ndola Hospital. "Please inform Léopoldville of the crash. Tell my wife and kids I'm alive before the casualty list is published."

Harry Julien entered the hospital with a good prognosis, but six days later he succumbed to renal failure. A. V. (Paddy) Allen, the police inspector who accompanied Julien to the hospital, was surprised because he did not think Julien's injuries were life-threatening, adding another odd element to an exceptionally odd case.

In the ambulance, Julien shared details of the accident with Allen and later with hospital personnel. A tape recorder in his room was supposed to document what he said, but either the machine was not turned on or the tapes disappeared, because the reports contain only the brief statements Julien made to the police, the nurses, and physician Mark Lowenthal.

"It blew up," he said, when asked what happened as the plane was making its pass over the runway. "There was great speed. Great speed."

Officer Allen asked him, "What happened then?"

"Then there was the crash," Julien replied.

Julien said the others were trapped on the plane. Autopsies showed they were all badly burned. This made it even more curious that Hammarskjöld's body, untouched by fire, was outside the airplane when witnesses saw it. The diplomat could have been tossed out of the plane and away from the blaze on impact, or someone might have moved him.

Hammarskjöld was not the only one found in an unexpected condition. One passenger was in the cockpit, an unusual place for him to have been on approach to landing, and then there were the two who had bullet wounds.

The Federation of Rhodesia and Nyasaland Commission of Inquiry under the director of civil aviation concluded that the bullet wounds had to have been the result of fire detonating the ammunition being carried on the plane. The experts consulted by Williams for her book concluded that this was not possible. "Ammunition for rifles, heavy machine-guns and pistols cannot, when heated by fire, eject bullets with sufficient force for the bullets to get into a human body," according to a Swedish explosives expert. Another said, "If bullets were found in the bodies of any of the victims of the air crash, they must have passed through the barrel of a weapon."

As to the cause of the crash itself, a dozen scenarios have been considered. In his book *Disasters in the Air*, Jan Bartelski weighs the theories and suggests one of his own.

A nearly undamaged instrument panel from the captain's position was found in the wreckage, and the static line to the altimeter was disconnected. In their report, the Rhodesian investigators discounted the significance of this, but Bartelski suggested that the bad instrument could have led the pilots to believe they were higher than they were as they approached the airport.

As in my MH-370 theory, Bartelski acknowledges certain assumptions. His scenario is based on his experience flying the DC-6. According to Bartelski, *Albertina* was a DC-6B, which had an idiosyncratic pressurization system. It did not always depressurize on landing. On one occasion a crew member was blown out the door because of the positive pressure differential—in a situation like what happened to American Airlines purser José Chiu in Miami in 2000. For this reason, pilots flying the DC-6B depressurized the aircraft before landing, at an estimated two thousand feet.

Capt. Per Erik Hallonquist arrived at the Ndola airport ten

minutes earlier than he anticipated and had to make a steeper and faster descent than planned, dumping the cabin pressure at a higher altitude by opening the emergency pressure-release valve. This sudden, drastic change "could have had a catastrophic effect on the flexible line" to the altimeter, Bartelski writes. Getting from a separated static line to making the approach sixteen hundred feet too low involves a number of missteps, combined with design features unique to the DC-6 and certain laws of physics.

"I'm not saying it couldn't have happened that way; it could," said Nick Tramontano, who piloted and worked on DC-6s during his career with Seaboard World Airlines.* When I asked him to analyze the altimeter-gone-bad theory, he said he'd take a look and compare it with DC-6 maintenance manuals.

Tramontano said that the pilot's and first officer's separate altimeters could have given the same and, in this case, incorrect altitude information if the captain switched the static source to alternate, the position in which the switch was found at the crash site.

Bertelski writes that investigators were not as familiar with the specifics of the DC-6B as they should have been, which caused them to dismiss this important evidence in the wreckage.

With the exception of Bertelski's detailed explanation, nearly every other theory has a malevolent element, in keeping with the violent and chaotic last days of colonialism in central Africa. Mercenary pilots have confessed to, or boasted in public about, shooting down the plane. These comments were plausible. On the flight just before the one to Ndola, *Albertina* had been hit with machine-gun fire by Katangan forces in

---

* Later Flying Tigers.

Elizabethville,* and the damage repaired. People at the crash site saw holes in the fuselage consistent with weapons fire. The Rhodesian inquiry, however, concluded that shots to the plane would not have disabled the flight controls enough to cause it to crash.

A separate team assembled by the United Nations was working at the same time as the Rhodesians. The UN team hired Max Frei-Shulzer, a Swiss microbiologist and forensic scientist, to answer the question of whether the plane had been attacked.

Why Frei-Shulzer was hired is puzzling. His work with the Zurich Police Department involved handwriting analysis and lifting evidence from surfaces with tape—think fingerprints and fiber residue—but he had no expertise in aviation or metallurgy. His technique for settling the issue of whether bullets were in the fuselage consisted of melting down four thousand pounds of fused aluminum and looking for the presence of other metals. Bartelski describes it as "an extremely critical metallurgical process requiring accurate temperature control." After Frei-Shulzer made soup of the plane, he said he could "exclude the possibility of hostile actions from the air and from the ground." He also discounted sabotage.

In 1962, the Rhodesian board of inquiry followed Frei-Shulzer's lead, concluding that the crash was "probably due to human failure." The complete discounting of overt action against the flight was not accepted by the UN then, or in its 2015 review. Yet these and other contradictions have been examined multiple times as people associated with the case have come forward with new information and as forensic tech-

---

* Now Lubumbashi.

nology advances. Still, some unexplored aspects of the accident cannot be reviewed half a century later.

For example, it would not be possible to reconstruct some of the critical factors impacting the pilots' performance, MacIntosh, the retired safety investigator, said. "The issue of making this nighttime approach, where everybody is looking out the window and nobody is looking at the altimeter, and you think you are flying level and you are not, those things are never going to be discussed." After flying multiple missions in the Congo for the U.S. Air Force, MacIntosh left the area two weeks before the Hammarskjöld crash. His interest in what happened has not waned.

Yet the person responsible for the most recent revival of the Hammarskjöld whodunit is not a scientist, aviation professional, or criminologist. Susan Williams is a British historian specializing in Africa. On every research trip to the continent, she would come across some thread of the mystery that begged to be pulled. And she pulled enough of these threads to weave her own complex tapestry that includes independent analysis of memos, witness statements, and photographs of the bodies. She makes a compelling case that during the conflict-ridden period marking the beginning of the end for colonialism in central Africa, what happened to the secretary-general was probably deliberate. The cover-up was possible only because the Federation of Rhodesia and Nyasaland was ruled by Britain, which was able to control every aspect of the investigation.

National, racial, political, and commercial biases all played a role, she said. To try to extract those intrusions from what is supposed to be the objective work of air crash investigators would be like trying to reassemble the *Albertina* after it was boiled down by Frei-Shulzer.

The Hammarskjöld Commission relied heavily on Susan Williams's work *Who Killed Hammarskjöld?* when it prompted the United Nations to launch the fourth inquiry into the crash early in 2015. After a review of the evidence that lasted nearly a year, a three-member panel of experts made one small step forward when it ruled out an uncontrolled descent and, therefore, a midair explosion. Controlled flight into terrain was the most likely scenario, the panel said, based on the swath of downed trees along the final flight path and the wreckage distribution. This small advance does not explain what caused the pilots to fly the plane too low. Still, Williams finds it heartening.

"The truth is starting to emerge, and I find it exciting," Williams told me, adding optimistically, "It would be hard to imagine that a cover-up like this could happen now."

Susan, read on.

The Dodge

On either end of 1985, air safety agencies in Bolivia and Canada were thrust into one of America's biggest political scandals when plane crashes in those countries were linked to wide-ranging Reagan administration programs to provide support to Nicaraguan rebels and arms to Iran in the Iran-Contra Affair.

American lives were lost on American-made airplanes operated by American airlines, but America's air safety agencies did not participate in the investigations in a significant way, and a probable cause was not satisfactorily determined. Two books suggest cover-ups intended to hide the relationship of the airlines to secret and perhaps prohibited U.S. government activity.

On December 12, 1985, a DC-8 operated by the Miami-based air charter company Arrow Air crashed fifteen seconds after takeoff from Gander, Newfoundland. Two hundred fifty-six people were killed, most of them U.S. Army soldiers from the 101st Airborne Division, the Screaming Eagles. The soldiers were on their way home for Christmas to the base at Fort Campbell, Kentucky.

In December 1985, Arrow Air wasn't just moving soldiers; it also had contracts to transport high-explosive incendiary ammo and forty-millimeter shells and weapons, according to Richard Gadd, who coordinated the movement of weapons for the CIA.

"There were layers and layers of intrigue associated with the crash," said Les Filotas, one of ten members of the Canadian Aviation Safety Board. There was evidence of mechanical, operational, and possible criminal elements in the accident. What Filotas found bizarre was that staff investigators at his agency didn't seem too interested in pursuing these bewildering leads.

"There was a lot of transportation of weapons from Egypt to the U.S. or from the U.S. to Egypt," Filotas told me, an allegation he made in *Improbable Cause*, his book about the bureaucracy and politicization of the Arrow Air crash investigation. Filotas couldn't say if the plane's flight history or the airline's relationship to the CIA were relevant to what happened, but he thought both should be checked out.

Under international agreements, it was the responsibility of the Canadians to look into the circumstances, but on either side of the border it was obvious this was a sensitive case. The flight was a U.S. military charter on an airline associated with the CIA. The cargo included mysterious boxes whose contents were never identified. In the cargo hold and the passenger cabin—if past flights were any indication—there was a supersize collection of weapons and ammunition, as soldiers stashed these kinds of combat souvenirs in their bags. Furthermore, the plane had been left unattended during extended stopovers in Egypt and in Cologne, its intermediate stop on the way back to the United States.

All this was going on during a sensitive time in American and Iranian relations, as the United States was negotiating for the release of hostages held in Lebanon. National Security Council staffer Oliver North had ticked off Iran by selling it weapons that were not the ones the Iranians expected. In a memo to National Security Advisor Robert McFarlane and McFarlane's deputy, Richard Poindexter, North urged them to fix the problem. Failing to get the Iranians the missiles they wanted would "ignite Iran fire—the hostages would be our minimum losses." Was the Arrow Air disaster a fulfillment of that warning?

What prevented a detour into the briar patch of spies and soured secret deals was the quick dismissal of terrorism, sabotage, or even an in-flight explosion on Arrow Air Flight 1285. After the disaster, claims of responsibility came from the group Islamic Jihad and the Independent Organization for the Liberation of Egypt, but the Canadian air accident investigator and a spokeswoman for the government were dismissive right away.

"A lot of groups will claim responsibility, and every claim will be looked into," Helene Lafortune, from the Canadian Department of External Affairs, told The New York Times. "They use that to promote their cause. I don't think it's a lead on anything," she said of the groups claiming responsibility.

Compare that to the October 2015 in-flight breakup of a Russian charter flight leaving the resort town of Sharm El Sheikh in Egypt with a load of holidaymakers headed back to St. Petersburg. The Metrojet Airbus A321 came apart and crashed into the Sinai Desert, killing 224. While American, British, and Russian politicians were quick to say the plane was felled by a bomb, Egyptian investigators insisted that there was no evidence of this. The Islamic fundamentalist group ISIS claimed to have been responsible for the disaster. Despite Egypt's reticence, news organizations reported as fact that the plane was bombed out of the sky.

In Canada thirty years earlier, however, all deference was paid to the official investigation. A team of thirty-two soldiers from the U.S. Army, under the command of Maj. Gen. John Crosby, arrived in Gander, as did a group of FBI agents. While the American soldiers were permitted to retrieve the victims, the FBI agents were confined to their hotel rooms by the Canadians. The Royal Canadian Mounted Police did not need the FBI's help to search for evidence of a crime.

The Canadians were handling the air accident investigation without America's help also, though the NTSB's George Seidlein was on hand as a designated representative. Soon, however, he would be replaced by the agency's chief of major investigations, Ron Schleede, who said he flew to Gander with someone from Pratt and Whitney at the request of NTSB chairman Jim Burnett. "Our chairman never trusted anybody," Schleede told me. "He wanted a second set of eyes, and I was sent to sort that out."

One early theory was that ice on the wings may have prevented the plane from climbing, sending it slamming into the trees less than a mile past the airport. Filotas wasn't yet a member of the Canadian Aviation Safety Board (CASB), but he had some idea of how this theory might have been generated, even though no ice was seen on the wings by the six people who serviced the plane before its departure, and only a small quantity of snow grains was observed at weather observation sites at the airport.

"I can imagine how this huge accident happens in Gander, and our board chooses investigators who might have investigated small accidents. They go down there. They meet the engineers of Pratt & Whitney, and they all have a meeting," he told me, describing the organizational session that kicks off any investigation. The airline, the airplane, engine makers, unions for the crew, and government aviation organizations are all represented.

"They're swamped by experts with a point of view, and they come up and say, 'It might have been an engine failure,' and the engine maker says, 'No, it's impossible.' And it goes around the room. 'Could have been ice?' And they all nod their heads [and] say, 'Yeah, it could have been ice.' Our investigators can be overwhelmed, and they convince each other."

Schleede told me that when the crash happened, an FBI agent hurried out to his car to drive to the airport and discovered that his windshield wipers were frozen to the glass. To Schleede, this was notable; the ice theory wasn't just a construct. Schleede told me, "I'm willing to admit when I'm wrong," but when it came to supporting the Canadian ice theory, he insists he was right.

It was an opinion that had him in conflict with Seidlein, who didn't think ice caused the crash. Seidlein, who died in 2008, was sent back to his office in Chicago, never to return to Gander, never more to champion the theory that contradicted that of Schleede and the tin kickers at CASB.

Filotas doesn't know how the ice idea started, of course. His round-the-table "Yeah, it's ice" scenario was speculation during one of several lengthy phone conversations about his book. Based on early news reports, ice on the wings at takeoff was mentioned as a possibility within hours of the crash, even before the first organizational meeting. Anyway, Filotas was being charitable about the initiation of the ice theory. On other matters, he was far more conspiratorial.

There were behind-the-scenes discussions between CASB and the Americans that he was not privy to, he tells me. He is politically savvy enough to conclude that "General Crosby was all over the crash site talking to investigators. And they don't have to tell anybody to hide anything. Somebody from the Justice Department just has to phone the chairman and say, 'It would be inconvenient for us if one of your board members starts shooting his mouth off about a bomb.'"

Filotas was so convinced that ice wasn't the cause that he and three fellow board members wrote a dissent to CASB's official probable cause. Filotas was an aeronautical engineer, as were members Norm Bobbitt and Dave Mussallem; member Ross Stevenson was a former DC-8 pilot with Air Canada. (A fourth man, Roger Lacroix, a former combat pilot and a member of the Royal Canadian Mounted Police, disagreed with the ice theory but resigned from the board before the final report and dissent were released.) When these men received the preliminary staff report in 1987, they found an overreliance on the scant data from the flight recorder. The witness statements were missing, and recordkeeping from the engine inspections was shoddy.

This deep level of scrutiny by political appointees who were not air safety specialists cannot be called unprecedented, because CASB was too new to have much of a history. It was created only a year before the Arrow Air accident, in an attempt to separate safety from regulation. Ironically, the controversy over Arrow Air and another crash in 1989 would prompt a second overhaul of the way Canada handled air accidents.

In the second half of the eighties, however, CASB's civil servants were not expecting to be cross-examined by board members over engineering minutiae such as engine teardown procedures and the limitations of data gathered from four channel flight data recorders.

"There was an ongoing dispute at the board level about what the role of the board member was," Peter Boag, the man in charge of the CASB investigation, told me of Filotas and the others who challenged the staff view of the evidence. "They wanted to be investigators, but that wasn't their role."

There's a lot of he said/he said at this point. Filotas claims to have begun a review of the staff's findings only because he found misrepresentations in it. Perhaps the investigation was too large and complex for Boag to handle, Filotas thought. On that impression, he was not alone.

Peter Boag had a "very thin background, extremely thin," the NTSB's MacIntosh said, calling the investigator in charge of the Arrow Air crash overconfident to a fault. "I can't imagine how you could approach him and get constructive suggestions going when his attitude toward everything was 'I can handle it, and I've done a good job.'"

During one particularly testy exchange recounted in *Improbable Cause*, the members promoting a theory other than ice were asking Boag for the plane's maintenance records from an earlier accident when Boag made it clear he had had enough. He stood up to leave, saying, "Frankly, gentlemen, the well is dry for me. I've done all I can do."

"Once the idea [of ice] got permeated, it was convenient, and all the departments thought it was a good idea," Filotas said. He was troubled that the official investigation had disregarded eyewitnesses' accounts and toxicological exams that suggested a fire or explosion.

Four bystanders who saw the DC-8 in its brief flight across the sky said they saw fire or a glowing light on the aircraft before it slammed into the woods. Yet information from these witnesses was dismissed. When CASB chairman Ken Thorneycroft explained why to Lynn Sherr for ABC News's *20/20*, it sounded as if the board were cherry-picking witnesses.

"We have taken evidence from two hundred or three hundred witnesses; obviously we can't call them all," the board chairman told Sherr. "So let's have a roundtable discussion, decide what evidence we want to have come out at the public hearing, and then select a group of witnesses who will provide that evidence."

The most disturbing contradiction concerned the autopsies. The bodies were taken to the Armed Forces Pathology Lab in Dover, Delaware, and examined by Dr. Robert McMeekin. He declared the deaths instantaneous, but no separate determination of cause was given beyond "plane crash." This misnomer was applied to all 256 victims, regardless of individual injuries.

The toxicology results produced by the Canadians showed that more than half the victims had carbon monoxide or hydrogen cyanide in their systems, which indicates smoke inhalation. This meant that "the soldiers were alive, and they breathed carbon monoxide. There was either a fire or something aboard the plane that emitted carbon monoxide prior to the plane crashing," wrote Cyril Wecht in his book *Tales from the Morgue* after examining the medical records. "These soldiers had to breathe in the CO while still onboard the plane because the autopsies show that the soldiers were dead on impact."

This is the "obvious evidence that this airplane was on fire and it came apart" that board member Roger Lacroix was talking about when he disparaged the ice-on-the-wings scenario in his interview with *20/20*.

In the final report, however, Dr. McMeekin's time-of-death determinations changed. They were no longer instantaneous.

Now death was estimated to have occurred between within thirty seconds to five minutes of the crash for 125 of the victims, which explained the presence of fire-related chemicals in 62 of them. The investigators' facts were changing to preserve the theory that there was no fire before the crash, Filotas said.

When he arrived in Gander for a private planning session with the CASB in the spring of 1986, the NTSB's Schleede had been instructed by NTSB chairman Jim Burnett about what to focus on: Arrow Air and FAA oversight of the airline. It may have seemed like a small matter then, but a 1989 House Judiciary Committee subcommittee hearing noted that of all the government agencies that should have been involved, it was left to the tiny and obscure NTSB to be the fig leaf for the U.S. position. "All the government agencies deferred to the NTSB. The NTSB deferred the question of terrorism to the Canadians," the subcommittee concluded.

"I was told by Burnett to be a hard-ass on Arrow and FAA," Schleede told me. Arrow Air was "a shabby operation," and the FAA hadn't been supervising it sufficiently. These issues appeared in CASB's majority report in December 1988. This was the report that the U.S. congressional subcommittee claimed did not receive sufficient scrutiny by the NTSB.

It doesn't take an overly active imagination to conclude that the United States was diverting attention away from the clues that the plane might have been lost because of a fire or explosion resulting from weapons or sabotage or a terrorist act. This paved the way for CASB's majority report finding that the plane had stalled on takeoff, probably from ice on the wing and a loss of thrust on the number four engine. It was the position Boag and his investigators had taken almost from day one.

Like ice crystals on a windshield in a Newfoundland winter, the ice deniers clung to their position in a dissenting report that said that a fire broke out while the plane was in flight.

Seven months later, Willard Estey, a retired Supreme Court justice in Canada, reviewed the reports and found both of them incredible. "Surmise and speculation inside and outside these proceedings abound, factual evidence does not. Nothing indicates any hope of uncovering explanations of this accident in those areas."

The judge's finding didn't dissuade Boag. A lawyer is looking for something different from an accident investigator, he told me. "I wasn't there, and you weren't there, and the people who were are dead," Boag said. "There could have been complicating factors. The potential power loss from a compressor stall in the engine might have been a complicating factor. Ice represented the most likely, the best if not a definitive finding as to cause."

Filotas called Estey's conclusion that a cause would never be found circular logic. "We shouldn't go on with the investigation because we wouldn't be able to find the cause, and dropping the investigation would ensure that we never did," he said.

And that's the way it was left.

This airplane was not lost in the sea or downed in a global hotspot. It crashed in a First World nation less than a mile from the airport, carrying American servicemen and women home to their families.

The United States "had to know what happened," Filotas said when we talked in 2015. He said it was only the second year since 1985 in which no journalist had been in touch to ask him about the case.

"The military had this tragic loss, and here we were bumbling along. If the U.S. didn't know [what happened to the plane] would they have let this controversy 'ice/no ice' alone or would they have tried to get involved?" He insisted, "They don't care what we do here because they knew what happened."

Judge Estey seems to have been correct in his dim prediction for finding the truth about Arrow Air. Filotas was equally convincing when he said that what the congressional subcommittee hearing called "a near total absence" of a U.S. investigation can only be seen as willful. Why wouldn't a country pull out all the stops in trying to uncover every detail of an accident with such a high toll unless the truth threatened some great scandal?

When Eastern Airlines captain George Jehn first delved into the controversy over the Arrow Air disaster, he was stunned by the similarities with an accident earlier that same year. "The Reagan administration had a definite modus operandi for handling potentially embarrassing air disasters," he told me. Jehn is convinced the mysterious crash of a Boeing 727 in Bolivia was another disaster the U.S. government didn't want to solve.

Eastern Airlines Flight 980 crashed on a mountain just outside La Paz, Bolivia, on New Year's Day 1985, killing twenty-nine people. By international agreement, the country where an accident occurs is in charge, which is why Canada handled the Arrow Air case. For Eastern Flight 980, it was a Bolivian investigation. Still, because everything about the accident except the location was American, people from the NTSB, Boeing, Eastern, and the airline's unions had a right to participate, and to some extent they did. A number of them went to Bolivia, but little of what they learned there shed light on what happened.

Barry Trotter, Eastern's then accident investigator, flew down to South America along with the airline's chief pilot and the VP of flight operations.

"We didn't sit around," Trotter told me. "We went to where the aircraft departed from to get information from ATC and the radar people, the en route radar people. I had a rep with me from the NTSB who was specialized in ATC centers and towers and so forth."

Trotter was talking about Michael O'Rourke, the NTSB's air traffic control expert. What O'Rourke found on visiting the tower at La Paz was a post–World War II–era setup. He was very concerned about the age of the equipment and the lack of maintenance.

"I insisted the FAA come down and flight-check all the nav aids," O'Rourke told me, remembering the on-site visit quite clearly. The equipment had been installed nearly forty years earlier and had never been checked. "It blew my mind," O'Rourke recalled.

In a story in *The New York Times* after the accident, reporter Richard Witkin zeroed in on this issue, writing that immediate attention would be paid to the "accuracy of navigation aids" on which the crew would have relied during the plane's descent over the mountains and on its approach to the airport. Witkin was partially correct. The FAA did test the airport with a specially equipped Boeing 727 and found everything in order, but there was no report on whether the equipment was accurate on the night of the accident.

In his book *Final Destination: Disaster*, Jehn writes that between New Year's and the FAA flight test a few weeks later, repairs had been made to the system. "A rep was there" from the company fixing things before the inspection, Jehn told me. "Of course it was going to pass."

The first attempt to get investigators to the site came about five days after the crash, when helicopter pilot Rus Stiles took a Sikorsky Black Hawk over Mount Illimani. The helicopter was on loan from United Technologies. The company's chief executive, Harry Gray, was a personal friend of Ambassador Arthur Davis, whose wife was killed in the disaster.

"All we could see was a cut in the snow that formed the shape of the wing," Stiles told me. "The plane was so buried, I don't remember any part of the airplane. I didn't see the tail at all." Stiles said he could hover, but landing or leaving people on the mountain was out of the question. Nearly a year would pass before investigators attempted to access the wreckage again.

Jehn read all the early news accounts and was struck by how many leads there were to follow: criminal, political, and operational. Initially, there was reason to suspect an in-flight explosion because people who lived nearby reported hearing "a roar of thunder" and seeing pieces of the plane falling from the sky. Another news story raised the possibility that Davis, the U.S. ambassador to Paraguay, might have been the target of an assassination attempt by the country's military dictator, Gen. Alfredo Stroessner.

Ambassador Davis was scheduled to be on the flight with his wife, Marian, but changed plans at the last minute. Davis and Stroessner had a sometimes contentious relationship, and there was more: Paraguay was earning the ire of the U.S. government for its involvement in drug trafficking. Two months before the crash, the Americans slashed financial aid to Paraguay, and the bulk of the remaining three-million-dollar appropriation went to the Peace Corps. By coincidence (or maybe not), the director of the Peace Corps in Paraguay was also killed on Flight 980.

Eastern Airlines' participation in the movement of illegal

drugs also had to be considered relevant, Jehn said. The airline had been in the news for repeated violations of drug trafficking laws. Drugs had been seized twenty-two times on Eastern's jets in 1984, and the contraband was always hidden in areas accessible only by aviation personnel. One pilot testified to a Senate committee during a hearing that he saw money being taken off planes at Eastern's Panama hub.

Based on the stories pilots told him and also reported to the FBI in Miami, Jehn suggests that Eastern Airlines may have been assisting the Reagan administration's clandestine effort to supply weapons to Nicaraguan rebels in the Iran-Contra, arms-for-hostages, drugs-for-rebels, it-has-a-lot-of-names scandal that dominated the fortieth president's second term from 1984 to 1988.

It wasn't all political intrigue, though. Like the questionable integrity of the navigational aids at La Paz, Jehn and the ALPA (Air Line Pilots Association) pilots who were part of the probe discovered alarming facts related to human error. None of the three men in the cockpit that night had any experience flying in South America, with its high terrain and low-tech navigation facilities. Company policy required a check captain to supervise the first flight into the region, but not the second. This trip back to Miami was the pilot's second flight; the supervising pilot was riding as a passenger.

Don McClure, an ALPA air safety pilot, flew a re-creation of Flight 980 and noted that the airline's radio-based navigational system, called Omega, "continually steered the aircraft off course approximately five miles to the east," or toward the direction of Mount Illimani. Jehn found errors on navigational charts.

Jehn's interest in Eastern Flight 980 was professional: an

airliner had crashed; colleagues were dead. Working separately on a parallel course was Judith Kelly, whose mission was more personal. William Kelly, her husband of sixteen years, was the Peace Corps director in Paraguay. He was traveling aboard Eastern 980 to Miami on business. Judith, who also worked for the Peace Corps, had stayed behind in Asunción. It didn't take her long to realize that her government wasn't pulling out all the stops to determine what had happened.

Six months after she was made a widow, Judith Kelly flew to Bolivia, hired a guide, and climbed Mount Illimani, arriving at nineteen thousand feet to the place where the wreckage of the plane was scattered. She took a few small pieces, left letters she had written to her husband, and climbed back down. Then she traveled to the United States and appeared on NBC's *Today* show to talk about what she'd done and to challenge the NTSB to get up there and have a look. "I made it, a woman, on my own," she explained to Jehn when the two met years later. Her message to the NTSB: certainly the U.S. government and Eastern airlines, with all their resources, could get up there and conduct a proper inquiry. She'd proven it could be done.

From her home in San Antonio, Texas, Alisa Vander Stucken, twenty-eight, watched Judith Kelly berate the NTSB on the morning news in the summer of 1985 and thought "it was awesome." Her husband, Mark Louis Bird, was the second officer on Flight 980. Like Kelly, Vander Stucken was discouraged, and puzzled at the lack of progress in the probe. "I expected both the government and the airline to get down there and investigate and find out what happened," she said. But after the crash faded from the news, Vander Stucken's only source of information was in the letters and phone calls from Judith Kelly. "I think it's pretty sad when a woman has to go up and try and do that for herself," she said of Kelly's hike up Mount Illimani, "instead of the airline or the government; the NTSB. I mean, that's what they're there for."

In his book, Jehn claims that then NTSB chairman Jim Burnett, a Republican appointee of President Reagan who died in 2010, was accommodating the interests of the White House or Eastern or both with this perfunctory investigation. No one I spoke with who was associated with the NTSB then agrees with that conclusion. Peter Kissinger, the board's managing director at the time, said he could not imagine why there would have been reluctance to look into the circumstances. "We truly live by the adage no stone unturned," he told me.

Still, Jehn's perception that Burnett was extremely political did square with that of others who spoke to me both on and off the record. Ron Schleede recalled disagreeing with Burnett over the handling of another accident investigation. "He wanted to have a hearing for some political reason," and Schleede was opposed, he explained. Ultimately Schleede prevailed, but "Burnett was pissed," the investigator said. "He said, 'Okay, can we get Mr. Schleede reassigned to the railroad division?'" It sounded like a joke to me, but that's not how Schleede saw it. "A lot of senior people left the NTSB because of Jim Burnett," he said.

At the time of Flight 980, the NTSB did have a close relationship with Eastern. Burnett's special assistant was a former Eastern pilot named John Wheatley. "Burnett, for some reason, he was really more in contact with Eastern than the other carriers," said Tom Haueter, the former director of aviation safety at the NTSB. "Why that was, I don't know, but it did seem to me that there were a lot of Eastern people around at the time."

Eleven years after the crash, NTSB investigator* Greg Feith

---

* Feith retired from the NTSB in 2001.

told a meeting of the International Society of Air Safety Investigators that politics can drive a case in one direction or another. He knew about it firsthand because when the NTSB finally acted on Judith Kelly's challenge, Feith was chosen to lead an expedition to the wreckage on Mount Illimani.

In late August 1985, quite out of the blue, Feith was part of an NTSB teleconference in which investigators were invited to volunteer to climb to nineteen thousand feet and look for the black boxes of the Boeing 727. Feith was just twenty-eight and new at the job. He lived in Denver, at an altitude of five thousand feet. His workouts kept him in good shape, and included hiking in the Rockies. Recognizing it would be good for his career, he volunteered to go. More experienced investigators had also stepped up, but it was Feith who was selected. Feith didn't know that the agency's interest in the accident had been dormant, but he knew the NTSB was being pestered by Judith Kelly.

The first indication that something was not right with his assignment was the timing. The climbing season, May to September, was over. It had been ten months since the crash, but all of a sudden it was rush, rush, rush. "It was thrown together at the last minute." Feith told me he was notified on September 25, arrived in DC on October 1 to plan the trip, and left for La Paz on October 2. "There wasn't a lot of planning time. It was more or less, 'You've got the go-ahead. See ya.'"

Feith was joined by two engineers from Boeing, Jim Baker and Al Errington, and two representatives of ALPA, pilot Mark Gerber and his brother Allen, who was not a pilot. The four men were experienced climbers. Royce Fichte, a diplomat at the American embassy in La Paz, and Feith would follow their lead and that of their professional guide, Bernardo Guarachi, who took Kelly up Illimani in June and had been the first to inspect the crash site on foot, in January, at the request of Col. Grover Rojas, the Bolivian air force's director of rescue operations.

The men had little time to acclimate even to the twelve-thousand-foot altitude of La Paz, and the lack of preparation was apparent immediately. The climb began on October 8 and was beset with problems. Errington succumbed to altitude sickness first, so he and Baker did not go on. The Gerber brothers, Fichte, and Feith continued up the mountain, but then Mark Gerber fell ill and Fichte also began to deteriorate. Feith made it to the crash site, but said he had just hours there to dig around in the snow. Though he found the plane's tail section, where the flight and data recorders should have been, he did not see the black boxes. Fearing for the health of the team, the group started back down the mountain to La Paz the following morning.

It was a frustrating experience. Errington suggests that the men were too eager, especially the experienced climbers. "We guided the team through youthful overexuberance," he told me. They were feeling good enough to push forward instead of remaining cautious. "We should have gone slower, and we realized it, but we really wanted to get things done. We could have slowed things down, but we didn't."

The Gerber brothers interpret the time pressure and the assortment of other planning and support blunders as a deliberate campaign to foil them. "The whole situation was rather bizarre," Mark Gerber said. "Looking back, we were there to do a job, yes, but it was a sham." The Gerbers agreed with Jehn. "There were political games going on," Gerber said.

Supporting their suspicion is this: even before the climbers left for La Paz, the Bolivian Board of Inquiry on Accidents and Incidents had written its report. It had been submitted on

September 4, and concluded that "the accident was apparently caused by the aircraft's deviation from its airway." It was a statement of the obvious that didn't include any of the information the NTSB had gathered. Of course it was a deviation from the airway—the airway didn't cut through the mountain. The question was why the plane was where it should not have been. If there was any effort made to find the answer, it wasn't in the report. The issues raised by McClure, the findings of O'Rourke, the reports of eyewitnesses—none of that made it in, either.

Considering how much information has come from armchair investigators, it is fitting that after thirty-one years, two adventurers from Boston should be the ones to claim to have discovered pieces of the black boxes. In May 2016, Dan Futrell and Isaac Stoner climbed Mount Illimani to a field of debris where they found uniforms, engines, human remains, and fragments of orange metal. On their return to the U.S., Stoner posted on the internet site Reddit, "There's a smashed up flight recorder on my kitchen counter!" Michael Poole, once the head of Canada's flight recorder laboratory, said data might be recoverable even after all this time. Even so, the NTSB had no plans to reexamine an accident that was the responsibility of the Bolivians, a spokesman said.

The inconclusive conclusion of the Bolivians is the only official record of a crash that was in every way an American catastrophe, just as Arrow Air had been. Just as with Arrow Air, the NTSB was satisfied to let the Bolivians have the only and final word.

In his role as chief international aviation affairs officer for the NTSB from 1988 to 2011, Robert MacIntosh navigated the complex and often delicate relationships between governments.

Even he was surprised at the noticeable lack of interest in pursuing the safety and security lapses exposed by the parties looking into the crash of Eastern 980. "It's not typical, and that's about all I can say."

Around Christmas 1985, as the first anniversary of the crash approached, a journalist asked the NTSB investigator in charge, John Young, about Flight 980. "Any secrets about the crash are buried beneath snow at an elevation where excavation is virtually impossible," he said.

Young, who died in 2005, might as well have written the script for many investigations to come, including MH-370, where reliance on recovering the airplane is so great that even the Royal Malaysian Police can't make progress without it. When asked for the status of the police probe into the disappearance of MH-370, Inspector-General Tan Sri Khalid Abu Bakar replied, "I'm not at liberty to reveal" any news "until at an official inquiry when the black boxes are discovered."

While everyone agrees that having the airplane is nice, not all investigations are so neatly presented. Without ever leaving his desk, George Jehn came up with enough clues to write a book filled with possibilities. Investigators never know what they're going to find when they start asking questions and digging through records. And before they give up, first they have to try.

Snow Job

Of all the air accidents linked to political intrigue, the Air New Zealand Flight 901 disaster over Antarctica seems the most incredible. Featuring lies, manipulation, document shredding, and burglary and set in one of the world's most inhospitable places, it is a tale worthy of any tinfoil hat–wearing conspiracy theorist, except that it is true.

In 1977, long before cruise lines started offering tours of Antarctica, Qantas and Air New Zealand inaugurated one-day sightseeing trips through which adventure seekers could spend a day on a first-class aerial tour. Antarctica and back in just one day—who wouldn't want to take that flight? On Air New Zealand, the flights were scheduled during the near-twenty-four-hour days of the austral summer on a McDonnell Douglas wide-body DC-10.

From altitudes as low as fifteen hundred feet, passengers could see the Ross Ice Shelf; McMurdo Sound; New Zealand's scientific and industrial research center at Scott Base; the Americans' McMurdo Station, with its ice airfield; and even expedition sled dogs and indigenous emperor penguins. Most impressive was the still-active Erebus Volcano, the twelve-thousand-foot-high exclamation point of Ross Island.

These weekly trips were conducted only one month a year, so there was not much opportunity for pilots to gain experience in this unusual environment. Of the eleven flights between February 1977 and November 1979, only one captain had flown to Antarctica more than once.

It was considered a plum assignment. Management pilots handled most trips, often with VIP guests of Air New Zealand or journalists on board. So line pilot Capt. Jim Collins was surprised to be rostered on the flight on November 28, 1979. Flying with Collins would be first officers Greg Cassin and Graham Lucas and flight engineers Nick Moloney and Gordon Brooks. Brooks was the only one of the five who had flown an Air New Zealand Antarctic flight before. For the others, their first "Antarctic Experience" would be this one.

Shortly after arriving over the ice, the jumbo jet slammed into Mount Erebus, instantly killing all 257 people on board. At the time, it was unfathomable that the experienced airmen would descend into this well-known high terrain. Yet that shocking event was eclipsed by what happened next. The airline figured out how the plane happened to be over Mount Erebus; it was a terrible, tragic data entry error, as simple as it was unintentional. Rather than confess, however, the people at Air New Zealand decided to hide the truth by incriminating the pilots.

When Captain Collins made the decision to descend from sixteen thousand to six thousand feet to give his passengers a better view of Antarctica, he was confident that he was approaching the continent over McMurdo Sound, a forty-mile-wide expanse of water that ended at landfall at the McMurdo waypoint.

He and the two first officers thought this because it was the route they had been shown at a mandatory preflight briefing nineteen days earlier. It was also the route Collins and Cassin flew at the flight simulation session that followed, according to the testimony of two other pilots who attended the session with them.* The night before the crash, Captain Collins, a bit of a cartography nerd, sat in the dining room of his home in Auckland with his daughters and showed them the path he would fly, moving to the living room floor when one of the maps proved to be too big for the table. He pointed out to his two elder daughters, Kathryn, sixteen, and Elizabeth, fourteen, the mountains of Victoria Land, about twenty-five miles to the west of his overwater course, and Mount Erebus, twenty-seven miles to the east.

When Collins checked in at Auckland Airport the following day, however, the information given him to program the flight plan into the plane's inertial navigation system had been altered. In an attempt to correct a data entry error made fourteen months earlier, Air New Zealand changed by two degrees of latitude a waypoint on the routing. Rather than approach the continent over the flat terrain of McMurdo Sound, the plane would fly directly over Mount Erebus, the twelve-thousand-foot volcano. Even though this made for a very different flight path, the crew was not notified of the change.

Neither the captain nor the first officers would have noticed the difference just looking at the numbers, which are latitude

---

* First Officer Lucas did not attend the briefing.

and longitude coordinates for a series of waypoints between Auckland and the continent of Antarctica. The pilots would have had to pull out maps and cross-check the routing to catch the switch, which they had no reason to do. They had been briefed on the route and had practiced it in the simulator. That was the purpose of their November 9 session, and that is what Captain Collins had reviewed so intently the night before.

By the time the plane neared Antarctica, Flight 901 had been in the air for about four hours and forty-five minutes. This wasn't normal air travel. Air New Zealand wanted to delight and awe its customers, so it staffed the flight with an Antarctic expert, who provided a running commentary. Sir Edmund Hillary, who along with Tenzing Norgay was the first to summit Mount Everest, was on some flights. On this one, though, was Hillary's friend Peter Mulgrew, retired from the New Zealand Navy. Mulgrew had accompanied Hillary on an expedition to the South Pole in the late 1950s. Passengers moved around the cabin with glasses of champagne, looking out the windows and listening to Mulgrew pointing out the sights. They could mosey up to the cockpit, where an open door invited them to see the view head-on.

Cameras clicked as the plane passed the ragged mountains of Victoria Land to the west. In total, more than nine hundred images taken on the flight were developed and studied, photos that would play an important role in exposing flaws in the official conclusion of what happened to Flight 901.

Two hundred eighty miles north of McMurdo Station, Collins was invited by air traffic control at McMurdo Center (Mac Center) to fly down to fifteen hundred feet via radar, through a layer of clouds below him at eighteen thousand feet. This was good news: it meant that the passengers could get their first close-up look at the scene below. Then Collins saw the clouds breaking up, so he descended in clear air instead. On the way down, he made a modified figure eight. First he flew a three-hundred-sixty-degree turn to the west and then to the east, ending up once again aiming south toward McMurdo Station.

After completing the second orbit, Captain Collins reengaged the autonavigation system to be sure he was back on the course the airline had provided and continued his descent. Had the DC-10 been on the track shown at the pilots' briefing, this latest group of airborne explorers would have had the same experience as the travelers on earlier flights. But once Collins reactivated the automatic navigation, Flight 901 was locked onto a path that would take it straight into the side of Mount Erebus.

The cockpit and flight data recorders recovered at the crash site reveal that the plane was flying at around fifteen hundred feet when the first alert sounded with *Terrain pull up!* Seconds later, Captain Collins instructed the first officer, "Go-around power, please." The recording ends six seconds after the initial warning.

There were two big questions for those assigned to investigate the crash: why was the plane flying so low approaching high terrain, and why had the pilots not seen the mountain in front of them? For Air New Zealand, the answer to the first question came within hours.

As soon as they learned that the plane was missing, flight dispatchers Alan Dorday and David Greenwood looked at the navigation information given to Collins and compared it with the previous Antarctic flight. They saw that the two paths were different. Captain Collins was not routed over flat sea ice, as the previous flight had been, but directly over land, and not just land, but the highest terrain for miles around. The pilots were flying low over a mountain because they thought they were over the sea. It was that straightforward.

Anyone who has ever screwed up probably understands wanting to escape the consequences, and it must be exponentially greater when lives have been lost as a result. People at the airline gave in to that impulse. It began with a decision to hide the route shift from investigators so that when the country's chief air accident investigator, Ron Chippindale, left New Zealand for Antarctica the following day, he was unaware of the critical error that led the pilots to make their fatal descent.

Accompanying Chippindale for the ten days of on-site investigation was the chief pilot of Air New Zealand, Ian Gemmell. Unlike Chippindale, however, Captain Gemmell knew about the change in flight path, because flight dispatcher David Greenwood had told him.

Gemmell was by Chippindale's side throughout the investigation, as a technical adviser. How much he influenced Chippindale's early view of the accident is a matter of opinion. What is not disputed, however, is that materials discovered at the crash site were tampered with, and some things just went missing. The most intriguing item was Captain Collins's small ring binder— and it was the absence of this item that led people to suspect that Gemmell was behind the disappearance of evidence.

Forty-five-year-old former air force pilot Jim Collins was a notorious list maker and note taker. He took his ring binder with him in his flight bag whenever he flew.

As they worked at the crash scene recovering bodies, two New Zealand police identification officers, Stuart Leighton and Greg Gilpin, found the ring binder not far from where Captain

Collins's body lay. The binder had about thirty pages, mostly blank, except for a few in the front, which contained numbers. Sergeant Gilpin characterized it as flight-related information. When the binder arrived in New Zealand, however, those pages were gone. No one could satisfactorily explain what happened until 2012.

On his deathbed, Captain Gemmell told documentarian Charlotte Purdy that the airline had removed the pages. Purdy, whose uncle was the flight engineer on Flight 901, was producing the film *Operation Overdue*, an account of the retrieval of the victims from Antarctica. That someone whom Gemmell did not name removed the pages made sense to Purdy, but by then, all of New Zealand already knew about how the airline sought to cover up its mistake by keeping the route change secret and blaming the pilots for flying too low.

Yet there on the ice in 1979, any indication that Captain Collins did not know about the route over terrain would have derailed that plan. This is why the question of Gemmell's access at the crash site and his influence over Ron Chippindale was so important.

Gemmell always insisted he did not know about the alteration of the flight coordinates until after he returned from Antarctica on December 8, but his coworkers told a different story. "I certainly told Ian Gemmell," said David Greenwood, the dispatcher, when testifying about sharing his discovery with the chief pilot the morning after the crash.

These conflicting recollections did not happen in a vacuum, and it wasn't just Collins's binder pages that went missing. His atlas and flight papers were never found, either. And in the days following the accident, items were taken from the home of First Officer Cassin. Anne Cassin told me her husband

Greg's body had not even been recovered from Antarctica when she returned home from an errand to find that her in-laws had handed over boxes of documents to an Air New Zealand pilot who had come to the house. "Insurance details, Greg's time sheets, bills, receipts, personal letters, bank statements, check stubs, flying books—everything had gone," she said, the memory still vivid more than thirty years later. "The person chosen to liaise with the dead air crews' families and Air New Zealand stole every single item that I'll call paperwork from my home."

When she realized what had happened, Anne Cassin went to the coffee table where her husband had left the folder containing notes on his Antarctica briefing. Most of the contents were gone. Anne Cassin was a thirty-one-year-old mother of three and a private pilot,* but this early in the probe, she couldn't imagine why details of her husband's last briefing mattered to the airline. In February, it became clear when Air New Zealand's mistake in changing the route to McMurdo without notifying the crew was leaked to a newspaper.

Cassin and the pilots at Air New Zealand understood for the first time: The airline was saying the pilots knew they were flying over Mount Erebus. But the briefing notes indicated otherwise. That's why they were being snapped up. Collins's notes were gone and so were Cassin's. And all this time, Air New Zealand's chief executive Morrie Davis was ordering the shredding of crash-related documents.

That odd request came within days of the accident, when

---

* Anne Cassin went on to become a flight instructor and commercial airline pilot for Mount Cook Airline, in Christchurch.

the airline boss said that all original relevant material should be collected and everything else destroyed. Davis later explained to the lawyer for the airline pilots union that he was motivated by a desire to prevent leaks to the media.

In June 1980, Chippindale, the chief air accident investigator, released his report. The probable cause of the disaster was "the decision of the captain to continue the flight at low level toward an area of poor surface and horizon definition when the crew was not certain of their position." The airline was cited for the inaccuracies in the briefing to the crew. The country's Civil Aviation Division, or CAD, was told it should have paid more attention to how Air New Zealand was operating the flights. But it was the pilots who dominated Chippindale's report.

Regardless of whether the pilots thought they were flying over high or low terrain, everyone would have returned home safely if the crew hadn't descended below sixteen thousand feet, Chippindale said. There was a certain logic to this, reinforced by what the airline told Chippindale: pilots were absolutely prohibited from flying below sixteen thousand feet on the Antarctic Experience flights until directly over McMurdo.

It had taken Chippindale six months to come to his conclusions. One month later, a special Royal Commission Inquiry would begin examining all his findings and the information from the airline on which it was based. The national disaster was on course to become a national scandal.

Peter Mahon, a Christchurch lawyer and longtime judge in Auckland, was appointed to conduct the evaluation. After ten months, the commissioner found fault with practically every aspect of the probable cause report. It was full of inaccuracies and supported by sloppy fact-finding techniques, Mahon found. Curious interpretations of the truth were exposed in Chippindale's conclusions.

In one example, Chippindale wrote that officials with McDonnell Douglas and Air New Zealand pilots told him that when approaching Erebus, the pilots would have seen the volcano depicted on the flight deck radar monitor, so they must have ignored the approaching mountain. Yet Bendix, maker of the radar, said the air in Antarctica was too dry for the mountain to be reflected on radar. When Chippindale was asked to provide names or notes to back up his contrary information, he could not.

After a committee assigned to transcribe the cockpit voice recorder spent a week at the office of the NTSB in Washington, DC, debating every utterance and sound on the tape, Chippindale and Gemmell replayed the tape in Chippindale's home and revised the transcript. Chippindale then went to the United Kingdom and had another go at the transcript alone, revising it yet again.

"That's just not done. You cannot do that," aviation safety specialist John Cox told me. In his years as an accident investigator for ALPA, Cox has listened to and participated in the transcription of half a dozen cockpit voice recorders and calls them the most subjective aspect of the investigation. If Chippindale thought he'd heard something new or different in the cockpit voice recording, Cox says the process would have been to recall the entire CVR committee. "You sit down and say, 'We've listened again. We think the following corrections need to be made.'"

That did not happen. When the words were published in the final report, fifty-five changes had been made to what the CVR committee had earlier agreed to. Words and phrases no other contributor heard had been added, and an entire exchange the committee had agreed to had been excised.

The all-important question was whether the pilots had truly been ordered to remain at sixteen thousand feet on approach to the continent. Controllers in Antarctica seemed to have been unaware of the restriction, because they cleared Flight 901 to fifteen hundred feet. Mahon was convinced the prohibition was never heeded because flights often operated between fifteen hundred and three thousand feet. Newspaper reporters who made the trip wrote about the low-level flights, as did writers for the airline's marketing material.

The official probable cause report and the report of the Royal Commission disagree on just about every key fact except one: Air New Zealand and the Civil Aviation Division, which was responsible for regulating the airline, did not take seriously the risks associated with flying in Antarctica.

When the flights began, there were a number of requirements designed to mitigate the dangers. The crews were to be provided with flight charts on a topographical map. They were not. Two captains were to be on each flight, but that requirement was swapped for one captain and two first officers. All captains were to fly one flight with supervision. That rule was abandoned because the briefings were supposed to be good enough to eliminate the need for actual flight experience.

Above all, the special circumstance ignored by CAD and Air New Zealand is the one that sent Flight 901 into the mountain: the failure to recognize and train the pilots for the singular nature of flying in Antarctica.

People who knew Collins and Cassin to be thoughtful and conscientious aviators were outraged at the lopsided way the accident was attributed to the pilots. Still, everyone was baffled by one question: why steer a course into the side of a volcano? The day was clear: the photos captured in the cameras of the passengers revealed expansive landscapes, and sunshine to the east and west. Presumably, the view was the same out the cockpit windows, or Collins would not have continued to note that he was flying in visual conditions.

In spite of that, the official accident report concluded that the pilots were flying in cloud and that descent was foolhardy. The CAD's chief, E. T. Kippenberger, had a theory that "Captain Collins must have been suddenly afflicted by some medical or psychological malady, which made him oblivious to danger looming in front of him."

Ultimately, a more sensible answer, one in keeping with the evidence, came from Gordon Vette, an Air New Zealand pilot. Vette had been a captain on an Antarctic Experience flight. He'd flown with every crew member who died at Mount Erebus. He knew the pilots had been fooled into believing they were over McMurdo Sound. Reading the cockpit voice recorder transcript, he learned how the ground references on approach to Mount Erebus bore an unlucky and uncanny resemblance to what the crew would have seen on the McMurdo Sound approach. So he wondered if another trick had been able to hide from the crew a twelve-thousand-foot obstruction. Remarkable as it seems, the answer was yes.

When Collins took the plane below the layer of overcast, the summer sun was behind the plane. Ahead were forty miles of unbroken white: the white of the sea ice stretching to the horizon, where it blended indistinguishably with a sky bleached white by the sun's diffused rays above the unbroken clouds. The powerful effect of light meeting white eliminated the visual borders created by texture, shadow, and depth. Under these conditions, there would be no perception of the lines that separate one item of the landscape from another.

Dr. Arthur Ginsberg, director of the Aviation Vision Laboratory at Wright-Patterson Air Force Base, confirmed Vette's hunch that there was a reason for the pilots' improbable and inexplicable flight into the side of a volcano. The flat white carpet in front of the plane rising at an inclination of thirteen degrees and then nineteen degrees would not have been perceived by the crew. A pilot not familiar with the illusion would have flown straight into it.

Whiteout was not unknown at the time of Air New Zealand's Antarctic Experience flights. In his report, Chippindale devotes a page and a half to it. But whiteout (and more specifically, sector whiteout, where visibility is affected in just one direction) was not part of the training of the Antarctic crews.

Several movies and even more books have been produced dissecting the Erebus scandal. In *Verdict on Erebus*, his book about the case, Peter Mahon says that when he accepted the assignment, he thought Chippindale's report to the Office of Air Accidents Investigations was solid. He went in thinking he'd rubber-stamp a well-researched, well-reported analysis, but he discovered that nothing was as it seemed. What Mahon, an aviation outsider, saw, like a mountain dead ahead, was a government-owned airline that had engaged in what he ultimately called an "orchestrated litany of lies."

Mahon did not have the final word on Air New Zealand Flight 901. Chief Inspector Ron Chippindale wrote a rebuttal, claiming Mahon's finding "abounds in errors," and to this day, two conflicting reports account for one disaster.

How different is that really from the Arrow Air crash in

Canada, where neither probable cause was considered credible, or the Hammarskjöld accident, investigated four times and still considered incomplete? These troublesome investigations show that the search for truth does not always result in certainty, and that ambiguity may be the best cover-up of all.

When the Metrojet flight from Sharm El Sheikh in Egypt to St. Petersburg, Russia, crashed on Halloween 2015, confusion reigned once again. Metrojet executives immediately announced that nothing was wrong with the plane or the pilots, and British prime minister David Cameron offered that it was likely that a bomb brought down the airliner. Under international agreement, it fell to the Egyptians to lead the probe into what had happened, and for months they said it was too soon to say.

That didn't matter, because a deluge of stories concluded that terrorism was involved; even a front-page story in *The New York Times* said the Egyptians could not be trusted to carry out an impartial investigation.

A few days after the crash, I spoke to National Public Radio's Robert Siegel on the program *All Things Considered*. I told Siegel this should be no mystery: all the tin was there; the flight data and cockpit voice recorders had been recovered. What I failed to consider were the external factors, how each government would posture.

The Russians were responsible for supervising the safe operation of the airline. Had they failed to do so? European airlines were frequent users of the Sharm El Sheikh airport. Had they paid enough attention to the security there? Egypt had the most at stake; its economy is largely reliant on tourism. Had it been diligent enough protecting the safety of the tourists at its airports? Would it bamboozle, as the *Times* incautiously suggested, or were its investigators acting responsibly by holding off on drawing conclusions?

As much as metal on the ground, these intangible elements of realpolitik become part of the story, and the growth of international air travel means that even more than in the past, an accident investigation will involve multiple governments. Their competing interests are thought to provide balance and to ensure an unbiased result. But what I say to Susan Williams, I say to you: these cases caution us to be judicious with our optimism.

PART THREE

Fallibility

It's slips, lapses, mistakes, and violations. It's tedious because it is so banal. It's like every day, it's like breathing, it's like dying. There's nothing remarkable about it.

—PSYCHOLOGY PROFESSOR JAMES REASON

Progress and Unexpected Consequences

In the summer of 2011, I spent a week in Dubai with a hundred enthusiastic twenty-somethings training to be flight attendants for Emirates Airline. I was writing a first-person article about how Emirates is changing the industry by bringing glamour back to air travel.

At the end of my stay, I flew back to New York on an economy ticket, but I didn't stay in the back of the plane for long. Recognizing a pin I was wearing that indicated I had attended a secret initiation ceremony for Emirates employees, a curious flight attendant moved me to an empty spot in business class. I was digging into a bowl of salted almonds and trying not to get too much grease on the controls of my wide-screen TV when the woman came back with even better news. I was being moved yet again, now into first class, with an even cushier seat and a bigger TV screen. I wasn't there long before the spa attendant—yep, you read that right—came to schedule my appointment to bathe in what was, at the time, the world's only commercial airline in-flight showers. Frankly, it didn't sound especially appealing, but I reasoned that such an opportunity would not likely come my way a second time.

Standing in the altogether in the narrow cylinder watching the timer-activated faucet counting down my five-minute water limit, I marveled at how much had changed in air travel. And you should, too.

The Airbus A380 on which I was flying takes off weighing as much as 1.3 million pounds. It carries 555 people in three classes, or as many as 853 in the all-economy version. It is a far, far cry from the first airliners, like the canvas-covered Avro 10 Fokker with wicker seats for eight passengers that was flown by Australia National Airways in the early '30s, or the Martin 130 flying boat with sleeping berths for the long transpacific routes flown by Pan Am just a few years later.

The twenty-first-century airliner soars seven miles above the earth, a warm bubble protecting travelers from the dry, frigid, thin troposphere just beyond the cabin walls. The French-built, shower-equipped Airbus A380; the equally revolutionary American-built Boeing 787 Dreamliner, which is so sophisticated it is called a computer network with wings; Canada's new Bombardier CSeries; and Brazil's growing menu of Embraer E-Jets, demonstrate what the best engineering minds can produce. Each new model adds to the knowledge base. Even when the engineers err, their mistakes become bricks in the foundation for the new and improved model.

Err is such a tidy word, suggesting manageability. But to err when you are an aeronautical engineer is to unleash mayhem. Planes that do not stop upon landing, that issue alerts that confuse pilots, that explode and catch fire or pitch down unexpectedly—these are the unanticipated products of progress in aviation, and it has been that way since Wilbur Wright told the Western Society of Engineers in Chicago in 1901, "If you are looking for perfect safety, you will do well to sit on a fence and watch the birds; but if you really wish to learn, you must mount a machine and become acquainted with its tricks by actual trial."

Those tricks beset the Wrights on September 17, 1908. During a demonstration flight of the Wright Flyer for the U.S. Army at Fort Myer, Virginia, Orville Wright lost control of the plane, and it hit the ground. He was injured, and his passenger, Lt. Thomas E. Selfridge, was killed. It didn't take long to figure out what happened: A propeller blade had split, hitting a bracing wire. That, in turn, tugged on the rudder, nosing the plane down. As planes became more sophisticated, the factors leading to catastrophe became more numerous and more difficult to diagnose.

No example is more cited than the fatal design defects built into the world's first jetliner, the de Havilland Comet. The British-designed mid-twentieth-century airplane wasn't just the first passenger jet; it was a spectacularly innovative design with four motors tucked smartly into the wings. Even today it looks futuristic.

The story of the Comet focuses on its propensity to burst apart in flight, its most dramatic and well-publicized flaw, but it had other design issues. Accidents prompted changes, and lessons were learned. What has not changed is how difficult it is for designers to know in advance all the ways an idea on the drawing board will function in reality.

This is not surprising. To create an airplane is complex, involving layers of decisions that become locked into systems that are inextricable parts of the whole. Undoing one feature is like trying to remove eggs after they have been beaten into cake batter.

In the case of the Comet, a number of problems emerged

soon after passengers started flying on it. On two occasions the plane failed to take off, careening instead off the end of the runway. Three more events were even more mysterious: the planes simply broke up in the sky.

De Havilland may have been the first jet maker to go back to the drawing board, but it was far from the last. The flap handle on the DC-8, the cargo door on the DC-10, the fuel tanks of nearly all Boeing airliners—these and other components have been reexamined, reconfigured, or redesigned.

In what must be one of the fastest redos in history, Boeing modified the battery system on its 787 Dreamliner after the worldwide grounding of the fleet for nearly four months in 2013. Relentless news coverage about the things Boeing overlooked prompted the chief engineer for the 787 Dreamliner, Mike Sinnett, to admit that revolutionary creations are never fully understood at the outset. "Unknown unknowns," as he called them, lurk within, and the process of transitioning to the known is a messy and sometimes unpleasant affair.

Nearly every mishap-induced airliner redesign features a Jeremiah, the early detector of the "unknown unknown" who voices concern about the problem, but who may or may not be heeded. For the Comet, the first Jeremiah was Capt. Harry Foote in 1952.

The thirty-six-year-old pilot flew for British Overseas Airways Corporation (BOAC).* He worked with aviation writer and fellow BOAC captain, the late David Beaty. In his book *Strange Encounters: Mysteries of the Air,* Beaty concludes that Captain Foote's suicide at the age of fifty-three was because of his role as the first pilot to crash the world's first jet-powered airliner.

---

* Now known as British Airways.

The crash happened just six months after the Comet's first flight with fare-paying passengers, on May 2, 1952. That historic event was followed just a few weeks later by the first Comet flight with royalty on board. Queen Elizabeth; her sister, Princess Margaret; and the Queen Mother had a four-hour fly-around as guests of de Havilland.

All this proclaimed that the Comet wasn't just a new airplane; it was the vehicle that was going to fly England into the future. The postwar nation was getting back on its feet and taking to the air. British products were flying into the global marketplace.

And why not? Jet technology originated in Britain, the invention of a young Royal Air Force cadet named Frank Whittle, who patented the idea for a gas turbine engine while still in his twenties. And though the Germans were the first to create a jet that actually powered an aircraft, Whittle went on to help develop the engine used for the DH-100 Vampire, England's first single-engine jet fighter. With this technological advantage, the British could overtake the American plane builders Lockheed, Douglas Aircraft, and Boeing, who were selling their slow and noisy propeller planes to airlines around the world.

In 1947 the British government turned to the Vampire's creator, Geoffrey de Havilland, to make the first jetliner. It took less than a year for the company to detail the new plane's attributes, and they were astonishing. The airplane would be light, with a thin aluminum skin. Some sections would be glued rather than riveted, saving the weight of metal connectors. And the plane would fly high. Where the DC-6s and DC-7s and the Lockheed Constellations cruised at twenty-four to twenty-eight thousand feet, the Comet would soar at thirty-six to forty thousand feet. In the thinner air of higher altitude, the plane would encounter less drag and would be more fuel efficient.

The downside of flying seven miles above the earth was that the cabin would require an unprecedented level of pressurization. An interior atmosphere equal to about eight thousand feet above sea level meant putting eight and a half pounds of pressure on every square inch of the walls separating outside from in.

More pressure and a thinner structure were two decisions that would factor in the disasters soon to come, but they were not the only ones. Those new jet engines would subtly alter some basic characteristics of flight and have their own repercussions.

When the war ended, military aviators filled the cockpits of BOAC's airliners. Among them was Harry Foote, who flew the four-engine Lancaster heavy bomber for the Royal Air Force. He had 5,868 hours in his logbook and was considered one of the airline's elite pilots, according to Beaty, who wrote that only the best were selected to fly the technological marvel that was the Comet 1. Of course, even the elite would have relatively few hours in the new plane. Foote had just 245 on the Comet on October 26, 1952, the day that would mark the beginning of the end for Harry Foote and for the Comet 1.

Unknown Unknowns

I t was just before 6:00 p.m. on October 26, 1952, the sun
had already set, and rain was falling when Captain Foote
began the Comet's takeoff roll for the second leg of a journey from London to Johannesburg. Eight crew and thirty-five
passengers were on board the plane, registered as G-ALYZ.
As the plane accelerated on the runway at Rome's Ciampino
airport, the pilots watched for the needle on the speed gauge
to reach eighty knots. When it did, Foote pulled back on the
yoke and felt the nose of the airplane rise. The main landing
gear was still on the ground, as it should have been, as the
plane continued to accelerate. At one hundred twenty knots,
Foote pulled the control column back again to lift the jetliner
into the air.

So far, it felt like every other takeoff, so he called for the
next step. "Undercarriage up," he said to the first officer. Before
the man had time to comply, however, the left wing dropped
and the plane turned left. The plane was no longer gaining
speed, and the pilots felt a buffeting sensation, the precursor to

a stall. The Comet flopped back onto the runway, forward momentum now propelling it into the darkness.

Foote pulled back on the throttle, cutting fuel to the engines as quickly as he could, but what had caused the plane to slow was the braking effect of the main landing gear being torn away by a mound of earth. The plane stopped just ten yards from the perimeter fence. Mercifully, there was no fire, though one wing had ruptured, spilling fuel onto the ground and sending fumes into the night. Passengers were shaken but uninjured.

By November, an accident investigation concluded that Foote's technique, lifting the nose too high on rotation, was the cause of the crash. The pilot argued that it hadn't happened that way. The airplane had become airborne after rotation, but had failed to climb and instead sank onto the ground, nose still high.

Many forces were working against Foote. The first crash of the highly touted Comet was the kind of news money can't bury. Banner headlines and news photos showed the gearless, semi-wingless, entirely hapless G-ALYZ as it lay on the far end of Ciampino airport. Even those at BOAC who sympathized with Foote's argument would not help him in his effort to reopen the examination, which had acquitted the plane in less than a month by convicting the pilot.

Then, just four months later, Capt. Charles Pentland of Canadian Pacific Airlines had a similar problem getting the plane off the ground. What started out as an uneventful takeoff roll from the airport in Karachi, Pakistan, ended in a deadly inferno. The plane was not carrying passengers, only four crew members who worked for the airline and six technicians employed by de Havilland, all of whom were killed.

Canadian Pacific was taking delivery of the plane it had

already named *Empress of Hawaii,* because it was going to provide the Sydney-to-Honolulu leg of the airline's transpacific service to Vancouver. The *Empress* was making a hopscotch journey. Day one was London to Karachi. The second day began at 3:00 a.m. On an already hot and steamy morning, the crew prepared for the flight from Pakistan to Rangoon, Burma.*

More than half a century later and after decades of research into how to enhance pilot performance, it is apparent how many aspects of the *Empress* flight created additional hazards for the pilots. Most significant, neither of the two men flying the *Empress* had even the little experience flying jets that BOAC's Comet pilots had.

Captain Pentland, the airline's manager of overseas operations, and Capt. North Sawle, thirty-nine, each had thousands of hours of flight time, but the Comet was their first experience in a jetliner.

In his book *Bush Pilot with a Briefcase,* the biography of Canadian Pacific's then-president Grant McConachie, author Ronald Keith describes Pentland's and Sawle's Comet training as a "crash course." The terrible pun notwithstanding, even the instructors at the de Havilland pilot school in Hatfield, England, considered the men novices during their time there.

Ironically, part of what made them weak in the Comet was the depth of their experience on other aircraft. Pentland had been a pilot with BOAC and Imperial Airways before joining CPA. Captain Sawle was CPA's chief pilot for overseas operations. He had been an aircraft mechanic, a plane builder, and a float and ski plane pilot who in his youth had flown mail,

---

* Now Yangon, Myanmar.

supplies, and passengers around some of the least hospitable areas of Canada's frozen north.

What Pentland and Sawle learned at Hatfield "clashed with flying instincts formed by many thousands of hours at the controls of conventional planes," according to Keith. On the night of the crash that killed them, Keith wrote that "neither had experienced a night take-off in the jet, nor had they flown it heavily loaded."

Yet the company not only selected these two to fly an unfamiliar plane on a globe-spanning delivery flight without any relief pilots, but McConachie had ratcheted up the pressure by trying to set a publicity-generating London-to-Sydney speed record. It was a decision Pentland called "bloody rough on us cockpit help."

Aviation at the time was a swashbuckling, take-no-prisoners business, with airline bosses such as Canadian Pacific's McConachie, Pan Am's Juan Trippe, TWA's Howard Hughes, and American's C. R. Smith. These men presided over equally driven superpilots who claimed to thrive on the knife's edge, impervious to the fatigue and fear that affected ordinary men. It was an unrealistic dynamic, ridden with risk. Suffice it to say, Pentland and Sawle were set up to fail even if the plane had not harbored the many design flaws it did.

Loaded with two tons of fuel in the wing tanks, *Empress of Hawaii* was taxied into position by Captain Pentland and prepared for takeoff. Pentland set the brakes and advanced the throttles, feeding fuel to the four engines. He watched the gauges, waiting for the engines to gain sufficient power so that when he released the brakes, the heavy plane would pop off the mark and begin the takeoff roll.

Moving down the runway, the plane passed eighty-five knots. Pentland pulled back on the yoke, raising the nose of the airplane. He expected the acceleration to continue, but the plane instead lumbered on at one hundred knots, twenty-two knots below what was required to get it into the air.

Whether because of fatigue or habit, Pentland seemed to have forgotten that takeoff in the Comet requires a different procedure. At rotation, the nose is elevated slightly, just three to six degrees: anything steeper risks making the airplane stall, even while it is still on the ground.

The plane had already consumed more than a half a mile of runway and was still far from achieving takeoff speed. Concerned, Pentland raised the nose even higher, but the plane went no faster. At that moment something must have clicked. Pentland lowered the nose, and the wheel hit the runway. Only then did the plane start to speed up. He needed just a few seconds of acceleration now, but those were seconds he did not have.

The plane was going too slow to fly and too fast to stop when the Comet reached the end of the runway. The right landing gear hit a culvert, causing the plane to pivot sideways into a dry canal and then slam against the forty-foot embankment on the other side. The brand-new Comet shattered into pieces and erupted into flames as two tons of fuel burst out of the broken tanks in an explosive mist.

This second event, now with fatalities, exposed to a wide audience the first of the Comet's "unknown unknowns." Harry Foote was aware that something was wrong from his first-hand experience of four months earlier. The official report may have blamed his piloting skills, but it was notable that de

Havilland revised the takeoff procedures for the airplane after his event.

The new procedures required the pilot to rotate at eighty knots and then lower the nose back to the ground while increasing speed. That was the takeoff procedure taught to Pentland and Sawle when they arrived for Comet training early in 1953.

In an article for *American Aviation*, William Perreault and Anthony Vandyk explained that unlike with piston planes, where the propellers "create a bubble of compressed air close to the ground that nudges the wing up," the Comet wing with its jet engines did not get the benefit of this cushion. The engineers at de Havilland had discovered "a downward push which can make it stall," the article said. Pilots were instructed to nurse the plane off the ground by raising, lowering, and then slightly raising the nose again at takeoff speed, a technique called the "Foote takeoff."

Despite these two accidents, the Comet was flying high among the traveling public, on a steady course to three more disasters and an aviation mystery that would command the world's attention.

While the Comet 1's propensity to ground-stall was unrelated to the design problem that would bring the plane to infamy, Foote's personal experience on the wrong side of the first design error turned him into the Comet's fiercest critic. He could never put his finger on what was wrong with the airplane, partly because the only other pilot who he knew had experienced the ground stall on takeoff was now dead. Foote was unaware of any other similar events. During a series of meetings with the British Air Line Pilots Association, in an attempt to reopen the investigation that had tarnished his reputation, Foote learned that eight other BALPA Comet pilots had been disciplined for their involvement in accidents during the brief but deadly year and a half the Comet 1 had been flying. He could also see that de Havilland was making changes associated with the ground-stall issue. The takeoff procedure had been revised a second time. Later versions of the airplane featured stall warning devices and a redesigned wing that provided more lift.

Foote's thoughts kept coming back to the Comet because events related to the plane were finding him like the proverbial bad penny. After his accident, BOAC had sent Foote back to flying propeller planes. He considered this a demotion, but he accepted it. A few months after his accident, Foote was visiting the training center at Hatfield; Captain Pentland was also there, for his Comet training. The two shared a car to the train station, but not a conversation. Foote told fellow BOAC pilot David Beaty that it was an uncomfortable ride.

Imagine the scene: two captains, one sanguine about his upcoming status as jetliner captain, the other humiliated for the flaws in that same plane and now sentenced to spend the rest of his career flying yesterday's piston-driven aircraft. It was a two-character Greek tragedy set in the backseat of a car.

Later, when Foote heard the news about the accident that killed Pentland, he shared his worries with Beaty, suggesting that if anyone had paid attention to what he had been saying about the odd takeoff characteristics of the plane, Pentland and the ten others on the *Empress* might still be alive. His argument was getting traction, because shortly after that, *Aeroplane* magazine made a similar point. The article said that after Foote's crash, the chance of "pilot error could be accepted" as one in a million, but with the *Empress* crash just four months later, the plane's design must be considered. When pilots repeatedly make the same mistake, it "must be presumed to be too easily possible."

On May 2, 1953, the first anniversary of the Comet's inaugural flight, Foote was in command of a four-engine York freighter headed to Calcutta. In the sky twenty thousand feet above him, a BOAC Comet was flying in the same direction. Foote's plane was carrying cargo; on the jet there were happy passengers being waited on by an attentive staff. After a stop in Calcutta, many of the travelers would continue on to London; several were going to the coronation of Queen Elizabeth, on June 2.*

Given the jet's speed advantage, the Comet landed to refuel for its journey to Delhi well ahead of Foote's lumbering York, but the two pilots met up at the airport. While the captain of the Comet, Maurice Haddon, waited for late-arriving passengers to board, he and Foote chatted briefly and then went their separate ways, Foote to his hotel, Haddon back to the flight deck of the airplane with the registration G-ALYV.

When the last of the Comet's passengers was seated, the plane departed. After takeoff, Captain Haddon confirmed clearance to climb to thirty-two thousand feet. That was the last message transmitted. Arriving at the hotel, Foote heard the news that the Comet had gone silent. BOAC tried to allay any fears. "We have not posted it as missing yet," a spokesman for the airline told the *Times of India* news service. "We hope that the [air]liner has come down at one of the emergency landing

---

* Queen Elizabeth had already taken the throne, but her coronation was delayed to observe a period of mourning for the death of her father, King George VI, in February 1952.

PART ONE: MYSTERY

Reporters fill the ballroom used for press conferences at the Sama-Sama Hotel at Kuala Lumpur International Airport. | *(Photo courtesy the author)*

From left: Malaysia Airlines CEO Ahmad Jauhari Yahya, acting minister of transport Hishammuddin Hussein, and director general of civil aviation Azharuddin Abdul Rahman at a news conference in Kuala Lumpur on March 31, 2014. | *(Photo courtesy the author)*

The 9M-MRO, an eleven-year-old Boeing 777, on approach to Los Angeles International Airport three months before it disappeared.
(Photo courtesy Jay Davis)

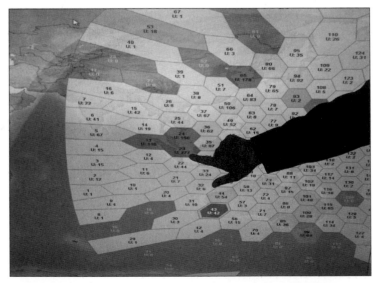

The region of Western Australia where the search for MH-370 was centered. Data from Inmarsat's satellite network led the company to conclude that the plane flew south, which assisted in the search effort. | *(Photo courtesy the author)*

Wreckage of GOL Airlines Flight 1907, which crashed after colliding with a private jet. | *(Brazilian Air Force via Creative Commons)*

PART TWO: CONSPIRACY

The *Hawaii Clipper* on the day it was christened in Pearl Harbor, Honolulu, May 3, 1936. Nine-year-old Patricia Kennedy (*seated on the plane, left*) poured coconut water over the flying boat's bow. Two years later the plane disappeared on a flight from Guam to Manila; it has never been found. | *(Photo courtesy Pan Am Historical Foundation)*

The Cuban pilot's license issued to Leo Terletsky in 1930. He was captain of the ill-fated *Hawaii Clipper*. | *(Pan Am Historical Foundation / courtesy University of Miami)*

The tail assembly of Helios Flight 522 rests on a hillside. | *(Photo from the Air Accident Investigation and Aviation Safety Board)*

An unidentified official at the scene in the forest where the Douglas DC-6 came down on September 18, 1961, killing the UN secretary-general and fourteen others. The sole survivor of the crash died in the hospital six days later. | *(Photo copyright Adrian Begg and used with permission)*

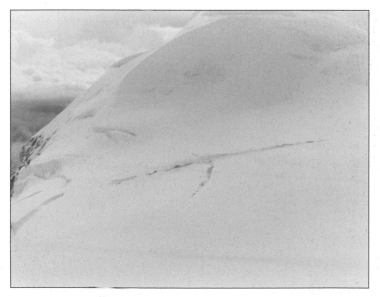

Snow on Mount Illimani, in Bolivia, shows signs of where Eastern Flight 980 hit the mountain on New Year's Day 1985.
| *(Personal photo courtesy Rus Stiles)*

The crash of an Arrow Air DC-8 in Gander, Newfoundland, on December 12, 1985, remains unsolved, and the official report remains controversial. | *(Royal Canadian Mounted Police photo)*

Two hundred fifty-six people were killed in the Gander crash, most of them members of the U.S. Army's 101st Airborne Division, the Screaming Eagles, who were on their way home from overseas duty.
| *(Canpress photo by Jann Van Horne)*

The Air New Zealand DC-10's tail-mounted engine lies not far from the jet's landing gear in the snow on Mount Erebus, in Antarctica.
(Photo courtesy New Zealand Police)

PART THREE: FALLIBILITY

Lt. Thomas E. Selfridge (*left*), seated next to Orville Wright, moments before Selfridge died in the crash of the Wright airplane undergoing trials at Fort Myer, Virginia, in September 1908. | *(Photo by Carl H. Claudy, National Air and Space Museum Archives)*

G-ALYP is greeted enthusiastically when it becomes the first jetliner to carry passengers. On January 10, 1954, it would break apart and fall into the sea near the Tuscan island of Elba. | *(Photo courtesy British Aerospace Hatfield)*

At the Royal Aircraft Establishment in Farnborough, England, workers test a Comet fuselage in a water-filled tank. | *(Photo courtesy British Aerospace Hatfield)*

The captain of ANA Flight 692 addresses passengers after the emergency evacuation of the 787. | *(Photo courtesy of passenger Kenichi Kawamura)*

ANA Flight 692 on the tarmac at Takamatsu Airport after its emergency landing. | *(Photo courtesy of passenger Kenichi Kawamura)*

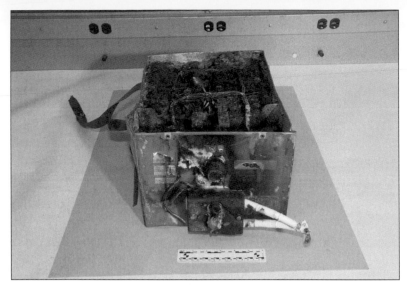

Investigators examined the lithium ion battery taken from a Japan Airlines 787 that appeared to have caught fire while the plane was on the ground at Boston's Logan International Airport on January 7, 2013. No passengers were on the plane at the time. | *(NTSB provided photo)*

NTSB investigator Mike Bauer examines the damage from the uncontrolled heating of a lithium-ion battery on a JAL 787. | *(Dreamliner NTSB photo)*

PART FOUR: HUMANITY

Capt. Dominic James was considered a hero after he successfully ditched a medical evacuation flight in the Pacific Ocean in 2009 with no loss of life. Later, top aviation officials in Australia vilified the pilot during an investigation that was itself subject to criticism.
| *(Personal photo of Dominic James)*

Pilots failed to remove locking devices on the Boeing 299's flight-control surfaces, and the plane crashed during a demonstration flight in Dayton, Ohio, on October 30, 1935. The accident prompted the creation of the pilot checklist. | *(US Air Force photograph)*

The Pel-Air medical evacuation jet that ditched off the coast of Norfolk Island, Australia, photographed where it lay on the floor of the Pacific Ocean in 2009. *(ATSB Photo)*

An artist's depiction of KLM captain Jacob van Zanten's attempted takeoff over the Pan Am 747 still taxiing on the runway. | *(Creative Commons)*

Adam Jiggins, a student at CTC Aviation, Hamilton, New Zealand, inspects his airplane under the supervision of flight instructor Sarah Jennings in 2011. | *(Photo courtesy the author)*

Lisanne Kippenberg during pilot training in Switzerland in 2013.
| *(Kippenberg family photo)*

The first powered, controlled, sustained flight. Orville Wright is at the controls while Wilbur runs alongside. | *(Photo from Library of Congress)*

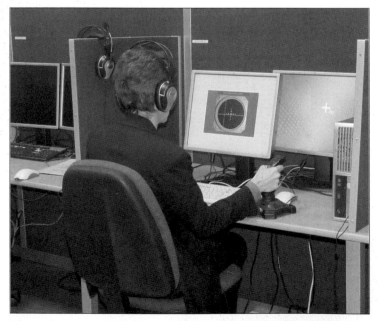

The author does a dismal job on a pilot aptitude test at CTC Aviation, a flight school for aspiring airline pilots in Hamilton, New Zealand.
| *(Photo courtesy the author)*

PART FIVE: RESILIENCY

The nose gear of Air Canada Flight 143 collapsed as the 767 glided to an emergency landing in Winnipeg in 1983. The pilots did not know that a sports car club was holding a rally on the abandoned airfield but, miraculously, no one on the ground was injured. | *(Wayne Glowacki / Winnipeg Free Press)*

First Officer Laura Strand *(far left)* and Capt. Cort Tangeman *(far right)* with the crew of American Airlines Flight 1740 in Chicago. | *(Personal photo of Cort Tangeman used with permission)*

British Airways Flight 38 lands short of the runway after losing both engines on approach to Heathrow Airport.
 | *(Photo courtesy Metropolitian Police Air Support Unit)*

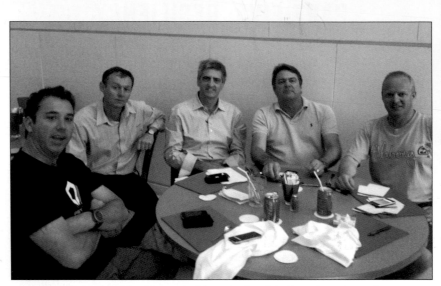

From left: Matt Hicks, Harry Wubben, Richard de Crespigny, Dave Evans, and Mark Johnson the morning after their brush with disaster in a severely crippled Airbus A380 over Singapore. None of the 459 aboard was injured in the emergency. | *(Personal photo of Richard de Crespigny)*

Nancy Bird Walton, the Airbus A380 flying as Qantas Flight 32, returns to Australia after repairs caused by an uncontained engine failure over Singapore in November 2010. | *(Photo courtesy Qantas)*

grounds between Calcutta and Delhi." Foote was not as optimistic.

At dawn the following day, his was the lone British airplane among those from the Indian Air Force taking off in search of G-ALYV. Twenty-five miles to the northwest, Foote spied the wreckage in an area accessible only by foot. So widely strewn was the debris that it appeared the plane had disintegrated while still in the air. According to his friend Beaty, when Foote heard of the plane's disappearance the night before, he was heard to have predicted, "It will have crashed."

The area where the plane went down may have been remote, but it was far from unpopulated. During an evening of sixty-mile-an-hour winds accompanied by dust storms and torrential rains, villagers reported explosions and flashes of light. One boy said he'd seen a wingless plane flying low. Where the pieces of the Comet hit the ground, a man told the *Times of India* news service that he heard human screams amid the fire, "but the heat was so intense that no one could approach."

The storm was immediately thought to have been the cause of the crash. A policeman in the town of Jangipara telegraphed the news to Calcutta, wiring, PLANE KNOCKED DOWN BY TEMPEST. When investigators began their work, they found both outer wings separated from the plane, explaining the "wingless machine" seen by the villagers. In the report the government issued a month later, the Indian inspector of accidents was circumspect, explaining that his panel had suffered from limited facilities and data and a lack of time to investigate adequately. A year or more would be needed, the report said. But they were clear about one thing: "the aircraft suffered a complete structural failure in the air" during a thunder squall. In a joint statement, BOAC and de Havilland challenged the Indians' conclusion that this was because of either "severe gusts or over controlling or loss of control by the pilot" as little more than theorizing.

To know what really happened, the Royal Aircraft Establishment, the British government's research-and-development agency, needed to determine the sequence of the breakup. While the official cause of the loss of the first two BOAC Comets had faulted the pilot, this time pilot action was an unlikely cause, the de Havilland/BOAC statement said. If it was an attempt to protect the reputation of the airline's pilot training and the integrity of a jetliner that had already been sold to airlines around the world, the effect was lopsided. Airlines were not reassured; orders from Japan, Brazil, and Venezuela were canceled. Among passengers, however, the plane remained popular. BOAC had no problem selling tickets to fly on the Comet.

Even before the Calcutta crash, de Havilland had been conducting additional research to determine if the plane was experiencing metal fatigue. The company had been prompted to do so based on what it was learning about age and fatigue on de Havilland transport planes used by the Royal Air Force. Initially, the primary focus was on the wings, but soon the U.K. Ministry of Supply, which oversaw the military planes, and the Air Registration Board, responsible for civil airplanes, asked de Havilland to broaden the study. De Havilland's chief structural engineer, Robert H. T. Harper, agreed.

The work began in July, with technicians repeatedly applying levels of pressure to the cabin greater than what it would experience in flight. By September, the engineers found that tiny cracks were developing in the aircraft skin at the corner of the plane's square windows.

This sounds like an aha moment, but hang on. Rather than causing alarm, the examiners found it reassuring. The amount of pressure applied to the cabin walls during the testing was so far beyond what the plane would experience in flight, "It was regarded as establishing the safety of the Comet's cabin with an ample margin."*

What de Havilland failed to realize was that the test setup provided additional support to the structure that would not be there in flight. This was a critical oversight, one that led investigators to have a false appreciation of the cabin's strength under pressure. This same kind of error would be made sixty years later, during the testing of the revolutionary Boeing 787 Dreamliner.

Pressure tests were also conducted on the wings of the Comet, and in December, in much the same way, tiny cracks began to appear. In this case, however, the engineers were alarmed. The pressure had been applied for the equivalent of six thousand hours, and that was not a lot of flight time. Many Comets had already flown more than that. BOAC immediately instituted an inspection program on its planes.

Throughout Christmas, the manufacturer and the airline discussed whether that was enough. Did the wings need to be modified? The debate continued until it was interrupted with another Comet bursting apart in the sky.

---

* "Report of the Public Inquiry into the Causes and Circumstances of the Accident Which Occurred on the 10th January 1954, to the Comet Aircraft G-ALYP, http://lessonslearned.faa.gov/Comet1/G-ALYP_Report.pdf."

This was the original plane—the first jetliner to carry passengers, the plane that had starred in the newsreel films. Now it was in pieces on the floor of the sea and thirty-five people were dead.

It happened on January 10, 1954, a clear, sunny Sunday. Capt. Alan Gibson, thirty-one, and thirty-three-year-old First Officer William John Bury had an uneventful takeoff from Rome for the last leg of a flight that originated in Karachi. Rome to London would have been a quick two hours and twenty minutes in the air.

Captain Gibson was ascending through twenty-six thousand feet and making a radio call to a BOAC pilot in another plane, but the transmission was cut off midsentence. At thirty thousand feet, the center of the passenger cabin ripped open. The tail, the nose, and the wings outward of the embedded engines blasted off with a downward force. The tail remained largely in one piece as the plane tumbled through the air and slammed open-end first into the water.

Before the rupture of the passenger cabin, travelers had been seated two by two on either side of the plane's center aisle in armchair-style upholstered seats that might have made them feel as if they were enjoying a cocktail in the living room of friends. With the breakup of the airplane, some of those travelers were shot out of the ruptured fuselage. Fifteen others slammed against what remained of the fractured front bulkhead, which was fitted with a library shelf and water dispenser. The torn wings exposed the engines and released flammable kerosene that quickly ignited. The fire spread inward, burning the bodies of those who remained in the cabin.

As in the in-flight breakup of G-ALYV outside Calcutta,

G-ALYP shattered into countless pieces, descending in a cacophony of explosions and smoke. In India, the witnesses had been jungle villagers. In Italy, they were fishermen who watched for three long minutes as the plane and its contents fell into the water near the Tuscan island of Elba. Racing out in their boats, they came across the only bodies that would be recovered, the fifteen trapped on board by the bulkhead.

Autopsies by the director of Pisa's Institute of Forensic Medicine, Dr. Folco Domenici, would provide important clues about what happened. The victims' organs showed the plane had experienced a split-second decompression at high altitude and blunt force injuries suggested they had died from slamming into the cabin divider.

It took awhile for investigators to recognize the value of that information, but its most immediate effect may have been to provide a shred of comfort to the victims' families: their loved ones could not have suffered. They died immediately.

Floating wreckage was gathered, including the rear fuselage, the engines, and the wing center section, but the rest of the plane lay six hundred feet below the surface of the Tyrrhenian Sea. At that depth it was twice what British salvage divers could descend to at the time.* Obtaining it would not be easy, and certainly it would not be quick.

Investigators from BOAC, de Havilland, and the Air Accidents Investigation Branch of the U.K. Ministry of Transportation focused instead on the airplanes to which they had access.

---

* Tony Booth, *Admiralty Salvage in Peace and War 1906–2006: "Grope, Grub and Tremble"* (South Yorkshire, U.K.: Pen and Sword Maritime, 2007).

All seven BOAC Comets were grounded in what the airline called a prudent measure "to enable a minute and unhurried technical examination of every aircraft in the Comet fleet."

De Havilland threw itself behind newer, safer versions of the airplane. The engineers examined the structures and the systems. They discussed all the possible scenarios. They designed modifications to guard against anything that could have happened, even if no proof existed that the potential problem had anything to do with the disaster. If the investigators found something that didn't happen but could have, it became a high-priority fix. Note that, because you don't see it happening every day.

Lord Brabazon, the chairman of the Air Registration Board and a member of the Air Safety Board, summed up the work by saying, "Modifications are being embodied to cover every possibility that imagination has suggested as a likely cause of the disaster. When these modifications are completed and have been satisfactorily flight tested, the Board sees no reason why passenger services should not be resumed." So even though the cause of the crashes remained a mystery, on March 23 the Comets returned to the sky.

Of the seven airplanes subjected to the alterations described by Lord Brabazon, one was a two-and-a-half-year-old Comet, registration G-ALYY, with twenty-seven hundred flight hours. In February, the plane had undergone an eleven-pounds-per-square-inch pressurization test to check its structural soundness. G-ALYY was leased to and operated by South African Airways to service the London-to-Johannesburg route. On April 2 and again on April 7, the plane was subjected to more inspections, perhaps one too many.

After a panel was removed from the plane to give access to a test inspector, the panel was not reinstalled correctly. The plane departed on its first leg to Johannesburg on April 7. On arrival in Rome, the mechanics were horrified to discover loose bolts inside the right wing and "an equal number of missing bolts" from the panel at the wheel well. Opening the plane up for inspection had created a hazard. That nothing had gone wrong as a result seemed a blessing, but the blessing was short-lived.

Other maintenance issues kept the plane in Rome for a day. At 6:32 the following evening, former South African military pilots Capt. Willem Karel Mostert, thirty-eight, and thirty-two-year-old First Officer Barent Jacobus Grove, took the plane and its fourteen passengers into the air. Next stop: Cairo, three hours away.

Radio calls were normal. The crew checked in at seven thousand feet, and then at eleven thousand feet. Then, on the way to thirty-five thousand, they made a transmission that also included telling controllers their anticipated arrival time in Egypt. Then nothing more was heard. Calls from Rome and Cairo went unanswered.

The scenario was all too familiar.

It took a day just to find the oil slick indicating that the flight had likely ended in the Tyrrhenian Sea off the coast of the volcanic island of Stromboli. Six bodies were found along with some airline seats, but in an area where the sea depth was thirty-three hundred feet, the downed plane was as inaccessible as if it had flown into outer space. Concluding that the wreckage would never be recovered, authorities realized that whatever they determined about this accident would be an extrapolation from what they found in the Elba crash.

Both planes had come apart on ascent at roughly the same altitude and with tremendous force. The plane that crashed at

Elba had flown 1,290 pressurized flights; the South African Airways plane had completed 900. Again, the autopsies were performed by Dr. Domenici, who confirmed that a rapid decompression had taken place. The question was why.

The British government pulled the airworthiness certificate of the Comet 1. This time the planes were on the ground for good.

Into this puzzle came one of the era's most provocative thinkers, Alan Turing, who broke Germany's Enigma code and was the subject of the 2014 movie *The Imitation Game*. Turing developed the Automatic Computing Engine, a machine that automated complex equations so that they could be completed faster than humans could solve them. Parts of G-ALYP retrieved from the sea were subjected to exhaustive testing and comparison to an undamaged Comet, and for that, Turing's Pilot ACE computer was used to run the many calculations required.

The investigators didn't rely entirely on that newfangled thing called a computer. At the Royal Aircraft Establishment in Farnborough, workers also constructed an enormous tank into which would fit the fuselage of an entire Comet 1 jetliner, with the wings protruding out on either side like arms out of an undershirt. Beginning in early June 1956, water was alternately pumped into and out of the cabin to create 8.25 pounds of pressure per square inch against the walls. This was to simulate the effect of flight at forty thousand feet. Each infusion and release of water lasted about three hours, a typical flight leg for a Comet. Every day, the test airplane accumulated virtual flights and experienced actual stress.

While that was happening, the wings were flexed up and down as if the plane were in flight. After one thousand applications, a "proving flight" was conducted and the pressure to the inside of the plane was increased to eleven pounds per square inch.

On June 24, as the water was being pumped into the plane for the proving flight, the needles of the pressure gauge passed 8. They climbed to 9 and then 10. But it got no farther than 10.4 inches of pressure, because the fuselage ruptured at the cabin ceiling. An eight-foot section gaped open as much as three feet at the widest part. The slice ran through an area that included the cutout for the emergency escape hatch.

That might sound like the end of the story, but was far from it. It was as if a light had been turned on a previously darkened path. Investigators could see where they needed to go, but not what they would find on arrival. The effort to retrieve wreckage from G-ALYP off the coast of Elba received new energy. Two months later, nearly 70 percent of it had been recovered, enough to show that there were several places where a fatigue crack could have originated.

It was not possible "to establish with certainty the point at which the disruption of the skin first began," the report of the Comet inquiry read, but the long, erratic, and oftentimes faint line charting the course of this mystery was soon to end.

When the Elba accident investigation was concluded, it was joined like a Siamese twin to the tragedy that followed four months later near Stromboli. The report lays out the whole sad story, justifying to the end the decisions by British aviation officials to keep the Comet in the air. Many, including me, would wonder about that. But when I ask those who have studied the history of the Comet, I find few skeptics.

Of the final decision to let the plane fly after the still-unsolved Elba accident, Graham Simons, aviation historian and author of *Comet! The World's First Jetliner*, writes, "It was all that could be done, for no one had any idea what had gone wrong" with the airplane. Hold on to that thought, because Simons has summarized not just the decision to let the Comet fly again, but the kind of risk-benefit analyses airplane manufacturers have been making ever since.

Deflection

The single aisle Boeing 737, introduced in 1968, is Boeing's best-selling airliner and has flown in nine different versions. On March 3, 1991, a United Airlines 737 crashed preparing to land in Colorado Springs, killing all twenty-five people aboard. It had been an uneventful flight until just after 9:43 a.m. Flight 585 was on approach, and First Officer Patricia Eidson was concerned about the turbulence experienced by the plane that had landed ahead of them.

"I'll watch that airspeed gauge like it's my mom's last minute," Eidson said to Capt. Hal Green. Indeed, the descent was dodgy, with the plane accelerating and Green complaining how hard it was to hold his airspeed.

"Wow," Eidson said, followed twenty seconds later by "We're at a thousand feet." The plane rolled to the right, and the pilots tried to regain control. The cockpit voice recorder suggests the captain was adjusting settings for a go-around, abandoning the present landing to go around and try again. The only communication between the pilots makes it clear they realized the plane was going to crash. "Oh God," the first officer says repeatedly. "Oh no," Green says the second before impact.

Investigators thought early on that the rudder, the hinged vertical panel on the tail that swings from side to side to control the plane's left and right motion, played a role. The week before the accident, two crews who flew the plane reported problems related to the operation of the rudder, including uncommanded movement. In July 1992, as the investigation was under way, a United maintenance worker reported finding an anomaly during a ground check of another 737 in the fleet. "The rudder had the potential to operate in a direction opposite to that commanded by the flight crew," the airline reported. The main rudder control valve was changed by Parker Hannifin, the company that designed it.*

Still, after nearly two years studying the evidence, Tom Haueter, the NTSB investigator in charge, could not say conclusively if or how the rudder factored in. The probable cause of the accident was left as one of two likely events: some mechanical problem with lateral control of the aircraft, or an atmospheric disturbance that caused the airplane to enter an uncontrollable roll. From that point on, though, Haueter took notice of any difficulties reported with the 737's rudder.

Among the family of Boeing airplanes, the 737's rudder design was unique in a number of ways. First, since it was smaller than the 727 and the 747, there was not enough room for two entirely separate and redundant power control units. That unit, known by the abbreviation PCU, takes the input of the

---

* This was the first of four modifications to the Parker Hannifin design.

pilot's foot on the rudder pedal and converts it through hydraulic action into movement of the swinging panel on the tail.

Boeing got the plane certified with a novel design that put both control of the rudder and a backup in the same unit. In what was to be a belt-and-suspenders plan, Boeing told the FAA that in the unlikely case of a loss of both primary and secondary rudder control, pilots could still control the movement of the plane with the use of panels on the wings called ailerons.

But two aspects of the device in operation went unappreciated when the FAA certified the plane in 1967. First, the two cylinders in the PCU were "hand-fitted and mated for life," according to Haueter. Because the space between the two cylinders was hair-thin, just enough to allow one valve to move within the other, particles trapped between the cylinders could cause a jam that could then make the rudder go in a reverse direction, as when a steering wheel is turned to the right and the car goes left. It wasn't often, and it wouldn't happen in all the units. "Some would never reverse," Haueter said when we talked about the case years later. "Some were extraordinarily sensitive to reversal because of the way they were made."

When the rare event did occur, the second unforeseen problem could reveal itself. At slower speeds the ailerons would not have sufficient power to offset the force of the rudder. This was discovered only in 1994, when another Boeing 737 crashed, also under puzzling circumstances.

On September 8, 1994, USAir* Flight 427 plummeted from six thousand feet during what was up until that point a normal flight from Chicago to Pittsburgh. The plane was crossing the

---

* USAir was renamed US Airways in 1997. In 2012 it merged with American Airlines.

wake turbulence of a Delta Boeing 727. Suddenly it rolled to the left, surprising both pilots. Then the nose of the plane went down. In his book, *The Mystery of Flight 427: Inside a Crash Investigation*, author Bill Adair gives a horrifying description of the sensation experienced by the 132 people on board. "It would have felt as if they had reached the top of a roller coaster and were starting the first, huge drop."

The pilots pulled back on the yoke, but the left wing remained pointed down, and the plane began spiraling to the left, picking up speed as it fell. From the initial upset to the plane's crash into the woods just outside Pittsburgh, the event took twenty-eight seconds.

It was a difficult investigation. Flight data recorders at the time contained just a few details, but no data about the position of the rudder or ailerons. Tests of the components that control the plane's lateral movement did not reveal any problem that could have caused the plane to act as it did.

Throughout the investigation, however, Boeing insisted there was nothing wrong with the plane or the rudder. "The rudder was doing what it was asked to be doing," chief 737 engineer Jean McGrew told investigators in January 1995. McGrew was saying the pilots had mishandled the controls, exacerbating the problem by slamming on the rudder pedal and pulling back on the yoke, effectively stalling the plane.

Boeing clung to that position for two years. Then, in October 1996, Ed Kikta, a young Boeing engineer, was reexamining data from an earlier test and discovered that a fail-safe mechanism in the rudder control unit did not work as it should. Kikta was simulating a jam when hydraulic fluid began flowing in the wrong direction, which would then cause the rudder to swing in a direction opposite to what the pilot expected.

After a few hastily arranged follow-up tests, Boeing notified the FAA, agreeing to redesign faulty parts and supply them to 737 operators. Boeing started a campaign to help pilots understand how to react to in-flight upsets. John Cox, a 737 captain for USAir and a member of the accident investigation team, was enthusiastic about the pilot training. But he disagreed with the notion that Boeing would not abandon: the pilots' actions caused the accident.

Cox listened to the cockpit voice recorder repeatedly. He told me each time he heard it it was clear the pilots "had no idea what was going on. They never understood what the aircraft was doing or why it was rolling uncontrollably, and they could not stop it."

During an interview at the time with John Purvis, who was a Boeing air safety investigator, he took a similar tack, spinning the rudder fix not as a remedy to a problem with the plane but as an additional precaution. He told me, "We're making a safe plane safer." I was to hear the same thing two more times over the next fifteen years as Boeing recognized, both times under duress, that its designs could sometimes harbor hazards.

"Go to the engineering folks. They'll say, 'It couldn't happen, it's perfect. I understand that," Haueter told me. It's like what happens when the police show up and say your straight-A student robbed a convenience store. You're not going to believe it. Engineers are so embedded into the system, they know the design so well, they can't see its flaws."

I was working as a correspondent for CNN in 1996 when I got a call in the middle of the night telling me about the crash of TWA Flight 800. It was a Boeing 747 with two hundred thirty people on board that exploded thirteen minutes after taking off from New York on its way to Paris. There had been no distress call, just normal cockpit conversation—and then, wham, the plane broke into three large sections, leaving a long trail of debris in the Atlantic Ocean. Where each of these sections landed would help investigators determine the timeline of events, but not what triggered the blast.

Federal law enforcement agents were concerned about an act of terrorism, but the tin kickers with the safety board concluded the blast had been triggered by a flaw in the design.

The 747 jumbo jet and many other models produced by Boeing feature a large fuel tank in the space between the wings— the structural center of the plane. This tank was designed to double as a heat sink for the air-handling equipment located below. But it worked that way only when there was fuel in the tank to absorb the heat. When the tank was empty, there was nothing but fumes, which would heat up as if the tank were a giant saucepan sitting on top of the stove. It could get hot enough to ignite.

In my book *Deadly Departure*, I write that the stunning news to emerge from the four-year probe into the disaster was that this flammability problem was well known. Engineers at Boeing, some of the airline's customers, and federal air safety regulators had been discussing it for thirty-five years, because of a number of similar events beginning in 1963. In those cases, Boeing concentrated on locating the specific ignition source rather than the greater hazard of operating with a fuel tank in an explosive state.

Studies carried out as part of the Flight 800 accident probe showed that fuel tanks with heat-generating devices below them can be like ticking time bombs as much as one-third of the plane's operating time.

In the 1960s and '70s, safety officials asked for devices to be installed in fuel tanks to preclude the possibility of explosion by eliminating the oxygen, a necessary component of fire. During the development of the 747, Boeing even tested some systems specifically designed to do this. The manufacturer ultimately dismissed the idea, however, citing concerns about the additional weight.

The recommendations for protecting the fuel tanks emerged repeatedly over the decades, but the FAA accepted Boeing's position that if the triggers for the explosion could be identified and fixed, the design would be safe enough. What the TWA 800 disaster showed was that there would always be unknown triggers. We would have to call them the "known unknowns."

In 2006 the U.S. Department of Transportation issued a new rule: all new airplane designs had to include a system to protect the tank from explosion. Boeing's newest airplane, the 787 Dreamliner, incorporates a fuel tank explosion-prevention system that is a direct result of the TWA crash investigation.

So it is ironic that after just fourteen months in service, the 787, which had already secured its place in the pantheon of revolutionary aircraft, was gracelessly sidelined for four months in 2013 because of a risk of fire and explosion from the plane's lithium-ion batteries.

The designers of the Dreamliner and the Comet shared an overconfidence in their creations. "The Comet embraced new technologies before they were fully understood," Graham Simons, the author of *Comet*, told me. "With the Dreamliner, Boeing pushed the same limits. They seem to have forgotten when you push the envelope, you open a greater area of risk."

Fever Dream

Among Boeing's worldwide customer base, there are few as loyal as Japanese carriers Japan Airlines and All Nippon Airways. ANA effectively launched the 787 Dreamliner by placing the very first order for fifty of them in 2004. Ten years later it remained the largest 787 operator.

There was much national pride in the 787 because of the number of Japanese companies making parts for it. Fuji Heavy Industries, Mitsubishi Heavy Industries, and Kawasaki Heavy Industries all turned out pieces that were shipped to Boeing's American assembly plants.

While these giants of Japanese industry made the big parts, in Japan's historic former capital of Kyoto, battery manufacturer GS Yuasa was churning out a much smaller and more obscure component that was on the cutting edge of transportation power systems. Lithium-ion batteries the size of a bread box and the weight of a dorm refrigerator were to ignite the biggest issue in aircraft design since the Comet.

The first time I saw a Dreamliner outside the factory, it was on its six-month world tour. The aircraft arrived at Bole International Airport in Addis Ababa in December 2011. Ethiopian Airlines captain Desta Zeru, dapper in a forest green uniform, was at the controls for the first flight of the new airliner into the African continent. Ethiopian was a launch customer, with ten 787s on order. Ethiopian was also a new member of the Star Alliance, the world's largest network of airlines, so the airline hosted a three-day extravaganza to celebrate. Boeing created a large meeting space on board the airplane and invited reporters in for a press conference and look-see.

Of course, everybody was delighted to have the plane on display. Three years late to customers, the plane was sometimes called the seven-*late*-seven, and Boeing had had it up to here with criticism of its inability to set a delivery date and stick to it.

In late October 2011, however, when the first Dreamliner began revenue flights for All Nippon Airways, the game-changing airplane was changing headlines, too. "The engines purred rather than roared." Travelers were "agog." The engines "sipped fuel," and the passenger cabin "glowed," and that's just one review* from among thousands written in a similar vein once the plane actually started flying. President Barack Obama called the Dreamliner "the perfect example of American ingenuity."

The Japanese are enthusiastic air travelers, and they embraced the Boeing 787, too. Kenichi Kawamura is a policy adviser to his father, a Japanese political official in Tokyo. His job required him to commute by air each week between his home in Yamaguchi and his father's office. A self-described aviation enthusiast, Kawamura knew he was traveling on a special airliner on January 16, 2013.

---

* John Boudreau, "In Praise of the 787's Emotional Experience," *San Jose Mercury News*, September 25, 2012.

Eighteen minutes into the ninety-minute flight on ANA's Flight 692 to Haneda Airport, the Boeing 787 Dreamliner nosed down precipitously. Kawamura grabbed his drink moments before it would have tipped off his tray table. He had never experienced such a rapid shift. "It was a sudden fall and very steep," he told me. Looking at the flight profile, an experienced airline pilot described it as being like riding in the backseat of a car racing down a highway and then suddenly having the driver hit the brakes.

"Then there was a smell like plastic burning," Kawamura said. The flight attendants were walking up and down the aisle purposefully, collecting the cups and bowls in which they'd recently served miso soup. As an attendant approached his row, Kawamura started to ask what was going on, but then stopped as a voice came on the PA. "This is the captain," Kawamura remembers hearing. In fact, it was the forty-six-year-old first officer, one of the airline's very first pilots to be certified to fly the Dreamliner.

"We have smoke, we smell smoke," Kawamura remembers being told. "We must make an emergency landing." That much was already clear. Kawamura was heartened to hear the pilot say that instruments in the cockpit indicated that there was no problem.

In truth, the pilots were worried that the flight instruments were giving bad information. As soon as the first officer was finished with the announcement, he told air traffic control that there was "thin smoke, possibly by an electric fire." The main battery had failed. The pilots wanted to land as "soon as practicable," he said.

The drama for the flight crew began sixteen minutes into the flight, as they were taking the plane through thirty-two thousand feet on the way to leveling off at forty-one thousand feet. Voltage dropped in the main battery used to provide emergency power in case of the loss of other systems. It was not a subtle decline, either, falling from thirty-one volts to eleven volts in ten seconds. The pilots were unaware of this, though. Their first alert was an advisory that emergency floor and exit lights had come on in the cabin.

The first officer had only moments to wonder what might have triggered the lights, because everything seemed to be working fine. Then he smelled something burning.

Pilots adopt an air of bravado about their work. But if there is a kryptonite for aviators, it is fire. That's a "no-shit problem," Capt. James Blaszczak, the retired Dreamliner captain, told me in reference to how the ANA crew would have reacted.

Nine days earlier, a Japan Airlines Boeing 787 (JA 829J) with just 169 flight hours and 22 landings was parked on the ramp at Boston's Logan International Airport when a maintenance worker called the airline's station manager, Ayumu Skip Miyoshi, reporting "smoke inside the cabin."

At first Miyoshi was confused. "So you mean one of the passengers smoked in the lavatory?" he asked. "Smoke inside the aircraft cabin" was the reply. Miyoshi hurried out to the tarmac, and as he approached, another maintenance worker was running toward the plane with a fire extinguisher in his hand. Smoke was billowing out of the electronics bay. When firefighters arrived, they said the battery was hissing, sputtering, and popping as flames leapt from the connectors on the blue battery case. It took an hour and forty minutes to get the smoke under control. The contents of the battery box continued to burn until all the fuel feeding the fire was exhausted.

Every operator of the Dreamliner heard about the Boston

event within minutes. I was interviewing former American Airlines chief Robert Crandall at his Florida home when his wife interrupted us with the news. CNN was carrying the story live. Forty-seven airlines around the world had already ordered the airplane. If Crandall's reaction was typical of other aviation executives, they were all glued to their TV sets.

A number of entry-into-service problems, including fuel pump leaks and engine fan shaft fractures, had been reported but were considered ordinary shake-out stuff that operators come to expect with new designs. The battery fire, however, was no minor issue.

Fire, smoke, and airplanes don't mix—ever. Or as Captain Blaszczak told me, "If there is any indication of smoke or fire, the definition of eternity is from now until we get this airplane on the ground."

Fire is not a common occurrence in air disasters. About 16 percent of commercial aircraft accidents involve fires; less frequently are they the cause. That is because a lot of effort has gone into minimizing the risk, which is a difficult task, considering that combustion is what makes the engines run. The attention paid to fire prevention is so great because an in-flight fire can quickly turn to catastrophe.

On a Swissair flight from New York to Geneva in 1998, pilots mistook smoke in the cockpit as a minor air-conditioning issue. Trying to identify the source delayed by four minutes how they dealt with what turned out to be an electrical fire in the space above the cockpit ceiling. Arcing, a high-temperature electrical discharge across a gap in wiring, had ignited highly flammable insulation material, and the fire spread quickly. Just twenty-one minutes passed between the first smell of smoke and the plane slamming into the Atlantic Ocean off the coast of Nova Scotia, killing all 229 aboard.

In its report on the accident,* the Transportation Safety Board of Canada concluded that pilots dealing with fire have between five and thirty-five minutes to get the plane on the ground. That's it.

Swissair 111 "was a seminal event in aviation history," said Jim Shaw, an airline captain who participated in the accident probe on behalf of the Air Line Pilots Association. There were a lot of lessons learned. One of the most important to Shaw was the error in the FAA's decision to allow McDonnell Douglas to continue to use metallized Mylar (polyethylene terephthalate, if you really want to know) to insulate the walls of its airliners, even after other safety authorities determined it was flammable.

It was a curious decision. In the decades leading to the accident, airplane manufacturers had been ordered to replace all sorts of interior fabrics and materials with those that were fire-retarding and flame-resistant. Seats, dividing walls, carpets, curtains—all these had to be made of substances that were slow to ignite and self-extinguishing, meaning that if a fire were to start, it could not spread more than a few inches. The rules went into effect on all planes built after 1990 and included the MD-11 that flew as Swissair Flight 111.

So, naturally, you are wondering if the metallized Mylar was flammable, why was it on the Swissair airplane in the first

---

* "Aviation Investigation Report A98H0003," Transportation Safety Board of Canada, http://www.tsb.gc.ca/eng/rapports-reports/aviation/1998/a98h0003/a98h0003.asp.

place. The answer is that it wasn't prohibited because it was used away from fire zones. Absent an ignition source, the flammability of the insulation material didn't matter, or so the thinking went at the time.

It did matter, though, because power cables, light fixtures, battery packs, and electrical wires all ran throughout the insulated area. A spark from any one of them could trigger a fire, which is what happened with Swissair 111.

After the crash, safety regulators said metallized Mylar had to be removed from twelve hundred airplanes. The effort took years, and by the time the last of it was being pulled out, Boeing was trying to convince the FAA that another highly flammable material, lithium-ion cobalt-oxide batteries, should be allowed to power the new plane the company was designing, the Boeing 787 Dreamliner.

Powerhouse

In the post-9/11 world, the twin-engine, mid-capacity, long-haul airliner on Boeing's drawing board was the most eagerly anticipated airplane since the Boeing 747, which had redefined travel in the 1970s by opening up the skies to everyone. Forty years later, the 787 was going to allow airlines to fly between far-flung secondary cities without having to rely on masses of passengers to fill the plane. Sure, any airline could sell four hundred fifty seats on a London-to-New York flight, but the markets between Houston and Lagos, Auckland and San Francisco, Toronto and Tel Aviv, would be thinner. A smaller and more fuel-efficient airplane that could fly eight thousand miles, nearly one-third of the way around the globe, would be a showstopper.

Two things made the Dreamliner different from any other airliner at the time. The first was that Boeing had eliminated vast amounts of aluminum in the plane's structure, just as de Havilland had done decades earlier. Where de Havilland simply used thinner metal (and wound up making it thicker in later models), Boeing replaced aluminum with stronger but lighter-weight carbon fiber.

The second differentiation was all twenty-first century: the plane would have an unparalleled reliance on electricity. Six generators would convert energy from the engines to electrical power, creating five times as much as any other airliner, enough to power four hundred homes, the Boeing press material claimed. The 787 would be a virtual power plant in the sky, supplying its own needs, and they were mighty. Boeing replaced mechanical flight controls and their heavy stainless-steel cables with electromechanical controls that activated cabin pressurization, brakes, spoilers, the stabilizer, and wing ice protection.

A critical part of this new energy production, storage, and distribution plan was the use of two powerful lithium-ion ships batteries, which would provide start-up power and supply some emergency electronics, lighting, and independent power for the black boxes.

Not all lithium-ion batteries are alike. There are manganese, iron phosphate, titanate, sulfur, iodine, and nickel. Each element or compound offered some benefit and some drawback. The names refer to the combination of materials used to move ions from one chemically coated thin strip of metal, through a thin permeable sheet, to another chemically coated strip, all of which is wound into a jelly roll shape and placed in a metal can, then sealed and called a cell. The motion of the ions generates electricity. The electricity is collected and stored until it is called on to deliver power. And now you know how batteries work.

Of all the lithium-ion battery recipes, the one called cobalt oxide had the best energy-to-mass ratio, meaning it gave the most energy for the least weight and size. It had other features that made it desirable: It charged quickly and held a charge longer than others. It was slightly more expensive than lead-acid batteries, but because it was already a widely produced item, the cost was below that of any of the other chemistries.

Jeff Dahn, a professor of physics and atmospheric science at Dalhousie University in Halifax, pointed out, however, that for what Boeing was trying to achieve, cobalt oxide was "not well suited" because it "has inferior safety properties compared to other alternatives." He was referring to what has been reported to be the largest industrial recall ever.

In 1991, Sony Energy Devices of Japan held the patent for one of the formulas used to produce cobalt-oxide lithium-ion. About thirteen years later, it was a multibillion-dollar product, powering all kinds of what are called 3 C devices: those used in computer, communication, and consumer electronics.

The batteries had a tendency to heat up on their own, progressing to fire and explosion, according to a paper produced for the International Association for Fire Safety Science in 2005. Some of the spontaneous combustion events had been filmed and uploaded to YouTube, where anybody could view alarming videos of cell phones and laptops sputtering and emitting tongues of flame in airport boarding areas and at office meetings.

At the time Boeing selected lithium-ion, in 2006, the U.S. Consumer Product Safety Commission was issuing recalls for the batteries powering the devices sold by Lenovo, Dell, Toshiba, Apple, and others. About four million battery packs sold by Dell alone were ordered off the market in August of that year. "Consumers should stop using these recalled batteries immediately and contact Dell to receive a replacement battery," one commission recall notice read.

This was all big news, but at the same time at the FAA, Boeing was pushing a plan to use lithium-ion batteries on the Dreamliner. It was progressing through the bureaucracy with some caution, but little public attention. The FAA told Boeing that if it wanted to use the technology, it would have to meet the terms of a special condition, because nothing in the existing regulations governing airliner design addressed this "novel technology."

There was limited experience, according to the FAA, and what experience there was wasn't good. When the FAA asked the public to chime in, just one organization did, the union representing the pilots who would ultimately fly the airplane.

"We got involved because we've always had issues," said Keith Hagy, the ALPA safety director, explaining why the union wrote several letters to the FAA during the process. Hagy wasn't so confident Boeing could achieve safety on the 787 while using batteries with such a troubled past. "Once they start burning, they never go out," he said.

ALPA was not standing on a deep well of research. So sparse was the material publicly available that it relied on just one document, the FAA's "September 2006, Flammability Assessment of Bulk-Packed, Rechargeable Lithium-Ion Cells in Transport Category Aircraft," and that wasn't even focused on powering an airplane with lithium-ion; it was about how airlines should pack the batteries if they were being sent as cargo. What struck Hagy is that even Boeing didn't know much about the batteries.

Whether the information wasn't there or the effort to get it was ineffective, people in the battery industry dispute the notion that lithium-ion batteries were a new frontier. Maybe they weren't being used on airplanes, but they'd been under review by NASA since 2000. Boeing's space division generates ten billion dollars a year, roughly 12 percent of the company's total revenues on average, but according to one scientist with knowledge of the battery development, no one from the company's space side was ever asked to provide information or expertise to the commercial airplane division or even to review the Dreamliner battery design until after the events in January 2013.

Nor does it seem that the experience of automakers was sought even though they had been working on electric cars for nearly a decade. The Tesla Roadster, a high-end electric car, was being developed in 2006 using the same cobalt-oxide formulation as Boeing, but the two companies were not sharing information.

Through the summer and into the fall of 2006, the Consumer Product Safety Commission's recalls continued. One computer company after another was telling customers to stop using the batteries that came with their laptops and to request a free replacement. And just as doggedly, Boeing kept working on the design of the lithium-ion battery system it would put on the Dreamliner. The day before Halloween, another round of recalls of nearly a hundred thousand batteries was announced. One week later, on November 7, 2006, the news became personal for Boeing.

A fifty-pound prototype, so expensive to produce and so chock-full of power it was called the "Ferrari of batteries," had been delivered to the Arizona headquarters of Securaplane Technologies from the Japanese maker GS Yuasa. It wasn't the final product, but it was what Securaplane was going to use to test the charger, its contribution to the power generation system on the Dreamliner.

Michael Leon, a technician at Securaplane, was one of those

assigned to work on the test, but the battery made him nervous. Earlier, there was a short circuit between the terminals. Workers immediately removed the current, but not quickly enough to prevent a second short circuit. Leon didn't want to use the battery again, but executives at GS Yuasa were untroubled. Analyzing the data sent by Securaplane after the first short circuits, the Japanese said that, with proper handling, the battery would be fine for continued use.

Then, on November 7, the battery ignited and exploded. Leon told the *Arizona Daily Star* that flames were leaping ten feet in the air. "The magnitude of that energy is indescribable," he said. No one was hurt, but the company's administration building was destroyed. For everyone involved, it was a multimillion-dollar lesson in unknown dangers. Boeing reevaluated its selection of lithium-ion and considered swapping it for lithium-manganese, but didn't.

Everyone went back to work: GS Yuasa on the battery, Securaplane on the charger, and the French company Thales, which had been hired by Boeing to oversee it all.

Primarily, everyone working on the battery design was concerned that in the process of charging the battery, too much power had been pushed into a cell, causing it to heat up and ignite. So they added a contactor that would disconnect the battery from the power supply. It would take the battery out of commission, bricking it for the rest of the flight, but that was considered the lesser of two evils.

In April 2007, the FAA published a two-page special rule in the Federal Register that would give Boeing the go-ahead to use lithium-ion batteries on its new airliner, provided it met certain conditions. The FAA addressed the battery's persnickety nature using aviation's four letter F-word, *fire*, and some other bad words, such as *flammability, explosion*, and *toxic gases*. Boeing would have to make sure cells didn't heat up uncontrollably, cause the failure of adjacent cells, catch fire, explode, or emit toxic gases. The plane maker was still a long way away from being able to claim it accomplished this, and in fact, it never could. Then, in July 2009, a new hurdle emerged.

Engineers at a Hamilton Sundstrand lab in Rockford, Illinois, were plugging together 787 hardware to see how it all worked as a system. The answer was "not well." One of the cells heated up uncontrollably, spewing electrolyte and causing the entire battery to fail. Boeing had a second round of second thoughts. Lithium-manganese and nickel-cadmium battery alternatives were briefly put back on the table. Yet, really, "ni-cad" offered only a little more than a tenth of the power for start-up as lithium-ion, and the company still didn't like manganese, so once again Boeing stuck with its original choice.

"If they understood the risks, they never would have done it," said Lewis Larsen, a Chicago entrepreneur and theoretical physicist whose work requires him to know about this chemistry. In 2010 he sent a presentation to Boeing and all the automobile companies with similar plans to use cobalt-oxide lithium-ion batteries for power. Through his company, Lattice Energy LLC, Larsen has been tinkering with lithium-ion because of the very characteristic that makes the batteries so inherently unsafe: the microscopically small, naturally occurring dendrites that grow inside cells over time, creating a pathway for internal electrical shorts called field failures. These miniature flash fireballs generate temperatures between five thousand and ten thousand degrees Fahrenheit. They are called LENRs, for "low-energy nuclear reactions." Larsen studies LENRs because he thinks they can be used as a source of green energy.

As a feature of a battery that will be used on an airplane, however, the idea of flash fireballs ought to set off alarm bells. Writing for the *Encyclopedia of Sustainability Science and Technology* in 2012, Brian Barnett said that field failures could create "violent flaming and extremely high temperatures" as well as explosive combustion. "Most safety tests carried out in the laboratory or factory do not replicate the conditions by which safety incidents actually occur," Barnett wrote.

This was the nature of the message Larsen sent off to Boeing. He told me, "We thought it was a moral issue to make some public statements about what Lattice knew technically at that time, so we did." Larsen said he heard back from a contact at the company, who told him that ten battery experts had assured Boeing that Larsen "was full of shit."

Thermal Fratricide

In the fall of 2011, the first Dreamliner was delivered to All Nippon Airlines, complete with the two ships batteries that had been the subject of so much tinkering. The following spring, the airline reported that not only was it pleased with the airplane, but its customers were also. Nine out of ten passengers said the 787 met or exceeded expectations, ANA reported. Who pays close attention to the model of airplane on which they fly? The Japanese. Eighty-eight percent of Japanese travelers surveyed were familiar with the Dreamliner when they boarded their flight.

Koichi Hirata, fifty-seven, was on his way to attend the InterNepcon electronics show in Tokyo on January 16, 2013, and, like those other happy ANA customers, he was looking forward to flying in the 787. He had a business-class window seat on the right side of the airplane, and he was listening to Rakugo, a traditional form of Japanese comedic storytelling on the in-flight entertainment system. He noticed right away when the plane turned and started to descend.

"The passengers didn't get into a panic, and cabin attendants seemed to be making emergency landing preparations with great efficiency," he recalled later. Once the plane was on the ground in Takamatsu and stopped in a cleared area of the taxiway, Hirata saw smoke being drawn into the engine on the right side, behind where he was seated. He didn't have much time to think about it because the flight attendants were telling the passengers to leave their things, take the emergency slides, and get away from the plane. Hirata said that between the smoke and the rapid rush to the exits, he wondered if the incident was "something far more serious." As far as he and his fellow passengers were concerned, the answer was no. Yet for Boeing, ANA, and the four dozen other airlines that had invested in this airplane, the answer was an unequivocal yes.

The JAL battery fire in Boston nine days earlier had been alarming, but until this ANA episode in Japan, the reaction of aviation officials had been to suggest that the battery meltdown was a one-off. The then-administrator of the FAA, Michael Huerta, had even gone so far as to hold a reassuring news conference with Boeing CEO Ray Conner by his side, at which he said that "nothing we have seen leads us to believe the airplane is not safe." That was January 11, five days before the emergency landing at Takamatsu. The second event resulted in the decision to ground the fleet worldwide.

In just over a week, the world's newest airliner experienced two incidents that the safety board's then-chairman characterized as unprecedented and serious. "We do not expect to see fire events on aircraft," then-NTSB board member Deborah Hersman told reporters.

It had become clear to Hersman that the lithium-ion cells

in the Dreamliner battery box—the cells Boeing was supposed to coddle like a temperamental child, the cells the FAA warned had characteristics that "could affect their safety and reliability"—had just done the very thing they were not supposed to do under any circumstances: heat up uncontrollably. In Boston, which was the incident the NTSB would investigate, this had caused a very-high-temperature chain reaction that destroyed the entire eight-cell assembly.

"These events should not happen as far as design of the aircraft is concerned," Hersman told reporters. "There are multiple systems to protect against a battery event like this. Those systems did not work as intended. We need to understand why."

This was not as easy as it sounded. Every air accident may be different, but there are common investigative themes: mechanical, operational, organizational. The mystery on the Boeing 787 wasn't about the physics of flight or the human operation of the plane. This was a puzzle about complex electrochemistry. When Hersman's investigators in America and their counterparts in Japan set about to educate themselves on the topic, they quickly found that many of the experts had already been hired by Boeing. Though it had eschewed outside advice during the development phase, the company was now assembling advisory committees and review boards and scooping up spare batteries for its own testing.

Dana Schulze, deputy director of aviation safety at the NTSB, said getting up to speed for her investigation was frustrating. Still, she showed remarkable understanding of Boeing's point of view.

"Our job is safety, but it's hard to argue that the priority was getting this plane back in the air," she told me. "At the same time, we had an investigation to conduct and wanted to be sure that the safety issues were addressed."

Judy Jeevarajan was one of those experts who found herself on the receiving end of a call from Boeing. From 2011 to 2015, she was battery group lead for safety and advanced technology at NASA. Part of her job was to study and publish articles on how to use lithium-ion batteries safely in a manned space environment. Because the batteries are so much larger and more powerful than those used on personal devices, when they go bad, they have the potential to trigger catastrophe. Jeevarajan's job was to manage those risks on the International Space Station by critically assessing the battery at three levels: the individual cell, the cells as a unit (the battery), and the electrical system into which they were integrated.

When the Dreamliner was grounded, Jeevarajan was recruited by Boeing to give an honest opinion about the battery design and function. On the day the experts got together in Seattle, the damaged battery from the JAL plane in Boston was wheeled into the room on a cart. Everyone crowded around for a look. Jeevarajan was surprised at what she saw. The cells were missing any bracketing substantial enough to keep them firmly in place, protected from vibration, and separated from one another. This observation was shared by Kazunori Ozawa, a battery engineer who was involved with the development of lithium-ion batteries many years before at Sony, but who was not part of the review. He had seen photos of the damaged battery.

"By looking at the inside of the pack after the accident, it can be easily understood that those cells were not clamped well," Ozawa told me. He was concerned that the cells would vibrate in an aviation environment, causing the jelly roll–like windings to move around inside the case, perhaps even triggering short circuits if the terminals touched.

Also, Jeevarajan noted that hot spots could develop inside each cell and within the foil/chemical roll if "used outside of manufacturer's specifications." Substantial heat could melt the film separating the cathode from the anode, a big no-no because it can trigger a short circuit and immediate thermal runaway.

Professor Dahn also thought that was a problem. Referring to tests by the NTSB during the investigation, he noted that "when the cells were discharged at their max-rated power, the terminals were hot," he said. "They became one hundred eighty Celsius [three hundred sixty degrees Fahrenheit] above the melting point of the separator. That's bad." As far as he was concerned, part of the problem was the size of the cells. At two inches each, the individual cell pack was just too thick. One failure might propagate and "set off the neighbors," as he put it.

GS Yuasa designed the Dreamliner battery based on one it produced for all-terrain vehicles. When I met with Dana Schulze at the NTSB's offices in Washington, I asked her if it had been a leap to suggest an ATV battery and a battery on an airplane were the same. She said GS Yuasa's experience could be applicable as long as the differences between the two were considered, something Schulze, a mechanical engineer, called a similarity analysis. In the NTSB's review of the battery design, "We couldn't find evidence that they had done a lot of that."

Locked in competition with Boeing with its same-size and same-range Airbus A350, it might sound like bragging when the French airplane maker Airbus points out the various differences between the 787 battery and the lithium-ion battery now powering the A350. But, actually, I called Airbus, not the other way around.

Airbus accounted for the possibility of an internal short circuit in one cell, according to Marc Cambet, a systems component architect for the A350. The design included precautions to prevent one failing cell from spreading to another. "On our side, the cells are insulated one from each other and insulated in terms of thermal insulation and in terms of vibration and in terms of separation between the cells," Cambet said.

Jeevarajan's review of the Boeing battery covered many issues, including propagation, insulation, and vibration. She had one overriding problem, though, and that was Boeing's safety philosophy when it came to the batteries. The company worried too much about overcharging them and ignored the potential for and response to internal and external short circuits. These could result from something such as the melting of the separator; the build-up of dendrites; or field failures, internal pressure, and deformations in the cell case.

It was not that Boeing failed to consider them, Jeevarajan said. The company had, but it had also dismissed the hazards. When it tested for external shorts, "every single cell" vented and emitted smoke. When she asked the company, "Why didn't you take that into consideration?" the answer was, "There was no fire. We didn't think it was a big deal."

"It blew my mind that they had every single cell vent with smoke," which was expressly prohibited under the FAA's conditions, she reminded me, "and they just ignored it."

"They had good protection for overcharge, but none for short circuits," Jeevarajan concluded, and overcharging wasn't a factor on either of the Japanese airliners. In the pages of notes she gave to Boeing, Jeevarajan spelled out what she saw as the design's many shortcomings, including the one that the Japanese investigators would seize on much later as the likely culprit for what happened on the ANA Dreamliner.

"If you want to charge at cold temperatures, you've got to reduce the charge current," she explained, or risk generating too much heat. It's harder for the ions to move when it's cold, so charging generates more heat in the battery.

On the A350, the battery temperature is taken into account, Cambet explained. "The charge is slowed when the temperature is too low," he said, because "if you try to charge full power at low temperatures you can build some risk of internal short circuit."

Moderating the rate was not possible on the Dreamliner battery system, and the fact that the ANA and JAL events happened in January was an interesting piece of the puzzle. Around this time, one of the government investigators (who asked not to be identified by name) summed it up, saying, "The cause was not found, but so many potential causes were found that [it] was pretty surprising."

In Tokyo, as in Washington, DC, the air safety folks were trying to solve a mystery while taking a crash course in electrochemistry. The Japan Aerospace eXploration Agency (JAXA) was advising, as were NASA and the U.S. Naval Sea Systems Command, which, like the space programs, is intrigued by the potential of these batteries, yet cautious about the hazards.

"It was quite difficult to take enough time to learn the new technology," said Masaki Kametani, fifty-three, one of the seven investigators assigned to the case in Japan. Their little department was the subject of international attention. While the Boston battery fire had taken place on the ground in a nearly empty plane, the ANA flight had been in the air with passengers. "What if" was on everybody's mind.

The investigations' official reports ran to hundreds of pages. Japan's took twenty months to complete, and the American version nearly two years. While the flaws in the design of the battery were many, neither agency could say specifically what initiated the incidents they'd investigated. The JTSB concentrated on the cold weather charging phenomenon. The NTSB thought a manufacturing defect in the cell case might have created a hot spot leading to a short circuit. In both cases the entire battery fell to what the industry and physicist Lewis Larsen graphically call "thermal fratricide."

In its report, the NTSB went beyond what had happened on the plane in Boston to review how Boeing had convinced the FAA that the battery would meet the special condition. There were dozens of tests with a mind-numbing collection of titles and findings. Yet later, when I interviewed the NTSB's Schulze, she explained it to me quite simply. It wasn't the number of tests that was relevant; it was the assumptions made by Boeing as to what actually needed to be tested and how closely those checks reflected how the battery would operate in an actual airplane. "The test in and of itself really didn't provide enough information to assume that an internal short circuit wasn't going to result in propagation to the other cells," Schulze said.

The parallel to the Comet was unmistakable. The de Havilland engineers sought reassurance by referring to demonstrations of the cabin withstanding twice the amount of pressure the plane would experience. Yet during testing, the structure had been given supplemental support. It was therefore not representative of the plane in flight.

By the time the investigators published their findings, the

Dreamliners had been back in the air for nearly two years, released to fly again after a number of changes that recognized the battery's newly exposed hazards, if not its suitability. Boeing also acted on the suggestions of experts such as Jeevarajan and put more insulation between the cells, placing them in a stronger frame and isolating them electrically with Kapton tape. These were precautionary measures. They didn't change the battery's volatile nature, so Boeing opted to cage the beast.

Each battery went into a stainless steel housing with a titanium vent tube. The box would contain and smother a fire and protect against heat. The vent would release outside the airplane smoke or fumes generated by a failure. The system was an insurance policy against more unknowns, known or otherwise.

Boeing opted not to talk to me for this book, rejecting repeated requests made in person and via e-mail. I didn't like it, but I certainly understood. The company might be concerned that the plane it spent a decade developing will be permanently associated with one particular design failure. Had someone at Boeing given an interview, I'm sure that person would have reminded me that the 787 is carrying out the mission for which it was created. Airline customers love it, and passengers do, too. One thousand had been sold by 2015.

What Boeing probably believes in its corporate heart, is akin to Wilbur Wright's thoughts about "mounting a machine and becoming acquainted with its tricks." Progress involves risk. Innovation will always have unanticipated consequences. The challenge for plane makers past and present has not been finding the guts to gamble, but balancing audacity with prudence before the plane moves from design to product.

The price of getting it wrong can be too high, as Rolls-Royce and Lockheed learned in the early 1970s during the development of the L-1011 jumbo jet.

Ask any airline pilot who has ever flown it to tell you about the Lockheed L-1011 and be prepared for a long soliloquy. "Best seat in the sky," one captain told me. Passengers enjoyed its unprecedented space and the quiet that had L-1011 customer Eastern Airlines calling the plane the "Whisperliner." Yes, everybody loved the three-engine Tristar, but unlike its competitors, the Boeing 747 and the McDonnell Douglas DC-10, the L-1011 is not seen flying anymore. Only two hundred fifty were made, and aviation analyst Richard Aboulafia, who writes the widely read industry newsletter *Teal Monthly*, cites an engine design gone terribly wrong with contributing to the ultimate failure of the L-1011.

We hear about the use of composite material in aviation all the time these days, as it replaces heavier metal in airplane structures and components in planes such as the Dreamliner, the Airbus A350, and the A380. Back in the sixties, however, when Rolls-Royce was designing a more powerful, lighter-weight engine to power wide-body aircraft, its plan to use woven layers of compressed and hardened glass fibers to replace the metal on engine fan blades was new. Using a composite called Hyfil for the blades would save three hundred pounds and make the engine 2 percent more fuel efficient, but it didn't work as planned.

In a 2012 *Royal Aeronautical Society* magazine story called "Blades of Glory," writer Tim Robinson called it "the blade that almost broke the company." While the engine was still in development, Rolls-Royce and Lockheed discovered that the Hyfil composite was prone to delaminate. The layers would separate, just like what happens when a laminate board is left out in the rain. The fan blades would also not withstand the assault of frozen poultry. That's not as bizarre as it sounds; to ensure that an engine will survive ingesting birds without coming apart, manufacturers shoot hard-as-ice frozen chickens into the core of a spinning jet engine. In this case, it was a battle the roasters won.

While Boeing and McDonnell Douglas churned out their wide-bodies, sending them to airlines so they could start flying to far-flung places, Lockheed's L-1011 was stuck on the ground waiting for Rolls-Royce to refit the engine with titanium blades. Unable to pay its bills, Rolls went into government receivership. Lockheed fared only slightly better; it required government loans to stay in business. It took years for Rolls-Royce to finally deliver the engine Lockheed had ordered for the L-1011.

Aboulafia says the bad bet on Hyfil was orders of magnitude worse for the companies involved than what Boeing faced with its lithium-ion batteries, even though the engines should have been an easier fix. "You have to distinguish between two types of design. On the Dreamliner the issue is fundamental, and on the L-1011 the problem was an accessory; an expensive accessory, yes, but it was a discrete system," he said. "Replace the engines, problem solved; it was not a fundamental design flaw."

The problem for Lockheed was that it was locked into the Rolls-Royce engines; it could not swap them out for the product of another engine maker. Lockheed had no choice but to wait out the delay. Once the composite blade was replaced with titanium, the RB221 became one of Rolls-Royce's best-selling engines. Updated versions still power the Boeing 747 and Boeing 767.

The Dreamliner battery saga does not have such an unequivocal finish or even a dignified one. Aboulafia calls the stainless steel containment box "inelegant," the opposite of a Rube Goldberg invention, where a comically over-engineered response addresses a simple quandary. "It's a simple solution to a complex problem," he said. And it is a problem that just won't go away.

On January 14, 2014, nearly a year to the day after the ANA Dreamliner made its emergency landing at Takamatsu Airport, maintenance workers in the cockpit of a Japan Airlines Dreamliner preparing to depart Narita for Bangkok saw white smoke coming off the plane. Checking the battery, they discovered that one of the eight cells had vented, leaking fluid into the box. The problem did not spread to other cells.

Ten months later, a Qatar Airways 787 had to make an emergency landing when one cell in the airplane's battery vented. Boeing notified the NTSB and the FAA, but neither agency conducted an investigation.

"The airplane performed as certified for this failure," FAA spokeswoman Laura Brown told me. When I asked by what means the air safety authority would know how the airplane performed since it had not investigated, Brown said that Boeing had taken a look and shared its findings.

Not only is the FAA not investigating when cells vent, but it is not even keeping count of how often it happens. Since the box contains the smoke, fumes, and presumably fire, the American aviation regulator's position is that a battery malfunction is no longer their concern. "We don't consider something an 'event' if the containment box performs as designed," she said.

Several battery scientists, including some who do not want their names to be associated with their opinions because they work with Boeing, say it is lunacy to dismiss the seriousness of continuing cell failures.

John Goodenough, a physicist and professor at the University of Texas who is considered the inventor of lithium-ion batteries, points out that by the time electrolyte vents, there is fire within the cell. "If you are hot enough to start boiling and needing to vent, the electrolyte will have caught fire by then."

Since it first approved Boeing's use of lithium-ion energy storage on the 787, the FAA went from saying that fire in any situation was unacceptable to calling containing a fire no big deal.

"Why play with fire when you don't have to play with fire?" asked Dalhousie University's Jeff Dahn. That cells vented on four or maybe five batteries in the plane's first three years of service means the GS Yuasa–produced cells were failing at an "astronomically high rate," Dahn said.

Here's how he figures this. Each plane has sixteen cells, and by the end of 2014 there were fewer than three hundred Dreamliners in service. If the cell events noted here are the only ones, and we can't know, because no one aside from Boeing seems to be counting, and Boeing's not saying, then the failure rate in the cells is one in every few hundred. By contrast, Dahn said, "for the cells used in laptops and phones, the failure rate is one in more than twenty million. It's irresponsible to continue with such a product."

The FAA is not alone in its conviction that Boeing has solved its battery problem. In Japan, JTSB spokesman Mamoru Takahashi told my researcher Takeo Aizawa that the safety board was not surprised or concerned by subsequent cases of cell venting. This was similar to what the board's Koji Tsuji had told me. "We cannot create the situation where no short circuit happens, but we have reached the point where we can control the heating, even if venting occurs," he said. "We can consider it a minor problem."

"Boeing has made all the conceivable improvements for their 787s to ensure the resumption of normal flight," including more than eighty modifications that "are desirable, but may not be necessary," Tsuji told me. It was eerily evocative of what was said about the Comet before it was returned to service with the source of its problem still a mystery.

PART FOUR

Humanity

An accident sequence is like someone slipping down a knotted rope. The pilot's decision may be the last knot in the rope, but there are many other events which set up the accident sequence. Pilot error is increasingly seen as far too simplistic.

—MAURICE WILLIAMSON, NEW ZEALAND'S
MINISTER OF TRANSPORTATION, 1999

The Right Stuff

Sometimes in the summer I go kayaking with my friend Pete Frey, a pilot for a U.S. carrier whom you met earlier in this book. For a man in his late fifties, Pete's in great shape. Still, it's hard for men of a certain age to pull off the baggy shorts and windblown hair look. Truth is, Pete doesn't even try to look hip.

In his pilot's uniform, however, Pete is a babe magnet. It's not just the navy jacket with the gold braid; it's his confidence, his completely unselfconscious "you're safe in my hands, baby" attitude. Pete the airline captain is all authority and competence.

Around the world, tens of thousands of airline pilots make a similar transformation. That harried blonde in line at Starbucks, the guy pumping gas into his pickup truck—when these suburban parents and weekend anglers don their uniforms, airlines trust them with multimillion-dollar airplanes and the companies' reputations. This is why the making of airline pilots is serious business. Airlines screen them before they hire them, test them once they're in, and train them repeatedly throughout their careers. The airlines want seemingly contradictory qualities in their pilots: decisive but open-minded, vigilant but flexible, experienced but constantly learning, adherence to standard procedure but with an ability to improvise when required.

Creating a "pilot-type person" is so important that 95 percent of the cadets hired by Lufthansa have not flown at all when they arrive at the company-owned Airline Training Center in Arizona, fifty-seven hundred miles from company headquarters in Frankfurt, Germany. The thinking at the carrier is that if they can find people with the right personality, they can "grow their own pilots," as Matthias Kippenberg, president and CEO of the training center, explained. I saw this process up close in the fall of 2010, when I joined class number NFF380 for a week.

Lufthansa might as well be looking for astronauts; that's how hard it is to get selected. And with good reason: at the time, it cost thirty-five million dollars a year to run the school that turns cadets into airline pilots. "Students are selected by the airline, trained and sponsored by the airline," Kippenberg said. "They have a job guarantee," he said. "All they have to do now is learn to fly."

Kippenberg graduated from ATCA in 1977 and has been running the program since 2002. He may not have appreciated how hard his students work to get accepted until his own daughter Lisanne applied at the age of nineteen to take an Introduction to Aviation course offered by the Swiss government. She qualified to apply because her mother is Swiss, but, like everyone else, she would have to take a series of aptitude exams. In preparation, she and her dad went online for guidance—only to be confounded by the very first practice test. On the screen were six three-dimensional cubes. An X was placed on one of the six sides of each cube. Lisanne had to listen as a voice instructed her to imagine the cube rotating up or down, right or left, back or front. Lisanne's job was to keep track of where the X ended up.

"My dad and I were looking at it, and then we looked at each other; we didn't know what was going on," she told me. The "nine clocks test" was equally baffling. I'll spare you the details.

The students in my dorm at ATCA told me they'd performed similar tests, and others in which they had to listen to long series of numbers and repeat them back in reverse order. It sounded like torture to me, and I had the chance to experience it myself when CTC Wings of New Zealand put me through my very own pilot aptitude evaluation.

This differed from the kind of screening conducted by airlines because applicants at CTC are paying their own way, with no assurances they will find a piloting job. The aptitude test is necessarily less selective and less intense. Even so, having to keep the wings of my simulated aircraft straight and level while flying through a series of yellow rectangles appearing on my computer screen, I was tense and sweaty even before the mental processing exam began.

My overall score suggests that as a pilot, I make a great writer. I could process information okay and even acquire data under time pressure, judging by how quickly I was able to make sense of an image of shattered glass. (Don't ask.) When it came time to handling a joystick while following a flight path and working math questions involving counting backward, I was fried.

Viktor Oubaid, head of the German Aerospace Center in Hamburg, told me that all these challenges are designed to test working memory. One could practice and get better, as Lisanne and the Lufthansa students did, "but the maximum possible performance depends on your original abilities," Oubaid said. "In other words: many people can learn to fly, but only some are able to work as airline pilots."

After several months spent practicing for the tests, Lisanne went to Dübendorf, outside Zurich, for her entrance exam. The setting was quiet, and she had a good feeling. "I did a lot better than I thought I was going to do," she told me. Sure enough, Lisanne was accepted. After two weeks of flying lessons, she said she was even more excited about a career as a pilot and more appreciative of what the tests were trying to determine about her cognitive abilities.

Lisanne's dad knows very well this aspect of her experience. Call it multitasking or workflow management—pilot aptitude tests are designed to detect this and other things because so much more than epaulets is riding on the shoulders of the men and women on a flight deck. This was made most evident five years later, when one of the students at Kippenberg's school passed right through the airline's tightly woven web of diligence.

Andreas Lubitz arrived in Phoenix right after I'd left, when he was twenty-three years old. He had aced five days of testing and had interviewed with confidence back in 2008, when he was selected to begin ground school in Bremen, Germany. Yet Lufthansa's notably tough standards may have proven to be too much, because after two months, he took a leave of absence. From January to October of the following year, he underwent psychiatric treatment for reactive depression that a German medical examiner told the FAA had been triggered by excessive demands.

By 2010, Lubitz was considered fit to continue his training, and so he did: ground school in Bremen, and then flight school in Phoenix, followed by jet training back in Bremen and a stint as a flight attendant. In 2013 he became a first officer on Lufthansa's low-cost carrier GermanWings.

In the spring of 2015, Lubitz would commandeer his own flight from Barcelona to Dusseldorf and fly it into a mountain, killing himself and 149 others. The thirty-four-year-old captain, Patrick Sondenheimer, had left the cockpit to go to the bathroom after leveling the plane at thirty-eight thousand feet. With Sondenheimer gone and the cockpit door locked, Lubitz put the Airbus A320 on an autopilot descent to one hundred feet, a path that would take the plane directly into the high terrain in the French Alps.

Lubitz overrode the captain's attempts to return to the flight deck and did not reply to radio calls from controllers. For eleven minutes the plane descended, until finally it hit a mountain near Prads-Haute-Bléone. It would soon come out that Lubitz's depression had returned, and that in the weeks before the event, his physicians had advised him not to work, according to notes found in the trash in the young man's home.

Suicidal and/or homicidal airline pilots are a special kind of scary, even though this is an exceedingly rare occurrence. During its investigation into the crash, the French air accident bureau reported six similar events in which commercial pilots had deliberately crashed planes with passengers aboard. Japan Airlines in 1982, Royal Air Maroc in 1994, SilkAir in 1997, EgyptAir and Air Botswana both in 1999, and Mozambique Airlines Flight 470 in 2013. These crashes were all believed to have been purposely initiated by one of the pilots. With more than 717 million flights since 1980, you can see how infinitesimal this particular flight safety risk is.

It is an entirely different story when you get to unintentional acts. Then the mistakes pilots make that contribute to disasters are everywhere you look.

Sole Responsibility

None of the six people on the private jet from Samoa to Melbourne on November 18, 2009, will ever forget the night they ditched into the choppy waters of the Pacific off the coast of tiny Norfolk Island. Capt. Dominic James and First Officer Zoe Cupit were piloting the medical evacuation flight, with patient Bernie Currall, her husband, Gary, and a medical team riding in the back. As the Israel Aircraft Industries Westwind jet approached the island where the plane was to refuel for the last leg to Melbourne, the weather was so bad that neither James nor Cupit was able to see the runway. After four missed approaches, James decided to put the plane down in the ocean before it ran out of fuel.

The jet split in two on impact with the rough sea. Only three of the six people on board had life jackets, but all got out of the plane. For ninety minutes, James played shepherd, swimming around them in a circle and keeping them together. Finally, a search party on a charter fishing boat spotted the light from the small flashlight James was waving toward shore, and the group was rescued.

"It gives me goosebumps still thinking about it," said Glenn Robinson, an island resident and one of the crew members on the boat that rescued the survivors. "They're all alive. You know they've ditched that plane into a rolling ocean in the middle of the night, and here they are."

Brainy, articulate, tenacious, and the spitting image of the actor Tom Cruise, James was a hero and a celebrity when he arrived back in Australia. "Gold standard" is how he and Cupit were described by John Sharp, the chairman of Pel-Air, the company whose airplane the pilots were operating that night. By Christmas Eve, however, the two had fallen from grace. The Australian Civil Aviation Safety Authority (CASA) suspended their licenses, claiming the two had demonstrated bad airmanship. The accident was entirely the fault of the captain, said John McCormick, CASA's chief.

A man who puts a jet aircraft into a dark and stormy sea on a moonless night and then, without a life preserver, keeps his passengers together for an hour and a half like some kind of aquatic sheepdog is not the kind of man to allow himself to be made a scapegoat.

In planning for the flight from Apia, Samoa, James said he had been hampered at every turn. Unable to get WiFi on his phone or at the hotel, he did his flight plan on his cell phone in the hotel parking lot. He fueled up the jet with the assumption that it would fly in reduced vertical separation minima airspace (RVSM), a horizontal slice of the sky between twenty-eight thousand and forty thousand feet that requires planes with highly calibrated altimeters and special certification, both of which this Pel-Air plane did not have. Because flying in RVSM airspace can reduce fuel consumption, pilots routinely beg their way in by explaining that they are on a medical flight. James said it was a company practice he had complained about the year earlier, but nothing had changed.

When weather deteriorated on the way, James did not have enough fuel to make it to an alternate airport. He was not required to, under the work rules that applied to air ambulances. This was a loophole that national safety authorities had been trying to close for years, but CASA had failed to take action.

Years later, when James got his license back and started flying for other operators, he realized that many tools were available that could have changed the outcome that night. "I had access to flight planning software wherever I went. I had access to performance data, so I could look at a destination and calculate weights, speeds, and options," none of which he had access to while flying for Pel-Air.

These shortcomings and others were noted in a special audit of the airline that CASA conducted right after the ditching. Thirty-one safety deficiencies were found. CASA noted a conflict between "the commercial objectives of the company and safety outcomes." That's bureaucrat-speak for saying the operator was "more worried about profits than safety." Nevertheless, the Australian aviation authority's position was that the operation of the airline was not relevant. The accident, it stated, had been "caused by poor fuel planning, poor decision-making" by the captain.

Two years before the Pel-Air mess, George Snyder wrote in an article for the Flight Safety Foundation's *AeroSafety World* magazine, "The assignment of blame artificially and *prematurely* restricts the investigation process" and can even stop the investigation in its tracks. It was a prescient bit of writing, because that's exactly what happened in the Pel-Air case. Even knowing the airline had safety lapses, the head of CASA, John McCormick, did not share them with the accident investigators because the ditching, he said, "was entirely the fault of the captain."

Captain James admits he made mistakes, but adds that none of the support that would have helped him do his job was there. "I didn't operate in a vacuum. I operated as a pilot who belonged to a company that was overseen by a regulator," he said. "You can't isolate one from another and say that's a fair appreciation of what took place."

An Australian television documentary program called *Four Corners* presented the full story in 2012, just as the ATSB was issuing its probable cause report. The program prompted several parliamentary hearings into the way the aviation agencies were doing their jobs. This intrigued me, because issues of safety can be nuanced, and that isn't always appreciated in politics. Yet here was a case where the politicians sounded reasonable while the aviation professionals were looking no further than the pilot.

"It is surprising and dismaying both," said John Lauber, a research psychologist in the field of human factors—essentially, trying to understand why people do the things they do. He had been a member of the NTSB, and he'd spent most of his career trying to improve support systems for pilots. "All human performance takes place in a context, defined by the technology, procedures, and training."

On a bright morning in October 2014, my sister Lee and I were on vacation in Darwin, the capital of Australia's Northern Territory. We'd booked a seaplane flight into the aboriginal territory called Sweets Lagoon. Outside our hotel, the bus to the airport was waiting, and out of the driver's seat bounded a tanned and attractive man who looked vaguely familiar.

"Christine Negroni?" he asked with a smile, extending his hand. "Dom James." By then I had recognized him. My surprise was seeing him driving a tour bus. When he'd told me his story over lunch at a restaurant in Sydney half a year earlier, he was dashing off for a pickup job he had flying corporate jets. By then, CASA had restored his pilot's license. He was hoping for full-time work, but he had been vilified by the nation's top aviation official, and that had taken a toll. He would go for job interviews, but it was always the same story. "All these people would say, 'the crash, the crash, the crash.' They didn't know about the senate inquiry. All they know is I'm some guy who crashed a plane," he told me. "You can't make someone be educated on the nuances of the accident."

Pilots err for many reasons, Lauber told me. "To say a pilot made a bad decision is not a reflection on that pilot, but a reflection on the overall design of the system that he is tasked with operating."

The Prevention System

There's a story about an airline captain who, having landed at the airport and parked the jet at the gate, announced to the departing passengers, "Welcome to your destination, ladies and gentlemen. The safest part of your journey has come to an end."

Flying is so safe that we can appreciate the joke. From the very first plane crash in 1908, attention has been focused on finding out what went wrong and how to fix it. For decades this meant modifying the airplane or engines, and sometimes both, as was the case with the Comet; or coming to grips with new technology, as with the Dreamliner. Dana Schulze had spent more than a decade as an air safety investigator when she started the two-year project to understand what happened on the 787. She told me it was rare to have a case where her team was concentrating solely on the machine. By the time the probe was finished, though, human errors had been discovered in quality control during the manufacturing of the battery cells and in the assumptions made by engineers during the certification of the airplane.

Still, Schulze's expectation demonstrates the transition over time to more reliable airplanes and engines. They simply don't fail as they did in the early days of air travel. What has not changed is the fallible human, unpredictable at every level except for how reliably he or she will make mistakes. Something had to be done about making people perform better. Mechanical engineers and aerodynamicists had their place, but beginning in the 1970s, a new kind of specialist was digging into the "soft" sciences of psychology, ergonomics, communication, and design. These people were practicing in a relatively new field called human factors. They worked on ways to help airlines select and train pilots. Programs widely used in the military were adapted for civilian airlines. They researched how to enhance the flight deck and improve communications—what, in the jargon of aviation, is called information transfer—so that misunderstandings could be averted and errors prevented before they ended in tears. When a disaster happened, it could be turned into a valuable learning opportunity. The three biggest developments in human factors were triggered by pilot error, including a development as simple as it is profound: the checklist.

In 1935 three airplane manufacturers were competing to provide the U.S. Army Air Corps with a bomber capable of carrying a ton of ordnance a distance of two thousand miles. Boeing thought it had just the thing: an all-metal, four-engine model it called the Boeing 299. A *Seattle Times* reporter named Richard Williams, upon seeing the enormous new airplane for the first time, reportedly exclaimed, "Why, it's a flying fortress!" and the nickname stuck.

Douglas and Martin were also in the running with twin-engine models. The Martin 146 and the Douglas 1B could carry the load, but neither could go the range. Even before the flying demonstration began, the army procurement officers were pushing to buy sixty-five Flying Fortresses. The competition was Boeing's to lose.

On October 30, the day of the fly-off at Wright Field in Dayton, Ohio, two army pilots, two men from Boeing, and a representative of the engine manufacturer Pratt & Whitney climbed in and took off. There were three pilots aboard, Ployer P. Hill and Donald Putt from the army, and Boeing's chief test pilot, Leslie Tower. Yet as they taxied across the airfield, none of them noticed that the elevators and rudder, movable panels that control the plane's up-and-down and side-to-side motion, were still secured with a gust lock that kept them in place so they did not swing in the wind and get damaged when the plane was on the ground. But when the plane took off it was locked into a configuration for a steep climb that the pilots could not correct in the air. The giant aircraft stalled and fell to the ground, erupting in flames. Two of the men died from their injuries.

Before that flight, the only negative about the Boeing 299 was that it might be too complex, but it was a simple oversight that brought it down, literally and figuratively. The plane was disqualified from consideration by the Army Air Corps, and the big bomber order went to Douglas.

What could be done to protect against forgetfulness? The army pilots got together and came up with a checklist. In twenty-four steps, from "before taxi" to "after takeoff," the pilot would be reminded of each critical task. Boeing went on to build the B-299, and the Army Air Corps bought it and flew it for decades. The Flying Fortress entered the history books. So, too, did the pilot checklist.

Checklists aren't a perfect solution. Every fix has unintended consequences. The same checklist read eight times a day might not be met with the same level of concentration, a phenomenon that former NASA scientist and human factors expert Dr. Key Dismukes calls "seeing but not seeing."

The number of checklists on an uneventful journey is about a dozen. On an eventful one, such as Qantas Flight 32, an Airbus A380 jumbo jet that experienced an uncontained engine failure shortly after takeoff in 2010, the pilots went through about one hundred twenty checks. Due to the way the Rolls-Royce Trent 900 engine exploded, Capt. Richard de Crespigny and his first officer, Matt Hicks, had one engine out; the three others not working properly; an inability to transfer fuel; problems with electrics, communication, flight controls, hydraulics, and pneumatics; and "a whole bunch of other stuff," as de Crespigny described it.

They were busy assessing the condition of the plane and planning their next steps while emergency checklists kept appearing on the flight display "like dinner plates at an all-you-can-eat buffet," according to de Crespigny. "I think I invented the term checklist fatigue," he said—but he hadn't. De Crespigny just had the most high-profile experience with the phenomenon of checklists overwhelming pilots, characterized as "stop interrupting me when I'm busy" and identified by Dismukes back in 1993.

Dismukes wasn't calling for an end to checklists, which, if used properly, might have prevented disasters such as Helios Flight 522, where pilots seem to have neglected to turn on the cabin pressurization switch; or the Spanair Flight 5022 crash that followed an attempted takeoff without flaps. He was recognizing that as machines grow in complexity, every part of how humans interact with them must evolve, too. "How complex is too complex?" is a question that would come up again and again.

In the summer of 2009, the sixty-year-old captain of a Continental Boeing 777 keeled over at the controls of a flight carrying 247 people from Brussels to Newark. Passengers heard flight attendants ask if there was a doctor on board. There was, but it was too late for Craig Lenell. All airlines are required to have two pilots, and on flights over a certain number of hours, there can be three or more: the crew flying and a pilot or crew in reserve.

"If something happens physiologically to one of the pilots, the other one is seamlessly able to carry on," ABC News aviation consultant and retired airline pilot John Nance said.

A pilot dying at the controls is pretty rare. The benefit of having two pilots is realized far more often in less dramatic circumstances. As Nance explained, two pilots provide "two brains and two sets of eyes" for the flight. At its best, a two-pilot crew operates as a precision team sharing a common view of the task before them, and separate views of each other. The terms *challenge and response* and *monitoring and cross-check* and the information transfer I mentioned earlier describe this relationship, which might also be called communication.

Entire books have been written on how to improve the way pilots communicate, because without special training, pilots can misunderstand each other as easily as any other two people who meet briefly and maybe for the first time and set out to accomplish a task together. Yet in the cockpit, the stakes are higher.

The deadliest aviation accident ever, the collision of a KLM Royal Dutch Boeing 747 with another 747 being operated by Pan American World Airways, made it very clear that more attention needed to be paid to the seemingly simple task of talking and the complex phenomenon of hierarchy on the flight deck. The crash happened on March 27, 1977, on a runway in Tenerife, in the Canary Islands.

Both planes and several others had been diverted from Las Palmas in Gran Canaria to the Los Rodeos Airport in Tenerife. A bomb at the Las Palmas airport terminal had shut it down, and three hours passed before it was reopened. When it was, airline crews started preparing to leave Tenerife for the short flight to their original destination, Las Palmas.

On the KLM plane the pilots in the cockpit were under the command of fifty-year-old Jacob van Zanten, head of flight training and, as the face on the airline magazine ads, something of a superstar in the Netherlands. The delay must have weighed on van Zanten, who was operating along with the other pilots under new flight time restrictions. If they were held up much longer, they would not be allowed to make the return flight from Las Palmas to Amsterdam.

If that happened, hundreds of travelers would have to be accommodated in hotels, and the jumbo jet would sit at the airport overnight instead of providing revenue to the carrier. And there was another factor to consider: the commander's ego. As Nance explained, there is "the embarrassment of a senior leader in being unable to make happen what he wanted to happen." In the years to come, this and other similarly subtle pressures would be explored more thoroughly for their impact on the decisions made that fateful afternoon.

There were far more planes at Los Rodeos than gates at which to park them, so planes parked on a few of the taxiways. But this created a new problem: they were blocking the way to the runway for departing flights.

Controllers told the departing crews to follow an unusual procedure known as backtaxiing. One plane was to taxi down the runway followed by the second. When the first plane arrived at the departure threshold, it would make a one-hundred-eighty-degree turn into takeoff position.

The following plane had to pull off onto a taxiway to get out of the way of the plane positioned for takeoff.

When the first plane departed the second crew would taxi their plane into position and go.

Two planes had already taken off, and Pan Am and the KLM wide-bodies were next. KLM led the way, followed by *Clipper Victor*, under the command of the coincidentally named Victor Grubbs, fifty-six. Robert Bragg was the first officer and George Warns was the flight engineer.

Rumbling down the runway, Bragg, 39 at the time, recalled that the skies were clear, but before the Pan Am plane could find the taxiway where it was to pull off to get out of the KLM's take-off path a dense fog rolled in. "Our visibility went from unlimited to 500 meters in under one minute. The tower even made a call stating, 'Gentlemen, be advised that runway visibility is 500 to 700 metres,'" Bragg, thirty-nine, wrote in an article for *Flight Safety Australia*. The fog was so thick that the Pan Am crew determined it was below the takeoff minimum and assumed that the runway was now closed. Grubbs, a pilot with twenty-one thousand flight hours, continued to steer the plane through the fog, but slowly. All three men strained to find the turnoff.

On the takeoff end of the runway, however, the fog had passed. Van Zanten pivoted the KLM airplane around to point in the direction of takeoff. His plane was now head to head with the slow-moving Pan Am jumbo, unseen in the cloud a half mile ahead. He pushed forward on the throttles—which seemed to startle his first officer, thirty-two-year-old Klaas Meurs. "Wait a minute, we don't have ATC clearance," Meurs said. The first officer had experience with this captain. It was van Zanten who had qualified him on the 747 just two months earlier.

Van Zanten pulled back the power and instructed Meurs to call ATC. The first officer radioed that he was ready for takeoff and waiting for clearance. The tower controller replied with departure and navigational information, but didn't issue the clearance to take off.

Just as Meurs was confirming the instructions, van Zanten said, "We go, check thrust." Once again, the captain fed fuel to the airplane's engines.

Meurs cued the mic and read back the controller's words, adding something that sounded like "We are now at takeoff."

In an analysis of the accident by the ALPA, this ambiguous phrase would receive a lot of scrutiny. The pilots concluded that the KLM first officer thought something was wrong with Captain van Zanten's decision and was "trying to alert everyone on frequency that they were commencing takeoff."

Captain Grubbs, on the Pan Am Clipper, heard the transmission and was surprised. "No," he said, followed a second later by the controller telling KLM, "Stand by for takeoff. I will call you."

"And we are still taxiing down the runway," Pan Am's First Officer Bragg added.

The Pan Am pilots must have thought they were making it

clear to KLM that the Pan Am 747 was still in the way, but these messages were drowned out by the dueling transmissions, which created a shrill noise in the KLM cockpit.

"Report when runway clear," the controller told the Pan Am crew, and Pan Am responded, "Okay, we will report when clear."

The KLM 747 was accelerating down the runway; its first officer, Meurs, and flight engineer, Willem Schreuder, heard this. It prompted Schreuder to ask, "Is he not clear, then?"

"What do you say?" Captain van Zanten asked.

"Is he not clear, then, that Pan American?" Schreuder repeated.

"Oh yes," van Zanten and Meurs answered at the same time.

Captain van Zanten had made his decision. "To reassess that decision at such a critical point in the takeoff may have seemed an intolerable idea," the human factors specialists at ALPA concluded in their report, citing the other factors that must have been on the captain's mind, including the heavy airplane, wet runway, and poor visibility.

The KLM Boeing 747 was closing in on the other jumbo jet still obscured in the soup.

On *Clipper Victor*, Captain Grubbs was startled to see the lights of the KLM airliner rapidly approaching through the mist.

"Goddamn, that son of a bitch is coming straight at us," he said. He applied power to the throttles and turned the nose wheel to the left in a desperate attempt to get out of the way.

At this point, KLM's van Zanten also saw the impending collision. With his aircraft moving too fast to stop, he pulled back on the yoke in a frantic effort to take off over the Pan Am Clipper. The tail of the KLM plane scraped along the runway as the front end lifted enough for the nose gear to clear the dome of the Pan Am 747.

Having been seated on the right side of the Pan Am flight deck facing directly toward the KLM jet, First Officer Bragg remembers his horror. "Get off, get off, get off," he screamed at Grubbs as the underside of the KLM plane rose above him.

"I ducked, closed my eyes, and prayed, 'God, let him miss us.' When it did hit our plane, it was only a very short, quiet shudder. I actually thought that he had, in fact, missed us until I opened my eyes."

As the KLM 747 dragged its undercarriage across the upper deck of the *Clipper Victor*, it tore off a huge section and then slammed back down onto the runway, skidding another fifteen hundred feet in a burst of sparks and explosions as the fuel spraying from ruptured tanks ignited.

All 249 people aboard the KLM flight were killed. Of the 396 people on the Pan Am jet, 70 survived the crash (though nine died later), a fact Bragg credits to Grubb's quick work getting at least the front end of the plane out of the way.

Among the survivors, some said the impact was like a bomb going off. Its effect on the airline industry was equally explosive. It was not that two airliners had collided; there had been others. But the number of casualties and the cascading series of communication failures was a loud wakeup call to the industry.

Everywhere one looked, errors had been made, most obviously by the three men on the KLM flight deck, who failed to communicate their concerns clearly. The collision also revealed the danger of aviation's long-established "right stuff" religion. The dogma consists of the belief that the captain is always right and that good pilots never make mistakes. In a 1990 article for the Flight Safety Foundation, Robert Besco, a retired airline captain and a consultant in human performance, wrote, "Pilots have adopted an attitude of risk denial." If the captain was considered God and everyone else a congregant, you can see how pilots would not/could not speak up even when they saw that something was wrong.

John Lauber, working at NASA's Ames Research Center in California at the time, had already spent several years noting the growing disparity between the reliability of the machine and that of the human flying it. He had visited airlines and spoken about a new concept he called cockpit resource management, or CRM. One of the airlines he visited was KLM Royal Dutch. One of the pilots he met was Captain van Zanten.

Lauber remembered, "He was a very impressive guy, a blond, steely-eyed airline pilot. He was a strong-minded personality." Lauber was pitching CRM as something airlines could use to train pilots to better manage their workplace. Yet they "had not done anything in terms of developing programs that address these issues," Lauber recalled.

CRM was about more than teaching communication and moderating hierarchy. It was intended to help pilots manage a wide array of pilot errors that Lauber had seen in a review of eighty accidents in the 1970s and '80s. The one that stood out was the flight into terrain of a brand-new Lockheed L-1011 in Miami in 1972.

Capt. Bob Loft was one of Eastern Airlines' most senior captains, with thirty thousand hours of experience. His first officer, former air force pilot Bert Stockstill, had six thousand hours and even more time in the L-1011 than Loft had. The flight engineer, Don Repo, was a twenty-five-year employee with Eastern with nearly sixteen thousand flight hours.

As Eastern Airlines Flight 401 approached Miami International Airport in late December 1972, the nose wheel landing gear indicator light did not illuminate. Without knowing whether the failure was of the light or of the gear, the captain did a go-around. Cleared to fly at two thousand feet, the crew began diagnosing the situation, and during the process of removing the light fixture and trying to reinsert it, someone inadvertently turned off the altitude hold. This went unobserved by the three pilots and the mechanic occupying the jump seat because all four men were trying to figure out whether the problem was with the gear or just the warning light.

As the plane dropped from its assigned altitude, an alert began to sound, but no one seemed to hear it. They were close to concluding that it was just a bad bulb when Stockstill noticed the plane's descent.

"We did something to the altitude," the first officer said.

"What?" said Captain Loft.

"We're still at two thousand, right?"

Loft's final words showed his confusion: "Hey, what's happening here?"

Flight 401 smashed into the Everglades, killing 111 of the 177 on board.

When John Lauber came across the detailed report he called it a "prototype" of an accident in which the crew does not manage the resources available. His cockpit resource management would teach pilots how to do this, in the same way businesses train their managers. "Pilots generally were well trained on aircraft systems and basic flying skills," he said. But nothing was done to teach them what they needed to know for decision making, communication, and leadership.

The Tenerife accident gave Lauber's work new energy, and in the years to come, cockpit resource management would be changed to "crew resource management," in recognition that other flight personnel such as mechanics, flight attendants, dispatchers, and air traffic controllers had a role to play in safe flights. As a bonus, the acronym, CRM, remained the same.

"So many incidents in life as well as [in] other industries have broken down because of the ambiguity in communications," said Christopher D. Wickens, a professor of psychology specializing in aviation human factors. "CRM is clearly one of the most important things that has developed in aviation over the past forty years."

CRM was sometimes dismissed by those who said it's a sissy notion, an "I'm okay, you're okay," touchy-feely exercise. Overall, resistance has subsided, though there remains a challenge in eliminating what Wickens calls the negative authority gradient, when differences in rank and experience in the cockpit create communication difficulties.

The power divide still restrains lower-ranked or less-experienced pilots from calling errors to the attention of a senior pilot. In a report for NASA, Dismukes and fellow human factors scientist Ben Berman discovered that captains would correct copilots when they made mistakes twice as often as first officers would when they saw the captain err.

"The cockpit traditionally was a strict hierarchy; the junior pilot never asked questions. Part of CRM training is to create an environment that, when [the junior pilot] has information that's critical to the flight, the captain will listen," Wickens said. Drawing a parallel to how rank is disregarded in safety-critical situations in the military, Wickens explained, "Landing on aircraft carriers, a low-ranking person can be in charge of things because they have the information that everyone needs. Authority shifts dynamically."

Pointing out errors can make for difficult conversations, and many inhibiting factors were in play on the night in 2009 when a Colgan Air turboprop crashed on approach to the airport in Buffalo, New York. Rebecca Shaw, the twenty-four-year-old first officer, had been flying for Colgan for one year. Marvin Renslow, the forty-seven-year-old captain, had four years with the company but only a hundred hours flying as a captain on the Bombardier Q400. While Shaw sniffled with a head cold and responded with a lot of "uh-huhs," the captain kept up a nearly one-way dialogue, even on approach to the Buffalo airport. Whether the first officer considered the banter a distraction isn't clear. She did seem worried about the difficult conditions in which they were flying: at night, in ice. A reading of the CVR suggests she was not inclined to assert herself. Even her apprehension about the ice was less than direct: "I've never seen icing conditions. I've never deiced. I've never seen any . . . I've never experienced any of that." She continued: "I'd have, like, seen this much ice and thought, 'Oh my gosh we were going to crash.'"

As the plane neared the airport, Renslow mishandled a stick shaker alert that the plane was flying too slow, presumably because it had accumulated ice, though in actuality it had not. Stalling protections on the plane caused the nose to go down to gain airspeed but the pilot pulled it back up, exacerbating the problem. The plane crashed into a house near the airport, killing everyone on board and one person on the ground.

It was an entirely different accident in terms of specifics, but a case of the same reticence to speak up, when Asiana Airlines Flight 214 landed short of the runway at San Francisco International Airport on a clear summer day in 2013. A series of misunderstandings about the way the automation worked meant that the flight was coming in too low and too slow, and the decision to go around and try the landing again came too late.

The plane hit a seawall at the edge of the runway bordering San Francisco Bay, slammed onto the ground, and pivoted up before hitting the runway a second time. Lee Kang-guk, the captain, in the left seat, had ten thousand total flight hours on other jets but just thirty-three on the Boeing 777. He was transitioning from the Airbus A320 narrow-body under the supervision of Capt. Lee Jung-min, who was in the right seat.

After the accident, Lee Kang-guk told investigators that he delayed initiating a go-around because he thought "only the instructor captain had the authority."

How open pilots are to asserting themselves, pointing out the errors of superiors, or acknowledging their own fallibility is highly influenced by culture. In an analysis in the *Journal of Air Transportation* in 2000, Michael Engle wrote that "there were extreme cultural differences" about whether "junior crewmembers should question the actions of captains" depending on where in the world they were from.

Forty years after the push to improve cockpit interaction and imbue the entire flight crew with a sense of shared responsibility, it seems the techniques work better in societies where individuality is valued more than rank. CRM may need to evolve to take into consideration the vastly different standards people have about interpersonal communication in parts of the world where aviation is experiencing the strongest growth, as in Asia, the Middle East, and South America.

The crashes of Colgan 3407 and Asiana 214 also shine a light on a hydra of issues that arrived like stowaways on the digital airplane: automation, complexity, and complacency.

Evolution

In the early days of flight, the cockpit was a busy and crowded place. The crew complement on the *Hawaii Clipper* in 1938 consisted of captain, first officer, second officer, third officer, fourth officer, engineer, assistant engineer, and radio operator—eight people required to fly six passengers. Each new generation of airplane incorporated advances that did better and faster a task formerly accomplished by the pilot. To fly as Wright had done meant to operate the machine with one's body and engage with one's senses. Each new advance made piloting less physical and more cerebral.

A normal crew consisted of three when Robert Pearson got his first job as an airline pilot in 1957. He was a first officer on the DC-3 for Trans-Canada Air Lines, which would become Air Canada in 1965. After flying the four-engine British Vickers Viscount, the DC-9, and the Boeing 727, Pearson was a forty-seven-year-old captain in 1983 when Air Canada went out and bought the world's most modern jetliner, the two-engine wide-body Boeing 767. This airplane was radically different because of the incorporation of technology that eliminated the need for a third pilot. The flight engineer (sometimes called the second officer) had been responsible for supervising the airplane's fuel, hydraulics, pneumatics, and electrical systems. But with the computers on the 767, the plane could monitor itself and present all that information to the pilots in bright, graphic, easy-to-read flight management system monitors.

The Boeing 767 was one step ahead of Airbus, which was producing an even more radical airplane, the first-generation fly-by-wire airliner that would put a computer between the flight controls and the control surfaces and create a protective flight envelope outside of which the pilot could not fly.

The digitization of flight started a new era, but were the airlines ready?

In February 1983, Pearson began a four-week course to qualify on the 767: two weeks of ground school and two weeks of flying the simulator. By April he was a captain. Sitting in the left seat, gazing at the array of gadgetry, he noted how many manual functions were now handled by the computer. "What did I know about computers? My experience with computers was using a Royal Bank of Canada ATM," he said. He was about to have a near-catastrophic experience on the Boeing 767, the origin of which was in not understanding the basics of the new airplane's technology.

On July 23, 1983, Pearson and First Officer Maurice Quintal were assigned to fly one of Air Canada's new 767s from Montreal to Edmonton. Due to a series of misunderstandings, the ground crew calculated the amount of fuel to load on the airplane by converting fuel volume to pounds, which is how they filled the other airplanes in the Air Canada fleet. But the 767's fuel system used kilograms. Since a pound is less than half a kilo, the error meant that only half the required fuel was pumped into the tanks for the four-and-a-half-hour transcontinental flight. The fuel quantity display was not working, so the crew manually entered the number 22,300 into the flight computer—without realizing that the plane's computer would consider it 22,300 kilos, or twice as much fuel as it actually contained. With the crew thinking the aircraft had enough fuel for the journey and then some, the plane departed.

Neither the pilots nor the fuelers realized their error, and the 767 no longer had a flight engineer managing the system whose job it would have been to ensure that the plane had the correct amount of fuel for the journey. "If everyone is trained and the lines are drawn as to who is responsible for what, there's no ambiguity," said Rick Dion, an executive with Air Canada maintenance who was a passenger on the flight. "In this case it was sort of open-ended. We weren't aware who was responsible for the final say on this fuel stuff."

Flight 143 was flying at forty-one thousand feet, about one hundred miles short of Winnipeg, when the first engine ran out of fuel, followed closely by the second. Without the engines to generate power, the pilots lost their flight deck instruments. They were seventy-five miles from the nearest airport. The riveting story of how experience and teamwork saved the day follows in part 5 of this book. The lesson here comes from Pearson, who said he and others learned that day that they were unprepared for the monumental leap in technology—and this from a man who had literally flown into the jet age.

"Transitioning from the noncomputer age to the computer age was more difficult than transitioning from propeller planes to jets, and it wasn't because they flew twice as high and twice as fast. It was all the big unknowns," he said.

After years of accidents attributable to pilot error, automating some functions was intended to make flying more precise, more efficient, and of course safer. A look at the decline in the rate of air accidents since the arrival of the digital airplane shows the benefits. The number of crashes resulting in the loss of the airplane, known as a "hull loss," has remained stable over the years, while the number of flights increased from half a million a year in 1960 to nearly thirty million in 2013. The third and fourth generation of automated airplanes, those with digital displays and computers that protect the airplane from maneuvers outside a predetermined range of safe flight parameters, are even more effective.

Automation's downside is that it creates both complexity and complacency. The complexity can cause pilots to misunderstand what the airplane is doing or how it works. It was complexity that caused half a dozen Air Canada employees to be unable to calculate how much fuel to pump into Flight 143. It was the opacity of the system that led the pilots to think that by entering the amount of fuel they thought had been loaded into the tanks, they would get an accurate reading of the fuel available for their flight. Recognizing the mistake afterward, Pearson said he understood for the first time the expression "Garbage in, garbage out."

Considering how automation can lead to confusion, it is a paradox that it can also contribute to crew obliviousness. With the L-1011 on autopilot, all three men on Eastern Flight 401 turned their attention away from the controls to work on changing a lightbulb. More recently, a Northwest Airlines flight from San Diego to Minneapolis made headlines around the world when the pilots got so wrapped up working on their laptops that they flew past their destination.

Flight 188 was one hundred fifty miles beyond Minneapolis International Airport with 144 passengers in October 2009 when a flight attendant called the pilots, curious to know why the plane had not begun its descent. For fifty-five minutes, the pilots had failed to acknowledge radio calls from air traffic control in Denver and Minneapolis or calls from the flight crew of another Northwest plane. To this day, people suggest that the pilots must have fallen asleep, because how else could they have missed hearing all the people calling them on the radio?

Robert Sumwalt was a member of the NTSB at the time. A former airline pilot, he was familiar with the troublesome issue of complacency. In 1997, Sumwalt and two others went through anonymous pilot reports and found that failure to adequately monitor what the airplane was doing was a factor in one-half to three-quarters of air safety events. Between 2005 and 2008 an airline industry group found sixteen cases similar to Northwest Flight 188, including one in which a captain returned from the bathroom and found the first officer engaged in a conversation with the flight attendant. The copilot's back was to the instruments, so he did not notice that the autopilot had disconnected and the plane was in danger of stalling. After losing four thousand feet of altitude, the captain was able to recover control of the airplane.

When Flight 188 made headlines, then-FAA administrator Randy Babbitt got on the evening news and castigated the flight crew. He pointed out that the Northwest pilots were on their laptops doing work unrelated to the flight, a prohibited activity. "It doesn't have anything to do with automation. Any opportunity for distraction doesn't have any business in the cockpit. Your focus should be on flying the airplane."

Tough talk sounds good, especially when stories such as

that of the Northwest Flight 188 get blasted all over the news, making air travelers nervous. Still, telling pilots to pay closer attention is too simple. It may not even be possible to give unrelenting focus to routine tasks, according to Missy Cummings, a systems engineer and director of Duke University's Humans and Autonomy Lab. "The human mind craves stimulation," she said. Failing to find it, the mind will wander.

Cummings, a former navy F-18 pilot, is a proponent of automation, and envisions a future with more of it, not less, if the problems identified by one of her former students at Massachusetts Institute of Technology can be resolved.

While working on her masters at MIT, Christin Hart Mastracchio conducted a study that showed that when automation reduces a workload too much, vigilance suffers. "Boredom produces negative effects on morale, performance, and quality of work," she found. Now an air force captain at Minot Air Force Base in North Dakota, Mastracchio is a pilot on the sixty-year-old, eight-engine B-52 Stratofortress, and automation is not her problem.

"The B-52 is on the opposite end of automation. It takes five people just to fly it," she told me. "It takes all of us working together to control the monstrosity. You need to find a center point where you have the right amount of automation."

On the day that Asiana 214's Lee Kang-guk was making his first approach to the San Francisco airport while training to be a captain on the Boeing 777, an electronic navigational aid that would normally have been used was down for maintenance. Since July 6, 2013, was a clear, sunny day, this might not have been a problem for many pilots, but it's the practice of some airlines, including Asiana, to use automation all the time.

After the plane's crash landing, Capt. Lee Kang-guk told investigators he'd found making a visual approach "very stressful." It was "difficult to perform," he said, in the absence of the electronic system that tracks a plane's glide path.

Capt. Lee Kang-guk was an experienced captain on the Airbus, though it is important to remember that he had just thirty-three hours on the Boeing 777. On approach, he made a series of errors while trying to get the airplane on the glide path to the airport. Neither he nor the pilot supervising him, Capt. Lee Jung-min, even discussed doing a go-around despite the fact that company policy required it when a plane was not at the appropriate height or speed approaching five hundred feet. In one respect, Capt. Lee Jung-min, with twelve thousand hours, was like Lee Kang-guk: it was his first flight as a training captain.

All these factors and others played a part in the accident. In its report, the NTSB concluded, "More opportunity to manually fly the 777 during training" would help pilots perform better.

In the process of writing this book, I had the chance to listen to a familiar story told from a new perspective. The tale begins the week prior to the historic flight of Orville and Wilbur Wright. Samuel Langley, the head of the Smithsonian Institution, had been given a government grant of $50,000 (equivalent to $1.2 million in 2016) to develop a powered airplane. Throughout the summer of 1903 he had been tinkering with this one-man contraption called the Great Aerodrome. It was to be catapulted from a track mounted on a houseboat in the Potomac River, but prototype flights had not gone well.

On December 8, 1903, with Langley's assistant, test pilot Charles Manly, on board, the Great Aerodrome was pushed from the top of the boat, but it never became airborne. It collapsed and fell into the icy waters of the river. Discouraged, Langley gave up. Sixty-nine at the time, he may never have expected to live long enough to see man fly. Yet nine days later, the Wright Brothers made history with a twelve-second controlled flight at Kitty Hawk in North Carolina. That's the story I knew.

The goose bump–inspiring and brilliant postscript was presented to me by John Flach, a professor and chair of the Department of Psychology at Wright State University in Dayton, Ohio: "Christine, the Wright Brothers learned that for a plane to work, it had to put control in the hands of humans. That's a metaphor."

It is a metaphor appropriate for aviation's first century. But what about the second? Flying has gone from the days of the Wright Brothers controlling the plane by shifting their weight to pilots who sit at keyboards typing instructions that command a complex system of computers. For a while the debate has been over who or what does the job better, the human or the machine. What is emerging is that each does the job differently

"The computer is a rule-based system," Flach told me. "What it means to be reasonable and human is to break the rules. A computer will continue to do its computing while the building burns around it. A human will adapt to the situation."

The aviation industry has spent decades creating support for the stresses that pilots encounter, from choosing the right candidates to teaching them how to manage resources. And on almost every flight, new technology and age-old human qualities mesh in just the right way so that flying is safer than the sum of these parts.

PART FIVE

Resiliency

Every day, somewhere in the air, a cockpit crew averts disaster by routinely dealing with equipment malfunctions, weather uncertainties, or unscripted situations.

—DR. KEY DISMUKES,
NASA HUMAN FACTORS SCIENTIST

The Control Metaphor

The scenario of MH-370's disappearance that I describe in this book is a tragic illustration of Flach's metaphorical look at the Wright Brothers flight: control had to be in the hands of the pilot. On MH-370, a rapid decompression triggered a chain of events that required human control, but hypoxia may have stripped the pilots of their mental ability.

Fallibility sometimes leads to disaster. Far more often, however, resiliency saves the day. Pilots interrupt errors and correct oversights. They find workarounds and reshuffle priorities. They avert problems they don't even know they have— and not just once in a while, but on nearly every flight, without the passengers even knowing something is amiss.

On occasion, however, the malfunction becomes obvious.

Alarms started blaring on the flight deck of Malaysia Flight 124 eighteen minutes after takeoff from Perth Airport on August 1, 2005. The plane was climbing through thirty-eight thousand feet when Capt. Norhisham Kassim and First Officer Caleb Foong were startled by two very conflicting warning horns. The

233

first alerted them that the Boeing 777 was flying too slowly and was in danger of stalling; the next indicated that the plane was flying too fast. Before either man had time to react, they were thrust back in their seats as the front end of the airliner abruptly turned up.

One experienced 777 captain told me that it had to have been a "WTF moment." Yet with great understatement, Norhisham recalled that he was "startled." The nose was high, about seventeen degrees, and rocketing farther skyward at a speed of ten thousand feet per minute. That's an ascent of more than one hundred miles per hour.

They had been flying on autopilot when the trouble started so Norhisham shut off the autopilot and pushed the yoke to get the nose down. That caused the autothrottle to rev, pumping more fuel into the engines and giving the descent an unexpected kick so that the plane started a four-thousand-foot dive. Moving the throttles to idle only made the plane bolt upward again, and the aircraft climbed two thousand feet before the confounded pilots could get it to stop.

The plane was shuddering violently, according to Kim Holst, a passenger from Australia. "A flight attendant dropped an entire tray of drinks and began crawling on his hands and knees back to his seat, and the other flight attendant began praying," Holst remembered.

For the pilots, "It was somewhat like riding a bucking horse," Norhisham said, adding, "As a passenger at the back-most seats, you definitely will feel worse than that."

Norhisham and Foong were facing a situation similar to Robert Pearson's experience on the Air Canada 767: a "garbage in, garbage out" encounter with the airplane's computerized brain.

All the fancy electronic gizmos feeding information to the pilots and enabling automated flight rely on sensors in the plane's air data inertial reference unit, called the ADIRU (pronounced ADD-uh-roo). The ADIRU consists of two sets of three accelerometers. Two accelerometers calculate the side-to-side/up-and-down movement of the wings called roll, two calculate the up-and-down motion of the nose called pitch, and two gauge the side-to-side/front-to-back motion on a horizontal plane called yaw. There are two sets of sensors for each; one is primary, and the second set is a backup. That redundancy provided such a feeling of security to operators of the Boeing 777 that no checklist was developed for what the pilots should do if there was bad information from the sensors. Yet this was what was causing MH-124's wild ride over Australia.

The crew knew that the plane was performing erratically, but not why. So as they prepared for a return to Perth, Norhisham hesitated to turn off the autothrottle. He had a handful of airplane, and he was hoping some part of the automation would help reduce the workload.

Like a bad driver pumping the accelerator, the lever controlling fuel to the engines kept "hunting up and down" as the two pilots struggled to get control of the flight. Norhisham and Foong were engaged in a kind of triage, dealing with the most critical problems as they nursed the 777 back to Perth. Faced with a confounding situation, Captain Norhisham had to give up diagnosing and concentrate on learning how to fly this plane with all its sudden idiosyncrasies.

Certainly they were relieved to see the approach to the airport, but that feeling was short-lived. They were about to get a last-minute surprise. As the plane descended through three thousand feet, another instrument in the orchestra of alarms began to sound. *Wind shear, wind shear,* the computerized voice called out, accompanying the shrill series of beeps.

Pilots are appropriately cautious about wind shear, which is a sudden change in the direction or speed of the wind. It is concerning close to the ground because it can cause a plane to lose lift, with little time for the pilot to recover. On the crippled Malaysia jet, the pilots were loath to get into a situation where they would have to rely on the plane performing as expected, considering how unpredictable it had been so far. Going around and trying the landing again, with all the uncertainties about the condition of the plane, also seemed risky.

Norhisham was worried. Was the alert real or another unreliable result from unreliable inputs to the ADIRU? The captain had to make a decision. The day was clear, visibility was good, and the wind was manageable, but the sun was going down. "We continued [toward the landing] with full caution," he said, keeping an eye out for any indication of wind shear.

"Thank God," Norhisham said when Flight 124 landed safely with no injuries, though everyone on board the airplane was shaken. Only then did Norhisham stop and think about the "very thin margin of survival." He had joined a fraternity of pilots who had knowingly broken the last link in the chain to calamity.

Three and a half years later, Chesley Sullenberger and Jeff Skiles ditched an Airbus A320 in New York's Hudson River after geese flew into the engines following takeoff from LaGuardia Airport.

In September 2010, Andrei Lamanov and Yevgeny Novoselov landed on an abandoned runway in northwestern Russia that was half as long as their aircraft required. A total power failure on a the Tupelov TU-154 caused all the fuel pumps to fail, starving the engines and leading to the loss of all navigation and radio equipment on what should have been a five-hour flight to Moscow.

Praising the actions of pilots like these, a writer for *New York* magazine called them "a dying breed." I don't think that's true. It is not that few can do what Norhisham and Foong, Sully and Skiles, Lamanov and Novoselov, did. It's that aviation's safety net is so expansive and robust that it is a blessedly rare occurrence when the pilots' full complement of talent, skills, and training is not enough to keep them from falling through it.

When pilots fail, it is headline news. When they succeed in addressing minor issues before they become major, however, it is for the most part invisible, making human resiliency the most mysterious of the many contributors to the industry's stellar safety record.

It is easy to see when things go wrong, writes James Reason in his book *The Human Contribution*. A professor of psychology and a pioneer in the study of human factors, Reason spent most of his career writing about why people screw up. At a conference in 2009, however, he presented what he considers the much more interesting flip side. Speaking to the annual Risky Business Conference in London, Reason called the subject of his life's work "human as hazard," a tedious subject. "It's banal; it's so everyday," he said. The octogenarian's attention had been turned to "the stuff that legends are made of," the qualities that allow humans to be heroes.

So much time has been spent learning from failure; what can be gleaned from studying the right stuff? This is not just Reason's question. From the icy day Sullenberger and Skiles ditched their plane in the Hudson, the public has clamored to hear their story. The same is true of the heroes who preceded them. The controlled crash landing of United Flight 232 occurred in 1989 and has been the subject of books and movies. The latest, Laurence Gonzales's *Flight 232: A Story of Disaster and Survival*, was turned into a play. People remain fascinated by the horrifying drama and uplifting conclusion.

To find out what qualities these pilots share, I analyzed five commercial flights that went terribly wrong but were saved from total disaster by the actions of the flight crew. I interviewed these pilots about their experiences, asking them what factors had led to the outcome. Their stories had several themes in common and I've grouped them under headings to show that. Innovation was one consistent theme and this should not be surprising. After all, machines do not improvise, and computers are not creative. What pilots bring to the cockpit is their humanity. It is their greatest contribution.

Knowledge and Experience

In the middle of an unseasonably warm winter in Australia, Richard de Crespigny and his adult son Alexander took me boating in Sydney Harbour. Windblown and athletic, the men were clearly in their element; in their nautical shirts and deck shoes, they could have been modeling for the Vineyard Vines catalog.

Then something went wrong with the engine, and de Crespigny had to strip down to his swimsuit and hang on from the fantail to repair the motor so we could get moving. Drenched and oil-spattered, he no longer looked like the man Australia has come to know as Captain Fantastic, but once again his mechanical know-how and experience saved the day.

Call it maturity, knowledge, or time at the wheel, when a pilot gets to a certain age, there's little he or she hasn't seen before. John Gadzinski, a pilot for a U.S. airline and a safety and hazard specialist, says, "You've already been vaccinated as far as your experience and reactions go. It's less and less a deer-in-the-headlights look and more 'Okay, this is what we're gonna do.'"

Still, many experienced airline pilots don't have de Crespigny's in-depth knowledge of the Airbus A380. That's what he was flying on November 4, 2010, when he led a team of five pilots to land a severely crippled airliner with 469 people aboard. For nearly two harrowing hours the jumbo jet circled above the Singapore Strait after an uncontained engine failure blew holes in the wing and fuselage and disabled multiple critical systems.

It was a clear, sunny morning when Qantas Flight 32 departed Singapore's Changi Airport. Then, while passing through seven thousand feet, passengers were jolted by a loud bang. Mike Tooke, seated on the left side of the plane, saw "a flash of white off the inner engine. Then there was an incredibly loud second bang, and the whole plane started to vibrate." Five seconds later, he said, "it felt like we were plunging out of the sky."

From below the wing, a stream of atomized fuel was hosing out of the tank. Some passengers took out their phones and recorded the terrifying sight, no doubt believing they were capturing the last moments of their lives.

On the flight deck, de Crespigny had been about to turn off the seatbelt sign when he heard the two bangs followed by the repetitive beeping of the master warning system. He pushed the altitude hold button, which reduced engine thrust and stress on the engines. It also lowered the nose, which was what caused Tooke to think the plane was "plunging out of the sky."

This simple response wasn't reflex on de Crespigny's part. He was reaching back to an experience he had had nearly a decade before, when he was a passenger on a Qantas 767 that had an engine explode as the plane was ascending after takeoff. In his book *QF32*, he writes that he was impressed by how quickly the 767 captain moderated the plane's violent shaking. Once back on the ground, de Crespigny asked the man what he had done to reduce thrust so quickly and was told, "I just hit the altitude hold button." The small lesson stuck with him. Remembering and deciding to heed it was the first of many decisions, sometimes quick and sometimes after achingly slow deliberation, that contributed to the happy ending of his own near disaster.

My friend David Paqua, a general aviation pilot, once told me, "A pilot can have a thousand hours of experience, or he can fly the same hour one thousand times." Pilots such as de Crespigny use each hour in the air, and even their hours on the ground, to become utterly familiar with the physics and the mechanics of flight. Heck, before QF-32, de Crespigny had visited the factories of both Airbus and Rolls-Royce, gathering material for a technical book he was writing about big jets, including the A380, the plane that gave him such a hard time on that fateful day in 2009.

By contrast, Robert Pearson, the Air Canada captain whom I wrote about earlier in the book, and whose brand-new Boeing 767 would run out of fuel halfway across Canada in July 1983, told me he didn't know enough about the plane he was flying on the day of his near catastrophe, and neither did his airline. "These airplanes came out of Boeing flown by test pilots who had known every rivet and bolt," Pearson said. They arrived at the airline to be flown by "guys like me who knew nothing" about the revolutionary design. His drama began with his not understanding the way the computers assisted the airliner. This complexity masked a very simple problem: the plane was out of fuel. "We didn't know what the problem was. Even when the engines were failing, we were wondering, 'How the hell can computers shut down engines?'" Pearson said.

At the same time, a lifetime of piloting all kinds of planes, including and especially unpowered gliders, enabled Pearson to land the 767 successfully without engines. Each hour in the air can teach something new to even the most experienced pilot.

When the fuel pump alarms started illuminating on Air Canada Flight 143 that summer day in 1983, Pearson said no one on the flight deck had any idea what could be wrong. The engines were still working, and the flight management computers indicated that there was plenty of fuel. Remember, the pilots had manually entered the pounds of fuel loaded, but the 767 flight management system interpreted the input as kilos, a unit of measurement roughly double that of a pound.

As a sign of just how confusing all this was to the crew, Pearson's first announcement to his passengers was that the plane's computer had gone kaput and the flight would divert to Winnipeg to get things sorted out.

When the engines spooled down, the pilots realized they could not spend any more time trying to figure it out. That was in the past. What was going to happen in the immediate future— that was up to them.

Pearson told me that he and the first officer, Maurice Quintal, who died in 2015, needed to focus on how and where they would glide the plane. Pearson was flying, but with only basic instruments. Quintal was doing the math, logging the distance to the closest airfields and comparing it to how quickly the plane was losing altitude.

"I believed we could make it" to Winnipeg, Pearson said, but Quintal's calculations showed otherwise.

While in the military, Quintal had trained at Gimli, an air force base fourteen miles off to the right of where they were flying. They had more than enough altitude to get there—too much altitude, in fact. As the plane approached the airfield, it was too high, and the pilots had no ability to slow it. Quintal lowered the landing gear, but it wasn't enough. So Pearson used a side slip (or crab) maneuver he had honed towing gliders in his off time. Using the rudder, the panels on the wings called ailerons, and the elevators, he turned the fuselage into the airstream so that the plane's bulky metal flank would work against its movement through the air. You can mimic the effect by putting your hand out the window of a moving car with the palm facing forward. You'll feel the resistance right away. That's what Pearson was counting on to help bring down his speed.

"We were using the fuselage as an airbrake," Pearson said. It gave everyone on board a bone-jarringly rocky ride, but it worked.

"I had total tunnel vision. I knew Maurice was beside me. I was one hundred percent concentrated on speed and our relationship to that piece of cement."

In the stories written about the "Gimli Glider," Pearson's

experience in gliders is credited for his inspired innovation that day. Pearson argues the point on two levels. First, the crab maneuver was used most often when he was towing gliders, not flying them. "When coming in on approach on a grass field with a metal rope hanging down [from the plane], you come in high because you don't want to catch the rope on the fence. I'd side-slip every time I came in, and I did a lot of glider towing." Anyway, Pearson points out, gliders have speed brakes, and without power the 767 he was flying did not.

More to the point, he says it was all the flying he did that prepared him for that day. Gliders and airliners, for sure, but also aerobatic planes and ultralights, floatplanes and ski planes on ice and snow—decades of experiences all came flooding back, he told me. "There's something to be gained from everything we do."

Synergy and Teamwork

The philosophy of crew resource management, or CRM, is to merge each pilot's separate strengths to create a more knowledgeable, more experienced team. With de Crespigny on QF-32 were First Officer Matt Hicks and Second Officer Mark Johnson. In what would prove to be fortuitous, two other captains, Dave Evans and Harry Wubben, were also on the flight deck. De Crespigny was being checked out on the A380, and the pilot checking him was being trained as a check captain (that is, learning how to assess whether a pilot meets government criteria). "So," de Crespigny explained, "we had a check captain checking a check captain who was checking me." A total of seventy-six thousand flight hours was represented by the five navy suits.

After reading about the flight of Qantas 32—and I promise, I'll get back to that story shortly—I called Denny Fitch, who told me that all that combined experience would have been an enormous asset for de Crespigny. He should know; he was a hero pilot himself.

In 1989, Fitch was a passenger aboard United Airlines Flight 232 from Denver to Chicago. One hour into the flight, the engine mounted on the tail of the DC-10 came apart at cruise altitude, and a piece of it sliced through a section at the back of the plane, where three separate hydraulic lines came together. Severing the lines caused the fluid to drain, leaving the pilots with no way to turn, slow, or brake the airplane.

Al Haynes was in command of the flight, with First Officer William Records and Second Officer Dudley Dvorak. "Somebody has set a bomb off" was Haynes's first thought when he heard the noise. He was so startled he dropped his coffee.

The pilots were still trying to figure out what happened when they were interrupted by another crisis. The plane began a descending turn to the right. The plane's right wing angled sideways at thirty-eight degrees, far steeper than commercial airline passengers are accustomed to. The DC-10 was on its way to rolling over. Haynes closed the throttle to the left engine and slammed open the lever controlling fuel to the right one. The uneven engine power brought the right wing back up. It was an act of instinct and creativity, gleaned from Haynes's early days flying. He was relying on his knowledge of basic aerodynamics. "You reduce thrust, and that reduces lift," he explained.

Right side up again, the plane began to nose up and down

in a near-constant cycle of ascents and descents called phugoids, which would last throughout the flight. Still, the successful righting of the airplane allowed Haynes to reframe his thinking about what just moments earlier had seemed an impossible situation. The crew could continue to maneuver the airplane using the only control mechanism available: fuel to the engines. Into this scene of spontaneous piloting walked Denny Fitch.

Fitch was a United DC-10 training captain, and he'd gone to the cockpit to see if he could help. He found the men focused on the technique Haynes had just thought up. The added complication was that they could not keep the thrust the same on both engines because that made the plane want to roll over.

"Take one throttle lever in each hand," Haynes told Fitch. "You can do it much smoother than we can." So, positioned between Haynes and Record, Fitch did as instructed. "The throttles became my assignment," Fitch said. None of the four experienced airmen on United 232 had ever tried to fly an airplane this way. No one had ever imagined an airliner losing all flight controls.

Haynes was the commander of the flight, but in the many talks he has given on this event since 1989, he has acknowledged that the skill, talent, and knowledge of all four combined worked to avert complete disaster. "Why would I know more about getting that airplane on the ground under those conditions than the other three?" he said.

When the plane slammed down onto the runway at Iowa's Sioux Gateway Airport three-quarters of an hour later, 185 of the 296 people aboard, including all four of the pilots, survived the crash landing and subsequent fire. One hundred eleven people died, so at best it was a mitigated calamity. It was also a demonstration of the Wright metaphor: a plane otherwise not flyable was wrestled through the air and down onto the runway because control was in the hands of the pilots, and not just any pilots, but a coordinated team whose knowledge, maturity, and experience had a synergetic effect.

Fitch died in 2012, but when I spoke to him about Qantas 32 in the fall of 2010, he reminded me that, as with United 232, those four men on the flight deck that day represented an abundance of hours at the controls of an A380, so it wasn't coincidence that things turned out so well. "You cannot have all the experience in your life to equal seventy-six thousand hours," he said when I told him the combined flight hours of the Qantas crew. The combined flight hours of the pilots on United Flight 232 was even higher: eighty-eight thousand hours. Machines will break, Fitch said, so "at the end of the day it is the human factor that counts."

Decision Making

When the number two engine on de Crespigny's A380 flew apart, the pressure turbine disk fractured into three crescent-shaped pieces, each roughly six feet long and a foot wide. They flew out of the engine like supersize medieval chakrams, taking the back end of the engine cowling with them. Other shrapnel peppered the fuselage and tore holes in the plane's left wing, puncturing the fuel tank and severing a number of wire bundles.

There was no mystery that the problem was with the number two engine, but everything else was uncertain, including why two of the three remaining Rolls-Royce Trent 900 engines were not performing properly. The pilots could not jettison or transfer fuel, and the pumps were not working. Fearful that the last engine might fail, de Crespigny made a request to ATC to climb to ten thousand feet. "I wanted enough altitude so we could glide back to Changi," he reasoned.

Nine months earlier, Captain Sullenberger found himself in a similar situation with even less altitude. He was at three thousand feet following takeoff from New York's LaGuardia Airport when geese flew into the engines, knocking them out. The A320 began a one-thousand-feet-per-minute descent. In his book *Highest Duty*, Sullenberger said he and Skiles knew in less than a minute that they were not going to get to any of the nearby airports. "We were too low, too slow, too far away and pointed in the wrong direction," he wrote. The Hudson River was "long enough, wide enough and on that day, smooth enough to land a jetliner." So he did.

Worrying about whether the Qantas A380 might also turn into a 550-ton glider, de Crespigny calculated just how much altitude he would need to get back to Changi Airport. He wasn't thinking about Sullenberger, he was thinking about the astronaut Neil Armstrong, remembering that when Armstrong was a test pilot flying the X-15 at NASA in the 1960s, he helped develop a technique for gliding the rocket-powered plane back to earth once its fuel was spent.

Armstrong reached altitudes as high as two hundred thousand feet, then glided back to Edwards Air Force Base in California, harnessing gravity to descend in an ever-diminishing spiral. This bit of pioneering aviation was something de Crespigny thought he might need to emulate.

"I was going to do a slow climb to ten thousand feet, to be in gliding zone using the calculation that I could get thirty miles" at that altitude, he explained. His unilateral decision alarmed the other pilots. They wanted to get the plane lower, not higher. For all his charm, de Crespigny is no pussycat. He is opinionated and sometimes stubborn, and he was perturbed that the other airmen did not agree with him. Still, de Crespigny yielded, realizing, as had Al Haynes, that when flying a plane with such grave damage, no one was an expert and everyone was.

"The total number of flight hours accumulated by pilots does not predict the quality of their decisions," Robert Mauro, a professor of psychology at the University of Oregon, wrote in a paper on pilot decision making. "It is experience within a situation that confers expertise." When everyone is a novice, communicating during decision making becomes even more critical.

James Reason describes this as "a willingness on the part of subordinates to speak up and a corresponding willingness on the part of the leader to listen." So concerned was de Crespigny that the three senior pilots on the flight deck not smother the input of the two younger men that he asked the most junior officer, Mark Johnson, to offer his opinions first, followed by his copilot, Matt Hicks.

Using past experience to guide a decision is called associative decision making. And while it can be a fast and effective method, the danger, according to Mauro, is that past experience may not be helpful in "unstable environments or ambiguous situations." Worse still is applying a reflective by-the-book response when creativity or innovation is needed.

As the crew of Qantas 32 flew in circles a mile and a half above the sea, they were consumed by the checklists that were constantly being generated by a computerized airplane trying to diagnose itself and guide the pilots through possible remedies. Fuel was draining overboard from the hole in the left wing tank, and this created several fuel imbalances. When the checklist for wing imbalance appeared, it called for the pilots to open the valves to send fuel from the good tank to the one that had been breached.

"Should we be transferring fuel out of the good right wing into the leaking left wing?" de Crespigny asked his crew. "No," they replied. Many airlines expect pilots to follow standard procedures strictly. Determining when to follow and when to ignore them requires knowledge, experience, logic, mindfulness, communication, and strength, but decision-making strategies are still evolving.

In *The Pilot's Handbook of Aeronautical Knowledge*, the FAA uses the mnemonic 3P, for *perceive*, *process*, and *perform*, to help pilots remember what steps ought to precede a decision. At Lufthansa, the cadets learn a different acronym, FORDEC, for *facts*, *options*, *risks*, *decisions*, *execute*, and *check*. That final C could also stand for *circle back* because the big lesson for pilots is that a decision isn't made and done; it's an ongoing cycle.

Captain Norhisham opted to keep the autothrottles engaged while maneuvering MH-124 back to Perth, but he had to revise that plan because of the constant revving and powering back of the engines. That's one example of reviewing a decision. On Air Canada Flight 143, Pearson and Quintal wanted to land at Winnipeg Airport because emergency equipment would be available and big-city hospitals were nearby. But it was too far away. They considered ditching the plane in Lake Winnipeg, but as Quintal continued updating his distance calculations, he realized they could glide to Gimli. The constant revising of the plan continued, leading to the innovative piloting that has made

Air Canada Flight 143 one of aviation's most talked about recoveries.

Airmanship

The day James Reason gave his presentation on heroic recoveries to the attendees of the conference on risk in 2009, he shared the stage with forty-five-year-old British Airways captain Peter Burkill. Burkill's crash landing in London the year before was the darkest swan among the flock because the 3Ps, FORDEC, CRM—all those intended-to-be-helpful alphabet formulas—were irrelevant. Burkill and First Officer John Coward were faced with a failure so sudden they had only seconds to react.

The pilots and the relief first officer, Conor Magenis, were at the tail end of the ten-hour flight of British Airways 38 from Beijing. As the plane flew over the outskirts of London, Burkill had no worry bigger than whether the gate would be available when they arrived at the airport. The captain could see where they would touch down, on runway 27L, off to the west, on the other side of the borough of Hounslow. Less than a minute before landing, Coward, who was flying the leg, said suddenly, "I can't get any power."

"I remember looking at his hands on the throttles, and I could see the demand: the autothrottle was fully forward," Burkill told me. He was still processing what was going on when Magenis chimed in from behind them, saying it looked like a double engine failure.

"I remember every second of that event. It seemed like the event was three minutes long," Burkill said. In truth, the time that passed from Coward's stunning discovery to the plane hitting the ground was just thirty seconds.

After realizing they would have to make a landing without power, Burkill first decided to leave Coward flying the plane while he concentrated on their options. Ahead loomed frightening obstacles: factories, multistory residences, the Hatton Cross tube station, and a gas station, all of which they would have to fly over to reach the airport. The airfield was surrounded by a high perimeter fence, and on the other side of that, a nine-foot-tall lineup of antennas and airport lights would block a too-low approach.

Burkill eyed the gauges showing ten tons of fuel still in the tanks and worried about fire. Again he checked the throttles, but there was no improvement. Then the first warning horn sounded in the cockpit. The autopilot had kept the flight on the approach path, but the lack of fuel to the engines was causing the plane to slow. The yoke started to vibrate in Coward's hands, and an audible airspeed warning sounded. The rate of descent increased until it was more than double the normal seven hundred feet per minute.

"I knew what it was supposed to feel like, and it was not this," Burkill said. The only way to keep the plane from slamming into the football-size two-story building dead ahead was to reduce the airplane's drag. The landing gear, which had been lowered before the crisis began, was slowing them down, but there wasn't enough time to retract it. Burkill thought it might also help absorb the impact of the inevitable crash landing. He kept thinking.

Before the trouble began, in preparation for the approach, Coward had asked Burkill to set the flaps to thirty degrees.

This makes the wing more comma shaped so the plane can fly at slower speeds. Burkill now considered whether slightly flattening the curved surfaces might be enough to keep the plane flying. He reached over to the flaps lever and, after a moment's hesitation, moved it from thirty to twenty-five degrees. He did not consult Coward; there just wasn't time. The effect was immediate: the descent slowed.

Gus Macmillan, a musician from Melbourne, was in a window seat just behind the wing on the right. "I remember thinking, 'We only just cleared that fence' as the grass of the runway unfolded beneath us," he told the Australian newspaper *The Age*. The plane hit the grass field 890 feet short of the runway, at 124 miles per hour.

Burkill's decision had given the plane an additional 164 feet in the air and enabled Flight 38 to fly over the ominous white building, pass the gas station, clear the highway, and cross safely over the imposing electrified metal barrier of antennas and runway lights. All 152 people on board survived.

"I wish I had time to actually communicate" with the others, Burkill told me later. A believer in the benefits of CRM, he says that not only did they face a situation for which they were never trained, but also there was no time to use any of their crisis management tools. It was nothing like the sessions in the simulator with all that time to talk to ATC and the cabin crew, glorious minutes to consider options with others on the flight deck. In a real-life emergency, he had to make everything up as he went along.

"I'm in this gray area," he said, "this gray area that no pilot wants to be in, with no checklists for my situation and nothing written down." In the modern jet age, the loss of all engines is so exceedingly rare that it is not a scenario practiced by pilots in their simulator sessions.

Without diminishing the horrifying experience, one that leads many hero pilots to wrestle with posttraumatic stress disorder long after the public accolades subside, this lack of guidance is where humans excel.

Uncertainty and Surprise

If you are wondering if I've forgotten you over the Singapore Strait in a noisy and unstable jumbo jet, flying a horse track holding pattern with the 469 frightened travelers on Qantas Flight 32, I have not. I left you to experience just a portion of the hour and forty-five minutes during which the pilots and their passengers flew on, uncertain of their fate.

One of the mighty plane's four engines was out, and two others were degraded. Imagine Second Officer Mark Johnson walking down the aisle of the airplane, straining to assess the damage by looking out the passengers' windows.

Perhaps, like me, you wonder why the pilots didn't just put that airplane back on the ground ASAP? This was a subject of discussion in the cockpit.

De Crespigny said, "We reconsidered this option every fifteen minutes in the air. This was not the time to panic and make irrational decisions. We were on a fact-finding journey; we had to understand how much of the A380 we had left before we could hope to land."

Yes, flying was a hazard. Still, before committing to landing a plane that was still too heavy because of all the fuel loaded for the flight to Sydney and only 65 percent of its braking power, de Crespigny had some questions he wanted answered. Could any of their many problems be fixed? How would those they could not solve affect their ability to land? They could not know the answers. Too much was wrong with the airplane.

Nearly an hour into the flight, Dave Evans and Harry Wubben set about calculating how much pavement the plane would need to stop. The longest runway at Changi Airport was 13,000 feet. Evans and Wubben calculated that the plane would need 12,700 feet of it, more than twice that for a normal landing. It was achievable, albeit with a very tight margin. That was good news.

When the wheels of the giant A380 touched the ground, de Crespigny jammed both feet on the brakes, and miraculously the plane slowed, stopping within the distance calculated by Evans and Wubben. Yet the drama was still a long way from over.

Fuel continued to dump out of the wing, but now it was pooling within range of the brakes that had just done all that stopping and were heated to sixteen hundred degrees Fahrenheit. The fire trucks could not approach the aircraft until the engines were powered down, but when the crew switched them off, the plane was thrown into darkness. Nine of the ten cockpit display screens had failed. Six of the seven radios were dead, and the number one engine kept on spinning.

For nearly an hour, everyone sat in the dark and sweltering airplane, while the crew worried about the ignition of the fuel and the threat posed by an engine that still whined as if it were in the air. Dave Evans told the Royal Aeronautical Society, "We've got a situation where there is fuel, hot brakes, and an engine that we can't shut down. And really the safest place was on board the aircraft."

It took three hours of dousing the engine with water and foam to finally get it to stop turning.

As with the other dramatic events described in this chapter, the pilots knew the uncertainty would come to an end—in hours for Qantas Flight 32, forty-five minutes for United Flight 232, half an hour for Malaysia Flight 124, a quarter of an hour for Air Canada Flight 143, and less than a minute for British Airways Flight 38. They did not know what the end would look like. It's easy to forget that.

All the pilots I've written about here were deliberate in their decisions, and they struggled to improve the odds weighing heavily against them—and they all had to contend with an eleventh-hour disruption. It was an engine that would not shut down and the ongoing risk of fire on Qantas 32; and it was a wind shear alarm that rattled Norhisham and Foong as the Malaysia Airlines 777 approached Perth. With United Flight 232, as the DC-10 approached Sioux Gateway Airport, another of the phugoids sent the jet plummeting just three hundred feet above the runway.

"That's where our luck ran out. We just ran out of altitude, trying to correct it," Haynes told a NASA conference on risk in 1991. "That close to the ground, we didn't have time." The right wing and tail section broke off, a fire erupted, and the body of the airplane bounced along the runway and broke apart. Most of the fatalities were in the back of the plane and in the first-class cabin behind the cockpit, which broke away during impact.

The most bizarre postscript came in the final moments of the Air Canada flight that came to be known as the Gimli Glider.

The nose gear collapsed as the plane touched down, and the front end of the plane hit the ground with "a hell of a thump," as Pearson recalled it. The dragging of the metal across the pavement acted to brake the plane, which was a blessing. For, unseen by either of the pilots as they approached what they thought to be an abandoned airfield, the former air base had been converted into a motorsports track. On that day, it was being used by the Winnipeg Sports Car Club and was crowded with spectators enjoying the summer afternoon. Miraculously, no one on the ground was injured.

After wrestling with perplexing calamities in the air, not getting a break in the final seconds just seems wrong, but hurdles right up to the end do not surprise retired airline pilot and air safety specialist John Cox. "Air accidents are complex," Cox explained. "In some cases, factors outside the original problem can come into play, and in others, there is so much going on that it is not possible to anticipate all the possibilities."

The Opposite of Despair

Norhisham Kassim praised God after his harrowing brush with disaster, and Al Haynes chimed in with his belief that "something guides us in all we do," adding that strength can be found by looking inward, a philosophy shared by Pearson and Burkill. This last component of resiliency is what James Reason calls "realistic optimism," the opposite of despair, a stubborn belief that things will be all right in the end.

"You have to believe in yourself. Every time you go to work you're doing something that not everyone on the street can do," Burkill told me. In managing emergencies, confidence is necessary, "for sure," he said. Pearson chimed in with the circular argument that experience makes a pilot confident, and confidence can lead to positive outcomes.

"Pilots should feel they can handle anything," Haynes told me. "If you don't have that feeling, you shouldn't be flying."

These nerve-racking flights are rare. The general public will never know just how often pilots avert disaster much earlier in the chain, but several airline executives say that safety threats are interrupted all the time.

Despite the ambiguities in how the increasingly complex airliner affects the pilots' ability to interact with it, one thing is clear: the amount of data available from new-generation airplanes is a remarkable tool. Hundreds of details on every routine flight are collected and analyzed as airlines try to determine how often their operations veer outside the safety envelope. Voice and data recorders offer an after-the-fact view, but information collected during normal trips can be downloaded, combined with others, and analyzed in order to discover hidden weaknesses in maintenance, training, or operational procedures.

"Even with a good outcome, every part of the story isn't perfect," said Billy Nolen, a former captain with American Airlines and now senior vice president of safety for the U.S. airline trade association Airlines for America. Reviewing large numbers of flights allows a carrier to understand how close to the edge uneventful flights get. "What is our data showing? What is our story?"

It's not exactly studying the silver linings instead of the clouds. Much more can be done to get there, according to Captain Fantastic (a.k.a. de Crespigny), who has taken on the study of human achievement with the same energy he has devoted to flying. "Many things improve when we mine the big data for successes," he said. From the few hero pilots who have accomplished dramatic saves to the many who overcome hurdles and safely bring their passengers to their destinations—these examples should be examined for the lessons they hold. "We'll be able to change our definition of safety from avoiding what goes wrong to ensuring things go right," de Crespigny said.

On a summer morning in 2006, Capt. Cort Tangeman and First Officer Laura Strand were approaching Chicago's O'Hare Airport. They'd taken an MD-80 airliner on the overnight flight from Los Angeles. Strand was flying the leg, and she called for Tangeman to lower the landing gear as they neared the airport, but Tangeman found that the nose gear doors would not open.

"At that point we had been up all night, and it's kind of like shock and awe," Tangeman said. "You're not sure what you're seeing, and you know it is not going to be solved between now and the time you land." The crew took the plane down to about five hundred feet, making an unusual flyby right down the runway of one of the world's busiest airports. From there, a tower controller eyeballed the plane using binoculars. This confirmed that while the main gear was down, the wheels under the plane's nose were not.

The crew was given an area off of the approach path to fly while they planned for landing. They were not immediately concerned about fuel, but soon they would be.

"I was alarmed at how much fuel we were burning, because flaps were down in early-approach mode setting, and the gear was down and we were low. Airplanes burn a lot of fuel at low altitude," Tangeman said. He had taken over the flying duties from Strand, who was now working the radios. "When that fuel light went on, that added another level to that event."

The pilots had talked to maintenance and tried to extend the gear manually, without success. Tangeman remembers the tension and finality that came with the realization that the emergency was real and that all their skills would be required to avert disaster.

"This is not a simulator, we can't step back and do it again; we're fuel low," he said he thought at the time. "We're not getting out of this."

As the plane touched down, Tangeman decided to stay on the main gear as long as possible without operating the thrust reversers. "When the aluminum skin of the MD-80 finally hit the tarmac, the sound was like running a Skil saw on a garbage can, and we stopped really fast at the seventy-five-hundred-foot mark, fully loaded, with no reversers." It was a landing so flawless that none of the 136 people aboard was injured, and damage to the plane was minimal.

A television news helicopter equipped with a camera had recorded the last thirty seconds of the landing, providing a riveting element to an already compelling story. Maybe this is the reason Tangeman's and Strand's performances that day became the subject of human factors training at American for the next eighteen months.

Tangeman was encouraged to share his story with his fellow pilots, and the subject to which he kept returning was the value of the lessons he'd learned from others. "There are no top guns" in the airline cockpit, he said. Senior pilots who share their expertise enable an atmosphere where pilots routinely save the day.

"The most influential thing in my life has been working with other great captains," Tangeman told me. "Nothing replaces great mentoring."

At a time, and in an industry, in which automation is preferable to the human touch, humanity's marvelous flip side is often overlooked and underappreciated, except in cases of hero pilots such as those you've read about here. Their stories are uplifting, but they are certainly not the only people contributing to the complex system that keeps flying safe. Aircraft and engine designers, airline workers and maintenance engineers, air traffic controllers and regulators—they all play a role; as do passengers when they note the closest emergency exit to their seat and keep their belts fastened throughout the flight.

When things go wrong, as they inevitably do, the crash detectives find the lessons in catastrophe. Our uniquely human ability to learn from mistakes, to think, create, and innovate, works better than we will ever know.

ACKNOWLEDGMENTS

Writing a book is an exercise in patience—not for me, but for everyone whose path has crossed mine over the past two years. I pestered them all. People I knew and people I didn't. An astonishing number of them provided assistance.

Some are quoted or profiled in this book. Others gave background help, research, guidance, fact checking, and provocation, all of which crystallized my thoughts. Without all these people, this book would be incomplete.

I am deeply grateful for the knowledgeable people mentioned here and also for those who, fearing negative consequences, asked that I not thank them by name. Their contributions infuse every page.

In the digital age, a librarian's job is constantly evolving. I had the opportunity to work with two stellar examples of this still-vital profession, Yvette Yurubi, who presides over nearly seven decades of Pan American Airways history at the University of Miami, and Nick Nagurney, from the Perrot Memorial Library in my hometown of Old Greenwich, Connecticut, who cheerfully searched the world for some very obscure titles. To the authors of the books and reports in my bibliography, thanks for making complicated subjects comprehensible.

Sometimes the written word isn't enough, so I relied on Bob Benzon, James Blaszczak, Mike Bowers, Barbara Burian, John Cox, Key Dismukes, Olivier Ferrante, Peter Fiegehen, Pete Frey, John Gadzinski, Darren Gaines, Mitch Garber, Keith Hagy, Tom Haueter, Guy Hirst, Kevin Humphreys, Judy Jeevarajan, Jim Karsh, Rory Kay, Lewis Larsen, John Lauber, Robert MacIntosh, John Nance, Michael O'Rourke, Kazunori Ozawa, David Paqua, Mike Poole, Helena Reidemar, Eduard M. Ricaurte, Donald Sadoway, Steve Saint Amour, Gary Santos, Ron Schleede, Patrick Smith, and Robert Swaim.

Working in an unfamiliar culture is always challenging. Providing assistance in Malaysia in too many ways to count were Maureen Jeyasooriar, Riza Johari, and Anita Woo. Although, like all Malaysians, they were dazed by the disappearance of Malaysia 370, these women worked with energy and dedication.

In Japan, Takeo Aizawa started off as my legman, became my translator, moved into the position of researcher, and then adviser, and will always be a dear friend.

For digging up old records and sharing stories of events from long ago, special thanks to Ed Dover of Albuquerque, and the late Nick Tramontano. Others deserving of a special shout-out are Stuart Macfarlane and Anne Cassin in New Zealand, Mick Quinn and Ben Sandilands in Australia, Samir Kohli in India, George Jehn in New York, Les Filotas in Ottawa, Guy Noffsinger in Washington, DC, Jeff Kriendler in Miami, and Graham Simons and Susan Williams in England.

Officials with the following organizations went out of their way to accommodate me in one way or another: Daniel Baker,

CEO at FlightAware; Perry Flint of the International Air Transport Association; and Markus Ruediger of Star Alliance. From Lufthansa, Matthias Kippenberg, Nils Haupt, and Martin Riecken (the latter two employed elsewhere now). Also thanks to Corey Caldwell of the Air Line Pilots Association; Martin Dolan, now retired from the Australian Transport Safety Bureau; Robert Garner of the High Altitude Chamber Lab at Arizona State University, Mesa; Mary Anne Greczyn at Airbus; Peter Knudson of the National Transportation Safety Board; James Stabile and James Stabile Jr. of Aeronautical Data Systems; and Mamoru Takahashi of the Japan Transport Safety Board.

Special thanks to ABC News for bringing me in to help with the network's coverage when air disasters happen. While I was in Malaysia, it was a gift to work with Mike Gudgell, Matt Hosford, David Kerley, David Reiter, Gloria Rivera, Brian Ross, Rhonda Schwartz, Ben Sherwood, Jon Williams, and Bob Woodruff.

Exercising patience is one thing, but there's little time for real exercise when writing a book. Thanks to Joanna Stark at Rebel Desk for enabling me to write on my feet; Steven Fiorenza of Advanced Physical Therapy of Stamford for stretching out my kinks; and M. J. Kim of Kida NYC for helping me feel pretty.

The two best critics in the world love me, if not everything I write. My sister Andrea Lee Negroni is a lawyer, but she slices sentences with such precision she could have been a surgeon. My husband, *New York Times* editor Jim Schembari, is an accomplished word polisher, but he had his work cut out for him in tackling mine.

I hope their efforts made my copy a little easier to handle for my editors, Shannon Kelly and Meg Leder, and the very clever Emily Murdock Baker, formerly of Penguin and now the head of EMB Editorial. Special thanks to them and to publicist Christopher Smith and to my agent, Anna Sproul-Latimer of Ross Yoon, who is prone to saying, "What can I do to help?" just when I need it most. Anna and I might never have met if not for the situational awareness of the beautiful and talented Dara Kaye, also of Ross Yoon. Thanks to my research assistant Chrissi Culver, whose tracking-down and following-up skills will surely be applied to the benefit of the flying public in her new position as an air traffic controller.

Women are a small part of the aviation geek community, but our numbers are growing. I'm so thankful that Chrissi, Emily, and Anna are among them.

Unending appreciation and love to my family: my husband, Jim, and my children, Antonio, Sam, Joseph, Marian, and her husband, Elliot Speed, for all their support. My undying gratitude to God for saving grace.

BIBLIOGRAPHY

Adair, W. *The Mystery of Flight 427: Inside a Crash Investigation.* Washington, DC: Smithsonian Institution Press, 2002.

Air Accident Report No. 79-139. Air New Zealand McDonnell Douglas DC 10-30 ZK-NZP. Ross Island Antarctica 28 November 1979. Wellington: Office of Air Accidents Investigation, Ministry of Transport, 1979.

Bainerman, J. *The Crimes of a President: New Revelations on Conspiracy & Cover-up in the Bush & Reagan Administrations.* New York: Shapolsky, 1992.

Bartelski, J. *Disasters in the Air: Mysterious Air Disasters Explained.* Airlife, 2001.

Beaty, D. *Strange Encounters: Mysteries of the Air.* New York: Atheneum, 1984.

Booth, T. *Admiralty Salvage in Peace and War 1906–2006: Grope, Grub and Tremble.* Barnsley, England: Pen & Sword, 2007.

Bragg, R. L. "Tenerife—A Survivor's Tale". *Flight Safety Australia*, September-October 2007.

Brock, H. *Flying the Oceans: A Pilot's Story of Pan Am, 1935–1955.* Lanham, Maryland: Jack Aronson, 1978.

Burkill, P., and M. Burkill. *Thirty Seconds To Impact*. Bloomington, Indiana: AuthorHouse, 2010.

Butler, S. *East to the Dawn: The Life of Amelia Earhart*. Boston: Addison-Wesley, 1997.

Choisser, J. P. *Malaysia Flight MH370—Lost in the Dark: In Defense of the Pilots: An Engineer's Perspective*. CreateSpace, 2014.

Crouch, G. *China's Wings*. New York: Bantam, 2012.

Davis, J. R., et al., eds. *Fundamentals of Aerospace Medicine*, 4th edition. Philadelphia: Lippincott Williams & Wilkins, 2008.

de Crespigny, R. *QF32*. Sydney: Pan Macmillian Australia, 2012.

deHaven-Smith , L. *Conspiracy Theory in America*. Austin: University of Texas Press, 2014.

Filotas, L. *Improbable Cause: Deceit and Dissent in the Investigation of America's Worst Military Air Disaster*. BookSurge, 2007.

Gawande, A. *The Checklist Manifesto: How to Get Things Right*. New York: Metropolitian Books, 2009.

Gero, D. *Aviation Disasters: The World's Major Civil Airliner Crashes Since 1950, 4th ed*. Stroud, England: Patrick Stephens, 2006.

Gonzales, L. *Flight 232: A Story of Disaster and Survival*. New York: W. W. Norton, 2014.

Griffioen, H. *Air Crash Investigators: The Crash of Helios Airways Flight 522*. Lulu.com , 2009.

Haine, E. A. *Disaster in the Air*. Cranbury, New Jersey: Cornwall Books, 2000.

Hill, C. N. *Fix on the Rising Sun The Clipper Hi-jacking of 1938 – and the Ultimate M.I.A.'s*. Bloomington, Indiana: 1st Books Library, 2000.

Hoffer, W., and M. M. Hoffer. *Free Fall: A True Story*. New York: St. Martin's Press, 1989.

Holmes, P. *Daughters of Erebus*. Auckland: Hodder Moa, 2011.

Inkster, I., ed. *History of Technology 2005*, volume 26. London: Continuum, 2006.

Jackson, R. *China Clipper*. Everest House, 1980.

Jehn, G. *Final Destination: Disaster: What Really Happened to Eastern Airlines*. Howard Beach, New York: Changing Lives Press, 2014.

Keith, R.A. *Bush Pilot With a Briefcase: The Incredible Story of Aviation Pioneer Grant McConachie*. Vancouver, Canada: Douglas & McIntyre, 1972.

Kemp, K. *Flight of the Titans: Boeing, Airbus and the Battle for the Future of Air Travel*. London: Virgin Books, 2006.

Kohli, S. *Into Oblivion: Understanding #MH370*. CreateSpace, 2014.

Langewiesche, W. *Fly by Wire: The Geese, The Glide, The Miracle on the Hudson*. London: Picador, 2010.

Levine, S. *The Powerhouse: Inside the Invention of a Battery to Save the World.* New York: Viking, 2015.

Lindbergh, C. A. *Of Flight and Life*. New York: Charles Scribner's Sons, 1948.

Long, E. M. and M. K. Long. *Amelia Earhart: The Mystery Solved*. New York: Simon & Schuster, 1999.

Mahon, P. *Report of the Royal Commission Crash on Mt. Erebus*. Wellington, New Zealand: Hasselberg Government Printer, 1981.

Mahon, P. *Verdict on Erebus*. London: Collins, 1984.

McCain, J., ed. *Aviation Accident Investigations: Hearing Before the Committee on Commerce, Science, & Transportation, U. S. Senate*. Darby, Pennsylvania: Diane Publishing, 1997.

McCullough, D. *The Wright Brothers*. New York: Simon & Schuster, 2015.

Medina, J. *Brain Rules*. Seattle: Pear Press, 2014.

Micklos, J. *Unsolved: What Really Happened to Amelia Earhart*. New York: Enslow, 2006.

Murphy, J. D. *Courage to Execute: What Elite U.S. Military Units Can Teach Business About Leadership and Team Performance*. New York: Wiley, 2014.

Reason, J. *The Human Contribution: Unsafe Acts, Accidents and Heroic Recoveries*. New York: Ashgate, 2008.

Reed, T. and D. Reed. *American Airlines, US Airways and the Creation of the World's Largest Airline*. Jefferson, North Carolina: McFarland, 2014.

Serling, R. J. *The Jet Age*. New York: Time Life Books, 1982.

Simons, G. *Comet!: The World's First Jet Airliner*. Barnsley, England: Pen & Sword Aviation, 2013.

Soucie, D. *Malaysia Airlines Flight 370: Why it Disappeared—and Why It's Only a Matter of Time Before This Happens Again*. New York: Skyhorse, 2015.

Sullenberger, C. with J. Zaslow. *Highest Duty: My Search for What Really Matters*. New York: William Morrow, 2009.

U.S. Department of Transportation, Federal Aviation Administration. *The Pilot's Handbook of Aeronautical Knowledge 2008*. Washington, DC: GPO, 2008.

Vette, G., and J. MacDonald. *Impact Erebus*. Lanham, Maryland: Sheridan House, 1983.

Wagner, A.H. and L.E. Braxton. *Birth of a Legend: The Bomber Mafia and the Y1B-17*. Bloomington, Indiana: Trafford, 2012.

Walker, J. *The United States of Paranoia: A Conspiracy Theory*. New York: Harper Perennial, 2014.

Wecht, C. H. and M. Curriden. *Tales from the Morgue: Forensic Answers to Nine Famous Cases*. Amherst, New York: Prometheus Books, 2005.

Wiggins, M. W. and T. Loveday, eds. *Diagnostic Expertise in Organizational Environments*. New York: Ashgate, 2015.

Williams, S. *Who Killed Hammarskjöld? The UN, the Cold War and White Supremacy in Africa*. New York: Oxford, 2014.

Wise, J. *Fatal Descent*. Amazon Digital Services, 2015.

INDEX

PELICAN

A

THE AZTECS

GEORGE C. VAILLANT

The Aztecs of Mexico

ORIGIN, RISE AND FALL OF THE AZTEC NATION

BY GEORGE C. VAILLANT

★

WITH A POSTSCRIPT BY
C. A. BURLAND
F.R.A.I.

PENGUIN BOOKS

Penguin Books Ltd, Harmondsworth, Middlesex

U.S.A.: Penguin Books Inc., 3300 Clipper Mill Road, Baltimore 11, Md

CANADA: Penguin Books (Canada) Ltd, 178 Norseman Street,
Toronto 18, Ontario

AUSTRALIA: Penguin Books Pty Ltd, 762 Whitehorse Road,
Mitcham, Victoria

First published in the U.S.A.
by Doubleday, Doran and Co. Inc. 1944
First published in Pelican Books 1950
Reprinted 1951, 1953, 1955, 1956

Made and printed in Great Britain
by Richard Clay & Company, Ltd,
Bungay, Suffolk

FOREWORD

THIS book is a history of the Indians of the Valley of Mexico and the civilizations which they wrought. It was a hard book to write. It will be a hard book to read. There are two reasons for this unfortunate circumstance. First, the Indians did not have the same goals in life as we have, so that their pattern of life is different from our own and difficult to understand. Second, Indian history has to be reconstructed from what we can find, so that much of the material, like techniques of making household implements, does not fall within the scope of our usual historical reading. The first four chapters deal with such reconstruction, and the reader is warned in advance that the going will be very difficult. These pages may be skipped if he is not particularly interested in such a historical background.

The remaining chapters are based on contemporary observations made by the conquering Spaniards and by the Aztecs themselves. They deal with people who were seen alive, their culture functioning. We can form an impression of what the Aztecs were like, and this makes easier reading, since we can envisage people in terms of what they did, not in terms of the objects which they made. Even so, this will not be a crystal-clear process, for their customs, habits and motives differed from ours. However, I hope that I shall be able to show that it was a perfectly good way of life and the result of considerable experience. Our Western civilization, on the social side, is nothing to boast of today, so we need not be scornful of the Aztecs.

I want here to express my thanks to some of the many people who helped me to write this book: to the authorities of the American Museum of Natural History for providing me with the sinews of research and the time to exercise them, to the authorities of the Mexican Government for their consistent courtesy and co-operation in making my work possible, to my colleagues in my own and other lands, who by their friendship, counsel and collaboration make one proud to be an Americanist. To my wife I owe especial thanks for her unfailing aid and comfort during the long hours spent in the field and laboratory and in the preparation of this book.

To Colonel Theodore Roosevelt, Mr A. P. Tedesco and Mrs Mary Slavin of Doubleday, Doran I am grateful for stimulation and counsel. To Dr Edward Weyer I am under deep obligation for permission to incorporate illustrations and articles from Natural History. I wish to thank Miss D. Levett Bradley for her excellent sheet maps of Aztec Mexico and, last, but by no means least, Miss Frances Jay for her unflagging patience and judgment in preparing this manuscript and smoothing the path of the reader who traverses the ill-marked trail of this aspect of Indian history.

To Mr Clarence L. Hay I am deeply indebted for collaboration in field and laboratory as well as for supporting much of my research, and to Mr Willard Carr for underwriting our last field season, which brought this book into being.

NOTE TO PELICAN EDITION

Recent studies of carbon dating and of Mixtec histories newly interpreted in Mexico have led to great alterations in our views of Mexican archaeological datings. It is now considered that the Mazapan period, equated with the historic Toltecs, lasted from about A.D. 550 to about 950, and that the Teotihuacan cultures II to IV cover a span of about A.D. 100 to 500. Other dates, including those for the Lowland Maya, should be adjusted accordingly (July 1950).

CONTENTS

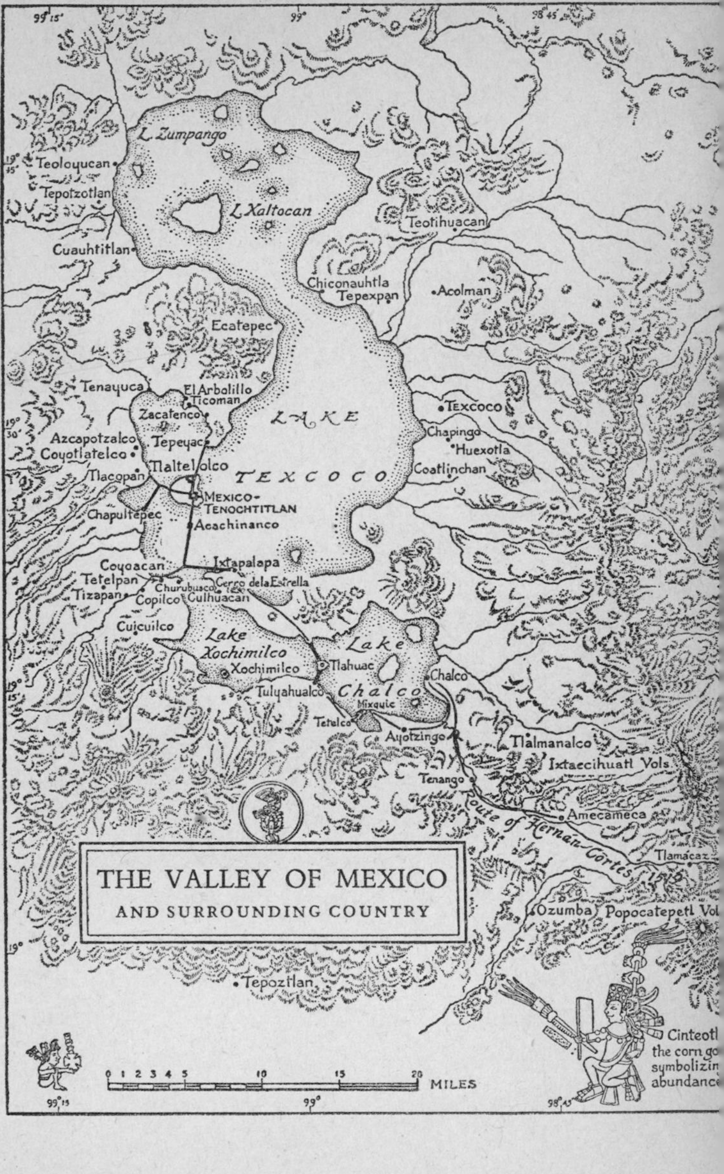
THE VALLEY OF MEXICO
AND SURROUNDING COUNTRY
L. Zumpango
L. Xaltocan
Teoloyucan
Tepotzotlan
Cuauhtitlan
Teotihuacan
Chiconauhtla
Tepexpan
Acolman
Ecatepec
Tenayuca
El Arbolillo
Ticoman
Zacatenco
Azcapotzalco
Coyotlatelco
Tepeyac
Tlaltelolco
Tlacopan
Chapultepec
MEXICO-
TENOCHTITLAN
Acachinanco
LAKE
TEXCOCO
Texcoco
Chapingo
Huexotla
Coatlinchan
Coyoacan
Tetelpan
Tizapan
Churubusco
Copilco
Culhuacan
Ixtapalapa
Cerro de la Estrella
Cuicuilco
Lake
Xochimilco
Xochimilco
Tlahuac
Lake
Chalco
Chalco
Tulyahualco
Mixquic
Tetelco
Ayotzingo
Tlalmanalco
Ixtaccihuatl Vol.
Tenango
Amecameca
Route of Hernán Cortés 1519
Tlamacaz
Ozumba
Popocatepetl Vol
Tepoztlan
Cinteotl
the corn go
symbolizin
abundanc
MILES
0 1 2 3 4 5 10 15 20
99°15'
99°
98°45'
19°45'
19°30'
19°15'
19°

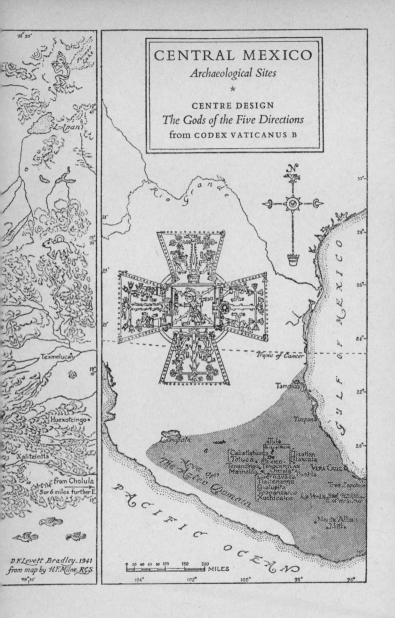

CENTRAL MEXICO
Archaeological Sites

★

CENTRE DESIGN
The Gods of the Five Directions
from CODEX VATICANUS B

D.F. Levett Bradley. 1941
from map by H.F. Milne. R.G.S.

ILLUSTRATIONS IN THE TEXT

TABLES

ACKNOWLEDGEMENT OF
SOURCES OF PLATES, PHOTOGRAPHS
AND ORIGINALS

THE writer acknowledges his deep obligation to the American Museum of Natural History for allowing him to use the blocks illustrating articles in the Museum magazine, *Natural History*, and other publication series of this institution. In some cases plates in other publications were copied, following general scientific procedure. The list below designates the source of the illustrations taken from such published material and later used in the magazine or guide-leaflet series. Where the photograph was made directly from a Museum original for the journal the term Natural History is used. Unless otherwise designated the originals are all in the Middle American collection of the American Museum. The writer, therefore, wishes to express his thanks to those scholars whose illustrations are copied here.

1. *Natural History*.
2. *Natural History*.
3. *Natural History*.
4. *Natural History*. Top: model in Peabody Museum, Cambridge, Mass. Middle: original photograph by Sylvanus G. Morley. Bottom: photograph by Lilo Hess.
5. *Natural History*.
6. Top, *left*: after Maudslay, *Biologia Centrali Americana*, 1889–1902; *right*: *Natural History*; original in Museo Nacional, Mexico. Bottom: after Totten, *Maya Architecture*, 1926; after Catherwood, *Views*, 1844.
7. Top: after Gordon and Mason, *Maya Pottery*, 1925–28; original in British Museum. Bottom: after Morris, Charlot and Morris, *Temple of the Warriors*, 1931; original fresco in Temple of the Warriors, Chichen Itza. Both *Natural History*.
8. Top: Wide World Photograph. Middle: after Batres, *Monte Alban*, 1912. Bottom: Musée de l'Homme, Paris.
9. Top, *left and right*: *Natural History*. Bottom: photograph by Miguel Covarrubias; original in Oaxaca Museum.

B

10. *Natural History.*

11. Top, *left*: A. Caso, Museo Nacional, Mexico; *right*: after Joyce, *Maya and Mexican Art*, 1927; original Codex in British Museum. Bottom: after Charnay and Viollet-le-Duc, *Cités et Ruines Americaines*, 1862–63. Museo Nacional, Mexico.

12. Top: after Morris, Charlot and Morris, *Chichen Itza*, 1931. Middle: *Natural History*; original in Merida Museum. Bottom: Museo Nacional; photograph by Department of Historical Monuments, Mexico.

13. *Natural History.*

14. *Natural History.*

15. Top: *Natural History.* Bottom: Archaeological Papers, American Museum of Natural History.

16. *Natural History.*

17. *Natural History.*

18. Top: *Natural History.* Bottom: *Natural History*; photograph by La Rochester, Mexico.

19. *Natural History.*

20. *Natural History.*

21. *Natural History.*

22. Top: after Gamio, *Teotihuacan*, 1922. Bottom: *Natural History*; photograph by Fairchild Aerial Surveys de Mexico, S. A.

23. After Lehmann, *Aus den Pyramidenstädten*, 1933. *Natural History.*

24. Top: *Natural History.* Bottom: after Gamio, *Teotihuacan*, 1922.

25. *Scientific Monthly.*

26. Top: *Natural History.* Middle: Museo Nacional, Mexico. Bottom: *Scientific Monthly.*

27. Top: after Lumholtz, *Unknown Mexico*, 1902. Middle and Bottom: *Natural History.*

28. Top: *Natural History.* Bottom: *Natural History*, photograph by La Rochester, Mexico.

29. *Natural History.*

30. *Natural History.*

31. *Natural History.*

32. Top: *Natural History.* Bottom three rows: Museo Nacional, Mexico.

33. After Keith Henderson, in Prescott, *Conquest of Mexico*, 1922.

34–35. After Codex Florentino, 1905. *Natural History.*

36. After Keith Henderson, in Prescott, *Conquest of Mexico*, 1922.

37. Top: *Natural History*; drawing by Ignacio Marquina. Bottom: *Natural History*; photograph by Ewing Galloway. Aerofilms Library.

38–39. After Codex Florentino, 1905. *Natural History.*

40. Museo Nacional, Mexico. Museum of Modern Art photograph by Sunami.

41. Top: after Codex Mendoza, 1738. Bottom, *left*: after Holmes, *Archaeological Studies*, 1895–97; *right*: after Codex Florentino, 1905. All *Natural History.*

42. Top: after Aubin, *Peinture Didactique*, 1885. Bottom: after Codex Florentino, 1905. All *Natural History.*

43. *Natural History.*

44. *Natural History.*

45. Top: after Heger, Federschmuck, 1908. Bottom: *Natural History.*

46. Top row: *Natural History.* Middle, *left*: Museo Nacional, Mexico, original in Oaxaca Museum; *right*: *Natural History*; original in Museo Nacional, Mexico. Bottom: after Codex Florentino, 1905, *Natural History.*

47. Museo Nacional, Mexico; original of upper left in Oaxaca Museum; bottom, Museo Nacional, Mexico.

48. After Saville, *Mosaic Art*, 1922; *left*: original in Prehistoric and Ethnographic Museum in Rome; *right*: original in British Museum.

49. *Natural History.*

50. *Natural History.*

51. Top: after Dupaix, *Antiquités Mexicaines*, 1834. Bottom: photograph from Ewing Galloway. Aerofilms Library.

52. Top: after Peñafiel, *Monumentos*, 1890. Bottom: *Natural History.* Both originals in Museo Nacional, Mexico.

53. Top: Museo Nacional, Mexico. Bottom: Museo Nacional, Mexico; photograph by Museum of Modern Art.

54. Top: *Natural History.* Bottom: original in Museo Nacional, Mexico.

55. Top, *left*: *Natural History.* Bottom, *left and right*: originals in Museo Nacional, Mexico.

56. *Natural History.* Top: original in Museo Nacional, Mexico.
57. Top, *left*: *Natural History*, after Caso, *Tizatlan*, 1927; *right*: Museo Nacional, Mexico; original ornament in the Oaxaca Museum. Bottom: *Natural History*, after Codex Florentino, 1905.
58. Top: *Natural History*; after Gamio, *Teotihuacan*, 1922. Middle: after Humboldt, *Vues*, 1814. Bottom: after Codex Florentino, 1905.
59. *Natural History*; after Spinden, *Ancient Civilizations*, 1928.
60. *Natural History*; after Codex Florentino, 1905. Top: British Museum.
60. *Natural History*; after Codex Florentino, 1905. Bottom, *left*: British Museum.
61. *Natural History*; after Codex Florentino, 1905.
62. *Natural History.*
63-4. *Natural History*; after Spinden, *Ancient Civilizations*, 1928.

THE AZTECS OF
MEXICO

*

TO MY WIFE

*

*One of the strangest feelings left to
us by prehistory is the sensation of
omen. It will always exist. It is like
an eternal proof of the non sequitur
of the universe. The first man must
have seen omens everywhere,
he must have shuddered
at each step.*

GIORGIO DE CHIRICO

CHAPTER I

THE HISTORICAL AND CULTURAL BACKGROUND OF AZTEC CIVILIZATION

A somewhat speculative summary of the social and economic factors which directed the rise of Indian civilization

THE history of the Americas records the colonization and settlement of a great continent. We take a just pride in our European ancestors, who, from the Vikings down to the most recent political exiles, set forth to find a new life in the changing conditions of a new land. Our histories and traditions describe the evolution of these colonies into the present group of American republics, and it is a remarkable episode in the story of mankind. Yet the European settlement of the Americas, for all its modern political significance, is just a late phase of the history of man on the American continent. The Asiatic colonization of the New World, which preceded the European infiltration by many centuries, has its own proud place in the annals of Continental America.

This immigration from Asia produced the American Indian. Without his preliminary development of the resources of the continent it is dubious whether the European occupation would have succeeded as it did. The great Indian civilizations of the Aztecs and the Incas challenged the European imagination and opened a rich life for their military conquerors. The humble farming skill of the tribesmen of North America's eastern seaboard sustained religious exiles until they could live off the land and create their own type of commonwealth. The Indian and his culture were soon ploughed under, but they enriched a soil which otherwise would never have produced the lavish harvest of Pan-American civilization.

The most violent clash between the Indians and the Euro-

23

peans took place in the Valley of Mexico during the early summer of 1520, when Cortés and his Spaniards achieved the Conquest of Mexico and overthrew the Aztec civilization, the most advanced Indian culture at that time. Cortés' success was the loadstone which drew to the Americas the iron might of Europe. Stone could not withstand steel, and the days of the Indian were numbered. The history of the Aztecs and their forebears is a synopsis of the rise of Indian civilization and its doom.

The Aztecs were a numerous group of independent Indian tribes who occupied a restricted section of central Mexico. Their history and social customs are better known than their neighbours' because their conquest had such a far-reaching significance for the European world. Spanish observers of military, priestly and civil status wrote careful accounts of the Aztec life and history, and Indian authors a generation later augmented these records, drawing on the tribal lore still only thinly veneered by Christianity. A few pictographic records, either prepared before the Conquest or copied afterwards, are precious additions to the Aztec annals. However, our chief data on Indian history come from archaeology, that branch of research which recovers social history through the study of the surviving remains of human handiwork in ages past.

Most of the American Indian tribes had not developed writing, so that archaeology is the one available medium for reconstructing their past, and the Aztec records reveal only a few centuries in the life of a single tribe. To sketch the broad background of Aztec culture before we turn our attention to the people themselves, we should realize that the earth must be our archive, the shovel our reading-glass, and that Nature, eternally destroying to create anew, has scattered our materials over mountain, plain and forest, from Greenland to Tierra del Fuego. Aztec history, like that of the American republics, begins with the discovery of this continent. (See Plate 1.)

Long before the Aztecs existed, the ice-sheets began to re-

treat northwards, as the last glacial era was ending. Those animals accustomed to cool climates gradually moved north, and
small nomadic bands of hunters followed the game on which
their lives depended. Some of these groups moved up through
Siberia and reached the shores of the Bering Strait. With so
much water held in suspension by the ice-sheet, the sea level
was probably lower than now, so that the islands were larger
and the extent of water between them less. In winter the sea
was doubtless choked with ice, and, crossing over this ice, hunters and hunted could reach Alaska. Thus man discovered
America and made his first settlements there (1).[1]

Other hunters may have constructed rafts and boats and passed from island to island until their ceaseless search for game
led them to the mainland. The process must have been slow
and the migrating units small. We can reconstruct conditions
from what we know of modern hunting tribes, who, as social
fossils, still pursue a precarious existence in the old, old way.
The primitive hunting group moved on foot and had no effective beasts of burden. Therefore they carried little in the way
of food or equipment. Their progress was no faster than that
of the oldest man or woman, or youngest walking child. Food
had to be secured even on the march, and hunting was a slow
and arduous process. Such conditions necessarily kept the
group units small, for a large cluster of people, when on the
march, besides requiring food in quantity, must also scare
away the very game on which its nourishment depends (2).

This nomadic hunting life had its effect on language and
physical type. The tendency for hunting groups to split into
smaller units whenever their numbers threatened the balance
between consumption and available food supply encouraged
the establishment of isolated bands. This loss of contact with
other groups intensified mannerisms of speech and thought, so
that profound differences of dialect resulted after several generations. Inbreeding also followed, and strains of physical type

1. See Notes, beginning on p. 279.

became established. Such conditions, already existent in the Asiatic life and continued under American conditions, probably account both for the linguistic diversity among the Indian tribes and also for their great physical variation within a more or less homogeneous frame of dark eyes, straight or wavy black hair and a yellowish skin colour (3).

When this infiltration took place, or how long it continued, has yet to be expressed in exact dates. No examples of Old World palaeolithic industry have been uncovered in the Americas, but excavations on the campus of the University of Alaska have turned up tools like those found in neolithic stations on the Gobi Desert. Other stone implements, defined by archaeologists as Folsom culture, occur in association with the remains of extinct bison at sites in Colorado and New Mexico. Far to the south, in a cave on the southern tip of the Argentine, the dung of an extinct sloth is mixed with the tools and refuse of men who hunted and ate an extinct type of American horse. Sloth dung also seals in the remains of Nevada hunters. These human vestiges may not have the great antiquity of geologic man in Europe, nor may the fact of extinct species have the same implication of age that obtains elsewhere, but man may well have come to America between ten and twenty thousand years ago (4).

Hunting techniques have thus been established as an early form of Indian life in America. Some of the first hunters fished with net and line and gathered shell-fish as their chief nourishment. Deep accumulations of discarded shells are found along the coasts of the Atlantic and Pacific and along some of the great inland rivers of North America. In one such heap in Tennessee the earliest layer disclosed bone implements, and no stone tools appeared until very much later. How old these heaps are we cannot guess, and we have no way of dating them by geology or palaeontology. Yet man, from his earliest beginnings, must have used these rich and relatively stable sources of food (5).

Another primitive livelihood is disclosed along the shores of dried-up lakes in California and Texas. Mortars and grinding stones found here indicate that the early people ground nuts and seeds into flour, while a lack of well-made stone points suggests that they found the gathering of vegetable foods a more reliable way to fill their larders than the hunting of game. These desert cultures are highly important, since they provide early evidence of an economy which led eventually to the development of agriculture (6).

These three early ways of life – hunting, fishing and gathering – were often combined in whole or in part. There is no hunting group in the Americas which does not take advantage of vegetable products to some extent, and in North America the properties of four hundred species were known and utilized. Some tribes found their hunting economy so satisfactory that they never abandoned it. Other peoples, like the Eskimos, were so situated geographically that they had to hunt or starve. The Plains tribes, when they acquired the domesticated horse from the Spanish colonies, turned from a successful if drab farming life to a highly dramatic existence, living off the wandering buffalo herds and exalting masculine virtues in war and the chase. Fishing groups, like the tribes of the North-west Coast, were able to live in sedentary villages and create an elaborate social and material culture on the rich abundance yielded by forest, stream and ocean. In California one of the densest populations in the Americas maintained itself by gathering wild nuts and fruits, supplementing this diet with shellfish and game. Yet in spite of these successful primitive techniques the Indian would have never attained really high cultures without the domestication of plants (7).

In the New World there were two centres of intense agricultural development, Middle America and the Andean region, which likewise represent the peaks of Indian social and material culture. There is considerable discussion among botanists as to which area first had domesticated plants, but the problem is not yet resolved. Perhaps the answer to this question may have a botanical rather than a social significance, since there are several other areas where plants not cultivated in Mexico and Peru are agricultural staples. The presence, early in the history of America, of peoples who lived largely by gathering must have led almost inevitably to the independent development of several different types of agriculture, based on the food plants common to particular regions (8).

The great staple of Brazil, for example, was manioc or cassava. Before the introduction of corn in eastern North America, sunflowers, the giant ragweed and other plants of prairie and savannah were cultivated for their seeds. The highlands of Peru yielded the white potato, but at the time of the Conquest the great basic American foods, corn and beans, were diffused over most of agricultural America. Whether they were first domesticated in Peru or Middle America is a point still arguable; each may have had its own separate point of primary cultivation. However, the great principle to bear in mind is that no plant cultivated by the American Indians was known to Asia, Europe or Africa prior to the white settlement of America. The introduction of these plants more than doubled the available food supply of the older continents.

The development of agriculture accomplished, in America as elsewhere, the liberation of man from the constant search for food. A permanent food supply which could be enlarged by bringing fresh land under cultivation allowed the tribal population to grow. The precarious equilibrium maintained by Nature between population and food supply became more stable, and man had leisure to invent techniques and to develop rules for societal behaviour. It became possible to support aggregations of people large enough for the individual to specialize according to his skill and for the community to carry out public projects like irrigation systems and temples.

The successful growth of agriculture was not paralleled in the raising of animals. True, the dog, which may well have come in with the immigrants from Asia, was almost universally domesticated. In the north it was a beast of burden; in Mexico an article of diet. The Mexican and Pueblo tribes tamed the turkey. The Peruvians ate guinea-pigs and raised llamas and alpacas for wool and transport; bees were kept for honey in Middle America and north-west Brazil; some southern Mexican tribes raised cochineal for dye. But the native horse, which might have proved as useful here as in the Old World, became extinct early in America, the cow and sheep were unknown, and the caribou and bison, which, if domesticated, might have taken their place, had their chief range in regions occupied by primitive groups who were content merely to hunt them (9).

This lack of suitable domestic animals prevented man's migration on an extensive scale, comparable to that of the great hordes from Asia which beat against the walls of Rome. At first the nomadic groups in the Americas were too small to threaten seriously the sedentary groups, and the question of population pressure, so often an indirect cause of war in the Old World, was virtually non-existent in Indian America. War techniques in consequence were little developed in the Indian cultures, and the killing and rapine which took place during the white colonization did not have their origin in the usual Indian political attitudes.

The invention of agriculture accentuated rather than changed the basic structure of Indian social organization. Those groups which gradually shifted their economic reliance from hunting to farming were in thinly populated country. As their population increased they could enlarge their fields without infringing on the rights of previous inhabitants. A growing population scared away game, forcing neighbouring hunting groups to withdraw to regions where wild life was more plentiful. If the available arable land became insufficient for the community a number of people drifted away to found a new settlement.

According to the environment, be it forested or semi-arid

and consequently open, there tend to be two types of settlement. In dry, open country the minerals which plants need remain near the surface, so that fields can be farmed over and over again. The people, therefore, can maintain a permanent village. Forest country, on the other hand, presents a serious problem to Stone Age people. To clear ground for planting, trees must be girdled and, after they die, burned. The soil therefore rapidly becomes exhausted and incapable of supporting crops. The Indians met this situation in two main ways: by moving the entire village, or by allowing each family group sufficient land so that crop rotation would permit exhausted fields to recover by lying fallow. This last method tended to decentralize the population except in very small communities (10).

The social implications of these two methods of life are highly important for reconstructing the genesis of American Indian culture. The food-plants used by the higher civilizations in the Americas seem largely derived from highland, open-country species, emanating from the kind of region permitting the maintenance of a permanent village. In a community where the village street was a forum, technical school and social centre, interests were pooled and techniques improved by emulation and inherited experience. The opportunity to store accumulated equipment, as opposed to the bare essential minimum of portable implements used by nomads, led to specialization in tools and techniques. The decorative arts became fixed according to style, since custom channels shapes and forms into directions approved by communal practice. Enterprises involving the man-power of the whole village could be undertaken with a resultant benefit to the whole community. The long stretches of relative leisure when crops did not need care afforded time for technical experiment and intellectual speculation.

The complete series of steps by which an early farming group converted itself into a high civilization has not been recovered in any one area. However, North America, which preserved so many tribes at various stages in the development of Indian civilization, yields, in the case of the history of Anasazi or northern Pueblo culture, an example of such an evolutionary process (11).

At the bottom of the scale are found the remains of people (called the Basket-Makers by the archaeologists) who lived by hunting, gathering and the cultivation of corn. They occupied shallow, dry caves in small units of twenty or thirty individuals. They were skilful weavers of fibres of apocynum, fashioning baskets, bags and sandals. They had no pottery, but constructed rude images of sun-dried clay and modelled trays and lined baskets with this material. They did not use the bow, but propelled long darts with the throwing-board or *atl-atl*. Their equipment in the way of nets, tools of stone, bone and wood, was relatively elaborate. In their later phases they learned how to make a hard, flinty pottery in simple forms, decorated with designs derived from their weaving.

About the year A.D. 700 a new people drifted into the South-west and changed the direction of the local economy. New varieties of corn enriched the larder, and the cultivation of beans supplied the protein content in a diet impoverished by lack of game. Cotton tended to supplant apocynum for weaving clothing, while the bow superseded the *atl-atl* for hunting. The underground house gave place to clusters of joined rectangular rooms, although the older form was retained for a men's clubhouse and ceremonial chamber. Pottery improved greatly in shape and design. There is every evidence of a considerable increase in population.

By the eleventh century the number of settlements decreased, but the towns became much larger. The Anasazi constructed great communal apartment houses of two, three and even four stories not only in the open, but also in shallow caves high in the canyon wall. Their arts and crafts changed in style, but not in character, and the manner of life developed

then has lasted to the present day, despite the infiltration of
nomadic groups like the Apaches and Navajos and the intrusion of white conquerors from Spain and the United States.

In Middle America and the Andean region the earliest *discovered* cultures begin where the Pueblo left off. Our investigations have not yet brought to light the early hunting and sedentary aspects of human history in this area. The cultural
level which the Pueblo attained in the eleventh century is represented in strata assignable to the centuries immediately preceding and succeeding the birth of Christ. This base discloses
people living in permanent villages, supporting themselves by
the cultivation of corn, beans and other vegetables. They
raised cotton and wove it for clothing. They made pottery for
the storage and service of food. They developed techniques
for the manufacture of tools of stone, bone and wood, as well
as ornaments for themselves and designs for their utensils.
They achieved a tribal government and evolved a religion
which centred around the natural forces that control the
growth of plants (12).

The term 'Middle Culture' best expresses this level of development, which is midway between the meagre resources of
a hunting group and the splendour of a ceremonial civilization. Dr Spinden and Mr Means defined this stage by the
broad term 'archaic', and the writer coined the clumsy phrase
'Early Culture' to describe this phase in Central Mexico.
Neither term allows for the naming of older or more primitive
cultures which will eventually be discovered. Consequently
the phrase 'Middle Culture' appraises more justly than the
other terms a cultural situation and emphasizes less strongly the
element of historical position.

In Middle America and the Andes man and his works progressed and prospered from a Middle Culture base, but in
somewhat different directions. The Andean peoples, to gener-
alize broadly, concentrated on the material technique of supporting life; the Middle American on spiritual or, more ac-

curately, supernatural methods. In the Andes, especially in the coastal valleys of Peru, enormous cities were built and vast irrigation systems watered the fields. Weaving was developed to a point unequalled by man in the whole course of human history, and pottery in excellence of construction and richness of design had no peer in the Americas. This civilization culminated in the Inca Empire, the original benevolent, monolithic state, unique in American annals as the only governmental system which combined territorial expansion with the amalgamation of conquered peoples into a social whole (13).

The Middle Americans, on the contrary, lived in independent tribal or civic groups and created a religious art and architecture without rival in the Americas (14). The ceremonial aspect of life dominated the civil structure, and the remains of temples, not cities, gauge the splendour of the past. The cause or causes of this difference are shrouded in the past, but the more primitive North American scene suggests that here again agricultural conditions played a part (15).

The Indians of the arid South-west, as we have seen, built permanent towns, but did not devise an imposing ceremonial architecture. In the south-eastern United States the more sophisticated tribes reared great earthen platforms to support their temples and the houses of their chiefs, and to serve as centres at which the community membership might congregate at specified times. The demands of a forest agriculture did not permit the occupancy of permanent towns like those of the Pueblo country, since the south-eastern tribes had to move their villages whenever the soil of their farm clearings was exhausted. A good part of the year saw the able-bodied men and women virtually abandon the villages to hunt and gather wild food. But they all united for tribal rites at the ceremonial centres, and thus strengthened the bonds of social solidarity, loosened and frayed by the conditions of their ecology. The ceremonial centre occurs late in the history of the South-east and bears the earmarks of a trait imported from Mexico. Yet it answered a very definite need for maintaining social unity in the growing population of a forest area.

Therefore it seems reasonable to suppose that some such ideas germinated centuries before in the lowland forests of Middle America, since the elaboration of this social and ceremonial requirement became a dominant theme in Middle American civilization. There is nothing strange in this practice, which characterizes the earlier culture patterns in the development of western Europe and the colonial United States. The great cathedrals of the Middle Ages loomed massively out of a countryside wherein miserable villages, set in tiny clearings, made a violent contrast between the poverty of man's individual material existence and the rich glory of his corporate spiritual life. In New England communities still survive where the church, the store and the town hall are the social centre for people scattered in isolated farms over the forested hills. The master artists who covered the miles of sculptured temple walls in Cambodia lived in flimsy towns now totally consumed by the jungle. Both the act and the fact of ceremonial building coalesce into a tangible expression the relationships of man to society and of society to the universe; so it is not surprising that different tribes have independently adopted this practice which, in the modern United States, we follow in structures like libraries, hospitals, colleges and governmental buildings, used primarily for the public benefit.

This assumption carries further weight when we examine the broad spread of Middle American cultural history. No evidence of truly primitive communities has been discovered as yet. The earliest materials represent a mid-point between the rude life of hunters and the complex society in developed American Indian civilization. From Salvador to Zacatecas, from the high mountain valleys to the forested coast, we find evidence of tribal cultures which had reached a competent plane of technical development and, implicitly, social adjustment as well. The surviving remains consist of ably-made implements of pottery, stone and bone. Hand-made clay figures show that the religions in vogue required simulacra of the gods as a part of worship. The flat grinding-stones and mullers, still used in Mexico and called *metates*[1] and *manos*, prove that the people relied on corn as their principal food. The regional differences in form and decoration of the figures, pottery and other utensils indicate that several different tribes remained at this Middle Culture stage for several centuries, to judge from the deep layers of refuse in the Valley of Mexico (16).

Between the Middle Cultures and the elaborate ceremonial civilizations which succeeded them there are transitions in the design and form of implements, a sure sign that the authors of the various Middle Cultures were the creators of the later civilization. Those transitions appear to be gradual and not abrupt, so that the impression is strengthened of cultural development *in situ*. The existing evidence gives no valid reason for assuming any source for the high civilization of Middle America except the inventiveness of the local population (17).

Monuments of these highly developed tribes are found between a south-eastern limit in western Honduras and Salvador, and a north-western boundary in the state of Zacatecas in Mexico. On the basis of their art styles and the reports of the Spaniards we can identify a number of distinctive tribal cultures. In the lowlands of Guatemala the Mayas had their imposing ceremonial centres, which in the mountain regions were much less elaborate. In the state of Oaxaca[2] in Mexico the Zapotecs were the authors of a rich civilization. The coastal region of Vera Cruz yields evidence of several high civilizations which archaeological research is just beginning to distinguish. Most notable among these are the works attributed to the Olmecs and the Totonacs. On the northern border the Toltecs and the Aztecs created the great civilizations of Central Mexico. North and west of them tribal cultures of lesser development represented in some cases persistences and survivals from

1. Me-tah'-tays.   2. Wah-hah'-cah.

the Middle Culture plane, in others distorted reflections of the
more elaborate civilizations (18).

Just as in fifteenth- and sixteenth-century western Europe,
where distinctive national and regional art styles were developed under the aegis of the Roman Church, so in Middle
America there was sharp stylistic differentiation in the arts and
crafts of tribes whose broad culture pattern was the same. This
civilization was grafted to a Middle Culture base, and comprised such elements of advanced culture as a polytheism based
on Nature-worship, the representation of various divinities
through drawing and sculpture, the erection of temples on
platforms to honour these gods, a system of writing for religious and tribal records, a calendar and an astronomy designed
primarily for ritualistic purposes. The Middle Americans probably did not develop these practices simultaneously, but evolved
and elaborated first one, then another, trait.

Other tribal units gradually absorbed and adapted these customs to suit their local needs. To maintain a civilization along
these lines a tribe had to be numerous, stable and successfully
adjusted economically. Men had to be freed to a very considerable extent from the bare struggle for existence to perform
and direct the elaborate ritual, to build the ceremonial structures and to develop the arts and crafts which gave the religion
its outward expression.

The Mayas of Guatemala, Yucatan, south-eastern Mexico
and western Honduras attained the greatest eminence in the
elaboration of this cult. Their temples and priestly dwellings
were built of masonry and roofed by means of the corbel or
false arch. The sculpture in stone and plaster adorning these
buildings has the elaborate sophistication of a matured art.
Their carefully pondered delineation of their gods and goddesses reflects theological maturity. Their writing is set forth
in conventionalized hieroglyphs, of which only the calendric
texts can be deciphered. It is this calendar which particularly
excites the admiration of our Western civilization, for it is

based on a highly evolved mathematical and astronomical system (19). (See Plates 4–7.)

The Maya calendar should be a great aid in reconstructing history, but opinions differ as to how it should be correlated with Christian dates. There are several calculations designed to reconcile the Maya with the Christian calendar, but each correlation involves a difference of some two hundred and sixty years in the expression of Maya dates in Christian terms. This lack of agreement has led to quite divergent interpretations of Maya history, although the main trends are well established (20).

The complexity and elaboration of the Maya civilization, barely touched on here, have challenged the imagination of explorers and students. Extravagant theories have been woven by seers and visionaries as to the origin of the Mayas in lost continents like Atlantis or Mu. Soberer judges see them as American in origin and credit them with the invention and spread of Middle American culture. However, in view of the unanswered correlation question it would seem more just to consider the Mayas as carrying to a higher degree, without implication of greater antiquity, a civilization shared by their neighbours (21).

The excavation and study of remains in Middle American sites discloses a symmetrical cultural development which began at Middle Culture plane and passed through a long period of highly stylized local development, only to be cut short by a sudden decline and the intrusion of cult practices from Central Mexico (Table I, p. 44–5). In the Maya area even the Middle Culture plane is not uniform at the several sites where it is represented. Pottery and figurines differ so strongly in style and ware as to suggest their manufacture by unrelated tribes.

These Middle Culture forms gradually became more sophisticated as the people began to build temples, erect stone time-markers and develop a mature religious art. The differences in style observable at the Middle Culture plane became

strongly accentuated in this civilized period. Yet pottery vessels made at one site have been found as trade objects in another, so that in the broad sense we know that the local cultures were contemporary. A vast amount of building and, in
places, deep refuse-beds suggest that a long span of time elapsed
during this period. Whenever this civilized epoch crystallized,
be it the years preceding the Christian Era, the early centuries
afterwards, or the fifth century A.D., according to the correlation one adopts for the Maya calendar, we do know from
traditional sources that about the twelfth century A.D. tribes of
Mexican stock moved into the Maya country, where they
founded various local dynasties. This movement is reflected in
the archaeological remains which show influences from the
Mixteca[1]-Puebla culture complex and reveal a degeneration
of the local tribal civilization (22).

The Maya region, prior to the twelfth-century infiltration
from Mexico, contained peoples speaking different dialects
and having distinctive regional styles in their material culture.
Their religion and calendar, however, were essentially the
same throughout the area. On the mainland of Mexico we find
that the regional populations had not only distinctive arts, but
also different theological conceptions. Yet these Mexican civilizations, like that of the Maya, had their roots in the Middle cultures and succumbed at the end to Mixteca–Puebla influences.

The recent discoveries in southern Vera Cruz and Tabasco
suggest a tantalizing explanation for the origin of Middle
American civilization. At the sites of Tres Zapotes and La
Venta great ceremonial centres occur, producing huge stone
heads and religious and calendric formulas inscribed on stone
door-jambs and stelae. Little clay figures made by hand
follow the aesthetic tenets of Middle Culture art, but some
types reflect the more matured modelling of the stone sculpture. The religious art portrays strange beings whose faces are
either swollen and infantile or else grotesquely reproduce the

1. Mish-te′ca.

visages of tiger-like monsters. This art has been called Olmec, after a gifted and civilized people whom the traditions say lived in the region, but whose handiwork has never been securely identified (23). (See Plates 3–4.)

The sculpture has relationships with other tribal arts that suggest great antiquity. The tiger-like mask has close analogies with the plaster decorations on the oldest temple at the Maya site of Uaxactun,[1] a building which exhibits none of the characteristic features of Maya art. Masks and infantile faces were also present in the earliest occupation of Monte Alban, the great ceremonial site of the Zapotecs of Oaxaca. The 'baby face' was repeated on figurines from Upper Middle Culture sites in the Valley of Mexico, and an associated type of figurine also marked the close of the Lower Middle Period in that area. (See Plates 3, 8.)

The associations between 'Olmec' art and early culture levels in the Maya area, Oaxaca and the Valley of Mexico would suggest that the first steps towards ceremonial civilization were taken in southern Vera Cruz and Tabasco, except for one very perplexing feature: the writing and calendar system were those used by the Mayas, but the dates expressed seem to be earlier than those they inscribed on their own monuments. Further excavations will undoubtedly resolve this problem, which is like the old one of which came first, the hen or the egg.

The majority of scholars consider that 'Olmec' art was later than early Maya, and that its creators understood so little of the complexity of the Maya calendar that they made errors, giving a fictitious impression of antiquity. Others claim that the early sculpture is a decisive argument for the antiquity of 'Olmec' art and that the inscriptions are contemporaneous. Furthermore, they argue that the position of the Olmecs in the midst of Maya, Zapotec and other tribes with different art styles and calendar systems indicates a centre from which such

1. Wash-ac-toon'.

elements were diffused. However, later research is bound to answer this question.

The excavation of Tres Zapotes discloses that after the first period the inhabitants developed a well-defined local style which had connections with the so-called Totonac cultures northwards up the Vera Cruz coast. This period seems to have been a long one, to judge from the amount of mound-building and the quantity of pottery and figurines dug up. In the final epoch Mexican influence seeped in, testifying to the spread of the Nahua-speaking peoples of the Central Plateau. Since the work at Tres Zapotes is still in progress, we cannot yet sum up the final conclusions as to the historical and cultural affiliations of the occupants of this site. None the less, the pattern of development followed the same lines we have noted before. (See Plate 10.)

On the uplands of Oaxaca, south-west of the Olmec country, another local civilization flourished, that of the Zapotecs. Their chief ceremonial site, Monte Alban, has been extensively excavated. It covers a small mountain, levelled and terraced into a gigantic natural platform which supports lesser artificial structures such as temples and ball courts. The five periods of occupation disclose the same sort of culture history that we have sketched previously, but Zapotec art styles and writing were quite different from those of their eastern neighbours (24).

Monte Alban in its earliest period was the home of a people who made pottery and figurines of Middle Culture quality. They were advanced enough to rear platforms for their temples and they carved in relief human figures reminiscent of 'Olmec' art to adorn their buildings. Hieroglyphs accompanied some of them, suggesting further connection with Vera Cruz; and two 'Olmec' divinities, the infantile god and the tiger god, were represented in ceremonial vases of the period. But a later phase showed a gradual shift away from 'Olmec' influence. Stones were inscribed in a distinctive writing, and calendric calculations were set forth, not in the elaborate long count of the Mayas, but in an abbreviated system which fixed a date in terms of a fifty-two-year cycle. The art also reveals a vague suggestion of Maya influence, and occasional vessel forms recall shapes found early in Maya history. (See Plates 8–9.)

The third and fourth stages of Monte Alban were of long duration. The Zapotecs grew less susceptible to foreign influence and developed a strongly regional theology and art. At the close of this era they appeared to be in contact with northern peoples, like the Toltecs of Central Mexico, and their culture underwent a transformation in its fifth and final period. A new people, the Mixtec, came into the Valley of Oaxaca, and brought with them a new art, new gods and a new type of calendar and writing.

This later religious civilization was also spread into the Maya country by members of a totally different linguistic stock, the Nahua, and it reached its zenith among the Aztecs of Central Mexico. Research has not progressed to the point where we can identify the formulators of this civilization. Its place of origin seems definitely to centre in the lands of the Mixtecs in northern Oaxaca and in the territory of Nahua tribes in Puebla. Thus to call the civilization Mixteca–Puebla and to identify its latest carriers under their tribal name, when this is known, seem the best ways to reconcile cultural with political history. In much the same way we use the term Western civilization to cover those culture elements shared by the nations of Europe and the Americas. (See Plates 7, 11, 12.)

In Central Mexico, at the north-western frontier of the zone of high civilization, we find the same sort of sequence which we have set forth for the Mayas, the Olmecs and the Zapotecs. First, there was a long Middle Culture occupation; second, a shift in culture whereby another group, basically Middle Culture, took on the beginnings of a civilized status as shown by the presence of mounds and the sculptural representation of one or two gods. Out of a branch of this Upper Middle Culture a third phase developed, a majestic ceremonial civilization called Teotihuacan[1] or classical Toltec, which was sur-passed by its southern contemporaries only through their superior development of sculpture and the religious calendar. A fourth interval in the history of the Valley of Mexico was known as the Chichimec[2] Period, and comprised a phase of decline when the Teotihuacan Toltecs disintegrated and mi-grant tribes vied with one another for supremacy. Finally a fifth phase saw the introduction of the ceremonial civilization, de-veloped by the Mixteca–Puebla peoples, which culminated in the domination of the Aztecs (25).

The Aztecs and their forebears grew up on the outer bor-ders of an intensely civilized area in which the cultural history of its various peoples seems to have been very similar. Out of a long period of exploration and experimentation, the pro-cesses of which we have to reconstruct from our knowledge of the archaeology and ethnology of surviving cultures in North America, some of the tribes developed the sedentary life based on agriculture, typical of the Middle Cultures. This economy persisted for many centuries, and in some places was never modified. However, somewhere in Guatemala or southern Mexico the conception of a ceremonial centre for religious practices changed the older pattern of life. Conditions in for-ested country, as we have noted, would seem to offer the most urgent reasons for such a practice, but it spread over the Highland area as well.

In the train of this ceremonial architecture followed closely the ritualistic definition of the gods and, elaborated in various degrees, a calendric system closely tied in with their worship. The development of these practices followed tribal lines, creat-ing regional art styles and special religious modifications. There seems to be a correlation between the evolution of these tribal styles and the spreading out of an increasing population. Yet these populations at first do not seem to have had close enough contact to modify specifically the patterns and styles of

1. Tay-o-tee-wah-can´.   2. Chee´-chee-mec.

each other's cultures. Eventually this protracted phase of independent civilization ended with a spread of ideas and peoples, derived from Central Mexico, which continued for the last four centuries before the Spanish Conquest.

Estimates of time are hard to make in the absence of specific dates. Yet to allow eight centuries for the duration of the independent civilizations does not seem excessive, and to assume a similar length of time for the Middle Culture phases appears to be well within the bounds of probability. However, several thousand years could have elapsed between the first immigrations to America and the establishment of sedentary agricultural settlements like those of the Middle Cultures.

Rhythms of development are obviously not the same in all areas. The conditions of the natural environment had a profound effect on the progress of the American Indians, and the causes which affect the rise and decline of the birth rate likewise played a part in their history. The forces leading to invention and to the development of techniques, the status of the various tribal societies, and many other important factors must have operated in this historical evolution, but it is next to impossible to reconstruct them from the mute evidence of archaeological remains.

Since the history of the Aztecs and their forebears is better known than that of any other American Indian population, it is worth while to see how closely we can reconstruct the social, economic and environmental forces which affected them. Indian and Spanish sources illuminate the Aztec period, and dim traditions shed a faint light on the decline and fall of the Toltecs of Teotihuacan. Only for the Middle Culture peoples do we have to rely solely on material remains; nevertheless, in the Valley of Mexico the deep refuse-heaps accumulated through the centuries present a record more detailed and capable of interpretation than are found elsewhere in Middle America. Therefore, the history of the Aztecs and their forebears presents in small compass the major trends which governed the rise of Middle American civilization.

TABLE I

PRINCIPAL CULTURE SEQUENCES IN MIDDLE, NORTH, AND SOUTH AMERICA

Approximate Dates	U.S. Southeast	U.S. Southwest	Central Mexico	Cholula	Oaxaca	Vera Cruz	Highland Maya	Lowland Maya	Peru North Coast	Peru South Highland	Approximate Dates
				Mixteca-Puebla Period							
1600		Pueblo V									1600
1500	Temple Mound II		Aztec 4	Cholula 5	Monte Alban 5		Chipal 3		Late Chimu plus Inca		1500
1400	Temple Mound I	Pueblo IV	Aztec 3			Cempoala		Chichen Itza 3	Inca Conquest / Late Chimu	Inca	1400
1300	Burial Mound II	Pueblo III	Aztec 2	Cholula 4							1300
1200	Burial Mound I		Aztec 1				Chipal 2	Chichen Itza 2	Black-White-Red	Inca Conquest	1200
1100			Mazapan	Cholula 3		Cerro Montoso					1100
				Late Independent Civilizations							
1000	Early Stages	Pueblo II	Teotihuacan 5		Monte Alban 4		Chipal 1	San José 3-5		Decadent Tiahuanaco	1000
900			Teotihuacan 4			Ranchito de las Animas	Chamá 4	Uaxactun 3	Tiahuanaco		900
800		Pueblo I	Teotihuacan 3			Tres Zapotes 3	Chamá 3	Holmul 5	Gallinazo-Chavin II	Chiripa	800

44

FULL INDEPENDENT CIVILIZATIONS

Date					Kaminaljuyú						Date
700		Early Chimu B								Basket Maker III	700
600	Pukara Classic Tiahuanaco								Teotihuacan 2 Cholula 2		600
500				San José 2 Holmul 2-4 Uaxactun 2	Chamá 2	Monte Alban 3					500
400		Early Chimu A		Holmul 1	Chamá 1	Monte Alban 2		(Teotihuacan 1 Cuicuilco Ticoman Gualupita 2	Basket Maker II		400

MIDDLE CULTURES

Date											Date
300	Early Tiahuanaco	Chavin I		Uaxactun 1b		Tres Zapotes 1	Cholula 1	Monte Alban 1	Gualupita 1	Basket. Maker I(?)	300
200				Uaxactun 1a		La Venta			{Copilco-Zacatenco		200
100					Miraflores				Early Zacatenco		100
0									Early El Arbolillo I		0
100											100
200											200

EARLY CULTURES

Date											Date
1000										Desert Cultures(?)	1000
2000										Cochise	2000
5000	Argentine Caves									Folsom	5000
10000											10000
20000											20000

45

THE MIDDLE CULTURES IN THE VALLEY OF MEXICO

An attempt to interpret the history and society of the earliest peoples found in Central Mexico through their archaeological remains

THE first peoples of whom we have a record in the Valley of Mexico lived on the Middle Culture plane in the centuries immediately preceding and following the birth of Christ. They occupied permanent villages, subsisted chiefly on the products of their fields, made adequate implements of stone, bone and clay, and fashioned little idols of terra cotta. Their level of development was about midway between a relatively primitive hunting or farming society and the more elaborate social and technical systems of the ceremonial civilizations. In the Valley of Mexico there were two occupations of this type, which we may distinguish as Lower and Upper. The people of the Upper Middle Cultures introduced the ceremonial mound or platform and made occasional images of gods, defined according to the laws of their ritual, while the Lower Middle population followed a simpler religious presentation (1). (See Plate 13.)

The Valley of Mexico was a superb place to live in at that time. Seven thousand feet above sea level high mountain chains walled in a fertile valley in which lay a great salt lake, Texcoco,[1] fed at the south by two sweet-water lagoons, Xochimilco[2] and Chalco; at the north-west by two more, Xaltocan[3] and Zumpango, and at the North-east by a sluggish stream, the Acolman River, which drained the fertile Valley of Teotihuacan.[4] The lakes were shallow, and their marshy shores, thick with reeds, attracted a teeming abundance of wild

1. Tes-co′-co.   3. Hal-to′-can.
2. Sho-chee-meel′-co.   4. Tay-o-tee-wah-can′.

fowl. On the wooded mountain slopes deer abounded. During the rainy season thick alluvial deposits, ideal for primitive agriculture, were washed down along the lake shores.

As village sites, the Middle Culture peoples selected points along the lake where they could take the greatest advantage of the natural resources of lake and forest, and cultivate most easily their crops of corn, cotton and other plants. Once located in a suitable spot, they stayed there for a long, long time, enough for 25 feet of refuse to accumulate at the site of El Arbolillo[1] and 15 feet at Zacatenco[2].

Their homes were impermanent affairs which left no remnants of foundations, floors or fire-pits. Little fragments of burned clay, impressed with stick-marks, suggest that the dwellings were of wattle, daubed with mud and covered by a thatched roof, like the homes of modern Indian communities in this very valley. The inhabitants were not troubled by ideas of sanitation or civic neatness, and threw their refuse on their own doorsteps. Broken pottery, animal bones, all the nameless trash that man rejects, found their way to the dumpheap, but its most conspicuous element was corn shocks, which, in the absence of domestic animals, had no possible use. This vegetable matter, disintegrating into earth, caused the middens to accumulate rapidly and, indirectly, has aided archaeological research, for an object dropped into this mess was as lost as the proverbial needle in a haystack. Even the dead found their way into the middens, not, however, because of their survivors' lack of respect, but because graves were dug more easily with wooden tools in the soft, churned earth of the refuse-heaps than in undisturbed soil.

Mexican myths and annals give no clue to the identity of these men or the language they spoke. The study of their skeletal remains reveals a people of medium height, composed of several physical strains; but not enough material has been amassed to trace these affiliations precisely. The middens, how-

1. El Arb-o-lee'-yo.   2. Za-ca-te'n-co.

ever, filthy and fly-blown as they may have been, are real historical documents. Laid down gradually through the years, the successive layers disclose the different types and styles of the people's tools and utensils (2).

Archaeological research refers to these Lower Middle remains in the Valley of Mexico as the Copilco–Zacatenco culture, named from the sites where the material was first studied. The stylistic sequences also receive their names from the places where they were first determined. Specimens of both the Lower and Upper Middle phases were referred to under various names until 1917, when the first real excavation defining the Lower Middle material was made under the lava quarry of Copilco. In the winter of 1928–9 excavations at Zacatenco showed that the Copilco remains were a late stage in the history of the Lower Middle occupation of the Valley. Two years later the excavation of El Arbolillo produced deep beds of Early Zacatenco material, enabling us to detect three stages, of which the earliest, El Arbolillo I, preceded Early Zacatenco (3). (See Plate 1.)

Thus archaeology works with two sets of factors, peoples in the past and their material remains; the terms used in distinguishing the one do not always apply justly to the other. A style of pottery may be very useful and important in defining the presence of a people at a given time, but it is a mere adjunct to the reconstruction of their history. The making of the style is not an important historical fact in itself. The technical literature of archaeological research must concern itself with the methods of reconstructing Indian history, but such findings appal the general reader, who quite reasonably wants to know the history itself.

This digression, it is hoped, will explain Table II (p. 63), in which is summarized the material evidence for the history of Lower Middle Culture peoples of the Valley of Mexico, the creators of the Copilco–Zacatenco culture. Their life-history seems to have been a peaceful one, without external indications of of war or revolution. They made numerous tools of stone, the forms of which were so satisfactory to them that there was little change through several centuries. For many purposes they used obsidian or volcanic glass. Hard but fragile, it could be chipped into projectile points or scrapers and flaked off into long, narrow blades. Discarded fragments could be used without re-touching, since the edges of a freshly broken piece are as sharp as a razor-blade. Projectile points, which required careful shaping, show changes through the years, caused by technical improvements. For example, the stone-workers of the later periods found that by notching the butt of an arrow-head it could be more firmly lashed to its wooden shaft. (See Plate 16, bottom.)

Metates and *manos*, the grinding-stones and mullers used to grind corn kernels into flour, were made of lava rock and, being efficiently developed for the purpose, were not changed through the centuries. Axes and celts were rare, and the examples recovered were made of serpentine, porphyry and jade, rocks not found in the Valley of Mexico. An occasional beautifully worked jade ornament, like an earplug or pendant, indicated trade and the existence of more advanced cultures south of the Valley limits.

The tribesmen found deerhorn and bone very useful for fashioning various kinds of tools, such as flakers for working obsidian and awls for perforating hide or aiding in weaving basketry, and they sometimes notched a deer shoulder-blade to beat out a rhythm by rasping a stick along the serrations. A few crude shell ornaments made from Pacific coast species testify to trade to the south and west. Wood and basketry have all disintegrated, so that we cannot tell whether the people used the bow or the *atl-atl*, or what their techniques of weaving were. However, we know that they did weave and possibly beat out bark cloth, for some of their little clay images are represented as wearing turbans. Furthermore, a tiny fragment of cloth, miraculously preserved, was woven

c

from cotton thread in one direction and apocynum fibres in the other (4).

These people were practical potters, but were not troubled unduly by an aesthetic urge. Ninety per cent of their vessels were solidly constructed storage and cooking-jars, ranging in colour from a light tan to the shade of a bay horse. At first they made black bowls with three little feet, and incised a rude geometric design, into which they rubbed red paint. Later they grooved a pattern before applying a slip or wash, a practice which led ultimately to handsome channelled designs. In their later days they gave up this practice, changed the vessel shape and, after the bowl was fired, took a piece of obsidian and etched a running pattern that had the same relation to the previous stiff geometric design that script has to block lettering. (See Plates 16, top; 17, top.)

Painted decoration was not very popular. At one village, Zacatenco, in the early period, there was a fashion of painting white geometric designs on red clay. Later on this style shifted to spreading white slip on vessels and adding a simple solid design in red. There was some further experimentation in trying out different types of slip, but the most conspicuous change was in the shape of the bowls which, in the later period, differed markedly from the earlier forms.

This impression of smug competence, uninspired by artistic yearnings, is borne out by the little baked-clay images which the people made in abundance. They were usually female, and may have represented a mother goddess, symbolizing growth and fertility – a conception common among the religious ideas of mankind. The figures were not valued in themselves, as they are almost always found broken and discarded in the refuse-heaps. Distinctive styles seem to have developed in different regions. Among the vastly more numerous locally-made figurines there are a few which are the standard types elsewhere, so that if the little idols were not traded they must have been brought in by pilgrims. When we consider how carefully, even if naïvely, the figures were made, and how clay idols were manufactured in later periods to represent specific gods, we must conclude that they had religious significance even at this early date.

The early sculptor did not work in stone or wood, but clay. His figures were small, seldom over six inches high. His method was to model the head and torso first and then add details, like arms and legs, nose, eyes and ears, by pinching on little pieces of clay. Later the figurine was fired, and often after firing the face and body were painted with ornamental designs. The sculptor strove for a naturalistic effect rather than follow a rigid convention. Yet standardized ways of doing things produced styles that vary according to tribe and to changes in fashion or in technical development and degeneration. (See Plate 14, top.)

In our modern world we are accustomed to sophisticated and self-conscious art forms. Seen objectively, these Early Middle Culture figurines are dumpy and gross. Short, fat bodies, blobby noses, protuberant eyes and stubby arms and legs are not attributes of a graceful form, according to our way of thinking. Yet handling one of these figurines and tracing each step in its formation, one is conscious of an intense seriousness and comprehends a whole world of thought dammed by the want of technical facility in expression. An intuitive person sometimes sees a populous world of shining fantasy behind the meagre scribbling of a child. Behind these figurines must have existed an austere realization of the complex rhythms of birth, growth and death in nature, epitomized in the miracle of woman and her bearing of children. (See Plate 14, bottom.)

The process of experimentation kept on throughout the early part of the Lower Middle Period. A careful observer can see how certain manners of presentation dominated the sculptor's interest from time to time. The work of one cluster of settlements differed from that of another, and figurines seem to have been exchanged between communities. Perhaps the most attractive type developed in this era had its centre in Puebla and Morelos, but was so liked by the people of the northern Valley of Mexico that a small but constant quantity has been found at almost every village. These figurines, in contrast to the matronly bearing of the local images, have something of a girlish grace. They are too distinctive and differ too sharply from the northern-Valley forms to have been copies made by the local artisans. (See Plate 15.)

However, as time went on, the importation of another new style (Type A) stimulated local adaptations. This sculpture reproduced in relatively accurate proportions the rounded contours of the Central American face. The artist, by sinking his wads of clay into slots, was able to reproduce the curves of the nose and lips more accurately in relation to the face planes. This new style had no discovered prototypes in the Valley of Mexico, and seems to have been evolved originally by Tres Zapotes sculptors during the early 'Olmec' occupation. Its introduction to the Valley also brought distinctive changes in the form and decoration of certain types of pottery bowls, and had a pronounced effect on the local tradition of clay modelling. The painstaking methods of the early work were neglected for the slap-dash fashioning of flat gingerbread forms, coarsely conventionalized. One contemporary style was so crude that it may have been made as an intentional grotesque. Another quaint concept evolved at the time was a two-headed being which must have represented some god or mythological personage. (See Plate 17, middle, bottom.)

Thus, to judge from the material remains, the Lower Middle Culture people existed for centuries, developing their own techniques without being affected very much by outside peoples. Then they suddenly showed signs of being strongly influenced by external groups from whom they borrowed an art style and new types of pottery. The social significance of this typological change is hard to interpret. (See Plate 17.)

The history of art is also the history of artists who, in a primitive community, are not a specialized class but the people themselves. When an art is created for religious purposes the development of the content of the religion and the requirements of ritual are as important as the evolution of the artistic technique. These little figurines, judged by the standards of the great arts of the world, are feeble and fumbling examples of the social process which, in our own culture, we designate as aesthetic. Even as the dissection of a frog leads to the understanding of the biology of more advanced organisms, so we can see how the plastic art of this Lower Middle Culture passed from a period of convention to one of experiment, and then settled back to convention again. Contact with a foreign source of inspiration brought in a new manner of presentation which may have withered interest in the older technique. Such rhythms appear over and over again in the history of art.

The religious significance of the figurines is less intelligible. A common concept in the religion of farming peoples is that of a female principle or generative force, tied up with growth and productivity. A goddess frequently symbolizes that belief, since man often invests the processes of Nature with his own attributes and motives. The little clay figures of Zacatenco and El Arbolillo always represent women, some of whom carry children in their arms, but no two wear precisely the same costume. A few exceptional examples have two heads.

Such evidence is little to build on, but it is all we have. We do not know what lay behind the sculpture in the way of theology, philosophy and ritual. The modern Pueblo Indians of our own South-west have few ceremonial objects which could survive destruction and decay, and such implements as they have by no means reflect the full complexity of religion and ritual which these people possess. We should not, therefore, leap to the assumption that the Lower Middle Culture people were lacking in religious development because of the crudeness of their surviving ceremonial equipment.

The only other index to the religious practices of this period is the treatment of the dead. They were buried, but seldom according to a set plan. Some were contracted, others extended; usually a single person was buried at a time. Yet group burials occurred, and the differences in the age and sex of the occupants of a single grave suggest a family interment. The skeletons exhumed show no marks of death by war or sacrifice. Disease has left no trace, but over a quarter of the dead were children, and few individuals reached old age. Offerings like pots, tools, weapons and ornaments often accompanied burials, but prosperity in life may have had something to do with the practice. At El Arbolillo one half of the dead, irrespective of age and sex, had offerings, but at Zacatenco, less than five miles away, only one out of eighteen was so honoured. The mourners covered a few of the corpses with red paint made from haematite; they left with one man his ornament of turquoise mosaic and endowed a tiny baby with two jade ear ornaments and two pottery bowls, an unprecedented gift, suggesting exceptional parental grief or wealth. Some of the dead they dumped into shallow pits, while they stretched others out in formal tombs, lined and covered with stone slabs and floored with clean beach sand (5).

The government of these Lower Middle Culture people is not told in this earthy record. The economics are only faintly outlined: hunting, farming and a little trade to the south. Status in society was apparently recognized, since the burials differed in richness of equipment, and most people grant honour to the dead in the same proportion as prestige to the living. The tenor of life was peaceful in the main, but Nature seems to have intervened with occasional violence. At Zacatenco the lake level suddenly rose just at the dawn of the late period. Whether the changes in art styles were brought in by refugees, driven from their homes by the rising waters, or were due to modes and fashions from farther afield, is still a moot question. Some communities, inhabited at the end of this period, were abandoned as local floods swept over them, sealing the remains under several feet of silt (6).

Yet abruptly the Lower Middle Culture people disappeared, and their stylistic traditions did not linger on into later periods. Immigrants took their place who were the makers of the Upper Middle cultures of Cuicuilco–Ticoman[1] (named from Cuicuilco, the great mound erected to honour their gods, and Ticoman, their most carefully studied village site) (Table III, p. 64).

The Upper Middle Culture throve in the Valley of Mexico, Morelos, Puebla, Michoacan and in Vera Cruz. It was already in existence during the later phases of the Lower Middle Culture, in Morelos, south of the Valley of Mexico. Whereas the Copilco–Zacatenco styles ceased abruptly, the Upper Middle techniques persisted into the later Teotihuacan civilization and the high cultures of western Mexico. The Upper Middle art, in contrast to the unity of the Lower, had strong local variations. Yet the Upper Middle Cultures were the scaffolding used to erect the ceremonial civilization of the Teotihuacan Toltecs, and as such take an important place in Mexican history (7). (See Plate 13.)

A meagre listing of objects found in the earth constitutes the historical record of the Upper Middle Cultures, but by contrasting these pots and tools with those of the preceding era social forces may be seen at work. At Ticoman, the most carefully studied village site, the population terraced their rocky peninsula to make level places for houses which were too perishable to leave traces for later archaeological reconstruction. In the refuse-beds deer bones are less in evidence than in the adjacent sites of the preceding period, indicating that game was gradually being hunted off. The Ticomanos made a greater variety of stone tools, both in shape and in purpose, and they found that the flakes of obsidian could be worked more easily than the more solid fragments used in Lower Middle

1. Kwee-kweel'-co-Tee-co-man'.

times. Yet as techniques became more complex the capabilities of the individuals differed. We found two graves of leather-workers who were buried with the tools of their trade; one carefully fashioned his implements, while the other contented himself with chips and flakes, as if he cared more about finishing the job than about taking pride in sheer workmanship. (See Plate 16, upper, middle.)

The potters showed this same interest in improving the manner of living. They made a much higher proportion of carefully fashioned vessels for the service of food than did their Lower Middle predecessors. They were attracted more by shape and finish than by painted designs. Not content with little tripods to hold the vessels steady, they modelled the legs with care, and often filled them with pellets to make them rattle pleasingly. At first they had trouble painting designs because the burnishing process caused the red paint to run. They tried to correct this after firing by outlining the blurred pattern with an obsidian blade. Later they found that painting a heavy white outline gave a pleasing trichrome effect, which at the end of the era they abandoned for simple polishing. (See Plates 19, 20, top.)

They also experimented with a new process, negative painting, the same technique as batik. A vessel was coated with wax or gum, which was then scraped away to make a pattern. The pot was next covered with paint, and when fired the gum burned away, leaving only the scraped portion coloured. This method of decoration may have had its origin in Central and South America, where the practice is more common, and the technique may well have passed from tribe to tribe until, at this early date, it reached the Valley of Mexico in an imperfect form. Archaeology does not reveal the use of an analogous method for textiles, but in the early days of Indian Peru garments were beautifully treated in batik (8).

Trade was much more extensive than in Lower Middle times. Shell was more abundant and more carefully worked, but the varieties were those of the Vera Cruz coast, in contrast to the west-coast origin of the Lower Middle shells. Ornaments and axes of jade, porphyry and serpentine also pointed to an eastern origin, but fragments of pottery seemed to disclose a wide radius of commercial activity.

The figurine cult was still very important, and the imaginative person can read into these little votive objects the art history of a forgotten people. Before the Upper Middle Culture spread out into the Valley of Mexico there was a little settlement in the present ward of Gualupita in Cuernavaca.[1] The inhabitants made clay idols, stiff and clumsy like the Lower Middle figurines of the Valley but distinct from them in style. Sporadic examples traded from one region to another show that early Gualupita was contemporary with the Lower Middle Cultures of the Valley. These Gualupita forms, obviously representative of a much more widely distributed art, later crystallized into a happy little style wherein the conventionalized treatment of the face was balanced by the variety of the head-dress and of the posture. This type was being made by the Upper Middle people when they filtered into the Valley of Mexico (9). (See Plates 19, 20, bottom.)

The wave of technical experiment that affected the other artisans also stimulated the sculptors, and they began to elaborate these shapes, making grotesques as well as naturalistic human beings, in which they tried to depict different positions and even actions. They polished the surfaces to enhance the form by the lustre of its finish. To our modern eye the results are not particularly impressive, but they marked a step in the technical development of the art. Finally out of this chaos in miniature two styles developed that must have been satisfactory to the tribal sculptors, since they were in vogue to the exclusion of all others. In one the figures were coated with a polished white paint, sometimes touched up in red. They were shown seated or standing, arranging their hair, covering their

1. Kwayr-na-va'-ca.

eyes, holding a bowl and performing various acts. In the other there was a return to applying pieces of clay in meticulous detail, emphasizing ornaments and hairdress, as well as the limbs and features of the individuals. While most of the figurines were female, a few were obviously male, a suggestion, even though tenuous, that the theology was becoming more complex.

Supporting this theory, we find two carefully individualized beings portrayed with some skill. One is a figure with a contorted mouth and the general lineaments of a baby. In the Valley of Mexico this personage was crudely conventionalized, but at Gualupita, a sculptor made superb and large-sized representations that stand far above the general artistic norm. They seem truly to reflect in clay the strange infantile beings, hewn out of gigantic boulders or graven on stone slabs, that dominated the religious art of the Olmecs in Vera Cruz (10). (See Plate 20, bottom.)

The other being, portrayed in both clay and stone, is an old man who sits with bowed head, supporting on his head and shoulders a bowl for burning incense. This god was also important in the Teotihuacan civilization and in Aztec times, when he was appropriately called Huehueteotl,[1] the Old God, and sometimes Xiuhtecuhtli,[2] Lord of Fire. Such a divinity is peculiarly fitting for a volcanic region, and his presentation as an old man suggests the manifest antiquity of mountains. His continuous worship for many centuries would seem to make him the oldest god ritualistically shown in Middle America, even though the mother goddess of corn and growth may represent an earlier concept (11). (See Plate 18, top left.)

Yet the full impact of Middle American religion on those Central Mexican villagers is symbolized by the great adobe mound of Cuicuilco. On the skirts of the volcanic range of Ajusco,[3] at the south-west of the valley, tribesmen built a massive oval mound, approximately 369 feet in diameter and 60 feet high, to the top of which led a wide ramp. They faced the

1. Way-way-tay′-otl.   2. Shee-oo-te-cootli′.   3. A-hoos′-co.

sides with river boulders to guard against the erosion of sea-sonal rains and, perhaps, to add to the effect of rugged majesty. They reared no stately temple on the summit but instead con-structed an altar, open alike to the sky and to the eyes of the congregation. With its lack of the stiff rectangles of formalized direction, the mound seems, to a modern, almost a spontane-ous evocation of the mass religious spirit. The altar is a direct contrast; here sloping rectilinear walls and a pair of steps flanked by low balustrades presage the developed architecture of a later day. The sides are faced with smoothed adobe to approach as nearly as possible the plaster-work of religious architecture fully developed elsewhere. The whole beautifully symbolizes the introduction of a cherished ritual, as exempli-fied by the altar, to the mass need of a large population, re-presented by the mighty mound (11). (See Plate 18, bottom.)

The people of Cuicuilco added twice to their temple, each time replacing the altar by setting another above it. Once they added a new facing to the structure, utilizing jagged blocks of lava instead of the river-boulders. They allowed refuse to pile up around the base, covering up a narrow passage of stones set on edge, which answered some forgotten purpose of the early builders. In time they paid little attention to their creation, and the rains weakened the stone veneer and let the sides slump down. Then a volcano, Xitli,[1] erupted, and molten lava poured down along the slopes and flowed over the country-side, creating the volcanic desert of the modern Pedregal Cooling, it left many feet of solid stone, sealing in the lower third of the platform. The flow was stopped by the lake after it had also covered up several abandoned sites of earlier date, like Copilco. However, the molten flood affected directly only a small part of the Valley of Mexico.

The desert of the Pedregal is a waste-land. The lava quar-ried from the congealed stream is now the principal building stone of Central Mexico and the ballast for its tracks and its

1. Shee'-tly.

motor roads. In exploring the quarries the early discovery of Copilco was made. Then the artificial mound projecting through the Pedregal challenged the imagination of Dr Gamio, who requested Dr Bryon Cummings to undertake the excavation of Cuicuilco. Finding traces of man underneath this impenetrable sheet of rock suggested a culture of immeasurable antiquity. When did the volcano erupt? On the answer to that question hinges the date of these Middle Cultures, first traces of man in Central Mexico.

The vast and precise learning of geology was brought into play, and the geologists concurred that the flow was recent, and gave it the trivial age of 2000 to 10,000 years, nothing in terms of the millenniums and multimillenniums in which they usually measure time. But 2000 to 10,000 years are enormous units by which to count the history of man. The oldest legendary history of Mexico reached back only to A.D. 500–700 for the founding of Teotihuacan. What happened between that date and the cataclysm of the Pedregal? That was a problem for archaeology to answer, if it could (12).

First the materials from Copilco and Cuicuilco, the two buried sites, were compared, and found to be different. Then these styles were discovered in other parts of the Valley in open sites, unaffected by the local eruptions which formed the Pedregal. Next several seasons of work in these open sites disclosed that not only was Copilco older than Cuicuilco but that Copilco–Zacatenco culture was represented by rubbish-heaps twice as deep as those at Cuicuilco–Ticoman. There is no way to measure the rate of accumulation of such heaps. However, on the basis of a deposit at Pecos,[1] New Mexico, the beginning and ending dates of which are more or less known, it does not seem unreasonable to compute six or seven centuries' duration for the Lower Middle Culture of Copilco–Zacatenco and 300 years or so for the life-span of the Upper Middle Culture of Cuicuilco-Ticoman (13). (See Plate 13.)

1. Pay'-cos.

The next step was to fit Cuicuilco–Ticoman to the later phases of Indian history in Mexico. Cuicuilco and Ticoman material is stylistically akin to pottery and figurines found at mound sites in Puebla and Morelos, suggesting that the massive shrine of Cuicuilco in the Valley was an outpost. The baby-faced divinity leads back to the highly ceremonialized 'Olmec' culture in Vera Cruz, and the Fire God occurs not only at Ticoman and Cuicuilco and the Upper Middle Culture site of Jalapazco,[1] in Puebla, but also very frequently at Teotihuacan.

Actual examples of Teotihuacan culture have appeared in Gualupita and Ticoman. Yet much more significant was the discovery at Teotihuacan that its earliest phase was closely affiliated to pottery and figurines commonly occurring at Cuicuilco, Ticoman and Gualupita. Thus the beginning of the Teotihuacan civilization was a part of the same cultural manifestation that we have characterized as the Upper Middle Cultures. The lava-flow of the Pedregal must be dated in terms of the continuous history of the Valley of Mexico tribes. Cuicuilco was abandoned before the flow took place and, to judge from the destruction, an appreciable time before. Six or seven hundred A.D. then is none too late a date for the eruption (14). (See Plate 21.)

Therefore, we must conclude that one or two centuries prior to the dawn of the Christian Era sedentary farmers were maintaining themselves in the Valley of Mexico. Their culture was sufficient for their needs, and very little in the way of outside influence affected them. Towards the end, influences in art or, more precisely, religious representation began to modify their culture. Finally, in the third or fourth century after Christ they seem to have withdrawn from the Valley, giving way before the pressure of a new people.

These new people may well have come from the regions east and south of the Valley of Mexico, now embraced in the states

1. Hah-lah-pah'z-co.

of Morelos and Puebla, and seem to have been in a ferment of technical and religious experiment. They showed greater interest than their predecessors in modelling and technique, and exercised something of an artistic independence between villages. Their most impressive contributions were the introduction of religious architecture and the beginnings of defined ritualistic art. Their contacts in trade and in intellectual inspiration were with the peoples of the east coast, but they worked out their styles in their own way. Some groups built clusters of mounds; others seem not to have taken up this type of architecture. They abandoned Cuicuilco, where they built their largest platform, possibly owing to warnings of the cataclysm that later took place when the Pedregal was formed. Another site, fifty miles away across the lake, eventually evolved into the great ceremonial centre of Teotihuacan, the first and mightiest of the temple cities of Central Mexico.

With the foundation of this new capital the frontier of Middle American civilization shifted from the south and east of the Valley of Mexico to the territory north and west of it. The Valley was no longer the haunt of tribes taking their first steps towards ritualized civilization, but the proud domain of the Toltecs, traditional founders of civilization in Central Mexico, who had their capital at Teotihuacan.

TABLE II

SUMMARY OF HISTORY
OF LOWER MIDDLE CULTURES

EARLY PHASE: Permanent villages, gradual evolution and changes in pottery and figurine types. Long occupation, stages of which are better defined at some sites than others.

Early El Arbolillo I: Figurines, C3a, C3b, C1–2, C2, pottery incised black with red paint.

Intermediate El Arbolillo I, Early Zacatenco: Figurines, C1–2, C2, pottery incised black, thick black, white, white on red, vague olla necks; laurel-leaf points.

Late El Arbolillo I, Early Zacatenco: Figurines, C1a, C1b, C3c, C3d, D1, early F; pottery as in intermediate period.

LATE PHASE: Permanent villages, sharp shift in figurine and pottery styles, introduction of new figurine style, type A; evidence of local floods at beginning and end of Late Phase, which seems shorter than Early Phase.

Transitional El Arbolillo I, Transitional Zacatenco: Figurines, B–C, B–F.

Copilco, Middle Zacatenco, El Arbolillo II: Figurines, A, B, F, C5; pottery thin black with etched design, red on white, red on yellow, trade wares; stone points with tangs.

TABLE III

SUMMARY OF HISTORY
OF UPPER MIDDLE CULTURES

EARLY PHASE: Permanent villages in Puebla and Morelos; pottery and figurines in distinctive styles; trade connections suggest contemporaneity with Late Phase of Middle Cultures of Valley of Mexico.

Gualupita I, Cholula I: Figurines, D1, D2, D3, K, O; pottery, simple silhouette bowls and bottles in brown and red ware.

LATE PHASE: Permanent villages, introduction of platforms and altars; evolution from Early Phase in Morelos and Puebla; replacement of Lower Middle Cultures in the Valley of Mexico without transition; distinctive figurines and pottery which go through gradual evolution; ritualized presentations; some sites better defined than others; first settlement of Teotihuacan; lava flow of Pedregal after abandonment of Cuicuilco.

Early Ticoman-Cuicuilco I: Figurines, E1, E2, E3, I3; red-on-yellow incised pottery; disc earplugs.

Intermediate Ticoman, Cuicuilco II: Figurines G1, G2, I1, I2, E4, J, M, N; red-on-yellow pottery with white outline; incised earplugs.

Late Ticoman, Cuicuilco III, Late Zacatenco, Gualupita II, Teotihuacan I: Other sites in Puebla and Morelos; figurines, H1-5; in Gualupita, C9 and hollow figures; fire gods at Cuicuilco and Ticoman; pottery polished and elaborate tripod supports; carved earplugs hollowed in centre.

CHAPTER III

TEOTIHUACAN AND THE
CLASSICAL TOLTECS

*A description of a civilization, the monuments of which are the wonder of
Mexico, and an attempt to reconstruct the history of its creators from the
meagre and distorted sources available*

THE Toltecs or Master Builders were the first people mentioned in the annals of the Valley of Mexico. Their customs and
achievements are so wrapped in the mystery which myth
draws over the raw facts of history, and so confusing and illogical are the references to them, that a leading Mexicanist
once challenged their very existence (1). The facts of the case
seem to be that, in the late migration period between the tenth
and fourteenth centuries, marauding tribes applied the term
Toltec to whatever settled population they met, and later assumed that name themselves as a badge of advertisement of
being civilized. In our own cultural history we have frequent
cases of the names of stately European capitals being similarly
applied in wistful hope to the tiny hamlets of the first settlers
of North America. (See Plate 21.)

One set of annals refers to an imposing civilization whose
creators we may call Toltecs of Teotihuacan from their majestic capital (2). Other histories recount the lineage of chiefs
of different tribes, which we may distinguish as Dynastic Toltecs (3). If the history of Europe were recounted in fragmentary
records without consecutive dates we should have a similar
difficulty in distinguishing between the Roman Empire of
Caesar and Augustus and, say, the Holy Roman Empire, which
one writer has defined as neither holy nor Roman nor an
empire.

The Teotihuacan Toltecs have been described as great architects, carpenters and mechanics. They were skilled likewise in

agriculture, cultivating corn, cotton, beans, chili peppers and all the other domesticated plants known to Mexico. From cotton they spun thread to be woven into cloth which ranged from the fineness of linen to the thickness of velvet. The men wore robes and breech-clouts, supplemented in cold weather by sleeveless jackets, and were shod with sandals of henequen, the fibre of a variety of maguey. Women dressed in *huipiles*,[1] sleeveless blouses, and *enaguas*, skirts made by wrapping a long strip of cotton around the waist and legs, a costume which still persists in the Indian villages of modern Mexico. Warriors wore armour made of quilted cotton, and used spears and wooden clubs set with blades of obsidian. The club-wielders carried shields, and Ixtlilxochitl [2] says that some soldiers had copper helmets, although no trace of this metal has been officially reported from Teotihuacan–Toltec sites. Priests were distinguished by a more elaborate costume composed of a headdress and a long black tunic which touched the ground (4). (See Plate 24, bottom.)

The 'kings' wore robes like the priests and adorned themselves with necklaces and earrings. They wore socks as well as sandals, a great elegance for sandal-wearing people. They distinguished themselves as much by conduct as by dress, rising early and eating only at daybreak and at nightfall. They spoke little, but to the point. A 'king' had one 'queen', and neither could remarry upon the death of the other, although commoners might take a second or even a third wife. A 'queen' could inherit the realm from her husband, and her legitimate sons succeeded her, a statement suggesting that the austerity of the martial ideal did not interfere with the royal pleasure.

The Toltecs built their palaces and houses of stone and mortar and used the *temascal* or steam bath, which still persists among the modern Indians. They held a market every twenty days, or each month in terms of the Middle American year. These markets were located in Tula, Teotihuacan, Tulancingo,

1. Wee-peel'-ess.   2. Eesh-tleel-sho'-cheetl.

Cuernavaca, Cholula, Tultitlan and several other towns where remains of Teotihuacan occupation may still be seen. There is additional evidence that the Toltecs counted their years and used the sacred almanac of 260 days, according to the pattern followed by their successors (5).

The religion of this bygone era is difficult to interpret, for both the sixteenth-century Christian mentality and the late Aztec theology distort for us its true structure. Ixtlilxochitl reported a supreme being, Tloque Nahuaque,[1] who surpassed all other gods. However, to a Sun God and his wife, the Moon Goddess, tradition persistently dedicates the two largest structures at the sacred city of Teotihuacan. Tlaloc,[2] a Rain God, was mentioned as highly important, and a Frog Goddess was also honoured by a sumptuous temple. Quetzalcoatl,[3] Feathered Serpent, was worshipped as the bringer of civilization, but the same name was used as a title for the chief priests. There were persistent myths referring to the conflict between an old worship and a new, symbolized by a struggle between Quetzalcoatl and the war and sky gods of the later Aztec religion (6).

Apparently a basic Nature-worship was transformed into an elaborate polytheism. Later history tells of the struggles between the votaries of one god as opposed to those of another. The elevation of a god to the role of tribal protector led to the domination of his worshippers in the community, and was as important to the ancient Mexican as the domination of an economic or political system is to our modern populations. There was then, as now, the same masking of desire for power with conviction of rectitude. Probably, too, there was the same confusion of motives in the individual.

The history of the Teotihuacan Toltecs is as tenuous as their sociology and religion. The two chief sources, Ixtlilxochitl and the *Annals of Cuauhtitlan*,[4] refer to different localities, one

1. Tlo'-kay Nah'-wah-kay.   3. Kayt'-zal-co-atl.
2. Tlah'-loc.   4. Kwow-ti-tlan'.

at Teotihuacan, the other at the west of the lake near Azcapotzalco.[1] (7). The eastern history, written by Ixtlilxochitl, began very properly with the creation of the world and the four
or five Suns, or eras, through which life has survived. The first
era, the Water Sun, was when the supreme god, Tloque Nahuaque, created the world; and after 1716 years floods and
lightning destroyed it. The second era, the Sun of the Earth,
saw the world populated by giants, the Quinametzin,[2] who
almost disappeared when earthquakes obliterated the earth.
The Wind Sun came third, and Olmecs and Xicalancas,[3] human tribes, lived on earth. They destroyed the surviving giants,
founded Cholula and migrated as far as Tabasco. A marvellous personage, called Quetzalcoatl by some, Huemac [4] by
others, appeared in this era and brought civilization and ethics.
When the people did not benefit from his teachings he returned to the east, prophesying the destruction of the world by
high winds and the conversion of mankind into monkeys, all
of which came to pass. The fourth age, the present, is called
the Sun of Fire, and will end in a general conflagration.

These four eras are mythological, with a small amount of
historical information incorporated (Table IV, p. 78). The
Aztec versions, which had five Suns, were more purely theological. Yet these mythical floods and fires may recapitulate
calamities, such as inundations and volcanic eruptions, which,
according to evidence found at Middle Culture sites, beset
man in Mexico.

Toltec history, when it breaks through the background of
myth, describes a people wandering through Mexico. Under
the guidance of an astrologer priest, Huemac, they founded
the city of Tollan and elected a king whose reign was fixed at
fifty-two years. This was the length of an Aztec year cycle, a
major time unit having the same function as our century. The
list of the nine rulers is given in Table V (p. 79), but tribal events

1. Az-ca-pot-zal'-co.   3. Shee-cah-lan'-cas.
2. Keen-a-met'-zeen.   4. Way'-mac.

were seldom recorded until the end of the period. Huemac died at the age of 300 in the reign of the second ruler, after compiling a book of history and prophecy. This observation may be a back-handed explanation of the introduction of established ritualistic practices, including a calendar and architecture. The sixth ruler, Mitl, broke the order of length of rule, enlarged his kingdom and built the splendid Temple of the Frog and many other sumptuous structures. Mitl's association with extraordinary building operations had a possible basis in fact, as we shall see in describing the Temple of Quetzalcoatl.

Significant events for the reigns of the last rulers are recorded. The eighth had a dominion extending over Toluca, Cuernavaca, Yolotepec, Cholula and Jalisco. The old gods were still worshipped, but the cult of two new ones, Tezcatlipoca,[1] the great Sky God, and Huitzilopochtli,[2] the War God, were introduced. During the reign of this king a lady, Xochitl,[3] popularized an intoxicating drink named pulque,[4] made from the fermented juice of the maguey, which is to-day the standard tipple of Highland Mexico.

Topiltzin, the ninth king, who introduced the ball court, had a reign fraught with disaster. In his time the domain of the Toltecs disintegrated because of local revolts, invasions and the bitter toll exacted by famine and pestilence. Teotihuacan was abandoned. When they could, the people emigrated south to Tabasco and Guatemala. Those who remained were absorbed into the new tribes, and their lineage was assumed as a mark of honour by the ruling houses of the succeeding Chichimec or Dynastic Toltec period. Such is the story of the eastern Toltecs as set forth by Ixtlilxochitl.

The dignity and awe in which tradition holds the Toltecs affect the modern visitor to Teotihuacan. Here in the valley which bears its name, a vast area, three and a half miles long and nearly two miles wide, was given over to clusters of im-

1. Tez-cat-li-po'-ca.   3. Sho'chitl.
2. Weet-zeel-o-potch'-tly.   4. pool'-kay.

posing buildings. The whole zone was paved with a plaster floor, not once but many times. This was no residential city but a great ceremonial centre given over to temples and houses for the people engaged in religious activity. There is little trace of the humble refuse of communal life. Teotihuacan is an impressive monument to the toll which men exact from themselves for their salvation (8). (See Plate 22, top.)

The architects built their city in several successive precincts, extending southwards from the mighty Pyramid of the Moon. This was not a true pyramid but was truncated at the top to give space for a temple, and the ascending planes were skilfully broken to provide terraces. A broad stair led up the south side from a wide rectangular court. Additional buildings flanked this plaza, and several hundred yards to the east and west two smaller precincts added to the symmetry of the plan.

Two rows of buildings of impressive size lead south from the Moon Plaza. Excavation of one revealed lovely frescoes, the content of which suggests a temple of Agriculture. Another group of small mounds lies off to the east, and directly south is a second large unexcavated group of temples, which, from the emplacements found in the vicinity, is called the Group of the Columns.

The Pyramid of the Sun dwarfs all the other buildings in Teotihuacan. This great truncated pyramid, almost 700 feet at the base, rises in four terraces to a height of over 200 feet. The slopes were varied by their builders to create an impression of greater mass. The exterior was faced with stone and covered with plaster, but the pyramid proper was built of adobe bricks, made from the refuse-beds of an earlier era. The fragments of pottery, figurines and tools, embedded in the interior, were transitional between the developed culture of Teotihuacan and the Upper Middle Culture group. (See Plate 22, bottom.)

The Pyramid of the Sun is surrounded by a wide platform, constructed of square cells, walled by adobe and filled with refuse and rubble. Outside the enclosure are situated the houses for the priests. Smaller mounds still unexplored extend southwards, until another great enclosure is reached, in this case surrounded by masonry dwellings. Rooms with pilastered porches open on inner patios. There are no two-storey buildings, but by means of platforms some apartments are raised higher than others.

A river makes a natural terminus at the south, but across it lies a magnificent platform, the walls of which are faced with carved stone blocks; but the crowning temple has disappeared. The feathered serpent is the dominant decorative motive, and great heads carved in rugged simplicity project from the balustrade and from the façades. These were originally painted, and some still glare at the onlookers through eyes of burnished obsidian. Along the façade the serpent heads alternate with those of a strange being, who may be Tlaloc, the Rain God. On the wall behind them the undulating bodies of the snakes are carved in low relief, and sea-shells, all Caribbean varieties, are used to fill the spaces left by the curves of the bodies. The effect is massive and awesome. Though lacking the sinuous grace of Maya relief, the decorative scheme, none the less, is that of an achieved art. There was no fumbling in this work of many craftsmen, labouring through the years, cutting stone with stone. This building, called by modern investigators the Temple of Quetzalcoatl, Feathered Serpent, the God of Learning, is splendid enough to qualify as the edifice for which Mitl was renowned. The ancient name, Temple of the Frog, may have arisen from the symbolic association of frogs with Tlaloc, the God of Rain. (See Plate 23.)

Once the city was completed in all its mighty scope, a transformation took place. From the Pyramid of the Moon at the north, to the Temple of Quetzalcoatl, every single building was rebuilt. Rooms were filled in and façades covered up to form platforms for new temples. Not even the gigantic hulks of the Pyramids of the Sun and Moon escaped the addition of new stairs and façades. The Temple of Quetzalcoatl, as was fitting, received the most extreme alteration. The original shrine became the core of a high platform which dominated a huge enclosure, surrounded by a broad rampart. This wall supported four lesser platforms on each of three sides, and on the eastern wall behind the main structure three such temple foundations.

The later building is less massive than the earlier. There is less use of hewn stone, and rubble is extensively employed. Although the reconstruction extended eventually to rebuilding the whole sacred area, no violent shift in the styles of pottery or figurines suggests conquest by new tribes. The new architecture has all the earmarks of a religious reformation which destroyed the symbolism of one cult to uplift a new. Moreover, in one sector of the city the filling between the late and the early pavements produced much burned material, such as charcoal, adobe, pottery and the like, as if the debris from incendiary fires had been utilized for foundation material. The events recounted in the annals seem to reflect this architectural change, and possibly the new religion of Huitzilopochtli and Tezcatlipoca replaced the old cult of Quetzalcoatl and Tlaloc. Certainly the levies of man power, time and materials sufficient to achieve the rebuilding of Teotihuacan would have been enough to bring about serious popular disorders.

People continue to live, though their religion change and their kingdoms perish. Their basic techniques for maintaining life persist likewise. Therefore, tools and pottery give a more continuous guide to tribal history than the annals of chiefs or the soaring bulk of religious architecture. The material culture of Teotihuacan is an important index to the history of the early Toltecs. The contrast between articles for household use and for ritual became sharper as the Teotihuacan culture reached its full development. The rhythms of change in different types of activity do not always synchronize, and in the Teotihuacan culture we distinguish two building periods, three ceramic phases and five successive styles in clay figurines.

The beginnings of Teotihuacan culture are revealed by the contents of the adobes in the Pyramid of the Sun. The pottery fragments and figurines show an amalgamation of four culture strains, one deriving from the Upper Middle Culture, another containing the germs of the later Teotihuacan periods, a third tying in with the tribes of western Mexico and a fourth of unknown provenience. The little clay figures are hand-made and closely affiliated with Upper Middle Culture types. The early Teotihuacanos developed a new kind of idol made of crudely incised stone. A combination of three-coloured pottery, like that of Ticoman, with a lost-colour process, resulted in a four-colour polychrome which was highly characteristic. Clay earplugs were as common at Teotihuacan as at the Middle Culture sites. While the early Teotihuacanos did not make, style for style and piece for piece, implements identical with those of their contemporaries at Ticoman or Cuicuilco or Gualupita, their material culture comprised specific elements drawn from each particular site. The early Teotihuacanos took part in the same Upper Middle Culture migration (9). (See Plate 21.)

When the Teotihuacanos began their first big building operations their handiwork had become more conventionalized and more stylistically unified. Polychrome pottery gave way to simple lustrous wares of black and brown or vases and large jars painted in red on yellow. A flourishing trade sprang up in the importation of a thin orange ware that attains at times almost an eggshell delicacy. For use in their religious rites the Teotihuacanos constructed cylindrical wares of black or brown which they carved in ritualistic patterns, utilizing such techniques as simple incision, champlevé and, very rarely, intaglio (10).

Their stone and bone tools were not capable of much elaboration. However, since abundant deposits of obsidian were close at hand, the Teotihuacanos used this material lavishly, flaking blades to a scalpel-like narrowness and chipping tools of every variety. They made little animals of this hard and brittle substance, and ground it to mirror-like smoothness to make eyes for their great stone idols. In addition they used lava, not only pecking out great blocks for facing their buildings, but also carving designs and creating a sculpture. The great step taken by the Teotihuacan Toltecs was to formalize their religious art. Clay figurines which carried the main trend of artistic development in the Middle Cultures became conventionalized into simple little figures of men and women whose faces were reduced to their bare anatomical essentials. Women were shown dressed in *huipiles* and *enaguas*, men in the *maxtli* [1] or breech-clout. The sculptors painted the faces and the costumes of both male and female figures. The growth of ritualistic definition may also be seen in representations of the Old God, of a god in a human skin, later known as Xipe [2] (Our Lord the Flayed One), and in composite figures, having attributes of men and animals among which the jaguar predominated (11).

Their mastery of stone sculpture was most evident at the Temple of Quetzalcoatl, where able presentation was subordinated to the decorative demands of architectural ornament. To make incense-burners, the sculptors embodied the idea of the Old God seated under his bowl. Other artists traded for jade and porphyry and wrought these hard substances into beautiful masks and figures, which stand out as masterpieces of Middle American sculpture. Much of the work in stone has disappeared, smashed by the Spanish priests or broken into building-stones, but two colossal examples still survive. One is the ten-foot statue of the so-called Goddess of the Waters, now in the National Museum. Jade ornaments, *huipil*, *enagua*, sandals, every detail is set forth, not as graceful accents to a suave naturalism but as the ornament to an architectural creation. This goddess is a monument, a sort of monolithic building, that symbolizes the implacable force of Nature. The other statue was never finished. It lies still anchored to its matrix of living rock in a ravine near Texcoco. [3] Larger by far than the

1. mahsh'-tly.   2. Shee'-pay.   3. Tess'-co-co.

Goddess of the Waters, battered by the elements, the deity of Coatlinchan [1] cannot fail to impress the modern visitor. Its concept is grandiose, but the engineering skill was lacking to cut the sculpture free of its base. Prometheus in his chains may symbolize the tragedy of European thought, but to me this goddess, still an integral part of the land that made her, represents the paralysis of Indian civilization. (See Plate 24, top left.)

Painting and drawing found an outlet in the requirements of ritual (12). The frescoes of the Temple of Agriculture show an appreciation of decorative design combined with a sense of natural values. One fresco which has now disappeared but which fortunately was copied at the time of discovery depicts a ceremony before two divinities like the Goddess of the Waters and confirms Ixtlilxochitl's description of the Toltec costume. Carved vases present in full ritualistic detail the attributes of tiger gods and other divinities, and little definitive symbols indicate that some sort of writing was in priestly use. Unfortunately no sacred books have survived. (See Plates 24, bottom; 58, top.)

A ceremonial centre like Teotihuacan must have exemplified the best work of which a culture was capable. The civil centres have been little explored. In the neighbourhood of Teotihuacan, some few miles from the sacred city, great communal dwellings were built, embracing fifty and sixty rooms set about patios connected by passage-ways. The rooms were made of adobe and rubble-work covered with plaster, and supported a life of comfort and security. There was also an altar prominently placed, for religious duty was not confined to the ceremonial zone (13).

Another huge settlement lay across the lake at Azcapotzalco. Here the land is tremendously fertile, so that the old buildings have been razed to level the fields for present-day agriculture. Modern excavations to get the clay used in brick and tile

1. Co-at-lin-chan´.

have yielded a rich stream of objects, and a few days' digging produces hundreds of specimens. Thus we may judge of the abundance of life in Toltec times from the quantity of human possessions.

At Azcapotzalco and at Xolalpan,[1] near Teotihuacan, hundreds of skeletons were buried under the floors of the houses. Adults were usually seated, and the quantity of pottery vessels accompanying them suggests the richness of the economy. At Azcapotzalco sometimes the people had great feasts, and after partaking they cast their dishes into pits prepared for the purpose. Since clay idols were thrown in likewise, we may be sure that these festivals were religious in character. Once we found a great red-and-yellow bowl in such a deposit. It contained the remnants of the *pièce de résistance*, the upper legs and hips of a human being, the most succulent portions for festive consumption. There is also other evidence of human sacrifice. At the Temple of Quetzalcoatl individuals were buried under the corners as foundation deposits. At both Teotihuacan and Azcapotzalco shallow dishes, cut from the top of skulls, testify to other rituals involving sacrifice and death.

The Toltec dominion had its widest extent in the first architectural and second ceramic period. Confirming the statement of the annals, remains are found in the Valley of Toluca, in Morelos, and most abundantly in Puebla. At Cholula the Toltecs constructed a whole temple site of enormous extent, which later peoples covered with the single great pyramid so renowned for its size. This Toltec site has produced no carving, but one temple had a fresco decoration portraying the Butterfly God, a mythological being important to Teotihuacan religion (14).

The third phase of Teotihuacan consisted of a tremendous reconstruction of the city, followed by a decline in the arts. The architectural activity evoked no corresponding elaboration in stonework or ceramic techniques, save in one respect,

1. Sho-lal'-pan.

the clay figurines. The idols of this period represent some of the finest modelling ever achieved in Mexico. The faces were so carefully constructed that some students have considered them portraits. At first handmade, later they were copied in moulds and retouched to bring them to a detailed perfection. Finally, like the other arts and crafts, the portrait style degenerated, to be replaced by mould-made heads of coarser workmanship. At this time, the fourth figurine period, Teotihuacan ceased to function as a sacred capital.

Ixtlilxochitl has related that religious conflict, revolt and crop failure contributed to the downfall of Teotihuacan. To some extent we can corroborate this statement from archaeological interpretations. The architectural change has the appearance of having been made simultaneously, in contrast to the gradual development of the original city. Teotihuacan was built over hastily with the maximum use of original construction. The abrupt change in figurine styles suggests that a new god was honoured by this new presentation. The drain on human resources, implicit in such large-scale construction, would lead readily to revolt under the strain.

Crop failure could have resulted from deforestation and the consequent drying up of streams. At Teotihuacan lime cement covered all the buildings and formed the entire paving. The modern Maya Indians burn ten times as much wood as the quantity of limestone to be reduced, and they have the advantage of steel axes (15). It is not too fanciful, therefore, to assume that the Toltec masons, lacking metal of any kind, found it easier to use hearths of charcoal, obtained by burning over the forest, than to try to obtain the requisite fuel by chopping out their logs with stone axes. If this interpretation is correct, the hills must have been widely denuded of timber, with a consequent drying up of streams and erosion of fields. Furthermore, the barren aspect of the hills of Teotihuacan to-day must be due to something more than the requirements for fuel and timber of the post-Conquest population. The Toltecs and their

TABLE IV

SEQUENCE OF TRIBES IN THE VALLEY OF MEXICO, ACCORDING TO VARIOUS AUTHORITIES

	Phillips [a]	Ixtlilxochitl I [b]	Ixtlilxochitl II [c]	Veytia [d]	Duran [e]	Muñoz Camargo [f]	Clavigero [g]	Sahagun [h]	de Jonghe [i]	Mapa Tlotzin [j]	Mapa, Quinatzin [k]	Codex Xolotl [l]	Motolinia [m]	Garcia Icazbalceta [n]
Maceguales (created by Gods)	1	–	–	–	–	–	–	–	–	–	–	–	–	–
Quinames (Giants)	2	1	1	1	1	–	–	–	–	–	–	–	–	–
Tarasco	–	–	–	–	–	1	–	–	–	–	–	–	–	–
Olmeca-Xicalanga	–	2	2	3	–	2	–	–	–	–	–	–	–	–
Zacateca	–	–	–	–	–	2	–	–	–	–	–	–	–	–
Toltec	4	3	3	4	–	–	1	1	–	–	–	–	–	–
Nomad Chichimec	3	4	4	2	–	–	2	–	1	1	1	1	1	1
Chichimec	–	–	–	5	2	3	–	2	–	–	–	–	–	–
Teo-Chichimec	–	–	–	–	–	4	–	2	–	–	–	–	–	–
Otomi	–	–	5	6	–	–	2	2	–	–	–	–	–	–
Acolhua I Tlailtoque	–	5	–	–	–	–	–	–	–	–	–	–	–	–
Chimalpanecs	–	5	–	–	–	–	–	–	–	–	2	2	–	–
Chalco-Toltec	–	–	–	–	–	–	–	–	–	2	–	–	–	–
Acolhua II Texcoco	–	6	5	6	–	3	3	–	(4)	3	–	–	2	2
Culhua { 7 Tribes	–	–	–	–	3	–	3	3	–	–	–	–	–	–
Tepanec	–	6	5	6	–	–	–	–	–	–	–	3	–	–
Culhua	5	–	–	–	–	–	–	–	–	–	–	3	–	–
Aztec	–	6	6	7	4	–	–	–	–	–	–	3	3	3
Huitznahua	–	6	–	–	–	–	–	–	–	–	–	3	–	–

[a] Phillips, *Codex Ramirez*, 1883, 618–19, 622–4.
[b] Ixtlilxochitl, *Relaciones*, 1891, 17–21, 75–103.
[c] Ixtlilxochitl, *Historia Chichimeca*, 1892, 21–45, 61–5, 69–71.
[d] Veytia, *Historia Antigua*, 1836, Vol. 1, 139–56; Vol. 2, 3–10, 39–46, 87–101.
[e] Duran, *Historia de las Indias*, I, 1867, 10–14.
[f] Muñoz Camargo, *Historia*, 1892, 5–116.
[g] Clavigero, *History*, 1787, 93–136.
[h] Sahagun, *Historia General*, 1938, Vol. 4, Book II, 106, 116–17, 138–47.
[i] de Jonghe, ed., *Histoire de Méchique*, 1903, 8–20.
[j] Aubin, *Peinture Didactique*, 1885, 58–74.
[k] Aubin, *Peinture Didactique*, 1885, 75–85.
[l] Radin, *Sources*, 1920, 41–5.
[m] Motolinia, *Historia*, 1914, 3–5.
[n] Origen in Garcia Icazbalceta, 1886–92, Vol. 3, *Origen de los Mexicanos*, 283–92.

TABLE V
SUMMARY OF TOLTEC HISTORY

TEOTIHUACAN I

Manufacture of materials inside adobes of Temples of Sun and Moon.

Eastern Lineage		*Western Lineage*	
Chalchiuhtlanetzin	510–62		
Ixtlilcuechahauac	562–614		
Huetzin	614–66		

TEOTIHUACAN II

Construction of first-period buildings at Teotihuacan, culminating in the Temple of Quetzalcoatl under Mitl; establishment of centre at Azcapotzalco (El Corral I); wide distribution of culture to Cholula, Morelos.

Eastern Lineage		*Western Lineage*	
Totepeuh	666–718		
Nacoxoc	718–70	Huetzin	869 (?)
Mitl-Tlacomihua	770–829	Totepeuh (?)	(?)–887

TEOTIHUACAN III–IV

Construction of second-period buildings; introduction of mould; complex ritual in figurines; trade with Mayas; introduction of new religion; abandonment of Teotihuacan; incursion of Chichimecs.

Eastern Lineage		*Western Lineage*	
Queen Xihuiquenitzin	829–33		
Iztaccaltzin	833–85	Ihuitimal	887–923
Topiltzin	885–959	Topiltzin	923–47

TEOTIHUACAN V

Shift of Toltec centre to Azcapotzalco, possibly under Topiltzin; great ritualistic development of figurines; influence from Oaxaca; new religion and destruction by Culhuas.

Eastern Lineage	*Western Lineage*	
	Topiltzin	923–47
	Matlacxochitl	947–83
	Nauhyotzin I	983–97
	Matlaccoatzin	997–1025
	Tlilcoatzin	1025–46
	Huemac	1047–1122

successors, Chichimecs, Acolhuas and Aztecs, undoubtedly contributed their fair share to this wastage of the forests.

Tradition ascribes the abandonment of Teotihuacan to the tenth and eleventh centuries, whatever the basic causes. However, Teotihuacanos still occupied the outlying villages, and across the lakes the enormous city of Azcapotzalco continued to flourish. Teotihuacan, however, was a city of ghosts. In Chichimec times the makers of the Mazapan [1] culture occasionally crept on to the ruins to bury their dead, but they never disturbed the silence by building houses in the zone. A persistent tradition describes the great Aztec ruler Montezuma as visiting Teotihuacan to make sacrifices, but no evidence exists in the shape of ceremonial equipment left behind (16). The three or four Aztec potsherds found among the hundreds of thousands of Teotihuacan fragments certainly cannot be testimony to the pomp and ceremony of Aztec worship.

Azcapotzalco was an enormous city, where dwelt a large population. The decline of Teotihuacan and the gradual abandonment of the eastern towns must have added substantially to its numbers. Its people did not follow the architectural practices of earlier times and have left no great monuments. It originally seems to have been founded at the time of the first great building period at Teotihuacan, because the same handmade figurines and pottery styles exist at both sites. However, the religious reformation at Teotihuacan suggested by the rebuilding of the city and the making of the 'portrait' type of figurines left no trace at Azcapotzalco. No true 'portrait' heads occur among the thousands of figurines found in the western district.

A fully-developed mould-made figurine cult replaced the older hand-made techniques, but this practice was absent from Teotihuacan. Just as Byzantium for centuries carried on the tradition of Rome after the barbarians had sacked the parent city, so, on a smaller scale, Azcapotzalco maintained the older

1. Ma-zah'-pan.

tradition of Teotihuacan. Yet the figurine cult was carried to an extreme development. The introduction of the mould led to mass production of images by skilled workmen. Thus the details of dress and ornament, which defined the gods represented, could be rigidly fixed. Each household could be equipped in miniature with the outward elements of a ritual previously confined to special centres. Elaborate incense-burners studded with moulded decorations reproduced the main temple altars with their ritualistic ornament. The origin of this practice may well have been in Oaxaca among the Zapotecs, who not only made elaborate incense-burners of this type, but, since fragments of Oaxaca wares are found in Toltec sites, also shipped pottery to be traded to these northern people (17).

This archaeological situation clears up a discrepancy in the annals that has made modern scholars tear their beards. The *Annals of Cuauhtitlan* recorded a list of Toltec rulers that only partially in name and not at all in date corresponds to Ixtlilxochitl's list of the rulers of Teotihuacan (Table V). It would seem highly probable that the lineage of Cuauhtitlan referred to the chiefs of this western settlement which endured after the parent site had been abandoned. The Azcapotzalco region was protected by the lakes from invaders on the east. There was no such tax on the population as at Teotihuacan, where the people had to carry out a religious reformation in architectural terms. Therefore, the pressures from within and without, which caused Teotihuacan to crumble, were not manifested in the west until over a century later.

Civil war, religious strife and the yielding of the Quetzalcoatl cult to that of Tezcatlipoca contributed to the downfall of the western Toltecs at the close of the twelfth century. A large cluster of baby burials at El Corral, Azcapotzalco, suggests that starvation with a resultant stepping up of infant mortality may have played its part as well. Yet the conquerors of the western Valley were the first to take the name of the conquered and aggrandize their lineage by the assumption of great

D

age. Toltec arts and crafts disappeared, and their styles had no continuation in the work of the later people. But the name continued, and so did that old, old cult of making images, though the idols were now in honour of a religion with a new personnel of gods.

The Toltec era, the classical period of the builders of Teotihuacan, saw the full emergence of a Middle American civilization. The culture was unified and seems to have been diffused by an increasing population. In the emphasis on ritual and the direction of technical skill towards the requirements of worship this frontier civilization recapitulated the culture history of Middle America.

CHAPTER IV

THE CHICHIMEC PERIOD AND THE DYNASTIC TOLTECS

In which are set forth the complex events, political, social and cultural, which led up to the formation of Aztec civilization

THE classical era of the Teotihuacan Toltecs was an age of cultural unity. The people of Central Mexico made the same things, lived the same way and worshipped the same gods for centuries. Dissolution set in as famine, religious disagreements and the incursions of strange peoples corroded the structure of Teotihuacan civilization.

The succeeding era in Mexican history, 1100–1300, was a chaotic one which eventually resulted in that mixture of cultural unity and political independence which we know as the Aztec civilization. A tempting analogy is to compare the Chichimec Period to the European colonization of North America, where groups of many conditions and sorts struggled to populate the land and eventually incorporated the sum total of their experience into the North American republic. (See Plate 25.)

Religions and social systems and peoples competed for domination of the Valley. Several of the powerful tribes at the time of the Conquest had their origin in this era of confusion, and from their tribal annals we may extract a fairly clear picture of what went on. As each tribe recorded its own affairs with relatively little attention to those of its neighbours, cross references are rare. History, in our modern sense of utilizing past trends to chart the present and the future, did not exist in the intellectual structure of ancient Mexico, and the traditions of the successive tribal immigrations are in confusing disagreement (Table IV, p. 78).

The histories of five towns summarize this period: Culhuacan,[1] Texcoco, Azcapotzalco, Cholula[2] and Tenochtitlan[3] (Table VI, p. 95–6). According to the *Annals of Cuauhtitlan*,[4] a long, confused record referring to Culhuacan, Tenochtitlan and the politically insignificant Cuauhtitlan, the Culhuas conquered the Toltecs and lived for a time at their ancient capital Tula. The location of this Toltec capital is not clearly stated, but it was on the west side of the lake and may have been either the late Toltec site of Azcapotzalco or the modern Tula, which has some late Toltec remains, but presents more evidence of a heavy Mazapan occupation (1).

The Culhuas later withdrew southwards to Culhuacan, where they established a lineage of chiefs, the length of whose reigns they carefully recorded in their annals. In the middle of the thirteenth century a new dynasty came in which the historians called 'Chichimec'; it replaced the older line which they called 'Toltec'. References were made to struggles with other tribes, chiefly at the northern end of the lakes, but there was trouble with the southern towns as well (Table VI, p. 95–6).

At the end of the fourteenth century civil war broke out and people deserted Culhuacan, which became weak and a shadow of its former self. The rise of a new power, the Tepanec, who had as allies the vigorous but ill-established Tenochchas,[5] contributed to its downfall. Yet before Culhuacan succumbed completely to vassalage under the new order, members of its reigning house had twice been sought to found the lineage of Tenochtitlan.

On the documentary evidences Culhuacan was an extremely important city-state. The consecutive reigns of its chiefs stretched from the time of the fall of the western Toltec Empire to that of the rise of the important Aztec state of Tenochtitlan. Culhuacan was considered a centre of civilization, and for three centuries was a major Power in the Valley of Mexico. Yet a visit to the modern town discloses no lofty re-

1. Cool-wah-can'.   3. Te-notch'-ti-tlan.   5. Te-notch'-cas.
2. Cho-loo'-la.   4. Kwow-ti-tlan'.

mains, for the ancient city is completely razed. Only the temple on the Hill of the Star, which rises behind the town and dominates the lakes, is a memorial to its past splendour. For here took place, even after the Culhuas had lost their power, the New Fire Ceremony which ushered in each new cycle of fifty-two years and epitomized the spirit of Aztec religion.

Texcoco, on the eastern shore of the lakes of Mexico, was the most civilized town in the Valley of Mexico at the time of the Conquest. Ixtlilxochitl, a descendant of the ruling house, had access to the annals of his people and left a full history, distorted though it was by his wish to make his lineage rival the noble lines of Castile; but he had a strong historical sense, doubtless absorbed from the Spanish priests who educated him. His ancestors were a nomadic group which lived mainly by hunting and eventually, under a chief named Xolotl,[1] occupied the territory around Teotihuacan. They pushed west to Tenayuca[2] and in the process learned agriculture and assumed a sedentary life. While there they met other tribes of varying degrees of culture and assumed the practice of choosing a chief from a special lineage instead of electing him directly from the clan leaders (2).

About 1300 two brothers were in line for succession to the chieftainship, and one Tlotzin, who was not selected, moved back to Texcoco and headed his own line. When he died and his son Quinatzin[3] took the throne two tribes moved into his territory from the Mixteca area in northern Oaxaca and southern Puebla. They brought with them the worship of the god Tezcatlipoca, the art of writing and many other useful skills. So completely did these people transform life at Texcoco that the picture manuscripts portrayed the local population clad in skins and the immigrants in woven clothing to emphasize the contrast between their own culture and the superior talents of the newcomers. Quinatzin, who was an extraordinarily competent ruler, extended his dominions greatly by conquering

1. Sho'lottle.   2. Te-nah-yoo'-ca.   3. Kee-nat-seen'.

many adjacent communities. The idea of absorbing conquered towns into the victorious state, so obvious to a modern member of western civilization, had not yet occurred to the Mexicans. Instead, defeated towns retained their local autonomy; but they paid a yearly tribute and their chiefs had to make a state visit to acknowledge their fealty to the conqueror. Quinatzin had some seventy towns as fiefs, and his dominion projected down to the shore of Vera Cruz. His successor, Techotlala, succeeded in unifying the Valley dialects into one language, Aztec.

Texcoco and Culhuacan never came into direct conflict, for they were situated at opposite ends of the Lake of Mexico. There is evidence, too, that the Valley was not completely settled, for in the mid-thirteenth century the Tenochca were able to thread their way south to Chapultepec [1] without coming into serious conflict with the settled populations (3).

However, in the mid-fourteenth century there was serious conflict. A tribe called the Tepanec, which lived at Azcapotzalco, outgrew its boundaries. Led by an able and vicious chief, Tezozomoc,[2] it began to extend its territories. Culhuacan felt the pressure first, and internal discord developed, as it must when a nation cannot feed itself and has no room to expand. Some of the Culhuas moved up to Texcoco along the eastern shore and added their long-practised skills to those of the Texcocan community. The Tepanec, blocked to the south by dense populations and to the west by high mountain walls, turned north and east to raid and occupy Texcocan lands. Otomi [3] tribes, whose territory lay on the islands and the eastern shore of Lake Xaltocan, were pinched between the opposing forces, who would brook no neutrality. They moved north, and the two great Powers, Tepanecs and Texcocans, came into direct contact and war ensued. Tezozomoc won a signal victory, broke Texcoco and alienated her vassals. He quickly dominated the rest of the Valley towns, almost obliterating the empty

1. Cha-pool'-tepec.　　2. Te-zoz'-o-moc.　　3. Ot-o-mee'.

shell of Culhuacan's former dominance. His son Maxtla [1] succeeded this vigorous and ruthless conqueror in 1427. Having
the northern Valley at his feet, he oppressed the conquered and
interfered in the affairs of former allies like Tenochtitlan.
Yet he was to enjoy his conquests only a bare two years (4).

Indian governmental practice extracted tribute from conquered tribes, but had not developed a technique for forcing
payment without declaring a new war and making a fresh
campaign. Consequently a bond of sympathy forged from
mutually shared ill-fortune grew up between otherwise somewhat hostile communities. Tenochtitlan and Tlacopan,[2] towns
at the backdoor of Tepanec territory, made a pact with Texcoco across the lake; and the allies, rising suddenly, overthrew
the new power. Maxtla was slain, his city burned and, contrary
to the practice of the time, his people incorporated into the
allied tribes. Land was apportioned to warriors who had performed notable feats of valour. So completely did the allies
break the Tepanecs, that all that remains of their history is the
memory of Tezozomoc and Maxtla and some petty local chieftains who succeeded them.

The Texcocans regained their prestige after this war, but the
Tenochcas, who had begun as mere vassals, grew so rapidly in
strength that at the coming of the Spaniards they had man-
aged to eclipse their former lords, as we shall see in the following chapter.

These events disclose a picture of expanding populations
and ensuing intertribal conflict. This cultural history shows a
diffuse background of tribal arts and practices gradually welded
into a closely similar whole, Aztec civilization. The process
was achieved before Tenochtitlan attained eminence, so at the
cost of academic tediousness the term Aztec has been reserved
for the civilization, Tenochca for the people who so conspicuously made it known.

The civilization of Teotihuacan disappeared before the in-

1. Mash'-tla.   2. Tla-co'-pan.

filtration of intruding tribes. The nomadic groups referred to in the chronicles have left no identifiable remains. Hunters reduced to the bare necessities which they can carry on their back do not leave much trace of their presence. Other immigrants came from established communities and, after founding their settlements, resumed building houses and making pottery, thus reverting to their normal life as sedentary Mexican villagers. There were two well-defined cultures of this type which are called Mazapan and Coyotlatelco,[1] after the sites where their remains were first discovered. What temples and towns the makers of these cultures constructed have disappeared during architectural revamping in the Aztec period, so that we have to rely on pottery and other imperishable equipment to find out their tribal connections and their significance for the history of man in Mexico (5).

The Mazapan culture was definitely later than Teotihuacan, for its graves penetrated through Teotihuacan floors and its refuse overlay deposits of Teotihuacan discard. These remains were strongly concentrated at the north-west of the Valley of Mexico, but extended to the west as well. While in general they seem to have been associated with villages, refuse-heaps did occur at the ceremonial site of Tula. In the modern town of that name stone sculptures in a distinctive style, neither Teotihuacan nor Aztec, may, by the process of elimination, be assigned to these people. The lavish equipment of their burials suggests that the Mazapan folk were prosperous and well-to-do. At Chiconauhtla,[2] a frontier town subject to Texcoco, the population, originally Mazapan in cultural affiliation, shifted to Aztec styles with no transition. (See Plate 25.)

The pottery of these people falls into three main types sufficiently distinctive to suggest that three independent groups were united. One ware comprises deep hemispherical bowls with decorations made in wavy parallel lines as if by a comb. Allied are other bowls with vaguely outlined maroon designs.

1. Coy-o-tlah-tell'-co.   2. Chee-co-now'-tla.

A second ware is used for heavy bowls with tripod support and floors scored for use in grinding pepper. A third consists of bowls with flat floors and slipped in distinctive colours of white or orange. Such vessels were traded to Puebla, to the slopes of the volcanoes and to other areas bordering on the Valley.

In return the Mazapan peoples received pottery from distant sources. From Puebla and Vera Cruz they acquired a popular fine orange ware that was commonly traded to Chichen Itza [1] in Yucatan, to Guatemala, and even as far south as Salvador. They had also the distinctive pseudo-vitreous ware called plumbate, which had a wide orbit of commercial distribution, centring in Salvador and Guatemala, but reaching south to Panama and east to Vera Cruz, west to Tepic and north to Tula. This ware is never found in classical Maya centres, but appears in the later sites. In the Valley of Mexico it never reached the Teotihuacan Toltec, and its distribution ceased in Aztec times. Wares decorated in plaster cloisonné were also esteemed by the Mazapeños, and a few examples appear far from their chief source of manufacture in northern Jalisco (6). (See Plates 26, top; 27.)

The Mazapan people made or acquired by trade beautiful spindle whorls with lustrous slips and stamped designs. Their obsidian work was excellent, and the scalpels flaked off by pressure were the finest in Mexico. Figurines were mould-made, but poorly fashioned, a mother god and a warrior god presaging the Tonantzin [2] and Tezcatlipoca of the Aztec period. They worshipped also the flayed god Xipe, who wears a human skin, and in his honour they broke through the lowly limitations of their clay sculpture to make two life-size representations of him, monumental examples of the potter's art. A smaller figure, carrying in his hand a little vase of Zapotec type, was prepared with closer detail. Thus archaeological evidence confirms the traditional origin of Xipe-worship in

1. Chi-chen' Eet-za'.　　　2. To-nan-tseen'.

Oaxaca, territory of the Zapotecs and Mixtecs. (See Plate 28.)

This Mazapan culture was cosmopolitan, and was in touch with the products of all civilized Middle America. Its basic wares indicate a western origin. The suggestion of fused tribal elements in the pottery hints at the tribal amalgamations mentioned in Ixtlilxochitl's accounts of the history of the Chichimecs of Texcoco. Thus archaeological evidence corroborates the native histories, assigning this period to the twelfth and thirteenth centuries, when Mexican influence spread south to the territories of the Zapotecs and Mayas.

The Coyotlatelco culture is confined chiefly to the western shores of the Lake of Mexico. Excavators have not had the luck to find clearly demarcated sites. It may well be old in origin, for fragments of simple vessels have been found at Tenayuca, underlying fully-developed Coyotlatelco ware; and similar fragments occur in Mazapan territory prior to that occupation. A collection in the American Museum of Natural History from somewhere near Tula suggests a cross-fertilization of this early ware with decadent Teotihuacan elements, resulting in a potential prototype of the full Coyotlatelco style. The developed ware comprises bowls with well-executed patterns in red, which reveal mastery of design (7).

The chronological position is a little uncertain. Beds of unmixed Coyotlatelco debris occur at Azcapotzalco and on the Hill of the Star, behind Culhuacan. Dr Tozzer, who named the ware, found it mixed with late Teotihuacan material at the type site, but my wife and I excavated a Teotihuacan site of the same period without finding a single sherd among the 200,000 fragments we examined. At one or two places west of Tenayuca, Coyotlatelco sherds have appeared with Mazapan material. Mr Noguera found the extreme limit in lateness at Tenayuca, where Coyotlatelco and Aztec II fragments were mixed. The geographical and chronological associations of this ware suggest that the makers were Culhuas or Tepanecs.

Culhuacan, so important in the annals as the seat of a famous line of chiefs, shows to-day little sign of its past greatness. Yet excavations undertaken twenty-five years ago prove that its historical importance was not over-estimated, for it seems to have been the base from which Aztec culture spread over the Valley. Pottery, so dismal to read about, so important in reflecting tribal patterns, tells the story of this process (8).

Aztec pottery is found everywhere in the Valley of Mexico, and, owing to the Aztec custom of destroying household goods at the end of each fifty-two-year cycle, it can be identified in terms of relatively exact periods: IV, 1507-19 (the date of the Spanish Conquest, which prevented the cyclical celebration of 1559); IIIb, 1455-1507; IIIa, 1403-55; II early and late, perhaps a century prior to 1403, and I. Periods III and IV are represented everywhere. Period II is common on the mainland, but less so in Tenochtitlan, which was politically insignificant until after 1400. To date, Period I is represented in quantity only at Culhuacan. The standard ware of Periods II-IV goes through a consecutive evolution, but has a close generic resemblance throughout, while Period I pottery is much closer to the fine orange wares of Puebla which were traded widely throughout south-eastern Mexico. There is also a trade connection between Aztec I and Mazapan (9). (See Plates 25, 29.)

In the history of Culhuacan digested on pp. 83-85 the fact was noted that there was first a Toltec dynasty, which was succeeded by a Chichimec or foreign régime. It may not be stretching the manipulations of the historian too far if we suggest that the Culhuas changed their culture with their dynasty. Coyotlatelco ceramics, which have vague affiliations with Teotihuacan pottery, may represent the material culture of the Toltec dynasty, while the Aztec I pottery, completely alien to the preceding styles, seems to embody the material presence of the new régime.

Seeming confirmation of this situation comes from the site of Tenayuca, where great Mexican archaeologists, like the late

José Reygadas Vertiz, Ignacio Marquina, Alfonso Caso, Eduardo Noguera, and others, have carried out a superb dissection of one of the temples. It was completely rebuilt five, or possibly six, times. The renovation answered the ceremonial requirement of rebuilding and refurnishing at the beginning of each fifty-two-year cycle in compensation for the destruction at the close of the previously elapsed period. As the site was occupied during the Conquest, the reconstructions probably followed the cyclical ceremonies of 1507, 1455, 1403, 1351 and 1299, with the first building erected some time earlier. The fourth, fifth and sixth constructions (1403, 1455, 1507) are purely Aztec; the third temple built (1351) is a transition between the Aztec style and the simpler, more archaic methods employed in the two earliest structures (1299 and the original temple). The three completely developed Aztec temples correspond closely to the distribution of Aztec III and IV pottery, between 1403 and 1519. The transitional temple and the second building suggest that cyclical renovations were adopted everywhere along with the Aztec II pottery of the fourteenth century. The original platform of this Tenayuca temple could have been constructed almost any time in the thirteenth century, since the building of a shrine did not entail the celebration of the beginning of a fifty-two-year cycle (10). (See Plates 25; 26, bottom; 29.)

The Aztec civilization was brought into the valley at Culhuacan, where it gradually supplanted the defined local cultures. Where, then, was its true source? The most probable answer is Cholula, in the state of Puebla, where still exists the largest structure in the world in terms of cubic content. The devoted group of Mexican archaeologists, whose co-ordinated efforts have organized the rich background of their Indian past, have been analysing this monument by excavation and archival research for many years. The results are important. (See Plate 26, top, middle.)

Originally Cholula was occupied by an Upper Middle Culture tribe which later fell under the domination of Teotihua-can-Toltec civilization. At this time the inhabitants built a large ceremonial precinct, a maze of temples, platforms and stairs, constructed of rubble covered with plaster. Eventually new-comers, possibly with the aid of the resident population, per-formed the stupendous task of converting the Toltec precinct into a single great platform, traditionally in honour of the god Quetzalcoatl. This mammoth construction entailed filling in every building and courtyard with adobe bricks. On its top they erected altars and quarters for the ceremonial personnel. In one of the altars, Altar de los Craneos, they buried two people and made a mortuary offering of pottery vessels, some of which resemble Aztec I in many respects, while others show affiliation with Mazapan types (11).

Later on the Cholulans gave up these forms for ornate cre-ations in polychrome, in which pure design and ritualistic de-coration were elaborated to an extraordinary degree. The skill of workmanship, the proliferation of ritual and the quantity of production from Puebla and the south surpass the work of the Valley tribes even though the content is the same. Therefore, it seems reasonable to assume that in Puebla lay the source and inspiration of Aztec civilization.

The few annals preserved relate chiefly to this period, and their pages are filled with the history of Teo–Chichimec and Tol-tec–Chichimec lineages. Breaking off from their parent com-munities, groups wandered away to found homes in new terri-tory. Occasionally they settled in unoccupied lands, but they usually imposed themselves as a ruling class on some already established tribe. Often the conquerors called themselves by the proud name of Toltec, usurping the title of the chief civilization they destroyed. Thus arose the confusion of the early annalists, who, without the countercheck of archaeology, were hard put to distinguish references to the classical Toltec of Teotihuacan from tales of the warlike interlopers who assumed the name of the vanquished civilization (12).

Most of these wandering groups spoke Nahuatl, the native tongue of the Aztecs, and of many other peoples in western Mexico. Some, like the conquerors of Oaxaca, spoke the unrelated Mixtec tongue. Yet, whatever their language, these invaders joined in spreading over southern Mexico, Guatemala, Salvador, even Nicaragua, such kindred cultural elements as chiefly lineage, formal war, distinctive gods and characteristic ceremonial practices, which we classify as Mixteca–Puebla culture. Other tribes moved north, leaving a strong imprint on the cultures of Sinaloa in the north-west, and elements of this religion affected tribal communities as far distant as the southeastern United States (13). (See Plates 11–12.)

This movement of people, in contrast to that of their civilized predecessors, was not the process of settling unexploited territory. Over-population seems the most logical cause, since it forces nations to risk the hazards of war rather than submit to the pangs of slow starvation. The vanquished, whose people had expanded into unpopulated territory during the previous epoch, had had no need to develop military techniques, and so fell easily under Chichimec domination. However, in view of the intimate relation between government and religion in ancient Mexican society, such conquest meant the worship of new gods as well as the acceptance of new chiefs. It is likely that some tribes adopted the new religion previous to actual physical contact, so that they could the better resist invasion. Yet the factor of conquest strongly influenced the spread of Mixteca–Puebla culture by tribesmen of Nahuatl and Mixtec speech.

War has its advantages when made on the unwarlike. The thin coating of Western civilization which Europe laid over the globe has its minor counterpart in the late Mexican influence spread over Middle America by these restless tribesmen. The winner's gods must be good gods, so cults of Mexican origin spread through the length and breadth of Middle America. Just so the Christian religion had a ready acceptance in Indian America when the missionaries were backed by such redoubtable exponents of our gentle faith as Cortés, Pizarro and their coadjutors.

TABLE VI

SUMMARY OF CHICHIMEC AND DYNASTIC TOLTEC HISTORY

950–1100, EARLY CHICHIMEC PERIOD

Eastern Phase: Contact with Toltecs at Tula (Teotihuacan) under Xolotl; Tenayuca I pottery; rude culture.

Western Phase: Teotihuacan V and western Toltec Empire at Tula (Azcapotzalco).

1100–1247, MIDDLE CHICHIMEC PERIOD

Eastern Phase: Tenayuca occupation by immigrants; replacement of Toltecs at Tula (Tula); tribal government; foundation of Texcocan Chichimec lineage in 1232; development of fiefs; introduction of Mazapan culture.

Western Phase: Destruction of Toltecs at Tula (Azcapotzalco); movement to Culhuacan; foundation of Culhuacan 'Toltec' lineage in 1114; adoption of Coyotlatelco ceramics; first Aztec cycle counted, 1143–95; second Aztec cycle counted, 1195–1247.

RULERS

Culhuacan	*Cuauhtitlan*	*Cuitlahuac*	*Texcoco*	*Tenochtitlan*
Nauhyotl (d. 1124 after 60 years)			Xolotl 1115–1232	
Cuauhtexpetlatzin 1124–81	Teiztlacohuatzin 1160–1226			
Huetzin 1181–1202				
Nonoalcatl 1202–1223				
Achitometl 1223–37	Quinatzin 1226–99			
Cuauhtonal 1237–51				

1247–99, LATE CHICHIMEC–AZTEC I PERIOD

Eastern Phase: Establishment of Texcoco as Chichimec capital under Quinatzin in 1298; persistence of Mazapan culture in east; penetration of Coyotlatelco and temple cult to Tenayuca(?).

Western Phase: Foundation of new dynasty at Culhuacan in 1251; introduction of Aztec I pottery at Culhuacan, with Pueblan origins; construction of Building I at Tenayuca(?); Cholula rebuilt (altar de los Craneos); Cholula III pottery; Tenochcas at Chapultepec; third Aztec cycle counted, 1247–99.

Culhuacan	*Cuauhtitlan*	*Cuitlahuac*	*Texcoco*	*Tenochtitlan*
New Lineage			*Lineage Begins*	
Mazatzin			Nopaltzin	
1251–74			1232–63	
Quetzaltzin		Coatomatzin	Tlotzin	Huitzilhuitl
1274–87		1282–88	1263–98	1235–98
Chalchiuhtlatonac				
1287–1304				

CHAPTER V

THE AZTEC PERIOD

In which is recorded the history of the Tenochcas and the political background of Aztec civilization

THE Chichimec period witnessed invasion of the Valley of Mexico by various tribes and the gradual domination of these tribes by a culture and manner of life that seems to have emanated from Puebla and northern Oaxaca. The basic political unit consisted of a tribe resident in a town supporting itself from its own land with the supplement, if possible, of supplies derived from the tribute payments of vassals. At the head of the State was a chief of lineage who also performed ecclesiastical functions. Craftsmanship was highly skilled, and trade flourished to furnish raw materials for the artisans. This productivity, however, was directed towards religion and ritual rather than the creation of personal wealth. Religion was an elaborate polytheism based on Nature-worship, with some god or gods singled out for special adoration, but the working of the *tonalpohualli*,[1] or sacred almanac, brought the full force of divine powers to aid man in his life on earth. (See Plate 29.)

The history of the Tenochcas, the Mexico City Aztecs, shows how a tribal body lived and acquired the position of an important State. According to their own records, the Tenochcas started their wanderings in A.D. 1168, though this date is arbitrary, and possibly represents the date of the invention of the calendar system in vogue in Central Mexico (1). At first they lived on an island in a lake in western Mexico and crossed in boats to the shore. In a hillside cave they found an idol of Huitzilopochtli (Hummingbird Wizard), which had the useful ability to speak and give them good advice. The accounts

1. to-nal-po-wahl'-li.

differ, and some have the Tenochcas starting off on their travels with several other tribes from a group of caves in which they originated. The names of the tribes are seldom the same in any two annals, but they always refer to important tribal entities at the time the particular history was inscribed (Table VII, p. 102–3). These beginnings may be considered as formalized origin myths without historical significance (2). (See Plate 62, top right.)

The Tenochcas carried their new god's image with them on their journey. At each stopping place they set him up to be worshipped, and in return he advised them. Their method of procedure was to stay a year or more at a given place, while pioneers searched the land for another site and planted a crop there to harvest when the whole tribe arrived. The list of stopping places is highly dubious, and the different traditions disagree. Not until the tribes reached the lakes of Mexico are the localities mentioned easily identifiable or in common accord.

The Tenochcas entered the lakes from the north-west, via Tula and Zumpango, so there may be a basis for believing their original home was in Michoacan.[1] They seem to have made every effort to avoid fighting, by keeping away from settled lands. At one place they split up, at another they sacrificed three individuals, according to the prescribed ritual of opening up the stomach and tearing out the heart, and at a third place they learned how to make pulque.

Their records make little reference to the tribes already in the Valley, and their own entrance was relatively unnoticed by the others. However, the hieroglyph of Tezozomoc in one manuscript suggests the obvious conclusion that they had to have Tepanec permission to pass through Azcapotzalco and settle at Chapultepec, where the beautiful park now is. Here they remained happily for nearly a generation. Their neighbours seem to have been small but growing communities, so

1. Mich-o-a-can'.

that conflict was inevitable. The Tenochcas began the strife because their young men went up the lake to Tenayuca to raid and steal wives, a common North American Indian method of gaining prestige. Their more powerful neighbours became irritated and made up a punitive expedition in which Tepanecs, Culhuas and Xochimilcas took part. The result was horrid; the Tenochca chief Huitzilhuitl [1] and most of the tribe had to go to Culhuacan territory to dwell in serfdom, while the rest escaped to the lake, where some low-lying islands offered refuge. The main body stayed in Tizapan, [2] near the present San Angel, where they were under the eye of Coxcox, [3] the chief of Culhuacan. The Tenochcas detested the waste, which was barren in all except poisonous snakes and insects. Huitzilopochtli they still enshrined, but his words had sunk so low that the Culhuas came to mock him at his shrine and toss nameless filth into the temple (3).

Finally, however, the tide turned. Coxcox became involved in a war with Xochimilco and called upon his vassals to aid him. When the Tenochcas reached the field of battle they rushed to the attack and took no less than thirty prisoners, from each of whom they detached an ear with their obsidian knives before sending him to the rear. After the battle Coxcox made a speech praising the valour of his forces in taking so many prisoners but denigrating the Tenochcas who came back empty-handed. The vassals waited until their lord had finished speaking, and then inquired of him why each captive was short of an ear. The attention of the Culhuas being riveted to this extraordinary circumstance, the Tenochcas opened their pouches and displayed the missing ears, proving beyond cavil the measure of their prowess. Clearly the war-sacrifice cult had reached the Valley by this time, for the emphasis set on the taking of prisoners indicates that this was one of the chief purposes of war. Furthermore, a drawing shows the later sacrifice of the prisoners, a cult practice the accomplishment of which was to

1. Weet-zeel'-weetl.　　2. Tee-za-pan'.　　3. Cosh-cosh.

make the Aztecs dreaded by other tribes throughout the length and breadth of Mexico.

So great had the prestige of the Tenochcas become that they went to their lord, Coxcox, and asked for his daughter as a wife for their chief so that they might found a dynasty. Coxcox granted their request, and the Tenochcas were so overcome with gratitude that they sacrificed the luckless girl and draped her skin on a priest to impersonate a Nature-goddess, Toci. Then, with something less than tact, they invited the father to the ceremony. He, expecting a marriage celebration, was utterly horrified, and summoned his warriors to exterminate the Tenochcas, who forthwith fled to the lake, rejoining their brethren already there.

There were two communities on the islands at the middle of the fourteenth century: Tenochtitlan, which seems to have become an entity in 1325, and Tlaltelolco,[1] which was founded about the same time. They were both havens for malcontents from the mainland, and about the middle of the century each was large enough to petition the mainland tribes for a chief to found a dynasty. Tlaltelolco received a leader from the Tepanecs, and the Tenochcas again induced Culhuacan to provide them with a chief, Acamapichtli.[2] The accounts vary as to whether or not he arrived as a lad accompanied by his mother. The *Annals of Cuauhtitlan* mention that at this time the Tenochcas were erecting houses of stone, an indication that a community had to reach a definite stage of development before enjoying the prestige of an important lineage (4).

In the time of Acamapichtli the Tenochcas were tributaries and allies of the Tepanec and fought successfully against Tenayuca and Culhuacan. Yet their field of operations was minute, and a morning's automobile ride will enable the curious to see the whole scene of Tenochcan history. Huitzilhuitl II succeeded Acamapichtli at his death, and prudently ensured the

1. Tlal-tel-ol'-co.   2. Ah-cam-a-peech'-tli.

future of the nascent state by marrying the daughter of Tezo-zomoc. He was chief during the final struggle between the two great lake-powers, the Tepanecs and the Texcocans, a war which ended in the death of the Texcocan chief, Ixtlilxochitl, and the dispersal of his fiefs.

Chimalpopoca [1] succeeded his half-brother Huitzilhuitl, and his reign was fraught with disaster. Tezozomoc died, and his son Maxtla succeeded him at the cost of murdering a brother. Maxtla was frankly out for power, and kept the city-states of the valley in a ferment of intrigue and oppression. Finally he murdered Chimalpopoca, and also the chief of the neighbouring town of Tlaltelolco, adding insult to injury, according to Indian thinking, by stepping up the tribute payments as well.

The people of Tenochtitlan were seething with indignation, and the small mainland town of Tlacopan (Tacuba) was sympathetic to the oppressed. Nezahualcoyotl,[2] the legitimate successor to the chieftainship of Texcoco, had taken to the hills after the defeat of his nation and was stirring up opposition to the enemy. He induced the Tenochcas under their new chief Itzcoatl [3] to attack Azcapotzalco through the back door of Tlacopan, while he rallied the Texcocans and their tributaries to assault the enemy with columns coming both by canoe and overland around the lakes. After a long war of several weeks the allies were successful. (See Plate 63.)

Nezahualcoyotl doubtless intended that his State should regain its position as the dominant Power in the northern lake country. But he did not realize that when he formed the triple alliance for mutual defence and offensive profit he laid the foundation for a rival State which would surpass Texcoco. The Tenochcas and the Texcocans were each to receive two shares of all loot, the Tlacopans one, but the division was probably liberally interpreted by whichever chanced to be the strongest of the three allies. The Tenochcas gained land on the

1. Chee-mal-po-po′ca.   2. Ne-za-wal-coy′-otl.   3. Eetz′-co-atl.

TABLE VII

MIGRANT TRIBES, ACCORDING TO VARIOUS AUTHORITIES, COMPARED TO CERAMIC GROUPS IN CENTRAL MEXICO

	Histoire Mexicaine [a]	Codex of 1590 [b]	Codex of 1576 [c]	Cubas–vd. Muñoz Camargo [d]	Historia de los Mexicanos [e]	Códice Ramírez [f]	Codex Boturini [g]	Duran [h]	Sahagun [i]	Codex Telleriano–Remensis [j]	Codex Vaticanus A [k]	Clavigero [l]	Motolinia [m]	Muñoz Camargo [n]	de Mendieta [o]	Suggested Correlation of Pottery Styles with Tribal Groups [p]
Aztec	x	x	(x)*	–	x	x	(x)*	(x)*	(x)*	–	–	(x)*	x	–	x	Regulation Aztec of Tenochtitlan [p]
Xochimilca	(x)*	x	(x)*	x	x	x	x	x	(x)*	–	–	x	–	–	*	(?)
Tepaneca	x	x	x	x	[x]†	x	x	x	–	–	–	x	(x)*	(x)*	*	Tenayuca II (?) [q]
Acolhua	x	x	x	x	x	x	x	x	x	–	–	x	(x)*	(x)*	*	Mazapan [r]
Culhua	–	–	x	x	x	–	–	x	x	–	–	–	–	–	–	Culhuacan (like Aztec) [s]
Cuitlahuaca	x	x^t	x	–	x	x	x^u	x	x	–	–	x	–	–	–	(?)
Chalca	x	–	x	–	–	x	–	x	x	–	–	x	–	(x)*	–	Some styles resemble Cholula wares [w]
Tlahuica	x	–	x	x	–	x	x	x	x	–	–	x	(x)*	–	–	Gualupita III [v]
Tlaxcalteca	–	–	–	–	[x]†	x	x	x	x	–	–	x	–	–	–	Some styles resemble Cholula wares [w]
Cholulteca	–	x^x	–	x	[x]†	x	x	x	x	–	–	x	–	x	x	Cholula wares [y]
Huexotzinca	x	x	x	x	–	x	x	x	–	–	–	x	–	–	x	Matlatzinca [z]
Matlatzinca	x	x	x	x	[x]†	x	x	x	–	–	–	x	–	–	–	(?)
Malinalca	x	x	–	–	–	x	x	x	–	–	–	x	–	x	–	(?)
Quauhquechollan–Xelhua	–	–	–	–	–	–	–	–	–	–	–	–	–	x	–	(?)

102

																	Monte Alban 5 [aa]	
Chichimeca	x	–	x	x	–	x	–	–	x	x	x	x	x	x	–	(x)*	–	(?)
Nonoalca	–	–	–	–	–	–	–	–	x	x	x	x	x	x	–	–	–	(?)
Michoaca	–	–	–	–	–	–	–	–	x	x	x	x	x	x	–	(x)*	–	(?)
Couixca	–	–	–	–	–	–	–	–	x	x	x	x	x	x	–	(x)*	–	(?)
Totonaca	–	–	–	–	–	–	–	–	x	x	x	x	x	x	–	–	–	(?)
Cuexteca	–	–	–	–	–	–	–	–	x	x	x	x	x	x	–	–	–	(?)
Xicalanga-Olmeca	–	–	–	–	–	–	–	–	x	x	x	x	x	x	x	(x)*	x	(?)
Mixteca	–	–	–	–	–	–	–	–	–	–	–	–	–	–	–	x	–	x
Otomi	–	–	–	–	–	–	–	–	–	–	–	–	–	–	–	x	–	x	(?)

* Implied but not specifically listed.

† "These people, say the Mexicans, and no more sallied forth, although those of Tezcoco and Tlaxcala and Huexotzinca boast . . . that they too . . . are also of that land." Phillips, Codex Ramirez, 1883, p. 625.

a Histoire Mexicaine in Boban, Documents, 1891, Pl. 60.

b Codex of 1590 in Boban, Documents, 1891, Pl. 24; Muñoz Camargo, Historia, 1892, p. 8, footnote.

c Codex of 1576 in Aubin, Histoire, 1893, p. 4, both of text and translation.

d Muñoz Camargo, Historia, 1892, p. 7. A footnote by Chavero gives a list taken from Cuadro Histórico-Jeroglífico de la Peregrinación de las Tribus Aztecas Que Poblaron el Valle de Mexico, No. 2, published in the Atlas Geográfico de Antonio García Cubas, Mexico, 1858, usually called the Codex Boturini.

e Phillips, Codex Ramirez, 1883, pp. 624–25. Forty tribes.

f Historia de los Mexicanos in Biblioteca Mexicana, 1878, p.18.

g Radin, Sources, 1920, p. 33, Pl. I taken from Kingsborough, Vol. I.

h Duran, Historia de las Indias, I, 1867, p. 10.

i Sahagun, Historia General, 1938, Vol. 3, Book 11.

j Codex Telleriano-Remensis, 1899, p. 34, Pl. 25.

k Codex Vaticanus A, 1900, Pl. 67.

l Clavigero, History, 1787.

m Motolinia, Historia, 1914, pp. 7–10.

n Muñoz Camargo, Historia, 1892, pp. 5–68. The list of tribes given under this authority has been extracted at random point from the text. Muñoz Camargo does not specify the list of migrants.

o de Mencieta, Historia, 1870, p. 145.

p Noguera, Características de Cerámica, 1930, Pl. 32.

q Noguera, in Tenayuca, 1935.

r Vaillant, Correlation, 1938.

s Boas, Album, 1911–12, Pls. 1–36; Brenner, Influence of Technique, 1931.

t Chavero, in Muñoz Camargo, Historia, 1892, p. 7, misreads this sign Cholula.

u Radin, Sources, 1920, misreads this sign Cholula.

v Vaillant and Vaillant, Gualupita, 1935, Figs. 19, 27.

w Noguera, Características de Cerámica, 1930, Pl. 31.

x Peñafiel, Nomenclatura Geográfica, 1897, gives this sign as Cholula.

y Noguera, Características de Cerámica, 1930, Pl. 31; 1937 b.

z Noguera, Características de Cerámica, 1930, Pl. 6.

aa Caso, Monte Alban, 1938.

TABLE VIII
SUMMARY OF AZTEC HISTORY BEFORE THE RISE OF TENOCHTITLAN

1299–1351, EARLY AZTEC II PERIOD

Eastern Phase: Introduction of picture writing and other arts at Texcoco by people from the Mixteca; adoption of Aztec IIa pottery.

Western or Culhua Phase: Cyclical reconstruction at Tenayuca, Building II; adoption of Aztec IIa pottery, retention of Coyotlatelco (?) pottery; revolt of Tenochcas at Chapultepec, settlement of Tenochtitlan; fourth Aztec cycle counted, 1299–1351.

Culhuacan	Cuauhtitlan	Cuitlahuac	Texcoco	Tenochtitlan
Cuauhtlix 1304–11	Tezcaltecutli 1299–1338	Miahuatonaltzin 1290–1300		
Yohuallatonac 1311–21		Axayaltzin 1300–08		Tenoch (?)
Tziuhtecatzin 1321–34	Vactli 1339–49	Atzatzamaltzin 1308–24	Quinatzin 1298–1357	
Xihuitlemoc 1334–52		Totepeuhtecutli 1324–43		*Lineage Begins*
		Epcoatzin 1343–54		Queen Ilancueitl 1349–83

1351–1403, LATE AZTEC II PERIOD

Eastern Phase: Unification of language by Techotlala; political and cultural dominance of Texcoco; Aztec IIb pottery and homogeneity of culture; Cholula IV pottery; cyclical dumps at Chiconauhtla.

Western Phase: Decadence of Culhuacan; rise of Tepanecs at Azcapotzalco; cyclical reconstruction of Tenayuca, Building IV, Aztec transition; captive Tenochcas escape to build in stone and adopt lineage pattern with Acamapichtli; fifth Aztec cycle counted, 1351–1403.

Culhuacan	Cuauhtitlan	Cuitlahuac	Texcoco	Tenochtitlan
Coxcox 1352–76	Queen Ehualyenitzin 1368–72	Quetzalmichin 1354–65		
				Acamapichtli 1375–95

Acamapichtli	Tematzacocuitzin	Mamatzin	Techotlala	
1376–88	1373–78	1369–89	1357–1409	
Achitometl	Tlacateotzin	Pichatzin		Huitzilhuitl II
1388–1400	1379–89	1389–92		1395–1414

TABLE IX
SUMMARY OF AZTEC HISTORY AFTER THE RISE OF TENOCHTITLAN

1403–55, EARLY AZTEC III PERIOD

Eastern Phase: Political elimination of Texcoco in first half of period with later recovery; prosperity and cultural advance under Nezahualcoyotl; expansion of palace at Chiconauhtla; Aztec IIIa pottery; Cholula V pottery; cyclical dumps at Chiconauhtla and Los Melones, Texcoco.

Western Phase: Political extinction of Culhuacan; rise and fall of Tepanecs; rise of Tenochtitlan with organization of Triple Alliance; growth of conquest and war-captive pattern; cyclical reconstruction at Tenayuca, Building IV; cyclical dump in Zocalo, Mexico City; broad diffusion of Aztec IIIa pottery; sixth Aztec cycle counted, 1403–55.

Culhuacan	*Cuauhtitlan*	*Cuitlahuac*	*Texcoco*	*Tenochtitlan*
Nauhyotl	Xaltemoc	Tepolozmayotl	Ixtlilxochitl	Chimalpopoca
1400–13	1390–98	1393–1415	1409–18	1414–28
	(1408)			
			Tepanec Tyrants	
			Tezozomoc	Itzcoatl
			1343–1427	1428–40
			Maxtla	
			1427–29	
			Texcocan Lineage	Montezuma I
			Resumed	1440–69
			Nezahualcoyotl	
			1418–72	

1455-1507, Late Aztec III Period

Eastern Phase: Continued development of culture at Texcoco; growth of Chiconauhtla palace; elaboration of ceramics; Aztec IIIb pottery; cyclical dump at Chiconauhtla.

Western Phase: Political power of Tenochtitlan; extension of conquest over Mexico and Guatemala; reconstruction of great temple; increase in captive sacrifice; elaboration of ritual; diffusion of Aztec IIIb pottery; cyclical reconstruction at Tenayuca, Building V; cyclical dump at Nonoalco, Mexico City; seventh Aztec cycle counted, 1455-1507.

Culhuacan	*Cuauhtitlan*	*Cuitlahuac*	*Texcoco*	*Tenochtitlan*
unimportant	unimportant	unimportant	Nezahualpilli 1472-1516	Axayacatl 1469-81
				Tizoc 1481-86
				Ahuitzotl 1486-1503

1507-1519 (Conquest) Aztec IV

Eastern Phase: Growing friction between Texcoco and Tenochtitlan; last expansion of Chiconauhtla palace; Aztec IV pottery styles with good life forms. Conquest.

Western Phase: Tenochtitlan domination with coercion of Texcoco; maintenance of old conquests rather than success of new ones; cyclical reconstruction of Tenayuca, Building VI; Aztec IV pottery with many life forms; eighth Aztec cycle counted, 1507-59, incomplete with Conquest.

Texcoco	*Tenochtitlan*
Cacama 1516-19	Montezuma II 1503-20
	Cuitlahuac 1520 (4 months)
	Cuauhtemoc 1520-24 (murdered on way to Honduras)

lake shore, which gave them a strong foothold for further conquest. Since this new territory was granted to the leading warriors, a caste of power and wealth was established. Thus outwardly the conquest brought the Tenochcas from the condition of a feudal tributary to that of an independent State. Inwardly there was a change of feeling, a shift from an inferiority to a superiority complex. Itzcoatl, the fourth Tenochcan chief, expressed this attitude by ordering all the historical picture manuscripts to be burned, 'as they were not appreciated by the ordinary people' (5).

From the time of Itzcoatl the State histories are in very close accord. Those written prior to his accession in 1428 exhibit considerable conflict, often resulting in discrepancies of a fifty-two-year cycle or more. I think this lack of agreement arose from the split in the tribal continuity at the time of the Chapultepec defeat in 1300. Part of the tribe refugeed to the islands in the lake and founded a town in 1325 or thereabouts, ruling it under a tribal council and a main chief. The other group was taken to Tizapan, and became civilized according to Culhuacan standards. The founding of Tenochtitlan, from their point of view, did not take place until they joined the original colony on the lake, where, as soon as possible, they erected stone temples, and tried to found a dynasty.

Itzcoatl enabled the Tenochcas to assume Aztec civilization. His historical reforms doubtless coincided with ritualistic regulations as well, for he undertook the construction of temples and the ordering of a religious hierarchy. He ordained the ranks of the civil government and superintended the building of the city, constructing causeways to the mainland to ensure easy access. Systematically Itzcoatl began to mop up those independent Valley tribes not subject to Texcoco; he also won victories and acknowledgments of supremacy from the powerful Chalcas and Xochimilcas, tribes culturally allied more closely to the Puebla groups than to those of the northern Valley. To show his independence Itzcoatl had a brush with Nezahualcoyotl's Texcocans, and thereafter the peace between the former allies was somewhat precarious.

Montezuma [1] I, surnamed Ilhuicamina,[2] the Wrathy, succeeded Itzcoatl after his death in 1440. This chief, already marked as a leader in the wars of Itzcoatl, extended the domination of Tenochtitlan even farther. He successfully fought the Chalcas, who detested the tribes of the northern Valley, and crossed the mountains to raid eastwards into Puebla and Vera Cruz and southwards to conquer towns in Morelos and Guerrero. A fairly close military co-operation must have existed between Texcoco and Tenochtitlan, for conquests claimed for Tenochtitlan by Tenochcan historians appear as gains for Texcoco in the Texcocan annals. Poor Tlacopan disappears from the scene, possibly independent still, but certainly unconsidered in the vision of pelf, a situation recalling that of Italy in 1918.

Under Montezuma I the cultural aspects of Tenochtitlan progressed mightily. He took measures to ensure the health of his people, building an aqueduct from the springs of Chapultepec to bring an abundance of sweet water to the city. Around the eastern rim of his capital he caused a great dyke to be erected to dam off the spread of the lakes during the rainy season.

The conquests into Puebla brought the Tenochcas in touch with the highly-developed religion of that area, so that many additional temples were built in honour of gods and goddesses which were revered by the conquered tribes. In times of relative peace he revived the War of Flowers, a ceremonial contest between warriors of two tribes or groups of tribes, in order that prisoners might be taken for sacrifice without the economic dislocation of formal war. This practice was known long before in the Valley, the Tenochcas participating in such struggles with the Chalcas in 1376–84, but the Tenochcas had been so continuously at war that they were accustomed to take their prisoners the hard way (6).

The crops failed from 1451 to 1456, owing to severe storms

1. Mon-tay-zoo'-ma.   2. Il-wee-cah-meen'-a.

and frost. Many people died, and others, unable to support themselves, adopted voluntary slavery in order to share the bounty of the more fortunate. Usually a famine led to increased military activity to replenish the empty larders with supplies exacted as tribute. But in this case the situation was so severe and the Tenochcas so weak that they had to be content with a War of Flowers.

Axayacatl [1] succeeded his father Montezuma I in 1469. He extended Tenochcan domination over a still wider area, spreading west into the Matlatzinca country and south to Oaxaca and Tehuantepec. He conducted a campaign into the Tarascan territory, and met with a dreadful defeat which ensured the independence of these tribes of Michoacan up to their conquest by the Spaniards. This was the only serious Tenochcan military disaster until the grim days of 1519 (7).

Neither Axayacatl nor his successors was able to transform domination of a region into dominion. He did succeed, nevertheless, in reducing the neighbouring town of Tlaltelolco, killing its chief and denying its council the right to meet with the Tenochcas in matters of tribal importance. Tlaltelolco up to that time had maintained its independence and had grown at the same rate as Tenochtitlan, aiding in many of the campaigns. It was famous for its merchants; and its market, even after its subjugation, was the greatest in Mexico. Local jealousy, however, did not lead to war until both towns competed in building temples to Huitzilopochtli, the War God. Apparently this competition for divine favour led to war, whereas economic conflict did not. Ridiculously enough, the open break was induced by the insulting behaviour of the Tlaltelolcan women, who flaunted their backsides at the enraged Tenochcan visitors (8).

The religious arts reached their full development under Axayacatl. In his time was made the great Calendar Stone, which weighs over twenty tons and is twelve feet in diameter. The

1. Ash-ay-ah'-catl.

block was quarried on the mainland, and the allied rulers sent help to drag this gigantic mass across the causeways. Designed to symbolize the Aztec universe, it is a masterly example of a pattern, the detail of which adds to, rather than detracts from, the spaciousness of the concept (9). (See Plate 52, top.)

In 1472, early in the reign of Axayacatl, the life of a great figure in American Indian history, Nezahualcoyotl, came to an end. This Texcocan chief had begun his manhood in political exile, fleeing from Tepanec vengeance, but had fought and intrigued his way back into power. He even restored the fortunes of his people, who, in the previous century, had rivalled the Culhuacanos in the formative years of Aztec civilization. Nezahualcoyotl had a broad judicial sense which enabled him successfully to elaborate the administrative structure of a far-flung realm. Since the Texcocans before the Tepanec domination in 1419–28 already had a chain of tribute-paying vassals, this resumption of control in after years was not so much a conquest as the forceful exercise of due rights (10).

He took a lively interest in the construction of temples and public buildings, so that, for all its tattered decay to-day, Texcoco was one of the most imposing cities on the Central Plateau. His palace nearby and his bath, hewn from the solid rock of Texcotcingo, are visible proof of the rich luxury of his life.

Nezahualcoyotl took a profound interest in religion and the arts. He transformed theological speculation into a philosophy of religion and worshipped a single god, the force through which Nature manifests itself and from which the lesser gods derived their power and being. He encouraged the arts, and in his own right attained great renown as a poet and orator. The lore of the stars fascinated him, and he had a deep knowledge of the astrological astronomy of his day and age. In contrast to the bleakly austere records of the Tenochca overlords, his career was a model of wise administration. Not the least of Nezahualcoyotl's achievements was his keeping the peace with his arrogant island ally, Tenochtitlan, which was ever ready by intrigue, murder or open warfare to add to its wealth and power.

Nezahualcoyotl was succeeded by his son Nezahualpilli,[1] who ruled until 1516. The length of his reign indicates the possession of an administrative skill equal to his father's. He successfully undertook a number of conquests, but they are not so dramatized as those of the Tenochcan chiefs.

Nezahualpilli had an interest in astrology, religion and necromancy, as would be natural in a chief whose religious obligations were as onerous as his civil and military duties. His later years were weighted with trouble with Tenochtitlan. He had married a sister of Montezuma II and, as she was unduly free in granting favours to the young men of the court, in 1498 he took advantage of his legal right to kill her. The Tenochcas took this act as a gross personal affront, and directed every effort, short of war, to overcoming their ancient ally (11).

Axayacatl of Tenochtitlan died in 1479, while Nezahualpilli was young in his rule, and his brother Tizoc, who had previously been the war chief, took his place. Tizoc's most important act of office was to begin the reconstruction of the great temple to Huitzilopochtli, the War God, and Tlaloc, the Rain God. In commemoration of his conquests he also had carved the so-called Sacrificial Stone. This monstrous-sized vessel for burning human hearts has a relief on the edge, depicting Tizoc dressed as Huitzilopochtli seizing captives representing tributary tribes. Most of the towns, unfortunately, must have been merely reconquered, since their names appear in the previous conquest lists of earlier rulers. It is not a complete surprise to read in some accounts that Tizoc died of poison administered by chiefs disgusted at his lack of military success (12).

Ahuitzotl [2] succeeded his brother Tizoc in 1486. His first task was to complete the great temple the others had begun, in the dedication of which the gathering of sacrificial victims played an important part. He invoked the aid of Nezahualpilli,

1. Ne-zah-wal-peel'-li.   2. Ah'-weet-zotl.

and the allies made a two-year campaign into northern Oaxaca, amassing no fewer than twenty thousand victims, the high point of the sacrificial cult in Mexico. At the start of the dedication the captives stood in two rows, and Nezahualpilli and Ahuitzotl began the grisly work of tearing out the victim's hearts. Lesser dignitaries succeeded each other according to rank, until the awful immolation was completed (13).

Ahuitzotl's military campaigns extended south into Guatemala and as far north as the Huaxteca in Vera Cruz. He was constantly engaged in putting down revolts, especially in Puebla, where the Tlaxcalans[1] and Cholulans had resisted Tenochcan domination. His capital, meanwhile, had grown so enormously that he had to construct another aqueduct, a fact which indicates that sheer pressure of population was an important cause for the military exploits of Tenochtitlan. An unusually disastrous flood beset the city in 1503, so that Ahuitzotl had to send to Texcoco for aid,in restoring the dykes. While superintending these public works he received a head injury which proved fatal. Ahuitzotl's personality was strong and vicious. He was passionately fond of war, being a vindictive and relentless foe. Likewise he had those traits which so often accompany military character, lust for women and fondness for display.

The luckless Montezuma II, surnamed Xocoyotzin [2] (the Younger), son of Axayacatl, succeeded his uncle. Not only had he to keep the conquered tribes in order, but also he had constantly to provide captives for sacrifice. This bloody cult, which to the Tenochcan mind had brought such eminence, had to be maintained lest disaster ensue. He approached his uncle's piety on one occasion when twelve thousand captives from a rebel province in Oaxaca were delivered up to the War God (14).

The last New Fire Ceremony took place in 1507. The years immediately preceding, with their threat of an ending world, were especially ominous, since in addition to earthquakes and other supernatural portents word came in of white strangers,

1. Tlash-ca'-lans.   2. Sho-coy-ot-seen'.

propelled in odd craft, who were ranging along the coast. But the ceremony took place, and the world continued. (See Plate 29, top.)

Montezuma fought an unsuccessful war against the Tlaxcalans, but at the same time he succeeded in avenging himself on his Texcocan allies for the death of his sister, by allowing their force to be ambushed and wiped out. In 1516, on the death of Nezahualpilli, he appointed his successor without recognizing the choice of the Texcocan council. The ousted candidate revolted and the already strained alliance was broken (15).

A year later Grijalva [1] reached Vera Cruz, and in 1519 Cortés started his march to Mexico. Montezuma died that winter, stoned by his own people, according to Spanish accounts; strangled by the Spaniards, in the Indian versions. Cuitlahuac succeeded him but died of smallpox in four months, and the last of the free chiefs, Cuauhtemoc,[2] conducted the heroic defence of Tenochtitlan, only to be hanged four years later on Cortés' march to Honduras (16).

Thus ends the bare record of Tenochcan history, without a description of the people, their government, their laws, their gods or their arts. Lacking, also, is an account of the clash between the two civilizations, Aztec and Spanish. The records are abundant, and we can form a lifelike picture of the time. Before we examine the nature of Aztec civilization and the causes of its downfall, let us recapitulate briefly the history of the valley tribes before the Conquest.

This chapter has covered the rise of the Tenochcas and how they came to be the greatest example of Aztec civilization. Yet the events set forth show quite clearly that they did not originate this civilization or, beyond the sacrifice cult, contribute much to it. During their migration period, from 1168 to 1248, they were simple primitive folk. In their sedentary period, from the settlement at Chapultepec in 1248 to the election of Acamapichtli in 1376, they were busily absorbing the culture

1. Gree-hal'-va.   2. Kwow-tay'-moc.

E

of their neighbours and overlords, especially that of the Culhuas. The tributary period, from 1376 to 1428, saw the Tenochcas under the control of the Tepanec, cautiously trying out
the formal Aztec city-state organization. Not until Itzcoatl assumed the chieftaincy in 1429 did Tenochtitlan really advance,
at which time the city took part in the general great rise of
Aztec civilization.

On the other hand, Culhuacan was associated with the earliest
phase of Aztec culture in the Valley and was contemporaneous
with such distinctive styles as Coyotlatelco and Mazapan. The
evolving Aztec culture in its ceramic aspect superseded and
obliterated these earlier folk arts and was well established
throughout the Valley at a date when the Tenochcas were
nonentities. The historical position of Culhuacan closely paralleled the archaeological record, yet this early Culhuacan phase
did not seem to be a spontaneous development so much as a
derivative from Puebla and the Mixteca.

The availability of annals and the existence of competent excavations in sites like Tenochtitlan, Texcoco and Culhuacan
have caused us to weight heavily the testimony of the people
on the northern half of the lakes. Chalco and Xochimilco, to
the south, whose annals have disappeared and whose sites are
largely unexcavated, may have had a far more important part
in the history of the Valley than appears here. Pueblan influence is far stronger in these southern city-states.

Aztec civilization, therefore, was a dynamic composite of
many elements, some developed as an answer to tribal needs,
others incorporated by contact with foreign peoples. Constant change took place, as in all other human societies, resulting from the continual adjustments man had to make to fresh
situations. Since individual men and women make up a community, let us in the following chapters begin with a single
person and work our way through his social obligations and
economics to his tribal organization and religion, finally reaching the Conquest and its aftermath.

CHAPTER VI

THE MAN AND THE TRIBE

In which are set forth the basic ideas of Aztec education, government, law and social customs

THE social organization of the Aztec tribes was in theory completely democratic. An individual was a member of a family which, in turn, belonged to a cluster of families or a clan.[1] Theoretically twenty of these clans made up a tribe, each of them regulating its own affairs, but in matters of tribal importance joining with the others in a council composed of all the leaders. The council appointed one chief to control civil and religious affairs and usually a second for war. Originally designed for simple farming communities and presumably of an antiquity dating back to Middle Culture times, this organization later ramified into the governmental complexity of a populous and highly complicated city-state (1).

The working of a community is best illustrated by the position of the individual in it, a process which is described in the third part of the Codex Mendoza. Immediately a child was born it was washed and swaddled by a midwife. Since the gods governed the fate of a man on earth, the parents consulted a priest who looked in the *tonalamatl*,[2] or book of fate, to see if the day of birth was lucky or unlucky. Four days later the child's family held a feast both to celebrate the birth and to name the child. If the day of birth proved to be unlucky, custom sanctioned a religious fiction whereby the naming ceremony was postponed to a more favourable period. At the feast the guests sprinkled food and pulque over the sacred fire, which had been kindled at the accouchement as an offering to the Fire God, the Old God, whose cult originated in the time of the Middle Cultures. The

1. The term clan is used to mean a tribal division without connotation of male or female descent.   2. To'-na-la-matl.

child, if a boy, was shown toy weapons and tools which the parents placed in his hands, guiding them in the motions of use. If the child were a girl the parents made her pretend to weave and spin with toy instruments. A name, that badge of identity so important to man, was given to the child at this time. A boy was often named from the date of his birth, One Reed, Two Flower, Seven Deer, or from an animal, like 'Nezahualcoyotl' (Hungry Coyote), or from an ancestor, like 'Montezuma the Younger', or from some event at the time of birth. Often the day name was given with an alternative animal title. Girls' names frequently were compounded with the word for flower, *xochitl*.

Education began after weaning in the third year. Its purpose was to induct the child into the techniques and obligations of adult life as promptly as possible. A world in which handwork is universal offers a child a chance to participate in adult activities far earlier than in our heavily mechanized culture. Fathers supervised the training of sons, and mothers instructed their daughters. Up to six years of age the children listened to frequently repeated homilies and advice, learned the use of the household implements and performed minor household chores (2).

The principle food was the tortilla, a flat cake of unleavened corn meal, which measured a good foot in diameter, to judge from the size of the clay griddles used in cooking them, in contrast to the modern tortilla, which varies from 4 to 6 inches. At three the child received half a tortilla a day; at four and five his ration was doubled; from six to twelve a tortilla and a half were prescribed, and at thirteen the allotment was two. Supplemented by beans and game, this diet was filling and nutritious.

The Mendoza manuscript reflects the current Aztec ideas on child psychology. Admonition was the chief method of discipline up to the eighth year. From then on a rigorous corporal punishment awaited the recalcitrant child. This discipline ranged from pricking the hand with the maguey spine to exposing the child, lying bound and naked in a mud puddle, to the chill rigours of a mountain night. In view of the almost universal kindness which Indian parents show to their children, they probably seldom applied these extremely imaginative native corrections for wrongdoing by the young.

This type of training, not unlike that of a modern farm child, initiated him directly into the economic life of the home. The satisfactions in playing a man's part by contributing to the family welfare compensated the child for the heaviness of his social obligation. At fifteen or sixteen most boys went through a special training before assuming the full rights of manhood; under certain conditions they were younger when they received this special instruction. There were two types of schools: the *telpuchcalli*, or house of youth, for standard training, and the *calmecac*, of uncertain etymology, for instruction in priestly duties. The *telpuchcalli*, maintained by the clan for the children of its members, offered instruction in citizenship, the bearing of arms, arts and crafts, history and tradition and ordinary religious observance. The *calmecac* was in the nature of a seminary for special training in priestly and chiefly duties, and several of them were maintained near the temples of important gods. The *calmecac* seems to have been an addition to ordinary training, required by the development of ritual, whereas the *telpuchcalli* carried on in special quarters instruction given in a simpler day by the old men of the clan. Other schools trained young women to be priestesses; they also learned to weave skilfully and to make featherwork for the preparation of priestly vestments. (See Plate 39, top left.)

A youth was ready for marriage at twenty, and a girl was deemed mature at about sixteen. The parents arranged the marriage with the consent of the boy and girl. A priest was consulted to decide whether or not the fates of the couple were harmonious. Incest laws like our own prevailed, with the further restriction that marriage must be outside the clan. Having satisfied these conventions, the father of the boy sent two elderly clanswomen with gifts to the girl's father, who, following custom, rejected the suit. The old ladies returned again to consult in earnest with the parents of the prospective bride. Such a discussion was necessarily intricate, since it involved the amount of the bride's dowry, which was to be balanced by the gifts of her suitor.

On the evening of the wedding one of the matchmakers carried the bride on her back over the threshold of the husband's house. Elaborate speeches were made by everyone, following which the mantles of the bride and groom were tied together, symbolizing the union. The old men and women gave tongue again in the form of long-winded homilies, and at last a feast, liberally lubricated with pulque, took place. The bride and the groom, after this merciless treatment, retired for four days of penance and fasting, and not until that period elapsed did they consummate their marriage.

As is often the case in a warrior nation which suffers from reduced man-power, polygamy was prevalent. Yet the first wife took precedence over the others, and her children alone had the right to inherit. Concubines were permitted and there was, likewise, prostitution. Desertion was frowned upon, but a court would grant a decree of divorce under certain conditions. A man could obtain the right to cast out his wife if she were sterile, were subject to prolonged ill temper or neglected the household duty. The wife could be freed from a husband who failed to support her or educate the children or who ill-treated her in the physical sense, for the Aztecs had not invented mental cruelty. A divorced woman could remarry as she chose, but a widow had to marry a brother of her deceased husband or one of his clansmen (3).

Women had definite rights, but they were inferior to those of men. They could hold property, enter into contracts and go to courts to obtain justice. In matters of sexual morality girls had to be chaste and wives faithful to their husbands. A man transgressed the rules of propriety only when his illicit relations involved a married woman. Otherwise his wife could not formally demand his fidelity. While the legal position of women was relatively low, judged by modern standards in the United States, personal influence was great, and there were several instances where a woman acted as regent when her son was too young to assume the office of chief. In matters of tribal alliance we have seen how the marriage of a chief's daughter or sister to another ruler cemented an alliance. Moreover, marriages were carefully arranged between families, so that for a husband grossly to neglect his wife's rights was a breach, if not of etiquette, certainly of social contract. The priesthood may have offered a modest field of influence and attainment to women. However, history records no mention of any advantage deriving from temple service.

Men had the chief opportunities, and these lay in various directions. The early chroniclers, conditioned by their mediaeval Spanish background, spoke of hereditary classes. In all probability, judging from Indian communities as a whole, there was *rank* but not *class* in the hereditary sense. As in our own society, a man could attain high *rank* through his own efforts, and through his eminence his children would consequently profit in their own social adjustment. Yet they could not reach their father's position unless they earned it through equivalent tribal service. *Wealth* did exist, and property in the form of rights to use land, tools and other possessions created a social and economic stratification. In theory and practice Aztec society was democratic, and the communal ownership of productive property was its economic base (4).

A man attained rank through the measure of his tribal service. The wise farmer, the wily hunter, the brave warrior or the dexterous artisan gained admiration from his fellows because of superior skill. If his wisdom and judgment were conspicuous he might be elected as the clan representative to the tribal council, or even as chief. Similarly an individual who dedicated himself to learning the magic rituals to placate the god, could become a medicine man or priest. However, in the populous and advanced city-states activities tended to become specialized, and greater opportunity led to a more finely graded scale of social eminence. (See Plates 33–6.)

A married man received a plot of land directly from the clan or else took over his father's fields if the latter were too old to work. Diligent husbandry, eked out by making stone tools, pottery or practising some such craft for barter, could produce a good living. Unmarried men helped their fathers and were able to add to their prestige by taking part in the numerous military campaigns.

Since the capture of victims for sacrifice was the chief glory of war, an able soldier who could subdue his enemies and drag them to the rear received much honour. According to the number of captives taken, a warrior had the right to wear an increasingly elaborate costume. Consistently successful warriors could enter an order, like the Knights of the Eagle or the Ocelot (often referred to as Tiger), which performed special dances and rituals. Sometimes a warrior of unusual prowess received additional grants of land or more often obtained an increased portion of the clan's share of tribute. Having reached an established position by this means, he had a more important voice in clan councils and might attain a seat in the council itself. A special honorific, *tecuhtli* (grandfather), which corresponds to chief among the North American Indians, distinguished these men. The title signified high social, but not official, rank, and from these men who had distinguished themselves by probity, bravery and religious observance, high elective and appointive posts were filled (5).

In this stratum there were many positions of honour and influence, which, like petty political offices in small North American towns, were held in connection with some other means of livelihood. There were officials who kept order in the markets and tribunals which settled disputes in clan affairs.

Men of proven wisdom and experience taught the young in the *telpuchcalli*, or houses of youth. Others kept the records of tribute and wealth in the clan storehouses, superintended the distribution of this communal property and even went abroad to supervise its collection.

Each clan had its elected officers whose positions dominated the administration of the tribe. One official, the *calpullec*, performed the duties of secretary-treasurer and kept economic order within the kinship, drawing upon the members of the body for as much administrative assistance as his task required. Ranking with him, the *teochcautin* acted as sheriff, preserving social order and enforcing it. In war-time he commanded the military forces of the clan. Linking the clans to the tribe were the *tlatoani*, or 'speakers', the supreme council, composed of a member from each clan and exercising judicial and directive functions. The wisest men and the most distinguished attained this post, for on them depended the well-being of the whole tribe. (See Plate 39, top right.)

Just as the clan had its executive officers, so this tribal body elected four officials who controlled the military forces of the four quarters, or phratries, into which the twenty clans were evenly divided. They maintained order among the clans and exercised tribal authority in disputes and crimes that could not be settled by the clan itself. Two were especially concerned with judicial matters; the third was an executioner, and the fourth acted as an intermediary between civil and military affairs (6).

These four offices were the proving ground to test the abilities of the supreme chief and the religious leader. In Tlaxcala [1] it appears that they jointly exercised the executive leadership. In Tenochtitlan the supreme chief, *tlacatecuhtli*, 'chief of men', was always chosen from the four and often occupied first the position of 'Snake Woman', a name also given to an important fertility goddess, Cihuacoatl.[2] The functions of these high

1. Tlash-ca′-la. 2. See′-wah-co-atl.

chiefs are difficult to interpret in terms of Western civilization. Roughly the 'chief of men' may be said to have represented the tribe in its external affairs, like war and alliances. As such the office had highest significance to the Spanish observers who saw its holder as the leader of the tribe. The 'Snake Woman' was the executive peak of the internal affairs of the tribe, where civil custom and religious demand governed almost every act. It is important to realize, however, that these chiefs could be deposed by the council at any time, if their services were unsatisfactory.

The continual election of such high officers from the same family or lineage, when democratic procedure obtained elsewhere, is harder to explain. Tradition is strong in primitive communities, and a family that produced one effective man might in the next generation produce another. The council in Tenochtitlan chose successive chiefs from a fairly wide range - brothers, sons, nephews and half-brothers were scrutinized in the rigid proving ground of public service. Furthermore, a wise council, exercising its tremendous powers, could make a puppet 'chief of men' seem effective as its representative in extratribal affairs. Even then, to be considered for election a person of privileged birth had to meet the long series of tests on which eminence was based.

Two other specialized fields were open to Aztec youth: trade and craftsmanship. Trade was a new development in a tribal economy which was based on living off the land. The opening up of intertribal contact through settlement and warfare and the growth of material and ritualistic wants led to the establishment of a class, the *pochteca*, whose members travelled all over Mexico, exchanging local for foreign produce. They had their own god, and apparently lived in a special quarter. From the valley they carried obsidian, cloth and rope, which in the hot country they exchanged for shells, tropical feathers, jade, cacao and other regional riches. In time they performed an important political function, spying out towns to conquer and reporting on the tribute which could be exacted. There is a very modern touch about the economic and political functions of these merchants who so often brought military conquest in their train (7). (See Plate 38).

Craftsmanship, with the growth of technique, must have attracted many men to whom straight agriculture seemed drab and unrewarding. Potters, jewellers, weavers and feather workers came to pursue these crafts to the exclusion of other labour. The enormous elaboration of the religion called into almost continual activity sculptors, masons and painters. The market, still important in Middle American Indian communities, had a profound social significance, for there, in addition to bartering his products for those of others, an Indian could hear the news and widen his social and intellectual horizons. (See Plates 34–5.)

The priesthood offered a relentless sort of career. Religion penetrated into every part of daily life, and the individual participated in great and complicated rituals. Civic eminence depended greatly on religious observance, and chiefs led in the direction of ceremonies. Therefore, it is hard to recognize a priesthood completely separate from civil officialdom; both were mutually dependent. There was a priestly hierarchy, it is true, but it probably operated in conjunction with civil position. Permanent positions may have existed, but in the chapters on religion we shall describe more fully how completely the realms of Church and State coalesced among the people of ancient Mexico, in contrast to the cleavage between them in our own society.

Mexican society existed for the benefit of the tribe, and each member was supposed to do his part in preserving the community. However, the bane of working social orders as well as hypothetical social schemes are those unfortunates who, by mischance, maladjustment or just plain devilry, do not do their part. The Aztecs, too, had this problem to cope with, and there developed a social class of people who had lost their civil rights and become slaves. This they might do voluntarily or because they were prisoners of war or were punished for crimes or were sold by their parents. Their treatment differed according to the circumstances of their enslavement (8). (See Plate 38, bottom left.)

Military captives usually were sacrificed, but those who demonstrated some unusual skill were sometimes bought for domestic service or put to work on some communal enterprise. Criminal slaves lost their free status for such offences as failure to denounce treachery, membership in a traitor's family, kidnapping for sale a free man, selling another's property without his consent, theft without restitution when over ten years old or hindering a slave from gaining the sanctuary of a chief's house. Penal slaves were privately owned, usually to make restitution to those whom they had injured.

Voluntary slavery was assumed by the poor and landless who needed food, by the indolent who were too lazy to provide for their own support, by gamblers and by prostitutes who wanted finery. Parents often sold a child, to be replaced by a younger one when the first was old enough materially to contribute to the family welfare. Sometimes destitute people offered a bondsman in return for a loan from a more fortunate neighbour. If the bondsman died in service or the master took any property unlawfully the debt was discharged. To avoid this contingency the owner made the slave live at home and perform only personal services. Slavery, except in the case of war prisoners, was not too exacting. A slave could control his family, own property or even have slaves of his own. His children were always born free. What the slave lost was his eligibility for tribal office, which depended, as we have seen, on public service and was negated by his reliance on the bounty of others or his commission of anti-social acts.

An important aspect of the legal code of the Aztecs involved the loss of civil rights as a result of flagrant anti-social acts. In general, custom dictated and regulated human behaviour.

Membership in the community brought safety and subsistence. To break away or to be cast off meant death at the hands of foes or isolation as a solitary wanderer, a prey to marauding beasts. Competition for rank and renown existed in the field of public service rather than in the acquisition of wealth. Hence the anti-social behaviour implicit in attaining many of our own higher grades or ranks was held to a minimum (9).

Growth of the community to a size where none but the great were known to society at large probably tended to break down the sense of membership and participation, so that theft and like petty crimes increased as mutual responsibility diminished. The increasing complication of tasks and manners of livelihood led to disputes and injustices. In a nation of warriors skilled in arms, personal animosity flared up into bloodshed. Thus the tribunals mentioned had to be set up to exercise their jurisdiction in affairs of clan and tribe and to reinforce the powerful influences of public approval and disapproval. (See Plates 35, 41.)

Religious crimes, like blasphemy or robbing temples, were rare, for the disfavour of the gods brought disaster on the community and on the individual as well. Religion, however, did not enter into the fields of ethics, and no post-mortem punishment awaited the sinner. Special heavens existed for warriors, for women who died in childbirth and for people who died in certain specified ways, but this belief had to do with the favour of particular gods. It was not a carefully defined system of rewards and punishments.

Restitution for the sinned-against was the chief basis of dealing with anti-social acts, in contrast to our pattern of punishing the sinner. Exile or death was the lot of the evil-doer who endangered the community. A random sampling of crimes and punishment will show the tenor of Aztec law, and why it was never necessary to resort to imprisonment as a means of enforcing expiation of a crime. Cages or detention pens, however, were used to confine prisoners before trial or sacrifice. (See Plate 34.)

Theft was punished either by slavery until restitution was made or by a fine of double the amount stolen, one part to the robbed, the other to the clan treasury. Highway robbery received the death penalty, and pilfering in the market-place meant instant death by stoning, since that petty crime militated against the social advantages of the gathering. To steal corn, the staple of life, when growing in the field, was a serious offence, demanding the death penalty or slavery, but a way-farer might with impunity satisfy his hunger by plucking ears from rows adjacent to the road. To filch gold, silver and jade, precious substances usually reserved for religious ornaments, was also a mortal crime.

Murder, even of a slave, brought the death penalty. Rebels and traitors received the same fate, but kidnappers were sold into slavery. Drunkenness was a serious crime except on pre-scribed ceremonial occasions. Social disapproval, public dis-grace, even death by stoning or beating, were penalties suffer-ed by the intemperate. However, the old of both sexes, who had fulfilled their tribal obligations, were allowed great lati-tude in their potations.

The witch or practiser of black magic was sacrificed, and death was likewise the lot of him who impersonated a high official. A slanderer had his lips cut off and sometimes his ears as well. Brawling and fighting in the market-place were dealt with severely, but in an ordinary case of assault the assailant paid for the cure of the assailed and for any damage done. Adultery, when committed outside the pale of the divorce laws, was punished with great severity, even death. Hanging was the usual penalty for violation of the incest laws, and sodo-my was punished with revolting brutality.

Thus reduced to cited instances, Aztec law was brutal. Actu-ally, from childhood on, the individual grew up into correct social behaviour; the violator of the code met with serious consequences. All people had some kind of personal property, but land belonged to the tribe, and only its produce to the individual. Therefore, the elaborate legislation surrounding our own property concepts was unnecessary.

There was little to harass the individual intellectually or economically. Existence was subject to divine favour, and a man fared much as did his fellows. Large as some towns were – Mexico City had 300,000 people – the sense of community was strong. Freedom of thought, individual liberty, personal fortunes, were non-existent, but people lived according to a code that had worked well and continuously for centuries. An Aztec would have been horrified at the naked isolation of an individual's life in our Western world.

CHAPTER VII

ECONOMY

The Domestic and Tribal Economy of the Aztec People

THE Aztec social system provided a means by which people could exist harmoniously together in considerable numbers. The domestic and tribal economy of the Aztecs offered the food, shelter, tools and clothing to which man largely owes his dominant position on earth. The measure of a human society may be gauged by the relationship between the organization of the people themselves and their use of materials to build houses and equip them. The Aztecs' economy had the same basic simplicity as had their social organization; likewise it had the same flexibility in expanding to meet the needs of a growing population (1).

Agriculture was the basis of Aztec life, and corn, *zea mays*, was the chief food plant. The cultivation of plants ensured a food supply near at hand, which was not subject to the fluctuations of game, and thereby enabled man to take thought for the morrow. The clan system, as we have seen, recognized that the fruits of the land supported the tribe. Therefore, it was only natural that the tribe should own and control the land which supported its members (2). (See Plate 38.)

The tribal council divided the land among the clans, and the leaders of each, in turn, apportioned its share among the heads of families justly and equitably. Sections were also reserved for the maintenance of the chief and the temple staff, for war supplies and the payment of tribute; these were worked communally, with some amount, no doubt, of slave labour. At the death of a tenant the land passed to his sons. If he died without issue the holding reverted to the clan for re-division, as was also the case if a tenant failed to cultivate his plot for a period of two years. Such a system could work equitably and profitably for all concerned so long as a society was relatively static and plenty of arable land was at hand. However, in the Valley of Mexico inequalities developed in the system.

The growing population of the Valley tribes used up all the available land, and families or clans had no way of adding to their farm holdings. A plot which produced ample supplies for a small family might yield a bare subsistence or less for a larger one. Normal variation in the richness of soil would result in similar injustices. Under such conditions the chiefs and priests who lived off the public lands would be far better off than the ordinary citizen whose holding, generation by generation, tended to diminish. Thus friction leading to foreign war and internal revolt was bound to result whenever a tribe could not expand its territorial limits to meet the needs of its population. The considerable migrations, like those of the Culhuas to Texcoco and Tenochtitlan or the Mixtec people to Texcoco years earlier, had their basis in a pressing economic necessity (3).

The Tenochcas, who came late to the Valley, at a time when land was at a premium, had, we have seen, a difficult time in withstanding their hungry neighbours. Forced to retreat to islands in the lake, they met the land problem in the same ingenious way as did the Chalcas, Xochimilcas and the tribes to the north-west, in Lake Zumpango.

This method was to create *chinampas*, the so-called 'floating gardens'. The *chinampa* was, in reality, a small artificial island, made by scooping up mud from the marshy borders of the lakes and at first holding it in place by a revetment of reeds and later by trees whose roots bound the earth solidly together. Water flowed into the narrow pits, making them into canals. Fresh mud was always added before planting, so that the fertility of the earth was constantly renewed. The Tenochcas and their neighbours thus converted great sections of otherwise unproductive marsh, flooded in the rainy season, into a grid of canals and fields, the fertility of which is equalled only by the river-flooded lands of the Nile Delta. *Chinampa* agriculture continues to-day in the districts of Xochimilco and Chalco, where most of the vegetables are grown for the modern metropolis of Mexico City. The inhabitants still use the Aztec language and occupy the same lands as did their ancestors, renewing them each year by the same methods as used in Aztec times. The outlines of former beds may be seen for a considerable distance round about, since the modern draining of Lake Texcoco has dried up much of the lake area of the Valley of Mexico (4). (See Plate 37, bottom.)

When the Tenochcas moved into the lake they achieved living room. As the city grew it could incorporate the adjacent garden-beds for house foundations, while the increase in population could be fed by building new *chinampas* on the outskirts of the farming area. Thus much of their success may be attributed to the freedom from internal strife achieved by the relatively unlimited possibilities of *chinampa* agriculture.

The Tenochcas supplemented their land hunger by another means. In conquered territories successful warriors received grants of land which were worked by members of the defeated tribe. Small colonies sometimes lived off this land to guard against revolt in the subjugated area. Such property passed from father to son, but if there were no heir it reverted to the tribal authority, not the clan in which the tenant had membership. Other such land must have been held for the benefit of the religious organization. Thus the central authority of Tenochtitlan, and presumably Texcoco as well, held considerable property to support the elaborate pomp of Church and State without straining the resources of the tribesmen. The relative fluidity of such real estate gave the tribal authority a wherewithal to adjust inequalities and dissatisfactions among the more ambitious tribal members. Naturally, as the Aztec peoples were less highly developed socially than ourselves, they did not attain our own elaborate system of rewards and adjustments by means of federal, state and municipal appointments (5).

A powerful Aztec tribe had another source of support: tribute. The levies often consisted of foodstuffs and raw materials, both native and foreign to the Valley, and also included warriors' and priests' costumes, mantles, pottery and other articles of craftsmanship. Distributed throughout the community these goods enriched both communal enterprise and private convenience (6). (See Plates 62, middle left, 64.)

Manufacture and trade were beginning to play an important part in Aztec economy, although not to the extent of societies which have developed media of exchange, like money, and therefore emphasize personal wealth in the possession of such a commodity. Manufacture was in the handicraft stage, carried on as a supplement to the main business of raising food. Most households were self-sufficient, making whatever they required in the way of tools, utensils or clothing. However, certain towns had access to natural resources which others had not and developed special skill in exploiting them. A town might have a good clay bed, for example, and its pottery would be far superior to that of surrounding communities. Another village would be especially successful in growing peppers, while a third might have in its territory a good quality of obsidian or flint for making stone tools. Thus such products would be exchanged by one town for the produce of another and even redistributed by the same process. Shells from the Caribbean have been traded from hand to hand as far as the central United States; pottery vases from Salvador were carried to distant Tepic [1] in Mexico; gold ornaments from Panama appeared as votive offerings in the Sacred Well of Chichen Itza in Yucatan (7). (See Plate 38.)

Such regional specialization was accompanied by the perfectly natural tendency of individuals to exploit what they made and produced with greater aptitude. As technical knowledge grew specialization increased, and the market became an important institution. Each town held one at specified inter-

1. Te-peek'.

vals to which people came from great distances. At Tlaltelolco
the daily market was a wonder of the Western world, exciting
by its lavish variety the admiring envy of the Spaniards. The
importance of the market still persists in Indian communities,
so much so that in Guatemala the people travel miles to exchange their produce, and so important is the market as a social function that a merchant will not dispose of his produce
except at that place, even though offered payment far in excess
of its market value (8).

Barter was the only means of exchange, and value was established by desirability and rarity. Money, an exchange
medium of fixed value, did not exist. However, something
had to be found which would balance an inequality of exchange by being not too valuable to use in adjusting small
transactions and at the same time universally wanted. The cacao bean answered this requirement and was easily portable as
well. The Aztecs were extremely fond of chocolate (the word
itself is of Aztec derivation), so that beans were gladly converted into the national luxury drink. Quills of gold dust were
sometimes used as an exchange medium, as were crescent-
shaped knives of thin-beaten copper. These last had not the
common acceptance or the utility of cacao beans, although
they represented easily portable value (9).

The most precious substance among the Aztecs was jade, or
stones resembling it in texture and colour. Both jadeite and
nephrite occur in the New World, and the American variety is
distinguishable from the Asiatic stone. Uncut stones are seldom seen to-day, for there is no lapidaries' market in modern
Middle America or the United States, whereas jade is still extensively worked in China, so that men find it worth their
while to search rivers in Burma for boulders of this rare substance. (See Plate 3.)

The testimony of the Conquistador Bernal Diaz is con-
clusive on this point of value. During the night when Cortés
retreated from Mexico, the leader, after taking off his share of

treasure, turned the surplus over to his troops. Many, burdened down with gold, drowned ignominiously in the canals. Diaz, however, noted Indian usage and confined himself to four jades which he was able to exchange later and which, in his words, 'served me well in healing my wounds and gathering me food' (10).

The Aztecs did not have our modern esteem for gold, so the Spaniards had great difficulty in getting it at first. The Mexican Indians responded to the invaders' demands for objects of value by offering jade and turquoise, those substances most precious to themselves. Such misguided compliance was highly irritating to Cortés and his men, who had no ethnological training; nor, it is only fair to say, would they have wanted such education, were it available. Gold was valuable to the Aztecs only for the ornaments which could be made from it, and silver may have had an even greater value, since nodules were rare and the Indians had no technique for smelting the ore (11). (See Plates 46–47.)

Thus the Aztecs did not hold our ideas of value and wealth. Yet they contributed much to our prosperity and well-being, partly through being forced as slaves to work the gold and silver mines, whose modern economic significance they so little understood, and even more through the enrichment of the world's supply of foods. In addition to corn of several varieties, the Aztecs developed many sorts of beans, a very nutritive addition to human diet because of the high protein content. Squash, gourds, *chia*, *camotes*, green and red peppers, alligator pears and tomatoes were products of the versatile Middle American farmer, enriching the Aztec diet and that of the modern world. Trade with southern Vera Cruz brought chocolate, vanilla and pineapples to the Aztec larder (12).

The maguey plant, or agave, was important to household economy for its sap, which was fermented to make a kind of beer. Not only was this pulque used both as a tipple and a ceremonial intoxicant, but it had an important nutritive effect as well in counterbalancing the lack of greens in the Mexican diet. The plant itself had many other uses. Its fibres could be twisted into twine or rope and woven into containers or even clothing. The thorns were excellent needles and had a more lugubrious use as instruments for mortifying the flesh in religious penances. The leaves as a whole were sometimes employed in constructing shelters or in roofing huts. Small wonder that the maguey and the corn plants were symbolized as goddesses and worshipped accordingly.

The Aztecs cultivated cotton in many varieties. Tobacco they smoked for the most part in hollow reeds as a sort of cigarette. Late in their history they also used elbow-shaped pipes, probably for some ceremonial purpose, much as our modern Pueblos restrict pipe-smoking to rain-inducing rituals. They consumed quantities of copal gum as incense during religious ceremonies and obtained rubber from Vera Cruz and the south, as well as from the dwarf guayule plant found in northern Mexico. The Aztecs, like us, found this material indispensable to their culture, for balls in their ceremonial game, *tlachtli*, and as a gum to fix feathers and other adornments to costumes. Bitumen, which came from the oil seepages in Vera Cruz, had its function as an adhesive and as a body-paint. In western Mexico the Indians prepared a serviceable lacquer which they used to coat gourds and wooden trays. This incomplete list of plants and substances cultivated and exploited by the Aztecs and their neighbours gives an idea of our deep indebtedness to these past civilizations. The original inventors and innovators are lost in the black obscurity of American history, but the fruit of their ingenuity plays an important part in our modern economy.

As opposed to this wealth of plants, the Aztecs were poor in domesticated animals. They had several varieties of dogs, one of which was bred for food, but they never used this animal for transport, as did Indians of our Northern plains. The turkey was their chief domesticated fowl, although there is some

evidence that they bred geese, ducks and quail also. In planta-
tions of the nopal cactus they carefully tended the cochineal
bug for the rich crimson dye it yielded when crushed. A second
insect, the maguey slug, still retains its place as a delicacy of
the Mexican table, served with another typically Aztec dish,
guacamole,[1] a thick mixture of tomato, alligator pear and chile.

Hunting, when possible, produced food, but as early as Upper
Middle Culture times the deer had been nearly all killed off.
The seasonal migration of the birds, which still visit the lakes
of Mexico, offered a profusion of geese, ducks and other wild
fowl. Small fish, netted or speared with a trident, were sometimes consumed, and the eggs which a certain fly lays on the
lakes were made into a paste still eaten in Mexican communities. The high functionaries, since they were supported by the
community, kept a much better table than the poor, who lived
meagrely off the produce of their own fields; the daily repast
of Montezuma was described by the Spanish conquerors as the
height of Lucullan luxury (13).

Tools showed relatively little variation from Middle Culture to Aztec times. The *coa*, or digging-stick, was the chief
farming instrument, and the *metate* and *mano* even now reduce
the kernels of corn to flour. Stone tools still persisted for cutting and grinding, and cold-beaten copper was beginning to
find favour as a material for needles, axes and ornaments. The
volcanic glass, obsidian, because of its sharp edges and its abundance, was as satisfactory as most of their edged metal tools.
The simple loom and the weighted spindle were sufficient
equipment for the weavers, and pottery had a variety of uses
in the storage and service of food. The bow, throwing-stick,
lance and club were the chief weapons. By and large, mechanical inventiveness was not conspicuous in Aztec culture, although craftsmanship, through the superior use of simple tools,
was developed to a high degree, as we shall show in the next
chapter. (See Plates 35, bottom left, 38.)

1. Wah-ca-mo´-lay.

The great cities of the Aztecs had their origin in the simple villages of sedentary tribesmen. Just as in their social organization and economy, there was a simple base, comparable to the settlements of some of our sedentary North American tribes. The houses on the outlying *chinampas* represented the primitive state of Aztec housing. These were huts with thatched roofs resting on walls of wattles smeared with mud, a type of shelter probably in use in Middle Culture times and persisting 2000 years later in the Indian villages of present-day Mexico. (See Plate 42.)

More imposing establishments graced the older portions of the city, where generations of successive residents had brought care, renovation and innovation to domestic architecture. Each house rested on a raised platform faced with stone, which gave some protection against floods. Rooms for social purposes, sleeping, cooking, storage and quartering slaves were arranged in a rectangular plan about a central court. The house walls had stone bases and, according to the wealth or taste of the owner, were finished in stone or adobe. The roof was constructed by covering crossbeams with small poles tightly fitted together and spreading a layer of lime-plaster over the whole. As there were no windows, the houses had to be shallow. To admit light and air the buildings were usually two rooms deep and prolonged according to taste and wealth. The back room, which contained a hearth for cooking, was completely enclosed save for the door to the outer chamber, which was left largely open on the patio side, columns or short wing walls supporting the rafters. Two-storey houses probably did not exist before the Conquest, but there are cases where, to have light and circulation of air, a rear court with its surrounding rooms was elevated on a platform to the height of the roofs of the rooms around the patio in front (14). (See Plate 41.)

Recent excavations in the palace of the chief of Chiconauhtla, a fief of Texcoco, revealed interesting data on the growth of a chiefly establishment. This palace was continually being rebuilt and expanded to meet the demands of a growing population and richer economy. Patios were arranged at different levels, according to the plan described above. The earliest rooms had the congested quality of a Teotihuacan plan, but the later chambers were more spacious and open to sun and air. Each renovation called for more space, so that, allowing a family of five to each hearth, the entourage of the chief more than trebled in a century and a quarter (15). (See Plate 43.)

The plan of an Aztec town tended to have a rectangular form, since the division of the land among the clans usually followed a more or less orderly rectilinear pattern. A central plaza was essential for communal gatherings; the market and the principal structures, like the main temple and the chief's quarters, were situated at this point. In Tenochtitlan, which was reported to have 60,000 fires or hearths, or, figuring on the same basis as above, 300,000 people, additional centres existed for each clan and for the four larger districts into which the city was divided for administrative purposes (16). (See Plate 37, top.)

We have been left a description of an Aztec city in 1524 by a Spanish monk, Fray Toribio de Benavente, called by the Indians 'Motolinia', or 'poor', in reference to his Franciscan simplicity of life. His first-hand observations have a fresh reality:

'They called these temples *teocallis*, and we found all over the land that in the best part of the settlement they made a great quadrangular court, which, in the largest pueblo, was one crossbow shot from one corner to another, while in the smaller places it was not as large. This court they enclosed by a wall, many of which enclosures were with battlements; the entrances looking towards the chief highways and streets, which all terminated at the court, and even, in order to still more honour their temples, they led their roads up to these in a straight line from two and three leagues' distance. It was a wonderful aspect, to witness from the top of the chief temple, how from all the quarters and the minor places, the roadways all led up in a straight line to the courts of the *teocallis* ... the devil did not content himself with the aforesaid *teocallis*, but in each pueblo and in each quarter, as far as a quarter of one league off, there were other small courts containing, sometimes only one, sometimes three or four *teocallis*...' (17).

The streets of Tenochtitlan were the canals bordered by foot-paths, and frequent bridges allowed easy access to all parts of the town. Three great causeways led north, west and south to the mainland, touching it respectively at Tepeyac, now Guadalupe, Tlacopan, now Tacuba, and Coyoacan. Canals paralleled these main roadways where they entered the city proper, following them as far as their terminus at the main plaza. Two aqueducts also joined the city to the mainland. The one to Chapultepec seems to have been constructed exclusively to carry water, and had two channels, so that when one was being cleaned or repaired, the other could remain in use. The Coyoacan aqueduct, built later by Ahuitzotl, may well have followed the great southern causeway. The problem of sanitation must have been serious, but boats were tied up at strategic points for public use, and when filled their contents were sold to fertilize the fields. Pottery vessels were kept in the houses to preserve urine, which the Aztecs used as a mordant in dyeing cloth. Hence sunlight and these simple methods for getting fresh water and disposing of offal kept down the pestilence that beset the city in Spanish times when the ancient methods of sanitation were abandoned (18).

A city so advantageously situated had no need of fortifications, and formal military architecture was rare. The temples, which dominated the city, were natural strong-points; indeed, the hieroglyph for the capture of a town was the burning of a temple, an indignity to which no people would submit unless driven from this last rallying point.

The temples had stone or rubble walls surmounted by a high roof, the construction of which consisted of a cribwork of logs, either thatched with straw or covered with plaster. Each temple usually had a chamber and an antechamber, and in some cases two or even three shrines rested on the same platform. This platform or substructure gave height and mass to the temple. The usual practice was to lay up rough stone, set in adobe or lime, into a truncated pyramid, the sides of which were broken up by three narrow setbacks and by a steep ramp leading to the top. The surface was of veneered cut-stone slabs, and additional blocks were laid along the ramp to make the stair. Wide balustrades bordered the staircase, and often ended in gigantic serpent heads. Aztec construction was the simplest type of engineering, but imposing architectural effects were gained by the consummate artistic sense and superb craftsmanship of the builders (19). (See Plates 50–1.)

The adequate, even imposing, housing of the Aztecs and their gods by no means eclipsed their dress. Clothing, besides protecting man from the weather, has an important social function. It is a guide to the sex, age, group, occupation, rank and even character of its wearer. The simple and standardized clothing of our modern society performs the same service, and with a moment's observation one can tell much about a stranger from his clothes. The Aztecs, like many peoples of the world, strove by their dress to accentuate the social differences between people, and pomp and panoply dominated their costume. On the barbaric splendour of high civilian dress was superimposed the fantastic garb of the priests and priestesses in their impersonation of the complex and ornately represented divinities in their pantheon (20).

The *macehual*, or ordinary tribesman, left his head uncovered, his hair long, and customarily wore a *maxtli*, or loin-cloth, a mantle knotted over one shoulder, and sandals of leather or woven maguey fibre in cold weather. Women wrapped about their loins a finely woven cloth, which they sustained with a narrow belt. A sleeveless slipover, or *kuipil*, completed their costume. They plaited their hair into braids, sometimes interlacing them with ribbons, and these they wrapped around their heads. This woman's costume may still be seen in many parts of Indian Mexico. (See Plates 33–6.)

The poor made their garments of maguey fibre or coarse cotton. The rich wore the same clothing fashioned from finer textures and decorated with elaborate embroidery. The many names given to the different kinds of mantles show their interest and importance to the wearers. Wool was almost never made into cloth, since dog-hair was all they had, but feather cloaks were highly esteemed. Chiefs wore a fillet of leather from which hung two tassels, and administrative chiefs had a sort of diadem of gold or jade and turquoise as a badge of office.

The warriors frankly gloried in their costumes. Rich mantles and ornate feather head-dresses were not enough for some, who carried on their shoulders a harness of wicker supporting an elaborate structure in feather mosaic. Others wore costumes modelled on the appearance of an ocelot or an eagle. On specified occasions the priests assumed the dress of the gods and goddesses, whose costumes were sumptuous and ornate and defined by exacting ritualistic marks of identification. (See Plate 61.)

Jewellery consisted of ornaments of copper, gold and silver, shell, various-coloured stones, like jade, turquoise, emeralds, opals or moonstone, and mosaics laid on a backing of clay, wood or reed. Large plugs were inserted in the ear-lobes of men and women alike. Men often wore ornaments passed through the septum of the nose or suspended from a slit in the lower lip. Elaborate necklaces and pendants, armlets and leg bracelets, gave brilliance to a costume for state occasions. Cosmetics were not used to touch up nature, as with us, but instead a lavish application of face and body paints in red, blue, yellow, green and black enhanced with prismatic richness the softer tones of their brown flesh. (See Plates 46–7.)

It is obvious that the Aztecs were no pitiable, craven savages. They lived upon variegated and delicious foods and dwelt in houses that were comfortable and airy. Their dress stimulated the exercise of merited self-satisfaction, not to be confused with the compensations of vanity. Their manner of life enabled them to take advantage of their personal aptitudes and exchange the products of their own creation for whatever they lacked. Articles for daily and ceremonial use were made with the loving care of master artisans, and rare indeed was the object that did not have the impress of some little decorative touch that makes a pleasant possession of a drab utensil. Their crafts deserve to themselves a complete chapter.

CHAPTER VIII

CRAFTSMANSHIP

A consideration of how the Aztecs attained a high degree of skilful craftsmanship with relatively few mechanical aids

CRAFTSMANSHIP allows an exercise of the creative impulse, satisfying the individual through his domination of the raw material. In our modern mechanized age most of us suffer from the lack of opportunity to create, since almost everything we use comes machine-made, and not even the skilled mechanic feels that his ingenuity and craftsmanship alone have produced a useful and attractive object. The ordinary modern floats like Mohammed's coffin, without contact with the earth on which he lives or the universe of which he is an infinitesimal part. The Aztec, however, lived in the most intimate contact with Nature in its finite and infinite manifestations. Because his conscious being was set in terms of the group mind, he seldom felt that sensation, common to the Western intellect, of having cut himself from the tree of natural existence with the saw of his own reason.

The home production of articles for daily use gave an impetus to craftsmanship, since wealth and prosperity lay in a man's possessions, not in the abstract ownership of rights to the work of others. Thus a successful man had a well-made house, finely fashioned and decorative clothing, carefully worked utensils and tools and well-tended and productive fields, while an unsuccessful man had a small and miserable equipment. Yet except for the intervention of natural disaster the differential was due largely to the ability of a man and his household to produce with their own hands the symbols of his wealth or to exchange his specialized product for equivalent superior equipment made by others. The entrepreneur and broker had small place in the undertaking of production and its distribution (1).

The gods also stimulated good craftsmanship. Every home had an altar, and every act was accomplished through the favour of some deity. Ceremonies to appease these custodians of natural force were of frequent occurrence. Thus the use of symbols, referring to the god whose favour was sought, came to exercise an important influence on design. Since a man does reverence with his most esteemed social attitudes and his best material possessions, each household must try to surpass its previous efforts to honour the gods. The temple equipment, therefore, tended to represent the cream of local craftsmanship.

Work in stone, the most durable natural substance available, is a common gauge of human ability. Since the tools last for ever, it is possible to compare the technical abilities of peoples over an enormous span of human history. However, for basic equipment like projectile points, axes, grinding stones, and the like, satisfactory forms are reached fairly early, and do not change in proportion to cultural advances in other directions. Thus the arrow or the dart points of Aztec times were not technically better than those used by the Middle Culture peoples. However, the technical demands of the sacrificial cult called for a heavy, broad-bladed flint that could tear through human flesh at a single stroke, and this type of knife, not found in earlier horizons, was produced commonly with the extra care in chipping which is to be expected in a ceremonial object. (See Plate 60.)

The three-legged *metate*, or grinding-stone, was not better made in Aztec times than before. In Middle Culture and Toltec times it had an edge, so that the *metlapil* (son of the *metate*, i.e., *mano*, or grinding stone) was bevelled and fitted within the confined space. The Aztec *metate* was flat, and the *mano* had swollen handles, projecting on either side of the grinding surface of the *metate*. I have never had the misfortune to break my back grinding corn in a *metate*, so that I have no way of knowing whether this represents a technical advance or a mere change in style.

The demands of ritual necessitated stone boxes for burning and storing human hearts. These boxes were pecked out of lava and lavishly decorated inside and out with reliefs, referring symbolically to the gods for whom the sacrifice was made. Some of these eagle vases (cuauhxicalli [1]) fall into that area of superior craftsmanship we designate in our own culture by the term 'fine art'. The great circular cup, ordered by Tizoc and miscalled the Sacrificial Stone, 8 feet in diameter and $2\frac{1}{2}$ feet thick, attained the stature of a monument. Stone incense-burners, often in the form of the Old God, were common in Toltec and rare in Upper Middle Culture times. The quantity of religious sculpture, produced chiefly in late Aztec times, to judge from the style, did not detract from the quality of the workmanship, so strong was the control of religious and social factors (2). (See Plate 55, bottom left.)

Obsidian must have had important economic value for the Valley peoples, and since volcanic glass is portable and very useful for its sharp cutting edge, it was widely traded to the tribes of non-volcanic regions. Techniques were established early in the Middle Culture, and the art of polishing this stone was known to the Teotihuacan Toltecs, who utilized it as eyes for the idols of the Temple of Quetzalcoatl. Ceremonial blood-letting called for a constant supply of thin blades (made by pressure flaking), some of which are exquisitely long and narrow. Yet scalpels of comparable fineness were made in Toltec and Mazapan times as well. Indeed, the principal innovation of the Aztecs was in fashioning vases from obsidian, a formidable task, owing to its hardness (3).

The making of mirrors called much ingenuity into play. They are so rare that they must have been used solely for ritualistic magic. Blocks of obsidian were sometimes polished to produce an eerie and mysterious reflection. However, iron py-

1. kwow-shee-ca-lli'.

rites, burnished and shaped, were more common; and rarer examples had thin pyrite flakes laid in a mosaic and glued to a background of wood or shell. In another technique used on the coast the artisan detached a surface of pyrites in its matrix of slate, burnishing one side and carving the other to fashion a mirror with a carved back. One example, at least, is known of a mirror of marcasite with its surface so ground as to produce a magnified reflection (4).

Stone sculpture we shall consider more conveniently under art, but the mass production of dressed stone for building must have required patience and skill to accomplish. Stone-working throughout Middle America was achieved without metal tools. Flaking and chipping for the hard stones, pecking and hammering for the softer ones, were the preliminary steps in every case. A final polishing with some simple abrasive like water and sand often completed the process. Some hard stones seem to have been detached from their matrix by applying the abrasive and sawing with a cord of rawhide or a tool of harder stone. The Middle American people also developed tubular drills of bone and reed, which, rotated by a bow and aided by an abrasive, could hollow out vases or bore out places that were otherwise inaccessible to the clumsy tools of the time (5).

Save for descriptions and drawings, the destruction of time and man has left us only a few examples of the weaver's art. Weaving of some kind is very old, and no people, however primitive, exist in the world to-day who do not make at least some kind of basketry. Textiles are made as a rule by higher groups, but they are found in the American continent as part of the material equipment of peoples who had not yet learned how to make pottery. An early example of cloth, combining threads of cotton with some fibre like yucca, was found in the Lower Middle Culture horizon of Zacatenco.

The long practice of weaving must and did have a significant effect on decoration, for the rectangular patterns, to which the weaver is confined, influence all of Indian art in Continental

F

America. Design and the arrangement of elements are more important than form in Indian art. While many geometrical patterns appear in pictures of Aztec clothing, fine embroidery could produce the effect of curvilinear designs or even naturalistic patterns drawn from the regional flora. Batik and tie dyeing also enriched the decoration of Aztec clothing. Other processes produced the effect of velvet and brocade, and some garments even imitated in texture and pattern the skins of animals. Judged on a visual basis, the designs on Aztec clothing were by no means inferior to those of the celebrated textile art of Indian Peru. However, we have no positive evidence that technical development of Aztec weaving was equal to Peruvian, for those ancient South American weavers knew and practised every method known to man and even a few unique to themselves (6). (See Plates 33–6; 62, middle left; 64.)

Feather mosaic is probably an old craft, since evidence seems to show that it was known to the Upper Middle Cultures. Feather- and the technically allied fur-cloth appear in primitive horizons in North America. The process consisted in tying the stems of feathers into a fabric during the weaving process. Feather-workers adorned shields in this way, dispersing the feathers to represent animals or else purely decorative designs. They made cloaks, too, and created sumptuous insignia worn on the head or harnessed to the body. In these objects the blending of colours was so delicate and perfect as to rival paintings. As late as the nineteenth century, although the art had declined, the Mexicans still depicted landscapes and scenes from daily life in this medium, and to-day they make charming pictures for the tourists with cardboard, feathers and glue (7). (See Plate 45.)

Feather mosaic had an early counterpart in stone and shell; we found a turquoise mosaic in a Lower Middle Culture grave. The wooden handles of sacrificial knives were sometimes ornamented in this way, as were masks, shields and even small gold ornaments. A *tour de force* of the mosaic worker is a wooden shield from the Mixteca, on which little pieces of turquoise were fitted together in a relief sculpture depicting a religious scene (8). (See Plates 48; 60, top.)

Mosaic workers utilized stones of different colours and shells of various kinds. Pure designs were common, but elements representing the costume or the body-paint were shown when the mosaic covered a figure in wood or stone. An application of mosaic on a larger scale was frequent in architecture, a veneer of cut stone being applied to the rubble of a platform or building. The temples of Mitla, Oaxaca, influenced by the same Mixteca–Puebla culture to which Aztec civilization owed its origin, are masterpieces of this technique, for individual blocks have their surfaces carved to fit together in an intricate geometric design (9). (See Plate 11, top).

The wood-workers, owing to the impermanence of their medium, have left little to exhibit their prowess, but the few surviving masks, idols, drums and *atl-atls*, or throwing-boards, bear ample witness to their superb craftsmanship. The very fact that they had to work wood with stone tools makes their achievement noteworthy. Their copper tools were dull and unserviceable in cutting even the softer woods, and these implements came into use relatively late in Aztec times (10). (See Plate 54, top.)

Wood was used extensively in buildings for roof-beams and door-jambs. A beam in the palace at Texcoco was 90 feet long and 5 feet thick, so that its preparation and transport must have been an arduous task. There was probably little use of planks in Aztec building, since it would be difficult to prepare them with the rudimentary equipment at Aztec disposal, and adobes and plaster were easier to make and just as serviceable. Wooden canoes, however, were essential for life in the lakes. Some were dugouts hollowed out by fire, but others, to judge from the type used by the Xochimilcan Indians to-day, were flat-bottomed punts, constructed of planks which were probably tied together in Aztec times rather than pegged, as they are to-day. The portable bridges used to cross the canals were also simple combinations of planks, or planks resting on beams. (See Plate 35, bottom left.)

Furniture, which in European culture has done much honour to the wood-worker, was little used in Mexico. Mats sufficed for beds and seats. High dignitaries sat on a sort of wooden throne which had legs and often a back and was called *icpalli*, from which the Mexican word *equipale* for a modern wickerwork and leather chair is derived. Mention is made of screens and chests and ornamental sheathing for room interiors, but no examples are left for us to judge their craftsmanship. (See Plate 39, top right.)

The wooden drums, on which musicians beat out ceremonial rhythms, were handsomely carved, as befitted their religious use. There were two types, a vertically cylindrical drum (*huehuetl* [1]), which had a skin head, and a horizontally cylindrical drum (*teponaztli* [2]), the top of which was slotted to form two tongues. While the notes differed, there was usually the same interval between the resonant sounds emitted when the tongues were struck. The task of reaching the pitch must have been excessively difficult, for the wood had to be hollowed by fire and then chiselled to a nicety. At times the artist fashioned these drums to represent a crouching man or animal. Masks were often used in temple ceremonies when a god was impersonated, and ceremonial staffs were part of this equipment. So, also, were the throwing-boards, or *atl-atls*, with which a warrior flung a javelin, the lengthening of the arm thereby giving the missile an increased propulsive force. Some of these *atl-atls* were most delicately carved and represent the best of Aztec design. (See Plate 54, top.)

Metallurgy was in its infancy. Copper was cold-hammered; the art of adding alloys to make bronze had not reached Mexico from the south, but the gilding of copper and mixing of gold and copper were adopted by Mexican goldsmiths. Cop-

1. way-waytl.   2. te-po-naz'-tli.

per was cast into bells and ornaments, and the process, used also for gold, was the cire-perdue, or lost-wax, method. The desired shape was modelled in clay, over which was dusted finely-ground charcoal, followed by an even layer of wax. This coating was also dusted with charcoal and the whole enclosed in clay, which was perforated at the top and bottom. The molten metal was poured in at the upper hole after the wax was melted and the lower orifice plugged. When the metal cooled the cast was broken and the finished object removed (11). (See Plates 46-7.)

Although most of the native goldwork found its way to the Spanish melting-pot, a few lovely ornaments survived; in 1932 the quantity was more than doubled by Dr Alfonso Caso's discovery of the undisturbed tomb of a high Mixtec official. The design and shape of these necklaces, earplugs and rings, by their sheer intricacy and bulk, make one realize that the Spanish decriptions of Cortés' loot understated the rich ability of the Aztec goldsmiths (12).

Metal-working, without much question, had its origin in Ecuador or Peru, and various techniques were transmitted up the Pacific coast to Panama and Costa Rica, where important gold-working industries were founded. Although the intervening area produced little metal, another centre was established in Oaxaca in Mixtec times. The Oaxacan ornaments, although deficient in some of the southern technical developments, surpass in design and workmanship the best of the older gold-work of Peru and Ecuador (13).

Metallurgy seems to have arrived late in Mexico, certainly not before the eleventh century. Mentions of copper in Toltec times refer more probably to the Dynastic Period than to that of Teotihuacan. I know of neither copper nor gold which comes from the early or middle periods of the great Middle American civilizations, although some hollow clay bells from the late Toltec occupation of Azcapotzalco tantalizingly suggest metal prototypes. Towards the close of the Independent

Civilization phase, and more especially during the domination of Mixteca–Puebla culture, there are consistent occurrences of metal objects.

Mining methods were rudimentary. Gold was collected in nugget form or panned as dust; copper also was mined as nodules or nuggets; silver, which seldom occurs pure in nature, was for this reason rarely converted into ornaments. The melting furnaces were heated with charcoal and their draught forced by a man blowing on the embers through a tube. The casting we have already described. This work in gold, one of the great wonders of the Conquest, was achieved by the same simple methods of all Aztec handiwork and was another triumph of sheer skill, unassisted by technical aids.

Pottery making was the greatest New World craft, and probably no other continent has such a complex range of form and design. The pliability of clay made it easy to work, and firing was simple, so that pottery products were an important part of Indian craftsmanship. In the Valley of Mexico we have no trace of people before the introduction of pottery, and in the chapters in Indian history we have seen how every tribe, almost every village, had its own particular style, which changed gradually through slow shifts in the popular taste as time wore on. In the absence of written records the archaeologists fortunately have been able to rely on pottery styles to peg out in time and space the relationships of these ancient and forgotten tribes, and thus lay a basis for New World history (14).

The Aztecs, like all the other New World peoples, did not use the potter's wheel, but built up their vessels with strips of clay, relying on their keen eye and sensitive fingers to achieve the desired shape. They did not use moulds to form their vessels, as was occasionally done in late Teotihuacan times; nor, apparently, did they make use of the *kabal*, a block on which Yucatecan potters rested their vessels and which they turned with their feet in shaping the raw clay.

The Aztecs had an abundance of finely-textured clay, orange after firing, from which they fashioned vessels for the storage and service of food. The potters of Culhuacan used this ware first, making plates with flat bottoms resting on cylindrical legs (15). On the floors they painted curvilinear designs which were sometimes faintly naturalistic. In the second period, when the manufacture of this ware became popular all over the northern Valley, the vessels were made more coarsely, and the hollow legs degenerated to thick, elongated cones (16). The decoration was converted into an abstract combination of curvilinear *motifs* that had the quality of European script-writing. In contrast to the usual rectilinear quality of Middle American design, it may be more than a coincidence that the introduction of this style at the beginning of the fourteenth century was contemporaneous with the traditional date of the diffusion of picture writing by the peoples from the Mixteca. (See Plate 29, third row.)

The third phase of this style, made during the fifteenth century, saw a gradual conversion of the line-work into crude, continuous patterns, but the construction of the vessels proper was much finer (17). A few potters rejected this slovenly manner and drew elaborate geometric designs. The closely parallel lines in some of these patterns were done freehand on the curved interior surfaces of the bowls, revealing extraordinary control in draughtsmanship. Perhaps in trade, perhaps in tribute, many foreign vases were introduced at this time and stimulated the local potters to develop new styles of their own.

In the fourth period, during the chieftaincy of Montezuma, the potters broke away from these extremes of concentrated meticulousness and slovenly linework. Naturalism found favour, with birds, fish and plants used as designs and executed with that careless finesse of brushwork which characterizes Japanese sepia drawing. After the Conquest draughtsmen accustomed to working in this style were able to copy accurately such elements of Spanish design as the double eagle of Charles V and the coats of arms of nobles (18). (See Plate 32, top).

Polychrome pottery was made locally, usually consisting of a red slip, or wash, adorned with a geometric design in black and white. Coarse construction with painfully careful, if crude, draughtsmanship characterized the fourteenth-century ware. In the fifteenth century the hands of the potters loosened so that they were able to paint more sophisticated designs on vessels as thin and delicate as any pottery ever made in the Americas. Trade wares were rare at first and emanated chiefly from Puebla, but in the fifteenth century the quality and quantity improved, indicating the effects of trade and tribute. The historical reports that Texcoco was culturally superior to Tenochtitlan are borne out by archaeology; the Texcocan wares, although following the same styles as the Tenochcan, were better made and had a greater variety of design. Also there is evidence of more trade with foreign tribes (19). (See Plates 30-2.)

Goblets were made for pulque; graters were made for grinding chilis, and clay vessels were made for every conceivable use; one form was a small oval platter with a special compartment for sauce, resembling the 'blue-plate special' dishes of our modern restaurants. The circular roaster or griddle for cooking tortillas came in with Mazapan culture and continued to be popular through Aztec times. The bottoms of griddles were roughened so that heat would penetrate rapidly and evenly to the dough on the smoothed upper surface.

Clay utensils had their use in weaving. The Aztec spinner rested the end of her distaff in exquisite little cups, often charmingly ornamented. Her spindle weights were also made of baked clay. In the fourteenth century these were heavy and had holes large enough for a heavy spindle. Often their burnished black or red surfaces were cunningly adorned with stamped or incised designs representing conventional patterns or human and animal figures. In the fifteenth century the spindle weights became much smaller, so that at times it is hard to distinguish them from beads. This reduction in size perhaps indicates the spinning of more delicate cotton threads.

The spindle weight, or whorl, has an important bearing on discussions as to whether or not the Aztecs knew the wheel. The weight had the function of a flywheel in accelerating the rotation of the distaff. The explorer Charnay apparently mistook spindle whorls for wheels which might have been attached to toy clay animals. His ingenuous explanation is not seriously considered to-day, for later research has proved the existence of jointed dolls in both Toltec and Aztec times. These had holes in their bodies through which strings were passed, attaching the arms and legs, which were similarly perforated. In 1940 Dr Stirling discovered some clay animals which rested on rollers, tubes of clay probably connected by wooden axles, socketed to holes in the legs. This knowledge does not seem to have been put to any efficient use. In the history of invention there are several similar cases, notably the Chinese discovery of gunpowder. They used it to make a noise in ceremonies, but not until the Europeans took over the substance did its application have any practical purpose.

In Aztec times stone sculpture was the usual medium used in reproducing the human form. The figurine cult, which in Middle Culture and Toltec times manifested the chief development of the plastic arts, became insignificant. The use of the mould did not induce superior craftsmen to fashion even the originals. Yet in these dull reproductions of gods and goddesses there still lurks that ability to capture the spark of essential vitality so characteristic of this field of art in earlier times. Curiously enough, the goddesses, more kindly and less ridden with abstract virtues than the gods, usually awoke a response in these ancient idol makers that resulted in perfectly charming little figures (20). (See Plate 29, bottom row.)

Pottery was not confined to household chattels; great roof ornaments of baked clay were made to adorn the temples.

Sun-dried adobes were commonly used for general house construction. However, they were sometimes fired into bricks which formed the back walls of fireplaces or were substituted for dressed stone in the corners of buildings. A temple at Tizatlan carries brick construction in the pillars before the altar, but rubble faced with cut stone was preferred as a general building material for temples. Before the great temples, braziers the height of a man combined ritualistic usefulness with architectural ornament. Cones of baked clay were used as studding to keep the plaster from slipping off the temple walls and to serve as a decorative element as well (21).

The Mexican craftsmen had at hand an abundance of good pottery clay, which from the earliest times provided a medium for plastic experiment and experience. Work in clay created the background for that sureness and security in creation that stands out in the later Mexican sculpture in stone and wood. According to our Western standards, clay is a substance inferior to wood or stone for plastic expression. However, the ancient Mexicans, like the old Chinese, considered it fit for the finest examples of their arts and crafts.

Mexican craftsmanship, whatever the tribe and whatever the era, was superb in that it answered the necessities and ideals of both the time and the people. There is little evidence of a wide gap between superior and inferior workmanship, as in our Western civilization, where there is less need or opportunity for high-grade handwork. In unindividualized societies the general skills of the tribesmen, so far as can be judged by their work, follow a more even course than in elaborated and specialized groups. To turn such craftsmanship into art required a mere flick of the switch of social demand. The arts, as considered in the next chapters, were just projections of the craft background.

The measure of Aztec civilization cannot be gauged solely by its technical achievements. The arts and crafts transcend the products of Old World peoples at the same mechanical level.

The spirit of the Aztec people, as exemplified in their religious art, soared to the lofty heights attained by the creators of all those ancient civilizations, like Egypt and Mesopotamia, whose monuments reflect the glory of their builders' religious devotion.

CHAPTER IX

THE FINE ARTS

*A consideration of those aspects of Aztec craftsmanship which we
segregate as Fine Art*

THE Aztecs did not have a term for 'fine arts', nor did they speculate about aesthetics, nor make objects to be contemplated for their beauty alone. They had none of the socially sterile attitudes towards art which we adopt in our own culture. Instead, they recognized the value of superior workmanship and used its products to honour the gods who were intermediaries between man and the infinite power of the universe. Aztec art, in this respect, is no different from the great traditions ancestral to our modern aesthetic. Religion has always evoked man's best in thought and deed so long as human society believed that religion was essential to its survival (1).

Aztec art was powerful in architecture and sculpture, weak in painting and drawing. The dance was more advanced than music, and literature, in the absence of an effective method of writing, was confined to the evanescent output of oratory. The years and the elements have left us only such examples as could survive the ravages of time, and we have no way, except by analogy with living groups, to ascertain the Aztec attitude towards their creations in those fields of endeavour which we moderns dignify as art.

The most impressive expression of architecture was in religious building. Houses might have a fortuitous beauty of proportion, but the main consideration was adequate shelter. Public buildings of a secular character, like the clan house or the chief's quarters, were large-scale projections of the domestic architecture. The addition of many apartments for attendants and concubines, a swimming-pool and a menagerie, such as composed the palace of Montezuma, did not alter structurally or in basic plan the scheme of rectangular rooms set about a patio.

The temple architecture, on the other hand, achieved real majesty. The great gods lived in the sky, so that their shrines and images were very naturally elevated above the level of worldly affairs. The climate contributed indirectly to the conversion of religious requirement into an impressive art form. It was not necessary to house the congregation or protect it from the weather. The altar or shrine alone needed to be elevated, and the worshippers stood in the plaza below. Thus the temple capped the substructure and was the culmination of a harmonious series of ascending planes, calculated to increase the illusion of height by emphasizing the effects of mechanical perspective (2).

Such aesthetic canons were probably not laid down as laws but were reached after centuries of experimentation had produced a standard procedure. The earliest temple found in the Valley was Cuicuilco, of Upper Middle Culture date, where the altar was exposed upon a massive oval mound (3). There is no trace of temple walls, and the use of fire precluded a canopy. However, at Teotihuacan, in the classical Toltec period, the temple had replaced the open altar, and in all probability it housed a representation of a god in wood or stone. In the whole of Mexico there is no more harmonious treatment of gigantic mass and planes than the substructure of the Temple of the Sun (4). (See Plate 18, bottom; 22, bottom.)

The floors of the temple survive, though the roof and walls were destroyed long ago, but the illusion of infinite height and space still remains. The planes between its terraces are so cunningly calculated that the observer standing at the foot of the great staircase cannot see people at the top. He is conscious only of the massive ascent disappearing into space. When the stair was used by a religious procession, in all its pomp and colour, the effect must have been stupendous. The elaborate hierarchy of a great civilization moved upward to meet, at a point unseen by the beholders, the infinity of the heavens, concentrated aloft in the god's image.

The plan of the sacred city of Teotihuacan was calculated to maintain the illusion of mass and height. The buildings were laid out in groups along a north–south axis, broken laterally by several precincts oriented to the east and west. From whatever angle one approached Teotihuacan the eye was led towards a point of interest, guided by the arrangement of the planes and masses. Thus the diminishing effect of distance was avoided. Within each precinct the surrounding walls insulated the observer from the rest of the city and emphasized the mass and height of the principal precinct temple. Not even the Pyramids of Egypt present so carefully calculated a plan to dominate the individual with the sheer weight of supernatural power. The modern visitor to Teotihuacan, now in ruins, cannot escape the ancient association of ideas that the greater his temple, the more powerful a god must be. (See Plate 22, top).

Teotihuacan was probably the result of the co-operation of communities scattered over a large part of the Valley. Its scale and vastness could not have been achieved by a single resident community. In Chichimec times, when there was no central authority, each community built its temple or temples as best it could, and few survived. Tenayuca still has a temple of this period, the platform walls of which ascend almost vertically. Apparently shrines to two gods rested on the summit. At this same time, across the mountains in Puebla, the Cholulans were piling sun-dried brick on sun-dried brick to make a man-made mountain. So huge is this structure that the priest' quarters as well as the temple were located on top of one of the platforms. A large colonial church founded on the pyramid has obliterated evidence of the ancient temple proper, which tradition dedicated to Quetzalcoatl. It would seem logical to assume that the priests' houses were on a lower level than the shrine, since the tenets of Aztec religious architecture required a dominating position for the earthly residence of the god (5). (See Plate 26).

However, in the Valley of Mexico the communities prospered and their peoples multiplied. As resources and manpower increased, the temples became larger and more numerous. Yet so complete was the destruction by the Spaniards and their Indian converts, who transformed many a temple on its platform into a large parochial church, that the modern visitor finds little to suggest the architecture of the past. Archaeology has abundantly confirmed, in fragmentary form, the amazed descriptions of the conquerors.

The last two reconstructions at Tenayuca bear witness to the excellent proportions and dramatic principles of Aztec architecture. Excavations in the hill above the railway station at Cuernavaca revealed a temple intact in all except its roof. The temple of the Tepozteco, perched high in the hills over Tepoztlan,[1] is another nearly perfect example of Aztec architecture on a small scale. A pit sunk in a vacant lot across the street from the cathedral in Mexico City reached the corner between the stair and the western wall of the great temple of Huitzilopochtli, War God of the Aztecs, and the massive size and ornate decoration prove that the startled descriptions of the Spaniards did less than justice to this tremendous monument. A recent excavation in a cliff over-hanging Malinalco, near Tenancingo, state of Mexico, brought to light a temple complex, hewed largely from living rock, which thrusts the famous Egyptian rock tombs of Abu-Simbel into the limbo of provincial opera-house scenery (6). (See Plates 28, bottom; 37, top; 50-1.)

The Aztec temple had a platform, the sloping sides of which were generally broken by three terraces. A steep, broad stair flanked by balustrades, occasionally with a third dividing it into two, gave access to the top. Carved stone blocks, projecting in rows from the sides of the platform, represented snake-

1. Te-pos-tlan'.

heads, skulls or some other symbolic form of the cult. At the foot of the balustrades huge serpent heads with gaping jaws added to the architectural design and created awe in the beholder. The stair rose broad and steep, focusing the attention on the sacrificial block at the top, over which victims were stretched to await the searching knives of priests.

Behind the block stood the temple or temples, which generally had a back room for the idol and an ante-chamber for the priests. The walls were usually of dressed stone and sometimes ornamented with carving or relief. The roof, which was thatched in poor or primitive temples, in important shrines was made of beams laid like a corncrib, growing smaller towards the top. Plaster laid on twigs or poles sealed the roof against the rain and was carved with designs symbolic of the god inside. The interiors were noisome places, coated with blood and smoke, for incense was burned in profusion, as were the hearts of sacrificed victims. The proportions of terrace to terrace, temple to platform, stair to façade, were maintained irrespective of size, producing an effect of height and mass which yet in no way detracted from either the platform or the temple. This sense of proportion extends into every aspect of Aztec art and craftsmanship.

Some temples were cylindrical and rested on square or circular platforms (7). These were dedicated to Quetzalcoatl, often represented as Ehecatl,[1] God of the Wind, to whose passage a rounded surface offered no obstacle. Sometimes the door of such a temple was fashioned in the form of a serpent head, while the circular building suggested its body. A superb temple of this type is part of the Malinalco group mentioned above, which is hollowed out of the living rock. The door is carved at either side in low relief to suggest a serpent head in profile, while the whole also can be visualised as a snakehead in full face, of which the open mouth constitutes the door. A bench circles around the walls within, and the *skins* of eagles and oce-

1. Ay'-hay-catl.

lots, emblematic of the rising and setting sun, are carved in relief as if they hung from the wall to drape over the bench. An altar in the centre of the room represents another eagle. This elaborate concept is carved from the solid rock cliff and is a marvellous blend of architectural design and sculptural skill (8).

The Aztec sculptors worked in relief and in the round, in heroic and in miniature size, and were equally able in symbolic and naturalistic conceptions, which they could execute in whatever medium was available. Our modern appreciation of their work is hampered by the prominence of religious *motifs* which often detract by crowded detail or grotesque fantasy from the clean lines of their basic proportions. Aztec art, we have insisted, was never completely secular. Yet, in compensation, the Aztecs allowed a lively appreciation of natural elements to enter purely religious conceptions wherever possible.

From the time of the Middle Cultures the Mexicans used baked clay extensively for sculpture and worked out in it their artistic standards. The few surviving examples of wooden sculpture suggest that this medium was carved in accordance with stone techniques and did not, as in Egypt and Greece, serve as a training ground for standards later transferred to stone. If anything, the plastic methods of Mexico had their origin in a long and continuous handling of clay. Both media entail an emphasis on surface and contour; and the technical process of reducing stone by pecking and polishing, if more laborious, is not, in the last analysis, very different from the final smoothing and finishing of a work in clay. Thus the sculptors achieved a delicate appreciation of the contours and lines of the human form.

Partly owing to the past tradition and partly because the images of the gods were set in the temples, the Aztec artists showed their figures in passive attitudes, more often seated than erect. The austerity of their life led the Aztecs to attribute similar attitudes to their gods, and, as a result, the soft emotionalism so characteristic of European art is almost totally absent. Thus Aztec sculpture is even more forbidding and gloomy than other Middle American arts, which have at first a depressing effect on observers accustomed to Old World aesthetics (9). (See Plates 40, 49, 52–6.)

The same sense of proportion so evident in Aztec architecture produced a monumental quality in their sculpture. The smallest piece has the same dignity that attends the most massive temple carvings. A photograph reveals no impression of the original scale, and in one case the head of a goddess was carved identically in a small piece of jade and a four-foot block of basalt, with no less of plastic or monumental values to either (10).

In relief sculpture the forming of the object and the disposition and subordination of details show the mastery of design inherited by eyes trained in centuries of weaving. The vast block of the thirteen-foot Calendar Stone is carved with as delicate an appreciation of the relative values of space as similar designs painted on pottery vessels or graven on jade. (See Plate 52.)

The finest Aztec sculpture, to the Western eye, reproduces the young gods and goddesses that presided over the crops. Thus the Aztec body, long of trunk, short of limb, softly rounded in its well-fleshed strength, is simply and accurately portrayed with passive grace. The patient and resigned features were perfect subjects for the sculptor and his medium. Some gods could assume the guise of animals, and the sculptors took full advantage of their close observation of nature to carve a coyote with ear atilt or to dignify a red basalt grasshopper with the armoured malevolence of an insect in heroic scale. The serpent, emblem of Quetzalcoatl, symbol of time and the year, representative of mystery and power, was frequently carved. The sinuous curves ending in the savage symmetry of the head offered a challenge which the sculptors accepted with a success that evokes the mysterious horror of the Aztec universe. (See Plates 53, 56.)

The grotesque gods are abstract and horrible to our modern eye. Coatlicue,[1] the 'Lady of the Serpent Skirt', and mother of Huitzilopochtli, was thought of as powerful and awesome, so the task of the sculptors was to transmute those qualities into stone. The great statue in Mexico, whose head is twin serpents, whose necklace human hands and hearts, whose feet and hands are viciously armed with claws and whose skirt is a mat of writhing snakes, brings into a dynamic concentrate the manifold horrors of the universe. A smaller carving, simpler and less detailed, produces this same effect, implying that the very essence of fear was honoured and worshipped. An altar of red lava, dug up in the street behind the cathedral, is grimly adorned with ranked skulls, but the design is so harmonious that death becomes an abstraction, part of a distant universe of fear, and not the imminent individual disaster which besets us moderns. (See Plates 54–5.)

The Calendar Stone embodies a finite statement of the infinity of the Aztec universe. In the centre is the face of the Sun God, Tonatiuh, flanked by four cartouches which singly give the dates of the four previous ages of the world and together represent the date of our present era. The twenty names of the days circle this central element, and they, in turn, are ringed with a band of glyphs denoting jade or turquoise, which give the idea of being precious and symbolize the heavens and their colour. This strip is girdled by the signs for stars, through which penetrate designs emblematic of the rays of the sun. Two immense Fire Serpents, symbolic of the Year and Time, circle the exterior to meet face to face at the base. Boring back through these forms to the significance behind them, we have a grandiose conception of the majesty of the universe (11). (See Plate 52, top.)

In recent years, under the Presidential Palace in Mexico City, a monolith over a metre high was found, which represented a platform and a stair crowned at the top by a similar solar disc.

1. Co-at-lee'-kway.

Reliefs on the sides show Huitzilopochtli, God of War, and Tezcatlipoca, God of the Smoking Mirror, symbolizing the sacred war between night and day. Probably the Calendar Stone was set up in much the same manner, and it is tantalizing to think of the lost reliefs which explained and ornamented the great disc when it was in position (12). (See Plate 52, bottom.)

The historical accounts record that the Calendar Stone was made in 1479 and the great eagle vase of Tizoc during his rule from 1481 to 1486. A trough, extending from the basin to the edge of the vase, has been explained as a drain for blood to run out. However, the design is not keyed to this drain, and the purpose of the basin is to burn hearts, not to receive blood. Therefore, the furrow was probably made by the Spaniards, who sought either to use the vase as a nether millstone or tried unsuccessfully to smash it as an example of idolatry (13).

The dates of these two monuments indicate that this was the time when Aztec civilization burst into flower. It is a tribute to Aztec artists that, originally fettered by the more lowly tasks of handicraft, they could accept the tremendous economic, social and religious stimulation of their sudden rise to power as a licence to convert craftsmanship into great religious art.

The Aztecs did not create their art forms or their religion, which seems to have seeped in from the Mixteca–Puebla country. There the religious manuscripts and the ritualistic concepts hewn in stone and painted on vases were more complex and better drawn than their Aztec equivalents. Unfortunately, as yet, archaeological investigation has not extended to more than a sampling of this potentially rich area of Mexican civilization. However, the Valley people, given the opportunity, eagerly accepted these forms and created their own versions of the parent art (14). (See Plates 57, top left; 58, 59.)

The same elements portrayed in stone monuments appeared in smaller objects. Wooden drums and *atl-atls* had relief carvings the equal of the temple ornaments in all except scale. The same divinities were graven in bone against a background of turquoise mosaic. The gold-workers reproduced in miniature the images of the gods and goddesses and the symbols of their cult, carrying out in costume ornament the elements of the ritual in which they were used. Lapidaries succeeded in reducing jade, obsidian, rock crystal, opal, moonstone and amethyst into tiny sculptures which carry the same emotional authority as the grand-scale art. The bulk of first-rate material is enormous. It would seem that the products of tribal craftsmanship had been raised *en masse* into arts. Virtually overnight a cluster of primitive villages had transformed themselves into great creative centres (15). (See Plates 45-8; 55, top left.)

Painting and drawing did not reflect this transmutation. True, we have recovered a few examples, but they come from sources which produced fine sculpture. The surviving frescoes at Tizatlan and Malinalco are in no way superior to the drawings in the codices or manuscripts. The use of colour is lavish, but the drawing is crabbed and conventional, confining itself to correct delineation of ceremonial elements rather than to the combination of composition, perspective and colour values into a significant emotional experience. Apparently the finer workers devoted themselves to sculpture, while drawing and painting, subordinated in the outward expression of ritual, fell to less skilful hands. Yet design was a requisite in a work in two dimensions, and, considered on this basis, the symmetrical disposition of the figures renders less serious the anatomical flaws and rigidity of presentation (16). (See Plate 57, top left.)

The pictographic annals often exhibit an engaging charm in the little historical scenes recorded. The humour cannot be entirely fortuitous. There is something inherently fascinating about drawing little men that impels a draughtsman to humanize his figures, with a resultant and welcome loss to their dignity. Even the supremely competent draughtsmen who decorated the Egyptian tombs in the Fourth Dynasty could not resist a casual impishness. Aztec drawing was hardier than the sculpture and was able to survive until the close of the sixteenth century. The Indians copied old records, and some annals were carried on in the same style until 1560. The friars used Indian artists to illustrate reports on indigenous affairs, and there are several manuscripts in which Indian and European drawing methods are inextricably and delightfully mingled. Pictured history has always had its appeal, to which emphasis of the essential and the suppression of the irrelevant, implicit in drawing, largely contribute. In our present day, with all the superb methods of photographic recordings and reproductions, the comic strip has a vogue unparalleled in our history (17). (See Plates 62, 63.)

Aboriginal music has largely disappeared. The friars quickly adapted the chants and dances of Europe to Indian needs and substituted Christian for Indian ritual practices, using song and dance as formulas easily understood by primitives. To judge from the instruments, Aztec music was strong in rhythm but lacking in tone. The two-tone and one-tone drums could emit sonorous rhythms, but the bone and clay flutes pipe pitifully and are not gauged to a fixed scale. The conch shell could be blown with varying notes, according to the intensity of the blast, although it was more suitable for summoning people than for making music. Whistles, rattles of clay and gourds, bells and shell tinklers enhanced the effect of carefully regulated rhythms. Notched bones, often human, were rasped with a stick and produced quite pleasant sounds. A strange type of drum, which seems to have been indigenous, had an amazing resonance attained by beating an inverted gourd floating in a large container of water (18). (See Plates 39, top right; 61, middle.)

The dance was highly important, but native steps seldom persist except in the most primitive outlying districts, for they were transformed by the friars into Christian patterns. The chroniclers describe dances of many types in which masses of people participated. It is impossible that the Aztecs, with their profound sense of design and form, should not have had elaborate rituals in which great bodies of people moved in complex patterns to complicated rhythms. Song was used to reinforce the ceremony, and the words of some chants survive without, alas, the musical notation. These dancers, acting out mythical events pertaining to the lives of the gods, must usually have been highly theatrical. Thus, as with other peoples of the past, religious service fulfilled the function of the drama (19). (See Plate 62, middle right.)

The pictographic writing of the Aztecs was too simple to record a literature. However, the many references to oratory and the wealth of allusions and synonyms referring to the gods and goddesses give a picture of rich fantasy and poetic imagination. The emphasis on the spoken word, the complex background of the religion, the closeness of the supernatural world, would not have produced lean, accurate prose. Rather a semi-poetic, highly symbolic verbiage came from the practice of oratory and the chanting of prayers. Thus a rhythmic and rich verbosity existed as a form of polite address that, given a system of writing, might have been transmuted into literature (20).

These activities, which we sanction in our own culture under the terms of arts and letters and to the practitioners of which we assign honour as creative artists, were existent in Aztec society. The status of these practices, however, was very different from their position in our own culture. Much of that area of our own life divided up into the infinite gradation of commercial, legal and governmental pursuits fell within the span of the individual Aztec's normal social life. That energy and activity which we exhaust in religion, art, belles-lettres and science were combined by the Aztecs in the observance of their religious requirements. An understanding of the nature of their religion and its position in Aztec life and social practice is fundamental to a realization of the nature of their culture.

CHAPTER X

RELIGION

A brief survey of the Aztec universe and the unpronounceable gods and goddesses who presided over it and ruled men's fate

AZTEC religion, in purpose and practice, tried to attract those natural forces which are favourable to human existence and repulse those which are harmful. Ethical control and spiritual perfection fell within the province of social custom, so that the moral goals of our own religion were largely absent; the Aztec religion had no Saviour of mankind, no heaven or hell to reward or punish the consequence of human behaviour (1).

The Aztecs and their forebears believed that the forces of Nature acted for good or evil very much as does mankind, so that it was logical for them to personalize the elements as gods or goddesses. The process of worship entailed offering presents, uttering prayers and performing symbolic acts to induce the divine powers to operate for the public benefit. The tribal intellect was mobilized, as it were, to sort out the processes of Nature, find out how they acted and devise magical procedures or rituals to win them to action favourable to man.

Nature operates in series of recurrences which give the effect of rhythms. Birth, maturity and death follow relentlessly in human life; night succeeds day; the stations of the year rotate endlessly through spring, summer, autumn and winter; the planets move in eternal sequence through the sky. Thus to discover what those rhythms were and follow their complicated but regular beat would, in Aztec philosophy, ensure the happy survival of the community. There was little thought of the perfection of the individual when vast powers hovered close, ready to destroy the whole tribe if it ceased its vigilant watch on Nature. Thus rhythm and form become an essential part of worship and found their outlet in ritual and religion, art, philosophy and science.

The growth of civilization, with the resultant ramification of social function and material equipment, led likewise to a more complex perception of the universe, expressed in the stratification of gods and goddesses and a specialization of their functions. This result led to a more intense observance of ritual, which consumed a great part of the material and intellectual produce of the tribe.

Aztec religion was an outgrowth of the recognition and fear of natural forces and the attempt to constrain them. The process by which man defines these forces and grades them in order of importance is as much a part of the evolution of culture as art, mechanics or social organization. The Aztecs developed a conception of the relationship of the supernatural forces to the universe that, given the precision of our method of thought, could have been developed into an imposing philosophy.

According to Aztec belief, the world passed through four or five ages, or Suns. Details differ, but the record on the great Calendar Stone may be taken as the official version in Tenochtitlan. The first era, Four Ocelot, had Tezcatlipoca as the presiding god, who, at the end, transformed himself into the sun, while jaguars ate up the men and giants who then populated the earth. Quetzalcoatl was the divine ruler of the second era, Four Wind, at the expiration of which hurricanes destroyed the world and men were turned into monkeys. The Rain God, Tlaloc, gave the world light in the third epoch, Four Rain, brought to a close by a fiery rain. Chalchihuitlicue,[1] 'Our Lady of the Turquoise Skirt', was a Water Goddess who presided appropriately over the fourth Sun, Four Water, wherein a flood came, transforming men into fish. Our present age, Four Earthquake, is under the control of the

1. Chal-chee-weet'-lee-kway.

Sun God, Tonatiuh, and it will be destroyed, in time, by earthquakes (2). (See Plate 52.)

While the versions vary from place to place, we seem to
have a recapitulation of the great disasters from flood, volcanic
eruption, hurricanes and earthquakes that beset the communities of ancient Mexico. Also there is a reflection of the
order in which the gods attained prominence in the local worship. In the history of the Mexican tribes there are references to
struggles within single towns between the devotees of two
cults as to which would have the mastery (3).

The universe itself was conceived in a religious rather than a
geographic sense, and was divided horizontally and vertically
into areas of religious significance. The horizontal universe,
possibly the older concept, recognized five directions, the four
cardinal points and the centre. The Fire God, old and fundamental in Mexican religion, controlled the central zone. The
east was assigned to the Rain God, Tlaloc, and the Cloud God,
Mixcoatl (Cloud Snake), and was a region of abundance. In
this idea geography was combined with ritual, since the intensely fertile Vera Cruz coast plain is the actual source of the
seasonal rains caused by the condensation of warm air when
the Gulf of Mexico is exposed to the chill winds of the Central
Plateau. The south was considered evil, possibly because of the
arid zones south of Morelos and Puebla, but had as presiding
deities gods associated with spring and flowers, Xipe (the
Flayed One) and Macuilxochitl [1] (Five Flower). The west,
however, had a favourable significance, being the home of the
planet Venus, the evening star, which was associated and even
identified with Quetzalcoatl (Feathered Serpent), the God of
Knowledge. The north was a place gloomy and awful, presided over by Mictlantecuhtli [2] (Lord of the Dead), who, in
one of those contradictions so frequent in Mexican theology,
was sometimes connected with the south as well (4).

The vertical world was divided into heavens and hells which

1. Ma-kweel-sho′-chitl.   2. Meek-tlan′-tay-coot-li.

had no moral significance, being merely overworlds and underworlds. The number of heavens varied up to thirteen and represented the dwelling places of the gods, according to their rank in the hierarchy, the original creator living in the topmost heaven, and so on down the scale. One of these heavens belonged to Tlaloc, who received those who died by drowning, lightning or other causes connected with water. One school of thought divided the heavens into east and west, according to the passage of the sun. The east was the home of warriors, whose death in battle or sacrifice nourished the sun, and the west the home of women who died in childbirth, thus sacrificing themselves in the bearing of potential warriors (5). (See Plate 57, top right.)

The rest of the dead passed to Mictlan, the underworld. They had to overcome several hazards before they could take up their life there, so they were equipped with charms and gifts for the journey, which took the sacred number of four days. The wayfarer had to travel between two mountains which threatened to crush him, avoid first a snake and then a monstrous alligator, cross eight deserts, surmount eight hills and endure a freezing wind which hurled stones and obsidian knives upon him. Then he reached a broad river, which he crossed on the back of a little red dog, sometimes included in the grave-furniture for the purpose. Finally arriving at his destination, the traveller offered gifts to the Lord of the Dead, who assigned him to one of nine different regions. Some versions make the dead spend a probationary period of four years in the nine hells before they take up their life in Mictlan, which was, like the Greek Hades, devoid of moral significance (6).

The Aztecs, as we have said, conceived of their universe as extending horizontally outward and vertically upward and downward. The world, as horizontally divided, implied the association of divine powers with the phenomena of geography and climate. This significance of direction is a familiar religious concept. The vertical arrangement of the heavens had rather more to do with rank and order than with a realization of natural phenomena. The hierarchy of the Christian saints, with its implicit recognition of position and authority, approaches closely to the point of view with which the Aztec peoples regarded their gods. Aztec and ritualized Christian worship have much the same attitude towards distinctions between philosophy and practice, and between the point of view of the instructed theologian and the humble worshippers.

At the head of the Aztec pantheon, in a theological sense, was a supreme and ineffable god, Tloque Nahuaque; but an active cult in his honour seems to have been restricted to a single temple, at Texcoco, which became a centre of religious philosophy under the stimulus of the great chief, Nezahualcoyotl. Ranking below this abstraction of divine power and far more widely recognized were a supreme couple, Tonacatecuhtli [1] and Tonacacihuatl,[2] 'Our Lord and Lady of Subsistence'. These gods were theologically important and fulfilled the functions of parenthood and origin for other divinities. They were not extensively worshipped, since their control of nature was remote. An equivalent being, Ometecuhtli,[3] 'Lord of Duality', occupied an analogous position, resulting from priestly speculation as to the ultimate origin of the gods who controlled man's destiny. The Sun God, Tonatiuh, who also discharged the functions of a heavenly overlord, was, however, more closely associated with the active expression of Aztec religion. The daily appearance of the celestial orb, so infinitely important to the existence of all life, made sun worship an essential part of the Aztec religion (7).

There were several gods who intervened in human affairs and were venerated above all others. Usually one of this group was the tutelary spirit of a community and had arrogated to him supreme powers. Such a god was honoured by

1. To-na-ca-tay-coo'-tli.   3. O-may-tay-coo'-tli.
2. To-na-ca-see'-watl.

the principal temple, synthesized the abstract position of the gods invented by the theologians and partook of all the supreme powers exerted by the chief god of other communities. This group, without exception, was composed of sky gods.

Tezcatlipoca, the 'Smoking Mirror', sometimes appeared on the scene as an adversary of the Toltec divinity Quetzalcoatl, the 'Feathered Serpent'. He was widely worshipped, and his powers were shared by other chief gods. His attributes, as depicted in the sacred manuscripts, showed him to be protean, and they were often assigned to the tribal divinities of other places. A Mixtec manuscript, which emanates from the probable centre of the Tezcatlipoca cult, shows the same divinity presiding over the four directions but with a different colour in each instance. The powers and dress of this great god passed to local tribal divinities with the spread of Mixtec religion and the Tezcatlipoca cult to the Valley of Mexico. (See Plates 57, top left; 61, top right.)

The red Tezcatlipoca of the west took the name of Xipe, or Camaxtli, the tutelary god of Tlaxcala. Huitzilopochtli, the great War God of the Tenochca, assumed the functions and dress of the blue Tezcatlipoca of the south and was a Sun God as well, but his adversary and opposite divinity of the night retained the name Tezcatlipoca and was shown as the black Tezcatlipoca of the north. Quetzalcoatl was sometimes depicted as a white Tezcatlipoca, associable with the east as a morning star and the west as an evening star. Under the name 'Feathered Serpent', but with the attributes and powers of Tezcatlipoca, he presided over the destinies of Cholula. Tezcatlipoca, as god of a favourable region, as surrogate of the sun and as the chief god of the original cult, was the chief divinity worshipped at Texcoco.

Tlaloc, the Rain God, is an ancient god, going back to Toltec times. His eye rings, his fangs and the volute over his lips render him an easily recognized figure in the Mexican pantheon. At Tenochtitlan he shared the great temples with Huitzilopochtli, and his control of rain made the attraction of his powers essential to survival on the Mexican plateau. (See Plate 59, middle.)

Quetzalcoatl, the 'Feathered Serpent', God of Civilization and the planet Venus, seems to have been widely venerated, but under different guises. In contrast to Tezcatlipoca, whose functions and appearance were assigned to tribal gods with different names, Quetzalcoatl had several forms shared by distinctive divinities. The sculptures of Teotihuacan and Chichen Itza show that a feathered snake was honoured, and the local records mention Quetzalcoatl and Kukulcan, Nahuatl and Maya names having the same meaning. At Tenochtitlan there is ample evidence of a feathered-serpent cult, but the records refer to Xiuhcoatl,[1] 'Fire Snake', as well as to the standard sacred variety. The term Quetzalcoatl applies as well to a bearded god with a projecting mask, also called Ehecatl, the 'Wind God'. In parts of the Mixteca–Puebla area and the Valley, as we have seen, there is evidence that the 'white' Tezcatlipoca had the name 'One Reed', the date name synonymous with Quetzalcoatl (8). (See Plates 23, 53; 59, bottom.)

In addition to this confusion over Quetzalcoatl, the God of Civilization, the annals and myths tell of Quetzalcoatl, the great king, who civilized the Toltecs and left for the east to return again. The friars seized upon this myth as evidence that St Thomas the Apostle had visited Mexico and converted its inhabitants, who later slid back into pagan ways. Therefore, the friars, to justify the Conquest, made much of a blonde god who, after taking leave of his people, promised to return from the east by sea. Yet the Quetzalcoatl of the Valley of Mexico manuscripts was never blonde but usually black in beard and face paint, when he was not shown as the masked Wind God, Ehecatl.

As if the confusion between a man and a god of many guises were not baffling enough for the historian, we find to our dismay that the title Quetzalcoatl not only was given to the rulers

1. Shee'-oo-co-atl.

of the Teotihuacan Toltecs but also was borne at Tenochtitlan by the chief priests who exemplified the learning of the time. Distinguished authority has supported the hypothesis that a Mexican named Quetzalcoatl went to Yucatan, where he attained high office and absorbed the civilization of the Maya. Later he returned to Mexico and taught a version of the calendar, as well as many other useful arts, to the peoples of the plateau. Others, more romantic, see in Quetzalcoatl an Irishman, Norseman or even Atlantean, who popped into Mexico and spread sweetness and light. I, personally, believe that the introduction of superior culture elements and the creation of local arts as well might not only lead to the invention of a God of Civilization, but also endow individual innovators with the name of that god. The conflicting data suggest to me that the name and concept did not originate in any one person, but resulted, rather, from the experience of many peoples over a long period of time in explaining and honouring the introduction of those benefits which ensured their corporal and spiritual well-being.

The great gods of the sky played an important part in the duality of the Aztec world in which an eternal war was fought symbolically between light and darkness, heat and cold, north and south, rising and setting sun. Even the stars were grouped into armies of the east and the west. Gladiatorial combats, often to the death, expressed this idea in ritual; and the great warrior orders, the Eagle Knights of Huitzilopochtli and the Ocelot Knights of Tezcatlipoca, likewise reflected the conflict between day and night. This Sacred War permeated the ritual and philosophy of Aztec religion (9). (See Plates 39, bottom right; 40.)

While the great gods, the chief deities of the tribe, tended to be associated with the heavens, there were many others who controlled growth and fertility. Often these gods had goddesses as wives or companions, as if the idea of reproduction of the male and female principles were dawning in Aztec theology.

Tlaloc, the Rain God, held sway over growth and vegetation, and his companion Chalchihuitlicue (Our Lady of the Turquoise Skirt) presided over lakes and rivers. This goddess was the centre of an important cult and is represented as a charming young girl beautifully dressed. Xipe (the Flayed One) symbolized spring, and his distinctive costume, a human skin, represented the new covering of vegetation with which the earth clothes itself each year. His priests, at the ceremonies in his honour, carried this symbolism into their costume by donning the skins of freshly flayed captives. (See Plates 28, top left; 59, middle; 61, top left.)

The corn goddesses were young and lovely and probably derived from the old cult of the Middle Culture goddesses. Chicomecoatl,[1] (Seven Snake), was the Goddess of Crops and Subsistence, represented by corn, the staple food. Xilonen,[2] 'Young Corn Mother', and Xochiquetzal,[3] 'Flower Bird', were the embodied spirits of young growth and, by analogy, youth and the games. These had as male counterparts such gods as Cinteotl, 'Maize God', Xochipilli,[4] 'Flower Prince' and Macuilxochitl, 'Four Flower', whose functions, identified with growth, youth and games, are almost synonymous. (See Plates 31; 56, bottom; 57, bottom.)

About the maguey plant revolved another cult embracing the goddess Mayauel, who represented the plant and whose 400 sons were associated with pulque. According to some accounts, the various styles of drunkenness were recorded in terms of these gods or their associated animal, the rabbit. Four hundred rabbits stood for complete drunkenness, while fifteen or twenty suggested mere conviviality. The chief of these pulque gods was called 'Two Rabbit', after his day in the almanac and another, Tepoztecatl, was the tribal god of Tepoztlan, honoured by a temple placed high in the mountains of Morelos.

The gods of the earth and death were highly important, since

1. Chee-co'me-co-atl.   3. Sho-chee-kay-tzall'.
2. Shee-lo'-nen.   4. Sho-chee-pee'-ly.

PLATE I

EXCAVATIONS
IN
CENTRAL
MEXICO

Top: *Left:* Excavation at Nonoalco. *Right:*
Clearing out a canal in the Nonoalco district
of Mexico City, which was filled with pots
from the cyclical destruction of 1507. Middle:
Dissecting a palace at Chiconauhtla, State of
Mexico; for plan see Plate 43. Bottom: *Left:*
Peeling layers of refuse at Zacatenco, D.F.
This work led to the formulation of the
Middle Culture sequence described in Chap-
ter II. *Right:* Deep pit at El Arbolillo, Federal
District, Mexico. The earliest discovered
figurine types (Plate 14) were found in the
bottom of this trench.

PLATE 2

CLAY FIGURES
FROM GRAVES
IN WESTERN
MEXICO

TOP: The dog is a hairless edible breed, the large ancestor of the modern dwarf Chihuahua. The accompanying figure shows a fresh vitality unobscured by ceremonial details. BOTTOM: Seated woman from western Mexico, a fine example of direct realism. The lack of sophistication is compensated for by the lively understanding of the subject matter.

SCULPTURES IN THE
'OLMEC' STYLE

Top: *Left:* Clay figure from Middle Culture site at Gualupita, Morelos. *Right:* Jade bead from Chiapas in similar style; note face marking. MIDDLE: *Left:* Jade tiger, Necaxa, Puebla, a superb example, in miniature, of the jade cutter's art. *Right:* Stone mask representing the same tigerlike god, see Plate 4. BOTTOM: Outline of jade tiger (above) with facial marking like that of the bead.

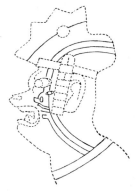

PLATE 4
SCULPTURES IN 'OLMEC' AND EARLY MAYA STYLES

TOP: Model of Temple E VII-sub Uaxactun, Peten, Guatemala. Later structures seal in the earlier monument of rubble covered by plaster. The second tier of masks closely resembles the sculpture at the bottom of the page. MIDDLE: Temple E VII-sub after excavation. The stela, or stone time marker at left, bears the earliest date found at Uaxactun. BOTTOM: Porphyry mask from Tabasco; note the simplification of the details of the tiger gods on Plate 3.

PLATE 5

MAYA
ARCHITECTURE
AND
SCULPTURE

TOP: *Left:* God, Co-
pan, Honduras. This
figure shows the com-
plete mastery which
the Maya sculptors
held over carving in
the round. *Right:* Gro-
tesque head from Co-
pan, Honduras. BOT-
TOM: Model of Temple
II, Tikal, Peten, Gua-
temala. The human
figures at the top give
an idea of the scale of
this monument. The
temple is almost com-
pletely decorative in
function, the massive
construction reducing
the room size to mere
slots.

MAYA ARCHITECTURE AND SCULPTURE,
LATE PERIOD

TOP: *Left:* Stela, 25 feet high, Quirigua, Guatemala. Stone time
marker bearing calendric calculations. *Right:* Figure in low relief, Jonuta, Tabasco. BOTTOM: House of the Dwarf, Uxmal,
Yucatan. Note large rooms and decorated façade.

PLATE 7

MAYA PAINTING

Top: Detail from a vase, Alta Verapaz, Guatemala. A high dignitary receives an offering. The inscription, being textual and not calendric, is undecipherable. Bottom: Detail from a Mexican period wall painting at Chichen Itza. Warriors are raiding a town and taking prisoners, suggesting the troubled days of the Mexican expansion.

PLATE 8

ZAPOTEC SCULPTURE AND
ARCHITECTURE,
OAXACA, MEXICO

TOP: Ruins of Monte Alban, near Oaxaca,
the Zapotec ceremonial centre, where a hill
was terraced to make room for temples and
tombs. MIDDLE: Relief from the earliest
period at Monte Alban. This art has certain
resemblances to the 'Olmec' style. Glyphs
accompanying some of the figures show that
a form of writing was known. BOTTOM: Jade
head, Oaxaca.

PLATE 9

ZAPOTEC
SCULPTURE
IN CLAY

TOP: *Left:* Mortuary urn depicting a rain god. Ritual demanded a formal and conventional treatment in defining this god. *Right:* This tiger god recalls the 'Olmec' divinity of Plates 2 and 3. It is a splendid example of the Zapotecan style combining the freedom and the conventionalization manifested in the sculptures at left and below. BOTTOM: This figure in the Oaxaca Museum shows how Zapotec sculptors could break through the bonds of convention to produce fine realistic art.

PLATE 10

'TOTONAC' SCULPTURE, VERA CRUZ

Impressive art forms have been found in this state and have been grouped inaccurately under the single term 'Totonac'. TOP: *Left:* Palmate stone, of undetermined use, representing a dead wild turkey. *Right:* Back of a slate mirror which probably had a reflecting surface of iron pyrites. BOTTOM: Model of the Temple of Tajin, Papantla. The niches held small idols, and the temple proper was at the top.

PLATE II

MIXTECA-PUEBLA ART

This culture became dominant after the eleventh century and had a wide influence on the established regional styles shown on the preceding plates. TOP: A temple or palace at Mitla, the largest roofed room in Middle America. BOTTOM: *Left:* Gold ear ornament representing a falling eagle, symbolic of the setting sun. *Right:* Page from the Codex Nuttall depicting warriors attacking a town in a lake. The band at the top represents the heavens, and the other symbols represent the name and number of the characters' birthdays.

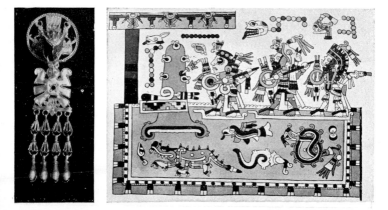

PLATE 12

MIXTECA-PUEBLA
INFLUENCE IN
YUCATAN

At the turn of the twelfth century Mexican tribes conquered Yucatan and built a ceremonial centre at the former Maya city of Chichen Itza. TOP: Reconstruction of the Temple of the Warriors by Kenneth Conant. MIDDLE: Head of the Mexican Rain God Tlaloc. BOTTOM: The Castillo at Chichen Itza, a majestic temple blending Maya and Mexican elements.

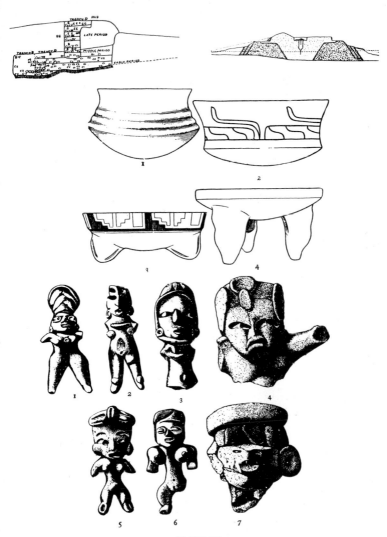

PLATE 13

CHART SHOWING NATURE OF MIDDLE CULTURE
ARCHAEOLOGICAL MATERIAL

Top: *Left:* Section of refuse heap, Zacatenco; figurine types noted. *Right:* Section of mound, Cuicuilco. Middle: 1–2, Lower Middle Culture pottery; 3–4, Upper Middle Culture pottery. Bottom: 1–4, Lower Middle Culture figurines, C3, C1–2, B–C, A; 5–6, Upper Middle Culture figurines, E, H2; 7, Teotihuacan I figurine, E4.

PLATE 14

LOWER
MIDDLE CULTURE
FIGURINES

TOP: Figurines (Type C 3) from earliest level. The features are made of applied bits of clay. Although the general appearance is crude, the technique shows long experimentation. BOTTOM: These figurines (Types C 1 and C 1-2) develop from those above. They seem to show a more slovenly procedure, but there is more variety in form than in the earlier style of female figures above.

TOP: A group of heads from Central Mexico, showing the variations within a single style. The scale is in centimetres. BOTTOM: The head (D1) in this much enlarged reproduction represents a style in which the craftsmen exercised skill and care. The source of the type seems to have been outside the Valley of Mexico, in Morelos.

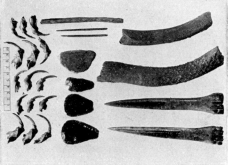

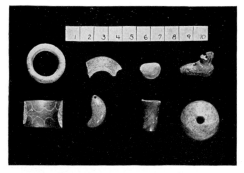

PLATE 16

MIDDLE
CULTURE
POTTERY
AND
IMPLEMENTS

TOP: Early Lower Middle
Culture pottery. L–R.
trade piece, red and orange
on white; bowls, white on
red; bowl, black ware.
MIDDLE: *Upper:* Upper
Middle Culture leather-
worker's tools, awls, grain-
ers, scrapers and rodent
teeth for cutting and
scraping. *Lower:* Lower
Middle Period ornaments,
earplugs, beads, and
whistle. Note jade orna-
ments, second in each row.
BOTTOM: Obsidian tools;
top row: Upper Middle
Culture; *two bottom rows:*
Lower Middle Cultures.

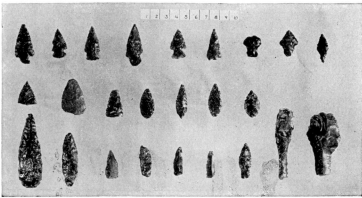

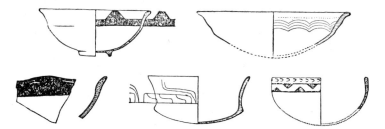

LATE LOWER MIDDLE CULTURE POTTERY & FIGURINES

Top: *First Row:* Red on yellow and incised black bowls. *Second Row:* Fragment and bowls, incised red on white, etched black, red on white. Middle: Figurines (Type A), from Zacatenco (?), Vera Cruz. Bottom: Figurines (Type B), same period.

PLATE 18

UPPER MIDDLE
CULTURE,
OBJECTS
AND
ARCHITECTURE

TOP: *Left:* Incense bur-
ner of lava, the oldest
stone carving found as
yet in the Valley of
Mexico. The bowl rests
on the back of a hunched
human figure. *Right:*
Ear-plug of carved baked
clay. A collar at the rear
was inserted in a per-
foration in the ear lobe.
BOTTOM: View of plat-
form of Cuicuilco. This
oval structure of adobe
faced with stone had
fallen into decay before
the lava (visible at upper
left) flowed over the
debris. At the left, circling the base of the platform, may be seen a
parallel row of stones of
unknown significance.

PLATE 19

POTTERY AND FIGURINES, UPPER MIDDLE CULTURE

Top: Three figurines (E) represent the early plastic art of this era. The bowl is polychrome and is ornamented with embossed birds. Bottom: The Type H figurines of the last phase of the Upper Middle Culture Era are covered with a white slip and painted. Their positions are lively and animated. The jar in the background is painted red on a brown background with a subsidiary pattern in black applied by the batik process. The small pot is of quartzite.

PLATE 20

POTTERY
AND FIGURINES,
UPPER MIDDLE
CULTURE

Top: These bowls from Ticoman show the standard shapes of this era. Note the elaborate tripod supports that distinguish these shapes from those of the preceding Lower Middle Culture era. Bottom: *Left:* This large seated figure of clay from Gualupita, Morelos, shows an individuality not found in the run of the sculpture. It belongs to the same school as the other figure (*right*), which appeared on Plate 3 in connection with 'Olmec' sculpture.

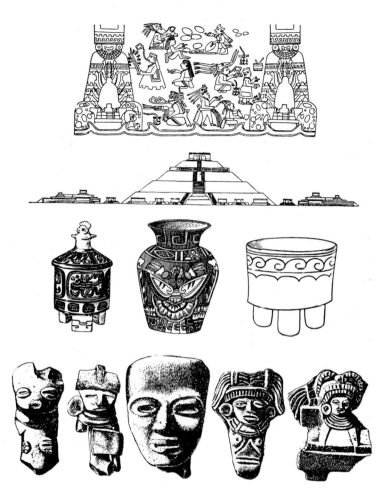

PLATE 21

CHART SHOWING NATURE OF TOLTEC
ARCHAEOLOGICAL MATERIAL

Top: Fresco from Temple of Agriculture, Teotihuacan, showing people taking part in an offering ceremony. Second Row: Reconstruction of the ceremonial precinct surrounding the Pyramid of the Sun. Third Row: Ceremonial vase, Teotihuacan II, in champlevé; ceremonial vase, same period, with fresco decoration representing a butterfly; vase, Teotihuacan V, polished red ware, with degenerate design. Bottom Row: Figurines representing the five stylistic stages of Toltec culture. The last two figurines are mouldmade.

PLATE 22

TOLTEC ARCHITECTURE

Top: Reconstruction of Teotihuacan by Gamio and Marquina. The long axis runs
north and south and includes, beginning with the Temple of the Moon, the Plaza
of the Moon, the Agriculture Group, the Group of Columns, the Pyramid of the
Sun, the Superimposed Buildings, and the Citadel Group. Note the arrangement in
terms of precincts and axes. Bottom: Air view of the Pyramid of the Sun, looking
east. The adjacent buildings show the size of this monster temple foundation made of
unfired bricks faced with stone.

PLATE 23

TOLTEC ARCHITECTURE

Detail from the Temple of Quetzalcoatl, which was later covered up to make the Citadel Group. The massive serpent heads had eyes of polished obsidian.

PLATE 24

TOLTEC ART

Left: This massive figure, ten feet tall, seems to be a water goddess. It is noteworthy for its monumental quality. TOP: *Right:* Mask of porphyry, showing a marvellous skill in reproducing the physical type. BOTTOM: This offering scene is a fresco. The figures at either side suggest the Water Goddess. Flames shoot up from the altars in front of them, while tribesmen and long-robed priests bring their offerings of feathers, food, jade, shell, and a bird. Note the speech rolls.

PLATE 25

CHART SHOWING NATURE OF CHICHIMEC
ARCHAEOLOGICAL MATERIAL

Top Row: Picture writings of this period. *Left:* Chichimec hunter from Mapa
Quinatzin. *Centre:* Tenochcas set forth on their wanderings and find their idol, from
Codex Boturini. *Right:* The eight tribes who settled Central Mexico, from Codex
Boturini (see Table VII). Second Row: The first three constructions at Tenayuca.
Note the sloping walls of the Aztec-influenced Building III. Third Row: Diagnostic
pottery styles of Mazapan, Coyotlatelco, and the Culhuacan Aztec I. Fourth Row:
Mouldmade figurines, Coyotlatelco style. Bottom Row: Mouldmade figurines,
Mazapan style.

PLATE 26

POTTERY AND ARCHITECTURE,

CHICHIMEC PERIOD

Top: Bowls of Aztec I–Cholula III type found at Chichen Itza, Yucatan. Middle: Temple of Cholula, Puebla. Note the large church resting on this ancient platform of adobe, which covers a ceremonial precinct of Toltec times. Bottom: Model of the Temple of Tenayuca, showing the original building and the five reconstructions, possibly corresponding to the cyclical ceremonies of 1299, 1351, 1403, 1455, and 1507.

PLATE 27

POTTERY, CHICHIMEC

PERIOD

TOP AND MIDDLE: Design from a vase, and another jar decorated in plaster cloisonné, from Jalisco. BOTTOM: Jar in plumbate ware, a quasi-vitreous ware, made in Salvador and in Guatemala. Pottery of this kind was traded extensively through Middle America in the twelfth and thirteenth centuries. The trade apparently ceased completely a century or so before the Conquest.

PLATE 28

POTTERY AND
ARCHITECTURE,
CHICHIMEC PERIOD

Top: *Left:* Life-size figure, Mazapan Culture, from Coatlinchan, Valley of Mexico, which represents the god Xipe dressed in a human skin. *Right:* Effigy vase, Mazapan Culture, from a grave at the type site. It seems to represent a dead man. Bottom: Temple at Teopanzalco, Cuernavaca. The later stairs and walls seen in the foreground are typically Aztec like the last three Tenayuca temples on Plate 29. The inner building is of the same style as the two earliest Tenayuca buildings (Plate 25), though larger.

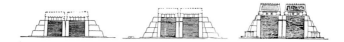

PLATE 29

CHART SHOWING NATURE OF AZTEC
ARCHAEOLOGICAL MATERIAL

TOP ROW: Historical picture manuscripts. 1. Arrival, in 1300, of the nations who brought knowledge of writing (Mapa Quinatzin); 2–4. New Fire Ceremonies (2) of 1403 (3) of 1455 (4) of 1507 (Codex Telleriano–Remensis); 5. Capture of Tenochtitlan, 1519 (Codex of 1576). SECOND ROW: Last three buildings at Tenayuca, corresponding perhaps to the cyclical renovations of 1403, 1455, and 1507. THIRD ROW: *First three:* Aztec pottery, Types II, IIIa, and IIIb, found respectively in the cyclical dumps for 1403, 1455, 1507; *fourth:* a type made from 1507 to the Conquest of 1520–21. FOURTH ROW: *First two:* Aztec figures (before 1403); *rest:* made between 1403 and the Conquest, representing Xochiquetzal, Xipe, Xochipilli, Tonantzin.

PLATE 30

TRADE
POTTERY,
AZTEC
PERIOD

Vessels like these from Puebla and Tlaxcala were much prized in Central Mexico and obtained by trade or tribute. At the top, a design composed of a feather fan and concentric circles, taken from a hemispherical bowl. The middle cup utilizes a simple grecque pattern, while at the bottom the hieroglyph for the day reed set against a black background decorates the neck of a vase, the body of which is painted a lustrous red.

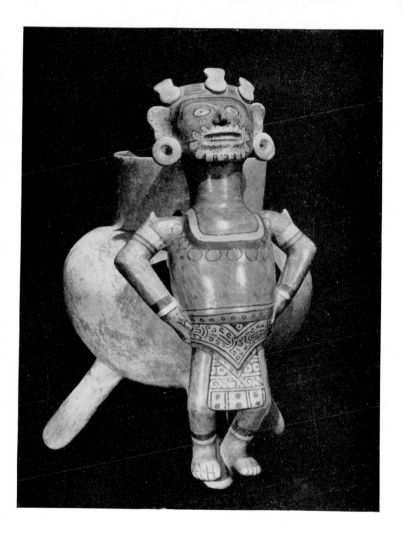

PLATE 31

CEREMONIAL VASE

Vase from Mihuatlan, Oaxaca, representing the god Macuilxochitl (Five Flower), God of Games and Feasting. His dress, necklace, and face painting are faithfully presented in polychrome, and above the left collarbone is a turquoise bead indicating the heart. Jade and turquoise were precious, and so was the heart of a god. There was therefore no symbolic conflict in showing as green an organ which is red.

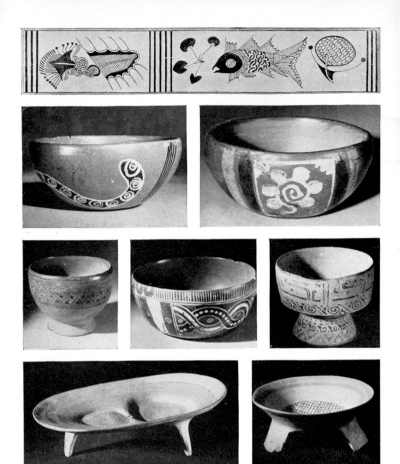

PLATE 32

AZTEC POTTERY

Top: Design from bowl of the Aztec IV period, representing a marine worm, water plants, and a fish. Second Row: Polychrome bowls, with, *left*, 'grecque type' decoration, and, *right*, figures of a snail in section, symbol of Quetzalcoatl. Third Row. *Left*: Cup, black and red; *centre*: Polychrome bowl, with stellar symbols; *right*: Cup with 'grecque type' decoration and symbols of fire, white and coffee colour. Bottom: *left*: Double bowl with fine black designs. *Right*: Aztec mortar, with symbol of summer.

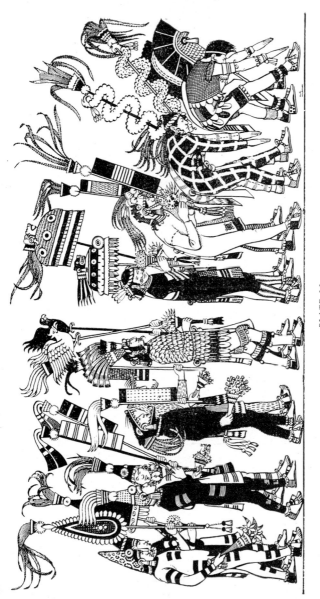

PLATE 33

PROCESSION OF NOTABLES, DOING HONOUR TO MONTEZUMA

This drawing by Keith Henderson, in the Henry Holt Edition of Prescott's *Conquest of Mexico*, was adapted from native picture records. The artist reconciles the crabbed fidelity of the Indian drawing with our own representational standards.

Rich Man

Poor Man

Beggar Man

Thief

Goldsmith

Feather Worker

Warriors

Doctor

Chief

Women

Merchant

Lawyer

Sailor, beware

Ant Bite

PLATES 34–5

AZTEC SOCIETY AND COSTUME FROM THE
CODEX FLORENTINO

In the middle of the sixteenth century the Spanish friar Bernardino de Sahagun made a famous study of the Aztecs, *Historia General de Neuva España*, which was not published until 1829. He got the Indians to prepare numerous illustrations, but they did not reach public circulation until 1905. The selections here show the various Aztec activities, seen with a fresh and humorous eye. Although some of the background details indicate that Spanish influence was already strongly felt a generation after the Conquest, the general details disclose a strong persistence of the Aztec way of life.

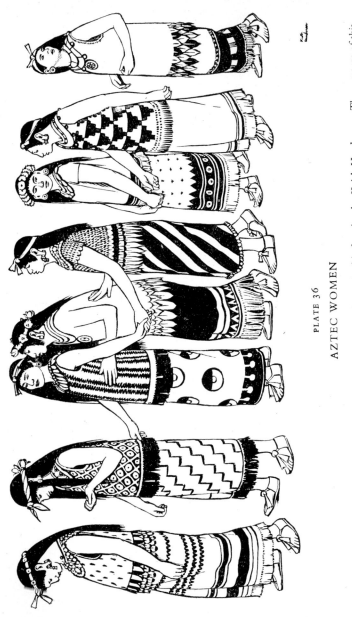

PLATE 36

AZTEC WOMEN

Rich embroidery enlivened the simple dress of Aztec women, as shown in this drawing by Keith Henderson. The measure of this artist's accuracy may be taken by comparing this plate and Plate 33 with the Codex Florentino paintings on Plates 34–5.

PLATE 37

THE AZTECS' MEXICO

Top: Ignacio Marquina's reconstruction of Tenochtitlan as it was in 1519. The reader looks slightly south-east. At the left looms the great temple; at the right stands the skull rack; in the foreground is the northern canoe basin. Left and right of the great temple may be seen the palaces of Axayacatl and Montezuma. The sacrificial stone, and behind it a round temple to the Wind God, Ehecatl-Quetzalcoatl, occupy the middle distance. Bottom: The 'floating gardens' of Mexico are much the same to-day as in pre-Conquest times. Xochimilco, where this picture was made, is occupied by the same Aztec-speaking people who lived there before the Tenochcas ever entered the Valley.

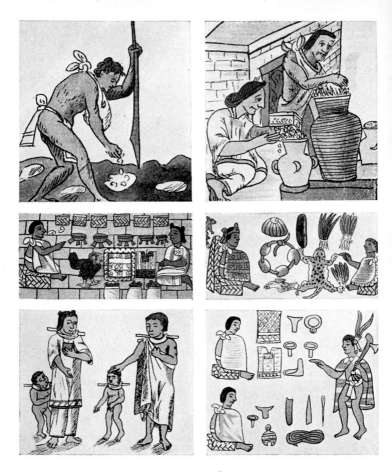

PLATE 38

AZTEC ECONOMICS AS SEEN IN THE
CODEX FLORENTINO

Top Row: A farmer plants his corn, using a digging stick, and later he and his wife store the harvest for the winter. These basic farming methods still persist among the modern Indians. Middle Row: *Left:* A produce market, which recalls the neatly arranged wares of a modern Indian vendor. *Right:* King Ahuitzotl receives produce of the coast: shells, jaguar skins, plumage, jade, and cacao. Bottom Row: *Left:* Members of a slave family wearing bars across their necks as a sign of bondage. *Right:* A merchant from the coast chaffers for such Highland products as cloth, gold ornaments, copper, obsidian tools, and maguey-fibre rope.

PLATE 39

SOCIAL OBLIGATIONS, REWARDS AND
PUNISHMENTS

TOP: *Left:* Boys are taken by their fathers to the school or Calmecac. These people
are of the poorer classes. *Right:* Montezuma has professional entertainers, hunchbacks,
jugglers, and musicians. MIDDLE: Four chiefs sentence criminals to death by noose
and clubs for outrageous crimes. BOTTOM: *Left:* A tribal ruler invests two leading
men with badges and trappings of rank. *Right:* Warriors of proven worth engage in
ceremonial combat. They wear the costume of warriors' orders or of chiefs.

PLATE 40

EAGLE KNIGHT, NATIONAL MUSEUM

This head represents the ideal warrior, steadfast, hardy, and devout. The 'very parfit gentil knight' of the Middle Ages would meet his peer in this noble Aztec. *Photograph by Sunami.*

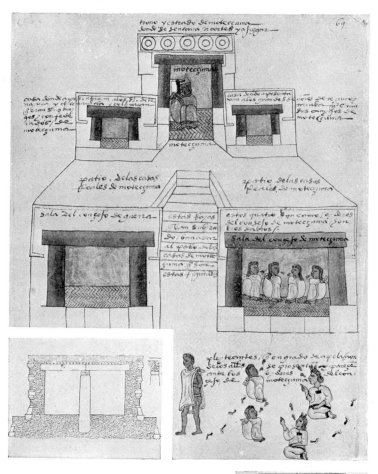

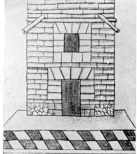

PLATE 41

AZTEC ARCHITECTURE

Top: Montezuma's palace, from the Codex
Mendoza. Note the ascending platforms, the
customary Aztec method of elevating rooms.
Montezuma's rooms are on the platform reached
by the stair, and are flanked by rooms for allied
chiefs, that on the left on the ground floor being
the war council's, and that on the right the
judges'. Middle: *Left:* Section through a temple
at Mitla showing the details of Aztec construction. Bottom: Two-storey house, probably of
post-Conquest date.

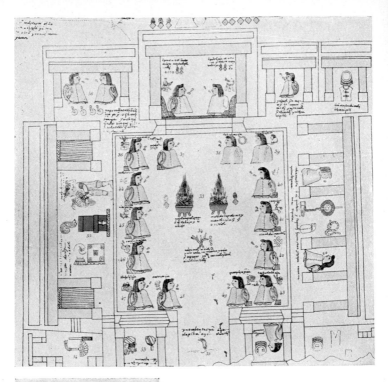

PLATE 42

AZTEC ARCHITECTURE

Top: An Aztec palace at Texcoco from the Mapa Quinatzin, drawn in elevation without perspective. Nezahualcoyotl and Nezahualpilli, father and son, face each other in the throne room. In the courtyard sit vassal chieftains, including the chief of Chiconauhtla (No. 46). The right side of the court is walled by storehouses for tribute; at the left is a temple, designated by the scribe as a hall of science and music. The top rooms are for the judges (*left*) and the arsenal (*right*). The bottom rooms house the war council and visiting ambassadors. Middle: House of wattle and daub, still used in Mexico. Bottom: A chief's house with adobe walls on stone foundations, wooden pillars for the anteroom and fresco painting on the façade.

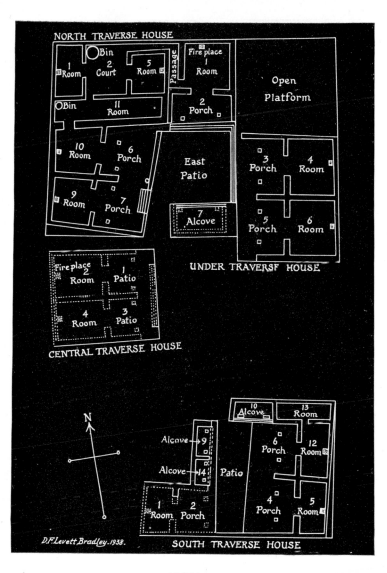

PLATE 43

AZTEC ARCHITECTURE

Palace at Chiconauhtla. Note how closely the plan resembles that of the Texcocan palace on Plate 42.

PLATE 44

AZTEC ARCHITECTURE

The Lienzo Chalchihuitzin Vasquez shows the chief and the founder of his line in the central house. The topmost row of figures discloses his descent, and the smaller houses joined to his palace by roads are those of his subjects. The people in the two large houses at lower right and left are allies. Post-Conquest painting on cloth.

PLATE 45

AZTEC

FEATHERWORK

Top: Montezuma's head-
dress, now in the Vienna
Museum. Cortés sent it to
the Emperor Charles V,
who gave it to his nephew.
Bottom: Nineteenth-cen-
tury survival of a famous
Aztec craft of which few
examples have resisted the
ravages of time.

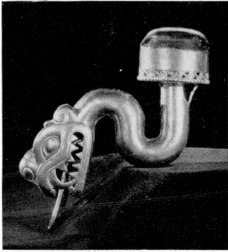

PLATE 47

AZTEC

GOLDWORK

Almost all Aztec gold-
work went into the Span-
ish melting-pot. Most surviving examples come
from Oaxaca, where the
supply was doubled by
Caso's discovery of Tomb
7 at Monte Alban, repre-
sented by top left and right
and opposite page middle
left. The lip ornament
(*below*) has a movable
tongue that makes it a very
lively serpent indeed.

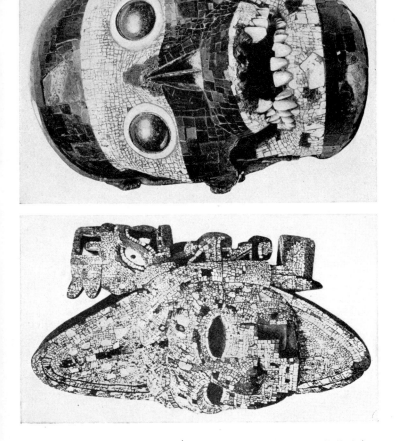

PLATE 48

AZTEC
MOSAIC
WORK

Mosaic work was one of
the most elegant crafts
and demands colour re-
production to give a just
impression. The mask in
jade and turquoise, now
in Rome, was part of the
original loot of the Con-
quest. The skull (*right*), a
British Museum trea-
sure, is composed of light
bands of turquoise and
dark bands of lignite, set
on a human skull, cut
away at the back to form
a mask, possibly repre-
senting Tezcatlipoca.

PLATE 49

AZTEC ART

Porphyry mask, Teayo, Vera Cruz. This mask is an outstanding example of Aztec art, even though it was made outside the borders of their domain. This carving and the Eagle Knight on Plate 40 are perhaps the finest secular sculptures from the Aztec period.

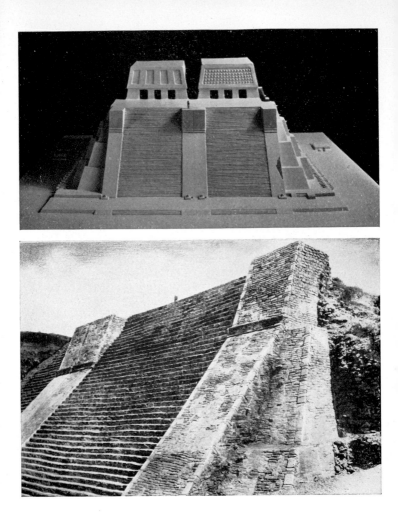

PLATE 50

AZTEC ARCHITECTURE

The temples were the most imposing aspect of Aztec architecture. Top: Model of the Temple of Tenayuca as it looked at the time of the Conquest. Bottom: The Temple as it looked during excavation. The suitcase focused the attention of the worshippers on the culmination of each ceremony, a human sacrifice. Compare Plates 60 and 61.

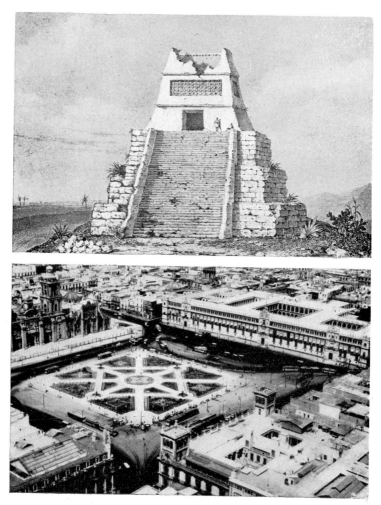

AZTEC ART

Top: This shrine in honour of the War God, one of the few Aztec buildings which have survived into modern times, is on the borders of the Aztec territory at Santiago Huatusco, Vera Cruz. BOTTOM: The Zocalo, Mexico City, looking north-east. This was the site of the great Plaza of Tenochtitlan. The president's palace (*upper right*) rests on the foundations of Montezuma's palace. The great temple to the Gods of War and Rain stood just east of the cathedral. At the road junction in the foreground a large disc like the Calendar Stone (Plate 52) still lies buried. The present square is built on the remains of the Tenochcan city, twenty feet above the ancient level.

PLATE 52

AZTEC ART

Top: The Calendar Stone, 13 feet in diameter, represents the history of the world. At the centre is the sun set within the sign Four Motion, the date of the present era. The dates of the preceding eras are given in the four arms of the Motion sign. The twenty day names, enclosed by glyphs for turquoise and jade, encircle the central symbols. Beyond are sun's rays and star symbols; the outer border consists of two great fire snakes, symbolizing time. Bottom: The National Stone, a monolithic block in the Mexican National Museum, suggests how the Calendar Stone was probably set on a platform. Its symbolism represents the Sacred War, the conflict between the opposing forces of nature.

PLATE 53

AZTEC ART

Top: The enormous snake at the foot of the balustrade to the great temple in Mexico is a dramatic architectural ornament, frequently employed in Aztec temple building. Snakes were the major ornament at Tenayuca (Plate 50) and many other Aztec buildings, appearing also far to the east in Mexican Chichen Itza. Bottom: This feathered snake in the Mexican National Museum may well symbolize Quetzalcoatl, God of Learning and the Priesthood. This representation differs from the fire snake in that it lacks a raised crest over the head.

Top: Wooden drum with two tongues (*teponaztli*) in the form of an ocelot. The smooth, simple outlines contrast with the macabre congestion of the presentation below. Bottom: Coatlicue, the Mother of the Gods, a highly important member of the pantheon. This representation, over eight feet high, displays her power in terms of such fearsome attributes as two snakeheads, a necklace of a skull, hands and hearts, a skirt of writhing snakes and claws on her feet. The bottom of the statue's feet is carved to represent the earth monster.

PLATE 55

AZTEC ART

Top: *Left:* Small rock-crystal skull representing the Death God. This is a fine example of Aztec lapidary work. Bottom: *Left:* A box, symbolically carved, to hold human hearts. Note the glyph for jade, i.e., 'precious', banding the sides of the container. *Right:* Another presentation of Coatlicue, the Mother of the Gods. An earth goddess, she is also associated with death, so that in this case her head is a human skull.

PLATE 56

AZTEC ART

TOP: A colossal head, nearly four feet high, of Coyolxauhqui, sister of the War God. She is shown dead. Simple handling of details enhances this monumental conception. BOTTOM: This Corn Goddess is envisaged as a young girl. Her soft Indian beauty is brought out with the same sure simplicity which characterizes the warriors on Plates 40 and 49.

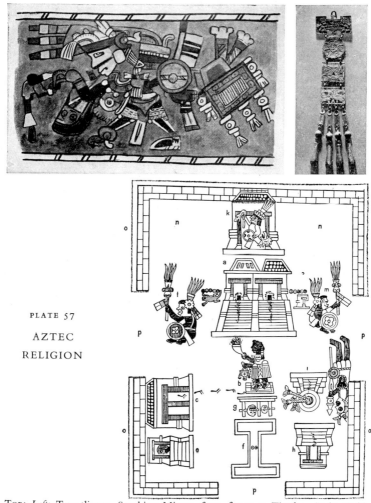

PLATE 57

AZTEC

RELIGION

TOP: *Left:* Tezcatlipoca, Smoking Mirror, from fresco at Tizatlan. *Right:* Gold ornament representing the vertical universe; at top gods play ball, symbolizing the sky and the movement of the planets, next the sun disc, then a flint knife, representing the moon, and finally the earth monster. BOTTOM: The Codex Florentino plan of Tenochtitlan (cf. Plate 37). a. The shrines of Huitzilopochtli and Tlaloc. b. Priest. c. Priests' quarters. d. Temple platform. e. Eagle Warriors' quarters. f. Ball-court. g. Skull rack. h. Temple of Xipe. i. Sacrificial stone. k. Old temple of Huitzilopochtli. l. Five Lizard (date) and Macuilxochitl, God of Flowers. m. Five House (date) and same god. n. Dancing places. q. Image of Xipe. p. Doors into sacred enclosure.

PLATE 58

AZTEC RELIGION

TOP: Altar at Teotihuacan with symbols of agricultural worship. Note glyph at top centre. MIDDLE: Vienna Codex, scene partly ceremonial and partly historical. Gods, dates, temples, chiefs, and fire making are shown. BOTTOM: Codex Florentino, special ceremony involving gods' descent to earth, with birdmen, snake dancers, rain-gods and priests dressed as the chief gods of the pantheon.

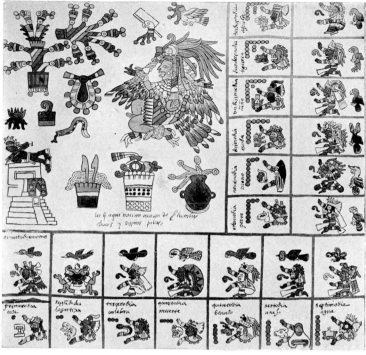

PLATE 59

AZTEC RELIGION

Top: Page from Tonalmatl of Codex Borbonicus. The goddess Itzapalotl, presiding over the fifteenth week, One House, is shown in the large division. The broken tree signifies Tamoanchan, a legendary homeland; the house below, with a man on top and the night sign in the door and the spider above, signifies the realm of darkness. The other symbols are offerings. The rectangular divisions refer to the days and their gods. A Night God is drawn in the middle of each day square. The squares above the bottom row and to the right of the vertical row reveal the gods of the Day Hours and their birds, beginning at the left with Xiuhtecuhtli. Middle: Tlaloc, God of Rain. Bottom: Quetzalcoatl, God of Learning, in guise of Ehecatl, God of Wind.

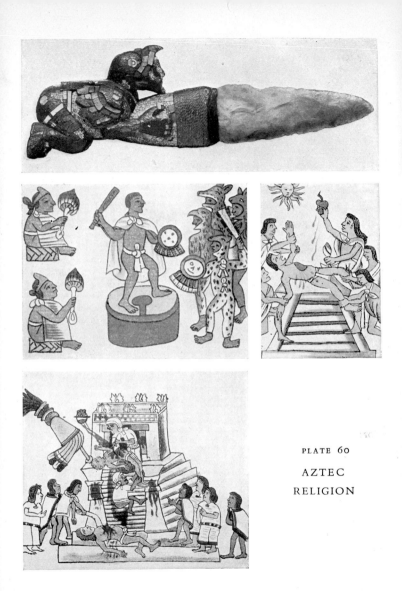

PLATE 60

AZTEC

RELIGION

Top: A sacrificial knife with a mosaic handle representing an Eagle Knight, in the British Museum. Middle: *Left:* A War captive on a sacrificial stone defends himself against warriors. *Right:* Sacrifice to the Sun. Bottom: Priests and laymen sacrifice two victims in honour of the War God. These pictures show the technique of using a stone knife to make an incision deep enough to reach the heart and tear it out.

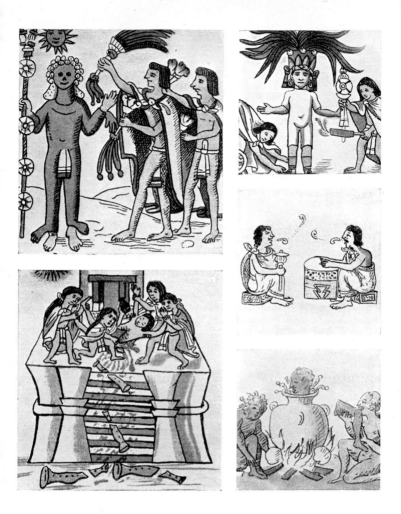

PLATE 61

AZTEC RITUAL

TOP: *Left:* Dressing a priest in the costume of Xipe, the Flayed God, who wears a human skin. *Right:* Dressing a victim and equipping him with the proper head-dress, shield and magical mirror to play the part of Tezcatlipoca. BOTTOM: *Left:* Sacrifice of the victim after a year. Note the flutes discarded by him as he ascended the stair. BOTTOM: Ceremonial cannibalism. The Codex Florentino artist had obviously never taken part in such a feast, fairly common before the Conquest. MIDDLE: Musicians with rattle and skin-covered drum, *huehuetl*.

Ｔｅｎｏｃｈｔｉｔｌａｎ．

PLATE 62

AZTEC RECORDS

Top: *Left:* Conquests of Montezuma
II; see plate 63 (Telleriano-Remensis).
Right: The Migration of the Aztec
tribes. They leave an island by boat,
reach Huitzilopochtli's cave, and
divide into migrant groups. Middle:
Left: Tribute Roll (Codex Mendoza).
Right: Monthly ceremony (Codex
Borbonicus). Bottom: Meeting of
Montezuma, Cortés and Marina
(Lienzo de Tlaxcala).

ano deso zeconegos y se 1426 segunla nra murio chimalpopoca y
fueelexido poes enor viz cohuatl krey nanzo eo te vizcohuatl ll sehal
garon. los mexicanos queno qui sieron seruir mas alos de azcapu
calco y asi quesaron ya aqui les entos ses tas voscobre grae
el capitaб gano azcapuçal ce sedezia maxtla
y fierra eclisada

PLATE 63

AZTEC WRITING

A page from the Codex Telleriano-Remensis describes the period from 1424–39.
The cartouches give the year names, indicating the succession of the four days with
the thirteen numbers. The sequence may be readily followed: Ten Knife, Eleven
House, Twelve Rabbit, Thirteen Reed, One Knife, Two House, etc. The death of
Chimalpopoca (Smoking Shield) is recorded for the year Twelve Rabbit (1426), as
is the accession of Itzcoatl (Snake of Knives). Each ruler is designated by his hieroglyph. The defeat of Maxtla (Breech Clout) is depicted, as well as an eclipse of the
sun shown by the disc obscured by a stone. The figures and descriptions were inserted
after the Conquest by two priests (to judge from the handwriting), who made use of
native informants. (Compare Plate 62, top left.)

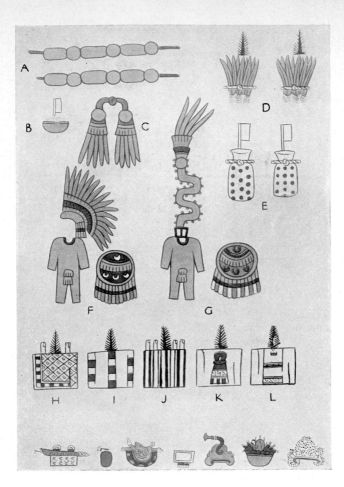

PLATE 64

AZTEC WRITING

A page from the Tribute Roll of Montezuma (after Spinden, 1928). The tributary towns are in the columns at bottom and right. The goods comprised: (*a*) two strings of jade beads; (*b*) 20 gourd dishes of gold dust; (*c*) a royal head-dress; (*d*) 800 bunches of feathers; (*e*) 40 bags of cochineal dye; (*f–g*) 2 warriors' costumes; (*h*) 402 cotton blankets of this pattern; (*i*) 400 blankets; (*j*) 404 blankets; (*k*) 400 blankets; (*l*) 400 blankets. Note the use of fingers for units, flags for twenties, and tree-like signs for four hundreds. The sign for eight thousand may be found on Plate 62 (*middle left*) in the top left-hand corner, designating the number of containers of honey.

growth takes place in the earth and the dead are received there. The sun on rising seems to be born in the earth and at its setting to be hidden by it, thus passing apparently to the world of the dead. The gods and goddesses associated with the earth had significance for the solar cults as well as for growth and fertility.

Tlaltecuhtli, 'Lord of the Earth', was depicted as a male monster of horrifying aspect, partaking of the attributes of a toad and an alligator. His open mouth could consume even the sun, since the setting sun passed into the earth, according to Aztec astronomical ideas. The goddesses, however, seem to have been worshipped more extensively, and the clay images made in their honour also continued in unbroken line the tradition of the Middle Culture figurines. Coatlicue (Our Lady of the Serpent Skirt) was the mother of the gods in their stellar aspect but also was honoured as the mother of Huitzilopochtli. The measure of her importance may be gauged by the great statue of her in Mexico which is a masterpiece of sacerdotal art and undoubtedly had a temple to itself. Coatlicue was also represented as a mother carrying a child in her arms. In this guise her function as a mother goddess brought her image into almost every home in the valley. Tonantzin (Our Mother), which may have been an aspect of this same goddess or of Cihuacoatl (Snake Woman), had a temple at Tepeyac, now the site of the shrine to the Virgin of Guadalupe, and her cult was transferred to the Virgin by the early missionaries, an act exemplifying their intelligent procedure in evangelizing the Aztecs. A goddess, Tlazolteotl (Eater of Filth), was extensively worshipped and was also synonymously known as the 'Mother of the Gods'. Primarily an earth-goddess, she, alone of the goddesses, had a moral significance, since in eating refuse she consumed the sins of mankind, leaving them pure. A rite of confession developed in her cult. (See Plates 54–5.)

Standing out from the numerous divinities associated with death were Mictlantecuhtli and Mictlancihuatl [1] (Our Lord

1. Meek-tlan-see′-watl.

I

and Lady of the Region of Death). They wore masks made from human skulls, and their ornaments were either human bones or representations of them. They presided over the northern regions and also ruled the hells below the earth. Theirs was no punitive function, for all who died, save in war or sacrifice, childbirth or drowning, passed upon death to their domain. (See Plate 55, top left.)

This incomplete description of the gods and goddesses who thronged the Aztec pantheon gives an idea of their variety of purpose and character, outlined more fully in Table X. For an individual to try to do honour to so many gods could result in an insupportable situation. Yet even the modern Navajos pass a third of their time in ceremonial activity, and they do not have half the economic wealth of the Aztec peoples. While the ancient Mexicans extended their ceremonialism to greater lengths than do the most ritualized Christian sects, yet the relationship between the Aztecs and their gods and the Christians and their saints is not so very dissimilar, different as are the ultimate concepts of the two religions.

The priests gave guidance and prescribed the ceremonies, and the worshippers gave heed to those especial divinities upon whose patronage their life directly depended, much as a devout Catholic selects certain saints for veneration above the list of those whose days are recorded on the calendar. In the same way the Aztec tribal god has his counterpart in the patron saint of country, town or craft. The Aztec, however, thought of his gods as having strong material powers, but their spiritual aspect counted little with him.

The ritual of Aztec religion was as complex as the theology. The organization of the priesthood followed the pyramided structure of the social order, but the ceremonies were worked out in accordance with the ritualistic requirements of the calendar and the seasons. In the following chapter we shall describe the priesthood, the ceremonies and also the Aztec methods of counting, recording and using time.

TABLE X
PRINCIPAL MEMBERS OF THE AZTEC PANTHEON, THEIR CHARACTER AND SPHERES OF WORSHIP

	Month	Week	Day	Day Hour	Night Hour
GREAT GODS					
Huitzilopochtli, Hummingbird Wizard, War and Sun God, chief god of Tenochtitlan	5* 9 15				
Tezcatlipoca, Smoking Mirror, chief god of pantheon, solar attributes, chief god of Texcoco	5 12		13 8	10	
Quetzalcoatl, Feathered Serpent, God of Learning and of Priesthood, chief god of Cholula, frequently shown as Ehecatl, the Wind God		2	2	9	
CREATIVE DEITIES					
Tloque Nahuaque, Lord of the Close Vicinity, creative spirit, theological abstraction					
Ometecuhtli, Lord of Duality, like Tonacatecuhtli and his wife					
Tonacatecuhtli, Lord of Our Subsistence, Creator God, chief of the gods		1	1		
Tonacacihuatl, Lady of Our Subsistence, wife of the above					
FERTILITY GODS					
Tlazolteotl, Goddess of Dirt, Earth Mother, worshipped under many synonyms	11	13	14	5	7
Teteoinnan, Mother of the Gods, synonym of Tlazolteotl					
Ixcuina, Four Faces, synonym of Tlazolteotl					
Toçi, Our Grandmother, synonym of Tlazolteotl					
Chicomecoatl, Seven Snake, Corn Goddess, ancient goddess dating from Middle Culture times	4 11				
Cihuacoatl, Serpent Woman, Earth Goddess, ruling childbirth and death thereby					
Tonantzin, Our Mother, synonym of Cihuacoatl					
Coatlicue, Serpent Skirt, Earth Goddess, associated with spring, mother of Huitzilopochtli					
Cinteotl, Corn God, son of Tlazolteotl, husband of Xochiquetzal, important				(12) (7)	4
Xochiquetzal, Flower Feather, Goddess of Flowers, of Craftsmen, important		19	20	(13)	
Xochipilli, Flower Prince, God of Pleasure, Feasting, Frivolity			11	(3) 7	
Macuilxochitl, Five Flower, synonym of Xochipilli					

* The numbers refer to the *Tonalamatl* of the *Codex Borbonicus*. Those in parentheses refer to variations found in the *Tonalamatl Aubin* and the *Codex Telleriano-Remensis*.

	Month	Week	Day	Day Hour	Night Hour
Xipe, Our Lord, the Flayed One, God of Seed-time and Planting, the red Tezcatlipoca, highly important	2	14	15	(11)(4)	
Xilonen, Young Maize Mother, Goddess of the Young Corn	8				
Ilamatecuhtli, the Old Princess, a goddess of ancient times, related to corn and the earth	17			13	

GODS OF RAIN AND MOISTURE

	Month	Week	Day	Day Hour	Night Hour
Tlaloc, He Who Makes Things Sprout, Rain God, very important	6 13	7	7	8	(8) 9
Tlaloques, minor rain gods, children or brothers of Tlaloc, a plural synonym	3 1 16				
Chalchihuitlicue, She of the Jewelled Robe, Water Goddess, very important	1	5	5	3	6
Huixtocihuatl, Salt Woman, Goddess of Salt and of the Dissolute	7				
Napatecuhtli, Four Times Lord, one of the Tlalocs					
Ehecatl, Wind, Wind God, a frequent guise of Quetzalcoatl					

FIRE GODS

	Month	Week	Day	Day Hour	Night Hour
Xiuhtecuhtli, Lord of the Year, Fire God, a divinity of ancient times, important	18 10	20 9	9	(7) 1	1
Huehueteotl, Old God, a synonym of Xiuhtecuhtli					
Chantico, In the House, goddess associated with the hearth and volcanic fire		18	19		

PULQUE GODS

	Month	Week	Day	Day Hour	Night Hour
Mayauel, She of the Maguey Plant, Goddess of the Maguey and also of Fertility		8	8		
Patecatl, He from the Land of Medicines, God of Medicine, husband of Mayauel		11	12		
Tezcatzontecatl, Straw-Covered Mirror, an important pulque god, identifiable with the Chac Mool figures in stone					
Centzon Totochtin, Four Hundred Rabbits, the many pulque gods					

PLANETARY AND STELLAR GODS

	Month	Week	Day	Day Hour	Night Hour
Tonatiuh, the Sun, Sun God with intimate connections with Huitzilopochtli and Tezcatlipoca				4	
Piltzintecuhtli, Young Prince, synonym of Tonatiuh					3
Metztli, the Moon, Moon God, sometimes identified with Tezcatlipoca					
Tecciztecatl, He from the Sea Snail, synonym of Metztli		6	6		(5)
Mixcoatl, Cloud Serpent, God of Stars and of Numbers	14				

	Month	Week	Day	Day Hour	Night Hour
Camaxtli, god of Tlaxcala, synonym of Mixcoatl, a War God					
Itzpapalotl, Obsidian Knife Butterfly, stellar and also agricultural goddess		15	16		
Tlahuizcalpantecuhtli, Lord of the House of Dawn, Venus, the morning star, variant of Quetzalcoatl		9		(1) (12)	
Coyolxauhqui, Painted with Bells, Moon Goddess, sister of Centzon Huitznaua					
Centzon Huitznaua, 400 Southerners, star gods of south					
Centzon Mimixcoa, 400 Northerners, star gods of north					
Tzitzimime, Monsters Descending from Above, stellar gods					

GODS OF DEATH, EARTH

	Month	Week	Day	Day Hour	Night Hour
Mictlantecuhtli, Lord of Region of Death, God of Death		10	10	11	5
Mictlancihuatl, Lady of Region of Death, wife of Death God					
Tepeyollotl, Heart of the Mountains, Mountain God, Jaguar God		3	3		8
Tlaltecuhtli, Lord of Earth, earth monster, personification of earth in contrast to sun				2	
Teoyaomiqui, God of Dead Warriors, a specialized Death God				6 (6)	
Huahuantli, the Striped, synonym of Teoyaomiqui					

VARIANTS OF GREAT GODS

	Month	Week	Day	Day Hour	Night Hour
Itztli, Stone Knife, a surrogate of Tezcatlipoca in guise of sacrificial knife		20			2
Itzlacoliuhqui, Curved Obsidian Knife, another variant of Tezcatlipoca		12	(13)		
Paynal, the Hasty, messenger of Huitzilopochtli					
Yacatecuhtli, Lord Who Guides, God of Travelling Merchants	15 12				
Chalchiuhtotolin, Jewelled Fowl, variant of Tezcatlipoca		17	(18)		
Yaotl, Enemy, synonym of Tezcatlipoca				(5)	

OTHER GODS

	Month	Week	Day	Day Hour	Night Hour
Xolotl, Double, Monster God, twin of Quetzalcoatl		16	17		
Ixtlilton, Little Black Face, God of Health and Cures from Ills				(2)	
Cihuateteô, Goddesses, witches, spirits of women dead in childbirth					
Huehuecoyotl, Old Coyote, backbiter or mischief-maker, god of Otomi		4	4		

CHAPTER XI

RITUAL

*In which are Summarized the Nature of the Religious Organization, the
Feasts, and the Relationship between Ritual, Calendar and Writing*

RELIGION was a general group activity necessary for the
social and economic safe-keeping of the tribe, and the priesthood was a highly important force in the direction of the communal life. In the early simple societies there were two executive chiefs, one for war and one for religious affairs. We do
not know whether the priesthood comprised laymen who performed the ritual acts of specific ceremonies, or whether it was
an established group whose whole life was devoted to religious
ends. It is probable that selected individuals originally carried
out the religious duties of the tribe in addition to their civil
obligations, but as Aztec culture became more elaborate, the
complexity of their functions moulded them into a body of
permanent officials (1).

In Tenochtitlan the Chief of Men and the Snake Woman
had double duties in respect of civil and religious affairs, the
former actively leading the services and the latter supervising
the temples, the form of the rites and the internal affairs of the
priesthood. Two high priests directed cult activities in honour
of the War God, Huitzilopochtli, and the Rain God, Tlaloc,
the chief divinities worshipped in this city. They were called
Quetzalcoatl-Totec-tlamacazqui [1] and *Quetzalcoatl-Tlaloc-tla-
macazqui*. The name Queztalcoatl was given them perhaps as
an honorific title in memory of the God of Civilization and
Learning, who was the archetype of the priestly ideal. The
second names refer to the gods of the respective cults, and the
third word means priest. Ranking below these two officials
was a third, *Mexicatl-Teohuatzin*, who, like a vicar-general, su-

1. Kayt'-zal-co-atl-To'-tec-tla-mah-caz'-kee.

182

pervised general religious business in the city-state and conquered towns. Two assistants looked after the instruction in the schools for citizen-warriors and for priests, and other officials supervised the pulque ceremonies (2).

Next in rank were the priests who were in charge of the worship, temple and ritual of each specific god or goddess and who, in the ceremonies, assumed the dress of the divinity, impersonating him on earth. They, in turn, had a host of assistants who were supplemented by aspirants to the priesthood, the bottom of the hierarchical scale. There seem to have been priestesses as well, and schools for their instruction were established in connection with certain temples. As might be expected as an accompaniment of a highly ritualized religion far above the comprehension of the masses, there was an active practice of magic carried on by male and female witch doctors. Undoubtedly many of these unsanctioned rites were rooted in the more primitive stages of the Aztec development; and in modern times, although the formal Aztec religion has been almost completely eradicated, the indigenous population continues many of the old magico-medical practices.

The priests, however, directed the intellectual life of the tribe. They elaborated cult ritual, and so instilled the realization of the power and proximity of the gods into the minds of the people that even their arts were dedicated chiefly to religious expression. The complicated astronomic and mathematical computations that kept the solar and religious calendars in harmony with the passage of the seasons were also the province of the priesthood. The priests arrayed the dancers, who, depicting mythological events, performed a type of mass drama. Aztec life under hierarchical direction became a pattern of rhythmic ritual, and this continued ceremony served the more firmly to establish the priests as interpreters of the divine order. One has the impression that the priests never overtly showed their temporal power. Situated as they were, with the instruments for interpreting the divine will in their own hands, they had to

TABLE XI

DAY NAMES AND NUMBERS OF THE AZTEC MONTH

1	Cipactli (Mythical Water Monster, Crocodile, Alligator)	
2	Ehecatl (Wind)	
3	Calli (House)	Year Name
4	Cuetzpallin (Iguana Lizard)	
5	Coatl (Snake)	
6	Miquiztli (Death's-Head)	
7	Mazatl (Deer)	
8	Tochtli (Rabbit)	Year Name
9	Atl (Water)	
10	Itzcuintli (Dog)	
11	Ozomatli (Howling Monkey)	
12	Malinalli (Grass)	
13	Acatl (Reed)	Year Name
1	Ocelotl (Ocelot)	
2	Cuauhtli (Eagle)	
3	Cozcaquauhtli (Vulture)	
4	Ollin (Motion, Earthquake)	
5	Tecpatl (Flint Knife)	Year Name
6	Quiauitl (Rain)	
7	Xochitl (Flower)	
8	Cipactli	
9	Ehecatl	
10	Calli	Year Name
11	Cuetzpallin	
12	Coatl	
13	Miquiztli	
1	Mazatl	
2	Tochtli	Year Name
	Etc. etc.	

TABLE XII

TONALPOHUALLI: SEQUENCE OF DAY NAMES, NUMBERS, AND WEEKS

Day	1	2	3	4	5	6	7	8	9	10	11	12	13
Crocodile	I · [1]	8	2	9	3	10	4	11	5	12	6	13	7
Wind	2	9	3	10	4	11	5	12	6	13	7	XVIII · [1]	8
House	3	10	4	11	5	12	6	13	7	XV · [1]	8	2	9
Lizard	4	11	5	12	6	13	7	XII · [1]	8	2	9	3	10
Serpent	5	12	6	13	7	IX · [1]	8	2	9	3	10	4	11
Death's-Head	6	13	7	VI · [1]	8	2	9	3	10	4	11	5	12
Deer	7	III · [1]	8	2	9	3	10	4	11	5	12	6	13
Rabbit	8	2	9	3	10	4	11	5	12	6	13	7	XX · [1]
Water	9	3	10	4	11	5	12	6	13	7	XVII · [1]	8	2
Dog	10	4	11	5	12	6	13	7	XIV · [1]	8	2	9	3
Monkey	11	5	12	6	13	7	XI · [1]	8	2	9	3	10	4
Grass	12	6	13	7	VIII · [1]	8	2	9	3	10	4	11	5
Reed	13	7	V · [1]	8	2	9	3	10	4	11	5	12	6
Ocelot	II · [1]	8	2	9	3	10	4	11	5	12	6	13	7
Eagle	2	9	3	10	4	11	5	12	6	13	7	XIX · [1]	8
Vulture	3	10	4	11	5	12	6	13	7	XVI · [1]	8	2	9
Motion	4	11	5	12	6	13	7	XIII · [1]	8	2	9	3	10
Flint Knife	5	12	6	13	7	X · [1]	8	2	9	3	10	4	11
Rain	6	13	7	VII · [1]	8	2	9	3	10	4	11	5	12
Flower	7	IV · [1]	8	2	9	3	10	4	11	5	12	6	13

follow the exactions of ritual far more exigently than did the masses. Were one to choose a single word to describe Aztec government, it would be theocracy. The gods ruled; the priests interpreted and interposed, and the people obeyed, not the priests, but the rhythm of action whereby the gods lived. (See Plate 58, bottom.)

At the core of the religion stood the calendar, which was arranged in two divisions: a ritualistic succession of days, the *tonalpohualli* (Tables XI–XVI, pp. 184, 185, 188–9, 190), and a solar calendar (Table XVII, pp. 192–3), divided into eighteen twenty-day months and a five-day unlucky period, in which the months' names related to crops and indicated the agricultural origin of this time count. A combination of the two systems permitted the numbering of years, which were counted not on an infinite scale, as with us, but in terms of a fifty-two-year cycle (3).

The *tonalpohualli*, sometimes erroneously referred to as *tonalamatl*, after the book in which it was recorded, was a sacred almanac. It covered a period of 260 days, the significance of which may have been magical or possibly of an astronomical origin, as yet unexplained. It was composed of the twenty day names of the Aztec month, combined with the numbers one to thirteen (Table XI, p. 184). Whenever the sequence of numbers ended, the series was repeated, and the same arrangement held true for the list of days. Thus the fourteenth day of the twenty in the list received the number one, and so on up to seven for the twentieth day. Then when the series of day names recommenced the first name was numbered eight. By this means within the 260-day period every day was distinguished by the combination of one of twenty names with one of thirteen numerals. At the close of each period another began immediately, as is shown in Table XI.

This sacred period was further divided into twenty weeks of thirteen days each (Table XII, p. 185). Every week began with the number one and the day name which came up according to the rotation of the sequence. Thus within the *tonalpohualli* period no day in one week could be confused with that of another, since the name and associated number precluded repetition (4).

A god or goddess presided over each of the list of twenty days (Table XIII, p. 188) and over each of the twenty 'weeks'

FIG. 1. AZTEC DAY SIGNS FROM CODEX

Cipactli Crocodile	*Ehecatl* Wind	*Calli* House	*Cuetzpallin* Lizard	*Coatl* Serpent
Miquiztli Death's-Head	*Mazatl* Deer	*Tochtli* Rabbit	*Atl* Water	*Itzcuintli* Dog
Ozomatli Monkey	*Malinalli* Grass	*Acatl* Reed	*Ocelotl* Ocelot	*Cuauhtli* Eagle
Cozcaquauhtli Vulture	*Ollin* Motion	*Tecpatl* Flint Knife	*Quiuuitl* Rain	*Xochitl* Flower

(Table XIV, pp. 188–9). The gods of the weeks followed the same order as the day gods, with this exception, that the god of the eleventh day was dropped from the list, moving the remainder in order up one place each. The resultant vacancy in the twentieth week was filled by two divinities who exercised joint control. Sometimes there was a further refinement whereby the

TABLE XIII

DAY GODS OF TONALPOHUALLI

Day	God	Name and Nature
1. Crocodile	Tonacatecuhtli	Lord of Our Subsistence, a Creator God
2. Wind	Quetzalcoatl	Feathered Serpent, Sky God, God of Learning
3. House	Tepeyollotl	Heart of Mountains, an Earth God
4. Lizard	Huehuecoyotl	Old Coyote, Mischief-Maker
5. Snake	Chalchihuitlicue	Lady of the Jewelled Robe, Water Goddess
6. Death's-Head	Tecciztecatl	He from the Sea Snail, Moon God
7. Deer	Tlaloc	He Who Makes Things Sprout, Rain God
8. Rabbit	Mayauel	She of the Maguey Plant, Pulque Goddess
9. Water	Xiuhtecuhtli	Lord of Year, Fire God
10. Dog	Mictlantecuhtli	Lord of Region of Dead, Death God
11. Monkey	Xochipilli	Flower Prince, God of Spring and Flowers
12. Grass	Patecatl	He from the Land of Medicines, God of Medicine
13. Reed	Tezcatlipoca or variant like Itzlacoliuhqui	Smoking Mirror, a Great God, cf. Gods of Weeks / Carved Obsidian Knife
14. Ocelot	Tlazolteotl	Goddess of Dirt, Earth Mother
15. Eagle	Xipe	Our Lord, the Flayed One, God of Seedtime
16. Vulture	Itzpapalotl	Obsidian Butterfly, a Stellar Goddess
17. Motion	Xolotl or variant	Double, Monster God
18. Flint Knife	Tezcatlipoca or Chalchiuhtotolin	Smoking Mirror, Great God, Jewelled Bird, a Week God
19. Rain	Chantico	In the House, Goddess of Hearth Fire
20. Flower	Xochiquetzal	Flower Feather, Goddess of Flowers

TABLE XIV

GODS OF TONALPOHUALLI WEEKS

Week Beginning	God	Name
1 Crocodile	Tonacatecuhtli	Lord of Our Subsistence, a Creator God
1 Ocelot	Quetzalcoatl	Feathered Serpent, a Sky God
1 Deer	Tepeyollotl	Heart of the Mountains, an Earth God
1 Flower	Huehuecoyotl	Old Coyote, Backbiter, old Otomi tribal god
1 Reed	Chalchihuitlicue	Lady of the Jewelled Robe, Water Goddess
1 Death's-Head	Tecciztecatl	He from the Sea Snail, Moon God

Week Beginning	God	Name
1 Rain	Tlaloc	He Who Makes Things Sprout, Rain God
1 Grass	Mayauel	She of the Maguey Plant, Pulque Goddess
1 Snake	Xiuhtecuhtli	Lord of the Year, Fire God
1 Flint	Mictlantecuhtli	Lord of the Region of the Dead, Death God
1 Howling Monkey	Patecatl	He from the Land of Medicines, God of Medicine
1 Lizard	Itzlacoliuhqui	The Carved Obsidian Knife, God of Cold
1 Motion	Tlazolteotl	Goddess of Dirt, Earth Goddess
1 Dog	Xipe Totec	Our Lord the Flayed One, God of Seedtime
1 House	Itzpapalotl	Obsidian Butterfly, a Stellar Goddess
1 Vulture	Xolotl	Double, Monster God
1 Water	Chalchiuhtotolin	Jewelled Fowl, variant of Tezcatlipoca
1 Wind	Chantico	In the House, Goddess of Hearth Fire
1 Eagle	Xochiquetzal	Flower Feather, Goddess of Flowers
1 Rabbit	Xiuhtecuhtli and Itztli	Lord of Year, Fire God Stone Knife, God of Obsidian Knife

TABLE XV

GODS OF THE DAY HOURS AND THEIR ASSOCIATED BIRDS

Day Gods	Name	Associated Bird
1. Xiuhtecuhtli	Fire God	White Hummingbird
2. Tlaltecuhtli	Lord of Earth, the Earth Monster	Green Hummingbird
3. Chalchihuitlicue	Water Goddess	Falcon
4. Tonatiuh	The Sun, Sun God	Quail
5. Tlazolteotl	Earth Mother	Eagle
6. Teoyaomiqui	Warrior Death, Death God	Screech Owl
7. Xochipilli	Flower Prince, God of Flowers	Butterfly
8. Tlaloc	Rain God	Striped Eagle
9. Quetzalcoatl-Ehecatl	God of Learning	Turkey Cock
10. Tezcatlipoca	Great God	Horned Owl
11. Mictlantecuhtli	Death God	Guacamaya
12. Tlahuizcalpantecuhtli	Lord of the House of Dawn, Venus God, variant of Quetzalcoatl	Quetzal
13. Ilamatecuhtli	Old Princess, ancient Earth Goddess	Parrot

nine gods and goddesses succeeded each other in governing the nights of the *tonalpohualli*, or sacred period (Table XVI). Finally thirteen of these gods influenced the thirteen stations of the Aztec day (Table XV, p. 189), and nine held sway over the night hours (Table XVI). The names and characters of these divinities are set forth in the accompanying tables.

The array of gods had to be placated and honoured at the appropriate time by the priesthood; but the individual, before embarking on an undertaking, could find out the proper divinity to appease on the date of that undertaking. It is impro-

TABLE XVI

GODS OF THE NIGHT HOURS AND THEIR ATTRIBUTES IN DIVINATION

Night Gods		Significance
1. Xiuhtecuhtli	Fire God	Good
2. Itztli	God of Obsidian Knife	Bad
3. Piltzintecuhtli	Lord of Princes, Sun God	Good
4. Cinteotl	God of Corn, Corn God	Indifferent
5. Mictlantecuhtli	Death God	Bad
6. Chalchihuitlicue	Water Goddess	Indifferent
7. Tlazolteotl	Earth Mother	Bad
8. Tepeyollotl	Earth or Jaguar God	Good
9. Tlaloc	Rain God	Good

bable that the ordinary communicant daily honoured each god any more than a Catholic layman prays daily to each saint in the calendar. He did reverence in terms of his own spiritual and actual necessity.

A number of the *tonalamatl* have survived. These reference books for priestly guidance are made of paper beaten from the bark of the amate or wild-fig tree, although some post-Conquest copies were composed of European paper. An ancient book consisted of a long paper strip which was prepared and coated to take paint and subsequently folded screen-wise to permit easy handling. Occasionally only one, but usually the two open pages were devoted to each week. A large coloured drawing depicted the divinity controlling the week, and other figures represented subsidiary gods and objects connected with their worship, such as thorns, incense-burners, altars, and the like. The rest of the space was ruled off into squares, in which were painted the requisite thirteen day names and numbers, the gods and goddesses associated with each and occasionally their *nahuals*, the bird or animal forms which the divinities could assume. Obviously only the initiate could make use of this information, which existed in the form of pictures without an explanatory text. However, it is the great good fortune of Mexicanists that some of the friars after the Conquest annotated a few of these manuscripts according to the explanations of Indian informants (5). (See Plate 59, top.)

The great Aztec ceremonies, however, took place in accordance with the solar year, composed of eighteen months of twenty days and a five-day period which was considered unlucky (Table XVII, pp. 192–3). The months had names having to do with farming, and the days of the month were distinguished by numbers, in addition to their *tonalpohualli* name and number described above. Years were identified in terms of the two methods, since they were named for the *tonalpohualli* day on which the year began (6).

Only four of the twenty day names could begin the year, as a simple mathematical calculation will prove. Three hundred and sixty-five (the number of days in a year) divided by twenty (the total of the day names) leaves a remainder of five. Thus, of the twenty day names, only four can begin the year. House, Rabbit, Reed and Flint Knife must always recur as New Year's Day, since they are the third, eighth, thirteenth and eighteenth days in the list, thus being separated from each other by five numbers. In that thirteen, the quantity of numbers available divides into 365 with a remainder of one, the number of the day increased by one each new year. Thus the years were numerically distinguishable – 1 Rabbit, 2 Reed, 3 House, 4 Flint Knife, 5 Rabbit, and so on, until the thirteen numbers and four day names began to repeat themselves, which occurred after fifty-two (13 × 4) years. This is the mathematical reas-

TABLE XVII

THE SOLAR YEAR, THE EIGHTEEN MONTHS, AND CEREMONIES

Months, seasonal character, approximate Gregorian dates, presiding gods and chief ceremonies

I Atlcoualco (want of water), ceasing of rain [Feb. 12–Mar. 3]. Chalchihuitlicue and Tlalocs. Ceremonies for rain; child sacrifice; Xipe sacrifice with blunt weapons.

II Tlacaxipeualiztli (boning of men), seedtime [Mar. 4–Mar. 23]. God Xipe. Impersonation of Xipe by priests wearing skins of captives; dances by priests wearing human skins; agricultural dances.

III Tozoztontli (short fast), rain desired [Mar. 24–Apr. 12]. Coatlicue and Tlalocs. Child sacrifice to Tlalocs to bring rain; end of Xipe rites which sometimes held over a month.

IV Huei Tozoztli (long fast), worship of new corn [Apr. 13–May 2]. Centeotl and Chicomecoatl. Ceremonial bloodletting; decoration of house altars with corn plants; young girls' ceremony with blessing of seed corn.

V Toxcatl (dry or slippery), rainy season begins [May 3–May 22]. Tezcatlipoca and Huitzilopochtli; god-impersonation ceremonies for either or both great gods (p. 197); scarification of children.

VI Etzalqualiztli (bean porridge), rain desired [May 23–June 11]. Tlalocs. Ceremonial robbing; rain ceremonies; fertility rite, drowning boy and girl in canoe filled with hearts of sacrificial victims.

VII Tecuhilhuitontli (little feast of princes), rain desired [June 12–July 1]. Huixtocihuatl. Ceremony of salt-workers, who leeched product from lake; women's dance with sacrifice of priestess impersonating goddess.

VIII Hueitecuhilhuitl (great feast of rulers), adoration of ripening corn [July 2–July 21]. Xilonen. Feast for Goddess of Young Corn; eight-day feast; women wear hair loose as sympathetic magic; sacrifice of slave girl impersonating goddess; after sacrifice people can eat new corn.

IX Tlaxochimaco (birth of flowers), first flowering [July 22–Aug. 10]. Huitzilopochtli. Feasts on turkeys and corn-meal cakes in honour of the god; great dance with both sexes taking part and men even touching the women; merchants' feast, honouring their patron god Yacatecuhtli.

X Xocotlhuetzi (fall of the fruits), heat for ripening [Aug. 11–Aug. 30]. Xiuhtecuhtli (Huehueteotl). Furnace sacrifice (p. 196); competitive climbing of high pole by young men to win special insignia at top.

XI Ochpaniztli (month of brooms), refreshment of Earth Mother [Aug. 31–Sept. 19]. Tlazolteotl or Teteoinan (Toçi). Sacrifice of woman impersonating Goddess of Ripe Corn; efforts to avoid sorrow by buffoonery, sympathetic magic to avoid rains at harvest; review of warriors and distribution of insignia of rank; drills and mock combats of Eagle and Ocelot Knights.

XII Teotleco (return of the gods), harvest [Sept. 20–Oct. 9]. Tezcatlipoca. Ceremonies honouring the return of the gods to the earth; Tezcatlipoca first to come; two absent, Xiuhtecuhtli, too old to travel, Yacatecuhtli, merchant wandering off beaten track; ceremonial drunkenness and furnace sacrifice.

XIII Tepeilhuitl (feast of the mountains), rain [Oct. 10–Oct. 29]. Tlalocs. Ceremonies for mountain rain gods, an aspect of Tlalocs; use of wooden snakes and figurines covered with amaranth paste; sacrifice of four women and a man with subsequent ceremonial cannibalism.

XIV Quecholli [bird, quail(?)], rain [Oct. 30–Nov. 18]. Mixcoatl. Making of weapons; general penance of four days; licensed old people abstain from liquor and husbands from their wives; ceremonial hunt with sacrifice of game and ceremonial feasting on the hill.

XV Panquetzaliztli (feast of the flags), winter solstice [Nov. 19–Dec. 8]. Huitzilopochtli. Festivals honouring War God; mock or staged combats; imprinting of hand impressions by captives.

XVI Atemoztli (fall of the waters), rain [Dec. 9–Dec. 28]. Tlalocs. Vigils and offerings to household gods; winter solstice at time of conquest; erection of poles with paper streamers coated with rubber.

XVII Tititl (severe weather), season of serenity [Dec. 29–Jan. 7]. Ilamatecuhtli. Sacrifice of woman impersonating goddess; sympathetic magic to bring rain by weeping, through children crying on first day of month and men and children beating women with straw-filled bags to make them cry.

XVIII Izcalli (resuscitation), toasting of corn supply [Jan. 18–Feb. 6]. Xiuhtecuhtli. Ceremonial hunt; killing of captives every four years; killing birds and arrow sacrifice at Cuauhtitlan.

Nemontemi (five unlucky days) [Feb. 7–Feb. 11].

193

on for the Aztec cycle or major time unit, and in the Valley of Mexico they did not go further and distinguish between cycles except indirectly. In consequence there is the same sort of confusion in referring to events as would result were we to designate years within the century without distinguishing the number of centuries before or after Christ. Thus the discovery of America would be recorded as 92 and the Declaration of Independence as 76, and only a detailed knowledge of history would enable us to fix the events in their proper relationship to the fifteenth and eighteenth centuries. (See Plates 62, top left; 63.)

The lag between the calendric and the solar year, for which we compensate by adding a day every four years as the twenty-ninth of February, was difficult to adjust by Aztec standards, since so much of the time count hinged on the orderly mathematical sequence of days. Some authorities believe that the Aztecs let the calendar drop behind, others that compensation was made during the unlucky period of five days. A third suggestion interprets the celebration of a feast held every eight years as a sign that a dateless day was introduced, unrecognized, in the *tonalpohualli* of the year, but honoured with special rites (7). (See Plate 58, bottom.)

However the matter of the leap year was settled, the close of one cycle and the beginning of a new one was celebrated with great pomp year Two Reed, chosen as the first day of each cycle for some ritualistic reason. In the Mixteca–Puebla area the *tonalamatls* show evidence that the priests observed the planet Venus and took note of a Venus Year of 584 days. At the end of two cycles (104 years) there was a tremendous ceremony of great ritualistic significance, for at the same time as the beginning of Venus count, a solar count, a fifty-two-year cycle, and a *tonalpohualli* all coincided. That four mystical rhythms, affecting such diverse aspects of the universe and the gods that dwelt therein, could meet must have produced great satisfaction and occasioned the utmost rejoicing among people for whom pattern and form had such great significance (8).

Although the Valley of Mexico Aztecs did not use the Venus count, they celebrated the cyclical change with the utmost ceremony. They thought of the change from one cycle to another as the death of one life and the beginning of a new one. The realization that nature could withhold the continuance of their existence endowed the ritual with profound solemnity. The New Fire Ceremony was symbolized by the extinction of the old altar fire, which had burned perpetually for fifty-two years, and the kindling of a fresh one in token of the new grant of life (9). (See Plate 29, top row.)

During the five useless days (*nemontemi*) of the final year the people let their fires go out and destroyed their household furniture. Fasting and lamentation were the order of the day while the populace awaited catastrophe. Pregnant women were shut up in granaries, lest they be changed into wild animals, and children were marched up and down and kept awake, for fear that sleep on that fatal evening would result in their turning into rats.

At sunset the priests, in solemn panoply, representatives of the whole array of the Aztec pantheon, ascended the Hill of the Star, anciently known as Huixachtecatl. This extinct volcanic crater rises abruptly from the Valley floor, and is visible from almost every quarter of the Valley of Mexico. From the temple on its summit the priests anxiously scanned the heavens as the night wore on, awaiting the hour when a certain star or stars, Aldebaran or the Pleiades, reached the centre of the heavens and gave the sign that their world would continue.

At the very moment when these stars passed the meridian the priests seized a wooden fire-drill and kindled a new fire in the open breast of a victim freshly slain for the purpose. The populace – priests, chiefs and commoners – thrilled to a great happiness. Runners lit torches from the new fire and re-kindled the altars in the temples of every town and hamlet, whence the people bore the flames to their hearths. Like fire-flies, the darting torch-bearers sped through the night, bringing the promise of a new life to every man, woman and child. With the dawn, more than ever gracious in its fulfilment of a nation's piety, the populace rallied, renovating their temples, refurbishing their houses and making new utensils for temple and household use. There was feasting on special food, and sacrifice, both by personal blood-letting and the immolation of captives, betokened the measure of popular gratitude.

Another striking ceremony fell on the day Four Earthquake (or Motion), the sign of the present age, and symbolized the passage of the sun through the heavens. At dawn a captive dressed as the Sun God, Tonatiuh, ascended the platform where the Calendar Stone was set. Four priests spread-eagled the victim, and a fifth opened his breast to tear out the heart as an offering to the god. The populace then feasted until noon, gashing their ears and parts of their bodies with blades of obsidian. In the afternoon the Eagle and Tiger Knights, votaries of the solar cult, took part in a dance dramatizing the sacred war wherein the sun was slain, to be reborn the following day. The dance culminated in a gladiatorial sacrifice. Selected Eagle and Tiger Knights, armed with real weapons, slew a captive warrior, chosen for his military distinction, who was tethered to a circular stone representing the sun's disc and who defended himself with dummy weapons only (10). (See Plate 60, top, middle left, right.)

A curious type of sacrifice took place in connection with the worship of the god Xipe, and may be the origin of the arrow sacrifice which is performed in honour of the morning star by the Pawnee of our Western plains. In the Mexican rite the victim was lashed to a scaffold, and priests, using bows or *atl-atls*, shot him to death (11).

The Aztecs performed a hideous ceremony in honour of the Fire God, Huehueteotl. Prisoners of war and their captors took part in a dance in honour of the god, and the next day the captives ascended to the top of a platform, where a powder, *yauht-li* (Indian hemp), was cast in their faces to anaesthetize them against their ghastly fate. After preparing a great fire, each priest seized a captive and, binding him hand and foot, lifted him on to his back. A macabre dance took place around the burning coals, and one by one they dumped their burdens into the flames. Before death could intervene to put an end to their suffering the priests fished out the captives with large hooks and wrenched the hearts from their blistered bodies (12).

In contrast to the callous brutality of the fire sacrifice, the ceremony in honour of the god Tezcatlipoca was strikingly dramatic, tinged with the pathos with which we view the taking of a life. The handsomest and bravest prisoner of war was selected a year before his execution. Priests taught him the manners of a ruler, and as he walked about, playing divine melodies upon his flute, he received the homage due to Tezcatlipoca himself. A month before the day of sacrifice four lovely girls, dressed as goddesses, became his companions and attended to his every want. On the day of his death he took leave of his weeping consorts to lead a procession in his honour, marked by jubilation and feasting. Then he bade farewell to the glittering cortege and left for a small temple, accompanied by the eight priests who had attended him throughout the year. The priests preceded him up the steps of the temple, and he followed, breaking at each step a flute which he had played in the happy hours of his incarnation. At the top of the platform the priests turned him over the sacrificial block and wrenched out his heart. In deference to his former godhood, his body was carried, not ignominiously flung, down the steps, but his head joined the other skulls spitted on the rack beside the temple (13). (See Plate 61, bottom left.)

Every one of the great monthly sacrifices had a dramatic significance, and a list of the principal feasts, the gods they honoured and the month of their occurrence is set forth on Table XVII (pp. 192–3). Several authors have availed themselves of

Friar Sahagun's matchless descriptions to set forth the elaborate rituals which we have lightly sampled here. The elements of time, training and elaborate preparation of costume, it can be readily seen, must have absorbed a large part of the resources of the tribe. The tentacles of ritual extended throughout the tribal activities, so that even games and sports were transformed into acts of religious meaning, although the participants undoubtedly derived a great deal of fun from their performance.

The ball game, *tlachtli*, was such a game, played in a court shaped like the capital letter *I*. Walls extended on either side of the stem of the *I*, and in the middle of each a stone or wooden ring was set vertically, in contrast to the horizontal position of a basket-ball hoop. The players tried to pass through this ring a hard rubber ball, which they could strike only with their elbows, hips or legs. There must have been some other method of scoring than by goals alone, since these, very naturally, were of rare occurrence – so much so that, in the event of one, players and backers had the right to snatch the wearing apparel of their adversaries. The game was played far and wide, courts having been found from the Republic of Honduras to south-eastern Arizona. It has a special interest for us in that the first description of rubber, so important in our modern economy, was when Oviedo, in the sixteenth century, wrote of the game and the ball used by its players (14). (See Plate 57, bottom; Fig. 3.)

There were also games of chance which were played with a semi-sacred significance. One such game, *patolli*, utilized a board shaped like a cross, with spaces ruled in the arms, not unlike a version of the old-fashioned parchesi of our childhood. Macuilxochitl, Five Flower, the god of all games, was sometimes portrayed in connection with players of *patolli* (15).

Another important entertainment involved the erection of a high pole at the top of which a movable platform was socketed. Men dressed as gods or the birds into which the gods transformed themselves, and, fastened by ropes wound around the platform, leaped off into space. As they did so, the ropes, unwinding, rotated the platform and gave the effect of flight to the circling performers. Each turn brought the birdmen nearer to the ground, and they were wont to alter their centre of balance and adjust their wings, producing the effect of the rise and fall of soaring birds. This modest application of the principle of gliding must have created a spectacle of colour and beauty. The ceremony is still performed in parts of Mexico, and the Volador, or flying place, of Tenochtitlan was, until very recently, the site of the 'Thieves' Market' in Mexico City (16).

The application of human sacrifice to the most simple ceremonial act of thanksgiving offers a grisly contrast to the spirit in which these rituals were carried out. However, social and religious behaviour are calculated to preserve human existence and ensure man's well-being regardless of how warped the method may become. It follows that the idea of sacrificing precious possessions to attain such ends would lead to the offering of the most precious gift of all, human life, since that is what man most ardently strives to keep intact. Thus instances of human sacrifices keep cropping up in the world's religious systems, and we preserve in our own culture the concept of martyrdom, achieved by voluntary or involuntary means, as an act of virtue. The very beautiful example of the Saviour transmutes to the highest spiritual plane this idea of sacrifice for the good of humanity.

The Aztecs did not reach this spiritual level, but the symbolism of their sacrifice has, none the less, its own barbaric beauty. They reasoned that for man to survive, the gods who permit his existence must also live and wax strong. These gods, however, received their best nutriment from the most precious of offerings, the hearts of men. Thus a vicious circle became established which led to sacrifice on an increasing scale. The gods manifested their favour and their strength to the Aztecs by letting them prosper, but the Aztecs, on their part, had to sacrifice hearts to the gods to maintain their good will. A good part of the tribal prosperity emanated from military success, so that the most acceptable sacrifices were the hearts of adversaries, which were the hardest to acquire, since prisoners could not be taken without military victory. A martial success, on the other hand, could be achieved only through the exercise of divine favour. Thus sacrifice led to war, and war back to sacrifice, in an unending series of expanding cycles. The effect that this practice had on foreign affairs we shall describe in the next chapter. (See Plate 60, middle left, bottom.)

War captives were the most esteemed offering, and the braver and higher in rank, the more valuable they were. Slaves were killed for minor ceremonies, and in rare instances women and children were slain in fertility rites to ensure growth in plants by the powers of sympathetic magic. Ceremonial cannibalism was sometimes practised, in the belief that the eater could absorb the virtues of the eaten, but this rite cannot be considered a vice. The letting of one's own blood was another way to ensure divine favour, and people did horrible self-penances, such as mutilating themselves with knives or drawing through their tongues a string on which were threaded maguey spines. The higher the social position of the individual and the more he consequently knew of ritualistic observance, the more arduously he performed the fasts, penances and tortures imposed by the religion. The priests, therefore, were strongly cognizant of their social responsibility, and by the rigour of their own lives strove to ensure the well-being of the tribe (17). (See Plate 61, bottom right.)

The picture-writings of the Aztecs take human sacrifice and penance as a matter of course, but seldom indicate the quantity of victims. Indeed, only one such manuscript records the monthly ceremonies, and a post-Conquest copy of another reveals a sacrifice of 20,000 people at the dedication of the enlarged great temple of Mexico (17). The Spanish accounts and those of the educated Indians agree, but whether Christian piety induced exaggeration, and how much, it is difficult to ascertain at this time and age. The Conquistador who counted thousands of skulls on the skull rack in Tenochtitlan apparently confirms these other statements, which the great humanitarian and Indian lover, Las Casas, discounted in his special pleading for decent treatment of the indigenous population of New Spain (18).

The priesthood, beside performing these bloodcurdling acts, had other more pacific duties; they also instructed youth in the mysteries of writing and keeping records. Aztec writing was pictographic, and was arriving at the stage of syllabic phonetics, which is an important part of the hieroglyphic writing of Egypt. There was no alphabet, but a picture of an animal or thing could be combined with the picture of another animal or thing to give a third meaning in terms of its sound value, much like our method of rebus writing. We could write: 'I can be hospitable', in terms of the sounds given to pictures of an eye, a tin can, a bee, a horse, a hole in the ground and a table. The Aztecs wrote the name of their capital by drawing stone *tena* from which sprouted a nopal cactus, *nochtli*, or the town Pantepec, by drawing a flag, *pantli*, on a conventionalized hill, *tepec*. Colour, position, puns and abbreviations all contributed to recording sounds by this means. Conventionalized signs, like footprints to show travel or movement, a shield and club for war, a bundled corpse for death, gave simple connotations of action (19). (See Fig. 2.)

Aztec writing offered no way of making general statements or expressing abstract ideas. Yet the full accounts of historical events, set down after the Conquest in Spanish or Nahuatl, indicate that oral traditions, possibly learned as a chant or saga, supplemented these ideographic records.

Their numerical system was vigesimal. The Aztecs counted by twenties where we count by tens. They indicated quantities up to twenty by the requisite number of dots, although in the Mixteca this method was abridged by using bars to represent groups of five. The Aztecs used a flag to indicate twenty, repeating it for quantities up to 400, while a sign like a fir tree, meaning numerous as hairs, signified 400 (20 × 20). The next unit, 8000 (20 × 20 × 20), was indicated by a bag, referring to the almost innumerable contents of a sack of cacao beans. (See Fig. 2.)

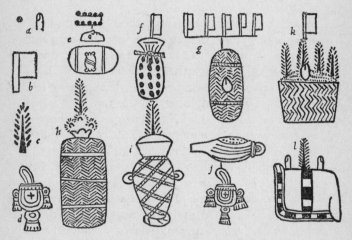

FIG. 2. AZTEC NUMBERS AND METHODS OF ENUMERATION.

(*a*) one, a dot or finger. (*b*) twenty, a flag. (*c*) 400, a sign denoting hairs. (*d*) 8000, a bag. (*e*) ten masks of precious stone. (*f*) twenty bags of cochineal dye. (*g*) 100 bags of cacao. (*h*) 400 bales of cotton. (*i*) 400 jars of honey of tuna. (*j*) 8000 leaf-bundles of copal gum. (*k*) twenty baskets each containing 1600 ground cacao nibs. (*l*) 402 cotton blankets of this type.

A post-Conquest manuscript shows devices that may not have been of native origin but European adaptations of the Aztec system. For example, fractions are shown by blacking in segments of a quarter, a half or three quarters of a disc. Similarly fives and multiples of five are indicated by colouring the requisite spaces in the flag of the sign for twenty, and hundreds by showing the proportionate lines in the four-hundred symbol (20).

Aztec histories consisted of annals of ancient times, contemporary events, year counts, accounts compiled yearly, specific records for each year, books of each day and day-by-day count or diaries (21). Some of the ancient and contemporary histories have been published, but none of the shorter records have reached print, even if they survive in some library. These histories followed two main styles. One, exemplified in the Mapa Tlotzin and Codex Xolotl, sets forth events, the people or tribes involved and the places, each designated by its hieroglyph. Year names were appended to give the dates. These Texcocan records are highly complicated to follow, but fortunately some have glossaries appended after the Conquest (22). (See Plate 25, top row.)

The other style recorded the succession of the years, one after the other, for the whole time covered by the history. Events, like conquests or the death of chiefs, were appropriately drawn near the proper year sign, and sometimes were connected by a line. This type of history seemed confined largely to Tenochtitlan. Since Tenochcan history is much more accurate after A.D. 1400 than before, one wonders whether the destruction of the books, ordered by Itzcoatl, did not really pave the way for a new style of writing (23). (See Plates 62, top; 63.)

In addition to the histories and the sacred almanacs, tribal records were kept. These are most useful to the modern student, for the names of the towns are inscribed in one column, while the rest of the page records the amount of gold, ornaments or cloth that was paid in as tribute. Since the geographical location of most of these towns is known, the chief products of each area can be determined. Other records showed lines of descent, lands occupied and other data essential to family economics (24). (See Plates 62, bottom right; 64.)

Fortunately, after the Conquest the Spaniards utilized the native methods of writing as well as their own in civil records, such as tax rolls, lawsuits, and the like, so that the Indians could understand the Spanish legal code and present their complaints (25). Friar Nicolas Tester even made an attempt to shift the picture-writing over to syllabic writing – the effect of the Lord's Prayer in Aztec glyphs is startling (26). This was too cumbersome a plan, and was soon abandoned for the recording of Nahuatl words in Roman characters. However, it is due to this usage of Aztec pictographs that so much survives of the records, many of which, with their oral accompaniment, were copied into Roman characters both in Spanish and Nahuatl. From these we derive such knowledge as we have of Aztec history and customs. (See Plate 44.)

The drawback of picture writing is its rigidity and its uselessness for the expression of abstract ideas. The cyclical count created great confusion as to the particular cycle in which an event took place. Exact and careful drawing was essential for the glyphs, and a slurred line might result in a totally different reading. However, the worst feature of Aztec history is its provincialism, for the scribes saw things only in terms of the tribe, and took no heed of internal events in other communities. The picture-writings show how communal interests extended vertically, as it were, from the tribe to the pantheon. There is no reflection of a horizontal interest outward to the lives and occupations of other peoples. The attitude of the Aztec communities to foreign affairs merits a chapter in itself.

CHAPTER XII

FOREIGN AFFAIRS AND WAR

The relationships of Aztec tribes to one another in peace and war, the nature of the Aztec domain and methods of military organization and warfare

THE community or tribe was the centre of the political and economic life of the Aztecs. Existence depended on the favour of the gods, who participated directly in the tribal fortunes, so that the degree of elaboration of the ceremonial structures was an accurate gauge of tribal prosperity. A man's position in the civil life of the community had a corresponding level in the hierarchy, since conspicuous fulfilment of civil obligations entailed an equal attainment in piety and observance of ritual. The basic design for living was a communal agriculture. The early tribal existence sought to achieve this pattern by avoiding other peoples and finding new land to settle. There is an essential affinity between agriculture and political isolation, just as commerce and manufacture require successively broader political contacts (1).

In the early history of the Valley of Mexico there appears to have been a series of small isolated settlements which carried on a vague process of exchange. The Toltec civilization seems to have attained uniform development over a wide area spread by a population which gradually filled up unoccupied territory. There was little to suggest war or conquest at first. Later civil disintegration caused the Toltec decline, and the character of the Valley was transformed. Formerly, tribes had slowly grown in numbers until dense occupation of a previously unpopulated territory took place. But in the Chichimec period men were driven from their home territories by various factors, of which over-population may have been one, vague unrest another, and set out in search of new land. While the goal of each group of immigrants may well have been to settle and farm in peaceful isolation, the very process of movement must have brought war and consequent readjustments in the social organization.

Throughout Chichimec times, and into the Aztec period as well, the political unit was a tribe, dwelling in its own village, supported by its own land. Even though a tribe might grow to thousands of members, the village become transformed into a city-state, and the communal lands cease to support the population, no real shift in political organization took place. No leader developed the concept of empire so successfully applied by the Incas of Peru. The group experience of the Indians was to colonize new land but, with perhaps the sole exception of Peru, never to incorporate, through conquest, weaker communities into their own tribe. However, when the tribe became too unwieldy to migrate *en masse*, an adjustment had to be made between population and food supply. One method was for part of the population to break away and join another community whose economic resources were relatively unexploited. As an illustration we have the case of the Chimalpanecs and the Culhuas, who joined the nascent community of Texcoco, to the vast benefit of its material and intellectual culture (2). (See Plate 29, top row; Fig. 1.)

The more usual means of adjusting food supply to population was the exaction of tribute from richer and weaker neighbours. Quinatzin of Texcoco instituted the system first in the northern Valley in the early fourteenth century, and it is an interesting point to speculate as to whether or not the Chimalpanec immigrants suggested this as a practice found successful in their homeland. Quinatzin, by force of arms or by persuasion, induced a number of towns to turn over to him supplies of various sorts. The local chiefs recognized him as an overlord, but maintained a complete political independence. He, in turn, granted the vassal chiefs the full measure of his military support. Yet these vassals had no sense of loyalty, and were quite ready to revolt or transfer their allegiance to a stronger suzerain (3). (See Plate 42, top.)

When Tezozomoc of Azcapotzalco saw his tribe develop to the point where it had to expand he found the southern Valley over-populated, so that he had to challenge the power of Texcoco. His first move was to create disaffection in the vassal states, after which he could move against his rivals with good hope of military success. Yet so light was Tezozomoc's tenure of control that it was relatively easy for the conquered tribes to combine later and wreck his domination.

Alliances like that formed by Texcoco, Tenochtitlan and Tacuba were so very rare that much is made of this combination as an example of the excellence of Aztec statecraft. It would seem that the division of spoils, two parts each to the larger states, and one part to Tlacopan, was in force only for that campaign. Later Texcoco and Tenochtitlan undertook wars for their mutual advantage, but there was constant intrigue in the hope that one of the two could overcome the other and derive the full benefits of the booty taken. By the mid-fifteenth century both Tenochtitlan and Texcoco had grown to the point where they had to have additional supplies or else starve, so, because of this common necessity, the alliance endured fairly well (4).

Despite their common background of language, thought, religion, custom and material culture, the Aztecs had no sense of unity. Tenochtitlan and Tlaltelolco, both of which are within the city limits of modern Mexico, existed side by side in complete independence for many years; not until 1473 did the Tenochcas make up their minds to conquer their neighbours. Each town and hamlet was sufficient unto itself, and its members felt no larger loyalty. In modern Teotihuacan this feeling still persists, and the members of one *barrio*, or ward, look upon those of the adjacent one as a congregation of the most horrible criminals. Not even the Spanish siege of Mexico brought unity to the Aztecs, and the Texcocans blithely joined the invaders to exterminate their former ally Tenoch-titlan.

Although community was potentially hostile to community, individuals could move freely about the countryside. Trade in simple commodities was carried on extensively from the early times of the Middle Cultures. In the Aztec period the travelling merchants became a special class, and their security of body and property, preserved at first for the advantages which each town could derive from their wares, was guaranteed by the force of Aztec arms. Pilgrims going to worship at special shrines had free and unmolested passage; and a suggestion that such journeys were made in the distant past is given by the Middle Culture figurines of foreign origin. One site especially, Tetelpan, produced so great a variety of idols from such a wide area that it must have been an important religious centre in Middle Culture times. However, neither trade nor religion broke down the sense of communal and political independence in Central Mexico. (See Plate 35; Fig. 2.)

Foreign relations centred around war, which, we have seen, was an important part of Aztec economy and religion. The same confusion of motives that we find in our modern culture affected the reasons for military action. We wage war for economic, territorial and political advantages and, while condemning the practice in our adversaries, justify our own participation by saying that we are fighting for freedom, to liberate someone, to extend civilization or to ensure peace. Soldiers on our own side are brave and attain glory, preserve our social virtues and sacrifice themselves for the public well-being. Those on the other side are aggressors, agents of evil and cowardly knaves. The Aztecs made war for defence, revenge and economic motives, which were inextricably confused with the need for the sacrificial victims requisite for proper adoration of their gods. Thus in warfare the great aim was to take captives, but behind this religious goal lurked the less holy urges of political and economic expediency.

The captive himself attained social status, since he went to a special warrior's heaven. A redoubtable Tlaxcalan chief, named Tlahuicol, was singled out for sacrifice to the sun, and fought so successfully with his dummy weapons that he killed some of his adversaries and wounded a number of the others. He was pardoned and offered a chieftaincy in the Tenochcan army. Tlahuicol, however, rejected his pardon, and gladly underwent sacrifice for the greater honour and glory in that death. This story illustrates the attitude of the individual warrior, which is not unlike that of the mediaeval knight or career soldier in our own culture (5).

The Aztec reasons for fighting and their social and moral sanctions for war were not so very different from our own, except that we have many more, owing to our superior rationalizations. The Aztec military technique, however, was definitely inferior, since it was not so completely developed a social tool as it is in our own culture. The basic organization of the army required the participation of every able-bodied man under the direction of the war chief. However, as Aztec society grew more intricate and greater numbers of warriors took the field, the military structure became more rigid.

The unit of organization was an aggregation of twenty men, several of which were combined into larger bodies of 200 to 400, roughly corresponding to our platoons and companies. Special detachments of from four to six men, who did scouting and raiding, operated much as do the squads of our own military system. The clan commander marshalled the larger bodies, much as a colonel handles his regiment. The clan troops were banded together in four divisions under the heads of the four municipal quarters, and the tribal war chiefs had the supreme command. In a very numerous army the troops from a given quarter, or *barrio*, were sometimes divided into brigades, composed of the forces from two or three clans (6).

The high tribal officers, the war chief, the chiefs of the quarters and the clan chiefs commanded the larger bodies. The or-

K

dinary chiefs and members of the warrior orders, the Knights of the Eagle and the Tiger and of a third infrequently mentioned order, the Arrow, according to their particular ability, took over the lesser units. In other words, the executive officials of the tribe in peace-time became its military officers in time of war. There was no distinction made between the civil and military offices, since the tribe operated as an entity in both peace and war, and standing armies did not exist. (See Plate 34, bottom left.)

The soldiers were the able-bodied men of the tribe. The *telpuchcalli*, houses of youth, through which boys passed at the age of fifteen for formal instruction in the duties of manhood, taught them the usage of different weapons. Drill, in the sense of the accurate movements of modern troops, did not exist, but the great monthly ceremonies called for military demonstrations in which warriors showed their abilities and performed sham manoeuvres. Each recruit followed an experienced warrior in battle, much as a mediaeval squire served an apprenticeship to a knight in full standing.

The chief offensive arms were wooden clubs, edged with sharp blades of obsidian, and the javelin, hurled by means of the *atl-atl*. Bows and arrows were used, but the heavier javelins were preferred for the close fighting of Aztec warfare. Slings and spears were weapons favoured by some. For defensive armour, shields of wickerwork covered with hide were most commonly in use, and some were elaborately painted or covered with feathers. The Aztecs also developed a body armour of quilted cotton, soaked in brine, which covered the whole body like a siren suit. This was so effective a protection against clubs and missiles that the Spaniards rapidly adopted it, extolling it as cooler and lighter than steel armour (7). Some warriors wore wooden helmets, which were elaborately carved to represent the insignia of the military orders. These had decorative rather than defensive values and added to the richness of costumes worn by the maturer warriors. A

tribesman had the right to elaborate his dress in accordance
with his prowess, and the great chiefs wore attached to their
backs immense frames covered with feathers. Tribes, and even
clans, wore special insignia, so that friend could be distinguished from foe and chief from common warrior. The term
uniform could hardly be used, since the rich variety and
indulgence in individual fancy produced a kaleidoscopic
effect in the motley array of bright colours and strange
forms (8).

To supply these forces was a very considerable task. Each
quarter of the town had its *tlacochcalco*, or house of darts, an
arsenal where the military supplies were stored. This was situated near the chief temple, the lofty sides of which made it a
natural strong point. At a call to arms the clan leaders could
rapidly assemble their men and equip them at these rallying
points, which were also centres of the religious and social life
of the community (9).

An offensive campaign was a more serious undertaking.
Having no beasts of burden, the warriors had to carry their own
food with them. Owing to the governmental system, wherein each town was independent, the armies did not dare live off
the country, for fear of inciting revolt, and also because most
communities lacked the food to sustain a large body of men.
Thus, prior to a war, negotiations had to be made whereby
supplies could be concentrated and allies brought together at a
point as near as possible to the zone of attack. Usually a single
battle decided the issue, since the attacking force could not
maintain itself in the field for more than a very few days. The
calculations necessary to fight a war 200 or 300 miles away in
Oaxaca, say, were highly complex, and much of the Aztec
force on such a campaign must have been composed of local
tribesmen, stiffened with a *garde d'élite* of Tenochcas and
Texcocans.

Owing to this difficulty in respect of transport, siege operations were virtually impossible, so that formal fortifications

were rare. Some towns were built in very strategic locations, high on a mountain-side or in the bend of a river, having access restricted to a narrow neck of land. Tenochtitlan, owing to its situation on the lake, was a natural fort. The causeways were penetrated by canals at intervals, so that removal of the portable bridges created natural barriers. The flat roof-tops offered good points from which to harry the enemy in the street below, and the many temples were strong points difficult to reduce. (See Plate 37, top.)

Miles of defensive walls surrounded a site in Tlaxcala, where a ditch backed by a wall enclosed an area of several square miles. At Huexotla,[1] a fief of Texcoco, a wall at least 15 feet high still exists, and must have had a strong defensive value, although its ostensible purpose was to enclose the area about the main temple. Xochicalco [2] is situated on a high hill which was intensively terraced, and it was further strengthened by a wide ditch cut through the point of easiest access. Sometimes a site was chosen between two ravines which made impassable obstacles to an attacking force. However, while defensive *purposes* were often taken into account in building towns, strictly defensive *works*, in the nature of fortifications, were seldom undertaken (10).

Open fighting, the difficulty of keeping up extended campaigns and the informal character of the military force were factors which stultified the development of tactics or strategy. In battle the howling mob which represented the collective strength of one tribe tried to route the yelling horde of its adversary, and the first to run lost the battle. Captives were taken, tribute imposed, the temple burned and the defeated group was then left alone again.

To attain victory more easily, surprise attacks, sometimes implemented by a little treachery, were instituted. However, the cumbrous process of getting an army on to the field of battle usually prevented this favoured method of warfare. More

　　　　1. Way-sho'-tla.　　2. Sho-chi-cal'-co.

often the Tenochcas and their allies would feint with a screen of warriors, who would be easily repulsed in a pretended rout. The main body would wait in a place of concealment until the pursuing enemy came into view, whereupon they would charge out and demolish them. Losses were chiefly felt in the number of captives taken, since these short hand-to-hand combats were not very damaging to the man-power of either side. The capture of a chief or the recognition of a sign of evil portent was sufficient to demoralize an army and, despite their bravery and constant experience in warfare of this type, the Aztecs were little fitted to resist soldiers trained in European techniques.

There was rather more opportunity for strategy than for battle tactics. Considerable planning, as we have said, was necessary to move troops upon the field of battle. The Aztecs won campaigns in Oaxaca, Puebla, western Mexico and along the Vera Cruz coast, as far north as Tamaulipas.[1] Having to move step by step and to intimidate or win over town after town, they needed patience and knowledge of geographical and political conditions. One reason for the honour in which merchants were held was the information of this character which they could furnish from their travels.

The triple alliance was a typical example of Aztec strategy. Nezahualcoyotl wanted to restore the hegemony of Texcoco and destroy Tezozomoc's Tepanec power, the centre of which was Azcapotzalco. The two towns were separated by the Lake of Mexico. To move troops overland would have required several days; to move them across the lake in canoes would have meant having a landing-base on the western shore. Nezahualcoyotl, therefore, induced Tlacopan and Tenochtitlan, which were at the back door of Azcapotzalco, and tributary to it as well, to declare war. Thus he had a base at which to land his canoes filled with troops, and, while his allies engaged the enemy strongly in this quarter, the Texcocan chief had

1. Ta-mow-lee'-pas.

time to bring reinforcements around the lakes by the overland route to attack another point.

The town of Chiconauhtla offers another example of these simple strategic ideas. This settlement dominated the straits through which the northern lakes of Zumpango and Xaltocan empty into Lake Texcoco. The people here could destroy any force in canoes moving east against Texcoco or west against Azcapotzalco. Their forces also could make a flank attack on land armies skirting the lakes against either of those two objectives. Early in the thirteenth century Chiconauhtla became a fief of Texcoco and participated, as a sort of guardian of the western marches, in campaigns against rebellious western tribes and in the great war with Tezozomoc. Later it seems to have become part of the Tenochtitlan chain of vassal towns, and its chief had the honour of sharing a royal apartment in Montezuma's palace with the rulers of far more important city-states. To confirm this documentary evidence, excavation of the site reveals, in the quantity and quality of the material culture surviving, evidence of participation in trade and booty far in excess of the apparent size and importance of the town (11). (See map, p. 8. Plates 41, top; 42, top; 43.)

The purely economic and military aspects of war are as crude, when judged by our modern technical standards, as the rest of the purely mechanical aspects of Aztec life. On the other hand, the ritualistic conception of war as the earthly re-enactment of the titanic struggle between opposing forces in nature has a quality almost sublime. The political and economic frictions that brought about conflict were welcomed by the warriors as an opportunity to vibrate to the deep rhythms of nature, rhythms which met in a celestial antiphony in the Sacred War which the Sun fights each day as he, by his own death and sacrifice, ensures the life of man.

The War of Flowers was undertaken to satisfy this yearning when no active campaign was in progress. In this incongruously named ceremonial combat the best warriors from several states met in a very real battle, so that feats of arms could be accomplished and captives taken to satisfy the hunger of the gods. One famous War of Flowers was repeated for several years, and the cream of the fighting men of Texcoco, Tenochtitlan and Tlacopan vied with the might of Cholula, Huexotcingo and Tlaxcala. If a warrior were captured, he met the most glorious of deaths in direct sacrifice to the Sun. If he lived, he gained renown. If he were slain, he was cremated, an honour reserved only for fighting men, and passed on to the special heaven where warriors dwell (12).

Such warfare had no place in a conflict with Europeans, but when reduced to fighting for their bare lives against the Spaniards, the Aztecs put up one of the most desperate defences in history. It was the last sacrifice, in which Aztec civilization offered up its very existence in an effort to survive. Aztec culture achieved, with Stone Age tools, a civilization patterned to balance the life of man against the dimly perceived forces of the universe. Its downfall was inevitable when confronted with that inexorable European world of steel, objective reasoning and a religion adjusted to meet such totally different concepts as the demands of the powerful and the needs of the weak.

We cannot tell what Aztec civilization might have become. Like all the nations of the past, and of the present too, which have flourished and ultimately withered in death, the Aztecs nurtured within themselves the seeds of their own destruction. But before we turn from their remote splendour to the preoccupations of our modern life, let us catch two last glimpses of Aztec civilization: one of the city of Tenochtitlan as the Spaniards first saw it, the other of the Aztecs in their ultimate war, profane and deadly on this final occasion.

CHAPTER XIII

GLIMPSES OF TENOCHTITLAN

What the Spaniards saw when they entered this great Aztec capital

THE history of the Aztecs and their forebears is the most complete record we have of the growth of any Indian civilization. Their conquest was the greatest feat in the European occupation of the American continent. The Aztecs were at their zenith in 1519, when Cortés and his 400 men first landed, and a description of Tenochtitlan, taken from the contemporary records of the conquerors themselves, will show us something of the external character of Indian civilization in America (1).

Bernal Diaz del Castillo, who left the most personal record of the Spanish Conquest, tells how his comrade-in-arms on first beholding Tenochtitlan, the ancient Mexico City, exclaimed, 'It is like the enchantments they tell of in the legend of Amadis ! Are not the things we see a dream?'

This is lyric language from hard-bitten men-at-arms, whose chief avocations, while engaged in converting the heathen, lay in acquiring booty and enjoying the charms of dusky Dulcineas. Yet, in contrast to the drab towns and tawny hills of Spain, Tenochtitlan must have appeared a paradise, for its green gardens and white buildings were set in the midst of blue lakes, ringed by lofty mountains. 'Gazing on such wonderful sights,' wrote Bernal Diaz, 'we did not know what to say or whether what appeared before us was real, for on one side in the land there were great cities and in the lake ever so many more, and the lake itself was crowded with canoes, and in the causeway were many bridges at intervals, and in front of us stood the great City of Mexico, and we ... we did not even number four hundred soldiers' (2).

Although socially and governmentally Tenochtitlan was distinctly an American Indian tribal town, outwardly it appeared the capital city of an empire. A bird's-eye view would have revealed an oval island connected with the mainland by three causeways which converged at the centre of the city. These roads were cut by waterways over which removable bridges extended. The edges of the island were fringed by the green of the 'floating gardens', while at the centre the shiny white of the houses predominated, and the verdure was reduced to tiny green squares in the patio gardens. Thrust above the quadrate masses of the roof-tops loomed the various clan temples, each set on its platform in the form of a truncated pyramid. The city had few streets or open spaces, but was gridded with canals crossed by portable bridges. The two principal plazas were those of the Temple of Tlaltelolco and of the religious centre of Tenochtitlan proper, open spaces which gave a welcome relief from the pyramids and official palaces clustered about them. There must have been a curiously living quality about this grouping, the temples seeming to ride like horsemen among the serrated ranks of the houses. (See Plate 37, top.)

Were a visitor to have traversed Tenochtitlan from south to north, he would have been struck by the rich variety of sights. Approaching along the causeway, the traveller of that time passed first between expanses of open water. Then gradually tiny islands of green appeared, made of masses of mud dredged up from the bottom of the shallow lake and held in place by wicker-work. White-clad farmers dexterously poled their tiny dugouts through the maze as they went about the cultivation of their gardens. These irregular islets merged gradually into a more orderly grouping where the accumulation of soil had become stabilized as the roots, striking downward, had established anchorage in the lake bottom and created solid ground. This artificially made land reduced the open water of the lake to mere canals. (See Plate 37, bottom.)

Save for the broad causeways, roads there were none; and along the canals the traveller saw, in increasing numbers, boatloads of produce headed towards the city. Here and there among the green of the crops and trees he caught glimpses of thatched roofs and wattled walls, the huts of the farmers. Then adobe walls of more substantial dwellings began to encroach on the gardens, and the waters of the lake shrank to a canal following the roadway. The adobe walls gave way to the fronts of more pretentious houses plastered white or washed with powdered pumice, a dull, rich red. Now the visitor could realize how the city expanded through the successive creation of artificial islands which bore first a crop, then a modest hut and finally became integral with the masonry of the city proper.

The causeway had now changed from a simple means of communication into a principal street with all its social complexity. Since canals took the place of roads, space for a saunter was so rare that the causeways were as much recreation grounds as arteries of traffic. Thus people out to see the sights, people on errands, people on their way to the myriad functions of religious import, swallowed up the long lines of trotting carriers who, bowed under their burdens, went to the city with produce and tribute or left with goods for barter. Not a wheel turned or a pack-animal neighed; transport was on the backs of men or in the bottoms of boats.

Outside the city limits the monotony of ant-like columns of laden folk had been but rarely relieved by the passage of a civil functionary, all pomp and feathers, or by a stern merchant with a handful of fighting men, followed by a chain of apprentices, showing the whites of their eyes as they peered from under the press of their tumplines. Now could be seen clan leaders wearing rich mantles and sniffing flowers as they watched the milling crowd, and black-robed priests whose ears were shredded and whose hair was matted with the blood of self-inflicted penance. There was little sound, little hurry, save for the carriers trotting to reach relief from their burdens. There was an intense vitality, none the less, that of a multitude of units participating in complex action, knowing each its allotted part, but never the substance of the whole. (See Plates 33–36.)

A glance into the doorway of a house gave welcome relief from the cold-blooded, almost insect-like quality of life outside. A shaded patio was flanked by buildings whose interiors were cool and spacious. Mats and straw cushions on the polished red of the cement floor welcomed the visitor to repose, while the rhythmic clap of hands and the scrape of stone on stone told that tortillas were being made and corn-meal ground in a kitchen at the back. Seated in a corner, an elderly man was talking to two small boys, whose serious faces showed that, already conscious of their participation in the tribal life, they heeded their uncle's precepts as to conduct befitting boys and men. A fat little girl squatting in the doorway vainly tried to imitate with her stubby fingers and toy implements the graceful movements of her mother as she produced fine threads by the cunning manipulation of her spindle. Lolling on a cushion, a young man idly smoked a cigarette in a cane holder as he picked thoughtfully at the scarcely healed lobe of his ear, tattered by penitential blood-letting with cactus spine and obsidian blade.

A fiesta was going on in another house, and one heard the rich vibration of wooden drums and the high squeal of reed flutes. The patio was full of people, gay in the bright colours of their holiday clothes, and the air was heavy with the cloying scent of lilies. The sharp smells of rich sauces cunningly mixed from many peppers embroidered this odour, and occasionally a light breeze wafted the cool, mystic scent of incense. Somebody was celebrating his birthday, since in the background one saw a painted figure adorned with amate paper, representing the god who presided over that event. A little apart from the feasters, who partook of their entertainment with dignified pleasure, was a group of old men whose clownish gestures and burlesque solemnity could be easily associated with the cups of pulque that a slave was industriously filling for them. Not for nothing had these elders passed through the rigid self-denial of young manhood; they were permitted alcoholic indulgence in their old age whenever a feast came to pass. A last backward glance revealed the musicians, garlanded with flowers, blowing their flutes and conch shells, while one man beat the head of a cylindrical drum and another the wooden tongues in the side of the two-toned *teponaztli*.

Farther up the street the priests seemed to increase in number. More individuals wore the trappings of high office, such as nodding panaches of quetzal plumes and cloaks, the designs of which were worked in feathers like the personal insignia on their circular shields. Evidently the visitor was near the centre of the town, and presently the causeway ended in a great open square, where the temples rose above the majestic planes of their pyramidal foundations. In the hard, bright light of early afternoon, heat-waves joined the smoke of incense in rendering indistinct and unearthly the outlines of the temples.

The short, black shadows suggested unspeakable things. Was it imagination or reality, that sickening smell of a filthy butcher shop, that hung in the air in revolting contrast to the immaculate pavement of the temple courtyard? Imagination is too personal and egocentric a sensation for an Indian community, and the great block of the skull-rack gave an answer founded only too firmly on fact. Thousands of skulls, threaded on poles, were piled up in orderly symmetry, and the black cavities of their orbits and nasal apertures suggested the marks on infernal dice. Undisturbed by this monument to human sacrifice, a few young men were practising in a ball court near by. They thrust at a solid rubber ball with agile hips and elbows, in an effort to drive it through two rings set transversely to the walls in the length of the court.

A circular stone placed a short distance away was the scene of a most cruel game. Here, on certain ceremonial days, a tethered captive was forced to defend himself with a wooden club against the onslaught of an adversary whose weapon was set with razor-sharp obsidian blades. Usually he was killed in the most honourable of deaths, that of sacrificial victim to the Sun God, Tonatiuh, but sometimes he would resist so successfully that he gained a pardon. Other disc-shaped stones were placed about the plaza. One, 13 feet in diameter, was set vertically on a special platform. Carved with a consummate mastery of design, it represented the symbolic history of the world. Another disc, set flat, was hollowed in the centre so that hearts wrung from war captives might be burned to nourish the great gods. This was carved on its surface and edge to commemorate the many conquests of War Chief Tizoc, who was shown dressed as a god with his captives before him.

In another part of the plaza a sacrifice was to be made. Before a small temple dedicated to one of the myriad Aztec gods a group was gathered, some in the gay panoply of merchants and others wearing the sinister black of the priesthood. A tightly pinioned slave stood in their midst and looked unseeingly before him, resignation, not fear, on his face. The priests rushed him up the steep steps of the temple, followed by the merchants at a more leisurely pace. Two priests seized the slave by either arm, forcing him backward, while two others pulled his legs from under him until his body curved, belly upward, over the altar. A fifth priest ploughed his flint knife in a long sweep from the breastbone to the base of the stomach and, reaching into the aperture, with a dexterous twist tore out the heart. This he burned, while it was still throbbing, in a carved stone vase, while the merchants, swinging long ladles of smoking incense, chanted their thanks for a safe and profitable excursion into the hot country. (See Plate 60.)

Paying only the most cursory attention to this pious little scene, knots of chiefs were converging on a large building at a corner of the plaza. The war chief, Montezuma, was planning an attack on a neighbouring town, remiss in its tribute payment, so there must be a gathering of clan leaders to prepare for war. Adorned with helmets like the heads of jaguars, eagles and wolves, girt with armour of wadded cotton brocaded in many colours or embroidered with feathers, their faces set with nose and lip ornaments of jade and gold, these fierce-visaged chiefs passed proudly through the door, but in an anteroom to the council chamber they stripped off their ornaments. Then, bareheaded and barefooted, with downcast eyes, they made their way to the throne, where sat the slim figure of Montezuma, simply dressed but for the gold crown and jade earrings of his exalted office. (See Plate 33.)

The austerity of the council chamber was not borne out by Montezuma's other apartments, which contained all the appurtenances of a sybaritic potentate. The war chief's two wives and his many concubines occupied magnificent quarters. Kitchens and storehouses were spread over another great space, for not only were there some 300 guests served at each meal but also a thousand guards and attendants. In contrast to the profusion within, outside the kitchen door squatted patiently a threadbare group of countrymen from whose carrying-bags swayed the mottled heads of the trussed turkeys which they had brought as offerings for the royal larder.

Other rooms in Montezuma's palace contained the tribal treasure, composed of the tribute wrung from many towns. Gold, jade, rich feather mantles, baskets of produce, were heaped in abundance. Clerks were listing the goods in picture-writing to see that each subject town had fulfilled its quota or else were calculating the share that should be turned over to the various clan stewards. Another patio presented a more animated scene. Here acrobats were practising their feats and poor, warped dwarfs were composing grosser contortions to win a chiefly smile. In another set of buildings was housed the zoo, where serpents undulated sluggishly and where, from behind wooden bars, peered the greedy, yellow eyes of jaguars and ocelots. In a side room a human arm projecting from a basket of raw meat showed how the bodies of some sacrificial victims were utilized.

The highway to Tlaltelolco extended north from this great plaza, which even to-day is the centre of the city. This wide road, with a canal beside it, was filled with the same indecisive multitude that thronged the southern artery. The setting sun had brought people out on their roof-tops. Some leaned over parapets to watch the crowd below, while idlers, squatting in a shaded bit of the street, took equal interest in the slow movements of the householders above them.

A path and a canal, debouching into the main avenue, led to a small square, in the centre of which loomed a pyramid. From the patio of an adjacent building shrill cries arose and the dull clash of wooden instruments. Within, a number of boys were receiving instruction in the manual of arms. Each equipped with a small buckler and a flat wooden club, they learned the art of cut and parry under the scornful eye of a warrior. They dealt and received hard blows, but the clubs were not toothed with wedges of obsidian, the volcanic glass that made hand-to-hand combat so vicious in war. Another group was practising with the *atl-utl*, or throwing-stick. The marksman laid his spear along a narrow wooden trough with a hook at the farther end, the nearer end being grasped in the hand. By lengthening the arm in this way it was possible to give a greater propulsive force to the spear.

On the other side of the plaza the boys in the religious-training school presented a less animated scene. Their little legs and faces lacerated by maguey spines, their bodies thin from fasts and penance and their eyes dulled by the monotony of self-denial, these children were chanting strophes from a ritual-istic chant. Their preceptor, who led the singing, showed by his own scarred and emaciated body that the propitiation of the gods was a relentless and never-ending task. Priest, chief, warrior or husband, every Aztec, from boyhood on, spent much of his life either in a kind of beseeching penance, to ensure his future, or in a state of grateful atonement for not having had a worse past. The Aztecs lived on intimate if uncomfortable terms with the supernatural powers.

Another aspect of this lack of individualism was to be seen in the *tecpan* or clan building. Here elders of the clan were arranging the affairs of the tribal unit, twenty of which made up the city-state of Tenochtitlan. One old man peered over picture-maps as he adjusted a question of land tenure between two contesting families and made his final judgment on the basis of how much land each family could cultivate by its own efforts. Another elder distributed pottery vessels, given up as tribute by a town across the mountains, to some of the poorer members of the community. None of these people, litigants or applicants, bestowed more than occasional glances into the back courtyard, where an adulterer was being stoned to death by members of the affronted family. Urban existence contained too many interests and life was too cheap for them to view as an excitement the inevitable result of wrongdoing.

Each of the twenty tribal divisions regulated its own affairs. The great plaza where Montezuma had his palace and where all the gods were worshipped in many temples was for the use of all the clans together; and was the civic centre for the 60,000 households of Tenochtitlan. Yet in spite of the importance of this centre of religion and government, the great plaza of Tlaltelolco near the northern edge of the islands was almost as striking. Once a Mexican tribe acknowledged the sway of another power it was supposed to furnish fighting men and tribute, but its government and economics were seldom modified.

Thus the recently conquered Tlaltelolco had a communal centre as majestic as that of Tenochtitlan. It seemed more dramatic to Spanish eyes because its great temple to the War God, Huitzilopochtli, was thrust into prominence by the widespread of the market-place, while in Tenochtitlan the great buildings were so close together that it was hard to gain an impression of their size.

The market-place of Tlaltelolco consisted of a large area of polished pavement, bordered by arcades which sheltered many of the merchants. At one edge a basin opened out from the canal beside the northern causeway, where boats bringing goods and produce could find an anchorage. Each kind of product was concentrated in a special place. Thus one section was completely devoted to vegetables, and compactly squatting women sat watching their goods, arranged before them in symmetrical heaps on woven mats. In another section cotton mantles were being sold, some spread to show the full design and others neatly folded. Elsewhere was a row of vendors of implements and tools, such as obsidian blades, carved and burnished pottery, spindle whorls, deer-horn awls, bone bodkins and a few copper axes and needles. A brilliant mass of colour characterized the booths of the feather salesmen. Some sold merely bunches of plumes, the lovely green of the quetzal, or trogon, and the multi-coloured plumage of parrots. At the other stands feather cloaks, mats and shields gave evidence of charming fancy in their design and patient toil in their execution. (See Plates 33-9.)

Jewellers displayed jade ornaments and gold worked into precious rings of filigree or massive beaten gorgets. It was the jade, however, that caught the envious eye and was produced with furtive circumspection as a material of great price. Other merchants sold ornaments of shell, and the pinks, whites and subtle mottled browns of sea-shells contrasted with the rich dark sheen of tortoise carapaces. At one booth a rich warrior earnestly bargained with the proprietor for an exquisite pair of earplugs, cunningly inlaid with a mosaic of turquoise and mother-of-pearl.

The smiling whispers and admiring glances of the crowd at the jeweller's abruptly changed in the slave quarters to appraising stares. Some of the chattels wore wooden collars, and their brutish faces had a hopeless expression. These had sunk to servitude long ago as a result of crime or of capture in war. Others were thin and emaciated but did not wear the collar of bondage. They had met with misfortune and were selling themselves for the first time to ensure food and shelter.

A low hum rose from the market-place; there was none of the strident shouting of the European fair. The bargaining for goods was carried on slowly, quietly, but, none the less, keenly. The Aztecs had no money, so that barter was the usual means of purchase. The cacao bean, however, had a standard value, and this, in equalizing exchanges, performed the nearest approach to the function of currency. Passing through the crowd were warriors who acted as police and, should a disagreement arise, haled disputants into a court, where a tribal elder settled the question in his capacity as judge.

Beyond the market was a double line of walls which divided the market from the temple precinct of Tlaltelolco. Rectangular buildings, with patios in their centres, housed the priests and the various schools and councils of the central organization of the community. Farther on were grouped the principal shrines. In their midst the great temple to the War God shouldered its bulk into the sky. There was a skull-rack here, like the one in Tenochtitlan, and another heap was made of the bones of the victims. Near the great pyramid stood a circular temple, the door of which was built to resemble the mouth of a serpent, the place of worship of the god Quetzalcoatl. The sacrificial block in front was black with the smoke of incense and the blood of victims. A pile of stone knives and axes gave a sinister indication of what rites were practised there.

Pools fed by the pipes of an aqueduct leading from the mainland gave an impression of quiet peace. The reflections of the temples, distorted occasionally by the breeze, intensified the brooding mysticism of the sacred enclosure. In contrast to the austerity of the priests, young girls, their eyes virtuously downcast, slipped back and forth, carrying out the various errands of their training-school within the enclosure. The great pyramid and the temple of the War God completely dominated the place. At regular intervals terraces broke the lines of the sloping sides and increased the impression of its size. A wide staircase of 114 narrow steps led up the western side, and so steep was this stair that not until one's head rose clear of the platform did the temple itself come into view.

The temple, in reality, comprised two shrines, built side by side, each having stone walls and soaring roofs of wood coated with plaster. Through the right-hand door one could clearly see the squat figure of Huitzilopochtli carved from the stone and covered with a paste in which were set jade, turquoise, gold and seed pearls. A girdle of gold snakes, picked out in precious stones, adorned his waist, and around his neck hung a string of gold masks covered with turquoise mosaic. By his side stood the statue of an attendant deity, equipped with a short lance and a gold shield, richly decorated with the customary mosaic.

In the adjoining shrine stood an image of Tezcatlipoca, one of the most prominent Aztec gods. His eye-sockets were inlaid with mirrors of obsidian, the black depths of which reflected the red gleams of the afternoon light. This statue, too, was adorned with gold and precious stones. High in the wooden roof of this temple perched a small figure of Xipe, the God of Seed-time. Braziers of incense discharged greasy coils of smoke which deepened the gloom of the temples, whose walls were already black with the blood of many victims. In dim corners stood heaps of ritualistic paraphernalia, conch-shell trumpets, knives, banners and baskets of shapeless lumps of meat, surplus human hearts which, for some reason, had not yet been placed upon the braziers. The priests who glided through this murk seemed fitting satellites to the diabolic images to which they ministered. In front of the temples stood the great drum which was soon to throb across the lake as a nation suffered its death-agony.

It was from this point that Montezuma showed Cortés his

empire, and Bernal Diaz, who witnessed the scene, left us this unforgettable description :

'Then Montezuma took Cortés by the hand and told him to look at his great city and all the other cities that were standing in the water and the many other towns and the land around the lake.... So we stood looking about us, for that huge and cursed temple stood so high that from it one could see over everything very well, and we saw the three causeways which led into Mexico ... and we saw the [aqueduct of] fresh water that comes from Chapultepec, which supplies the city, and we saw the bridges on the three causeways which were built at certain distances apart ... and we beheld on the lake a great multitude of canoes, some coming with supplies of food, others returning loaded with cargoes of merchandise, and we saw that from every house of that great city and of all the other cities that were built in the water it was impossible to pass from house to house except by drawbridges, which were made of wood, or in canoes; and we saw in those cities Cues [temples] and oratories like towers and fortresses and all gleaming white, and it was a wonderful thing to behold ' (3).

CHAPTER XIV

THE DEATH-THROES OF THE AZTEC NATION

A chapter in which are set forth the factors which brought about the success of the Spaniards and the downfall of the Aztecs

THE romantic circumstances which attended the fall of the Aztec civilization have long captured the fancy of the European world. A whole nation submitting to a handful of desperate Spanish soldiers offers a dramatic situation, seldom paralleled in our annals. Yet, given the unflinching generalship of a Cortés, the collapse of the Aztec tribes was inevitable. The psychological conditions inherent in this type of Indian culture could not withstand European military technique, any more than could the varied civilizations which became colonies of Europe in every continent on the face of the globe (1).

There are times in the histories of all peoples when the national will seems to disintegrate before intangible factors individually insignificant. All students of military affairs are familiar with these sudden routs affecting the high courage of victors as well as the grim fortitude of those who previously have unflinchingly endured successive defeats. The Aztecs' war against the Spanish Conquistadors is an elusive example of the paralysis of the national morale, followed by a defence carried on with that courage found in forsaken men, in this case abandoned by their very gods. We have seen, in the bitter year of 1940, the same pattern repeated when France collapsed and England found a new strength in despair.

An examination of the Mexican social structure in relation to the psychological state of the Aztec mind shows that the Spaniards arrived at a time very favourable for conquest. Comparison of the Aztec military technique with the European discipline and armament of the day reveals an exceptional opportunity for the triumph of European tactics. To explain the familiar tale of the Conquest from the Indian point of view may throw into sharper relief this conflict between two systems of civilization.

Aztec war was highly ceremonial, and fought in a spirit very different from the realistic calculation of European strife. The *technical* equipment of the Indians did not meet the requirements of a conflict waged in terms of European military *practice*. Moreover, Cortés arrived at the end of the summer, when the tribes of Mexico were too busy harvesting the crops essential for their survival to think seriously of military affairs. A final factor dooming the Aztecs to inevitable defeat was the political structure of Indian Mexico, which provided no way of converting military success to the establishment of a powerfully consolidated state.

The Aztec theocracy did not lend itself to governing or absorbing conquered peoples, although in time a social mechanism might have been developed. While the Aztecs received tribute from over a wide territory, there were constant revolts and betrayals. Probably this same process went on among the other tribal groups in Mexico, so that the political organization of the region as a whole was far from that of an empire. In reality a multitude of independent city-states seethed with intrigue and war, and were further disunited by differences in language, dialect, physical type and geographic economy. An invader, with a strongly disciplined force small enough to live off the country, and thus to stay in the field, could have an astonishing success, particularly if he had a taste for intrigue. Cortés, as events proved, was the ideal man for such a purpose, and he was further favoured by the psychological reaction of the Aztecs to his arrival.

The years before the Spanish Conquest had to the Aztecs been full of portents suggestive of future evil. There seems to have been in the air that same sense of paralysis that the French knew to their cost in 1939 and 1940. Montezuma, the war chief of the Aztecs and an amateur of witchcraft, had had an experience calculated completely to shake his nerve. He and Nezahualpilli, the chief of Texcoco, had fallen to arguing about the respective merits of their soothsayers, since the Texcocan held that strangers were going to rule the land of Anahuac. So convinced was Nezahualpilli of the correctness of his interpretation that he wagered his kingdom against three turkey cocks, the result to be decided by a ritualistic ball game with Montezuma. The latter won the first two

FIG. 3. The years before the Spanish Conquest had been full of evil omens for the Aztecs. To determine whether the dire predictions of Nezahualpilli, chief of Texcoco, were correct, Montezuma played and lost a ritualistic game of 'basketball' with him as depicted above. *Codex Florentino.*

games, but Nezahualpilli took the last three in a row. The defeat must have been disheartening to Montezuma, not only because he had so much to fear from the future, but also because his own experts had been held so cheap. (See Fig. 3.)

In close succession followed a series of phenomena, each bearing its message of woe to come. A column of fire was seen every midnight throughout the year; two temples were destroyed, one by a sudden fire, the other by lightning unaccompanied by thunder. A comet was seen by day, and sudden waves came up on the Lake of Texcoco. A sixth sign was a woman's voice crying, 'My children, we are

FIG. 4. Montezuma views the magical bird in the head of which was a mirror, showing first the heavens, then hosts of armed men, foretelling, according to tradition, the Spanish Conquest. *Codex Florentino.*

lost.' Monsters appeared and were brought before the chief, only to disappear as soon as he had seen them. Most sinister of all was a bird brought in by some hunters. This bird had a mirror in its head, revealing the heavens, and when Montezuma peered at it a second time a host of armed men was disclosed. When the chief brought his soothsayers to witness this augury and to explain its significance, the bird flew away. Distorted as these occurrences seem to us, they must have had a most upsetting effect on the population of the Valley of Mexico (2). (See Figs. 4, 28A–B.)

Consequently the emotional condition of the people was peculiarly receptive to the rumours, drifting in from the south-east, which told of four-legged monsters with human bodies issuing from their backs. As these strange beings moved up the coast, Montezuma's spies and ambassadors began to bring back more precise reports as to their nature, and even presents and messages for their chief. (See Fig. 5.)

The strangers were human, for they were vulnerable, re-ceiving wounds and dying from assaults upon them. They had new and strange weapons, noisy and lethal, for cannon, mus-kets, crossbows and steel swords were unknown to the Aztecs. Also novel and dreadful adjuncts of war were the horses and the savage mastiffs of the Spaniards. In battle the strangers were invincible, operating in a manner completely foreign to Indian principles of war. The simple Indian methods of mass attack were of little avail against the manoeuvring of a well-drilled force, for the native tactics could bring only the merest fraction of their fighting force in direct contact with the enemy.

The Spaniards also resisted witchcraft on the occasion when Montezuma seriously applied it. However, sorcery, according to native standards, was at best a two-edged weapon, so that it is doubtful if this failure had any other than a confirmatory bearing on the Indian attitude of mind toward the supernatural quality of the Spaniards. The problem that beset Montezuma was not that the invaders were themselves gods, but that they were the symbols, the vicars on earth, as it were, of vast un-earthly forces bent on establishing a new social order. As such the Spaniards required to be handled most gingerly (3). (See Fig. 6.)

FIG. 5. The Spaniards land in 1519 at the site of Vera Cruz. Their ships and equipment are carefully shown. At the right, Marina, Cortés' interpreter, is exercising her diplomacy on a native. *Codex Florentino.*

When the Spaniards were approaching the capital a political problem entered to complicate the spiritual one. The city-states, or *pueblos*, between the Valley of Mexico and the coast were independent communities and, even if tributary to the Valley powers, were often reluctantly so. Therefore, many of these tribes, like the Totonacs, welcomed the invaders as the spearhead for an open revolt. Others, like the completely inde-pendent and war-like Tlaxcalans, put the power of Cortés to a practical test in open battle and, when the Spaniards won, became the most loyal of Cortés' supporters. Cholula, a large town loosely allied to the Aztecs, met the Spaniards as friends, plotting to overcome them by treachery, a good Indian political manoeuvre instigated, perhaps, by Montezuma. The Spaniards, suspecting such a move, counteracted its efficacy by a judiciously executed massacre, thus, if not gaining a friendly community, at least creating a noncombatant one. (See Figs. 7–9.)

FIG. 6. Aztec sorcerers, sent from the highland, offer bewitched food to Cortés and his staff, who disdain the viands. *Codex Florentino.*

Montezuma and his more cautious counsellors watched this slow ascent from the coast with apprehensive interest. He has been condemned by many commentators as an appeaser and has been made the scapegoat of this great debacle of Indian civilization. Yet consider his position. While the leading man in his community, he was not an authoritarian monarch. For mass action he had to rely on the group decision of the clans comprising his tribe, as well as on the very doubtful allegiance of the vassal states, whose immediate needs transcended any sacrifice of a far-reaching political nature. Thus not only the demands of the harvest season but also the fear of damage to the communal property made communities loath for war. Montezuma had no method of enforcing a long-range diplomatic policy, such as is so characteristic of European and

Fig. 7. Cortés and his army, on passing the great volcanoes southeast of Mexico City, ask the way. Note the smoke issuing from the crater of Popocatepetl. *Codex Florentino.*

oriental political history. Nor must the extraordinary gifts of Cortés and his Indian mistress Marina be underrated. The pair played on Indian psychology as master pianists would execute a duet on the piano.

His hands tied by both practical and psychological considerations, Montezuma received Cortés and the Spaniards without having struck a positive blow. Then ensued a new chapter in the story. Cortés promptly seized Montezuma as a hostage, and the latter's power to influence his tribesmen disintegrated. A mass revulsion against the invaders slowly began to crystallize, but it was confined to the city itself, without extending to the neighbouring towns. People kept themselves within their houses; the market closed, yet no overt act was

Fig. 8. Montezuma, upset by the magical premonitions of disaster and by the failure of his sorcerers, does not know whether to flee or hide in a cave. *Codex Florentino.*

done. Cortés was allowed to leave for the coast to subjugate his new commander Narvaez, without open hostilities on the part of the Aztecs. (See Figs. 10–13.)

The storm broke during Cortés' absence. Some inhabitants of Tenochtitlan had assembled to celebrate the feast of the god Huitzilopochtli. Alvarado, a tough soldier, lacking all Cortés' gifts of intrigue, scented trouble in this gathering, the actual innocence of which he had no way of knowing. Following the Spanish technique at Cholula, he fell upon the celebrants and killed them all. The city rose like one man and drove the garrison to cover. Actuated by the single motive of revenge against the invaders, the Aztecs were ready to destroy the Spanish garrison. However, the structural weakness of the Indian government became bitterly evident when the chiefs permitted Cortés

Fig. 9. Cortés meets high dignitaries from Tlaxcala, the pueblo most loyal to the conquerors. Marina interprets while supplies of corn, tortillas, turkeys, etc., are accumulated. *Lienzo de Tlaxcala.*

and his reinforcements from the army of Narvaez to join the beleaguered troops of Alvarado. The ceremonial aspect of war in Indian Mexico did not envisage the splitting of an adversary's army and the separate destruction of its weakened parts, a rudimentary law of European military tactics.

Yet once the Spaniards were united in the city they ceased to be a military problem and became the emotional focus of

FIG. 10. The Spanish forces reach Tenochtitlan, the modern Mexico City, and Montezuma and his nobles come to greet Cortés. *Codex Florentino.*

FIG. 12. A great aid to the Spanish military success was the use of cavalry. Here we see mounted cross-bowmen, whose weapons were no less deadly than the firearms of the day. *Codex Florentino.*

FIG. 11. Marina's value to Cortés cannot be underestimated. Here she is ordering an Aztec to perform some duty. To judge from the speech scrolls, he complies with ill grace. *Codex Florentino.*

FIG. 13. Cortés seizes Montezuma as a hostage. The Aztec chief tries to calm his rebellious subjects who treat him with the contempt due to a traitor. *Codex Florentino.*

the Indians' wrath and fear. They had to shut themselves up in the palace of Axayacatl to resist the force of this uprising in which the whole tribe participated. The Aztecs, having immobilized their enemies, visited their hate and rage in a man-

FIG. 14. Following a series of outrages committed by the invaders, the citizens rise in arms against the Spanish. The Spaniards and their Tlaxcalan allies are besieged in the palace of Axayacatl. In this scene a field piece is shown in action, while the horsemen are held in reserve for a sortie. *Lienzo de Tlaxcala.*

ner unparalleled in the annals of Indian campaigns. Every citizen joined in hurling missiles at the besieged invaders, and masses of warriors blocked every sally the Spaniards made from their refuge. (See Figs. 14–5.)

The Spaniards could not manoeuvre in the narrow footpaths along the canals, and the portable fortresses they constructed of wood, the first tanks used in the New World, were useless against enemies on housetops and in canoes (4). (See Fig. 16.) The Spaniards lost heavily, and the unfortunate Montezuma met his death either at the hands of his own people, whom he was trying to calm, or, as two excellent authorities

ycqtla ti tetzavitl
yn mal ques.

FIG. 15. Here the Spanish are dislodging the Aztecs from a temple, where the Indians had gathered to enfilade them. *Lienzo de Tlaxcala.*

have it, at those of the Spaniards (5). After having passed a week shut up in the palace, Cortés decided to withdraw from Tenochtitlan. Just before dawn his forces made their way through the hushed streets out along the causeway to Tacuba.

A woman getting water from a canal saw them and raised the alarm. The whole male population surged forth along the roofs and through the streets. Some seized canoes and attacked the flanks of the marching column. The Aztecs tore up the bridges, and many Spaniards, laden down with gold, sank ignominiously beneath the waters or, while trying to keep afloat, were clubbed to death by warriors in boats. Alvarado, ever the precipitous man of action, confronted by a wide gap

FIG. 16. Wooden tanks were built by Cortes to protect his men when Aztecs took up positions on the housetops out of reach of the sallies of Spanish cavalry. This spirited picture reveals the tanks separated by a canal into which a horse had fallen. The Aztecs on the roofs impede its rescue. *Lienzo de Tlaxcala.*

in the causeway, plunged his lance into the lake bottom and in full armour vaulted over to the other side (6). The panic increased, and order was not restored until the Spaniards reached Tacuba. Cortés sat under a giant cypress and wept as he took toll of his losses. Three-quarters of the Spanish army had been lost in this rout and in the preceding siege. (See Fig. 17.)

The Spaniards found a temporary sanctuary on the hill of Los Remedios. Their adversaries, instead of following up their advantage, plundered the dead and tried to recover the booty stolen by the Spaniards from the Aztec treasury. They lost a precious opportunity to destroy the remnants of the Spanish army by not carrying their attack to its logical conclusion. (See Fig. 18.)

However, the Indians did make some effort towards con-

FIG. 17. Supplies run low and Cortés secretly tries to reach the mainland along a causeway. His retreat is discovered and the Aztecs, massing their forces in canoes, wreak havoc on the Spanish forces. Tearing up the bridges, the Aztecs further hindered the retreat and all but destroyed the invading army. *Lienzo de Tlaxcala.*

certed action later. The Texcocans, formerly the principal allies of the Aztecs, gathered their forces together and tried to intercept the Spaniards as they made their way cross country to the homeland of their allies, the Tlaxcalans. At Otumba battle was joined. The Indians in their battle formation could not overcome the mobility and tactical sense of the Spaniards. Wounded as every man was, and exhausted from lack of food and sleep, they kept their discipline; and a desperate charge by the cavalry reached the chiefs, who fell before the Spanish swords. Once their leaders were slain, the scant Indian discipline dissolved, and the tribesmen took flight. The Spaniards made their way to Tlaxcala to recuperate and to await reinforcements.

Montezuma was succeeded by his brother Cuitlahuac, and he, dying of the fever after four months, was replaced as war chief by their nephew, the heroic Cuauhtemoc. This strong and courageous leader was unable to overcome the mutual distrust of the Indian communities for one another. When the Aztecs might have joined together with other tribes to overwhelm the Spaniards by sheer weight of numbers, they did nothing.

Fig. 18. A handful of the Spaniards reach the mainland. The Aztecs, instead of following up their advantages, plunder the bodies of the killed and drowned. Be it remembered, however, the Spanish carried off the entire Aztec treasure. *Codex Florentino*.

In the meantime Cortés, having rested his army, began to consolidate his position. He made two series of campaigns, one eastward to the sea and the other in a south and westerly direction in the present state of Morelos. Utilizing Indian allies both as carriers and as a screen to conceal his more serious tactical movements, he subjugated town after town. In each case the Indian war convention of a single decisive mêlée proved worthless against the versatility of the Spanish attack. Cortés

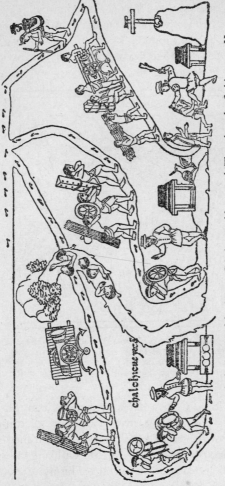

chalchcuapa

Fig. 19. Owing to the hesitancy of the Aztecs, Cortés was able to reach Tlaxcala and refit his army. Here we see military supplies being brought from the coast. In the left centre a minor disaster, involving the drowning of several Indian allies, is depicted. *Lienzo de Tlaxcala*.

soon pacified the eastern country sufficiently to try to regain Tenochtitlan. (See Fig. 19.)

Typical Indian perfidy, from our point of view to-day, but common sense to the people of that era, virtually accomplished

FIG. 20. Cortés' plan to retake Tenochtitlan involved isolating the island city from the mainland. Tenochtitlan is shown in the centre of the picture, surrounded by the lake on which float the war canoes of its defenders. The Spanish forces devote themselves to reducing the mainland towns. *Lienzo de Tlaxcala*.

the downfall of Mexico. The Texcocans, closest allies of the Aztecs, and for that reason perhaps the most jealous of their success, resented the part Montezuma had taken in forcing the election of a war chief. When the Aztecs had had a strong chance of maintaining their supremacy after Cortés' retreat from Mexico, the Texcocans valiantly took the field at Otumba. Now they switched to the Spanish side, seeing a chance of assuming a dominant position in Valley of Mexico affairs. Their defection gave the Spaniards a base on the Lake of Mexico and a means of mopping up whatever tribes remained unsubjugated in the previous campaign.

FIG. 21. Cortés built brigantines to defend his flanks while moving along the causeways into Tenochtitlan. In this picture a brigantine comes to the aid of Cortés and his allies, who are beset by Aztecs afoot and in canoes. *Lienzo de Tlaxcala.*

Having quieted the countryside, Cortés put into effect his plan of siege. He launched a fleet of small galleys armed with cannon, which had been constructed in Tlaxcala and brought piecemeal across the mountains, to be assembled on the lake. These ships were to sweep the lake clear of canoes and protect the Spanish flanks as they moved in across the three causeways to the island city, Tenochtitlan. Cortés divided his forces in three parts to move along these approaches and close in on the capital. (See Figs. 20, 22).

FIG. 22. The Spanish flotilla puts to sea. These galleys, equipped with oars and a sail and armed with a cannon in the bow, could play havoc with the Aztec war canoes. *Codex Florentino.*

The galleys soon cleared the lake of any hostile fleets of canoes, and the Spaniards began to invest the city. The Aztecs, fighting for their lives, stubbornly defended their position. Every night they sallied forth to destroy the bridges the Spaniards had made across the canals during the day. In fighting of this kind the Spaniards could not manipulate their troops, and

FIG. 23. The Spanish military problem was to raze enough of the city to permit the use of cavalry. The drawing at the left shows the gunboats taking part in an offensive with this end in view. *Codex Florentino.*

neither side had any great advantage. The Aztecs, however, still persisted in trying to take prisoners to sacrifice to their War God, instead of exterminating their enemies whenever the occasion offered. To offset this gain the thousands of Indian allies, who flocked to the Spanish side to participate in the expected victory, jammed the causeways and hampered rather than helped the besiegers. (See Fig. 21.)

FIG. 24. Time and again the brigantines relieved situations like this where armed tribesmen in canoes sailed up to attack the Spanish rear. *Codex Florentino.*

Cortés decided to change his manner of campaign, and his solution, while reasonable to us, must have been little short of miraculous to the tribesmen. He sent the Indian allies forward to tear down all the houses they could find and fill the canals with the debris. When counter-attacked, the allies retired, leaving room for the Spaniards on horse and foot to deal with the Aztecs. Each day the Spanish forces gained more room to manoeuvre, and thus could count on recovering more ground on the morrow. The Aztecs, animated by a rare unity, fought desperately but without avail. (See Figs. 23–4).

Towards the end of the siege an event occurred which indicated to the now-desperate Aztecs hope of eventual release in a common rising against the invaders. The people from the islands at the south of the lake, the Xochimilcas and their neighbour tribesmen, filtered through the Spanish galleys by night and told the Aztecs that, as neighbours, they would

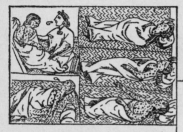

FIG. 25. Pestilence was a formidable ally on the Spanish side. Colds, smallpox, measles, and the like were unknown to the Indians who, lacking any sort of immunity, died by the thousand. *Codex Florentino.*

FIG. 26. A factor in the downfall of the Aztecs was their custom of taking captives for sacrifice rather than kill in direct battle. The heads of the sacrificed victims, both men and horses, were displayed in front of the temples. *Codex Florentino.*

make common cause against the whites. Overjoyed, Cuauhtemoc and his chiefs loaded them with ornaments, fine mantles and cacao beans, precious for the favourite drink of the Aztecs, chocolate. When night closed in again on the beleaguered city the Aztecs were startled by a great commotion. The new allies were trying to drag off the Aztec women and children as slaves. It is pleasant to record that this knavery received its just reward, and the Xochimilcas were all either slaughtered or disposed of in sacrifice (7).

Only when its members were too weak to resist and could no longer deal wounding blows did the garrison yield. Cuauhtemoc and his family took to the lake in a canoe, as did many others. He was picked up by one of the Spanish galleys and brought before Cortés, where his dignity and chiefly demeanour received the respectful attention of the Spanish general staff. The request for treasure brought the answer that there was none: it lay under the lake with the Spaniards who were

FIG. 27. Cuauhtemoc, who conducted the defence of Tenochtitlan, is received with all the honours of war by Cortés and his consort, Marina. In the upper right Cortés may be seen greeting Cuauhtemoc's wife and family. The legend translated reads: 'With this event, the Mexicans were finished.' *Lienzo de Tlaxcala.*

slain the preceding winter in their disastrous flight from the city. Cuauhtemoc then underwent prison and torture, to be murdered years later on Cortés' march to Honduras. He is now revered in Mexico as a national hero. (See Figs. 25-7.)

The downfall of the Aztecs cannot be explained in terms of European history, and the standard reasons give a false picture. Montezuma, singled out by European authors as a weak and

FIGS. 28A–28B. The story of the Conquest of Mexico in native characters. In the cartouches are to be seen the symbols One Reed and Two Knife, the Aztec names for the years 1519 and 1520. Under One Reed is a Spaniard below whose horse's feet are the shield, club and arrows symbolic of war. At the right the

bearded Cortés sits in the temple of Tenochtitlan, represented by the cactus. An Indian with the glyph of Montezuma offers a tribute of gold beads. Under Two Knife we find Alvarado massacring the Indians at the great temple and at upper right a comet in the sky. *Codex Vaticanus A.*

vacillating monarch, was a tribal leader devoid of the consti-
tutional rights of a European sovereign. His empire is also a
European creation, since it consisted, in reality, of communities sufficiently intimidated to pay tribute, but in no wise
bound to Aztec governmental conventions. Warriors the
Aztecs were, but not soldiers in the European sense. Given, as
we have said, the requisite leadership and organization, any
European expeditionary force could have taken Mexico. The
tragically courageous resistance at Tenochtitlan was not a military defence so much as a heroic group action by individuals
fighting for their lives.

Hunger and thirst, plagues and wounds, had so weakened the Aztecs that they could not resist. The horrors of the
last stand made by these desperate people are too awful to
describe. For long after, the memory of the tragedy lingered
about the place, a sort of exhalation of spiritual uncleanliness
like that of a haunted house or the scene of a crime. All
through the Colonial era, and even up to now, the northern
district of Mexico has found favour neither as a residential
quarter nor as a business centre. To-day there are railroad
yards and slums where the Aztec civilization bled to death.
The ghosts of its heroic defenders still haunt the place.

CHAPTER XV

THE AZTECS AFTER THEIR CONQUEST

*The history of the Aztecs after the Conquest and suggestions
for a tour through their domain*

AZTEC civilization died, but the Aztecs still live. Remove the
pure-blooded Indian from Mexico, and you lose two-fifths of
the population; take out those with Indian blood in their veins,
and a bare twentieth of the population will remain. The face
of Mexico is an Indian face. Yet travel in Mexico and read its
history, and you will see, as if in strata, the impress of the
colonial period, the republic, the empire of Maximilian, the
dictatorship of Diaz and the modern social thinking of the Revolution. The Indian civilization you do not see, except for its
descendants, who are everywhere, who are the Mexican people.
Though their outward aspect and their material and social culture are European, the stamp of the Aztec character is on their
minds, just as the masonry of broken Aztec temples is built into
the walls of their churches (1).

The original purpose of the Crown and the Church was to
convert the Indian population into Spanish citizens with full
civic rights. For two generations the authorities almost succeeded in their intent; but finally the individualism so emphasized in European culture broke through their legislative
controls, and the white conquerors reduced the Indians to
slavery. Now, after 400 years, it seems that the present Republican government might achieve by means of their Indian education programme the humane purpose formulated under the
colonial system.

After 1520, when the Conquest was established, the Spaniards began the process of converting a matured Indian culture
into a European one. The conquerors were granted lands, and

in return were supposed to exploit the new territory for the economic advantage of Spain. The Church had in its custody the education of the Indians and their spiritual and corporal welfare. The different monastic orders undertook the control of the Indians in specified localities. Their first steps were to eradicate the local idolatry and to learn the language and customs of their new charges, the better to accomplish conversion (2).

The friars, especially selected for the task, showed great understanding. They immediately replaced one theological structure with another. The Indians tore down their temples to build churches and monasteries in their place. The use of statues and paintings in Catholic ritual answered so well the requirements of Aztec worship that the friars had great trouble in preventing adoration of the images themselves. (See Plate 26, middle.)

The studies that the friars made of the Indian customs were admirable, with the Franciscans and Dominicans showing exceptional abilities (3). The children of Indian tribal leaders were educated in schools to spread the gospel. Under this Spanish control there was no recognition of the old communal land tenure, so the Aztecs were frozen into possession of the lands that they occupied by tribal sanction. The chiefs who had held the usage of the official lands found themselves the owners of extensive estates by which their descendants could profit. The Spaniards married into chiefly families, which they believed hereditary, according to their own cultural pattern. In some cases chiefs, like those of Tlaxcala, received coats of arms and patents of nobility from the king for their service in the Spanish cause. Out of 190 coats of arms presented for services during the Conquest of Middle and South America, at least twenty were granted to Indians. In consequence there took place a modest renascence of Indian culture. Indian authors like Ixtlilxochitl and Chimalpahin set forth, in Spanish or Nahuatl, the annals of their forebears as proof of their descent from great Indian nobles and of their right to Spanish honours as well (4). (See Plate 44.)

The old culture died slowly. In the Indian towns the records were kept in both Spanish and the old Aztec pictographic system to avoid dispute. Dress maintained its old form, except that the friars insisted on trousering the Indians. The rich agriculture was a great boon to the conquerors, who modified it little except for the addition of fruit trees and wheat. Household utensils, like pottery, revealed an engaging fusion of Indian and Spanish ideas, and glazing delighted the Indians, who applied the flux to purely aboriginal forms. Some enchanting little sculptures in clay reveal the old gods and goddesses masquerading as saints in a very thin disguise.

The Indians were used to building temples, and it seemed to them perfectly fitting that they should labour long hours in great numbers to rear structures honouring the new gods. The conversion was so popular that the churches were too small to hold the worshippers, and several conventual temples, like Acolman, Actopan and Tlalmanalco, had chapels which opened on a large court to accommodate converts who gathered literally in tens of thousands. Indian craftsmen found steel tools a superb improvement on their stone hammers and chisels. After the original plateresque architecture shifted into baroque they revelled in shaping the blocks into ornate shapes, for it was as easy as cutting cheese in comparison to the labour of their aboriginal days (5).

This period of fusion lasted for almost a century. In the meantime the original Conquistadors and their descendants, together with later immigrants to the new colony, had encroached more and more on the natives. The development of the mining industries absorbed thousands of Indians, lured to work for a pittance under noisome conditions which brought sickness and even death. The exercise of the *encomienda*, an arrangement whereby a man had the right to a native's labour in return for his care and the assurance of his religious in--

struction, led to abuse of the privilege, and the luckless Indians were reduced to serfdom. European diseases, like smallpox, measles and tuberculosis, wiped out great sections of the population, which had no hereditary resistance to such maladies. The Crown and the Church, through its Council of the Indies, sent questionnaires and enacted ameliorative legislation on the basis of the information received, but such laws were more honoured in the breach than in the observance. Many of the whites who went to New Spain wanted to get rich and enjoy an easy old age in the homeland. Others who had settled in the country enjoyed an almost feudal existence, no part of the profits and comforts of which they wished to yield, either for the betterment of the Indians or for the enrichment of the Crown. When the British destroyed the Armada in 1588 and weakened Spanish sea-power, the communication between the mother country and the colonies became increasingly difficult. Control was loosened, and laws for the benefit of the Indians were ignored. They became, indeed, an inferior majority, labouring as peons without hope of legal or social justice (6).

Most of the Indians lost their land and laboured on *haciendas* or in the mines. Some communities like Tlaxcala, having performed notable service to the Crown during the Conquest, kept their land, although they had lost social status. Other groups, like the lake peoples of Xochimilco and Chalco, occupied territory which the Spaniards considered unsuitable for their own purposes. A fourth group lived relatively unmolested in primitive little villages tucked away in the mountains. These refugees had taken to the hills not only because of the white conquerors, but also to avoid the rising Indian powers in the centuries before the Conquest. The several score languages and dialects spoken in Mexico are preserved in these tiny villages where the inhabitants are only lightly veneered with Christianity.

What remains of Indian culture to-day is largely the blend of early indigenous practices with the teachings of the friars in the sixteenth century. Yet the physical type and the languages have resisted absorption for four centuries. In Mexico there is hardly a group which remains as completely Indian as some of the North American tribes, but they, after all, have for the most part been conquered and put on reservations only in the last three generations. The groups who had earlier contact with the whites were exterminated many years ago (7).

The Mexican Indians have endured and have done the work of Mexico for four centuries. They have seen the whites struggle for the right to consume the fruits of their labour. They probably do not realize that the unmixed group of the ruling class gets smaller each generation, having in the last century dropped from thirteen per cent to seven per cent of the population. Individuals, like Juarez the Liberator, and Diaz, the greatest of Mexican dictators, shouldered their way from the anonymous Indian mass to lead the country and modernize its culture. The men of the Revolution had Indian blood in their veins, and one of them, former President Lazaro Cardenas, has made superhuman efforts to drag the Indians out of bondage into participation in the active and political life of the country.

The crafts of Mexico are the product of Indian hands. Humble artisans have handed down from generation to generation the love of the old days, the traditions of form and pattern. This background, like that of the social make-up of the people, was illumined in the Mexican Renascence, when during the Revolution Mexican painters like Orozco, Rivera and Goitia, and foreigners like Charlot, became conscious of Mexico's native American background. It is beside the point that Mexico's art is technically derivative from Europe. Socially and emotionally it is the only really national art which lives in the world to-day (8).

The visitor to Mexico is strongly conscious of the Indian. Sometimes he is appalled by the apathy of the people who have been oppressed for so many years, whose nations and whose temples have been levelled to make the foundations of a new society. Yet in these days, when our American world has greater meaning for us, we can think more deeply of those earlier colonists from another continent who, like ourselves, built a new world.

Mexico, the most American of American nations, opens a thrilling perspective down the corridors of time. One can read widely and yet completely miss the sense of a still-living past which affects the visitor to this extraordinary country. To take a car and drive through the rich valleys, hemmed in by their mountain ramparts, is to absorb the full flavour of our Indian past. A fortnight so spent will enable a visitor to survey much of the Aztec domain (9).

The first day one should visit the Museum, just to realize the bulk and quantity of the infinitesimal part of Indian work-manship housed there. A block away, near the Cathedral, yawns an excavation which reveals a corner of the Great Temple's stair. The street behind the Cathedral, running east and west, produced myriads of ceremonial objects, cast out from the temple by the outraged conquerors. The *Zocalo*, the great Plaza de la Constitución, covers the main square of Tenochtitlan. Its 20 feet of foundation are made of the temples torn down for the greater glory of God, and heaven knows what incomparable masterpieces of Aztec art are buried there. The Presidential Palace on the west rests on the ancient halls of Montezuma. A few blocks north the murals of the Ministry of Public Education show the tragedy of the Indian and his libera-tion, painted in the full tide of Rivera's genius (10). (See Plate 51, bottom.)

After lunch in the neighbourhood the visitor may well drive west past the Palace of Bellas Artes, built just beyond the an-cient shore of Tenochtitlan in the former lake bottom. The hill and park of Chapultepec merit a visit, for the cypresses, hoary with Spanish moss, date from Montezuma's time. Here the Tenochcas made their first settlement, the elder Monte-

zuma built the aqueduct for his city and the younger had a relief carved in his honour. Crowning the hill stands the palace
of the Austrian Maximilian, emperor of all the Mexicans during our Civil War, and at this place a few years previously a
handful of Mexican military-school cadets stood off a brigade
of United States Regulars in their one unhappy conflict with
their southern neighbour.

Turning south, one may visit the little palace of the chief of
Mixcoac and go on through the Villa Obregon (San Angel) to
see the remains of the Lower Middle Culture peoples buried
under the lava of Copilco. Then, turning west and south, one
may pass through Tizapan, where the Tenochcas spent the unhappy years of their captivity, and drive out over the Pedregal
to Cuicuilco. Here the oval temple of the Upper Middle peoples emerges from the surrounding lava waste, a dismal and
uncanny background, appropriate to this earliest monument
of Mexican religion. Then the visitor can return to Mexico via
Tlalpam and Coyoacan, on a road built over the same causeway which Cortés followed into Tenochtitlan. (See Plate 18,
bottom.)

The second day, equipped with lunch or self-control, the visitor might drive out on the Calle de Tacuba, which follows the
old western causeway to ancient Tlacopan. Here Cortés made
his dismal retreat, and two blocks are named from Alvarado's
famous leap. The cypress beneath which Cortés wept is worth
a glance, and the church in the main plaza of Azcapotzalco,
capital of Toltec and Tepanec chiefs, squats heavily on the remains of a once-lofty platform. The votive temple of Los Remedios on the hills behind was built where Cortés re-formed
his shattered army and has a wonder-working statue of the
Virgin, patroness of the Conquistadors.

Descending the hill, the visitor can pass through Tlalne-
pantla, where the church is built from the ruins of temples, and
go on to Tenayuca. Here the Mexican archaeologists have dis-
sected, as with a surgeon's knife, the six temples that epitom-

ize the history of that town from its Chichimec foundation until its conquest in 1520. On the hills to the east, at the foot of which runs a Spanish aqueduct, are strung the Middle Culture sites of El Arbolillo, Ticoman and Zacatenco. (See Plates 1, 50.)

It would be worth while to visit, on returning, the Villa de Guadalupe, built in honour of the apparition of the Virgin to Juan Diego. Her portrait, miraculously painted, is preserved in the church; and in December the Indians come from miles around to honour their special patroness, just as before the Conquest they made pilgrimages to this very spot to do honour to Tonantzin, the Aztec Goddess of Motherhood. Returning by way of the ancient northern causeway, the visitors should turn right at Peralvillo and pass by the grubby railroad yards and slums which cover Tlaltelolco and its famous market-place and the site of the Aztec Cuauhtemoc's last stand against the Spaniards.

On the third day the tourist should visit Teotihuacan, re-traversing the northern causeway and passing through Guadalupe. The road skirts the salt Lake of Texcoco and crosses, on a causeway of Spanish construction, the straits between it and the now-drained Xaltocan. The strategic site of Chiconauhtla at its northern terminus offers little to see, but farther on it is well to turn right and visit the great Acolman Indian School, or Convent, 'convento', as the Spaniards called any establishment where the friars educated the Indians. In the distance loom the pyramids of Teotihuacan; a short drive through Indian villages brings the motorist to this site, the most imposing in Mexico. The ruins are a tribute to the cultural interests of the present government, which has expended much time and money in interpreting and uncovering the remains. There is a good museum where one can see the craftsmanship of the builders of this magnificent sacred city, which still retains much of the grandeur of its ancient days. (See Plates 21–4.)

There is a good restaurant at Teotihuacan, and after lunch

the visitor should go back as far as Tepexpan and take the abominable road to Texcoco, except in the rainy season, when the town can be reached only by the main road from a point south of Mexico City. On the way one should visit the remains of Nezahualcoyotl's palace, where magnificent cypresses border a garden, and in their shade one can evoke memories of the life of the poet king. Some rough miles farther on, Texcoco reflects none of its former grandeur. It is an old, sad town, dim and ruined. A few mounds at the eastern entrance are gloomy reminders of its ancient splendours. One passes Huexotla and its great wall as one returns to Mexico by the main road, and hard by at the agricultural school in the *hacienda* of Chapingo are some of the best of Rivera's frescos, symbolizing the growth and fertility of the Mexican earth and translating Aztec ideas into modern painting.

An alternative procedure would be to give a fourth day to the Texcoco region. Leaving Mexico by the eastern road, pass south along the desolate salt marshes of Lake Texcoco and turn east at Los Reyes on the main road to Texcoco. At Coatlinchan a tip will command the services of an Indian to take one to see the massive Toltec monument to the Goddess of the Waters, which lies unfinished in a gulley, a long half-hour's walk from the town. Returning to the car, go to Chapingo and Huexotla, and at Texcoco turn off to see the rock-cut baths of Nezahualcoyotl, built into the hill behind Texcotcingo. The countryside is dotted with little towns, and the Indian and Colonial periods are very close to the surface.

The fourth day (or fifth, if a day each is given to Teotihuacan and Texcoco) could start a profitable two-day tour to Cuernavaca. The motorist will have an unforgettable experience if he takes the back road via Xochimilco, Tulyahualco and Chalco, where direct descendants of the ancient tribesmen occupy their old lakelands and till them as did their ancestors. Still speaking Nahuatl, they pole their canoes through the network of canals surrounding their *chinampas*, or garden plots.

Leaving the lakes, one climbs high into the mountains, approaching the great volcanoes of Popocatépetl (Smoking Mountain) and Ixtaccíhuatl (White Lady) by the nearest route. Tlalmanalco is the first stop, and here a fine open chapel combines pure elements of Indian and European sculpture in a church built from the stones of a destroyed temple. The road ascends past the shrine of Amecameca, through Ozumba, and drops into a new world, the hot Valley of Morelos, home of the Tlahuicas. The motorist goes past sugar *haciendas* burned during the revolution, through Yolotepec, seat of a Tlahuica tribe and home of the feared revolutionary leader Zapata, and ascends again to reach Cuernavaca for lunch.

Here the Conquest is starkly represented by the huge fortified church and Cortés' palace, now the seat of the state government, where Rivera has painted an exciting fresco of the conquest and subjugation of the once-powerful Tlahuicas. At the railroad station is a cluster of temples, one of which is extraordinarily well preserved and represents the dramatic values of Aztec architecture. Later one can drive in half an hour to the Nahuatl-speaking village of Tepoztlan, whose people blend the material and spiritual cultures of Indian Mexico, colonial Spain and the modern republic. The great convent towers over the shattered sculptures from the ancient temples, but, high in the mountains and easily accessible to those sound in wind and limb, the temple of the Tepozteco stands battered but unsubdued. Returning to Cuernavaca, a few mounds on the right of the road at Tlaltenango are a furtive monument to the Upper Middle Culture people whose remains at Gualupita were studied in a brickyard near the Hotel Selva. (See Plate 28, bottom.)

After passing the night in one of the many good hotels in this charming resort of Cuernavaca, one can drive down the Taxco road and turn at Alpuyeca to visit the hill city of Xochicalco. The main temple has a superb carved façade which would suggest a Maya origin were it not for the fire-snakes, dates and ritualistic symbolism of Mixteca–Puebla Culture. Probably of eleventh-century origin, this may have been a main outpost of those people whose culture originated Aztec civilization. The site is almost untouched, and the uncovered mounds and terraces undoubtedly contain sculptures and pottery that will illumine many dark places in Indian history. Taxco can be fitted in for lunch and Mexico City reached by nightfall over a fine road across the mountains. The traveller will realize how the mountain chains sealed off one group of people from another, so that language, art and culture could develop along special lines without outside influence. Coming down from the heights, the panorama of the southern Valley is laid out below one: the lakes, the valley floor and, looming up in the centre, the Hill of the Star, where each fifty-two years the Aztecs received the promise of continued life.

On the sixth day (seventh in the alternative schedule) the rugged traveller who can maintain this schedule might take a dramatic two-day trip to Puebla. Driving down the southern shore of Texcoco, where 'the sedge is withered from the lake and no birds sing', he crosses the mountain chain to the southeast, close under the snow-covered shoulders of the great volcanoes. As he emerges from the pine forests on the other side, the rich Valley of Puebla opens before him. At San Cristobal a mound crowning a big hill on the left was the chief offertory of a group of Middle Culture mounds at the base, but they are not worth the time available, so that the motorist pushes on to Texmelucan, where he turns left on the road to Tlaxcala. Here the Indian population is prosperous because Spain recognized the services of its most effective allies and did not let them be despoiled. The town itself is old and charming, little affected by change since the eighteenth century. The oldest church in Mexico, where the first Indian baptism took place, is on an eminence near the centre of the town. Across the river at Tizatlan there is a little temple whose painted altars, their colours still preserved, depict the great god Tezcatlipoca and some of the symbolism of the ancient religion. Nearby a former open chapel, delightfully naïve, is screened by an atrocious nineteenth-century church. There are also the dubious remains of an early sixteenth-century house, said to be the residence, after the Conquest, of Xicotencatl, who led the armies of Tlaxcala. Nearby can be seen the spot where Cortés built his brigantines to be transported, piecemeal, to the lakes of the Valley. (See Plate 57, top left.)

Returning to Texmelucan for lunch, one regains the Puebla road and stops at the once-important city-state Huexotcingo. The earliest civilization is obliterated by a marvellous old Franciscan convent, where simple, honest construction reflects the virtues of these holy men who accomplished the conversion of the Indians. The measure of their success can be gauged by the huge court, or *atrio*, where the Indians congregated in thousands to hear Mass.

Back to the road, in less than an hour Cholula looms on the horizon. Hundreds of little churches, whose coloured tiles shimmer in the sun, bear witness to a dense population which once had a temple in each place where a church is now. One can see why people from this region made their way to the Valley to get living space. Even to-day every field is cultivated. The people themselves are very Indian, and the strange sounds of Nahuatl often break in on the smooth syllables of Spanish. The big temple of Cholula is incredible. It seems like the counterpart of Babel, to which the friars compared it. On top the church rests proudly, and on a terrace below are the remains of rooms and the altar enclosing human burials, all carefully excavated by government archaeologists. Within the big mound run more than a mile of tunnels, which the archaeologists hollowed from the adobe bricks to follow the walls and stairs of the Toltec ceremonial precinct of earlier times. Deep inside frescoed representations of the Butterfly God are awe-inspiring in the dim lantern light. (See Plate 26, middle.)

Passing on to Puebla itself, one finds a large provincial town, whose dull respectability is leavened by the burst of inventive creativeness reflected in the ornate church architecture. Examination of Puebla and its museum can be made during the morning of the next day, after which the return to Mexico City is accomplished leisurely.

Another variation is to drive past Puebla to Tepeaca, the old Segura de la Frontera of the Conquest, and thence through a desolate waste to Tehuacan. Here one may turn up over the hills to Orizaba and down into the moist, tropical regions of Córdoba, through populous Indian territory. Or one may leave one's car and take the train to Oaxaca, if the road has not yet been completed.

Oaxaca is a charming provincial capital, unchanged since colonial days. The lofty hill which dominates the city is completely transformed by the terraces, temples and tombs which constitute the great Zapotec site of Monte Alban. Another valley, another culture, another language, make this region into one more Indian world. The ruins of Mitla are exquisite great buildings, and their intricate wall carvings attest the skill of their Mixtec architects. The regional museum in Oaxaca houses, besides collections drawn from Mitla and other parts of the state, the superb jewel collection found in Tomb 7 at Monte Alban. Indian life is near the surface at Oaxaca, and at the market one can hear not only the Zapotec and Mixtec of the rival groups who contested the hegemony of the valley, but the language of other mountain traders who bring their own obscure tongues to this modern babel. (See Plates 8-9, 11.)

A trip easily accomplished from Mexico City leads over the mountains to Toluca, the capital of the state of Mexico, where an enlightened governor constructed a State museum, showing the varied handiwork of the Matlatzincas, the Indian group who held this valley. Beyond Toluca the ruins of Calixtlahuaca boast a round temple to the Wind among the structures reared in honour of their gods. The more venturesome motorist who has no fear of bad roads should drive down past Metepec to Tenancingo, and from there go by car, by horse or on foot to Malinalco. These rock-cut temples are really thrilling, both because of the fine carving and for the strangely remote effect they produce on the visitor. In this mountain niche one can look far down the valley and back to the temples which, hewn from the rock, were cognate to their gods, envisaged in the manifold variety of nature.

If our visitor has not yet been overwhelmed by these skeletons of a once-lively civilization he can fly to Yucatan. Chichen Itza, Uxmal, Labnah, are great white ceremonial centres that thrust themselves from the enveloping bush. Half-hidden in thatched villages, growing their corn in little clearings, the modern Mayas carry on their ancient life, but their religion has lost much, and a simple Catholicism tinged with magic provides a slender bond with the supernatural. A visit to Yucatan will enhance the conception of the variety of the Mexican world, where once men of many tongues and many tribes wrought out their destinies. (See Plates 6–7, 12.)

The civilization of the Indian may not offer a direct inspiration to us modern individualists, yet we have profited from their labour in our food plants and the wealth produced by our neighbour republics to the south. In this world, torn with hate and war, adrift without an anchor or a compass with which to chart our course, we may well consider their example. The Indians worked together for their common good, and no sacrifice was too great for their corporate well-being. Man's strength lay in the physical and spiritual welfare of the tribe, and the individual was honoured only inasmuch as he contributed to that communal good. The Indian civilization may have been powerless to resist the culture of the Western world, but it did not consume itself, as we are doing, in the expression of military power.

The American countries to-day share the ideal of the republic and individual freedom. We share also an older tradition left us by our Indian forebears, that of mutual service for the benefit of man. With our continents spread before us, we have boundless opportunity to create on earth a wider life for everyone, an American civilization where old and new contributions to human welfare may be fused and amalgamated for the benefit of all.

POSTSCRIPT

BY C. A. BURLAND, F.R.A.I.[1]

SINCE this book was completed many archæological investigations, then in progress, have reached unexpected conclusions. New discoveries have been made. Some problems have been solved, and raise in their turn new problems. And George Vaillant has died.

This Postscript is, therefore, something of a memorial to a great scientist. The careful reader will note how some of Dr Vaillant's more startling theories have been amply justified; how new excavation has clarified problems which he was the first to bring to the attention of scientists; and how his painstaking excavations at Zacatenco, Ticoman and El Arbolillo have established a typology still in force for the 'Archaic' Middle Cultures of Mexico – and have been the models on which many a subsequent researcher has conducted his explorations. For many a year to come Dr Vaillant's book will remain a classic. It is the best general introduction to its subject, and will remain of permanent value to serious students, as well as providing fascinating reading for all who chance to turn its pages.

For our short review of the position of Mexican archaeology up to 1948, we will begin in the land that the Aztecs so emphatically made their own, the Valley of Mexico. Long before the Aztec days, perhaps 10,000 years ago, the fertile Valley had passed through a period of desert conditions; but before that the Lake had been larger than ever it was in historic times. Not far from Teotihuacan is the small town of Tepexpan, where in prehistoric time elephants and the extinct American horse browsed on the rushes of the swampy shore. Here Indian hunters chased the animals and slew them with weapons pointed with flakes of chalcedony. In February 1947 Dr Helmuth de

1. Author of *Art and Life in Ancient Mexico*, Bruno Cassirer, Oxford, 1948.

Terra found human remains at this site in apparent association with the extinct Archidiskodon elephant. If this were so a new chapter of physical anthropology had been added to Mexican prehistory. Scientific examination in Washington proved that this man was very like the more 'primitive'-looking Indians of the Mexican plateau to-day. Since the discovery these remains have been questioned, but nevertheless there is little doubt that in Mexico men were living a hunting life in this area about 15,000 years ago, contemporary with the late Palaeolithic cave paintings of Europe.

Further investigations of cave sites as well as of the Lake deposits of the Mexican Plateau have yielded stone flaked implements somewhat similar to those found in the South-western U.S.A. at Sandia and Folsom. Later, a local stone-flaking industry developed. It is named the Chalco culture, and must have lasted a long time until hunting as a means of livelihood slowly gave place to agriculture and such villages as those excavated at El Arbolillo and Zacatenco arose to bear evidence that man had discovered an easier means of living.

An even more sensational development in Mexican archaeology has been associated with the excavations at Tula, in the State of Hidalgo, some 30 miles north of Mexico City. Tradition had always referred this rather unimpressive group of mounds to Tollan, capital of the Toltecs. Fifty years ago both Teobert Maler and Désiré Charnay had noted that the few fragments of sculpture visible at Tula were like the work seen in the ruins of Chichen Itza in Yucatan. Chichen was known to be the centre of the Xiu family, who claimed to be descended from the Toltec Lords of Tula. Their remarks were lost in travel books that were soon outmoded by new and more serious works, and their idea was not revived because researchers in Yucatan thought their field had no connection with the archaeology of the Mexican Plateau. The Toltecs themselves were involved in the philosophy of the nineteenth-century materialism, which interpreted all ancient folk-legend as sun-

myths. Not many people of scientific standing were willing to
believe that the ancient records of pre-Spanish Mexico had any
basis in fact. Those who believed in the Toltecs as a real people
eventually triumphed. Dr Vaillant, in particular, was one of
the earliest of modern researchers to appreciate the value of the
ancient written records. The records however, described the
Toltecs as 'The Architects' *par excellence*. Where in Mexico
was to be found any ruin that might be constructed by such a
people? The obvious, and only, site was Teotihuacan, with its
astounding pyramids of the Sun and Moon. To confirm the
surmise, the connection of Toltecs with Cholula was known,
and excavations in the pyramid at Cholula had brought to
light pottery, buildings and frescoes like those of Teotihuacan. So it came about that every well-educated Mexicanist
was taught that Teotihuacan was once Tollan, capital of the
mighty Toltecs.

In 1941 Mexican archaeologists set to work on a project for
the excavation of Tula. The enterprise is by no means completed yet, but as the results have accumulated year by year,
it has become clear that Tula was indeed an important city.
Even in minor details of art work and costume the sculptures
of Tula resembled those of Chichen Itza. This was a fair cri-
terion of the Toltec art style, accepted by all the experts. But
the pottery of Tula was mostly the pottery of the Mazapan
culture, and included plumbate and yellow-glazed wares of
types that spread far and wide over Middle America, and was
known to be later than that of Teotihuacan. Thus was resolved
the riddle that had led the best thinkers among the students of
Mexico's past to postulate the two kinds of Toltec – Toltecs of
Teotihuacan and Toltec–Chichimecs. The Toltecs of the traditions were the people who lived at Tula; and excavation has
fully justified their reputation as architects. From the unimpressive Monticulo (Mound) B at Tula has emerged a very
jewel of a temple pyramid, far better proportioned and more
richly decorated than anything that came later, and far more

delicate than any of the massive monuments of Teotihuacan. Alas, it cannot be proved to be the House of the Frog that Ixtlilxochitl so often praises. It deserves a better name than just 'Monticulo B'.

Of course Tula has provided another puzzle – foreseen by Dr Vaillant in his Puebla–Mixteca complex. For in the vestibule of Monticulo B have been found pottery vessels of distinctively Mixtec type, and a painted relief frieze that might have been taken from one of the painted Codices made by the Mixtecs of Oaxaca four centuries later in time. It seems, then, that the Mixtecs were descended from an important section of the Toltec people, and that in truth some echoes of Toltec tradition may still be deciphered in the paintings of such books as the great Codex Vindobonensis now in Vienna and the Codices Bodley and Selden in the Bodleian Library at Oxford. The whole excavation has amply justified the relation, in pottery sequences, of Mazapan (Toltec) – Aztec I, II, III, etc. The early 'Aztec' periods belong to the time when warring city-states of Chichimec people, led by Toltec families surviving from the civil war, fought for the overlordship of the Valley of Mexico. The Aztec III and IV represent the rise of the Aztecs themselves as final victors in the struggle.

Well, now that we know Tollan to have been situated at Tula, what are we going to do about Teotihuacan? This greatest of all ruined sites in Mexico is an embarrassingly heavy baby to be left on archaeologists' hands. But that is just what has happened. We do not know how this great city began, nor why it was abandoned half-ruined by its nameless builders. Were they the 'Xicalancas' of the old chronicles? We cannot tell, so, for the sake of clear thinking, we just call these people the Teotihuacanos. They built other great centres, as you know, at Cholula and at Azcopotzalco. These all included temples and courtyards, and many-roomed houses with frescoed walls. There has been no trace of metal reported from a Teotihuacano site – yet there is some evidence that the con-

M

temporary Maya people of the sixth and seventh centuries A.D. may have known the rudiments of casting gold and copper.

Teotihuacano art is not like that of the Aztecs, and has few points of contact with that of the Toltecs. It is on the whole an architectural and very formal art, dealing with severe planes and masses rather than delicate ornament. There is a welcome relief in the little pottery figurines, which are often quite charming, even when their faces have been made in a mould. In the representation of gods there is some contact with Maya conventions; and Teotihuacan in its great days had a very great influence on the arts of the developing Zapotec culture on Monte Alban, as we know from the intensive researches conducted by Dr Alfonso Caso at that famous site.

Historically all the contacts of Teotihuacan seem to have been with the south and south-west of Mexico. A beautiful jade plaque and other artifacts of the classical Maya period have been found near Teotihuacan; and here and there Teotihuacano pottery types occur in Chiapas and the Peten. There must have been considerable trade going on when the great ruined city was in its heyday of the Teotihuacan III period. Other evidence comes from still farther afield. In 1947 was published the record of several years' painstaking research by Dr Kidder and his associates at Kaminaljuyu, near Guatemala City. The Teotihuacanos had been there, too. In one level of the excavations Teotihuacan III pottery occurred in such great quantities that, rather than postulate trade exchange on such an overwhelming scale, Dr Kidder is driven to conclude that there may have been an actual occupation of Kaminaljuyu by Teotihuacano people. Whether it was the result of war or not we have no clue.

There is a history to be unravelled by the excavator in Teotihuacan, the City of the Rain God, Tlaloc. In Teotihuacan I, its figurines continue some of the traditions of the old Middle Cultures of the neighbourhood, but in a new dress, as if the potters were interpreting a new civilization which had reached them from outside. Later the city develops to great richness of ornament and architecture ... it is obviously the centre of a great civilization with leisure for the refinements of art. Every new find, including the newly-uncovered frescoes of the 'Earthly Paradise', emphasizes the importance of the water-gods to the Teotihuacanos. Everywhere one sees the strange, spectacle-eyed, tusked-mouthed figure of Tlaloc. The great monolithic statue of a goddess has symbols on her feet that can be read as the later glyph we know to mean 'water'. These people trade far and wide in Middle America, and at the height of their civilization they end. Images are smashed. House walls are broken down. At Xolalpan, Dr Sigvald Linné found a Toltec (Mazapan) burial which had been made in an older mound. The grave had been dug through ruined mud walls as if the Toltec workmen had no knowledge that a ruined building lay there. How long was the time gap between the ruin of this suburb of Teotihuacan and the coming of the Toltecs? Or was there any real gap? Perhaps the burial was late, and the Toltecs themselves smashed Teotihuacan when they were founding Tula – the dates in the chronicles would give colour to such an idea.

To turn from the Mexican Plateau we may briefly review the results of excavation in other parts of the country. Work on sites in Southern Mexico has extended our knowledge of the culture revealed at Tres Zapotes and La Venta. Since this part of the country was occupied in historic times by the Olmecs (People of the Rubber Country) it has been common to describe the new culture as Olmec, but scientists have agreed that, with no written history to check, it is better to use the term 'La Venta Culture', and so avoid misconceptions such as occurred with the use of 'Toltec'. Painstaking research at many small sites in Tabasco and southern Vera Cruz, together with considerable study of the specimens in Museums and collections which show traces of the typically 'La Ventan' art styles, has revealed this as an independent civilization. It seems to have flourished in the first few centuries B.C. and A.D. and penetrated the Isthmus of Tehuantepec, and even influenced sculpture well into the mountains of Oaxaca and Guerrero.

The La Venta culture was the first 'High Culture' of Mexico proper; its echoes are seen on the earliest carvings of the 'Danzantes' at Monte Alban. Whether it was earlier or later than the earliest development of a high culture among the Maya people is unknown, but on balance at the moment it seems that the two developments were parallel and had many features of art and iconography in common. Its artists had an uncanny skill in working jade, especially a peculiar bluish variety that takes a high polish, and seems to have become extremely rare in later times. Its place of origin has not yet been determined. Their art is characterized by areas of high relief (figures, or heads) surrounded by flat surfaces with incised line decoration. Immense human heads were carved and altars erected before them. Paved courtyards may have been the first ball-courts. Jaguar gods were of great importance, and for some reason human faces were often distorted so as to present an everted upper lip and a forehead cleft to depict some resemblance to the symbol for jaguar. Something about the water-creatures also seemed to influence the superstitions of these people who represent turtles and toads, with human characters. That they bandaged babies' heads to give them a high cylindrical form is almost certain. What is missing almost completely is any cross references to other areas that give a clue to the origin of the La Venta culture.

Not much La Venta pottery has been reproduced in colour, but that little shows affinities, as Dr Vaillant pointed out before anyone else, with pottery from the Totonac of Vera Cruz. This is much later in date, because it is found at Sacrificios Island in association with plumbate wares of Toltec (Mazapan) style. There is evidence that this developed Totonac culture is later than that found at the pyramid of Tajin, near Papantla.

The art of the Tajin culture has many strange conventions, particularly the use of double outlines; but it has close resemblances to Toltec art in its iconography, and also some relation with Mayan art. It is associated with stone 'axe blades' made in the form of human faces, which also occur in Guatemala. Some of the parallels with its art are also to be found at Santa Lucia Cozumahualpa in circumstances which seem to date it as immediately later than Teotihuacan. Similar dating can be postulated for the little pyramid of Xochicalco in Central Mexico, based on its art which includes the double outline, figures with latest Teotihuacano costume, and a few day-signs that parallel the later system used by the Toltecs and Aztecs. It seems as if these cultures (represented by but few remains that are the result of properly conducted excavation) may fill the gap at the end of Teotihuacan, and perhaps even prove to be the origin of Toltec culture. The pieces from Sta. Lucia Cozumahualpa in Guatemala have been shown by Mr J. Eric Thompson to have some kind of connection with a tradition that the Nahua-speaking people who made them had migrated because they were oppressed by the 'Olmecs'. What Olmecs? Teotihuacanos? La Venta people? We can prove nothing except that the glyphs on the monuments are closely akin to those used by the Nahua-speaking Toltecs of later times, with the exception of one or two which are very reminiscent of Teotihuacan. The whole matter is an excellent illustration of the kind of puzzle presented by archaeological fact to one who would expound it as history.

In Western Mexico Dr Vaillant's judgment has again been vindicated; the beautifully modelled pottery figures and dogs which have proved so attractive to modern artists and collectors are pre-Tarascan in date. The modern practice is to ascribe them to the 'Colima Complex', a culture of quite highly civilized type lasting through a long period. It shows many variations in type, which are not satisfactorily determined as yet. The Tarascans, who have been credited with the art works of this earlier culture, arrived only a century or so before the Spanish Conquest, and had a distinctive pottery polychrome style of their own.

A minor excavation of some interest to students of Aztec history has been the discovery of the foundations of the great temple of Tlatelolco in Mexico City. The state of these ruins is sufficiently good to prove that the pyramid had been enlarged seven times. If the assumption that these enlargements took place every fifty-two years is correct, the city of Tlatelolco goes back to the end of Toltec times – and is older than the Aztec arrival at Tenochtitlan! Either the temples were rebuilt at more frequent intervals than had been supposed (one document has very slight evidence of a twenty-year celebration of building the city of Tenochtitlan), or else the Aztecs falsified their history for propaganda purposes!

There will yet be many works on ancient Mexico, because so much of the record of the past of the fascinating peoples of Central America has yet to be dug out of the earth. It is a valuable study to those who would understand human civilization as a whole, for the weight of evidence is on the side of those who claim that these fantastic cultures of Middle America are a native invention. They show by their parallels and divergencies from Old World civilizations just how much variation and how much similarity the human race displays in its course from savagery to civilization. Whatever may be written in the future will be written with some influences from Dr Vaillant's book, which has done a great service in clarifying our ideas, and forms a very solid basis for students to build on for years to come.

July 1948

NOTES

CHAPTER I

The recent dates of authorities cited indicate how rapidly ideas on the genesis of Indian culture are changing. New finds, new conclusions, new datings, appear each year. The summary in Chapter I is frankly interpretative, and no one will be more ready than the author to change his views as fresh evidence appears. The four works listed here: *Swanton Essays ; Maya and Their Neighbors ;* Wissler, *American Indian,* and Means, *Ancient Civilizations,* give a broad background for New World archaeology. Their detailed references are listed under their appropriate footnote number. The full titles of the four background volumes are:

Essays in Historical Anthropology of North America. Published in honor of John R. Swanton (Smithsonian Miscellaneous Collections, Vol. 100, Washington, 1940).

The Maya and Their Neighbors, New York, 1940.

Means, Philip, *Ancient Civilizations of the Andes,* New York, 1931.

Wissler, Clark, *The American Indian,* New York, 3rd ed., 1938.

(1)Howells, *Origins,* 1940. Nelson, *Antiquity of Man,* 1933. MacCurdy, ed., *Early Man,* 1937. Howard, *Evidence of Early Man,* 1935.

(2)Wissler, *American Indian,* 1938.

(3)Howells, *Origins,* 1940. Hooton, *Racial Types,* 1933. Dixon, *Racial History of Man,* 1923. Hrdlicka, *Origin and Antiquity of American Indian,* 1923.

(4)Nelson, *Antiquity of Man,* 1933. Roberts, *Pre-Pottery Horizon,* 1940. Howard, *Evidence of Early Man,* 1935. Bird, *Antiquity and Migrations,* 1938.

(5)Wissler, *American Indian,* 1938. *Swanton Essays,* 1940. Kroeber, *Cultural and Natural Areas,* 1939.

(6)Gladwin, *Snaketown,* II, 1937. Sayles, *Survey of Texas,* 1935.

(7)Kroeber, *Cultural and Natural Areas,* 1939.

(8)Sauer, *American Agricultural Origins,* 1936. Yanovski, *Food Plants,* 1936. Mangelsdorf and Reeves, *Origin of Maize,* 1938.

(9)Wissler, *American Indian,* 1938.

(10)Linton, *Crops, Soils and Culture,* 1940.

(11)Roberts, *Survey of South-western Archaeology,* 1935. Kidder, *Introduction to Southwestern Archaeology,* 1924. Gladwin and others, *Snaketown,* I and II, 1937.

(12)Spinden, *Ancient Civilizations,* 1928. Means, *Ancient Civilizations,* 1931. Vaillant, *Early Cultures,* 1935.

(13)Means, *Ancient Civilizations,* 1931.

(14)Spinden, *Ancient Civilizations,* 1928. Spinden, *Maya Art,* 1913.

(15)Linton, *Crops, Soil and Culture,* 1940. Vaillant, *Patterns in Culture,* 1940.

(16)Spinden, *Ancient Civilizations,* 1928. Vaillant, *Early Cultures,* 1935.

(17)Vaillant, *Patterns in Culture*, 1940.

(18)Spinden, *Ancient Civilizations*, 1928.

(19)Gann and Thompson, *History of the Maya*, 1931. *The Maya and Their Neighbors*, 1940. Thompson, *Civilization of the Mayas*, 1932.

(20)Morley, *Introduction to Maya Hieroglyphs*, 1915. Spinden, *Reduction of Mayan Dates*, 1924. Teeple, *Maya Astronomy*, 1931. Thompson, *Maya Chronology*, 1935. Andrews, *Chronology and Astronomy*, 1940.

(21)Donnelly, *Atlantis*, 1882. Le Plongeon, *Queen Moo*, 1896. Churchward, *Lost Continent of Mu*, 1926.

(22)Vaillant, *Chronology and Stratigraphy*, 1935. Gann, *Mounds in Northern Honduras*, 1900. Tozzer, *Maya and Toltec Figures*, 1930. Bancroft, *Native Races*, 1883. Butler, *Alta Vera Paz*, 1940.

(23)Stirling, *Great Stone Faces*, 1940; *Initial Series from Vera Cruz*, 1940; *Oldest Dated Work*, 1939. Weiant, *Manuscript*, 1939. Vaillant, *Bearded Mystery*, 1931; *Pre-Columbian Jade*, 1932. Ricketson and Ricketson, *Uaxactun*, 1937. Caso, *Exploraciones*, 1931–32, 1934–35, 1936–37. Holmes, *Nephrite Statue*, 1907.

(24)Batres, *Exploraciones en Monte Alban*, 1902. Caso, *Exploraciones*, 1934–35, 1936–37. Dauterman, *Pottery Yard Stick*, 1938.

(25)Vaillant, *Correlation*, 1938.

CHAPTER II

There are no really popular accounts of the Middle Cultures. Dr Spinden's excellent *Ancient Civilization of Mexico and Central America* sketches a broad outline; the author's *Early Cultures* sums up the results of the most recent excavations. The Middle Cultures are at that stage where technical studies have made great progress, but the subject matter has not passed into the hands of social and historical thinkers for intellectual rather than technical appraisal.

(1)POPULAR: Vaillant, *Threshold of Civilization*, 1929; *Beginnings of a History*, 1930. Beyer, *Antiguedades del Pedregal*, 1917.

TECHNICAL: Cummings, *Ruins of Cuicuilco*, 1923; *Cuicuilco*, 1923; *Cuicuilco*, 1926; *Cuicuilco*, 1933. Gamio, *Excavaciones del Pedregal*, 1920. Kroeber, *Archaic Culture Horizons*, 1925. Vaillant, *Zacatenco*, 1930; *Ticoman*, 1931; *El Arbolillo*, 1935; *Early Cultures*, 1935. Vaillant and Vaillant, *Gualupita*, 1934.

(2)Vaillant, *Early Cultures*, 1935.

(3)Vaillant, *Early Cultures*, 1935.

(4)Vaillant, *Prehistoric Cotton*, 1939.

(5)Vaillant, *El Arbolillo*, 1935.

(6)Vaillant, *El Arbolillo*, 1935.

(7)Cummings, *Cuicuilco*, 1933. Noguera, *Teotihuacan*, 1935. Vaillant, *Ticoman*, 1931. Vaillant and Vaillant, *Gualupita*, 1934.

(8)Linné, *Teotihuacan*, 1934, pp. 162–67.

(9)Vaillant and Vaillant, *Gualupita*, 1934.

(10)Vaillant and Vaillant, *Gualupita*, 1934. Stirling, *Stone Faces*, 1940.

(11)Cummings, *Cuicuilco*, 1923a, 1923b, 1926, 1933.

(12)Cummings, *Cuicuilco*, 1933. Mena and Hyde, *Antiguedad del Hombre*, 1922. Nuttall, *Aztecs and Their Predecessors*, 1926.

(13)Kidder, *Introduction*, 1924, pp. 16–35; *Pottery*, I, 1931. Vaillant, *El Arbolillo*, 1935, pp. 160–67.

(14)Vaillant, *Early Cultures*, 1935.

CHAPTER III

The so-called Toltec question is covered by an enormous speculative literature and a relatively small number of reports on excavations scientifically carried out. The extensive work of the Swedish archaeologist Linné has appeared in part only, and much of the modern Mexican work and the results of the writer's excavations have not yet reached print. The interpretation given here explains a number of features, but further work will correct and expand many of these opinions.

(1)Brinton, *Essays*, 1890, pp. 83–100.

(2)Ixtlilxochitl, *Relaciones*,1891; this sixteenth-century writer is underestimated. He was a descendant of the old Texcocan lineage and had access to many of the ancient records.

(3)*Anales de Cuauhtitlan*, 1885; *Historia Tolteca-Chichimeca*, 1937, and Muñoz Camargo, 1892, describe these later lineages. The great writer on customs and religion, Father Bernardino Sahagun, was confused by this double usage. History was difficult for him, while ethnology was an open book.

(4)Ixtlilxochitl, *Relaciones*, 1891; *Historia Chichimeca*, 1892. Bancroft, *Native Races*, 1883, Vol. 5. This historian is a veritable mine of information, but he worked from written records without the archaeological check accessible to modern students. Krickeberg, *Alten Kulturen Mittel-Amerikas*, 1937, an excellent summary of current and past interpretation of history. Beyer, in Gamio, *Teotihuacan*, 1922. Vaillant, *Correlation*, 1938, an effort to tie in historical with archaeological information in the Valley of Mexico.

(5)Caso, *Conocimiento del Tonalpohualli*, 1937.

(6)Sahagun, *Historia General*, 1938, Vol. 1, Book 1, p. 8; Vol. 2, Book 8, Chap. 5; Vol. 3, Book 10, Chap. 29, paragraph 1, 12. *Anales de Cuauhtitlan*, 1885. Ixtlilxochitl, *Relaciones*, 1891.

(7)Ixtlilxochitl, *Relaciones*, 1891. *Anales de Cuauhtitlan*, 1885. Bancroft, *Native Races*, Vol. 5, 1883.

(8)Linné, *Teotihuacan*, 1934, the best English work on Teotihuacan. Gamio, ed., *Teotihuacan*, 1922, the three-volume Mexican study on the archaeology, history and sociology of modern and ancient Teotihuacan. Charnay, *Ancient Cities*, 1888, an early account of the ruins and some excavations. Seler, *Teotihuacan-Kultur*, 1915, the standard scholarly work on this culture, now outdated by Gamio and Linné.

(9)Noguera, *Antecedentes de la Cultura Teotihuacana*, 1935, the single exhaustive study on this epoch.

(10)Linné, *Teotihuacan*, 1934.

(11)Linné, *Teotihuacan*, 1934.

(12)Chavero, *Monolito de Coatlinchan*, 1903.

(13)Linné, *Teotihuacan*, 1934; *Expedition to Mexico*, 1936.

(14)These Cholula excavations are still incomplete and reports on them unpublished.

(15)Morris, Charlot and Morris, *Temple of the Warriors*, 1928.

(16)Nuttall, *Teotihuacan*, unpublished; cf. Noguera, *Conclusiones*, 1937.

(17)Seler, *Teotihuacan-Kultur*, 1915. Tozzer, *Santiago Ahuitzotla*, 1921, a complete study of a building. Vaillant, *Correlation*, 1938.

CHAPTER IV

This era is just emerging from darkness and confusion. Recent definition of the Mazapan culture reinforces Dr Tozzer's work at Coyotlatelco by giving archaeological checks on the annals.

The writer's suggested identification of ceremonial dumps helps to clarify the confusion in the annals. The author believes the new finds corroborate Orozco y Berra's correlation of tribal rulers, but the late Dr Lehmann's exhaustive research does not agree. New data, worked out from newly discovered documents by Wigberto Jimenez Moreno, will clarify the picture when published fully.

(1)Joyce, *Mexican Archaeology*, 1914, gives a straightforward interpretation. *Anales de Cuauhtitlan*, 1885. *Relacion de Genealogia* and *Origen de los Mexicanos* are abridgments of the *Anales de Cuauhtitlan*. Lehmann, *Geschichte von Colhuacan und Mexico*, 1939, is a careful, analytical translation of the Annals of Cuauhtitlan. Orozco y Berra, *Ojeada de Cronologia*, 1878, is a useful critique. Kirchhoff, *Pueblos*, 1940, is important for interpretation of annals. Vaillant, *Correlation*, 1938, gives a résumé of the basis of this chapter.

(2)Ixtlilxochitl, *Historia Chichimeca*, 1892. *Mapa Quinatzin*, *Mapa Tlotzin*, *Codex Xolotl*; important picture manuscripts for this period.

(3)*Codex Ramirez*, *Historia de los Mexicanos*, in Radin, *Sources*, 1920. *Codex Boturini*, *Codex of 1576*; picture manuscripts.

(4)Bancroft, *Native Races*, Vol. 5, 1883, Chaps. V–VII cite early authorities. Orozco y Berra, *Historia Antigua*, 1880, cites early authorities and picture writings. Radin, *Sources*, 1920, an invaluable series of translations of early Mexican records.

(5)Vaillant, *Correlation*, 1938. Linné, *Teotihuacan*, 1934; *Mazapan Grave*, 1938.

(6)Vaillant, *Chronology and Stratigraphy*, 1935. Butler, *Alta Vera Paz*, 1940.

(7)Tozzer, *Santiago Ahuitzotla*, 1921. Boas, *Album*, 1911–12. Noguera, in *Tenayuca*, 1935.

(8)Boas, *Album*, 1911–12, Pls. 1–10. Gamio, *Texto*, 1921. Brenner, *Influence of Technique in Culhuacan*, 1931.

(9)Vaillant, *Correlation*, 1938; *History and Stratigraphy*, 1937.

(10)Marquina, Reygadas Vertiz and Noguera, in *Tenayuca*, 1935.

(11)Noguera, *Altar de los Craneos*, 1937; *Conclusiones*, 1937.

(12)Preuss and Mengin, *Historia Tolteca-Chichimeca*, 1937. Lehmann, *Geschichte von Colhuacan und Mexiko*, 1937. Muñoz Camargo, *Historia*, 1892. Sahagun, *Historia General*, 1938, Vol. 3, Book 10, Chapter XXIX. Bancroft, *Native Races*, Vol. 5, Chapters XI–XIII.

(13)Ekholm, *Results*, 1939; *Archaeology*, 1940.

CHAPTER V

The picture is much clearer for Aztec times; the archaeology is better known, and the historical records are more in accord. The cyclical constructions and destructions of the Aztecs are especially helpful. A confusing point is the foundation date of Tenochtitlan, for which the author provides a theory.

(1)EXHAUSTIVE ACCOUNTS OF AZTEC HISTORY: Bancroft, *Native Races*, 1883, Vol. 5; Orozco y Berra, *Historia Antigua*, 1880.

POPULAR ENGLISH DIGESTS: Thompson, *Mexico before Cortes*, 1933; Joyce, *Mexican Archæology*, 1914. Radin, *Sources*, 1922, gives translations and reproductions of important native sources, as well as a superb critical analysis.

OTHER SOURCES: Torquemada, *Monarquia*, 1723; Clavigero, *History of Mexico*, 1783.

PICTURE WRITINGS: the codices of 1560, 1590, Boturini, Mendoza, Siguenza, Telleriano-Remensis, Vaticanus A, Tepechpan.

DIGESTS OF PICTURE WRITINGS IN SPANISH AND NAHUATL: *Anales de Cuauhtitlan*, 1885; Chimalpahin, *Anales*, 1889; *Codex Ramirez*, 1878; Tezozomoc's *Cronica*, 1878; *Histoire Mexicaine*, 1891; *Historia de los Mexicanos*, 1886; Ixtlilxochitl, *Historia Chichimeca*, 1892; Duran, *Historia de las Indias*, 1867, 1880.

Tenayuca, 1935, is the great work of the Department of Monuments of the Mexican Ministry of Public Education, which blends archaeology and history in a masterly exposition of the Aztec past.

(2)*Codex Boturini*.

(3)*Historia de los Mexicanos*.

(4)*Anales de Cuauhtitlan*, 1885, p. 49, Year 8 Rabbit. Palacios, *Fundacion de Mexico*, 1925, résumé of historical evidence for founding of Mexico. Codex of 1590 shows Acamapichtli being crowned by the chief of Tlatelolco in the presence of the Tenochca clan council; cf. Vaillant, *Correlation*, 1938, p. 563.

(5)Sahagun, *Historia General*, 1938, Vol. 3, Book 10, Chap. XXIX, pp. 137–8.

(6)Bancroft, *Native Races*, 1883, Vol. 5, quotes early authorities on pp. 414–15.

(7)Bancroft, *Native Races*, 1883, Vol. 5, p. 434; Tezozomoc, Chapter LIV. Duran, *Historia de las Indias*, I, 1867, Chapter XXXII.

(8)Tezozomoc, *Cronica*, 1878, Chapters XLI–XLII.

(9)Tezozomoc, *Cronica*, 1872, Chapter LI. Duran, *Historia de las Indias*, I, 1867, Chapter XXXVI.

(10)Ixtlilxochitl, *Historia Chichimeca*, 1892.

(11)Bancroft, *Native Races*, 1883. p. 449, quotes Torquemada, Clavigero and Ixtlilxochitl.

(12)Saville, *Tizoc*, 1929.

(13)Bancroft, *Native Races*, 1883, pp. 439–40, quotes Ixtlilxochitl, Duran, Torquemada and *Codex Telleriano-Remensis*.

(14)Bancroft, *Native Races*, 1883, p. 471, quotes Tezozomoc, Torquemada and Duran.

(15)Bancroft, *Native Races*, 1883, p. 507, quotes Ixtlilxochitl.

(16)Diaz del Castillo, *True History*, 1908–16. Cortes, *Letters*, 1908.

CHAPTER VI

The customs of the Aztecs were a source of great interest to the conquerors and their palliative companions, the friars. The system of controlling the conquered depended on knowledge of the native methods of life. Consequently there is a full literature based on contemporary reports sent back to Spain by her civil and ecclesiastical administrators in the new colony.

(1)EXCELLENT POPULAR ACCOUNTS: Thompson, *Mexico before Cortes*, 1933; Biart, *The Aztecs*, 1883; Joyce, *Mexican Archæology*, 1914; Prescott, *Conquest of Mexico*, 1922.

EXHAUSTIVE ENGLISH STUDIES: Bandelier, *Social Organization*, 1880; Bancroft, *Native Races*, 1883, Vols. 2 and 5.

MEXICAN STUDY: Orozco y Berra, *Historia Antigua*, 1880.

BEST CONTEMPORARY ACCOUNTS: Sahagun, *Historia General*, 1938; Pomar, *Relación*, 1891; Zurita, *Breve Relación*, 1891; Motolinia, *Historia*, 1914; Torquemada, *Monarquia*, 1723; Clavigero, *History of Mexico*, 1787.

PICTURE WRITINGS: *Codex Mendoza*, *Codex Florentino* (illustrations for Sahagun's *Historia General*).

The transition from the tribal council to the domination of the chiefs is shown by the presence of individual members in the early times and their disappearance after the foundation of the lineage; cf. Vaillant, *Correlation*, 1938, pp. 563–4; Bandelier, *Social Organization*, 1880, pp. 576–88; Mapa de Siguenza, *Codex of 1590*; *Histoire Mexicaine*; *Codex Mendoza*, and *Codex Telleriano-Remensis*.

(2)*Codex Mendoza*; Sahagun, *Historia General*, 1938, Vol. 2, Book 6.

(3)Bandelier, *Social Organization*, 1880, cites early authorities.

(4)Bandelier, *Social Organization*, 1880; Bancroft, *Native Races*, 1883, Vol. 2.

(5)*Codex Mendoza*.

(6)Bandelier, *Social Organization*, 1880; cf. Waterman, *Bandelier's Contribution*, 1917, for a critique of Bandelier.

(7)Sahagun, *Historia General*, 1938, Vol. 1, Book 3, Appendix; Vol. 2, Books 6, 9: Vol. 3, Book 10; see also *Codex Florentino* and *Codex Mendoza*.

(8)Bancroft, *Native Races*, 1883, Vol. 2; Bandelier, *Social Organization*, 1880.

(9)Ceballos Novelo, *Instituciones*, 1935. Kohler, *Derecho de los Aztecas*, 1924. Moreno, *Organización de los Aztecas*, 1931.

CHAPTER VII

This aspect of life is fully covered in the contemporary literature of the Conquest.

(1)POPULAR AUTHORS: Thompson, *Mexico before Cortés*, 1931; Joyce, *Mexican Archæology*, 1914; Biart, *The Aztecs*, 1883.

EXHAUSTIVE ENGLISH STUDIES: Bandelier, *Tenure of Lands*, 1878; Bancroft, *Native Races*, 1883.

EXHAUSTIVE MEXICAN STUDY: Orozco y Berra, *Historia Antigua*, 1880.

CONTEMPORARY ACCOUNTS: Sahagun, *Historia General*, 1938; Torquemada, *Monarquia*, 1723; Clavigero, *History of Mexico*, 1787.

PICTURE WRITINGS: *Codex Florentino* (illustrations for Sahagun's *Historia General*), *Codex Mendoza*, *Tribute Roll of Montezuma*.

(2)Bandelier, *Tenure of Lands*, 1878.

(3)*Mapa Tlotzin*. Cortés, *Letters*, 1908, p. 221, referring to Valley of Puebla, 'Such is the multitude of people who live in these parts that there is not a palm of land which is not cultivated ... many places they suffer for want of bread.'

(4)Nuttall, *Mexican Gardens*, 1925.

(5)Bandelier, *Tenure of Land*, 1878.

(6)*Tribute Roll of Montezuma, Codex Mendoza, Tribute Roll*.

(7)Articles on Shell and Commerce in Hodge, *Handbook*, 1907. Lumholtz, *Unknown Mexico*, 1902, plumbate ware in Tepic. Lothrop, *Coclé*, 1937, gold in Yucatan.

(8)Diaz del Castillo, *True History*, 1908–16, Chapter XCII. McBryde, *Solola*, 1933.

(9)Blom, *Commerce of the Maya*, 1932.

(10)Nuttall, *Chalchihuitl*, 1901. Diaz del Castillo, *True History*, 1908–16, Chapter CXXVIII.

(11)Saville, *Goldsmith's Art*, 1920. Sahagun, *Historia General*, 1938, Vol. 5, pp. 193–219.

(12)Sahagun, *Historia General*, 1938, Vol. 3, Book 11. Emmart, *Badianus Manuscript*, 1940. Sauer, *Agricultural Origins*, 1936. Hernandez, *Historia Plantarum*, 1790. Spinden, *Ancient Civilizations*, 1928.

(13)Alcocer, *Comidas*, 1938.

(14)Bancroft, *Native Races*, 1883, Vol. 2, pp. 160–74, 553–74; cites authorities.

(15)Vaillant, *Twilight of Aztecs*, 1938.

(16)Anonymous Conqueror, 1917, narrative.

(17)Motolinia, *Historia*, 1914, Book 1, Chapter XII; Bandelier's translation in *Art of War*, 1877, p. 104.

(18)Bernal Diaz, *True History*, 1908–16, Chapter XCII, p. 72.

(19)Bancroft, *Native Races*, 1883, Vol. 2, pp. 553–74; cites authorities on temple architecture. *Tenayuca*, 1935. Marquina, *Estudio Arquitectónico*, 1928.

(20)*Codex Mendoza, Codex Florentino*. Seler, *Altmexikanischer Schmuck*, 1904. Peñafiel, *Indumentaria Antigua*, 1903.

CHAPTER VIII

There are abundant data on crafts and craftsmanship to be drawn from the contemporary authorities and from museum collections. Examples of the textile art, however, are conspicuously lacking, since few fabrics have survived natural disintegration or have survived from collections made by the Conquistadors. Pictures in the manuscripts do give the impression, none the less, that this art was on a par with the others.

(1)POPULAR ENGLISH DIGESTS are found in Thompson, *Mexico before Cortes*, 1935; Joyce, *Mexican Archæology*, 1922, *Maya and Mexican Art*, 1927; Spinden, *Ancient Civilizations*, 1928; Vaillant, *Artists and Craftsmen*, 1935.

SERIOUS SPECIAL STUDIES: Saville, *Goldsmith's Art*, 1920; *Turquoise Mosaic Art*, 1922; *Woodcarver's Art*, 1925.

(2)Saville, *Onyx Jar*, 1900. Holmes, *Handbook*, 1919. Nuttall, *Penitential Rite*, 1904.

(3)Holmes, *Masterpieces of Aboriginal Art*, 1914-19.

(4)Mason, *Mirrors*, 1927.

(5)Saville, *Onyx Jar*, 1900. Holmes, *Handbook*, 1919.

(6)Sahagun, *Historia General*, 1938. Peñafiel, *Indumentaria Antigua*, 1903. *Codex Mendoza*, *Codex Magliabecchiano*, *Tribute Roll of Montezuma*.

(7)Nuttall, *Feather Work*, 1895; *Standard or Headdress*, 1888. Seler, *Feather Ornaments*, 1904. Sahagun, *Historia General*, 1938. *Codex Florentino*.

(8)Saville, *Turquoise Mosaic Art*, 1922.

(9)Holmes, *Archæological Studies*, 1895. Saville, *Cruciform Structures*, 1909.

(10)Saville, *Woodcarver's Art*, 1925.

(11)Saville, *Goldsmith's Art*, 1920. Sahagun, *Historia General*, 1938, Vol. 5, orfebreria.

(12)Caso, *Monte Alban*, 1932; *Reading the Riddle*, 1932.

(13)Lothrop, *Coclé*, 1937.

(14)Noguera, *Decorative Aspects of Pottery*, 1930; *Características de la Cerámica*, 1930; in *Tenayuca*, 1935. Boas, *Album*, 1911-12. Brenner, *Influence of Technique*, 1931. Vaillant, *History and Stratigraphy*, 1937; *Correlation*, 1938, Figs. 3 and 4.

(15)Boas, *Album*, 1911-12, Pls. 1-10.

(16)Boas, *Album*, 1911-12, Pls. 11-24.

(17)Boas, *Album*, 1911-12, Pls. 25-31.

(18)Noguera, in *Tenayuca*, 1935, Pl. 58; *Cerámica del Templo Mayor*, 1934.

(19)Vaillant, *History and Stratigraphy*, 1937. Noguera, in *Tenayuca*, 1935.

(20)Vaillant, *Correlation*, 1938, Figs. 2 and 5-x.

(21)Noguera, *Ladrillo como Material*, 1928; *Tizatlan*, 1927.

CHAPTER IX

The study of Middle American art is in its infancy. We are only just realizing, in this and other American fields, the great contribution which the Indian has made. There are few publications dedicated especially to this purpose. I am including under footnote 1 a few books which cover the field of American Indian Art.

(1)NORTH AMERICA: Douglas and d'Harnoncourt, *Indian Art*, 1941. Vaillant, *Indian Arts*, 1939.

MIDDLE AMERICA: Caso, *Thirteen Masterpieces*, 1938. Cahill, *American Sources*, 1933. Castro Leal, *Twenty Centuries of Mexican Art*, 1940. Holmes, *Masterpieces*, 1914–19. Marquina, *Estudio Arquitectónico*, 1928. *Escultura Mexicana Antigua*, 1934. Spinden, *Maya Art*, 1913. Totten, *Maya Architecture*, 1926. Vaillant, *Artists and Craftsmen*, 1935.

SOUTH AMERICA: Lehmann and Doering, *Kunstgeschichte des Peru*, 1924. Nordenskiöld, *Archéologie de l'Amazon*, 1930.

(2)Marquina, *Estudio Arquitectónico*, 1928. *Tenayuca*, 1935. Holmes, *Archæological Studies*, 1895–7. Vaillant, *Artists and Craftsmen*, 1935.

(3)Cummings, *Cuicuilco*, 1933.

(4)Gamio, *Teotihuacan*, 1922.

(5)Noguera, *Altar de los Craneos*, 1937.

(6)*Tenayuca*, 1935. Saville, *Tepoztlan*, 1896. Seler, *Tepoztlan*, 1904. Larsen, *Malinalco*, 1938. Marquina, *Estudio Arquitectónico*, 1928. Pollock, *Round Temples*, 1936.

(7)Pollock, *Round Temples*, 1936.

(8)Gallop, *Ancient Monuments*, 1938. Larsen, *Malinalco*, 1938.

(9)Vaillant, *Artists and Craftsmen*, 1935.

(10)Vaillant, *Artists and Craftsmen*, 1935.

(11)Spinden, *Ancient Civilizations*, 1928.

(12)Caso, *El Teocalli*, 1927.

(13)Saville, *Tizoc*, 1929.

(14)Caso, *Reading the Riddle*, 1932. Compare the Mixtec Codices *Cospi, Vaticanus B, Borgia*, with the Aztec Codices *Telleriano-Remensis* and *Borbonicus*.

(15)*Goldsmith's Art*, 1920; *Turquoise Mosaic Art*, 1922; *Woodcarver's Art*, 1925.

(16)Caso, *Tizatlan*, 1927. Vaillant, *Artists and Craftsmen*, 1935.

(17)PRE-CONQUEST MANUSCRIPTS: *Codex Borbonicus, Codex Boturini, Tonalamatl Aubin.*

POST-CONQUEST MANUSCRIPTS: *Codex Telleriano-Remensis, Codex Vaticanus A, Codex of 1576, Codex of 1590, Manuscrit Mexicaine.*

POST-CONQUEST DRAWINGS TO SPANISH ORDER: *Codex Mendoza, Codex Florentino, Lienzo de Tlaxcala.*

(18)Castañeda, *Pequeños Percutores*, 1933.

(19)*Codex Borbonicus.*

(20)Orozco y Berra, *Historia Antigua*, 1880. Spinden, *Ancient Civilizations*, 1928. For oratory, Sahagun, *Historia General*, 1938, Vol. II, Book 6. Brinton, *Ancient Nahuatl Poetry*, 1887.

CHAPTER X

Aztec religion is a fascinating and confusing subject. Ritualism ran wild, and the early Spanish observers, trained in rigorous Christian theology, found the subject interesting but baffling. Sahagun is far and away the best contemporary source. He checked his data in three different localities and spent many years in the process. The late Eduard Seler was the great modern authority, bringing a philosophical background to aid a meticulous interest in ritual. Spence, the best English writer, was his disciple, as was the infinitely learned Hermann Beyer. Alfonso Caso, the distinguished Mexican scholar, has combined brilliantly the meticulousness of the German school with the long-continued Mexican tradition, passed on by many sympathetic and learned minds. Among modern American students J. Eric Thompson is outstanding.

(1) POPULAR ENGLISH ACCOUNTS: Thompson, *Mexico before Cortes*, 1933. Spinden, *Ancient Civilizations*, 1928. Caso, *Aztec Religion*, 1937.

MORE DETAILED STUDIES: Bancroft, *Native Races*, 1883, Vol. III. Spence, *Gods of Mexico*, 1923, standard text. Mrs Bandelier's translation of Sahagun, *Historia General*, Books 1–4, 1932.

FOREIGN LANGUAGES: Beuchat, *Manuel d'Archéologie Americaine*, 1912. Caso, *El Teocalli*, 1927. Paso y Troncoso, *Descripción del Codice Pictórico*, 1898. Seler, *Gesammelte Abhandlungen*, 1902–23; Commentaries on Codices Borgia, 1904–09, Fejervary-Mayer, 1901–02, Vaticanus B, 1902, and Tonalamatl Aubin, 1900–01.

(2) Caso, *El Teocalli*, 1927. Spence, *Gods of Mexico*, 1923. Official version of Calendar Stone.

(3) At Teotihuacan, Azcapotzalco, Culhuacan.

(4) Spence, *Gods of Mexico*, 1923.

(5) Spence, *Gods of Mexico*, 1923.

(6) Spence, *Gods of Mexico*, 1923.

(7) For definitions of gods: Caso, *Aztec Religion*, 1927; Spence, *Gods of Mexico*, 1923; Seler, *Commentaries*.

(8) Bandelier, *Archaeological Tour*, 1884.

(9) FOR FURTHER DEFINITIONS: Caso, *Religión Azteca*, 1938; *El Teocalli*, 1928. Spence, *Gods of Mexico*, 1923. Seler, *Commentaries*.

CHAPTER XI

The religious organization of the Aztecs is relatively clear. The ritual and the identification of deities is much more perplexing, as a certain amount of interpretation is involved. The working of the calendar has puzzled many a distinguished scholar, but its main principles are known. So elaborate a system of worship must have led to considerable local variation, so the student need not too greatly despair over the lack of agreement among authorities. The methods of pictographic writing are well known.

(1) POPULAR ACCOUNTS: Thompson, *Mexico before Cortés*, 1933; Joyce, *Mexican Archaeology*, 1922; Spinden, *Ancient Civilizations*, 1928.

More detailed studies: *for the priesthood:* Bandelier, *Social Organization*, 1880; *for ritual:* Spence, *Gods of Mexico*, 1923; Seler, *Commentaries*, 1900–09; Bancroft, *Native Races*, 1883, Vols. 1, 3; Del Paso y Troncoso, *Codice Pictórico*, 1898; Beuchat, *Manuel*, 1911; Robelo, *Diccionario de Mitologia*, 1905; *for calendar:* Caso, *Correlación*, 1939; De Jonghe, *Le Calendrier Mexicaine*, 1906; Orozco y Berra, *Historia Antigua*, 1880; Palacios, *Fundacion de Mexico-Tenochtitlan*, 1925; Seler, in *Bulletin 28*, 1904; *Gesammelte Abhandlungen*, 1902–23; Spence, *Gods of Mexico*, 1923; Spinden, *Indian Manuscripts*, 1933; *Diffusion of Maya Astronomy*, 1940; *for writing:* Aubin, *Mémoires sur la Peinture*, 1885; Orozco y Berra, *Historia Antigua*, 1880; Peñafiel, *Nombres Geográficos*, 1885; *Nomenclatura Geografica*, 1895.

Contemporary: Sahagun, *Historia General*, 1938; *Codex Florentino;* Torquemada, *Monarquia*, 1923.

(2)Bandelier, *Social Organization*, 1880; cites early authorities.

(3)Thompson, *Mexico before Cortés*, 1933; Beuchat, *Manuel*, 1911; De Jonghe, *Calendrier Mexicaine*, 1906; Spence, *Gods of Mexico*, 1923; Spinden, *Indian Manuscripts*, 1933; *Diffusion of Maya Astronomy*, 1940; Caso, *Correlacion*, 1940; Morley, *Introduction to Maya Hieroglyphs*, 1915; Orozco y Berra, *Historia Antigua*, 1880; Seler, in *Bulletin 28*, 1904; Commentaries on *Codex Vaticanus B, Fejervary–Mayer, Borgia,* and *Tonalamatl of Aubin Collection*, 1900–09.

(4)Seler, *Commentaries on Tonalamatl Aubin, Codex Fejervary–Mayer, Codex Vaticanus B;* Paso y Troncoso, *Codice Pictórica (Borbonicus).*

(5)Aztec records: *Tonalamatl Aubin, Codex Borbonicus, Codex Florentino, Codex Telleriano-Remensis, Vaticanus A.*

Mixteca–Puebla records: *Vaticanus B, Borgia, Bologna (Cospi).*

(6)Caso, *Correlacion*, 1940; Duran, *Historia de las Indias*, II, 1880; Sahagun, *Historia General*, 1938; *Codex Borbonicus;* Beuchat, *Manuel*, 1911.

(7)De Jonghe, *Calendrier Mexicaine*, 1906. *Codex Mariano Jimenez.* Sahagun, *Historia General*, 1938. Fewkes, *Central American Ceremony*, p. 285, 1893.

(8)Seler, *Venus Period*, 1904.

(9)Bancroft, *Native Races*, 1883, Vol. 3, pp. 393–6; cites authorities.

(10)Duran, *Historia*, II, 1880, pp. 155–60.

(11)Linton, *Pawnee Sacrifice*, 1926. Wissler and Spinden, *Pawnee Sacrifice*, 1916.

(12)Bancroft, *Native Races*, 1883, Vol. 3, pp. 387–8.

(13)Sahagun, *Historia General*, 1938; *Codex Florentino.*

(14)Bancroft, *Native Races*, 1883, Vol. 3, pp. 422–5. Blom, *Maya Ball Game*, 1932. Duran, *Historia de las Indias*, II, 1880, Vol. 2, Chapter CI. Oviedo, *Historia General*, 1851, Vol. I, p. 165.

(15)Caso, *Patolli*, 1927.

(16)Clavigero, *Historia Antigua*, 1787, Book 7, Section 46. Larsen, *Volador*, 1937.

(17)Bancroft, *Native Races*, 1883, Vols. 2 and 3. Nuttall, *Penitential Rite*, 1904.

(18)*Codex Borbonicus* for monthly ceremonies.

Telleriano-Remensis and copy *Vaticanus A* record this sacrifice in year 8 Reed (1487).

Bancroft, *Native Races*, 1883, Vol. 2, pp. 585–6; cites authors.

(19)Orozco y Berra, *Historia Antigua*, 1880; Spinden, *Ancient Civilizations*, 1928; Peñafiel, *Nomenclatura*, 1897; *Nombres Geograficos*, 1885; *Codex Mendoza; Tribute Roll of Montezuma.*

(20)*Memorial de Tepetlaostoc.*

(21)Chimalpahin, *Anales*, 1889, Introduction, pp. vii–viii.

(22)TEXCOCAN STYLE: *Mapa Tlotzin, Mapa Quinatzin, Codex Xolotl, Mapa de Siguenza.*

TENOCHCAN STYLE: *Codices Boturini*, 1576, 1590, *Telleriano-Remensis, Vaticanus A, Histoire Mexicaine, Mapa de Tepechpan.*

(23)Sahagun, *Historia General*, 1938, Vol. 3, Book 10, Chapter XXIX, pp. 137–8, paragraph 12.

(24)*Codex Mendoza, Tribute Roll of Montezuma.*

(25)*Codex Chalchihuitzin Vasquez*, in Vaillant, *Aztec Twilight*, 1939. Boban, *Documents*, 1891. *Tlaquiltenango Manuscript*, in American Museum of Natural History.

(26)Tozzer, *Value of Manuscripts*, 1912. Boban, *Documents*, 1891.

CHAPTER XII

The post-Conquest native historians approached Aztec history from an annalistic point of view. Only occasionally did economic and political ideas enter in. Bancroft's and Orozco y Berra's recapitulations of the early history give fullest materials for a detailed scrutiny of Aztec foreign affairs and war. Bandelier's technical study of their method of warfare is the best general outline of Aztecan procedure in this field.

(1)Bancroft, *Native Races*, 1883. Orozco y Berra, *Historia de la Conquista*, 1880. Bandelier, *Art of War*, 1877.

OLDER AUTHORITIES: Duran, *Historia*, 1867, 1880; Ixtlilxochitl, *Relaciones*, 1891, *Historia*, 1892; Tezozomoc, *Crónica*, 1878; Torquemada, *Monarquía*, 1723; Clavigero, *History of Mexico*, 1787.

(2)*Mapa Tlotzin.*

(3)Ixtlilxochitl, *Historia Chichimeca*, 1892.

(4)Commentary of Hamy in *Codex Telleriano-Remensis*. Aragon, *Expansión del Imperio Mexicano*, 1931.

(5)Bancroft, *Native Races*, Vol. 5; cites versions of various authorities.

(6)Bandelier, *Art of War*, 1877.

(7)Diaz del Castillo, *True History*, 1908, Vol. 1, Chapter IX, p. 43; Chapter XX, p. 74; Chapter XXIII, p. 85.

(8)*Codex Mendoza.*

(9)Bandelier, *Art of War*, 1877.

(10)Bandelier, *Art of War*, 1877.

(11)Vaillant, *Correlation*, 1938, footnote 81. *Codex Mendoza.*

(12)Bancroft, *Native Races*, 1883, Vol. 2, pp. 603–23.

CHAPTER XIII

This chapter was adapted from *Natural History*, Vol. 33, No. 1, pp. 17–30, January–February, 1933. It is based on contemporary accounts of Tenochtitlan and on various later archaeological studies on the topography of Tenochtitlan, the ancient Mexico City.

(1)CONTEMPORARY ACCOUNTS: Cortes, *Letters*, 1908; Diaz del Castillo, *True History*, 1908–16; Anonymous Conqueror, 1917; Mendieta, *Historia Eclesiástica*, 1870; Motolinia, *Historia de las Indias*, 1914; Sahagun, *Historia General*, 1938, Vol. 4, Book 12; *Codex Florentino*.

LATER STUDIES: Prescott, *Conquest of Mexico*, 1922; Maudslay, *Great Temple Enclosures*, 1912; Peñafiel, *Destrucción del Templo Mayor*, 1910; Alcocer, *Mexico-Tenochtitlan*, 1935; Maps reproduced in Maudslay's edition of Bernal Diaz del Castillo, *True History*, 1908–16, Vol. 3: *Plan on Maguey Paper, Map of Alonso de Santa Cruz*, 1560.

(2)Diaz del Castillo, *True History*, 1908–16, Vol. 2, Chapter LXXXVIII.

(3)Diaz del Castillo, *True History*, 1908–16, Vol. 2, Chapter XCII.

CHAPTER XIV

Prescott has unforgettably told the story of the Conquest of Mexico. This chapter seeks to stress the Indian side of the Conquest, as told by Sahagun, Duran and others and as illustrated in the *Codex Florentino* and the *Lienzo de Tlaxcala*. The latter was prepared as a memorial to show the services Tlaxcalan warriors rendered the cause of Spain. This chapter is adapted from *Natural History*, Vol. 39, No. 3, pp. 185–95, March, 1937.

(1)Prescott, *Conquest of Mexico*, 1922. Orozco y Berra, *Historia Antigua*, 1880. Cortes, *Letters*, 1908. Diaz del Castillo, *True History*, 1908–16. Anonymous Conqueror, 1917. Duran, *Historia*, 1867, 1880. Ixtlilxochitl, *Horribles Crueldades*, 1829. Sahagun, *Historia General*, 1938, Vol. 4, Book 12. *Codex Florentino*. *Lienzo de Tlaxcala*.

(2)Sahagun, *Historia General*, 1938, Vol. 4, Book 12, Chapter I. *Codex Florentino*.

(3)Sahagun, *Historia General*, 1938, Vol. 4, Book 12, Chapter VIII.

(4)*Lienzo de Tlaxcala*, Pl. 17.

(5)Sahagun, *Historia General*, 1938, Vol. 4, Book 12, Chapter XXIII. Duran, *Historia*, II, 1880, Chapter LXXVI, p. 50.

(6)Diaz del Castillo, *True History*, 1908–16, Vol. 2, Chapter CXXVIII, p. 247, says no! Bancroft, *Conquest*, Vol. 1, p. 480, says yes! on authority.

(7)Sahagun, *Historia General*, 1938, Vol. 4, Book 12, Chapter XXXIII.

CHAPTER XV

This chapter is the merest résumé of what the visitor to Mexico may see of the Indian past. Very properly one may insert here, as footnote 1, the twelve English books on Mexico, which, in the writer's judgment, are best suited to prepare the visitor for what he may see.

(1)Henry Bamford Parkes, *History of Mexico*, Houghton Mifflin Co., Boston, 1938. A history devoted chiefly to colonial and republican Mexico.

Herbert Joseph Spinden, *Ancient Civilization of Mexico and Middle America*, American Museum of Natural History, Handbook Series, No. 3, New York, 1928. A masterpiece of exposition, short and simple, incredibly packed with knowledge, a sine qua non for the understanding of Indian civilization.

Charles Flandrau, *Viva Mexico*, D. Appleton & Company, New York, 1908. An enchanting series of impressions of Mexico under Diaz.

Bernal Diaz del Castillo, *The True History of the Conquest of New Spain*. Hakluyt Society, Series 2, Vol . 23-25, 30, 40, London, 1908-16. This old warrior, a soldier under Cortés, gives the most personal account of the Conquest.

William Hickling Prescott, *The Conquest of Mexico*, Henry Holt and Co., New York, 1922. Not only a brilliant account of the Conquest as seen through Spanish eyes, but one of the masterpieces of American literature.

J. Eric Thompson, *Mexico before Cortés*, Scribners, New York, 1933. An intimately alive picture of the Aztec civilization.

George C. Vaillant, *Artists and Craftsmen in Ancient Central America*, American Museum of Natural History Guide Leaflet Series 88 and 103, 1935. A survey of Middle American art, fully illustrated, for a very low price.

Anita Brenner, *Idols behind Altars*, Payson and Clarke, Ltd., New York, 1929. A superb picture of the Mexican artistic renaissance of 1918 and the essential continuity of Indian life.

Ernest Gruening, *Mexico and Its Heritage*, the Century Co., New York, 1928. A carefully documented study of the conflicts inherent in modern Mexican economic and social life.

C. S. Braden, *Religious Aspects of the Conquest of Mexico*, Duke University Press, Durham, N.C., 1930. The theory of the evangelization of the Mexican Indian, showing the humanitarian theories behind the consolidation of the Spanish Conquest.

Madame Calderon de la Barca, *Life in Mexico*, E. P. Dutton and Co., New York, 1931. The Scottish wife of the Spanish ambassador to Mexico in 1828 writes a most entertaining account of contemporary habits and customs. A classic.

Stuart Chase, *Mexico, A Study of Two Americas*, Macmillan Co., New York, 1931. A succinct, slightly *simpliste* account of contemporary Mexico with special emphasis on the virtues of unmechanized life.

(2)Braden, *Religious Aspects*, 1930. Ricard, *Conquête Spirituelle*, 1933.

(3)The amount of writing by the different monastic orders is interesting as a reflection of direct interest in Indian affairs: Franciscan, 68; Jesuit, 19; Dominican, 18; Augustinian, 3; parish priests, 18; civilians, 6; cf. Clavigero, *History*, 1787, and Ricard, *Conquête Spirituelle*: Spanish

Friars, 61; Indians and Mestizos, 61; Spanish Civilians, 6; Foreign Friars, 7.

(4)Indian authors and approximate dates of composition: Tezozomoc, before 1561; *Anales de Cuauhtitlan*, 1570; Duran, 1581; Ixtlilxochitl, 1600; Chimalpahin, 1613.

Post-Conquest picture writings and closing dates: *Codex Telleriano-Remensis* and *Vaticanus A*, 1563; *Codex of 1576*, 1607; *Codex of 1590*, 1590; *Histoire Mexicaine*, 1521.

(5) —, *Tres Siglos de Arquitectura Colonial*, 1933, p. 27. Garcia Granados y MacGregor, *Huexotcingo*, 1934.

(6)Nuttall, *Official Reports*, 1926. Del Paso y Troncoso, *Papeles de Nueva España*, 1905–06.

(7)Redfield, *Tepoztlan*, 1930. Parsons, *Mitla*, 1936.

(8)Brenner, *Idols behind Altars*, 1929. Chase, *Mexico*, 1931.

(9)The perfect guide for Mexico has yet to be written. Terry, *Guide*, 1927, the most full, approaching Baedeker. Brenner, *Your Mexican Holiday*, 1932, good for the traveller. Marett, *Archaeological Tours*, 1934, good for a person interested in archaeology, since many ruins are not on beaten path. —, *Tres Siglos de Arquitectura Colonial*, 1933, brief illustrated guide. —, *Monumentos Arqueológicos*, 1933, brief illustrated guide.

(10)The index will provide references to descriptions of the sites given in the text.

BIBLIOGRAPHY

ALCOCER, I.
  1935 *Apuntes sobre la Antigua Mexico-Tenochtitlan* (Instituto Pan-
       americano de Geografía e Historia, Tacubaya).
  1938 'Comidas de los Mexicanos', in Sahagun, *Historia General*, Vol.
       3, pp. 365–74.

DE ALVA IXTLILXOCHITL, F.
       See Ixtlilxochitl, F. de Alva.

ANALES DE CUAUHTITLAN (CODEX CHIMALPOPOCA)
  1885 *Anales del Museo Nacional de Mexico*, Tomo 3, Appendix,
       Mexico.
       See also Lehmann, *Die Geschichte von Colhuacan und Mexico*,
       1938.

ANDREWS, E. WYLLYS
  1940 'Chronology and Astronomy in the Maya Area' (in *The Maya
       and Their Neighbors*, pp. 150–61, New York).

ANONYMOUS CONQUEROR
  1917 *Narrative of Some Things of New Spain and the Great City of
       Temestitan, Mexico.* Translated into English by Marshall H.
       Saville (Documents and Narratives Concerning the Dis-
       covery and Conquest of Latin America, No. 1, The Cortés
       Society, New York).

ANTIGUEDADES MEXICANAS
  1892 *Antiguedades Mexicanas.* Publicadas por la Junta Colombino de
       Mexico en al Cuarto Centenario de Descubrimiento de
       America. Mexico.

ARAGON, JAVIER O.
  1931 'Expansion Territorial del Imperio Mexicano' (*Anales del
       Museo Nacional de Arqueología, Historia y Etnografía*, 4a
       Época, Tomo 7, pp. 5–64, Mexico).

AUBIN, J. M. A.
  1885 'Mémoires sur la Peinture Didactique' (*Mission Scientifique au
       Mexique et dans l'Amérique Centrale: Recherches Historiques et
       Archéologiques. Première Partie – Histoire*. Paris).
  1893 *Histoire de la Nation Mexicaine* (Reproduction du Codex de
       1576, Paris). *See also* Codex of 1576.

BANCROFT, HUBERT HOWE
  1883a *The Conquest of Mexico* (3 vols., New York).
  1883b *The Native Races* (5 vols., San Francisco).

BANDELIER, ADOLPH F.
  1877 'On the Art of War and Mode of Warfare of the Ancient
       Mexicans' (*Tenth Annual Report of the Peabody Museum of
       American Archaeology and Ethnology*, Vol. 2, pp. 95–161,
       Cambridge, Mass).

1878 'On the Distribution and Tenure of Lands, and the Customs
with Respect to Inheritance, among the Ancient Mexicans'
(*Eleventh Annual Report of the Peabody Museum of American
Archaeology and Ethnology*, Vol. 2, pp. 385–448, Cambridge).

1880 'On the Social Organization and Mode of Government of the
Ancient Mexicans' (*Twelfth Annual Report of the Peabody
Museum of American Archaeology and Ethnology*, Vol. 2, pp.
557–699, Cambridge).

1884 'Report of an Archaeological Tour in Mexico in 1881' (*Papers,
Archaeological Institute of America*, American Series, Vol. 2,
Boston).

BATRES, LEOPOLDO
1902a *Explorations in Escalerillas Street, Mexico City*. Mexico.
1902b *Exploraciones de Monte Albán, México*. México.
1904 *Exploraciones en Huexotla, Texcoco, y El Gavilán, México*.
México.

BEALS, RALPH L.
1932 'The Comparative Ethnology of Northern Mexico before
1750' (*Ibero-Americana:* 2, University of California,
Berkeley).

BENNETT, WENDELL C., AND ZINGG, R. M.
1935 *The Tarahumara*. Chicago.

BEUCHAT, HENRI
1912 *Manuel d'Archéologie Américaine*. Paris.

BEYER, HERMANN
1921 'Sobre Antiguedades del Pedregal de San Angel' (*Memorias de
la Sociedad Cientifica 'Antonio Alzate'*, Tomo 37, pp. 1–16,
Mexico).

BIART, LUCIEN
1913 *The Aztecs*. Translated by J. L. Garner. Chicago.

BIBLIOTECA MEXICANA
1878 *Crónica Mexicana escrita por D. Hernando Alvarado Tezozomoc
... anotada por el Sr. Lic. D. Manuel Orozco y Berra, y precedida
del Códice Ramirez, Manuscrito del Siglo XVI intitulado:
Relación del Origen de los Indios que habitan esta Nueva España
según sus Historias, y de un Examen de Ambas Obras al cual va
anexo un estudio de Cronología Mexicana por el mismo Sr.
Orozco y Berra*, Biblioteca Mexicana, José M. Vigil, editor,
Mexico).

BIRD, JUNIUS
1938 'Antiquity and Migrations of the Early Inhabitants of Pata-
gonia' (*Geographical Review*, Vol. 28, pp. 250–75, New
York).

BLOM, FRANS
1932a 'Commerce, Trade and Monetary Units of the Maya' (*Middle
American Research Series*, pub. no. 4, pp. 531–56, Tulane
University, New Orleans).

1932b 'The Maya Ball-Game *Pok-ta-pok* (called *tlachtli* by the Aztecs)' (*Middle American Research Series*, pub. no. 4, pp. 485–530. Tulane University, New Orleans).

BOAS, FRANZ
1911–12 *Album de Colecciones Arqueológicas* (Publicaciones de la Escuela Internacional de Arqueología y Etnología Americanas, México). *See* Gamio, Text, 1921.

BOBAN, EUGENE
1891 *Documents pour servir a l'Histoire du Mexique*. Catalogue Raisonné de la Collection de M. E. Eugène Goupil (2 vols. of text and atlas, Paris).

BRADEN, C. S.
1930 *Religious Aspects of the Conquest of Mexico* (Duke University Press, Durham).

BRAND, DONALD
1932 *See* Sauer and Brand.

BRENNER, ANITA
1929 *Idols behind Altars*. New York.
1931 'The Influence of Technique on the Decorative Style in the Domestic Pottery of Culhuacan' (*Columbia University Contributions to Anthropology*, Vol. 13, New York).
1932 *Your Mexican Holiday*. New York and London.

BRINTON, DANIEL G.
1887 *Ancient Nahuatl Poetry*. Philadelphia.
1890a *Rig Veda Americanus*. Philadelphia.
1890b *Essays of an Americanist*. Philadelphia.

BULLETIN 28
1904 *Mexican and Central American Antiquities, Calendar Systems and History*, Papers by Seler and others (Bureau of American Ethnology, Bulletin 28, Washington).

BUTLER, MARY
1940 'A Pottery Sequence from the Alta Verapaz, Guatemala' (in *The Maya and Their Neighbors*, pp. 250–67, New York).

CAHILL, HOLGER
1933 *American Sources of Modern Art* (The Museum of Modern Art, New York).

CALDERON DE LA BARCA, MADAME
1931 *Life in Mexico*. New York.

CASO, ALFONSO
1924–27 'Un Antiguo Juego Mexicano: El Patolli' (*El Mexico Antiguo*, Vol. 2, pp. 203–11, Mexico).
1927a 'Las Ruinas de Tizatlan, Tlaxcala' (*Revista Mexicana de Estudios Históricos*, Vol. 1, pp. 139–72, Mexico).
1927b *El Teocalli de la Guerra Sagrada*. México.

1928   *Las Estelas Zapotecas.* México.

1932a   'Monte Albán, Richest Archaeological Find in America' (*The National Geographic Magazine*, Vol. 62, pp. 487–512, Washington).

1932b   'Reading the Riddle of Ancient Jewels' (*Natural History*, Vol. 32, pp. 464–80, New York).

1932c   *Las Exploraciones en Monte Albán, Temporada 1931–32* (Instituto Panamericano de Geografía e Historia, pub. no. 7, México).

1935.   *Las Exploraciones en Monte Albán, Temporada 1934–35* (Instituto Panamericano de Geografía e Historia, pub. no. 19, México).

1937a   *The Religion of the Aztecs.* Mexico.

1937b   'Tenian los Teotihuacanos Conocimiento del Tonalpohualli?' (*El Mexico Antiguo*, Vol. 4, Nos. 3–4, pp. 131–43, Mexico).

1938a   *Exploraciones en Oaxaca. Quinta y Sexta Temporadas 1936–37* (Instituto Panamericano de Geografía e Historia, pub. no. 34, Tacubaya).

1938b   *Thirteen Masterpieces of Mexican Archaeology.* Mexico.

1939   'La Correlación de los Años Azteca y Cristiano' (*Revista Mexicana de Estudios Antropologicos*, Vol. 3, No. 1, pp. 11–45, Mexico).

CASO, ALFONSO, WITH RUBIN DE LA BORBOLLA, D. F.
1936   *Exploraciones en Mitla, Temporada 1934–35* (Instituto Panamericano de Geografía e Historia, pub. no. 21, México).

CASTAÑEDA, D., AND MENDOZA, V. T.
1933   'Los Pequeños Percutores de las Civilizaciones Precortesianas' (*Anales del Museo Nacional de Arqueología, Historia y Etnografía*, 4a Epoca, Tomo 8, pp. 449–576, Mexico).

CASTRO LEAD, ANTONIO, AND OTHERS
1940   *Twenty Centuries of Mexican Art.* Mexico.

CATHERWOOD, FREDERICK
1844   *Views of Ancient Monuments in Central America, Chiapas and Yucatan.* London.

CEBALLOS NOVELO, R. J.
1935   *Las Instituciones Aztecas.* Mexico

CHARLOT, JEAN
1931   *See* Morris, Charlot and Morris.

CHARNAY, DÉSIRÉ
1887   *The Ancient Cities of the New World.* Translated by J. G. and H. S. Conant. New York.

CHARNAY, DÉSIRÉ, AND VIOLLET-LE-DUC, E. E.
1863   *Cités et Ruines Américaines* (1 vol. text and atlas of plates, Paris).

CHASE, STUART
1931   *Mexico, A Study of Two Americas.* New York.

CHAVERO, A.
 1887 'Historia Antigua y de la Conquista' (Vol. 1 of V. Riva
        Palacio, *México a través de los Siglos*, Mexico and Barcelona).
 1904 'El Monolito de Coatlinchan' (*Anales del Museo Nacional de
        México*, 2a Epoca, Tomo 1, pp. 281–305, Mexico).

CHIMALPAHIN
 1889 *Anales de Chimalpahin Quauhtlehuanitzin, Sixième et Septième
        Relations*, publiées et traduites par Remi Siméon (Biblio-
        thèque Linguistique Américaine, tome 12, Paris).

CHURCHWARD, JAMES
 1926 *Lost Continent of Mu*. London.

CLAVIGERO, FRANCESCO SAVERIO
 1787 *The History of Mexico*. Translated by Charles Cullen (2 vols.,
        London).

CODICES
        See also Lienzo, Mapa, Tonalamatl and Tribute Roll of Mon-
        tezuma.

CODEX OF 1576
        A Post-Columbian Codex in the Goupil Collection, National
        Library, Paris.
        See Aubin, *Histoire*, 1893.

CODEX MEXICANUS OF 1590
        See Boban, *Documents*, 1891, Pls. 23–4.

CODEX BOLOGNA
        See Codex Cospi.

CODEX BORBONICUS
 1899 *A Pre-Columbian Codex Preserved in the Library of the Chamber
        of Deputies, Paris.*
        See Paso y Troncoso, *Codice Pictórico*, 1898, and Vaillant, ed.,
        Sacred Almanac, 1940.

CODEX BORGIA
 1898 *A Pre-Columbian Codex Preserved in the Ethnographical Museum
        of the Vatican, Rome.* Published by le Duc de Loubat, Rome.
        See also Kingsborough, *Antiquities of Mexico*, 1830, Vol. 3, Pt.
        I, pp. 1–76; and Seler, *Commentary*, 1904–08.

CODEX BOTURINI (TIRA DEL MUSEO)
        See García Cubas, *Atlas*, 1858; Radin, *Sources*, 1920, pp. 11–12,
        33–5, Pls. 1 and 2; Orozco y Berra, *Historia Antigua*, 1880,
        Vol. 3, Chap. 4; Kingsborough, *Antiquities of Mexico*, 1830,
        Vol. 1, Pt. 3, pp. 1–23.

CODEX CHALCHIHUITZIN VASQUEZ
        See Vaillant, *Twilight*, 1939.

CODEX CHIMALPOPOCA
        See Anales de Cuauhtitlan.

CODEX COSPI (BOLOGNA)
1898   *A Pre-Columbian Codex in the Library of the University of Bologna.* Published by le Duc de Loubat, Rome.
        Kingsborough, *Antiquities of Mexico* 1830, Vol. 2, Pt. 3, pp. 1–24.

CODEX FEJERVARY-MAYER
1901   *An Old Mexican Picture Manuscript in the Liverpool Free Public Museum.* Published by le Duc de Loubat, Paris.
        See Seler, *Commentary*, 1902.

CODEX FLORENTINO
1905   Illustrations for Sahagun's *Historia de las Cosas de Nueva España.* Published by Francisco del Paso y Troncoso, Vol. 5, Madrid.

CODEX KINGSBOROUGH
1912   *See Memorial de los Indios de Tepetlaostoc.*

CODEX MAGLIABECCHIANO, XIII-3
1904   *Manuscrit Mexicain Post-Colombien de la Bibliothèque Nationale de Florence. Reproduit au frais du Duc de Loubat.* Rome.
        See Nuttall, *The Book of Life,* 1903.

CODEX MARIANO JIMENEZ
n. d.   *Codice Mariano Jimenez.* Edited by Nicolas Léon, Mexico.

CODEX MENDOCINO
        See Codex Mendoza.

CODEX MENDOZA (MENDOCINO)
1938   *Codex Mendoza.* Edited and translated by James Cooper Clark (3 vols., London).
        See also Museo Nacional de Arqueología, Historia y Etnografía, Mexico, 1925; Kingsborough, *Antiquities of Mexico,* 1830, Vol. 1, London.

CODEX NUTTALL (CODEX ZOUCHE)
1901   *Ancient Mexican Codex belonging to Lord Zouche of Haryngworth. Introduction by Zelia Nuttall* (Peabody Museum of American Archæology and Ethnology, Cambridge, Mass.).

CODEX RAMIREZ
        See Historia de los Mexicanos por sus Pinturas.

CODEX TELLERIANO-REMENSIS
1899   *A Post-Columbian Codex published by le Duc de Loubat,* Paris. Commentary by E. T. Hamy.

CODEX VATICANUS 3738 (VATICANUS A) (RIOS) (Copy of Codex Telleriano-Remensis).
1900   *A Post-Columbian Codex Preserved in the Library of the Vatican, Rome.* Published by le Duc de Loubat, Rome.
        See Kingsborough, *Antiquities of Mexico,* 1830, Vol. 2, Pt. 1, pp. 1–149.

CODEX VATICANUS 3773 (VATICANUS B)
  1896 *A Pre-Columbian Codex Preserved in the Library of the Vatican.
    Rome.* Published by le Duc de Loubat, Rome.
    See also Kingsborough, *Antiquities of Mexico*, 1830, Vol. 3,
    Pt. 4, pp. 1–96; Seler, *Commentary*, 1903.

CODEX VIENNA
    See Codex Vindobonensis.

CODEX VINDOBONENSIS (VIENNA)
  1929 *Codex Vindobonensis Mexic. I.* Facsimile. Text by Walter Leh-
    mann and Ottokar Smital. Vienna.
    See Kingsborough. *Antiquities of Mexico*, 1830, Vol. 2, Pt. 4,
    pp. 1–66.

CODEX XOLOTL
    See Boban, *Documents*, 1891, Pls. 1–10; Radin, *Sources*, 1920,
    pp. 17–18, 41–5.

CODEX ZOUCHE
    See Codex Nuttall.

CORTÉS, HERNANDO
  1908 *Letters of Cortés.* Translated and Edited by F. A. MacNutt (2
    vols., New York and London).

CUMMINGS, BYRON C.
  1923a 'Ruins of Cuicuilco May Revolutionize Our History of
    Ancient America' (*The National Geographic Magazine*, Vol.
    44, pp. 203–20, Washington).
  1923b 'Cuicuilco, The Oldest Temple Discovered in North America'
    (*Art and Archaeology*, Vol. 16, nos. 1–2, pp. 51–8, Wash-
    ington).
  1926 'Cuicuilco and the Archaic Culture of Mexico' (*The Scientific
    Monthly*, Vol. 34, no. 8, pp. 289–304, Lancaster, U.S.A.).
  1933 'Cuicuilco and the Archaic Culture of Mexico' (*University of
    Arizona Bulletin*, Vol. 4, no. 8, Social Science Bulletin, No.
    4, pp. 1–56, Tucson).

DAUTERMAN, C. C.
  1938 'The Pottery Yard Stick at Monte Alban' (*The Scientific
    Monthly*, Vol. 46, pp. 157–65, Lancaster, U.S.A.).

DÍAZ DEL CASTILLO, BERNAL
  1908–16 *The True History of the Conquest of New Spain.* Translated by
    A. P. Maudslay (Hakluyt Society, 5 vols., London).

DIXON, R. B.
  1923 *The Racial History of Man.* New York.

DONNELLY, I.
  1882 *Atlantis, the Antediluvian World.* New York.

DOUGLAS, FREDERIC C., AND D'HARNONCOURT, RENÉ
  1941 *Indian Art of the United States* (The Museum of Modern Art,
    New York).

DUPAIX, GUILLELMO
  1834   *Antiquités Mexicaines* (2 vols. and atlas, Paris).
DURÁN, D.
  1867, 1880   *Historia de las Indias de Nueva-España* (XVI Century) (2
          vols. and atlas, Mexico).

EKHOLM, GORDON F.
  1939   'Results of an Archæological Survey of Sonora and Northern
          Sinaloa' (*Revista Mexicana de Estudios Antropológicos*, Vol. 3,
          no. 1, pp. 7–10, Mexico).
  1940a 'The Archæology of Northern and Western Mexico' (in *The
          Maya and Their Neighbors*, pp. 320–30, New York).
  1940b 'Prehistoric "Lacquer" from Sinaloa' (*Revista Mexicana de
          Estudios Antropológicos*, Vol. 4, nos. 1–2, pp. 10–15, Mexico).

EMMART, EMILY W.
  1940   *The Badianus Manuscript. An Aztec Herbal of 1552.* Baltimore.
  1934   *Escultura Mexicana Antigua.* Mexico.
  1936   *Essays in Anthropology presented to Alfred Louis Kroeber.* Berke-
          ley, Cal. (*See* Lowie.)
  1940   *Essays in Historical Anthropology of North America. Published in
          honor of John R. Swanton* (Smithsonian Miscellaneous Collec-
          tions, Vol. 100, Washington).

FEWKES, J. WALTER
  1893   'A Central American Ceremony Which Suggests the Snake
          Dance of the Tusayan Villagers' (*American Anthropologist*,
          o.s., Vol. 6, pp. 285–306, Washington).

FLANDRAU, C. M.
  1908   *Viva Mexico.* New York.

GALLOP, R.
  1938   'Ancient Monuments of Mexico' (*The Geographical Magazine*,
          Vol. 7, pp. 321–38, London).

GAMIO, MANUEL
  1910   'Los Monumentos Arqueológicos de las Immediaciones de
          Chalchihuites' (*Anales del Museo Nacional de Arqueología,
          Historia, y Etnología*, 3a. Epoca, Tomo 2, pp. 469–92,
          México).
  1920   'Las Excavaciones del Pedregal de San Angel y la Cultura Ar-
          caica del Valle de México' (*American Anthropologist*, n.s.,
          Vol. 22, pp. 127–43, Lancaster).
  1921   *Album de Colecciones Arqueológicas, Texto* (Publicaciones, Escuela
          Internacional de Arqueología y Etnología Americanas,
          México).
          See Boas, 1911–12.
  1924   'The Sequence of Cultures in Mexico' (*American Anthropolo-
          gist*, n.s., Vol. 26, pp. 307–22, Menasha).

GAMIO, MANUEL, AND OTHERS
1922 *La Población del Valle de Teotihuacan* (Secretaría de Agricultura y Fomento, Dirección de Antropología, 3 vols., México).

GANN, THOMAS
1900 *Mounds in Northern Honduras* (19th Annual Report, Bureau of American Ethnology, Pt. 2, pp. 655–92, Washington).

GANN, THOMAS, AND THOMPSON, J. ERIC
1931 *The History of the Maya.* New York.

GARCIA CUBAS, A.
1858 *Atlas Geográfico y Estadístico de los Estados Unidos de Mexico.* Mexico.

GARCIA GRANADOS, R., AND MACGREGOR, L.
1934 Huejotzingo. *La Ciudad y el Convento Franciscano.* Mexico.

GARCIA ICAZBALCETA, J.
1886–92 *Nueva Colección de Documentos para la Historia de Mexico* (5 vols., Mexico).

GLADWIN, HAROLD S.
1937 'Excavations at Snaketown: Comparisons and Theories' (*Medallion Papers*, Gila Pueblo, No. 26, Globe).

GLADWIN, HAROLD S., GLADWIN, NORA, HAURY, EMIL, AND SAYLES, E. B.
1937 'Excavations at Snaketown: Material Culture' (*Medallion Papers*, Gila Pueblo, No. 25, Globe).

GORDON, G. B. (editor)
1925 *Examples of Maya Pottery in the Museum and Other Collections* (The University Museum, University of Pennsylvania, Philadelphia).
See Mason, *Maya Pottery*, 1928.

GRUENING, ERNEST
1928 *Mexico and Its Heritage.* New York.

D'HARNONCOURT, RENÉ
1941 *See* Douglas and d'Harnoncourt.

HAURY, EMIL W.
1937 *See* Gladwin, Gladwin, Haury and Sayles.

HEGER, FRANZ
1908 'Der altamerikanische Federschmuck in den Sammlungen der anthropologisch-ethnographischen Abteilung des k. k. naturhistorischen Hofmuseums in Wien (*Festschrift herausgegeben anlässlich d. Tagung d. XVI. Internationalen Amerikanisten-Kongresses in Wien*, September 1908, vom Organisationskommittee, Wien).

HERNANDEZ, F.
1790 *De Historia Novae Hispaniae Plantarum*. Madrid.

HISTOIRE DU MÉCHIQUE
See de Jonghe, ed., *Histoire*, 1905.

HISTOIRE MEXICAINE
See Boban, *Documents*, 1891, Pls. 59–64.

HISTORIA de los MEXICANOS por sus PINTURAS (CODEX RAMIREZ)
1886 *Anales del Museo Nacional, 1a Epoca*, Tomo 2, pp. 83–106, Mexico.
See also Phillips, *Notes*, 1883; Radin, *Sources*, 1920, pp. 57–66; *Garcia Icazbalceta Nueva Colección*, 1886–92, Vol. 3; *Biblioteca Mexicana*, 1878, *Codex Ramirez*.

HISTORIA TOLTECA-CHICHIMECA
1937, 1939 *See* Preuss and Mengin.

HODGE, F. W.
1907 *Handbook of the American Indian* (Bureau of American Ethnology, Bulletin 30, 2 vols., Washington).

HOLMES, WILLIAM H.
1895–97 *Archaeological Studies among the Ancient Cities of Mexico* (Field Columbian Museum, Anthropological Series, Vol. 1, no. 1, Chicago).
1907 'On a Nephrite Statuette from San Andres Tuxtla, Vera Cruz, Mexico' (*American Anthropologist*, n.s., Vol. 9, pp. 691–701, Lancaster).
1914–19 *Masterpieces of Aboriginal American Art* (*Art and Archaeology*, Vol. 1, pp. 1–12, 91–102, 242–55; Vol. 3, pp. 70–85; Vol. 4, pp. 267–78; Vol. 5, pp. 39–49; Vol. 8, pp. 348–60, Washington).
1919 *Handbook of Aboriginal American Antiquities. Pt. 1. Introductory.* The Lithic Industries (Bulletin 60, Bureau of American Ethnology, Washington).

HOOTON, ERNEST A.
1933 'Racial Types in America and Their Relations to Old World Types' (in Jenness, ed., *American Aborigines*, pp. 131 63).

HOWARD, EDGAR B.
1935 *Evidence of Early Man in North America* (Museum Journal, University Museum, University of Pennsylvania, Vol. 24, nos. 2–3, pp. 61–175, Philadelphia).

HOWELLS, WILLIAM W.
1940 'Origins of American Indian Race Types' (in *The Maya and Their Neighbors*, pp. 3–9, New York).

HRDLIČKA, ALEŠ
1903 'The Region of the Ancient "Chichimecs", with Notes on the Tepecanos and the Ruin of La Quemada, Mexico' (*American Anthropologist*, n.s., Vol. 5, pp. 385–440, Lancaster).

1923 *Origin and Antiquity of the American Indian* (Annual Report of the Smithsonian Institution for 1923, pp. 481–94, Washington).

HUMBOLDT, A.
1810 *Vues des Cordillères et Monuments des Peuples Indigènes de l'Amérique.* Paris.

HYDE, G.
1922 *See* Mena and Hyde.

IXTLILXOCHITL, FERNANDO DE ALVA
1829 *Horribles Crueldades de los Conquistadores de Mexico.* Mexico.
1891–92 *Obras Históricas* (XVI Century); *Relaciones, Vol. 1; Historia Chichimeca,* Vol. 2. Mexico.

JENNESS, D. (editor)
1933 *The American Aborigines. Their Origin and Antiquity.* Toronto.

JOHNSON, FREDERICK
1940 *See* Mason and Johnson.

DE JONGHE, E.
1906 'Le Calendrier Mexicain' (*Journal de la Société des Américanistes de Paris,* n.s., Vol. 3, pp. 197–227, Paris).

DE JONGHE, E. (editor)
1905 'Histoire du Méchique, Manuscrit Français inédit du XVIᵉ Siècle' (*Journal de la Société des Américanistes de Paris,* n.s., Tome 2, pp. 1–41, Paris).

JOYCE, THOMAS A.
1914, 1920 *Mexican Archaeology.* London.
1916 *Central American and West Indian Archaeology.* London.
1927 *Maya and Mexican Art.* London.

KIDDER, A. V.
1924 *An Introduction to the Study of South-western Archaeology with a Preliminary Account of the Excavations at Pecos* (Papers of the Phillips Academy, Andover, Southwestern Expedition, No. 1, New Haven).
1931 *The Pottery of Pecos, Vol. 1, The Dull-Paint Wares* (Papers of the Phillips Academy, Andover, Southwestern Expedition, No. 5, New Haven).

KINGSBOROUGH, EDWARD KING, LORD
1930–48 *Antiquities of Mexico* (9 vols., London).

KIRCHHOFF, PAUL
1940 'Los Pueblos de la Historia Tolteca-Chichimeca: sus Migraciones y Parentesco' (*Revista Mexicana de Estudios Antropológicos,* Vol. 4, nos. 1–2, pp. 77–104, México).

KOHLER, J.
  1924   *El Derecho de los Aztecas* (Spanish Translation. Edición de la
        Revista Juridica de la Escuela Libre de Derecho, México).

KRICKEBERG, W.
  1918-22, 1925 'Die Totonaken' (*Baessler Archiv*, Vol. 7, pp. 1-55;
        Vol. 9, pp. 1-75, Berlin. Spanish Translation, Mexico, 1933).
  1937 'Berichte über neue Forschungen zur Geschichte der Alten
        Kulturen Mittel-Amerikas' (*Die Welt als Geschichte*, 3.
        Jahrgang, pp. 194-230, Stuttgart).

KROEBER, ALFRED L.
  1925   *Archaic Culture Horizons in the Valley of Mexico* (University of
        California Publications in American Archæology and Eth-
        nology, Vol. 17, pp. 373-408, Berkeley).
  1939   *Cultural and Natural Areas of Native North America* (University
        of California, Publications in American Archæology and
        Ethnology, Vol. 38, Berkeley).

LARSEN, H.
  1937 'Notes on the Volador and Its Associated Ceremonies and Su-
        perstitions' (*Ethnos*, Vol. 2, no. 4, pp. 179-92, Stockholm).
  1938 'The Monolithic Rock Temple of Malinalco, Mexico' (*Ethnos*,
        Vol. 3, nos. 2-3, pp. 59-63, Stockholm).

LEHMANN, WALTER
  1909 'Methods and Results in Mexican Research' (Translated by
        Seymour de Ricci from *Archiv für Anthropologie*, Vol. 6, pp.
        113-68, Paris).
  1920   *Zentral-Amerika* (2 vols., Berlin).
  1933   *Aus den Pyramidenstädten in Alt-Mexiko*. Berlin.
  1938 'Die Geschichte der Königreiche von Colhuacan und Mexico'
        (*Quellenwerke zur Alten Geschichte Amerikas*, Ibero-Ameri-
        kanisches Institut, Berlin). *See also* Anales de Cuauhtitlan.

LEHMANN, W., AND DOERING, H.
  1924   *Kunstgeschichte des Alten Peru*. Berlin.

LEÓN, NICOLÁS
  1904   *Los Tarascos. Pt. 1. México.* (Reprinted from *Boletín del Museo
        Nacional de México*, 2a Epoca, Vol. 1, August, 1903 to June,
        1904, México).
  1903, 1906 'Los Tarascos.' Pts. 2 and 3 (*Anales del Museo Nacional de
        México*, 2a Epoca, Vol. 1, pp. 392-502, 592, México; and
        Vol. 3, pp. 298-479, México).
        See also Codex Mariano Jimenez.

LEON Y GAMA, ANTONIO
  1832   *Descripción Histórica y Cronológica de las Dos Piedras que se
        Hallaron en al Año 1790 en la Plaza Principal de Mexico.*
        Mexico.

N

LE PLONGEON, AUGUSTUS
1896 *Queen Moo and the Egyptian Sphinx*. New York.

LIENZO DE TLAXCALA
1892 'Lienzo de Tlaxcala' (in *Antiguedades Mexicanas*, Junta Colombino, Pls. 66–175, Mexico).

LINNÉ, S.
1924 *Archaeological Researches at Teotihuacan, Mexico* (The Ethnographical Museum of Sweden, New Series, pub. no. 1, Stockholm).
1937 'The Expedition to Mexico, 1934–35' (*Ethnos*, Vol. 1, no. 2, pp. 39–48, Stockholm).
1938 'A Mazapan Grave at Teotihuacan, Mexico' (*Ethnos*, Vol. 3, no. 6, pp. 167–78, Stockholm).
1939 *Zapotecan Antiquities and the Paulsen Collection in the Ethnographical Museum of Sweden* (Publications, Ethnographical Museum of Sweden, n.s., Vol. 4, Stockholm).

LINTON, RALPH
1924 'The Significance of Certain Traits in North American Maize Culture' (*American Anthropologist*, n.s., Vol. 26, pp. 345–49, Menasha).
1926 'The Origin of the Skidi Pawnee Sacrifice to the Morning Star' (*American Anthropologist*, n.s., Vol. 28, pp. 457–66, Menasha).
1940 'Crops, Soils and Culture in America' (in *The Maya and Their Neighbors*, pp. 32–40, New York).

LOTHROP, SAMUEL K.
1924 *Tulum* (Carnegie Institution of Washington, pub. no. 335. Washington).
1927 'Pottery Types and Their Sequence in El Salvador' (*Indian Notes and Monographs Museum of the American Indian, Heye Foundation*, Vol. 1, no. 4, pp. 165–220, New York).
1933 *Atitlan. An Archaeological Study of Ancient Remains on the Borders of Lake Atitlan, Guatemala* (Carnegie Institution of Washington, pub. no. 444, Washington).
1936 *Zacualpa. A Study of Ancient Quiché Artifacts* (Carnegie Institution of Washington, pub. no. 472, Washington).
1937 *Coclé. An Archaeological Study of Central Panama* (Pt. 1, Memoirs, Peabody Museum of American Archæology and Ethnology, Harvard University, Vol. 7, Cambridge).

LOWIE, ROBERT L. (editor)
1936 *Essays in Anthropology presented to Alfred Louis Krober*, Berkeley.

LUMHOLTZ, C.
1902 *Unknown Mexico* (2 vols., New York).

MACCURDY, G. G. (editor)
1937 *Early Man*. Philadelphia and New York.

MANGELSDORF, P. C., AND REEVES, R. G.
1938 'The Origin of Maize' (*Proceedings of the National Academy of Sciences*, Vol. 24, pp. 303–12, Lancaster).
1939 'Origin of Indian Corn and Its Relatives' (*Texas Agricultural Experiment Station, Bulletin 574*, College Station, Texas).

MAPA QUINATZIN
1885 *See* Aubin, *Mémoires*.

MAPA DE SIGUENZA
See Radin, *Sources*, 1920, pp. 12–13; Kingsborough, *Antiquities of Mexico*, 1830, Vol. 4; Orozco y Berra, *Historia Antigua*, 1880, Vol. 3, pp. 131–53; Garcia Cubas, *Atlas*, 1858.

MAPA DE TEPECHPAN
1887 *See Anales del Museo Nacional* (Tomo 3, 1a Epoca, Entrega 2, p. 368, Mexico).

MAPA TLOTZIN
1885 *See* Aubin, *Mémoires*.

MARETT, R. H. K.
1934 *Archaeological Tours from Mexico City.* London and Mexico.

MARQUINA, IGNACIO
1928 *Estudio Arquitectónico Comparativo de los Monumentos Arqueológicos de México* (Secretaría de Educación Pública, México).

MASON, J. ALDEN
1927 'Mirrors of Ancient America' (*The Museum Journal*, Museum of the University of Pennsylvania, Vol. 18, no. 2, pp. 201–9, Philadelphia).
1935 'The Place of Texas in Pre-Columbian Relationships between the United States and Mexico' (*Bulletin of the Texas Archaeological and Palaeontological Society*, Vol. 7, pp. 29–46, Abilene).
1937a 'Further Remarks on the Pre-Columbian Relationships between the United States and Mexico' (*Bulletin of the Texas Archaeological and Palaeontological Society*, Vol. 9, pp. 120–9, Abilene).
1937b 'Late Archæological Sites in Durango, Mexico, from Chalchihuites to Zape' (*Twenty-fifth Anniversary Studies, Philadelphia Anthropological Society*, Vol. 1, pp. 127–46, Philadelphia).

MASON, J. ALDEN (editor)
1928 *Examples of Maya Pottery in the Museum and Other Collections* (The University Museum, University of Pennsylvania, Philadelphia).

MASON, J. A., AND JOHNSON, F.
1940 'The Native Languages of Middle America and the Linguistic Map of Central America' (in *The Maya and Their Neighbors*, pp. 52–114, New York).

MAUDSLAY, A. P.
1889–1902   *Archaeology* (*Biologia Centrali Americana*, 4 vols. plates. 1 vol. text, London).
1912   *A Note on the Position and Extent of the Great Temple Enclosure of Tenochtitlan.* London.
1940   *The Maya and Their Neighbors.* Dedicated to Alfred M. Tozzer. New York.

McBRYDE, G. McC.
1923   *The Land Systems of Mexico* (Research Series, American Geographical Society, No. 12, New York).

McBRYDE, WEBSTER
1933   'Sololá, a Guatemalan Town and Cakchiquel Market-Center. A Preliminary Report' (*Middle American Research Series*, pub. no. 5, pp. 43–152, Tulane University, New Orleans).

MEANS, PHILIP AINSWORTH
1931   *Ancient Civilizations of the Andes.* New York and London.

MEMORIAL DE LOS INDIOS DE TEPETLAOSTOC
1912   (*Codex Kingsborough.*) (Editor, F. Paso y Troncoso, Madrid).

MENA, R., AND HYDE, G.
1922   'Antigüedad del Hombre en el Valle de México. Nueva Orientación Arqueológica e Histórica' (*Conferencias dadas en el Museo Nacional de Arqueología, Historia y Etnología, la noche del 27 diciembre de 1921.* México).

DE MENDIETA, FRAY GERÓNIMO
1870   *Historia Eclesiástica Indiana* (XVI Century). México.

MENDOZA, V. T.
1933   *See* Castañeda and Mendoza.

MENGIN, E.
1937, 1938   *See* Preuss and Mengin.
1939   *Unos Anales Históricos de la Nación Mexicana; Pt. 1.* (Baessler Archiv, Vol. 22, Berlin).

MERWIN, R. E., AND VAILLANT, G. C.
1932   *The Ruins of Holmul, Guatemala* (Memoirs, Peabody Museum of American Archæology and Ethnology, Harvard University, Vol. 3, no. 2, Cambridge).
1933   *Monumentos Arqueológicos de Mexico.* Departamento de Monumentos, Secretaría de Educación Pública. Mexico.

MORENO, M.
1931   *La Organización Política y Social de los Aztecas.* Universidad Nacional de México Autónoma. Sección Editorial. México.

MORLEY, SYLVANUS G.
1915   *An Introduction to the Study of Maya Hieroglyphs* (Bureau of American Ethnology, Bulletin 57, Washington).

1920 *The Inscriptions at Copan* (Carnegie Institution of Washington, pub. no. 219, Washington).

MORRIS, ANN A.
1931 *See* Morris, Charlot and Morris.

MORRIS, EARL H., CHARLOT, JEAN, AND MORRIS, ANN A.
1931 *The Temple of the Warriors at Chichen Itza, Yucatan* (Carnegie Institution of Washington, pub. no. 406, Washington).

MOTOLINÍA (DE BENAVENTE, T.)
1914 *Historia de los Indios de la Nueva España* (XVI Century). Barcelona.

MUÑOZ CAMARGO, D.
1892 *Historia de Tlaxcala* (XVI Century). México.

MURDOCK, G. P.
1934 *Our Primitive Contemporaries.* New York.

NELSON, N. C.
1933 'The Antiquity of Man in America in the Light of Archæology' (in Jenness, ed., *The American Aborigines*, pp. 87–130).

NOGUERA, EDUARDO
1927 *Ruinas de Tizatlan, Tlaxcala* (Publicaciones de la Secretaría de Educación Pública, Mexico).
1928 'El Ladrillo como Material de Construcción entre los Pueblos Nahuas' (*Revista Mexicana de Estudios Históricos*, Tomo 2, pp. 64–8, Mexico).
1930a 'Decorative Aspects of Certain Types of Mexican Pottery' (*Proceedings, XXIII International Congress of Americanists*, New York, 1928, pp. 85–92, New York).
1930b 'Algunas Características de la Cerámica de México' (*Journal de la Société des Américanistes de Paris*, n.s., Vol. 22, pp. 249–310, Paris).
1934 'Estudio de la Cerámica Encontrada donde Estaba el Templo Mayor de México' (*Anales del Museo Nacional de Arqueología, Historia y Etnografía*, 5a. Epoca, Tomo 1, pp. 267–81, México).
1935 'Antecedentes y Relaciones de la Cultura Teotihuacana' (*El México Antiguo*, Vol. 3, nos. 5–8, pp. 1–81, México).
1937a *El Altar de los Cráneos Esculpidos de Cholula.* México.
1937b *Conclusiones Principales Obtenidas por el Estudio de la Cerámica Arqueológica en Cholula* (Mimeograph, México).

NORDENSKIÖLD, ERLAND
1930 *L'Archéologie du Bassin de l'Amazone* (Ars Americana, I, Paris).

NUTTALL, ZELIA
1888 *Standard or Head-Dress?* (Papers, Peabody Museum of American Archæology and Ethnology, Harvard University, Vol. 1, no. 1, Cambridge, Mass.).

1901 'Chalchihuitl in Ancient Mexico' (*American Anthropologist,* n.s., Vol. 3, pp. 227–37, New York).

1903 *The Book of Life of the Ancient Mexicans. Pt. 1, Introduction and Facsimile.* Berkeley.

1904 *A Penitential Rite of the Ancient Mexicans* (Papers, Peabody Museum of American Archæology and Ethnology, Harvard University, Vol. 1, no. 7, Cambridge).

1910 'The Island of Sacrificios' (*American Anthropologist,* n.s., Vol. 12, pp. 257–95, Lancaster).

1925 *Gardens of Ancient Mexico* (The Smithsonian Institution, Annual Report, 1923, pp. 453–64, Washington).

1926 *Official Reports* (on Mexican towns) sent by Castañeda to Philip II in 1580, translated and edited (Papers, Peabody Museum of American Archæology and Ethnology, Harvard University, Vol. 11, no. 2, Cambridge).

1926 'The Aztecs and Their Predecessors in the Valley of Mexico' (*Proceedings, American Philosophical Society,* Vol. 65, pp. 242–55, Philadelphia).

ORIGÉN DE LOS MEXICANOS
1886–92 *See* Garcia Icazbalceta, *Nueva Colección,* Vol. 3, pp. 281–308.

OROZCO Y BERRA, MANUEL
1864 *Geografía de las Lenguas y Carta Etnográfica de México.* México.
1878 'Ojeada de Cronología Mexicana', in *Biblioteca Mexicana,* pp. 151–222.
1880 *Historia Antigua y de la Conquista de México* (4 vols. and atlas, México).
1887 'El Tonalamatl' (*Anales del Museo Nacional,* 1a Epoca, Vol. 4, pp. 30–44, Mexico).

PALACIOS, ENRIQUE JUAN
1925 'La Fundación de Mexico-Tenochtitlan' (*Anales del Museo Nacional de Arqueología, Historia y Etnografía,* 5a Epoca, Tomo 1, No. 3, pp. 230–54, México).

PARKES, HENRY B.
1938 *A History of Mexico.* Boston.

PARSONS, ELSIE C.
1936 *Mitla, Town of Souls.* Chicago.

DEL PASO Y TRONCOSO, F.
1898 *Descripción Histórica y Exposición del Códice Pictórico de los Antiguas Nauas que se conserva en la Biblioteca de la Camara de Diputados de Paris* (Commentary on Codex Borbonicus) Florence.

DEL PASO Y TRONCOSO, F. (editor)
1905 *See Codex Florentino.*
1912 *See Memorial de los Indios de Tepetlaostoc.*

PAYÓN, J. GARCÍA
    1936   *Zona Arqueológica de Tecaxic-Calixtlahuaca*, Pt. 1 (Departa-
            mento de Monumentos, México).

PEÑAFIEL, ANTONIO
    1885   *Nombres Geográficos de México* (Secretaría de Fomento, Mexico).
    1890   *Monumentos del Arte Mexicano Antiguo* (1 vol., text; 2 vols.,
            plates; Berlin).
    1897   *Nomenclatura Geográfica de Mexico* (1 vol. and atlas, Mexico).
    1903   *Indumentaria Antigua* (Secretaría de Fomento, Mexico).
    1910   *Destrucción del Templo Mayor de Mexico Antiguo*. Mexico.

PHILLIPS, H.
    1883   'Notes upon the Codex Ramirez, with a translation of the
            same' (*Proceedings, American Philosophical Society*, Vol. 21,
            pp. 616-51, Philadelphia).

POLLOCK, H. E. D.
    1936   *Round Structures of Aboriginal Middle America* (Carnegie In-
            stitution of Washington, pub. no. 471, Washington).

POMAR, JUAN BAUTISTA
    1891   'Relación de Tezcoco' (García Icazbalceta, *Nueva Colección de
            Documentos para la Historia de México*, vol. 3, pp. 1–69,
            Mexico).

PRESCOTT, WILLIAM H.
    1843   *The Conquest of Mexico* (3 vols., New York).
    1922   *The Conquest of Mexico* (edited by T. A. Joyce and illustrated
            by Keith Henderson, 2 vols., New York).

PREUSS, K. T., AND MENGIN, E.
    1937   'Die mexikanische Bilderhandschrift Historia Tolteca-Chichi-
            meca. Pt. 1' (*Baessler Archiv*, Beiheft 9, Berlin).
    1938   'Die mexikanische Bilderhandschrift Historia Tolteca-Chichi-
            meca. Pt. 2' (*Baessler Archiv*, Vol. 21, Berlin).

RADIN, PAUL
    1920   *The Sources and Authenticity of the History of the Ancient Mexicans*
            (University of California Publications in American Archæ-
            ology and Ethnology, Vol. 17, no. 1, Berkeley).

REDFIELD, ROBERT
    1930   *Tepoztlan*. Chicago.

RELACIÓN DE GENEALOGÍA Y LINAGE DE LOS SEÑORES QUE HAN SEÑOR-
    EADO ESTE TIERRA DE LA NUEVA ESPAÑA
            See García Icazbalceta, *Nueva Colección*, 1886–92, Vol. 3, pp.
            263–81.

RICARD, R.
    1933   *La 'Conquête Spirituelle' de Mexico* (Université de Paris, Tra-
            vaux et Mémoires de l'Institut d'Ethnologie, Vol. 20,
            Paris).

RIVA PALACIO, VICENTE (editor)
1887–89 *México a Través de los Siglos* (5 vols., México and Barcelona).

ROBELO, CECILIO A.
1911 *Diccionario de la Mitología Nahuatl*. México.

ROBERTS, FRANK H. H., JR.
1935 'A Survey of Southwestern Archæology' (*American Anthropologist*, n.s., Vol. 37, pp. 1–35, Menasha).
1940 'Developments in the Problem of the North American Paleo-Indian' (in *Essays in Historical Anthropology in North America*, pp. 51–116, Washington).

RUBIN DE BORBOLLA, D.
1936 *See* Caso with Rubin de Borbolla.

DE SAHAGUN, BERNARDINO
1829 *Historia General de las Cosas de Nueva España* (3 vols., Mexico).
1905 *Codex Florentino: Illustrations for Sahagun's Historia General de las Cosas de Nueva España*. Edited by Francisco del Paso y Troncoso, Vol. 5, Madrid.
1932 *Historia General de las Cosas de Nueva España*. Books 1–4 translated by Fanny Bandelier. Nashville.
1938 *Historia General de las Cosas de Nueva España* (5 vols., Mexico).

SAUER, CARL ORTWIN
1932 *The Road to Cibola* (Ibero-Americana: 3, Berkeley).
1936 'American Agricultural Origins: A Consideration of Nature and Culture' (*Essays in Anthropology in Honor of Alfred Louis Kroeber*, pp. 279–97, Berkeley).

SAUER, CARL, AND BRAND, DONALD
1932 *Aztatlan, Prehistoric Mexican Frontier on the Pacific Coast* (Ibero-Americana: 1, Berkeley).

SAVILLE, MARSHALL H.
1896 'The Temple of Tepoztlan, Mexico' (*Bulletin, American Museum of Natural History*, Vol. 8, pp. 221–6, New York).
1899 'Exploration of Zapotecan Tombs in Southern Mexico' (*American Anthropologist*, n.s., Vol. 1, pp. 350–62, New York).
1900a 'A Shell Gorget from the Huasteca, Mexico' (*Bulletin, American Museum of Natural History*, Vol. 13, pp. 99–103, New York).
1900b 'An Onyx Jar from Mexico in Process of Manufacture' (*Bulletin, American Museum of Natural History*, Vol. 13, art. 11, pp. 105–07, New York).
1901 'Mexican Codices, a List of Recent Reproductions' (*American Anthropologist*, n.s., Vol. 3, pp. 532–41, New York).
1909 *The Cruciform Structures of Mitla and Vicinity* (Putnam Anniversary Volume, pp. 151–90, New York).

1916 'Monolithic Axes and Their Distribution in Ancient America' (*Contributions, Museum of the American Indian, Heye Foundation*, Vol. 2, no. 5, New York).

1917 *See* Anonymous Conqueror.

1920 'The Goldsmith's Art in Ancient Mexico' (*Indian Notes and Monographs, Museum of the American Indian, Heye Foundation*, New York).

1922 'Turquoise Mosaic Art in Ancient Mexico' (*Contributions, Museum of the American Indian, Heye Foundation*, Vol. 6, New York).

1925 'The Wood-Carver's Art in Ancient Mexico' (*Contributions, Museum of the American Indian, Heye Foundation*, Vol. 9, New York).

1928 'Ceremonial Axes from Western Mexico' (*Indian Notes, Museum of the American Indian, Heye Foundation*, Vol. 5, pp. 280–93, New York).

1929a 'Votive Axes from Ancient Mexico' (*Indian Notes, Museum of the American Indian, Heye Foundation*, Vol. 6, pp. 266–99, 335–42, New York).

1929b 'Tizoc, Great Lord of the Aztecs, 1481–86' (*Contributions, Museum of the American Indian, Heye Foundation*, Vol. 7, no. 4, New York.

SAYLES, E. B.

1935 'An Archæological Survey of Texas' (*Medallion Papers*, Gila Pueblo, No. 17, Globe).

1936 'An Archæological Survey of Chihuahua, Mexico' (*Medallion Papers*, Gila Pueblo, No. 22, Globe).

1937 *See* Gladwin, Gladwin, Haury and Sayles.

SELER, CÄCILIE

1900 *Auf alten Wegen in Mexiko und Guatemala.* Berlin.

1922 'Alterthümer des Kanton Tuxtla im Staate Veracruz' (*Festschrift Eduard Seler*, pp. 543–56, Stuttgart).

SELER, EDUARD

1901 *The Tonalamatl of the Aubin Collection. Commentary.* Translated by A. H. Keane. London.

1902 *Codex Fejervary-Mayer. Commentary.* Translated by A. H. Keane. London.

1902–23 *Gesammelte Abhandlungen zur Amerikanischen Sprach- und Alterthumskunde* (Vols. 1–5, Berlin).

1903 *Codex Vaticanus 3773. Commentary.* Translated by A. H. Keane. London.

1904a *Ancient Mexican Feather Ornaments* (Bureau of American Ethnology, Bulletin 28, pp. 57–74, Washington).

1904b *The Temple Pyramid of Tepoztlan* (Bureau of American Ethnology, Bulletin 28, pp. 339–52, Washington).

1904c *The Venus Period in the Borgian Codex Group* (Bureau of American Ethnology, Bulletin 28, pp. 353–92, Washington).

1904*d* 'Altmexikanischer Schmuck und soziale und militärische Rangabzeichen' (*Gesammelte Abhandlungen*, Vol. 2, pp. 509–619, Berlin).

1904–09 *Codex Borgia*. 'Eine altmexikanische Bilderschrift der Bibliothek der Congregatio de Propaganda Fide.' 3 vols. Berlin.

1915 'Die Teotiuacan-Kultur des Hochlands von Mexico' (*Gesammelte Abhandlungen zur amerikanischen Sprach- und Alterthumskunde*, Vol. 5, pp. 405–585, Berlin).

SOUSTELLE, JACQUES
1937 *La Famille Otomi-Pame du Mexique Central* (Institut d'Ethnologie, No. 26, Paris).

SPENCE, LEWIS
1923 *The Gods of Mexico*. London.

SPINDEN, E. S.
1933 'The Place of Tajin in Totonac Archæology' (*American Anthropologist*, n.s., Vol. 35, pp. 271–87, Menasha).

SPINDEN, HERBERT J.
1913 *A Study of Maya Art* (Memoirs, Peabody Museum of American Archæology and Ethnology, Harvard University, Vol. 6, Cambridge).

1916 *See* Wissler and Spinden.

1924 *The Reduction of Mayan Dates* (Papers, Peabody Museum of American Archæology and Ethnology, Harvard University, Vol. 6, no. 4, Cambridge).

1928 *Ancient Civilizations of Mexico and Central America* (Handbook Series, American Museum of Natural History, No. 3, 3rd edition, New York.)

1933 'Indian Manuscripts of Southern Mexico' (*Annual Report of the Smithsonian Institution for 1933*, pp. 429–51, Washington).

1940 'Diffusion of Maya Astronomy' (in *The Maya and Their Neighbors*, pp. 162–78, New York).

STARR, F.
1908 *In Indian Mexico*. Chicago.

STAUB, WALTER
1933 'Zur Übereinanderschichtung der Völker und Kulturen an der Ostküste von Mexiko' (*Mitteilungen der Geographisch-Ethnographischen Gesellschaft in Zürich*, Vol. 33, pp. 3–26, Zürich).

STIRLING, M. W.
1939 'Discovering the New World's Oldest Dated Work of Man' (*The National Geographic Magazine*, Vol. 76, no. 2, Washington).

1940*a* 'Great Stone Faces of the Mexican Jungle' (*The National Geographic Magazine*, Vol. 78, no. 3, pp. 309–34, Washington).

1940*b* *An Initial Series from Tres Zapotes, Vera Cruz, Mexico* (National Geographic Society, Contributed Technical Papers, Mexican Archæology Series, Vol. 1, no. 1, Washington).

STREBEL, H.
1885–89 *Alt Mexiko* (2 vols., Hamburg und Leipzig).

STRONG, WILLIAM DUNCAN
1935a *An Introduction to Nebraska Archæology* (Smithsonian Miscellaneous Collections, Vol. 93, no. 10, Washington).

STUDLEY, CORNELIA
1887 'Notes upon Human Remains from Caves in Coahuila (*Reports, Peabody Museum of American Archæology and Ethnology*, Vol. 3, 1880–86, pp. 233–59; cf. also pp. 10, 21, 32, Cambridge).

SWANTON, JOHN R.
1911 *Indian Tribes of the Lower Mississippi and Adjacent Coasts of the Gulf of Mexico* (Bureau of American Ethnology, Bulletin 43. Washington).
1911b See Thomas, Cyrus, and Swanton, John R.

SWANTON ESSAYS
1940 *See Essays in Historical Anthropology of North America.*

TEEPLE, JOHN E.
1931 'Maya Astronomy' (Carnegie Institution of Washington, pub. 110. 403, *Contributions to American Archæology*, Vol. 1, no. 2, pp. 29–115, Washington).
1935 *Tenayuca* (Departamento de Monumentos, México).

TEZOZOMOC, H.
1878 'Crónica Mexicana (XVI Century)' (in *Biblioteca Mexicana*, México).

THOMAS, CYRUS, AND SWANTON, JOHN R.
1911 *Indian Languages of Mexico and Central America and Their Geographical Distribution* (Bureau of American Ethnology, Bulletin 44, Washington).

THOMPSON, J. ERIC
1927 *A Correlation of the Mayan and European Calendars* (Field Museum of Natural History, Anthropological Series, Vol. 17, no. 1, Chicago).
1932 *Civilization of the Mayas* (Anthropology Leaflet 25, 2nd edition, Field Museum of Natural History, Chicago).
1933 *Mexico before Cortes.* New York.
1934 *Sky Bearers, Colors and Directions in Maya and Mexican Religion* (Carnegie Institution of Washington, pub. no. 436, pp. 209–42, Washington).
1935 *Maya Chronology: the Correlation Question* (Carnegie Institution of Washington, pub. no. 456, contribution no. 14, Washington).
1935 *See* Gann, Thomas, and Thompson, J. Eric.

1939   *Excavations at San José, British Honduras* (Carnegie Institution of Washington, pub. no. 506, Washington).

TONALAMATL AUBIN
1900   *A Pre-Columbian Codex Preserved in the National Library, Paris.* Published by le Duc de Loubat, Paris.
    See Orozco y Berra, *El Tonalamatl*, 1887 (*Anales del Museo Nacional*, 1a Epoca, Vol. 4, pp. 30–44 and end of book, Mexico).

TORQUEMADA, JUAN DE
1723   *Los Veinte i un Libros Rituales i Monarchía Indiana* (3 vols., Madrid).

TOTTEN, GEORGE OAKLEY
1926   *Maya Architecture.* Washington.

TOZZER, ALFRED M.
1912   'The Value of Ancient Mexican Manuscripts in the Study of the General Development of Writing' (*The Smithsonian Institution, Annual Report for 1911*, pp. 493–506, Washington).
1918   'The Domain of the Aztecs and their Relation to the Prehistoric Cultures of Mexico' (*Holmes Anniversary Volume*, pp. 464–8, Lancaster)
1921   *Excavation of a Site at Santiago Ahuitzotla, D. F. Mexico* (Bureau of American Ethnology, Bulletin 74, Washington).
1927   'Time and American Archæology' (*Natural History*, Vol. 27, pp. 210–21, New York).
1930   'Maya and Toltec Figures at Chichen Itza' (*Proceedings XXIII International Congress of Americanists*, New York, 1928, pp. 155–64, New York).
1937   'Prehistory in Middle America' (*The Hispanic American Historical Review*, Vol. 17, pp. 151–9, Durham).
1933   *Tres Siglos de Arquitectura Colonial* (Departamento de Monumentos, Secretaría de Educación Pública, Mexico).

TRIBUTE ROLL OF MONTEZUMA (See CODEX MENDOZA)
    A Pre-Columbian Codex Preserved in the Museo Nacional, Mexico.
    See Peñafiel, *Monumentos*, 1890, Vol. 2, Pls. 228–59; *Transactions of the American Philosophical Society*, Philadelphia, 1892, n.s., Vol. 17, Pt. 2, Philadelphia.

VAILLANT, GEORGE C.
1929   'On the Threshold of Native American Civilization' (*Natural History*, Vol. 29, pp. 530–42, New York).
1930a   'Excavations at Zacatenco' (*Anthropological Papers, American Museum of Natural History*, Vol. 32, Pt. 1, New York).
1930b   'Reconstructing the Beginning of a History' (*Natural History*, Vol. 30, pp. 606–16. New York).
1931a   'A Bearded Mystery' (*Natural History*, Vol. 31, pp. 243–52, New York).

1931*b* 'Excavations at Ticoman' (*Anthropological Papers, American Museum of Natural History*, Vol. 32, Pt. 2, New York).

1932*a* 'A Pre-Columbian Jade' (*Natural History*, Vol. 32, pp. 512–20, 557–8, New York).

1932*b* *See* Merwin and Vaillant.

1934 *See* Vaillant and Vaillant.

1935*a* 'Excavations at El Arbolillo' (*Anthropological Papers, American Museum of Natural History*, Vol. 35, Pt. 2, New York).

1935*b* 'Early Cultures of the Valley of Mexico: Results of the Stratigraphical Project of the American Museum of Natural History in the Valley of Mexico, 1928–33' (*Anthropological Papers, American Museum of Natural History*, Vol. 35, Pt. 3, New York).

1935*c* 'Chronology and Stratigraphy in the Maya Area' (*Maya Research*, Vol. 2, pp. 119–43, New York).

1935*d* *Artists and Craftsmen in Ancient Central America* (American Museum of Natural History, Guide Leaflet Series, No. 88, New York. Supplement: Chart in Vaillant, 1936, Guide Leaflet No. 103).

1936 'The History of the Valley of Mexico' (*Natural History*, Vol. 38, pp. 324–40, New York. Accompanying chart reprinted as Guide Leaflet No. 103, American Museum of Natural History).

1937*a* 'History and Stratigraphy in the Valley of Mexico' (*The Scientific Monthly*, Vol. 44, pp. 307–24 New York).

1937*b* 'The Death Throes of the Aztec Nation' (*Natural History*, Vol. 39, pp. 185–95, New York).

1938 'A Correlation of Archæological and Historical Sequences in the Valley of Mexico' (*American Anthropologist*, n.s., Vol. 40, pp. 535–73, Menasha).

1939*a* 'The Twilight of Aztec Civilization' (*Natural History*, Vol. 43, pp. 38–46, New York).

1939*b* *Indian Arts in North America*. New York.

1939*c* 'An Early Occurrence of Cotton in Mexico' (*American Anthropologist*, n.s., Vol. 41, p. 170, Menasha).

1940 'Patterns in Middle American Archæology' (in *The Maya and Their Neighbors*, pp. 295–305 New York).

VAILLANT, GEORGE C. (editor)

1940 *A Sacred Almanac of the Aztecs* (*Tonalamatl of the Codex Borbonicus*) (American Museum of Natural History, Limited Edition, New York).

VAILLANT, S. B. AND VAILLANT, G. C.

1934 'Excavations at Gualupita' (*Anthropological Papers, American Museum of Natural History*, Vol. 35, no. 1, New York).

VEYTIA, MARIANO

1836 *Historia Antigua de México* (3 vols., México).

VIOLLET-LE-DUC, E. E.

1863 *See* Charnay and Viollet-le-Duc.

WATERMAN, T. T.
  1917 'Bandelier's Contribution to the Study of Ancient Mexican Social Organization' (University of California Publications in American Archæology and Ethnology, Vol. 12, no. 7, pp. 249–82, Berkeley).
  1924 'On Certain Antiquities in Western Guatemala' (*Bulletin of the Pan-American Union*, April, 1924, pp. 1–21, Washington).

WEIANT, C. W.
  n. d. *Manuscript on Ceramics of Tres Zapotes.*

WEYERSTALL, A.
  1932 'Some Observations on Indian Mounds, Idols and Pottery in the Lower Papaloapam Basin, State of Vera Cruz, Mexico' (*Middle American Research Series*, pub. no. 4, pp. 23–69, Tulane University, New Orleans).

WISSLER, CLARK
  1938 *The American Indian* (3rd edition, New York).

WISSLER, CLARK, AND SPINDEN, HERBERT J.
  1916 'The Pawnee Human Sacrifice to the Morning Star' (*American Museum Journal*, Vol. 16, no. 1, pp. 49–55, New York).

YANOVSKI, E.
  1936 *Food Plants of the North American Indians* (U.S. Department of Agriculture, Miscellaneous Publications, No. 237, Washington).

ZINGG, R. M.
  1935 *See* Bennett and Zingg.

ZURITA, A.
  1891 'Breve y Sumaria Relación de los Señores de la Nueva España (García Icazbalceta, *Nueva Colección de Documentos para la Historia de México*, Vol. 3, pp. 71–227, México).

INDEX

The rules for the pronunciation of Aztec names are simple despite the horrifying assemblage of consonants and vowels. X in general has a Sh sound; Qu has a K value; Hu and Gu have a W sound when preceding a vowel. All consonants and vowels are sounded as in Spanish. Rough English phonetic equivalents have been provided in the text and the index to guide the errant tongue.

THE ETRUSCANS

M. Pallottino

A 310

Before the Romans could establish their empire they had first to conquer and unify the other cities and peoples in Italy. The most powerful and highly civilized of these other peoples were the Etruscans. In this study Professor Pallottino discusses the origins, culture, religion, and language of this ancient and little known civilization which flourished so brilliantly 2,500 years ago, and whose history has been neglected for so long.

This translation by J. A. Cremona of the third Italian edition contains maps and diagrams and an inset of 32 plates, showing some of the wonderful objects that have survived the neglect of succeeding generations.

'This is an admirable introduction to the study of a subject little known to the general reader.' – *The Times Literary Supplement*

'*The Etruscans* is a good introduction to the subject because he can communicate his own interest in it with his learning … Professor Pallottino's chapters on the Etruscan language are exceptionally good and clear.' – *Manchester Guardian Weekly*

ISLAM

Alfred Guillaume

A 311

The cultural background of the Arab peoples, who are playing an ever larger and larger part in the modern world, has been formed as much by a great missionary religion, Mohammedanism, as has that of Europe and America by Christianity. The great awakening of the Muslim world which is now in progress, the emergence of new Muslim states such as Pakistan, Libya, Jordan, Saudi Arabia, and the ever closer contact between West and Middle East makes an understanding of the spirit of Islam essential to the informed Westerner.

Professor Guillaume provides the essentials for such an understanding in this book. He deals in turn with Mohammed, the founder of Islam; the Quran, its holy book; the evolution of Mohammedanism as a system of faith, law, religion, and philosophy; the varying schools of thought and the intense devotional life that have grown up within it; and he discusses the changes which are now taking place in the Islamic viewpoint as the Muslim peoples prepare to take their full part in the modern world.